Coaching the Dark Side of Personality

COACHING THE DARK SIDE OF PERSONALITY

RODNEY WARRENFELTZ, PhD
TRISH KELLETT, MBA

EDITORS

HOGAN PRESS

Rodney Warrenfeltz, PhD
Trish Kellett, MBA

Hogan Personality Inventory ™
Hogan Development Survey ™
Motives, Values, Preferences Inventory ™

are the exclusive registered trademarks of
Hogan Assessment Systems, Inc.

www.hoganassessments.com

First printing August 2016

ISBN 978-0-9975169-4-4

HOGANPRESS

CONTENTS

PART IV: COACHING TECHNIQUES FOR THE DARK SIDE

CASES

TABLES AND FIGURES

FOREWORD

In the 1980s, when Dr. Robert Hogan, the founder of Hogan Assessment Systems, introduced his theory that personality really does matter in leadership and, in fact, is the primary driver, he was considered a renegade by mainstream psychologists. Over the last 30 years, his views on leadership have gained more and more credibility and acceptance. They have inspired an entire field of study around personality-driven behaviors and their role as enablers and derailers of a leader's reputation, performance, and effectiveness.

Even with the recognition of Dr. Hogan's theory and the subsequent body of knowledge it fueled, until now, no one has written a definitive reference about Dark Side behaviors—how they manifest in the real world, how to recognize them, their impact on a leader's own reputation and on the people he or she works with, and most importantly, specific recommendations around what to do about them. With the publication of *Coaching the Dark Side of Personality*, we at last have a go-to guide for reining in Dark Side behaviors so that leaders can accomplish real change in their behaviors and reputations.

The editors and members of the Hogan Coaching Network who contributed to this book have created a rich, comprehensive resource that will have great value to a number of people:

- Individual contributors and leaders who want to gain insights about their own vulnerabilities or potential derailers.
- Leaders who want to identify development needs and provide coaching tips to their team members.
- Experienced coaches who will discover hundreds of easy to learn, practical suggestions for improving the performance of those they coach.

I am particularly impressed that there is a focus on how aspects of personality pose risks to performance (effectiveness) and career progress. Perhaps in a pure meritocracy there would be no need for this focus. More effective leadership and better results would automatically translate into advancement. My experience as an executive coach since 1986 reveals that, unfortunately, numerous factors besides merit determine how far someone goes in his or her career.

I have had the good fortune to coach almost 2,000 individuals and track many of them throughout their careers. I have observed those who reached their full potential and those who derailed or topped out. Here are some of the lessons I have learned:

- The most deserving person does not always get promoted.
- There is no guarantee that the company will make an informed decision about an individual with accurate knowledge about an individual's talent, contributions, and potential.
- Many of my coaching clients underestimated the impact that their reputation and the perception of others can have on their careers.

A popular axiom fits here: "The difference between reality and perception is that people make decisions based on perception." How does this apply to careers? Imagine a talent review at your company with your manager, his or her peers, and human resources executives talking about you, and you are not in the room. You are not there to provide missing information or correct misperceptions, and your reputation plays a central role in the discussion. *Coaching the Dark Side of Personality* will help you understand how you will be perceived by various constituencies and where those perceptions might present problems.

Let me give you an example. Fifteen years ago I worked with a company that initiated a high-potential program. Ten leaders were identified. They met quarterly with the CEO, Michael, and the COO, Kevin, in two-day offsite meetings. In addition, they were assigned an executive coach, and I was assigned to Steven.

Steven's Hogan scores were quite low on the Bold and Colorful scales. Halfway through the year, I checked in with Michael and Kevin to review Steven's progress. When I asked how Steven was doing in the program, Michael said, "Marty, I like this guy. At our meetings, he does not talk just to hear himself talk. When he does say something, it is well reasoned and fits with the flow of the conversation." Kevin's feedback about Steven was quite different. "Marty, I'm very disappointed. This guy has more experience than almost anyone in the program, but he is not a thought leader. I went on a market tour with him and he was invisible. I like someone who leads from the front."

Steven's approach to leading others could best be described as "servant leadership," which meshed well with his personality. People loved working for him. His engagement scores were outstanding, and his results were good. Yet, in this company, Kevin, the COO, was a key decision maker regarding Steven's career.

I was left with the question, "How should I proceed with Steven's coaching?" Coaching him about leadership did not seem appropriate as he was probably better than most in that area. The key to coaching Steven was to be found in the personality characteristics that were negatively impacting the way he was perceived by at least one key decision-maker. My coaching with Steven addressed four areas:

- Helping him understand how low Bold, low Colorful behaviors are perceived by someone like Kevin.

- Encouraging him to learn Kevin's "scorecard," the lens through which Kevin evaluates leaders.

- Helping him to adapt his meeting behavior to speak earlier in meetings, use a stronger voice, and use more language of conviction.

- Increasing his visibility in market tours with Kevin.

These are precisely the kinds of coaching insights that can be gained from *Coaching the Dark Side of Personality*. In Steven's case, he made modest adjustments to his low Bold and low Colorful behaviors to keep his career on track.

So I encourage all those interested in improving their career outcomes to take these steps:

- Deepen their self-awareness.

- Discover their "buzz" (i.e., their reputation and how they are perceived).

- Learn the scorecard of the decision-makers around them.

- Erase their performance challenges.

The insights, coaching tips, and techniques covered in *Coaching the Dark Side of Personality* offer a comprehensive roadmap for individual contributors and leaders interested in improving their performance and the guidance needed for coaches to help these individuals along their career journey.

Marty Seldman, PhD
Best-selling author of *Survival of the Savvy*
Founder of Optimum Associates

PREFACE

EVOLUTION IN OUR THINKING

Personality has become a central point of focus in understanding the performance of leaders over the past 25 years. This growth has been accompanied by an increasing realization that the behaviors driven by personality can be developed. Moreover, focused development of *personality-related behaviors* can change a leader's reputation in the workplace, alter the way a leader builds and motivates a team, and even improve how a leader makes business-related judgments.

Hogan Assessment Systems (Hogan) has been at the forefront of this shift in understanding the role of personality in the performance of a leader. In the early 1990s, personality assessment was just entering the workplace as an accepted area of evaluation when hiring employees. Throughout the 1990s and into the early 2000s, Hogan accumulated performance-related data demonstrating that hiring the right employees required a systematic consideration of personality characteristics. These data also began to demonstrate three other important facts. First, personality characteristics were just as important to leader behavior as they were to employee behavior. Second, building Strategic Self-awareness of one's personality profile represented a critical factor in a leader's development. Third, combining Strategic Self-awareness with focused development can substantially alter a leader's reputation in the workplace.

It is this last point that became the foundation for the evolution in our thinking. Reputation change is real change. If leaders (or anyone for that matter) change their reputations, they have in essence made behavior changes that others have observed. Consider a hypothetical salesman named William who is being considered for a sales management position. William regularly yells at employees, overreacts to difficult situations, and exhibits significant mood swings. His workplace reputation may be one of a person who lacks the necessary executive disposition needed to lead others. It is the perceived reputation that will have a deleterious effect on William's potential for promotion to a leadership position.

Furthermore, if William manages to make the behavior changes necessary so that others do not observe the overly emotional behaviors, the perceived reputation might be entirely different. William might be seen as calm, cool, and collected despite the fact that inside he might be a seething cauldron of boiling emotion. No one will be concerned with what is going on inside the person. The only thing that matters is that the perceived reputation is one of an individual who possesses the emotional demeanor necessary to lead others. In essence, the barrier to promotion (overly emotional behaviors) is removed by William's actively engaging in changing his reputation to be perceived by others as calm, cool, and collected.

Does this mean that William actually changed his personality? It probably does not, at least in the short term. William likely has the same natural tendencies to become overly emotional as before he managed to make changes to his behavior. However, what really matters is that his reputation is one of being calm, cool, and collected. It also means that he will have to remain vigilant and not let the overly emotional behaviors creep back into his repertoire and rekindle a reputation that is more closely aligned to his natural tendencies. Over time, it is the case that a degree of personality change will occur as the substituted behaviors increasingly become a part of the individual's natural tendencies. Such a transformation likely takes considerable time and essentially involves the individual's thinking of himself as calm, cool, and collected; but, such a transformation is really not important. What is important is the perceived reputation.

Robert and Joyce Hogan were the first psychologists to focus on the assessment of personality from the standpoint of reputation. It was this step that brought personality to the forefront of understanding and predicting behavior in all walks of life, including the workplace. Suddenly, the "you that you know" was hardly worth knowing. It was the "you that we know" that was responsible for life's successes (or failures). Moreover, the "you that we know" is observable, behavioral, and most important, able to change with focused development. This attention to reputation transformed the notion of personality from a topic reserved for the clinical couch to a topic that could form the foundation of personal development.

Purpose of the Book

The purpose of this book is to build upon the notion that it is reputation that drives success in the workplace. Reputation is the accumulation of past behaviors observed by others that are used to form their opinion of an individual. Reputation is driven by one's natural tendencies as measured by Hogan personality assessment inventories. Reputation, because it is rooted in behavior, can be measured and developed with focused behavior-change efforts.

Over the past 25 years, as we have taken this approach to personality assessment, we have accumulated a massive database regarding behavior in the workplace. Our foundation in research has resulted in hundreds of validation studies covering virtually every job associated with the Dictionary of Occupational Titles. Furthermore, our research archive allows us to build a success profile for these jobs. We know the behaviors that drive success and the ones that are responsible for failure.

Early in 2000, we added a significant focus on leader behavior when we implemented the Leadership Forecast Series of reports based on the assessment results of the Hogan Personality Inventory (HPI), the Hogan Development Survey (HDS), and the Motives, Values, Preferences Inventory (MVPI). We implemented a feedback process for leaders based on the results of these reports. It was designed to raise leaders' self-awareness regarding their reputation in the workplace based on their natural tendencies as measured by our assessments. It was not long before leaders who experienced this type of feedback not only appreciated the increased self-awareness, but they also wanted to learn about tips and techniques they could use to remediate behaviors that were hurting their reputation and strengthen those behaviors that led to improvement in their reputation.

This focus on reputational leadership pushed Hogan (traditionally an assessment firm) directly in the path of coaching and leadership development. Leaders wanted us to provide them with the coaching needed to help them develop and refine their leadership behaviors. Organizations wanted to use our assessments as a foundational component in their leadership development programs. Throughout the 2000s, we accumulated considerable knowledge regarding the development of leaders both at an individual and organizational level. As our expertise grew, it became clear that we could not hire consultants fast enough to keep pace with the growing need for experts who could help individuals and organizations utilize our assessment inventories to improve leader performance. The best way to meet this growing need was to establish the Hogan Coaching Network (HCN), a group of independent consultants fully trained in Hogan assessment inventories with expertise in developing leaders.

The combination of Hogan assessment consultants with external independent consultants resulted in a powerful combination of skill sets. The Hogan assessment consultants helped organizations build world-class leadership development programs, and the HCN provided the expertise needed to support the leaders attending the programs from a feedback and development standpoint. The knowledge accumulated through this partnership is the focus of this book. It includes perhaps the clearest understanding to date of what it takes to be a successful leader, our approach to coaching leaders based on personality assessment results, and a comprehensive description of the development techniques that can help leaders overcome performance challenges to reach their full potential.

STRUCTURE OF THE BOOK

One of the greatest challenges in writing a book of this type is maintaining an overall focus while integrating the thoughts and ideas of a broad array of experts who bring to the table their own perspectives on the topics of coaching and leadership development. Our overall focus for the book was clear from the outset. We wanted to create the definitive guide for using personality assessment as the foundation for helping leaders improve their performance. To achieve this, we believed the book needed to address four objectives:

- Define a leadership philosophy that is rooted in personality psychology.
- Provide a specific description of the mechanisms linking personality to leadership.
- Outline best practices for using personality as a foundation for developing leaders.
- Offer leaders and coaches detailed guidance for ameliorating unsatisfactory leader performance.

These objectives guided the development of each of the five parts of the book. The contributors to each part were selected on the basis of their general expertise in the field of leadership development and for their specific knowledge of the subject matter covered in the various chapters. The result is an essential reference guide for anyone interested in the general topic of leadership development and, more specifically, anyone who views personality as the driving force behind success as a leader.

Part I—Setting the Stage

Robert Hogan has been a life-long student of the topic of leadership. From his early days in the Navy to today as the leader of Hogan Assessment Systems, he has studied and written prolifically on what makes a successful (and unsuccessful) leader. Throughout his life he has been building a model based on the notion that personality is the driving force behind effective leadership. His views came under enormous criticism through the 1970s, 80s, and 90s. Even today, his views continue to be controversial and often challenged by those in the mainstream of psychology. Throughout all of these challenges, he tenaciously held to the belief that human survival depends on groups, leaders drive group success, and leader effectiveness is rooted in personality.

Part I has only one chapter—"The Hogan Leadership Model." The chapter formally outlines Robert Hogan's model of leadership. It directly ties the personality assessment inventories Dr. Hogan has spent a career developing to the measurement of leader effectiveness and potential. The chapter is so fundamental to understanding the rest of the book that we decided to set it apart from the remaining chapters. It represents Dr. Hogan's most comprehensive description of his model of leadership and is the culmination of a lifetime of work studying the topic.

Part II—Role of Personality in Coaching

Increasingly, the business community is recognizing the key role personality plays in the performance of a leader. Cognitive ability continues to play an important role in that it does take a certain level of intelligence to process the complexities a leader may be faced with in the challenging business environment that exists today. Pure intelligence only goes so far, and a case could easily be made that it is actually business knowledge or competence that is the true variable in play. However, the literature is replete with examples of really smart leaders who have failed miserably. In many, if not most, of those cases a sober examination of the facts will reveal that personality is at the core of the explanation for these derailed leaders.

Part II provides a systematic overview of the personality mechanisms at work in the performance of a leader. We focused on the personality characteristics measured by the Hogan Development Survey (HDS), the industry's leading inventory for assessing characteristics most often associated with leader derailment. We decided to focus on the HDS for two reasons. First, the HDS provides a comprehensive taxonomy of personality-related behaviors most often associated with the success or failure of leaders. Second, there is a growing body of evidence that leaders can improve their performance when armed with the insights derived from the HDS that result in focused development. For these reasons, the HDS provides the perfect foundation for structuring a personality-based approach to improving leader performance.

Chapter 2 uses actual results of coaching interventions to highlight how leaders can change. The examples illustrate the power of the HDS to point to development issues and guide the implementation of coaching interventions where positive behavior change was achieved. Chapter 3 provides a systematic description of the concept of Strategic Self-awareness. This concept is so central to behavior change that it deserved a thorough discussion of the Hogan perspective in relation to leadership development.

The remaining chapters in Part II provide a comprehensive look at the HDS from a development standpoint. The HDS has taken on a dominant role in the assessment industry as a necessary component in any serious program designed to improve leader performance. The inventory has recently undergone its fifth revision. The latest version, covered in Chapter 4, includes expanded interpretive content (including the implications of low scores) and newly designed subscales. In Chapter 5, interpretation of HDS results is extended to include Situational Context. This chapter uses a series of nine fully developed case studies to illustrate the role that context can play in determining the impact of HDS-identified leadership derailers. The case studies are carried throughout Part IV of the book in which coaching interventions are tied to HDS-identified leadership derailers.

Part III—Building the Coaching Foundation

When Hogan inventories in general, and the HDS specifically, started showing up in programs designed to develop leaders, there was enormous pressure on the company to move into fee-for-service consulting and especially executive coaching. We resisted this pressure for two reasons. First, our core business is personality assessment, and we wanted to remain true to our core. Second, we work with and supply many of the best consultants and consulting firms in the world that provide leadership development services that leverage our assessments. That said, we recognized that our expertise in developing leaders, especially as it relates to personality, was second to none in the industry. In order to take advantage of this expertise, we founded the Hogan Coaching Network (HCN). The HCN is a highly talented group of professional consultants vetted by Hogan to offer consulting services around our inventories. The HCN is a partnership with individuals and firms that believe as strongly as we do that personality is central to leader performance.

The HCN has evolved over the past 10 years, and much has been learned through that period of time. At the top of the list is a set of practices that all professionals should follow in working with leaders to improve their performance. Part III draws upon the knowledge of some of the best HCN executive coaches with respect to the practices that should be part of any effort to improve leader performance, especially those that include a focus on personality.

Personality data remain some of the most sensitive information available regarding a leader. For that reason, we felt a chapter was needed to establish how a coaching relationship should evolve when it includes personality assessment. Chapter 6 outlines many of the best practices associated with a coaching agreement, and while a coaching agreement may not guarantee a coaching relationship will unfold without problems, we are certain that implementing the type of coaching agreement advocated in this chapter will go a long way toward ensuring a positive experience for the leader and the coach.

Chapters 7 through 9 cover the nuts and bolts of working with leaders from a coaching standpoint. Chapter 7 addresses what personality says about the learner. Perhaps one of the most under-discussed topics when it comes to coaching a leader concerns how a coach should approach a leader from a learning standpoint when the individual's personality profile is known. Chapter 8 offers our most comprehensive discussion to date regarding the topic of delivering effective feedback. The HCN coaches have delivered tens of thousands of feedback sessions. This chapter contains the insights gained from that experience.

Organizations vary dramatically regarding the way they plan, monitor, and calibrate leader development. Chapter 9 covers some of the best practices we have observed in each of these areas. Although it is more descriptive than prescriptive, this chapter should provide those who have opportunities to influence work in these areas with a starting point.

We titled Part III "Building the Coaching Foundation" because every coach in the HCN has experienced what happens when the foundation work is not in place at the outset of the coaching engagement. We believe in the principles that are espoused in Chapters 6 through 9. They are used in all coaching engagements where our HCN coaches are working with leaders. We also believe that they would work well for any coach or leader looking to help others improve their performance.

Part IV—Coaching Techniques for the Dark Side

The most frequent question asked by a leader after receiving feedback based on Hogan inventories is "What's next?" The answer to this question was often dependent upon the person providing the feedback. Experienced coaches had their own development suggestions that they would use to enhance general recommendations found at the end of assessment reports. Leaders participating in more sophisticated company-sponsored programs would often participate in a development planning group session. Some companies even offered their leaders subsequent sessions with coaches dedicated to exploring development alternatives. All of these and other alternatives added value, but it became clear that there was no single authoritative source for development information related specifically to personality-based assessment results.

In Part IV, we systematically address the "What's next?" question with respect to personality and leadership development. The task was daunting from two perspectives. First, there is no shortage of leadership development content. In fact, it is overwhelming and has nearly reached the point of saturation between the Internet, thousands of books, course work, and many other sources too numerous to mention. The problem we faced was that content was not in any way tied to personality-based assessment results or our philosophy regarding the role of reputation change as the key to leadership development.

To address this challenge, we called upon the experts who are part of the HCN. They represent a resource that is unmatched in terms of their understanding of our personality inventories, experience working directly with leaders to improve performance, and accumulation of content that has a proven track record of success—after all, their livelihoods depend on their ability to help leaders improve their performance. The best development content we could possibly offer would be coaching tips and techniques used by the experts in the HCN.

The next major challenge was figuring out how to organize development content in a way that could easily be accessed and employed to improve leader performance. There were all kinds of ideas ranging from a pure competency approach to approaches involving the grouping of similar learning techniques. In the end, the best answer was the most obvious answer. If the scales of the HDS provide a sound taxonomy for understanding leader performance, they should be equally effective in organizing development content. As an example, if a leader is faced with a reputational challenge associated with the Excitable scale, then it would make sense to organize appropriate development content around that scale.

Over a period of nearly three years, we held focus groups with the HCN coaches, engaged them in conference calls, asked them to submit tips in writing, and built a coach evaluation system that included a mechanism for evaluating the effectiveness of development content offered to leaders by HCN coaches. We gathered hundreds of tips and techniques that HCN coaches had employed to help leaders across every scale of the HDS. Next, we assigned a coach champion to each scale on the HDS and charged that person with writing a chapter dedicated to improving leader performance as it related to the scale. We provided them with guidance on what we wanted to achieve in each chapter and gave them a common structure to follow in writing their respective chapters. We also identified a small cadre of coaches (four to six per scale) who were self-identified experts at working with leaders to improve performance related to that scale. These coaches served as advisors and reviewers for each coach champion to ensure the best development content possible was contained in each chapter.

The result of this effort is the first and only vetted compendium of development content dedicated to improving leader performance as it relates to the scales of the HDS, or what has often been referred to as the Dark Side of personality. It spans 11 chapters (one per scale) and covers the full range of challenges at the high and low end of each scale.

Part V—Beyond the Dark Side

The coaches in the HCN treat our inventories much like a prism with three sides: the Hogan Personality Inventory (Bright Side), the Hogan Development Survey (Dark Side), and the Motives, Values, Preferences Inventory (In Side). When discussing the information these inventories bring to the table as a group, our coaches will educate leaders on what each side of the prism addresses:

- Motives, Values, Preferences Inventory (In Side)—Identifies what leaders want out of a job or career.

- Hogan Personality Inventory (Bright Side)—Covers the personality characteristics most important in helping leaders get what they want.

- Hogan Development Survey (Dark Side)—Addresses the personality characteristics responsible for getting in the way of what leaders want.

It should come as no surprise that from a coaching standpoint, behavior change that most readily improves leader performance has its roots in the Dark Side. It should also come as no surprise that viewing a leader's profile from the Bright Side and the In Side can be of enormous value when structuring an effective coaching intervention.

In Chapters 21 and 22, we go beyond the Dark Side to reveal the value the Bright Side and In Side can bring to the performance improvement equation. We decided that we did not want these chapters to cover development content per se. Rather, we wanted them to help further enlighten what is getting in the way of a leader's performance as measured by the Dark Side—HDS. We achieved this objective by focusing on the relationships between the Dark Side scales and their counterparts on the Bright Side and the In Side.

From a content standpoint, we also recognized that there are some excellent general techniques that can add value regardless of the specific performance challenges facing a leader. The HCN coaches would describe these as their go-to techniques that they have come to rely on as part of any engagement. They are also techniques that the customers or sponsors would easily recognize as adding value in helping leaders improve their performance. Chapter 23 outlines these techniques as appropriate for Any Side when working with leaders.

We close Part V with a short chapter outlining some of our final thoughts when it comes to coaching leaders based on personality characteristics. Chapter 24 offers our closing thoughts on what was covered, why we believe it is important, and why leaders who address their derailers will enhance their own career prospects and the lives of those they lead. This book is a long journey. It was not meant to be a paperback novel with a surprise twist at the end.

AUDIENCE

This book is the most comprehensive treatment of the role of personality in coaching and leadership development to date. It outlines the Hogan position on leadership and the way personality impacts leadership performance (topics covered in Parts I and II). The book establishes the best practices for working with leaders when personality is a central component in the development equation. Part III goes into great depth on this topic followed by Parts IV and V, outlining in detail the tips and techniques that can be used to improve leader performance.

We set out to create a book that would have appeal to a broad audience. We wanted it to be a reference guide that could be found on the desk of anyone interested in the topics of personality and leadership. For those working directly with leaders to help them improve their performance, we wanted to provide a practical guide that is useful in supporting their coaching efforts. For leaders who are interested in improving their own performance or the performance of those around them, we wanted them to have access to the same tips and techniques that have worked so well for professional coaches. Finally, we wanted to leave no doubt as to where Hogan sees the role of personality as it relates to coaching and leadership development.

We hope this book will have a positive impact on the performance of all leaders touched by its content.

ACKNOWLEDGMENTS

This book was first conceptualized more than four years ago during the annual conference of the members of the Hogan Coaching Network (HCN). The focus of the conference was to begin organizing coaching content that could effectively address development issues identified for leaders who had completed Hogan inventories. The coaching content collected during the conference from some of the best coaches in the world was truly amazing. We identified hundreds of coaching tips and techniques that had been proven to be effective in improving leader performance. It was clear following the conference that an opportunity existed to create a reference book that would be of considerable value to leaders and coaches engaged in leadership development activities.

We discussed at length how best to complete the book, and we decided to enlist the support of the HCN members. Those who made major writing contributions are acknowledged as contributors in the book. We also want to thank a number of other members of the HCN who offered their insights and helped shape our thinking over the past three years. These coaches include David Brookmire, Margaret Butteriss, Cheryl Cerminara, Ben Dattner, Andrea Facchini, Jorge Fernandez, Karin Fulton, Jill Geehr, Fraser Clark, Dale Hayden, Bill Hector, Terry Hollon, Andreas Janz, Jennifer Johnson, Warren Kennaugh, Ed Marks, Sid Nachman,

Mary Nelson, Pradnya Parasher, Tom Patterson, Mirna Perez Piris, Diarmuid Ryan, Mitch Shack, Julie Shuman, Alan Siegel, and Kristie Wright.

A book of this scope also requires a great deal of work behind the scenes with respect to layout, formatting, and editing. We would like to thank Natalie Tracy and Sheryl Melton for their editing support on early drafts. In addition, we want to thank Kelly Thomas, Julie Warrenfeltz, and Steve Nichols for their diligence in helping us through the final editing process.

Finally, we would like to thank our colleagues for their willingness to review the book and provide us with their thoughts and ideas. Their contributions helped us to make significant improvements to the final version of the book and ensure that the content fully aligned with the theory and philosophy that are central to the success of Hogan Assessment Systems.

Many thanks to all those who helped!

Rodney Warrenfeltz   Trish Kellett

April 2016

ABOUT THE EDITORS

RODNEY WARRENFELTZ, PhD

Rodney Warrenfeltz, PhD, is a managing partner with Hogan Assessment Systems. He has more than 25 years of consulting experience in leadership assessment and development. He joined Hogan in 2000, focusing primarily on the selection and development of leaders.

Prior to joining Hogan, Dr. Warrenfeltz was executive vice president and national practice leader for coaching and consulting services at Manchester, Inc. He was also a vice president at Development Dimensions International (DDI) and was responsible for establishing a consulting business focused on the assessment and development of executives. In this role, Dr. Warrenfeltz developed one of DDI's most successful practice areas, which included a worldwide consulting team of more than 50 professional psychologists and executive coaches.

Dr. Warrenfeltz's early career included talent management positions at PepsiCo, Lockheed Martin, Colorado Department of Transportation, and IBM. Also, as program director from 1978 to 1980, he helped to establish Progressive Directions, Inc., one of Tennessee's largest and most successful centers for supporting those with intellectual disabilities.

Dr. Warrenfeltz has more than 100 publications to his credit, including coauthoring *The Hogan Guide: Interpretation and Use of Hogan Inventories*. He is also the author of *The Legend of the Princess Heart Crystal*, a leadership novel for middle grade and young adults. He has an MS in psychology from Vanderbilt University and a PhD in industrial psychology from Colorado State University.

TRISH KELLETT, MBA

Trish Kellett is the director of the Hogan Coaching Network (HCN), an elite team of consultants who are experts in interpreting Hogan inventories and coaching leaders. Since joining Hogan in 2010, she has grown the HCN from 15 domestic coaches to more than 50 coaches worldwide.

Prior to joining Hogan, Ms. Kellett spent 15 years in the leadership assessment, development, and coaching industry. She was a consulting practice leader for Manchester, Inc., where she developed their certification program for executive coaches. At Manchester and later in her own practice, she worked with leaders across myriad industries and functions to enhance their own effectiveness and that of their teams.

Before becoming a consultant, Ms. Kellett was an accomplished executive at AT&T and National Service Industries. She successfully led organizations as large as 2,000 people and managed annual revenue streams as large as $650 million. Ms. Kellett brings to client organizations both a line manager's perspective and understanding of their issues and a consultant's expertise to develop solutions.

Ms. Kellett is a Phi Beta Kappa, Magna Cum Laude graduate of Duke University, with a BA in mathematics, and she received her MBA from the University of Miami. While at AT&T, she completed the Program for Management Development (PMD) at Harvard Business School.

ABOUT THE CONTRIBUTORS

LISA S. ARONSON, MBA, PCC

As an executive coach with more than 20 years of experience, Lisa Aronson has partnered with many organizations to ensure that executives achieve their leadership aspirations and maximize their impact. Considered an expert in expanding leadership capability, developing high-potential talent, and implementing behavioral change, Lisa works as a coach to make certain that the skills leaders need and their approaches align with their intentions. Lisa is sought out for a style that includes direct, honest, and actionable feedback offered in a supportive framework.

Lisa's broad experience includes working with multinational clients in many industries—financial services, technology, consumer products, and pharmaceuticals—and in many disciplines—finance, marketing, law, operations, and the sciences. Additionally, Lisa is a coach at the Wharton School at the University of Pennsylvania, working with visiting senior global executives and MBA students. She holds an MBA from the Fox School of Business at Temple University and has completed post-graduate work leading to certification as a Professional Certified Coach by the International Coach Federation.

RONALD M. FESTA, PHD

Ron Festa, president of New Heights Consulting, has over 20 years of experience developing and implementing practical, business-driven solutions. Ron holds an undergraduate degree in psychology, a master's degree in industrial psychology, and a PhD in industrial/organizational psychology. Ron's training in psychology, coupled with over 17 years of corporate experience and more than 15 years as an organizational consultant, provides a strong foundation for delivering highly impactful leadership solutions to complex business challenges. In addition to his organizational consulting activities, Ron has been a featured speaker at numerous conferences and workshops.

Ron is a recognized expert in the areas of leadership development, executive coaching, assessment/selection, board/team development, change management, and organization development. He has achieved significant levels of success in helping executives achieve breakthrough performance through a business-oriented focus to leadership development, while addressing key organizational challenges.

Ron is a member of various professional associations, including the American Psychological Association and the Society for Industrial and Organizational Psychology.

RAYMOND P. HARRISON, PHD

Ray Harrison has over 20 years of experience as an executive coach, consultant, author, and psychologist. Ray is managing director of Executive TransforMetrics LLC (ETM), an organization founded in 1999 and devoted to helping executives and their teams create *meaningful* and *measurable* impact. ETM provides services worldwide to assist organizations in executive assessment, coaching, executive search, career development and transition, and team leadership.

Ray received his PhD in psychology from Pennsylvania State University. His postdoctoral education has included advanced study at the Wharton School at the University of Pennsylvania, where he taught for 10 years. Prior to founding ETM, he served as a regional general manager and as national practice leader for Executive Development and Career Services at Manchester, Inc.

Ray is a past president of the Industrial/Organizational Division of the Pennsylvania Psychological Association. He is also on the coaching staff of the Center for Creative Leadership (CCL). He is a long-time user/coach/consultant to Hogan Assessment Systems in its ongoing effort to link assessment with effective executive performance.

ROBERT T. HOGAN, PhD

Dr. Robert Hogan, president and founder of Hogan Assessment Systems since 1987, is an international authority on personality assessment, leadership, and organizational effectiveness. His theory-based work in personality measurement contributed to the development of socio-analytic theory, which maintains that the core of personality is based on evolutionary adaptations. He is widely credited with demonstrating how personality factors influence organizational effectiveness in a variety of areas, ranging from organizational climate and leadership to selection and effective team performance.

As an iconoclastic observer of American psychology, Dr. Hogan maintains that personality is best examined from the perspective of the observer (reputation) rather than the actor (a person's identity). As a consequence, he asserts that personality tools should be evaluated in terms of how well reputations (defined by personality tests) predict behavior on the job and in relationships.

Dr. Hogan is the author or coauthor of more than 300 journal articles, chapters, and books including *Personality and the Fate of Organizations*. His recent author, coauthor, and editing credits also include: *The Hogan Guide, Personality: Theories and Applications, The Handbook of Personality Psychology, The Perils of Accentuating the Positive*, the Hogan Personality Inventory, the Hogan Development Survey, the Motives Values and Preferences Inventory, the Hogan Business Reasoning Inventory, and the Hogan Judgment Inventory.

Dr. Hogan received his PhD from the University of California, Berkeley, in 1967, specializing in personality assessment. He served as McFarlin Professor and chair of the Department of Psychology at The University of Tulsa for 17 years. Prior to that, Dr. Hogan was professor of Psychology and Social Relations at the Johns Hopkins University. He is a fellow of the American Psychological Association and the Society for Industrial and Organizational Psychology. Dr. Hogan participated in grant review panels and committees for the National Science Foundation, National Institutes for Mental Health, National Institute for Education, National Endowment for the Humanities, Spencer Foundation, and the MacArthur Foundation.

RONALD M. JOAQUIM, MS, MBA

Ron Joaquim has more than 30 years of business experience during which he held executive positions in sales, service, information technology, materials logistics, and technical support. An accomplished executive with profit and loss experience, his achievements include running a business with over $1 billion in annual revenues, leading groups as large as 4,000 people through complex business transformations, and leading a worldwide consolidation project that resulted in $200 million in annual savings. He now uses his broad business background and perspective to provide results-focused consulting services in the areas of executive assessment and coaching, leadership development, organizational development and effectiveness, strategic planning, and change management. He understands the challenges his clients face, the pressures they are under, and the behaviors that are required to be an effective leader.

Ron received a BA in marketing from Providence College, and an MS in marketing and an MBA from the University of Rhode Island. He attended the INSEAD International Executive Development Program and the Dartmouth College Executive Management Program.

Elaine Kamm, MS

Elaine Kamm is an experienced leadership coach, consultant, and group facilitator. Once the head of a corporate talent development function for a Fortune 100 organization, she went on to establish her own consulting practice, EKGroup, where she has worked with thousands of professionals, managers, and executives in multiple functions, levels, and industries in both the for-profit and not-for-profit sectors, nationally and globally. In addition to her extensive leadership development and executive coaching work in organizations, she has developed and taught leadership development programs for Cornell University's ILR School for 15 years and is on the faculty of Rutgers's Program for Executive and Professional Education. Elaine's specialty is working with clients to leverage the talents and experience they already possess to achieve their goals and address their challenges, and then provide value added, tangible strategies and support.

Elaine received her master's degree from Stevens Institute of Technology in organizational behavior and holds numerous professional certifications, including being a Certified Physician Development Coach. She is a member of the Hogan Coaching Network and is a Hogan Assessment Certification Workshop facilitator.

Douglas Klippel

Doug Klippel is an experienced human resources consultant who is currently the president of People Development Partners LLC, a Florida-based management consulting firm. Trained as an industrial psychologist, Doug has served in a variety of corporate and private consulting roles, including eight years of employment at Hogan Assessment Systems. For several years, Doug also served as a member of the teaching faculty at the University of Tennessee College of Business. Doug has over 20 years of experience using the Hogan tools for both management development and employee selection purposes as well as helping craft the Hogan LEAD series of reports while a member of the Hogan team.

Doug's consulting work focuses on executive coaching, succession planning, selection systems for executives and managers, and executive retreats. He also provides expert-level interpretations of Hogan profiles for consultants who are more casual users. He has been a member of the Hogan Coaching Network for over six years and uses the Hogan tools extensively in his consulting practice.

Patrick Lagutaris, BS

Patrick Lagutaris is a professional leadership coach with over two decades of real-world business experience. After 15 years of coaching Hewlett Packard leaders, he opened his own practice in 2006 to make a difference in the lives of leaders.

Patrick has a strong track record working with leaders at all levels across diverse industries. He uses cutting-edge assessment tools and a customized, collaborative approach to grow their skills and to help them develop new strategies to tackle challenges head on—from finding the right talent for the team and instilling a culture of innovation to driving performance and exceeding the status quo.

Patrick's approach is honest and straightforward, and he holds up the mirror to uncover leadership strengths and liabilities. Together with his clients, he develops a plan to put leaders on a fast track that gets them from where they are today to where they want to be.

Joy McGovern, PhD

Joy McGovern is an accomplished industrial/organizational psychologist who helps leaders achieve their goals through assessing, consulting, coaching, and facilitating. She has over 20 years of experience, spending the first half of her career working in leadership development for corporations and working for consulting firms since then. Currently, she is the managing principal of her own firm, the McGovern Group. Her areas of expertise include preparing leaders for global roles, innovation, assessment centers, team development, and culture change.

Joy is an enthusiastic and energetic presenter who is often an invited speaker at conferences and special events. She has been quoted in *The Wall Street Journal* and *The New York Times* and has been interviewed on numerous other local, national, and international media outlets. Early in her career she won the annual Yoder-Henneman award for Creative Applications of Personnel Research from the Society for Human Resource Management. She was the key author of a groundbreaking study on the return on investment of coaching and a major contributor to *Developing Your Global Mindset: The Handbook for Global Leaders.*

Daniel Paulk, PhD

As senior designer for Hogan Assessment Systems, Dan Paulk develops and delivers comprehensive certification training programs for Hogan Assessment Systems on their proprietary assessment tools.

His career history reflects a combination of business and organizational psychology experiences. Dan is a licensed applied psychologist with particular expertise in pre-employment evaluation, assessment center evaluation, executive coaching, career development, adult learning, and professional development issues.

Dan has a PhD in industrial/organizational psychology from Georgia State University and has published extensively on a variety of business psychology topics. He has won several prestigious awards for multimedia programs he created and produced.

ELIZABETH REEDER, MBA, PCC

Betsy Reeder is an executive coach with extensive experience in the pharmaceutical, health care, and consumer product industries. Before starting her own executive coaching practice in 2002, Betsy spent more than 20 years in a variety of human resources leadership roles for Bristol-Myers Squibb. While there, she also played a lead role in the creation of the Center for Leadership Development and the design and implementation of a comprehensive array of leadership development programs and tools.

In her executive coaching practice, Betsy has worked successfully with senior and high-potential leaders in many Fortune 100 organizations. The primary areas of focus for her coaching include enhancing leadership impact and influence, strengthening stakeholder relationships, leading organizational change, and building high-performing teams.

Betsy holds a master's in business administration and a bachelor's degree in commerce and industrial relations from Rider University and has completed additional graduate studies in evidence-based coaching at Fielding Graduate University. She is a Professional Certified Coach through the International Coach Federation.

SUSAN TOBACK, PhD

Susan Toback is a psychologist with 20 years' experience working in psychological assessment and development. Drawing from her extensive background in human development, psychology, linguistics, and communications, Susan has a deep understanding of human capital and the issues business executives face today. Although Susan has expertise as a psychologist, coach, and consultant, her specialty is working with international and U.S.-based senior executives and high performers.

In addition to her client and consulting work, she has regularly facilitated Hogan Assessment Certification Workshops, the Hogan Assessment Advanced Workshops, and team development sessions utilizing the Hogan instruments. Susan has successfully developed two private psychotherapy practices, taught human development and personality theory at Duquesne University, and run several qualitative research projects.

Susan holds a PhD in clinical psychology from Duquesne University, an MA in psychology from Seattle University, and a BA in rhetoric and communications from the University of Virginia.

AUDREY WALLACE, MS

As the senior manager of Hogan's Independent Consultants team, Audrey Wallace works hand in hand with Hogan's network of independent consultants, coaches, and practitioners who leverage Hogan as their assessment provider. She was influential in the creation of this network and acts as a business strategist through consultation around client engagements, assessment interpretation and coaching, and business applications. Since 2012, she has grown this network to include over 600 coaching and consulting firms.

Audrey brings over a decade of consulting experience to provide strategic direction around incorporating psychometric tools into coaching, employee selection, on-boarding, team building, high-potential, and leadership development engagements. She facilitates project deployments for many Fortune 500 companies and partners with clients to explore business development opportunities, design assessment-based talent management solutions, and facilitate team and leadership development workshops.

Audrey holds an MS in industrial/organizational psychology and is certified as an executive and organizational coach through Columbia University's Coaching Certification Program.

VALERIE WHITE, PhD

Valerie White is a global assessment and leadership development specialist and an executive and life coach. She has been a decades-long partner with several Fortune 500 companies, helping them enhance their leadership pipelines, and she serves in advisory roles to consulting organizations. A member of the Hogan Coaching Network, she is also a trained facilitator for Hogan Assessment Certification Workshops. She is a licensed clinical psychologist who has extensively studied energy psychology and medicine methodologies. Valerie uses these approaches to assist her clients in attaining their professional and personal goals.

She is coauthor of *First Impressions: What You Don't Know About How Others See You*, published in 17 languages and a Books for a Better Life nominee. She is also a contributing author to *Developing Your Global Mindset: The Handbook for Successful Global Leaders* and to a number-one Amazon best seller, *Pathways to Vibrant Health and Well-Being*. Valerie has been interviewed by NPR, the *Today Show*, MSNBC, *Good Morning America*, the BBC, *The Times* of London, and numerous other media outlets.

NICOLE ZUCKER, MA

Nicole Zucker has over a decade of internal and external consulting experience, including six years as a member of Hogan's research and consulting teams, respectively. For the last seven years, Nicole has been a member of the Hogan Coaching Network and served as an expert reference and content creator for consultants who use the Hogan assessments to support a wide variety of talent management initiatives.

Nicole has extensive experience providing developmental feedback, and her written work forms the basis for many consulting firms' and corporations' reports. Trained in industrial/organizational psychology, Nicole particularly enjoys assisting clients with all matters related to psychological assessment, report design, content creation, data integration and interpretation, leadership development, and competency modeling.

COACHING THE
DARK SIDE OF
PERSONALITY

PART I

SETTING THE STAGE

CHAPTER 1

HOGAN LEADERSHIP MODEL

ROBERT HOGAN

BACKGROUND

Two experiences explain my obsession with leadership. The first concerns my career in the U.S. Navy. I worked my way through college and then signed up for the Navy. When I reported aboard ship, I thought I knew how to manage blue-collar employees. The other officers seemed to think working-class people were social inferiors. I was frequently criticized for treating sailors with respect, even though my department performed well. My unorthodox personnel approach stimulated a lifetime concern for understanding the best way to treat employees.

The second experience concerns my academic career. In graduate school, I learned that social psychology had shown that there are no individual differences in leadership effectiveness. In 1968, Vincent Lombardi, the legendary coach of the Green Bay Packers, joined the Washington Redskins, a team that had been terrible for years. I vividly recall thinking that if leadership was real, Lombardi would fix the Redskins, and indeed, Washington made the playoffs in his first year. At that point I became determined to demonstrate to academic psychology that leadership matters.

My thinking about leadership was shaped by (1) social psychology, (2) small group research, (3) sociology, and (4) psychoanalysis. Social psychologists study how people behave in public. They claim that what people do depends on their circumstances, not on their character or personality. This thought process creates a "shit happens" theory of leadership—if leadership depends on situational factors, then how well groups perform is a random walk—and the Lombardi anecdote repudiates this view. Later, in the early 1990s, I studied small group research, looking for lessons about leadership. Small group research concerns how people behave in formal groups. Research shows that leadership, in fact, affects how people behave in groups, which is progress; however, the research never asks about differences in between-group performance (i.e., why some groups perform better than others), which seems to be the bottom line.

Sociology has some important lessons for psychologists. Psychology studies individuals who create culture; sociologists study culture, which they believe creates individuals. Specifically, sociology argues that people are born into preexisting social structures (families, groups, religions, economies, educational systems, etc.) that shape their thinking in profound but unconscious ways through values. People have deep, organic needs for their culture, and when cultures fail, people become confused, alienated, and lost. People need their groups, and they only become individuals in the context of group identity—for example, Jersey girl, hipster, and metro-sexual are all forms of group identity. Sociology also argues that leadership is real and that social groups create the leaders they need, but sociology never asks why some groups, societies, and cultures thrive while others fail.

Freud (1913) provides some important insights about leadership. He believed that (1) leaders powerfully shape societies and history, (2) leaders have distinctive personalities, and (3) followers' personalities determine how they respond to leaders. Freud mistrusted political leaders in general and revolutionary leaders (e.g., Napoleon Bonaparte) in particular. He also believed that most people crave external guidance, a need that is potentiated during crises. Revolutionary leaders exploit these needs to assume leadership roles. Freud described revolutionary leaders as narcissistic, psychopathic, egoistic, and demanding; yet, their followers "fall in love" with them. As Nicholson notes,

> When leaders evoke such visceral feelings in followers, we are in the territory of pure animal instinct. The leaders know what they are doing—they get a deep animal satisfaction from their dominance—Hitler, Pol Pot, Gaddafi, Idi Amin, Saddam Hussein, Stalin, and many more . . . . It is a model of leadership that has its roots in the deepest areas of animal response—where the most basic emotions of fear and need reside. (2013, p. 20)

Freud provided a good starting point for a realistic discussion of leadership.

Defining Leadership

Academic psychologists use data to support their views, which is fruitful when they ask the right questions and collect the right data. However, when they ask the wrong questions (which often happens), they rarely produce useful practical conclusions about leadership. For example, researchers usually define leadership in terms of the people who are in charge. But the people in charge of large, hierarchical, bureaucratic, male-dominated organizations are the survivors of intense political competition who may or may not have a talent for leadership. The only thing people at the top of different organizations have in common is that they have won political tournaments, and different skills are needed to win different tournaments.

Humans are the products of evolutionary history. In broad terms, human evolution was shaped by two forces. Within groups, evolution was shaped by sexual selection, which concerns characteristics that make females attractive to males and vice versa; these characteristics also promote individual status within groups. Between groups, evolution was shaped by warfare; every aspect of human culture, from medicine to architecture, began as a response to warfare. Over the millennia, the warfare between groups was deadly—ethnic cleansing is an ancient human technology. In a climate of intense conflict, better organized groups have an advantage. People are inherently self-centered; leadership is needed to persuade self-centered people to work together to deal with existential threats to their groups. In this sense, leadership is a resource for a group and a crucial component of effective group performance, and this is how I define leadership—as the ability to build and maintain effective teams. Similarly, leadership should be evaluated in terms of the performance of a team compared to other teams engaged in the same activity.

The distinction between competition within groups and competition between groups parallels the distinction between leadership emergence and leadership effectiveness (Kaiser, Hogan, & Craig, 2008). Leadership emergence involves standing out in a group; organizations reward people who stand out with high-potential nominations, salary raises, and senior titles. In contrast, leadership effectiveness concerns inspiring a winning team, unit, or organization. Most leadership research focuses on people who stand out, but the attributes associated with standing out are different from the attributes associated with helping organizations prosper. For example, in a study of executive career success in Europe and the United States, Boudreau, Boswell, and Judge (2001) found that being selfish, self-centered, and arrogant predicted managers' promotion and compensation, yet the opposite characteristics are needed to inspire high-performing teams (Collins, 2001).

I want to emphasize the fact that being promoted—managing one's career—is different from being a leader—inspiring a team. Luthans, Hodgetts, and Rosenkrantz (1988) studied 457 managers and collected evaluations from their subordinates. They defined two groups: (1) successful managers (people who were rapidly promoted in their organizations) and (2) effective managers (people whose subordinates were satisfied and committed and whose organizational units performed well). They then catalogued the behavior of the two groups. They found that (1) successful managers spend most of their time networking, defined as "interacting with outsiders" and "socializing and politicking" (p. 38); (2) effective managers spend most of their time "keeping people informed," "managing conflict," and "persuading people to cooperate" (p. 70); and (3) 10 percent of the managers in their sample were both successful and effective. This research shows that those who stand out behave differently from those who inspire their teams. Most leadership competency models fail to distinguish between leader success and effectiveness, and this oversight has implications for leader selection and development, employee engagement, and organizational culture.

Leadership Lessons Learned

If we review the leadership literature from the perspective of team effectiveness, we find six practical lessons.

The first lesson concerns the characteristics that people want to see in their leaders. The constant warfare of human pre-history (Van Vugt, Hogan, & Kaiser, 2008) suggests that people may naturally expect certain characteristics in leaders. Kouzes and Posner (2010) devised a simple paradigm for studying leadership qualities: ask people to describe the best and the worst managers they have ever had, using a standardized format. This research reveals that people evaluate leaders in terms of four broad categories (Hogan & Kaiser, 2005).

- The first is integrity (Kaiser & Hogan, 2010). Followers need to trust their leaders. Followers' ratings of the degree to which they trust their leaders are the best single predictor of engagement and team performance (Dirks & Ferrin, 2002).

- The second thing followers want in leaders is evidence of good judgment. Lyndon Johnson's decision to attack North Vietnam and George W. Bush's decision to invade Iraq permanently damaged their reputations for judgment.

- Third, followers expect their leaders to be competent and experts in the business. Terry Semel, one of several failed CEOs of Yahoo, was the only chief executive in Silicon Valley with no background in technology. Leo Apothecker, a failed CEO of Hewlett-Packard, had no background in computers.

- The fourth thing that followers want to see in leaders is vision—the ability to explain why a team is doing what it is doing and why it matters. Vision provides teams with a sense of purpose, inspiring them to work hard to achieve their goal.

These four themes emerge in descending order—integrity is the most important attribute and vision is the least important—but all four are crucial components of leaders' reputations (Lord, Foti, & De Vader, 1984). Conversely, leaders who lack integrity, good judgment, competence, and vision will surely lead their followers to failure.

The second lesson concerns personality and leadership. In the early 1990s, researchers finally agreed that personality has an impact on occupational performance (Barrick & Mount, 1991). Ten years later, researchers agreed that personality predicts leadership emergence (Judge, Bono, Ilies, & Gerhardt, 2002). Across organizations, industry sectors, hierarchical levels, and thousands of managers, people who seem confident, socially appropriate, outgoing, dutiful, and bright stand out from the crowd. The data are perfectly clear: personality is the best single predictor of leader performance that we have.

Collins's book (2001) is a milestone in leadership research because he compared successful versus mediocre companies. Collins studied 11 companies on the Fortune 1000 list between 1965 and 1995 that had 15 years of below-average performance, followed by a transition year, and then 15 years of performance substantially above their industry average. He then identified the factors that separated the 11 winning companies from the others. Collins found that it was new CEOs who turned mediocre companies into great ones. In addition, his 11 highly effective CEOs were a blend of extreme personal humility and "intense professional will"—a fierce and relentless drive to win. Moreover, the new CEOs (in Collins's terms) put the right people on the bus, removed the wrong people from the bus, and put the right people in the right seats—that is, they built high-performing teams by using proper employee selection. Finally, Collins demonstrated that effectiveness always trumps emergence. He gleefully contrasted his humble, self-effacing, but highly effective CEOs with their high-profile, publicity-seeking (emergent) counterparts in poorer performing companies. His research confirms that personality predicts leader performance and that we should say goodbye to the myth of the charismatic, ego-driven CEO.

The third lesson from the literature concerns leadership and employee engagement. Engagement is "a relatively persistent psychological state associated with behaviors that are beneficial to an organization" (Macey & Schneider, 2008). In separate landmark studies, Huselid (1995) and Harter, Schmidt, and Hayes (2002) show that (a) managers' behavior predicts employee engagement and (b) employee engagement predicts business-unit performance. Engagement is a function of how people are treated by managers. When engagement is low, productivity, client satisfaction, and unit financial performance are low and vice versa. Specifically, the quality of the relationship between leaders and followers creates engagement. Gerstner and Day (1997) summarize the consequences of good relationships for organizational performance, and Christian, Garza, and Slaughter (2011) show that relationships are the aspect of leadership most correlated with engagement. Conversely, Townsend, Phillips, and Elkins (2000) show that low quality relationships not only degrade performance but also lead subordinates to retaliate against bad leadership.

The fourth lesson concerns the financial consequences of good and bad leadership performance. Collins's research shows that well-led companies are more profitable than those with average leadership. Research on managerial succession also shows a relationship between leadership and financial performance (Barney, 1991; Barrick, Day, Lord, & Alexander, 1991; Bertrand & Schoar, 2003). Although the estimates vary from 14 percent (Joyce, Nohria, & Roberson, 2003) to 29 percent (Mackey, 2008) to 38 percent (Hambrick & Quigley, 2013) to 40 percent (Day & Lord, 1988), several studies conclude that CEOs account for a significant proportion of variance in the financial performance of large organizations. In comparison, McGahan and Porter (1997) estimate that the industry in which a firm competes accounts for about 19 percent of the variation in financial performance.

Again using organizations as units of analysis, Bloom and Van Reenen (2007) also show that leadership and organizational performance are linked. They evaluated 700 manufacturing firms in the United States, the United Kingdom, France, and Germany in terms of management practices (internal communications, transparency of goal setting, monitoring individual performance, links between pay and performance) and company performance (profitability, sales growth). Country and industry effects explained about half the variance in firm performance. The authors attributed the remaining explainable variance to the quality of the management within organizations (see Collins, 2001). A subsequent study replicated these results with 4,000 Asian manufacturing firms (Bloom, Sadun, & Van Reenen, 2012).

The fifth lesson concerns managerial incompetence. In another milestone paper, Bentz (1967; 1985) reported on a 30-year study of managers at Sears. Sears used a good assessment battery to hire new managers, thereby assuring that they were bright, well adjusted, and socially skilled; nonetheless, half of them failed. Bentz broke the mold—his research shows that the failure rate for managers in American business is substantially higher than anyone expected, and it shows that managers fail for personality-based reasons.

How many bad managers are there? Hogan, Hogan, and Kaiser (2010) identified 12 published estimates of the frequency of management failure which range from 30 percent to 67 percent, with an average of about 50 percent. Note that these estimates concern the number of managers who are actually fired. Many bad managers are never caught. I believe that about two-thirds of existing managers are ineffective, but fewer than half will be caught because they are good at internal politics.

The misery that bad managers create for their staffs has morale consequences. About 75 percent of working adults say the most stressful aspect of their jobs is their immediate boss (Hogan, 2007, p. 106). The National Institute of Occupational Safety and Health (NIOSH) reports that (1) 40 percent of American workers think their jobs are very or extremely stressful and that (2) stress at work is the major cause of health complaints in American life, more than finances or family problems (NIOSH, 1999). Kelloway, Sivanathan, Francis, and Barling (2005) review the effects of bad management on employee health. Bad managers are a mental health menace that imposes huge medical costs on society and ruins the quality of life of many working people.

Finally, the sixth lesson tells us that bad managerial behavior primarily originates in the Dark Side of personality (Hogan & Hogan, 2001). As Bentz (1967) noted, managers fail for a consistent set of reasons: emotional immaturity, arrogance, micromanagement, dishonesty, indecisiveness, poor communications, and so on. Hogan and Hogan (2001) proposed a taxonomy containing the most common counterproductive managerial behaviors. Although the behavior patterns are different, they have the same effect on employees: they erode trust, increase stress, and degrade employee performance. Emergent leaders—those who stand out—are less concerned about their relations with their subordinates, and at the same time, certain Dark Side personality characteristics actually help them stand out.

Assessment Implications

The lessons learned lead to the inevitable question, "What is the profile of an ideal leader?" I start with Peter Drucker's observation that leadership is really about followership, that leadership should be understood in the context of what the followers expect from their leaders. My literature review suggests that followers want to see six characteristics in their leaders, and those characteristics (all with direct links to personality) provide a guide to an optimal assessment profile:

- **Integrity**—Integrity is the single-most important quality for leaders. People with integrity keep their word, honor their commitments, do not play favorites, and work for the good of the team. These behaviors create trust in subordinates. Trust is eroded when people lie, play favorites, self-deal, and behave in unpredictable ways. Low scores on the Hogan Personality Inventory (HPI) Adjustment and Prudence scales powerfully predict delinquency and bad behavior. These tendencies can be moderated by high scores on the HPI Ambition scale. For example, people with low scores on Adjustment and Prudence scales and high scores on the Ambition scale (sales people) have an investment in their careers that damps down their otherwise delinquent tendencies. People with high scores on the Hogan Development Survey (HDS) Excitable, Bold, Mischievous, Colorful, and Imaginative scales and low scores on the Cautious scale tend to be impulsive and unpredictable—qualities that erode their subordinates' trust.

- **Judgment**—Judgment represents an interesting intersection between cognitive ability and personality characteristics. The role of cognitive ability can be captured in the way a leader processes verbal and numeric information. The role of personality is more complex and encompasses decision-making tendencies and style as well as reactions to feedback. The Hogan Judgment Inventory combines measures of cognitive ability and personality characteristics to assess judgment.

- **Competence**—Followers expect leaders to know what they are doing and to be subject-matter experts. Some leaders come to their jobs with a background in the business, but some do not. In the latter case, high scores on the HPI Inquisitive and Learning Approach scales predict the capacity and willingness to learn on the job.

- **Vision**—Followers expect leaders to provide a sense of mission and a hopeful view of the future and to explain why they are doing what they are doing and why it matters. People with high scores on the HPI Inquisitive scale and (especially) on the HDS Imaginative scale are seen as visionary.

- **Humility**—People who are arrogant are always self-confident; however, people who are self-confident may or may not be arrogant. Humble leaders are confident but not arrogant. The HPI Adjustment scale predicts self-confidence—the higher the score, the stronger the self-confidence. The HDS Bold scale predicts arrogance, suggesting that humble leaders have high scores on the HPI Adjustment scale and moderate scores on the HDS Bold scale. Higher scores on the HPI Interpersonal Sensitivity scale and lower scores on the HDS Reserved scale predict sensitivity to social feedback, which also contributes to humility.

- **Fierce Ambition for Collective Success**—Bad leaders are selfish, self-centered, and out for themselves, whereas good leaders work toward collective success. Good leaders are competitive, driven, persistent, focused, and resilient, which are characteristics that can be captured by high scores on the HPI Ambition; Motives, Values, Preferences Inventory (MVPI) Power, Commerce, and Altruism scales; and by lower MVPI Recognition scores.

These six characteristics represent the foundational qualities that followers look for in their leaders. Leaders who seem to come up short on any of these characteristics may struggle in their efforts to obtain subordinate buy-in. At the same time, strengths in these six areas will afford leaders forgiveness when their subordinates detect other weaknesses. These strengths can also help leaders through difficult times with respect to business unit performance. Interestingly, these characteristics also tend to mitigate context or situational variables.

My emphasis on these six characteristics threatens to bring us back to the discredited Great Man theory of leadership. Consider Vincent Lombardi, whom I discussed earlier. Although he exemplified these six foundational qualities, other aspects of his personality also contributed to his success—for example, his ability to deal with the politics of the Green Bay Packers' Board was a crucial element of his success. These six characteristics are necessary but insufficient determinants of leadership effectiveness. Unique circumstances always play a role. For example, leaders who are surrounded by powerful rivals and enemies will always struggle—unless the competitors can be removed.

There are three implications for this view of effective leadership from an assessment standpoint. First, personality is at the center of leader performance. Second, leader performance can be predicted only by using carefully constructed and validated personality inventories. Finally, a comprehensive leadership model must be structured around personality with associated assessments that evaluate and predict leader behaviors that impact business unit (team) outcomes.

The Hogan Leadership Model

The foregoing discussion outlines the Hogan Leadership Model. We can summarize our view by saying that (1) personality drives leadership performance (who you are determines how you lead) and that (2) leadership performance drives business unit performance. Figure 1 illustrates the structure of the Hogan Leadership Model. The model assumes that personality predicts how leaders treat their subordinates. The manner in which leaders treat their subordinates follows three broad paths defined by behavior, values, and judgment:

- Leader behavior mostly concerns providing employees with structure and consideration. The Hogan Personality Inventory (HPI) and the Hogan Development Survey (HDS) predict leader behavior. The HPI concerns people's behavior when they are paying attention and behaving in a socially appropriate manner. The HDS concerns people's behavior when they are not paying attention—when they are tired, frustrated, bored, or just being themselves. Each scale on the HPI and HDS has positive and negative consequences for leader performance, and reviewing these data creates Strategic Self-awareness.

- Leaders' values determine what they pay attention to and what they ignore, what they reward and what they sanction. The MVPI predicts leaders' values, and leaders' values in turn create team or group culture. Certain cultures (e.g., greed and entitlement) are dysfunctional, while other cultures (e.g., quality products and good customer service) are functional. Leaders are often unaware of the kinds of cultures they create, and data from the MVPI can enhance Strategic Self-awareness.

- The decisions that organizations make accumulate over time and create their destinies. Senior leaders' decisions mostly concern projects and people: what to do and who to do it, as in, "Let's invade Iraq and put Donald Rumsfeld in charge." People have different decision-making styles, each of which has characteristic strengths and shortcomings. People also react quite differently to feedback regarding their bad decisions, and some of these reactions are more productive than others. The Hogan Judgment Assessment (HJA) concerns individual differences in decision-making. Because leaders are often unaware of their decision-making biases, the HJA can refine Strategic Self-awareness even further.

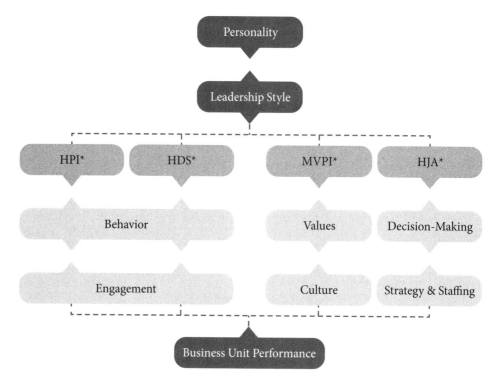

*HPI—Hogan Personality Inventory; HDS—Hogan Development Survey;
MVPI—Motives, Values, Preferences Inventory; HJA—Hogan Judgment Assessment

Figure 1   The Hogan Leadership Model**

In our model, the bottom line for evaluating leadership is business unit perfor-mance. Implicit in the model are not only those personality-driven behaviors, values, and decisions that impact business unit performance directly but also many associated leader characteristics that contribute to a leader's reputation and, ultimately, success in general. Perhaps the best known among these are emergent characteristics, which I referred to earlier in this chapter. While emergent char-acteristics are distinct from the effectiveness characteristics that directly impact business unit performance, they can play a significant role (positive or negative) in defining a leader's career and are a necessary part of the Hogan Leadership Model.

SUMMARY

My views on leadership are based on a lifelong concern for the consequences that lead-ership has for virtually all collective human endeavor. I have outlined the personality characteristics that determine effective leadership. Strategic Self-awareness involves learning to leverage personality-based strengths and manage shortcomings. The Hogan Leadership Model defines the path leaders can follow to achieve Strategic Self-aware-ness. The chapters that follow provide the guidance needed to make the journey.

** For more information about Hogan inventories, research, or support materials, visit www.hoganassessments.com

PART II

ROLE OF PERSONALITY IN COACHING

Part II focuses on the information necessary to begin formulating an approach to develop leaders that has its roots in personality. Chapter 2 sets the stage with clear examples of leaders who make dramatic changes resulting in improved performance based on insights gained through personality assessment. There are several important commonalities worth highlighting in reference to the examples reviewed. First, in each example reputation change was a critical part of the change equation. Reputation change is what occurs first after a leader begins implementing changes to behavior. Second, there is a cascade effect that often goes unnoticed or unrecognized when leaders make positive changes. Those around the leader can be profoundly impacted by both the effort and the results of behavior change. Finally, the 10 lessons learned that are outlined at the end of the chapter not only can be seen in the examples reviewed but also are pervasive in the approach we advocate for helping leaders develop.

Chapter 3 provides a systematic description of the concept of Strategic Self-awareness. This concept is so central to behavior change that we felt it deserved a thorough discussion of the Hogan perspective in relation to leadership development. Decision-making, a pervasive competency associated with nearly all models of leader performance, is used to illustrate the importance of Strategic Self-awareness from the leader perspective. The chapter also highlights the role coaches play in helping leaders build Strategic Self-awareness using a variety of assessment techniques.

The Hogan Development Survey (HDS) has become one of the most important tools available to coaches when working with leaders. In Chapter 1, Hogan and Hogan (2001) point out that "bad managerial behavior primarily originates in the Dark Side of personality." Chapter 4 is devoted to exploring the Dark Side of personality as measured by the HDS. It includes an overview of the development of the HDS and some of the more technical aspects of the tool from a psychometric standpoint. More importantly, this chapter sets up the interpretive content that coaches must possess if they are to use the tool effectively in coaching engagements.

We close Part II with Chapter 5, focusing on the concept of Situational Context. For the purist, Situational Context muddies the waters of the role of personality in effective leader performance. It is true that effectiveness driven by the personality characteristics outlined in Chapter 1 can mitigate the impact of Situational Context. It is equally true that Strategic Self-awareness, essential for leadership success, requires a thorough understanding and vigilant monitoring of one's Situational Context. Furthermore, for effective coaches, it is an essential ingredient in any attempt to fully understand and help leaders improve their performance. We rely upon a series of nine case studies in this chapter that we carry through the remainder of the book in developing our views on coaching content. These cases more than illustrate why Situational Context must be understood for coaching to truly be of value in helping leaders improve their performance.

CHAPTER 2

LEADERS CAN CHANGE

INTRODUCTION

Every year, the American Society for Training and Development (ASTD) releases its annual report on the state of the training industry, and every year the estimated amount of money organizations spend on employee education and development is staggering (e.g., $162.4 billion in the United States alone in 2012). Consistently, they estimate that 15 to 20 percent of that number is spent on some form of leadership development. Furthermore, professionals across the industry are quick to lament that not enough is being spent, it is being spent in the wrong way, the wrong behaviors are being targeted, and on and on. The driving force behind this huge allocation of resources can be found in three basic points.

First, it takes high-quality leaders to drive the success of an organization. Collins (2001) and Bloom et al. (2012) demonstrate convincingly that companies with effective leaders outperform companies with weak or ineffective leaders. Hogan, Curphy, Kaiser, and Chamorro-Premuzic (in press) state that "leadership is one of the most consequential subjects in human affairs." It absolutely matters who is in charge, and it often dictates the success of an organization.

Second, the Conference Executive Board (Kantrowitz, 2014) points out that identifying future leaders is a new global top priority, and Development Dimensions

International (Sinar, Wellins, Ray, Abel, & Neal, 2014) found that among the top challenges faced by CEOs was that their leaders were simply not ready to deliver on needed results. The conclusion is fairly simple. Organizations throughout the world do not have enough effective leaders, and the leaders they do have are not ready to face the challenges that confront them.

Third, leaders themselves are questioning their readiness to take on the challenges they face. Development Dimensions International (Sinar et al., 2014) found that less than two-thirds of leaders said they were either "highly confident" or "very confident" in their ability to be effective in today's volatile, uncertain, complex, and ambiguous world. Unfortunately, these leaders might be more accurate than they know when characterizing their own abilities. About a third of human resources (HR) professionals in the same survey viewed their organization's leaders as incapable of meeting the challenges they face in today's world.

These three points represent the fuel that will drive the leadership development industry for many years to come. The only barrier to growth is a failure to produce results—that is, results in the form of developing leaders who are effective. There are two sides to the results equation: the leaders themselves and the approaches used to coach and develop those leaders. We leave the question of effective approaches to later chapters. The purpose of this chapter is to address the leader side of the equation with a very simple question: "Can leaders change for the better, and how does change come about?"

CAN LEADERS CHANGE FOR THE BETTER?

As frustrating as it may be, probably the best answer is "it depends." Few would argue that leaders *can* change for the better. More often than not, the real challenge is in getting a leader to see the need for a change and then to be willing to put in the effort necessary to make the change. The parallels between individuals making a change and organizations making a change are striking. In both cases, it nearly always requires an unfreezing event, and the scope of the unfreezing event has to be in proportion to the size of the change under consideration. For example, achieving a culture change in an organization that is performing according to plan is extremely difficult compared to one that has just gone through bankruptcy. Similarly, getting leaders to change their interpersonal style when their bosses are telling them they are doing a great job is nearly impossible compared to leaders who have been told they are in danger of losing their jobs without making changes. While these examples are a bit extreme, they underscore the importance of readiness in the change equation. Furthermore, in a study examining the return on investment (ROI) for coaching engagements, McGovern et al. (2001) determined that the most significant factors detracting from a leader's ability to be successful in making a change were related to individual readiness.

The following examples are drawn from the experiences of professional executive coaches who are part of the Hogan Coaching Network (HCN). These examples were selected to illustrate that leaders can change for the better and that those changes can have dramatic career implications. The examples were also selected because they illustrate many of the success factors associated with leaders making changes and the role readiness consistently plays when a change process is undertaken. For each example, there is a situational overview, identification of development targets, analysis of how the engagement unfolded, and a brief discussion of the career impact that resulted from the change. The leaders and organization names have been altered to protect confidentiality.

Example 1—Jane, Vice President and General Manager

Situation

Jane was the recently promoted, sole female member of the executive team of the chemicals division of a large global conglomerate. The company had its roots in engineering and technology. The culture was described as "macho" with a "take no prisoners" approach. Jane, who had a chemical engineering degree and an MBA, had been promoted rapidly through the organization and was known as the "best strategic mind" in the chemicals division. As a mid-level manager in chemical sales, she had excellent relationships with global customers and was able to penetrate markets successfully that had previously been closed to the company. She was known as being relentless in her pursuit of results and being tough on her direct reports. Her peers groused that she was a control freak, a loner, overly aggressive, and hard to deal with. Prior to promoting her to the vice president/general manager role, executive management was aware of her reputation, but they felt that her strategic perspective and ever-increasing revenue numbers trumped her lack of people skills. However, once she was a peer on the executive team and they were dealing with her themselves, her inflexibility and confrontational style became more problematic.

Development Targets

The focus of the behavior change Jane needed to make was on improving her ability to function as a member of the executive team. If Jane could not make serious changes, there was every chance that she would derail in her first executive role. Three development targets were identified:

- Loosen up—Jane needed to be less intense, smile more, make small talk, and in general, not take herself or situations so seriously.

- Not require closure on everything (even the most insignificant items)— Jane had a need for everything to be tied up with a bow. In meetings, she would give her peers her laser stare and grill them with "Who's in charge of this?" "When will you have this done?" "If you won't commit to this, I'll just do it myself," and the like. She had to learn to choose her battles.

- Build relationships—Jane needed to get to know her peers on a personal level. She was a very private person, and she had no interest in a more personal relationship with her peers, but she had to build relationships proactively to survive. She needed to treat her internal relationships the way she treated the external customers, with whom she had excellent relationships.

How the Assignment Unfolded

At first, Jane struggled because the new behaviors were so foreign to her. Her executive team peers laughed behind her back that a "kinder, gentler Jane" was an oxymoron, and they took bets on how long she could possibly sustain the new behaviors. However, when they saw how committed she was to the behavior changes and once they got to know her better personally (due to her reaching out to them proactively), they gradually were won over. The process took over a year, and there were several instances of backsliding on Jane's part, but those instances became less frequent as the behaviors became more natural to her and as she saw that they were yielding positive results. Her direct reports benefitted from the new Jane as well, as she carried over the modified behaviors to her interactions with them. In addition, she became a true believer in coaching and development, and she started employing what she had learned with her staff. The employee engagement scores for her unit climbed significantly.

Career Impact

About two years later, Jane was promoted to lead a larger organization of the chemicals division. About a year after that, the company merged with another global company, and Jane left to become the CEO of a well-known consumer products company.

Example 2—Raphael, Vice President, Brand Management

Situation

Raphael, a Spanish national, was a seasoned multilingual executive with a worldwide Fortune 500 consumer goods company. He had successfully completed assignments in several foreign countries. He was seen as having the potential to be a corporate officer and was brought to the company's U.S. headquarters for further development, and he was given a challenging assignment overseeing all branding activities for a high-volume product line. His strong suits were viewed to be his extensive business knowledge and a hard-driving management style that focused on achieving results quickly. Soon after Raphael's arrival, it became readily apparent that his people management and relationship skills were lacking. His subordinates and peers viewed him as being brusque and unreceptive to the ideas and points of view of others. Additionally, he was reluctant to delegate work and recognize the contributions of his direct reports. The "take no prisoners" management style that served Raphael well in his field assignments was a detriment in his new headquarters position, where collegiality and teamwork were essential for success.

Compounding the situation was the fact that his manager, also a foreign national, was reluctant to give Raphael feedback on his shortcomings. Instead, the manager decided to engage an executive coach for Raphael. While Raphael was the primary beneficiary of the coaching, guidance also had to be provided to the boss to attain the objectives of the coaching engagement.

Development Targets

Identification of development targets for this coaching engagement was challenging because of the lack of feedback and involvement by Raphael's manager. However, the focus was clear: Raphael's management style needed to change in order for him to be successful in a headquarters setting. Three initial targets were identified:

- Heighten self-awareness of undesirable behaviors:
  - Failure to delegate.
  - Always in transmit or "tell" mode.
  - Always working at a frenetic pace and never reaching closure on tasks, resulting in confusion and redundancy.
  - Reluctance to praise or recognize the good work of others.
  - Failure to establish goals and objectives with direct reports and provide timely feedback.
  - The need to develop a more strategic focus.
- Adopt a more professional and refined approach when dealing with senior management.
- Build good working relationships with peers and subordinates, and strive to identify key stakeholders required to be successful.

How the Assignment Unfolded

The coaching engagement was positioned by Raphael's manager as a key factor for him to get promoted to corporate officer. No mention was made of his shortcomings. As a first step, the coach asked Raphael to provide his development goals, and they were significantly different from what others thought needed to happen. Raphael also completed personality assessments. The coach then conducted interviews with key stakeholders, and the difference between Raphael's perceptions and those of others was reinforced. Therefore, considerable time was expended working through specific examples of undesirable behaviors while developing plans and opportunities for Raphael to demonstrate that he had gotten the message. While exhibiting a willingness to change, Raphael resorted to his old behaviors when under pressure. A key incentive for improvement was the fact that a promotion was out of the question unless he demonstrated a much changed *modus operandi*.

The coaching engagement took 15 months, and gradual improvement was realized. The litmus test for judging success was the assessment of Raphael's behavior by his peers and subordinates. The coach also spent considerable time assisting Raphael in preparing for meetings and presentations with senior management. For much of the coaching engagement, Raphael's manager was not actively engaged, although the coach kept him apprised of key developments. Consequently, it was critical that those who experienced Raphael's changed operating style provide feedback to his manager. Upon conclusion of the coaching engagement, it was universally recognized that Raphael had made a marked improvement in the targeted areas.

Career Impact

Within six months following completion of the coaching engagement, Raphael was promoted to a corporate officer position with responsibility for branding strategy development and execution covering five major product lines.

Example 3—Suzanne, Training and Development Professional

Situation

Suzanne was a tenured, experienced, and valued training and development professional in a large insurance company undergoing massive changes. She was struggling with the expectations for her role resulting from the vision of the newly recruited head of HR. Suzanne was a skilled group facilitator and a creative thinker with strong interpersonal skills, and she was respected and extremely well liked by her colleagues and clients. Suzanne was also seen as someone who approached her role as an "implementer" rather than as a strategic business partner, thought leader, and champion of change that the head of HR wanted in the role. The behavioral changes being asked of Suzanne were not familiar or comfortable, and she doubted her ability (and questioned her motivation) to make them. She was also seen as thin skinned and defensive, which were personal characteristics that she had been aware of for many years but had never been able to change. Changes were needed if Suzanne were to retain her position, and the head of HR had serious doubts about Suzanne's ability to make those changes.

Development Targets

The purpose of the coaching engagement was to help Suzanne make the changes necessary to stay relevant and remain satisfied in her changing role. The following development targets were identified for Suzanne:

- Become more of a strategic business partner and consultant, as opposed to an implementer and order taker.

- Become more agile in adjusting to change and managing her defensiveness.

- Find ways to more fully leverage her expertise and relationships in the service of facilitating change in the organization.

- Earn the trust and support of the new head of HR.

How the Assignment Unfolded

A strength-based coaching strategy was selected that would allow Suzanne to capitalize on her passions and natural talents and translate these qualities into actions and initiatives that supported the vision of the head of HR. With the assistance of a comprehensive assessment strategy (personality assessment, multi-rater feedback, structured interview with biographical data) and exploration with the coach, Suzanne put together a development strategy that she fully embraced and that her new manager and the head of HR endorsed and supported.

The plan included Suzanne's channeling her natural inquisitiveness, creativity, and analytical thinking into more strategic and visionary directions. The plan also leveraged Suzanne's passion for supporting others and her strong collaborative and relationship-building skills to become more focused on addressing client business needs. Interpersonally, she was coached to deal more effectively with change, especially with respect to reacting less defensively and learning how to listen and respond to feedback. Lastly, Suzanne was asked to look for ways to use her natural passion and energy to help increase the morale of her coworkers and encourage the participants in her classes to practice new and challenging skills. The coaching engagement included skill building that supported her development goals, and it also provided structured support and guidance for Suzanne as she planned for and implemented new actions and behaviors. Suzanne also leveraged her love of formal learning. With input from her manager and the head of HR, she selected two professional seminars that focused on subject matter that could increase her value to the organization. In fact, she enrolled the head of HR as an internal guide and mentor in her plan.

Career Impact

Suzanne met with the head of HR frequently to solicit ongoing feedback, input, and guidance. She became more comfortable and successful in meetings, discussions, and initiatives that were centered on business issues and that took her into areas where she was reluctant to go before. She began to make significant contributions to her team and her colleagues in the implementation of organizational change. She also became adept at managing her defensive tendencies. Her relationship with the head of HR improved dramatically, and she became a valuable contributor in her newly configured role.

Example 4—Andrew, Change Management Specialist

Situation

Andrew was brought into a company with a very old, entrenched organizational culture and was asked to take on a role as change agent. He was professionally disliked by his team and peers and had been told directly how disliked he was on a professional level. Several people who were interviewed said that they liked him personally but could not stand working with him. He had worked with an on-site coach over the past year with little behavior change in spite of very specific feedback about what was not working and what should be done. Needless to say, Andrew's efforts at facilitating change were not meeting with success.

Additional interviews revealed that Andrew's interpersonal style was abrupt and often rude, and people felt disrespected and actively resisted him at every turn. Several individuals mentioned that they did not want to come to work because of him and that they were tired of providing feedback and not seeing it put to any good use. Aside from Andrew's interpersonal style, the organizational culture was one where being polite was highly valued, and people never wanted to hear bad news. Furthermore, there was considerable resistance to the culture changes that Andrew was supposed to be facilitating.

Development Targets

The focus of this coaching engagement was to help Andrew develop an interpersonal style that worked given the organizational culture. The development targets included the following:

- Taking a step back from the internal coaching he had received, which involved so many suggestions that it was overwhelming for Andrew.

- Ensuring positive interactions in key circumstances.

- Avoiding the need to win at all costs, even at the expense of interpersonal relationships.

How the Assignment Unfolded

It was surprising that Andrew even wanted to continue at the company, given what had been said to him. Furthermore, he was told there was a great likelihood that even if he did make significant changes, they would not be positively received because of the length of time that had transpired and all of the previous feedback he had received. To his credit, he insisted that he wanted to persevere in spite of everything.

The starting point was to build on the fact that many people liked Andrew on a personal level, and the assessment results revealed that he had a strong foundation for exhibiting effective interpersonal skills. The assessment results also revealed that he had a strong interest in helping others grow and develop and that this interest was not being fulfilled. Using this interest as a starting point, Andrew worked at making interpersonal goals a priority. He worked to ensure that people felt respected, valued, and appreciated as part of all interactions and emails. He also worked to demonstrate respect and interest in the ideas of others in working to meet his business goals. It was doable for him to keep one thing in mind, making sure the other person left feeling good after the interaction.

Career Impact

In spite of everyone's doubts that Andrew would be able to make any changes or would ever be bearable to work with, he started receiving feedback from people who were noticing a difference. As a result, Andrew started feeling better and actually started making progress in getting people's buy-in to the changes. He continued to hit bumps, but he became more effective at catching himself and recognizing when he was starting to go off track. The impact on his career was that he actually survived in the company and was an important part of the company's efforts to change the culture.

Example 5—William, Chief Operating Officer

Situation

William was recently promoted from vice president of marketing to chief operating officer for one of the companies in a restaurant conglomerate. He was very young and had made a rapid climb through key positions with virtually no setbacks. In fact, the reason for the coaching engagement was largely a function of concerns about his experience level as opposed to any particular performance issue. Personality assessment and stakeholder interviews were completed at the start of the coaching engagement. The assessment and interviews produced fairly clear results. William was described as a strong leader with a great deal of potential. He was viewed as being innovative with a good strategic perspective on the business. Most of the concerns raised were associated with his interpersonal skills and leadership style. While possessing strong and polished interpersonal skills in general, there were numerous challenges cited with respect to his ability to really connect with people. The most significant challenges surfaced through the interviews and the assessment results. The results revealed the following:

- **Relationship Building**—William's approach appeared to others as utilitarian, lacking a true connection with people. This detachment was noted with respect to direct reports, lower-level employees, and even franchisees.

- **Trust Building**—A related topic was cited regarding William's ability to build trust with people. Again, it was not an issue of his being untrustworthy but whether or not he would be able to reach out and build trust with others.

- **Leadership Legacy**—The company had a significant history of leaders who built a strong legacy. William had observed this trend and believed it was important to build his own legacy within the company.

Development Targets

The coaching engagement was designed around four key elements intended to significantly enhance William's reputation as a leader in a demanding new job:

- **Work-Life Balance**—Maintaining a positive work-life balance, given the demands that were placed on William's time in his new role.

- **Relationship Building**—Recognizing key internal and external stakeholders and making time to nurture those relationships to create an effective network of resources.

- **Trust Building**—Using trust-building skills to repair or build trust among key stakeholders.

- **Legacy Creation**—Identifying a long-term leadership legacy and structuring a development plan that could be executed over time to build his leadership legacy.

How the Assignment Unfolded

This coaching engagement was particularly difficult because of William's self-image. He had not had any setbacks in his career and had just been promoted to a very senior position at a very young age. His perspective was "Why do I need a coach? My career is going great!" As is often the case, the assessment and interview data painted a different perspective. His team viewed him as often disengaged, and a key stakeholder was posing a real problem for him because he had been promoted over her. Additionally, people generally did not know what he stood for other than rising through the ranks with his eye on the CEO position. The coaching engagement started in a fairly simple manner by getting William to understand that simple changes can have a big impact. He had a habit of texting during his team meetings, which left the impression he was disengaged. He was instructed to leave all electronics out of his meetings and request that others do the same. Almost immediately, he started getting positive feedback about the productivity that was being achieved in meetings. This affirmation energized William to want to tackle additional aspects identified through the assessments and interviews. The biggest challenge was a trust issue between William and the key stakeholder. William wanted to see her fired but realized that with trust building on his part, she could become a key ally. Finally, he decided that he wanted to build his leadership legacy around people development. He worked with his HR team to fully revamp the people development programs throughout the company.

Career Impact

The next 12 months were nothing short of amazing. William built the company into the lead revenue producer among the other companies in the conglomerate. His CEO was selected to be the overall CEO of the conglomerate, and William was promoted to the CEO position for his company. He also turned the relationship around with the key stakeholder he was having problems with and ended up helping her get promoted into a key position in the conglomerate.

LESSONS LEARNED

These five coaching examples do an excellent job of representing the types of challenges leaders typically encounter that a professional executive coach can help ameliorate. In a review of these examples, 10 lessons emerge that are critical to ensuring that, when leaders are ready, they can learn:

- Unclear demands or changing job circumstances often create the necessity for learning and, perhaps, the need for professional assistance. The old adage "what got you here won't get you there" exists for a reason. The most successful leaders are those who pursue lifelong learning, recognizing that each new challenge represents a growth opportunity.

- Initial reluctance to incorporate a new behavior because of the past success they have had with old behaviors is a problem for leaders. Incorporating a new behavior is not easy and takes work.

- Assessment data and interview data can play a critical role in unfreezing behavior and in providing guidance to calibrate behavior as learning and development occur.

- It is not always necessary to focus on weaknesses. Sometimes, turning a strength into a towering strength and using a strength to overcome a weakness are more effective strategies to facilitate learning.

- Discomfort and awkwardness are common when leaders start using new behaviors. The feedback is not always positive and may even be negative. It is important to power through the early stages of behavior change to accurately evaluate effectiveness.

- When leaders display a sincere interest in making a behavior change, those around them will inevitably offer their support and help. People have a natural tendency to root for a person trying to improve, especially a person who has a direct impact on their life.

- It does not always have to be a massive behavior change to have a big impact. Sometimes a change that is implemented with sincerity and noticed by those around the leader can produce amazing results.

- Reputation is central to the learning process. Regardless of the perspectives leaders have of their own reputations, their reputations among others are critical to success in their current position and for future opportunities.

- Successfully adopting new behaviors and incorporating them as natural tendencies can be central in leaders' thinking differently and more positively about their leadership abilities.

- Backsliding is perhaps the biggest challenge a leader may face after learning a new behavior. The only safeguard is vigilance in an ever-changing business environment in which the leader is the only constant.

HOW CHANGE COMES ABOUT

The collective experience that Hogan coaches have gained, over more than 25 years of experience working with leaders, has resulted in considerable insight regarding how leaders learn. Perhaps one of the most controversial aspects of the learning process from a Hogan perspective is the focus placed on reputation. The behaviors that combine to form a person's reputation are observable by others. This is particularly true when it comes to learning. It is the observable behaviors that count. People form opinions about a leader based on observable behavior. Those opinions might or might not be accurate, but it is indisputable that those opinions accumulate to form a leader's reputation. It is true that it is a perceived reputation, but perception is reality whether the leader agrees or disagrees with it. Therefore, it should make sense that a development cycle from a Hogan perspective centers on reputation change.

A second unique aspect about the Hogan perspective on learning is that it is couched in terms of a development cycle. Educators often talk of lifelong learning. The concept of a development cycle is that it is continuous learning. It goes on throughout our daily lives whether we are aware of it or not. The key is raising awareness to actively incorporate worthwhile lessons into our behavioral repertoire and, ultimately, into the development of our reputation. Keep in mind that not all learning contributes to a positive reputation. It can be a difficult challenge to determine the impact behavior will have on a person's reputation. For this reason, you will see considerable emphasis placed on awareness in the development cycle and the important connection we make between behavior and reputation.

Finally, we emphasize the importance of internalizing change. One of the most common questions that we receive regarding personality in general and leadership in particular is "How stable is personality or leadership style over time?" It is our contention that such stability requires changes to be internalized to the point that they impact reputation; one's reputation is then modified to the point that not only do others think about the individual differently, but the individual also thinks about himself or herself differently. One of the reasons leaders' results on a personality assessment are so stable is that they truly have to think differently about themselves before those changes will be reflected in the results. This transformation can take a considerable amount of time and is not something that happens in months but in years.

Figure 2 illustrates the Hogan Development Cycle. It contains five steps that operate continuously throughout a leader's career. Change behaviors are happening at all different stages of the model and at many different levels of awareness. The steps we describe below are from an active learning perspective in which it is assumed that the leader is actively pursuing learning or behavior change as would be the case in a coaching engagement or a learning event.

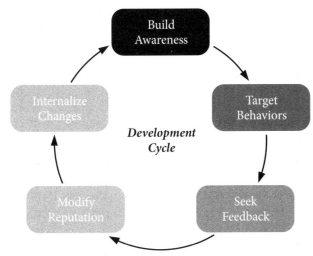

Figure 2   Hogan Development Cycle

Building Awareness requires a person to fully understand "the what and the how" associated with a development need. Targeting Behaviors involves the identification of behaviors to be changed and the development techniques that will be brought to bear in making the change. Seeking Feedback is necessary in order to calibrate progress. Reputation Modification will occur as others observe the changes and begin to respond or act differently around the person. These changes are often subtle, but they do accumulate over time. Finally, a person will begin to internalize the reputation changes, allowing them to become a part of the person's identity. Internalizing the changes is not something a person does actively. It comes as a consequence of the reputation modifications the person has achieved. Internalizing the changes comes as others treat the person in ways that are consistent with the reputation modifications.

For example, consider a common coaching engagement in which a leader (we will call her Christine) has a problem with being argumentative and not taking time to understand the position of those who interact with her. Perhaps she has had some general feedback that has caused her to understand her reputation and, as a result, wants to make a change. A coach, in working with her, might provide some specific examples of the problem behavior gathered through interviews. The coach might also conduct a personality assessment that suggests that Christine is very outgoing but lacks interpersonal sensitivity. Christine has now built considerable awareness around the problem behavior, including what the offending behavior is, how it is manifested, and even the behavioral tendencies that underlie the behavior. The coach then helps Christine target specific behaviors that she needs to change (e.g., overusing "tells" during interactions) and provides alternative behaviors (e.g., using more soft "seeks" and clarifying behaviors to understand the position of others).

Initially, the new behaviors may look forced and somewhat unnatural. Seeking and listening for feedback will allow Christine to begin to calibrate the effectiveness of using the new behaviors. Those around Christine will see the effort and the changes and begin to consider the possibility that her behavior is changing. As Christine's new behavior becomes more consistent, those around her start to form a different opinion of her that slowly accumulates in the form of a reputation change. Others begin to think of and talk about Christine as someone who is truly interested in their views, seeks their opinions, and works to understand their positions. They may even come to expect these behaviors from her. Such changes will inevitably result in Christine's thinking differently about herself to the extent that even her own identity becomes one of a person who looks to seek and understand before considering a "tell."

This description is quite linear and rarely happens that way in the real world. As stated at the outset of this section, the Hogan Development Cycle is a continuous process that happens at many levels across many types of behavior. However, the cycle serves as a way to consider learning as a discrete set of steps that can be actively planned out and executed by a leader to make positive changes. Furthermore, the validity of the cycle can be easily demonstrated from an empirical standpoint using before and after multi-rater assessments built around a professional coaching engagement with a leader. Even something as fuzzy as internalizing changes can be seen in a leader's self-ratings.

SUMMARY

We began this chapter by asking the question, "Can leaders change for the better, and how does change come about?" The evidence is overwhelming that not only can leaders change, but they must change if they are to remain effective in a world marked by volatility, uncertainty, complexity, and ambiguity. The coaching examples presented underscore the kinds of changes leaders can achieve and the lessons that emerge when the process of change is scrutinized. The Hogan Development Cycle is an outgrowth of these lessons. It offers a useful heuristic to guide the change process for leaders and coaches alike. At the foundation of the process is the need for Strategic Self-awareness, which drives readiness. In the next chapter, we will review the concept of Strategic Self-awareness in detail and explore the techniques leaders can use throughout their careers to maintain the high degree of Strategic Self-awareness necessary to meet the challenges of an ever-changing world.

CHAPTER 3

STRATEGIC SELF-AWARENESS

INTRODUCTION

Self-awareness is arguably one of the oldest terms ever associated with the field of psychology. It is typically thought of as becoming in touch with one's feelings and emotions that are trapped in the unconscious waiting to be brought to the surface. This view has its roots in the intrapsychic approaches to personality dating back to the early 1900s. For example, it is the cornerstone of traditional psychotherapy, which continues to flourish in clinical training programs throughout the world. More recently, self-awareness has been defined by social psychologists as "a psychological state in which people are aware of their characteristics, feelings and behavior" (Crisp & Turner, 2010). Unfortunately, even this view of self-awareness does not go far enough in bringing the concept out of the recesses of the mind to a place where it is a useful component in the process of leadership development.

Hogan and Benson (2009) argued that despite its dominance in the mainstream of psychology, the popular view of self-awareness is incorrect. In fact, they go further, stating, "it takes the process of guided individual development in the wrong direction." Their view of self-awareness takes a decidedly different direction that is much more behavioral and, for that matter, measurable.

Self-awareness, or as Hogan and Benson (2009) refer to it, "Strategic Self-awareness," involves knowing your strengths and weaknesses in comparison to those of your competitors in various activities. There are two important distinctions between Strategic Self-awareness and the view of self-awareness held by those who adhere to intrapsychic approaches to personality. First, strengths and weaknesses must be understood in behavioral terms and, as such, can be observed and measured. This is quite different from feelings or emotions, which are the purview of intrapsychic approaches to self-awareness where understanding comes through various forms of introspection.

Second, for self-awareness to be truly strategic, strengths and weaknesses can only be fully understood when compared with those of others, particularly those who form a defined reference group. For example, a soccer player playing at the high school level may be viewed as having superior ball-handling skills. At the college level, those same ball-handling skills might be viewed as average. At the European Premier League level, those same ball-handling skills might not even get the player a tryout. For our soccer player to gain true Strategic Self-awareness, ball-handling skills would have to be evaluated in terms of the level to which the individual aspires, or at least to the level of a defined reference group.

Interestingly, the roots of this view of Strategic Self-awareness actually date back to the writings of Socrates. Hogan and Benson (2009) describe this early take on Strategic Self-awareness among Greek philosophers as follows:

> Socrates' maxim was "know thyself"; he also famously maintained that the unexamined life is not worth living. However, Socrates and the ancient Greeks meant something very specific by self-knowledge. They were a practical people and they defined self-knowledge in terms of understanding the limits of one's performance capabilities—i.e., knowing one's strengths and shortcomings vis-à-vis one's competitors in various activities. (p. 120)

This view of Strategic Self-awareness has considerable utility as the starting point in any leadership development effort. It forms the baseline from which to evaluate current performance and establish a target for future performance. It is important to understand that Strategic Self-awareness cannot be acquired through introspection as mainstream psychology would have you believe. It can only be acquired through systematic, performance-based, behavioral feedback.

FEEDBACK AND STRATEGIC SELF-AWARENESS

Performance feedback comes to us in all different forms. Perhaps the biggest challenge for people trying to improve their performance is determining the useful feedback versus the feedback that is just noise, or worse, inaccurate. Hogan and Benson (2009) suggest that the only useful feedback is negative feedback, which comes via frustration, failure, and defeat. They go so far as to say that there is "no news in good news." This point of view seems to be a somewhat limited perspective and is even a bit inconsistent with the notion that Strategic Self-awareness involves knowing one's weaknesses *and* strengths. (Are people supposed to assume that their strengths are those things for which they have not received negative feedback?) It would also run counter to the training received by most coaches, in that accentuating the positive has a clear role in achieving behavior change.

An alternative view that has a better fit with the notion of Strategic Self-awareness is that feedback has a motivational component that can be positive or negative and an informational component that can be either quantitative or qualitative, or both. According to Connellan and Zemke (1993), "Quantitative feedback tells us how much and how many. Qualitative feedback tells us how good, bad, or indifferent" (p. 102). This approach can be illustrated using the soccer example. Consider the following 2 × 2 matrix (Table 1), which a coach might draw upon to give a player feedback regarding ball-striking ability with the left leg.

If the player is interested in improving ball-striking ability with the left leg, any of the four cells would provide useful feedback. The Informational component clarifies the focus of the feedback. Combining qualitative with quantitative information typically enhances the feedback simply by virtue of the specificity and behavioral nature of the feedback. Equally important is the fact that the Motivational component of feedback can be quite important to the player's Strategic Self-awareness in that the player can gauge the fact that the work being done to improve ball striking with the left leg is producing results. When the Motivational component is positive, it encourages the player to build upon what has been accomplished. When the component is negative, it sets up a performance gap that needs to be closed.

Informational Component		
	Qualitative	**Quantitative**
Positive	**Feedback**—I am pleased with the improvement in your ball-striking ability with your left leg. **Impact**—Qualitative guidance is provided that left leg work was needed and that results are being achieved, and motivation is provided to build on the performance improvement.	**Feedback**—I am pleased with the 20% improvement in your ball-striking force with your left leg. **Impact**—Quantitative guidance is provided that left leg work was needed, a 20% performance improvement has been achieved, and motivation is provided to build on the performance improvement.
Negative	**Feedback**—Your ball-striking ability with your left leg still needs more improvement. **Impact**—Qualitative guidance is provided that left leg work was needed and that results are being achieved, and motivation is provided to close the performance shortfall.	**Feedback**—The ball-striking force with your left leg still needs to improve by 20%. **Impact**—Quantitative guidance is provided that left leg work was needed and that results are being achieved, and motivation is provided to close the 20% performance shortfall.

Table 1   Components of Feedback

The question is, "Which type of feedback is more important from the stand-point of Strategic Self-awareness?" First, specific behavioral feedback from an In-formational standpoint is better in nearly every feedback situation. Beyond that, individual differences start to play a significant role. Some people respond better to positive Motivational approaches and may even shut down when negative ap-proaches are overused. Other people are perfectly fine with negative approaches and tire of the overuse of positive approaches, viewing them as just a form of "blowing smoke." One thing for certain is that Strategic Self-awareness is critical to the process of guided individual development, and feedback is the only way an individual acquires it.

STRUCTURING STRATEGIC SELF-AWARENESS

It is most certainly the case that most leaders do not think about structuring Strate-gic Self-awareness. When seasoned leaders are asked about the feedback they have received during the course of their careers, they will typically point to particular assignments or a mentor or coach who was very helpful. Occasionally, they will cite a particular assessment experience or learning event that they found helpful, but leaders do not describe a structure for cataloging the learning and experience they have acquired during the course of their careers, despite the fact that there have likely been literally thousands of pieces of information that have gone into shaping their awareness.

This failure to consider data presents a problem for three reasons. First, with-out some type of heuristic, the probability of retaining many potentially impor-tant pieces of performance-related feedback is very low. The information just gets mentally stored in a random fashion. Leaders with higher Strategic Self-awareness tend to structure the information in thematic ways regarding their strengths and weaknesses. Second, most experts would suggest that responsibility for personal development begins with the individual. That perspective only works throughout a person's career if he or she is able to maintain a clear, structured understanding of what is needed to improve or build upon. Finally, without structure, pursuing development is like throwing darts at a dartboard blindfolded. You might have a general sense of improvement, but it is doubtful that the improvement efforts will be as effective as they could be with a Strategic Self-awareness structure in place.

One approach for a leader to structure personal Strategic Self-awareness would be to use leadership competencies. This procedure would be a sound alternative if there were any consensus regarding *the* best set of competencies for a leader. Or-ganizations, if they have a competency model, typically use different models at dif-ferent levels, overcomplicate the models, change the competencies over time, and often confound the purpose of the competencies with the need for a communica-tion mechanism for leader performance. Also, leadership competencies are always different across organizations. Because it is becoming increasingly rare for a leader to spend an entire career in one organization, competencies will change each time the leader makes a career change.

An alternative to competencies is to structure Strategic Self-awareness around domains of effective leadership. Competency Domains are clusters of competencies that tend to go together. Hogan and Warrenfeltz (2003) proposed such a model that is based on four domains, including Business Skills, Leadership Skills, Interpersonal Skills, and Intrapersonal Skills. They have demonstrated that this model is quite robust in that it captures most of the competencies that are commonly related to leadership effectiveness (Hogan, Hogan, & Warrenfeltz, 2007).

Hogan et al. (2007) describe the four domains as follows:

- **Business Skills** include competencies that can be done on one's own and usually involve information processing.

- **Leadership Skills** include competencies used in managing others.

- **Interpersonal Skills** encompass competencies used in getting along with others.

- **Intrapersonal Skills** refer to self-regulatory competencies considered to be at the core of how one approaches any work assignment.

The Competency Domains in this model have an important developmental relationship to one another. Intrapersonal Skills develop early in life, followed by Interpersonal, Leadership, and Business Skills. The earlier in life a skill is developed, the more difficult it is to change. For example, it is much easier to develop problem-solving skills (Business Skills Domain) than work attitude (Intrapersonal Skills Domain). This distinction should be considered when choosing development targets. Figure 3 illustrates the four Competency Domains with examples of competencies aligned to them.

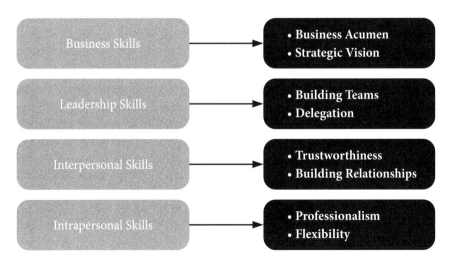

Figure 3   Competency Domains

While this model was originally developed to organize competencies across organizations to compare assessment information, it is equally useful as a mechanism for structuring Strategic Self-awareness. It is built on a foundation of individual development over the full span of a career. It is sufficiently robust to organize any competency model a leader might encounter in any organization. It also can be used to organize development targets and activities.

We have established the importance of Strategic Self-awareness to career development and the role feedback plays in improving awareness. The domain structure offers a robust way to systematically consider awareness needs, target improvement areas, and evaluate progress over time. The following section illustrates how this might work with perhaps the most critical of leadership competencies—decision-making.

DECISION-MAKING AND STRATEGIC SELF-AWARENESS

Decision-making shows up in one form or another in virtually every comprehensive model of leader performance. In some organizations, it might be referred to as Judgment, while in others, it might be referred to as Decisiveness. Regardless, it is a perfect candidate to illustrate the importance of Strategic Self-awareness to career development, the role feedback plays in improving effective performance, and the value a domain structure can play in organizing feedback information over time.

Decision-making in all its forms fits nicely into the Business Skills Domain as defined earlier. It is largely an information processing activity that goes on inside a person's head, with results defined solely in terms of outcomes. Most competencies that purport to define decision-making neglect to consider that it is really a process that requires Strategic Self-awareness in order for performance to improve. Figure 4 illustrates decision-making as a process.

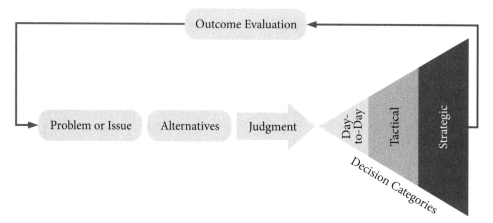

Figure 4   Decision-Making Process

Components for the process include:

- **Problem or Issue**—Anything that creates the need to consciously select among available alternatives.

- **Alternatives**—The known (or unknown) options from which one could select a course of action to address a problem or issue.

- **Judgment**—The act of selecting a course of action from among available alternatives to address a problem or issue.

- **Outcome Evaluation**—Gathering data and monitoring the impact of a selected course of action to calibrate all aspects of the decision-making process.

The outcome of the process is a decision. Decisions vary with respect to two parameters. The first is the amount of **time** that transpires between a decision and the outcome. It can range from immediate (Day-to-Day Decisions) to years (Strategic Decisions). The second is **impact**, which refers to the scope of consequences that result from a decision. It can range from very narrow (Day-to-Day Decisions) to far reaching (Strategic Decisions). Time and impact are continuous variables, meaning that there are an infinite variety of decisions. However, these parameters do provide a framework for classifying decisions into categories. For the purpose of this discussion, decisions are grouped according to three categories: day-to-day, tactical, and strategic.

- **Day-to-Day**—routine emails, scheduling meetings, daily tasks:
  - Some conscious evaluation of alternatives.
  - Impact rarely extends past self and immediate others.
  - Impact is usually narrow in scope.
  - Outcome evaluation occurs in minutes, hours, or days.
- **Tactical**—hiring employees, resource allocations, process changes:
  - Made with a reasonable consideration of alternatives.
  - Impact is often unpredictable, with varying risk.
  - Impact can have considerable scope.
  - Outcome evaluation may require weeks and months.
- **Strategic**—product mix, marketing approaches, make/buy decisions:
  - Made with careful consideration of alternatives.
  - Impact is very unpredictable, with high risk.
  - Impact will have far-reaching scope.
  - Outcome evaluation may require years.

The essential component of this model that is needed to improve decision-making effectiveness is outcome evaluation. It is at this point in the process when Strategic Self-awareness is impacted. Each decision offers a wide range of feedback through outcome evaluation. Some feedback is obtained passively by simply observing outcomes and mentally filing them. Other feedback can be obtained actively by seeking it from those familiar with the decision.

How important is decision-making to a leader's career, and, therefore, how important is it for a leader to possess Strategic Self-awareness regarding his or her decision-making ability? This question was addressed in a groundbreaking study by Brousseau, Driver, Hourihan, and Larsson (2006). They examined the decision-making styles of 120,000 individuals at five levels of management. They were interested in *if* and *how* the decision-making styles change at each level of management. Furthermore, they wanted to know if decision-making styles had a measurable impact on career success. They classified decision-making styles into one of four categories:

- **Decisive**—Those using this style value action, speed, efficiency, and consistency. They stick with a decision and move on to the next decision. Time is an important commodity for those using this style.

- **Flexible**—This style also focuses on speed, but emphasizes adaptability. Individuals using this style will gather just enough data to make a decision and quickly change course if the circumstances call for it.

- **Hierarchic**—Those using this style do not rush to judgment. They are methodical and meticulous in gathering and analyzing data. They expect those around them to contribute, and they are more than willing to challenge the views and decisions of others. The key to this style is that decisions are meant to stand the test of time.

- **Integrative**—Those using the integrative style do not necessarily look for a single solution. They tend to frame situations broadly and take many elements into account. Decisions resulting from this style tend to be broad and may consist of multiple courses of action. This is an inclusive style that is strongly process oriented.

Brousseau et al. (2006) make a number of important points to consider with respect to these styles. First, there is no one best style. An individual may have a dominant style, but is just as likely to move between styles as circumstances dictate. Also, styles tend to vary depending on whether they are being used in a public setting or in a private setting. Brousseau et al. (2006) refer to the public mode as the leadership style and the private mode as the thinking style. Apparently, the presence of people creates situational demand characteristics (e.g., the need to explain a decision, justify a decision, etc.) that can influence which decision style is employed.

The Brousseau et al. (2006) results go beyond statistical inference and are close to being a statistical fact. Figure 5 illustrates the results for the 20 percent of the sample who demonstrated the greatest career success. Career success was defined in terms of highest compensation, which, while not a perfect outcome variable, would certainly pique the attention of most individuals interested in climbing the leadership ladder.

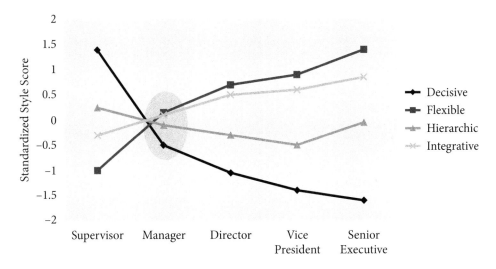

*Adapted from K. R. Brousseau, "The Lens of Success: Perspectives on Climbing the Spiral Staircase"
  (presentation delivered in Thousand Oaks, CA, in 2005).

Figure 5   Average Style Scores for Highest Compensated Leaders

These results clearly indicate that different styles are dominant depending on the management level one occupies. Supervisors' dominant style tends to be Decisive, while that of a senior executive tends to be Flexible. Furthermore, style dominance seems to change at the manager level for these highly successful executives, and the greatest variability in style use appears at the senior executive level.

The results for the lowest performing 20 percent of this sample are in stark contrast to the 20 percent with the greatest career success. Figure 6 illustrates the results for the lowest compensated leaders.

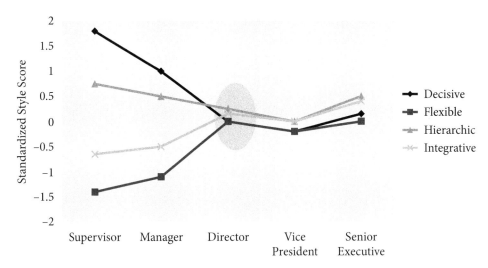

*Adapted from K. R. Brousseau, "The Lens of Success: Perspectives on Climbing the Spiral Staircase"
  (presentation delivered in Thousand Oaks, CA, in 2005).

Figure 6   Average Style Scores for Lowest Compensated Leaders

At the supervisor level, the dominant decision-making style is Decisive, and the order of dominant styles followed that of the highest compensated leaders; however, the greatest variability in style was found at the supervisor level. There are two striking departures for the lowest compensated leaders. First, all styles seem to be equally represented at the senior executive level. Second, the dominant styles converge at the director level and remain constant at higher levels.

These results have far-reaching implications for Strategic Self-awareness as it relates to decision-making. It behooves an individual interested in climbing the leadership ladder to fully understand these styles and how they impact the decision-making process. Furthermore, potential leaders who have a firm understanding of their dominant decision-making style, regularly seek feedback on their decision-making, and develop flexibility using all four styles would appear to have a clear advantage over their less "strategically aware" counterparts in achieving career success.

This advantage can be illustrated using a hypothetical high-potential leader progressing through the ranks to achieve a C-Suite position. As a supervisor, the leader would likely be confronted with a preponderance of day-to-day decisions. Many of these would be associated with people management, where efficiency and consistency would be of considerable value. These decisions would have near-term consequences and are tailor-made for developing Strategic Self-awareness. The key to success at this career stage would be to gain a broad experience base, filing away outcomes and being able to draw upon them as a backdrop for subsequent decisions. Keep in mind that decision categories (illustrated in Figure 4) are, in reality, a continuum. Some of these day-to-day decisions will bleed over into tactical decisions. The leader building Strategic Self-awareness will not only evaluate short-term consequences but will begin to build a mental file of long-term consequences. This type of personal development is in essence like stretching his or her decision-making portfolio into the realm of the tactical.

What is being described for the hypothetical high-potential leader is a very active process of developing Strategic Self-awareness using feedback and structured filing of information for future use. There is no doubt that learning can take place passively through repetition alone. However, the data suggest that leaders with greater career success build decision-making Strategic Self-awareness more quickly and do a better job of recognizing the need for styles other than Decisive as they accumulate and mentally file outcome data. Active building of this type of awareness would seem to have a clear advantage over a more passive approach.

This view is even more accurate as a leader progresses up the ranks. Examining a high-potential leader as a director shows the increasing need for active building of Strategic Self-awareness. At the director level, a leader is likely to be responsible for both a function and the people performing in that function. Decisions will become much more tactical in nature with a time horizon stretching into weeks, months, and even years. Some examples include budgeting, staffing, resource allocation, and so on. Unlike the day-to-day decisions of the supervisor, the time horizon for outcome evaluation will be much longer, and the scope of impact will be much broader. Also, there will be much less tolerance for mistakes, so information will have to be gleaned from successes or even from situations with no clear outcome. Passive building of awareness will become less and less effective under these circumstances. The most successful leaders will actively monitor their decisions, seek feedback, and reflect on the style used to arrive at a decision (i.e., they will actively build Strategic Self-awareness regarding their decision-making process).

As our hypothetical leader moves into a senior executive role, the challenge of building awareness around decision-making becomes even more difficult. Senior executives regularly describe how difficult it is to get good feedback. They often find themselves in a bubble, insulated from feedback. Their decisions move from tactical to strategic, stretching the time horizon and scope of impact even further. There is the added problem of frequency or volume of decisions. Back at the supervisor level, the challenge is often just keeping up with the sheer number of decisions that have to be made. Feedback is regular and easily incorporated into building Strategic Self-awareness. Successful senior executives, where Flexible and Integrative styles dominate, are faced with lower-frequency big decisions that are complex with many moving parts. Clear feedback on outcomes becomes increasingly rare, and active monitoring of the decision-making process as a whole is critical to success.

This hypothetical example clearly shows the importance of Strategic Self-awareness in decision-making. To turn Strategic Self-awareness into a competitive advantage, leaders need to approach it as we have framed it throughout this chapter. First, leaders need to take active control over building their self-awareness. While it is true that self-awareness grows to a large extent in a passive way as we interact with our environment, Strategic Self-awareness requires a leader to become much more active in the process for it to become a competitive advantage. Considering the amount of information a leader is inundated with on a daily basis, active awareness building is an essential filter for learning to occur.

Second, feedback is the cornerstone of building Strategic Self-awareness. Early in a leader's career, feedback comes regularly and is often quite specific to performance. As a leader's career progresses, specific feedback becomes increasingly difficult to obtain, especially with a competency such as decision-making. The only way to counter this phenomenon is to become an ardent champion of feedback and to pursue it actively on a regular basis.

Finally, systematically building Strategic Self-awareness can be much more efficient and useful if a leader does it with a structure in mind, versus just a random gathering of information. The Domain Model provides an ideal structure that can be applied throughout a leader's career. It is flexible enough to cover virtually any type of performance-related information. It can be applied regardless of the job situation or the way information is obtained. Most important, it is simple enough for a leader to use as a mental filing cabinet that structures information for easy retrieval.

COACHING AND STRATEGIC SELF-AWARENESS

Up to this point, we have focused exclusively on the role of Strategic Self-awareness from the perspective of the leader, but it is equally important to the effectiveness of a coach. Consider what happens to feedback as a leader progresses through the ranks to more senior-level positions. The short tale by Hans Christian Andersen titled "The Emperor's New Clothes" is worth recounting here. The plot is essentially the story of two weavers who promise an Emperor a new suit of clothes that is invisible to those unfit for his position or those who are hopelessly incompetent. It took the voice of a child to speak the truth that the Emperor was wearing no clothes for the Emperor to recognize how foolish he had been. Parables that stand the test of time often do so because of the honesty and truth that they convey. This particular parable is right on point when it comes to characterizing feedback to leaders.

It is absolutely the case that as a leader rises through the ranks, feedback slows to a trickle. Actually, it is not that feedback has slowed. There is plenty of feedback out there. It is simply that the feedback does not reach the leader. It is much like the parable in which those around the Emperor mumbled among themselves without daring to speak the truth for fear of the consequences, and the Emperor was unable to face the truth until a child spoke up. At that moment, the Emperor experienced the true meaning of Strategic Self-awareness.

The role of a coach in raising a leader's Strategic Self-awareness is not unlike the role of the child in raising the Emperor's awareness. However, there is an important distinction. Coaches have many methods available to help leaders raise their Strategic Self-awareness. Three of these methods are particularly important: detecting feedback, using multi-rater assessment and structured interview, and examining signs or samples of behavior.

Detecting Feedback

The first method involves raising the bar on a leader's ability to detect feedback. As mentioned earlier, the feedback is out there if the leader is vigilant enough to detect it. A coach can help a great deal by providing an honest and truthful sounding board for the leader and by directing the leader to areas in need of greater focus. This type of assistance has always been the bread and butter of the coaching profession. In theory, a coach is unfettered by consequences, and as long as the coaching is done with the appropriate tact, it can provide an honest and truthful take on a leader's performance. Beyond that, a coach can raise the leader's vigilance regarding specific areas of performance (a subtle, but critical discipline). A coach is only around for a finite period of time. Successfully raising a leader's Strategic Self-awareness depends on raising the leader's own ability to detect feedback independent of the coach. Failing to raise the leader's ability to detect feedback, especially as it relates to performance challenges, opens the door for Strategic Self-awareness to decline.

The following example illustrates just how important it is for a leader to detect feedback and remain vigilant because it does not take much to ruin a reputation.

Tim was a Marketing Vice President who was asked to take over as general manager of a restaurant chain. Tim possessed plenty of marketing experience but very little experience as a general manager. The situation was clearly a turnaround as the restaurant chain was seriously underperforming. Tim took over and made some minor changes to the rest of the leadership team but basically kept the old team intact. Tim was quite outgoing and tended to be longwinded at times. His team meetings were becoming lengthy, and he began to notice he was doing a lot of talking and other team members were disengaging and using laptops and cell phones. As the business challenges mounted, the CEO decided that Tim could use a coach. The coach did a number of interviews and began to hear a theme that Tim was arrogant and seemed more interested in hearing himself talk as opposed to hearing what others had to say. Tim was shocked when he got that feedback from the coach. He reported that he was never thought of as arrogant. The coach went back to his previous team members to check for the behavior, and sure enough, the last thing they considered Tim to be was arrogant. They did report, however, that he could be longwinded at times. After discussing this with Tim, two things became apparent. First, he recognized that he could be longwinded. Second, he admitted that he was probably trying to prove himself too much in the new role and was going too far in explaining and justifying his thoughts and actions to the members of his team.

Tim's failure to recognize the impact his behavior was having on his team members resulted in his garnering a reputation for being arrogant. He did not pick up on the fact that his efforts to try to prove himself in conjunction with his tendency to be longwinded had almost the opposite impact. Not only did he fail to detect the feedback from his team members in the form of their disengaging, he compounded the situation by stepping up his tendency to talk too much. Furthermore, Tim's team members misinterpreted the behavior as his being arrogant and self-absorbed.

With a bit more vigilance and greater awareness regarding the potential impact of talking too much, Tim could have avoided the negative impact to his reputation. A simple change of behavior involving the use of more seeks in place of his tells helped Tim to turn the situation around. While this is certainly not an elaborate behavior change, the improvement cannot take place without Tim's being vigilant regarding his tendency to talk too much and self-monitoring his seek versus tell behavior.

Multi-rater Assessment and Structured Interview

One of the most powerful methods coaches can use to raise the Strategic Self-awareness of a leader is gathering performance information from various stakeholders and providing it to the leader in the form of feedback. The two most common approaches for coaches to gather performance information are the multi-rater assessment and the structured interview. Both approaches have their strengths and weaknesses.

Multi-rater assessment approach involves submitting a rating form to stakeholders and asking them to rate various behaviors and, in some cases, provide written comments regarding the leader's performance. The advantage is the ease with which data can be collected on a wide range of behaviors. If the questions in the assessment have been well designed, this approach can provide valuable feedback. As with any rater-based assessment, this approach is subject to rater error, and written comments are often vague or lack behavioral information. Here are five of the most common problems coaches cite in reference to the multi-rater assessment approach:

- Halo or inflated ratings that provide little information.
- Poorly designed questions that confound multiple behaviors.
- One or two raters who skew the results.
- Conflicting results across raters.
- Poor or missing norms.

Despite the potential problems, the multi-rater assessment approach is still very valuable. It also is one of the few approaches that can be used to quantify performance improvement at the end of a coaching engagement.

Almost all coaches use some form of a structured interview of stakeholders to gather feedback on a leader's performance. Structured interviews are time consuming and often restrict the amount of information that can be gathered; however, if the interview guide is well constructed, if the stakeholders who are interviewed are candid, and if the coach has decent interviewing skills, there is probably no better way to get specific, behavioral information about a leader.

The case involving Tim is a perfect example of when the interview approach can be invaluable. The first round of interviews with stakeholders suggested that some thought Tim was quite arrogant, and it turned them off to the point they disengaged. It is important to remember that the stakeholders observed a behavior but misinterpreted it as arrogance. It took the coach's having a conversation with Tim and conducting follow-up interviews with members of Tim's previous team to uncover precisely which behaviors were creating the problem and how they could be addressed to improve the situation. It is doubtful that this type of accuracy could be obtained using any approach other than interviewing stakeholders. Moreover, the coach went beyond a first round of interviews to ferret out the facts in a way that fit with Tim's ability to understand and successfully address the problem behavior, which demonstrates the flexibility and precision that can be achieved with this approach.

Signs or Samples of Behavior

A third method for helping a leader raise Strategic Self-awareness and obtaining performance information involves gathering samples or signs of behavior. Samples involve the observation of a leader's performance in actual situations or by creating situations that require a leader to demonstrate performance. Signs involve the leader's completing an assessment tool that has been shown to correlate with performance. The specific tools or techniques that are categorized under this method are truly vast. For example, there are more than 2,500 test vendors in the United States alone. For the purpose of this discussion, we will focus on three points along the samples-to-signs continuum: direct observation, the assessment center method, and the personality assessment.

Coaches often choose to observe a leader directly to gather feedback information. They may sit in on team meetings, attend employee gatherings, or even observe a leader doing a performance review. There is no question that direct observation will produce plenty of information that can be used in feedback. However, there are two problems with this approach that are difficult to overcome. First, the coach may be in the situation to observe, but once in the situation, the coach becomes part of the situation. Because the mere presence of the coach alters the situation, there is no way to know how the presence of the coach changes the behavior of those in the situation. Second, many times the behaviors in need of improved Strategic Self-awareness are low-frequency behaviors, meaning that they do not occur often and may occur only under certain circumstances. The coach would have to be present at the right place and at the right time to observe the behavior.

An alternative to direct observation is the assessment center method. It falls somewhere in the middle of the samples-to-signs continuum. While inventories or tests may be part of an assessment center, the cornerstone of the method is behavioral simulations. Simulations put the leader in a situation where he or she has to demonstrate performance, which is observed and rated in terms of effectiveness. For example, to ascertain a leader's ability to conduct a performance appraisal discussion with an employee, have the leader do a simulated performance appraisal with a person trained to role play the employee. Since the 1940s, when assessment centers were used to train spies in World War II, assessment centers have consistently been shown as an effective way to measure leader performance. The challenge with using this method is the resource requirements needed to do it effectively. It is costly, time consuming, and typically requires a group of trained professionals.

There is little doubt that the shortcomings of methods involving samples of behaviors help to give rise to methods that measure signs of behavior. The earliest among these were measures of IQ, but today there are all types of methods measuring everything from Emotional Intelligence (EQ) to Organizational Savvy. Many of the methods, if not most of them, have been developed with little attention to professional standards for test construction. Worse yet, the ease with which they can be used often leads to misapplication of them by people with little or no training. Personality assessment has become the most prolific of the sign methods used by coaches in providing feedback to leaders. It is interesting that the rise in prominence of personality assessment nearly parallels the rise in professional coaching. Prior to the 1980s, personality assessment was largely the purview of clinical psychology. In the 1980s, the Hogans started using personality assessment to select employees. As coaching came out from under the umbrella of outplacement as a legitimate means of helping leaders with performance issues, many coaches latched on to personality assessment as an effective way to understand leader behavior. Three decades later, the coaching profession is thriving, and most coaches use some form of personality assessment in providing leaders with feedback that is important in raising their Strategic Self-awareness.

Looking across the full gamut of techniques and tools available to coaches to gather performance-related information, one combination stands out as the most efficient and cost effective: personality assessment in conjunction with a multi-rater assessment. In study after study, this combination consistently produces some of the highest validity coefficients when predicting leader performance. Furthermore, the combination is tailor made for use by a coach. The multi-rater assessment indicates what a leader does and how the leader does it. The personality assessment indicates why a leader does something, or, more accurately, indicates what the natural tendencies are that underlie the behaviors demonstrated in the workplace. This combination has incredible power in raising the Strategic Self-awareness of a leader when it is delivered by a professionally trained coach. That is not to say that the other tools and techniques discussed are not valuable. It is simply a fact that personality assessment combined with multi-rater assessment produces the highest quality of information at the lowest cost with the least drain on resources.

Summary

The concept of Strategic Self-awareness stands as the cornerstone in the development of a leader. Leaders who use it to calibrate personal growth throughout their careers tend to do much better than those who ignore it. Coaches who employ it as a core component in communicating with leaders do a better job of relating to those leaders and helping them engage in meaningful behavior change. Building Strategic Self-awareness is not an event; it is a journey. Leaders must take an active part in the journey by recognizing useful feedback and cataloging it in a way that it can be retrieved as experience. Coaches, if they are to be of the greatest value to leaders, must use the most effective techniques for raising Strategic Self-awareness and, at the same time, build the capacity of leaders to be awareness consumers. The Hogan Development Survey (HDS), described in detail in Chapter 4, is an inventory coaches must master to reach their maximum effectiveness in helping leaders develop, and leaders who are true awareness consumers will eagerly embrace their own HDS results.

CHAPTER 4

UNDERSTANDING THE HOGAN DEVELOPMENT SURVEY

INTRODUCTION

The Hogan Development Survey (HDS) is the industry standard for assessing dysfunctional behaviors related to performance in the workplace. Leaders throughout the world understand the value of the HDS for increasing their Strategic Self-awareness. Coaches rely on the HDS as an essential tool for identifying behaviors that disrupt or interfere with leader performance. They also know that systematic coaching techniques can be very effective in helping leaders make changes to these dysfunctional behaviors. The growth and popularity of the HDS directly reflect the measurable performance improvements leaders have achieved and the success coaches have experienced using the HDS inventory as a foundation for developing leaders.

There are numerous well-documented technical descriptions of the HDS (Hogan & Hogan, 1997, 2009; Hogan et al., 2007). This chapter briefly reviews some of that descriptive work to introduce the basic concepts behind the HDS inventory; however, the primary purpose of this chapter is to examine the HDS as a tool for enhancing Strategic Self-awareness as the foundation for improving leader performance. This approach will challenge some conventional thinking regarding how to interpret HDS scales. It will also expand upon the meaning of scale scores at all ranges regarding behaviors that disrupt or interfere with the performance of leaders.

BACKGROUND

Leadership is one of the most intensely studied topics in psychology and business. However, reviewing the morass of research, thousands of books, and countless opinions leads to only one conclusion: there is no consensus regarding what constitutes effective leadership. The roots of the HDS date back to this conclusion when Robert Hogan began studying leadership in the 1980s. He came away with two perspectives on the topic, which are entrenched in the history of Hogan Assessment Systems and the HDS:

- Effective leadership should be defined by the outcome it seeks to achieve, which is building and maintaining an effective team.

- The published literature largely ignores flawed leadership, which might be a more productive and useful avenue of inquiry, especially from a measurement and development standpoint.

The second point was particularly important in the creation of the HDS. One of the most disturbing findings in any critical review of leadership literature is the surprising rate of management failure. Although the definition of management failure varies greatly, there is little argument that it is characterized as the inability to build and maintain an effective team. The rate of management failure has been estimated to be between 50 percent and 70 percent (Hogan et al., 2010). As far back as 1983, when Robert Hogan began developing the HDS, management failure was seen as near epidemic in corporations across the United States (McCall & Lombardo, 1983). Such discussions were largely confined to the academic community and were only whispered about in corporate America. Looking back, it is possible to draw a near perfect regression line from those early discussions of management failure to the multi-billion-dollar leadership development and coaching industry of today.

The true seriousness of this academic discussion of management failure began to take shape in a multitude of high-profile failures beginning in the 2000s. Ken Lay (Enron), Bernie Ebbers (WorldCom), Jimmy Cayne (Bear Stearns), and Angilo Mozilo (Countrywide Financial) became the poster boys for management failure. Firings and high-profile criminal trials became front-page news and marked nearly a decade in which management failure went from the closet to more commonplace than management success. The serious repercussions of management failure peaked in 2008 when Lehman Brothers, one of Wall Street's most respected firms, triggered a nationwide financial panic (Portfolio, 2009). The banking meltdown that followed continues to plague the world economy to this day.

No one knows the full financial impact of management failure; however, in a review of the literature, the Hogan Research Division (2011) concluded the following:

Organizations continue to speculate about the cost of bad managers. If adjusted for inflation, a 1988 estimate of $500,000 amounts to $1 million in 2010. Other estimates range from $1.5 million to $2.7 million for each failed senior manager (Hogan, Hogan, & Kaiser, 2010). These estimates exclude hidden costs such as golden parachutes, severance costs, missed corporate objectives, and a disengaged workforce. Moreover, employee stress created by bad managers contributes to increased medical costs and reduced quality of work life.

How widespread is the problem of managerial incompetence in the United States? Reviewing 12 published estimates of the base rate of managerial failure, Hogan et al. (2010) concluded that 50 percent of managers will fail, and at least half of those will be fired. Organizations recognize this talent crisis as evidenced by the fact that the current global leadership development and coaching industry is estimated to exceed $2 billion annually (Hoagland-Smith, 2009).

By almost any metric, management failure is a serious problem and has had a detrimental impact on the lives of nearly every working adult in the world at one time or another. Not surprisingly, the growth in popularity of the first inventory designed to evaluate a leader's risk of failure, the HDS, has paralleled the public discussion of managerial misbehavior.

EARLY DEVELOPMENT

While early versions of the HDS were not commonly in use until the mid-1990s, the roots of the inventory date back much further. In the early 1980s, Robert Hogan wrote about the concepts of socioanalytic theory and the need for people to "get along" and "get ahead" (Hogan, 1983). The HDS is essentially an assessment of the barriers to getting along and getting ahead. Also during the 1980s, Hogan was doing extensive development work on the Hogan Personality Inventory (HPI) (Hogan & Hogan, 2007). Between 1979 and 1984, Hogan assessed more than 1,700 working adults with the HPI. This research legitimized the use of personality inventories in the workplace, and showed how to go beyond the Five-Factor Model (FFM) to gain insights into the personality characteristics associated with managerial failure (e.g., Hogan, Hogan, & Busch, 1984).

The original model for the HDS was the PROFILE, developed by Warren Jones (1988) shortly after the appearance of the DSM-III, Axis 2 personality disorders (American Psychiatric Association, 1987). Jones intended to use the PROFILE as a psychometrically defensible alternative to the inventories of personality disorders available at the time. Hogan used the PROFILE for about five years, conducting validity studies with business clients. This research revealed associations between high-risk PROFILE scores, managerial misbehavior, and indications of failure in achieving full career potential.

The data from the PROFILE led Robert and Joyce Hogan to conclude that there was a role for the assessment of performance risks in the workplace. However, they had concerns about the PROFILE's emphasis on anxiety and depression. The Americans with Disabilities Act of 1990 (ADA, 1990) indicated that the PROFILE would be seen as an evaluation of mental disabilities, which is prohibited for pre-offer employment inquiries. At this point, the Hogans decided to develop a nonclinical inventory to assess interpersonal behaviors that adversely affect the performance or reputation of people at work. They envisioned a tool to be used primarily for professional development and coaching, although even that vision has since expanded to include managerial selection—particularly in light of the high-profile executive derailments over the past decade.

The Hogans began working on the HDS in the fall of 1992. They developed items one scale at a time. They created an initial set of items, tested samples of people, computed internal consistency reliabilities and correlations with other well-established measures, reviewed the data, and revised the items so as to (a) enhance internal consistency reliability and (b) sharpen convergent and discriminant validity. They also received valuable input from colleagues in the United States and Europe concerning the content of the scales. The HDS is the product of six cycles of item writing, revision, testing, and further revision. The final set of items was defined during the summer of 1995. From 1995 to 1996, Hogan assessed more than 2,000 people, including employed adults, job applicants, prisoners, and graduate students. The ages in these samples ranged from 21 years to 64 years with a mean of 38.5 years. There were 1,532 men and 322 women, 620 Caucasians, and 150 African Americans.

The inventory that emerged from this research was an assessment of 11 dysfunctional personality characteristics. From the beginning, the HDS was never intended to be used only with leaders. Rather, the characteristics can be found in employees at any level and can negatively impact performance. The characteristics are not discrete behaviors; they are patterns of behavior that disrupt performance and tend to arise when a person (employee) fails to self-monitor and exert active behavioral control. All employees experience such moments to some degree. When leaders have these moments and one or more of the characteristics emerge, they can destroy morale, derail a team, or even degrade an entire organization.

The potential impact of personality on leader performance led Rodney Warrenfeltz, PhD, founder of Development Dimensions International's (DDI) Executive Development Practice, to conclude that personality assessment was essential in providing leaders with development feedback. Between 1992 and 1996, Warrenfeltz incorporated the HPI; the Motives, Values, Preferences Inventory (MVPI); and the PROFILE into a comprehensive executive-assessment program based on a wide range of behavioral simulations. The inventories quickly became a standard component of the assessment battery. In 1996, Warrenfeltz substituted the new HDS for the PROFILE. This was important for two reasons. First, DDI, a world leader in behaviorally based assessments, had adopted the HDS as a standard component of its Executive Development Practice. Second, it was the beginning of widespread acceptance of the HDS as an essential tool for understanding the development needs of leaders. The partnership between DDI and Hogan Assessment Systems continues to this day, and data resulting from this partnership show clearly that the combination of personality and behavioral assessment sets the standard for providing leaders with the development information (Strategic Self-awareness) necessary for performance improvement.

GROWING ACCEPTANCE

For 15 years following the development of the HDS, Hogan research demonstrated that performance risks are common among all working adults. Furthermore, it has been well documented, using coaching data collected after most HDS administrations, that (1) leaders gain considerable insight regarding their performance risks and (2) focused development efforts can reduce the career impact of these risks.

To date, nearly 2 million employed adults have taken the HDS. They represent every sector of the global economy, including manufacturing, communications, health care, retail, banking and finance, construction, transportation, security, law enforcement, and many others. The research involves more than 200 validation studies covering a wide range of job categories. Most of these studies link HDS scores with ratings of managerial/professional incompetence and demonstrate the ability of the inventory to account for unique variance beyond that obtained with traditional Five-Factor personality inventories.

The accumulated research regarding the HDS has been well documented in the technical manual (Hogan & Hogan, 1997, 2009). Perhaps more impressive is the way the HDS has been embraced by the business community. Much of the growth of Hogan Assessment Systems domestically and internationally can be attributed to customer demand for the HDS. More than 70 percent of Fortune 100 companies and more than 50 percent of Fortune 500 companies have used the HDS.

CONTINUOUS IMPROVEMENT

The success of the HDS has not been one of an inventory that was initially created and simply gained in popularity. The inventory has been subjected to virtually continuous scrutiny since its inception and represents a classic example of the Hogan approach to test construction known as Kaizen Psychometrics. In 2010, an initiative was undertaken to do a complete revision of the HDS. This initiative resulted in the HDS Form 5, which is the most significant upgrade to the inventory since its original design in the late 1980s and early 1990s. The critical challenge faced in this effort was maintaining full congruence between the original HDS and the HDS Form 5, while improving item content and adding subscales to the interpretation of each of the 11 main scales.

The technical effort that went into meeting this challenge was substantial, involving nearly five years of research aimed at achieving both the technical standards that Hogan is known for, as well as the user standards necessary to complete a seamless transition to the new Form 5. All of the technical documentation detailing the development work that went into the HDS Form 5 is available in the *HDS Technical Supplement: Form 5* (2014). Suffice it to say, the challenges associated with transitioning to HDS Form 5 have been fully achieved. The HDS Form 5 is fully congruent with the original HDS from a statistical standpoint.

Equally important to statistical congruence has been the congruence achieved between the HDS and the HDS Form 5 from an interpretation standpoint. The expert coaches in the Hogan Coaching Network (HCN) played a key role in ensuring interpretative congruence. The coaches had the opportunity to compare interpretive results between the HDS and the HDS Form 5 across hundreds of Hogan Assessment Certification Workshop participants. Across all scales, the HDS Form 5 was found to be as accurate or more accurate for 91 percent of the participants. Furthermore, the coaches found that the new subscale information (a key component of the HDS Form 5) added interpretive value for 28 percent of the participants.

The HDS Form 5 transition was completed in 2014. The new items removed virtually all concerns related to the content of HDS items. The subscales broaden the understanding of scale-level results and provide those responsible for interpreting inventory results with a deeper understanding of scale-level performance implications. From a leadership development standpoint, we are at an early point in our understanding of the role subscales will play in development content. However, given the refinements that have been achieved from an interpretation standpoint, it is likely that the subscales will prove equally valuable in targeting the development needs of leaders.

EVOLUTION IN HDS INTERPRETATION

For most of its history, the HDS has been positioned as a risk assessment. Higher scores on a given scale indicated that a person was at greater risk for the negative behaviors associated with that scale to emerge, particularly under stressful conditions. The issue with this perspective is not that it is incorrect but that it is simply far too narrow for the predictive power the HDS adds to the understanding of leader behavior. There are two interpretation aspects of the HDS that need to be expanded in order to gain a more robust understanding of what a particular score indicates for a leader: self-monitoring and low HDS scores.

Self-monitoring

The first area that needs to be expanded concerns the conditions under which a person might display negative behaviors. Conditions that increase stress absolutely open the door for negative behaviors to occur. A simple example would be to increase a person's workload over an extended period of time without a sufficient break or recovery time. Conditions such as this increase the probability that a problem behavior might surface in the workplace. A person with a high Excitable score is more likely to have an emotional outburst or a person with a high Bold score is more likely to blame others if something goes wrong, and so on. However, to fully understand what is going on under such conditions, it is important to consider that increasing the stress in a situation is not a guarantee that a negative behavior will emerge. It just increases the probability of an occurrence. Furthermore, a very high score on an HDS scale in conjunction with higher stress simply adds to the probability of an incident but is by no means a guarantee that the negative behavior will be displayed in the workplace. Therefore, it must be asked why an individual does not demonstrate a negative behavior under stressful conditions despite an elevated HDS scale score. It is this question that forces a more expansive view of what opens the door for a derailing behavior to occur.

The fact is, any condition that causes individuals to reduce their self-monitoring behavior opens the door for negative, derailing behaviors to emerge. Stress is only one of many conditions that could allow derailers to enter their behavioral repertoire. When people are heavily engaged in self-monitoring, they can often control or at least minimize the impact of a derailer.

Perhaps one of the best examples can be found in an interview situation. Generally speaking, during a job interview, people attempt to put their best foot forward. They are in a heightened state of self-monitoring and will do their best to make sure the interviewer only sees the Bright Side of their personality. That is not to say that the derailing behaviors are not lurking in the background. It just means that for a period of time, the person's heightened state of self-monitoring is standing guard, attempting to make sure that certain behaviors do not emerge. A job interview is a microcosm of what goes on in everyday life. The only difference is the degree to which people monitor their behavior. When self-monitoring goes up, the risk of a derailing behavior emerging declines. When self-monitoring goes down, the risk increases.

The implementation of self-monitoring is actually very good news from a leadership development standpoint. Leaders who possess self-awareness regarding their derailers and can effectively self-monitor these behaviors have an excellent chance of maintaining control over them. In fact, when you talk to effective leaders about their derailers, you will often hear stories about how the derailer might have impacted them early in their career and how they learned to control it. It is even better news for coaches because it offers a clear path on how to help leaders improve their performance over time. This point will be covered in detail in Part IV.

Low HDS Scores

The second area of expansion concerns the interpretation of low scores. There has been a lot of interest recently regarding the impact of low HDS scores on performance. Much of the interest has been generated because of a Hogan/Seldman Learning workshop titled "The Leadership Formula." The workshop is designed for leaders, and combines the power of Hogan assessment insights with behavior changes that can be achieved by applying high-impact coaching tips developed by Marty Seldman and John Futterknecht of Optimum Associates.

Early in the development of the Leadership Formula workshop, there were extensive discussions about a number of executive coaching cases that had been conducted over the past few decades and the role derailing behaviors (as measured by the HDS) played in these cases. Many of the cases involved typical HDS elevations (percentile scores above 80%) and highlighted behaviors that executives needed to control if they were to be successful. One case stood out as particularly intriguing. It involved a C-suite executive who had virtually no elevations on any

HDS scale, but this executive still described an ongoing struggle with a tendency to be overly trusting. That dichotomy led to a discussion about his Skeptical score, which was in the low single digits. It was apparent that certain behaviors associated with high to moderate risk levels on the Skeptical scale (such as "being insightful about the motives of others") were missing, or at least underused, in his day-to-day performance. In other words, he was at no risk of derailing because he was overly distrustful. His performance was suffering because he was unable to benefit from the skeptical tendencies that lead to insight about the motives of others.

The behaviors associated with low HDS scores have never been a secret. Robert Hogan described them from the very early days of interpreting HDS profiles, and they are well documented in *The Hogan Guide: Interpretation and Use of Hogan Inventories* (Hogan et al., 2007). This case was different. It was not that this executive was failing to demonstrate the positive behaviors associated with a low Skeptical score. The problem was that he was overly trusting when a "trust, but verify" set of behaviors often associated with mid-range HDS scores was called for to support effective performance. This case forced a consideration that low HDS scores could indicate the absence of certain behaviors necessary for effective performance. And with that realization, a whole new set of HDS challenges was born.

To understand the concept of a low HDS score, you have to begin with a reasonably precise understanding of an elevated or high score. Eighty percent or higher is the benchmark for concern about potential derailment. At this level, the interpretation usually goes something like, "Under certain conditions of stress or pressure, you are at high risk for demonstrating the derailing behaviors associated with the scale, and those behaviors could result in damage to your career." There are variations of that general theme, almost all of which emphasize the potentially harmful nature of the behaviors and the importance of getting them under control. Consistent with our discussion earlier, we have expanded the interpretation of the causes of derailing behaviors to include anything that causes people to let their guard down or reduce their self-monitoring. In other words, derailing behaviors show up as natural tendencies unless we guard against them.

This issue brings us to the next point about derailing behaviors. They are not really discrete behaviors. In fact, they are behaviors mixed in with an overall pattern of behavior. The pattern has many positive behaviors as well as negative behaviors, and even the negative behaviors have positive elements that can work to one's advantage if they do not go over the top. For example, everyone has encountered people when they are experiencing an excitable moment. They may talk fast, use words that convey passion, use hand gestures, and so on. When they go over the top, they may yell, bang desks, or throw things. These are all behaviors associated with the Excitable scale, but at some point an acceptable level of excitable behavior becomes a derailing level of behavior. This variance leads inevitably to the conclusion that for each scale on the HDS, there is an acceptable level of behavior that may, in fact, be important in a leader's performance.

Now let's extend this line of thinking to low scores. **A low score should be considered anything below 20 percent, and a really low score to be anything below 10 percent.** We have described a certain pattern of excitable behavior that would likely be acceptable under many circumstances and, potentially, a strength when it appears as something as acceptable as passion. What happens if a person demonstrates few (if any) excitable behaviors even when the situation calls for it? This is precisely what you might get with a low score on the Excitable scale and would almost expect from someone with a very low score. For all practical purposes, it is the absence of certain excitable behaviors that becomes the problem. Simply put, a high score on a scale indicates the potential for associated behaviors to be overused or demonstrated in negative or inappropriate ways. A low score on a scale may indicate the underuse or even the absence of the associated behaviors.

The throwaway line that captures the essence of the low-score versus high-score discussion is "high scores can get you fired, and low scores can get you passed over." Although a simplistic view, it is not too far from the truth. If coaches were asked to give behavioral examples of executives who have been fired, they would quickly fill up a flipchart. Furthermore, if they took enough time, they would find examples that touch every scale on the HDS with behaviors that sound as if they came right out of *The Hogan Guide: Interpretation and Use of Hogan Inventories* for scores at 80 percent or above (Hogan et al., 2007). If those same coaches were queried about executives fired for their low Excitable behaviors or their low Bold behaviors, they likely will have very little to report. That is not to say it does not happen. People can certainly come up with examples of individuals with low scores who were fired. However, it is much more likely that the circumstances that led to these individuals' being fired went beyond the absence of behaviors marked by a low HDS scale score.

When recalling people who were passed over for a promotion or who have had their career hit a plateau, it is worth considering the impact of a low score on an HDS scale. It is not a stretch to think about a person with a low Excitable score being passed over for a promotion because he or she did not seem to have the passion necessary to motivate a team. How about the low Bold individual who missed out on a career-changing assignment because that person did not verbalize sufficient self-confidence to convince the decision-maker that he or she could handle the job? It is examples like these that really bring low scores on the HDS into focus. They certainly do not create the high-profile events that often come from elevated scores; however, the damage they may do to a career could be just as devastating.

The role of self-monitoring and the impact of low scores should not be regarded as changes in interpretation. Rather, they are part of a continuing evolution in the understanding of the behaviors predicted by the HDS. They are the direct result of using the inventory with many leaders over an extended period of time and observing leader behavior through feedback and coaching and in the workplace. It is likely that the evolution in interpreting the HDS will continue as its power as an assessment tool is explored and coaches gain ever more experience using it with leaders.

INTERPRETATION, PERFORMANCE, AND CAREER IMPACT

When low-score interpretation is added to HDS scales, a continuum of behavior emerges rather than an inventory with scales that only gauge risk at the high end. It also becomes apparent that scores in the mid-range on the scales suggest behaviors that are not only ever-present, but they are often essential for effective leader performance.

The following is a scale-by-scale interpretation of the HDS at the high and low ends. It includes a general scale definition with a description of the range of behaviors possible at both ends of the main scale and the associated subscales. Leadership implications are outlined as a way to provide coaches with some major watch-outs they should consider when working with leaders. Finally, the watch-outs are summarized, indicating how behaviors may impact a leader from a career and performance standpoint. This chart is not an exhaustive summary of scale-by-scale interpretation information. Rather, it is designed to set the stage for considering the coaching tips and techniques outlined in Part IV that can be used with leaders to address performance challenges across the range of behaviors measured by the HDS.

EXCITABLE

Description: The Excitable scale not only concerns working with passion and enthusiasm, but also being easily frustrated, moody, irritable, and inclined to give up on projects and people.

Low scorers seem calm to the point of appearing to lack passion or urgency	⬅ Behavior Range ➡	High scorers display dramatic emotional peaks and valleys regarding people and projects

Subscale	Low Score	High Score
Volatile	Self-controlled; demonstrates strong emotional regulation but may seem overly restrained	Tempermental, easily angered or upset, tendency to lose control of emotions and react in interpersonally harsh ways
Easily Disappointed	Tolerant, steady, and resilient, but may seem to lack passion or "fire in the belly"	Demonstrates initial passion for people and projects, but becoming easily disappointed, frustrated, and losing interest
No Direction	Seems steady, self-assured, and clear about beliefs; unlikely to dwell on past mistakes	Cooperative and helpful, but may lack focus or have few well-defined beliefs or interests; tends to regret past behavior

Leadership and Reputation Implications

Leaders are expected to motivate and inspire others. Highly effective leaders are able to call on their emotions as part of delivering a message in either group or one-on-one situations as a way of adding excitement and urgency. They also are able to dial-it-back or avoid overusing their emotions as a motivating force. Without this versatility, leaders are at a deficit when it comes to motivating and inspiring others.

The Excitable scale suggests how even-keeled or steady a leader is across a variety of task and people situations. All leaders vacillate to one degree or another with respect to emotional highs or lows. When the amplitude of a leader's emotional sine wave is too great or too narrow regarding task or people situations, it can negatively impact his or her reputation. Too great, and people will regard the leader as unpredictable. Too narrow, and people will regard the leader as repressed or lacking passion. In colloquial terms, the latter is often referred to as "no fire in the belly."

Emotionality and steadiness are usually quite visible to those who work closely with a leader; however, that may not be the case with respect to beliefs as measured by the No Direction subscale. At the high end, a leader may just feel adrift with little clear sense of direction. At the low end, a leader may lack reflection, especially regarding mistakes, because of an entitled sense of direction. In both cases, reputational impact may be slow in coming but potentially just as problematic as more visible Excitable behaviors.

Risk Summary

	Low Scores	High Scores
Career	May be challenged to inspire people as a leader	Emotional outbursts may intimidate or alienate others
	Lack of emotion or flat affect may be misread as distinterest or a lack of concern	Emotional "roller coaster" may cause people to disregard opinions or concerns
Performance	Superiors may wonder if there is any "fire in the belly"	Superiors may see moodiness as "high maintenance" or a lack of executive maturity
	Peers may look to others for passionate support on important issues	Peers may be concerned about consistency and predictability
	Direct reports may have trouble reading the urgency of situations	Direct reports may avoid delivering bad news or avoid situations that create stress
	Opponents may fuel a misperception of no passion or urgency	Opponents may "press one's buttons" to provoke inappropriate emotional responses

Skeptical

Description: The Skeptical scale concerns being alert for signs of deceptive behavior in others and taking action when it is detected.

| Low scorers seem trusting to the point of naiveté | Behavior Range | High scorers are negative or cynical and expect to be betrayed |

Subscale	Low Score	High Score
Cynical	Seems positive and steady, but may not examine others' true intentions carefully enough; prone to naiveté	Perceptive about others' intentions but tends to assume they have bad ulterior motives; prone to negativity; quarrelsome
Mistrusting	Generally trusting; seems practical, cooperative, and follows through, but may get taken advantage of by others	Generalized mistrust of people and institutions; worrisome and alert for signs of perceived mistreatment
Grudges	Forgiving of others and understanding; others may take advantage of this accepting nature	Prone to holding grudges and unwilling to forgive real or perceived wrongs; unsympathetic and fault-finding

Leadership and Reputation Implications

One of a leader's most valuable assets is the ability to accurately size up people, an expertise that applies to everything from identifying talent to reviewing job performance. Leaders who approach the tasks associated with evaluating people from a "trust, but verify" standpoint typically outperform those who are ever on the watch for the Dark Side or, perhaps worse, tend to start from an unrealistic and stubbornly persistent Bright Side view.

The Bright Side versus Dark Side perspective that is measured by the Skeptical scale actually cascades across most situations for leaders. Leaders who start from the Bright Side tend to uplift people as long as they are viewed as sincere and not gullible. Leaders who start from the Dark Side usually do not fall victim to deception, but their questioning inclination can drain the energy out of people because of their often negative perspective. Behaviors associated with either extreme on this scale can be quite damaging to a leader's performance; however, it is probably fair to say that a healthy dose of skepticism should serve a leader well.

Interestingly, the subscales give some really useful insights regarding leader challenges at the low end of the scale. It is easy to see how people who are not cynical, who trust others, and who do not hold grudges would generally be held in high regard. Unfortunately, there are times when leaders have to be negative, and certainly there are times when they should not trust people. There are even times when leaders need a long memory of past transgressions to make sure history does not repeat itself.

Risk Summary

	Low Scores	High Scores
Career	May be taken advantage of by those who lack integrity or have an agenda	May be viewed as a negative force who drags people down
	May go too far in looking for the best in people who do not deserve it	May spend too much time looking for the Dark Side rather than for opportunities
Performance	Superiors may perceive a degree of naiveté	Superiors may tire of the negative or cynical views
	Peers may look for opportunities to advance their own agenda	Peers may use the negativism to advance their agendas
	Direct reports may prey on trust by taking performance liberties	Direct reports may have their morale depressed or lowered
	Opponents may feel comfortable using deception to achieve their interests	Opponents may prey on distrust to divide and conquer

Cautious

Description: The Cautious scale concerns risk aversion, fear of failure, and avoiding criticism.

| Low scorers are willing to take risks without adequate risk assessment | Behavior Range | High scorers are reluctant to take risks regardless of risk assessment |

Subscale	Low Score	High Score
Avoidant	Open, warm, enthusiastic, and eager to meet new people but may overpower others or seem uninhibited	Avoids new people and situations to avoid potential embarrassment; may seem aloof, inhibited, uninterested in others
Fearful	Willing to try new things; seems original, inventive, and confident; may be overly forceful when expressing opinions or ideas	Afraid of being criticized for making mistakes and reluctant to act or make decisions independently; prefers to cooperate rather than assert oneself; may seem unoriginal
Unassertive	Decisive, assertive, and willing to express opinions; may come across as abrasive, inconsiderate, or unsympathetic	Unwilling to act assertively; tendency to be indecisive and slow to act; may seem cooperative but overly compliant

Leadership and Reputation Implications

Decision-making is an essential part of being a leader. It is a process that includes the consideration of alternatives, selecting from among those alternatives, and taking action (or not taking action) on the basis of the alternative selected. Behaviors associated with the Cautious scale can impact a leader's decision-making process at any or all steps along the way. Overly cautious behavior can limit alternatives, slow the selection from among alternatives, and even thwart a leader's willingness to take action. In contrast, risky or low Cautious behavior can result in impulsive actions that stem from a lack of rigor in the decision-making process.

Perhaps more than any other HDS scale, the leadership implications of the Cautious scale can potentially impact the entire organization. Furthermore, behaviors associated with the scale are significantly impacted by the Situational Context in which they occur. This makes it difficult to pin down general leadership implications for low or high scores without the gratuitous "it depends." Nonetheless, behaviors at either extreme are not helpful to leaders under most circumstances. It is also true that others learn to take advantage of a leader's behavioral patterns at either extreme—at the low end to obtain agreement for action without due diligence and at the high end as a means to gain endorsement for no action.

The Avoidant subscale suggests a social cautiousness or fear of interacting with people, while the Fearful subscale tends to be more task focused or associated with decision-making fear. Both subscales will cause leaders to either approach or avoid situations based on the potential for failure. The Unassertive subscale tends to be driven more by a leader's self-confidence, and can be moderated to an extent by interpersonal skills in terms of how the assertiveness (or lack of assertiveness) is expressed.

Risk Summary

<table>
<tr><th></th><th>Low Scores</th><th>High Scores</th></tr>
<tr><td rowspan="2">Career</td><td>Decision-making may seem impulsive or overly risky</td><td>May miss career opportunities because of the potential risk</td></tr>
<tr><td>A history of bad decisions could be associated with poor judgment</td><td>May be seen as a blocker and not a mover in getting things done</td></tr>
<tr><td rowspan="4">Performance</td><td>Superiors may be concerned about due diligence in decision-making</td><td>May not be consulted by superiors regarding important decisions</td></tr>
<tr><td>Peers may be reluctant to support decisions that are seen as impulsive</td><td>Peers who want to get things done will find work-arounds</td></tr>
<tr><td>Direct reports may delay implementing decisions as a safety net</td><td>Direct reports may use slow decision-making to avoid work</td></tr>
<tr><td>Opponents may use risky decision-making as cover for their own risk taking</td><td>Opponents may use slow decision-making to stop initiatives they do not like</td></tr>
</table>

RESERVED

Description: The Reserved scale concerns seeming tough, aloof, remote, and unconcerned with the feelings of others.

Low scorers are too concerned about the feelings of others	Behavior Range	High scorers are indifferent to the feelings of others

Subscale	Low Score	High Score
Introverted	Socially engaging, enthusiastic, and enjoys being around others; may be seen as socially boisterous	Values private time and prefers to work alone; may seem withdrawn, unapproachable, or lacking in energy
Unsocial	Relationship-oriented, accessible, warm, and highly cooperative; may seem conflict-avoidant	Keeps others at a distance; limits close relationships, and seems generally detached, aloof, and potentially harsh/argumentative
Tough	Sympathetic, sensitive to others' feelings, but may seem overly diplomatic or too soft on people issues	Seems indifferent to others' feelings and problems; focused on tasks rather than people; may seem cold or unfeeling

Leadership and Reputation Implications

Leaders have to make tough calls on a daily basis. Often these decisions involve placing the good of the organization above the desires of individuals. Behaviors associated with the Reserved scale concern how leaders deal with these calls. At times, leaders need thick skin. Low-score behaviors may cause leaders to delay people calls or avoid delivering bad news. Higher score behaviors generally enable making tough calls as leaders will see people concerns as only one of a number of considerations.

High-score behaviors primarily impact a leader's communication style. Leaders displaying high-score behaviors often avoid interacting with others, and when they do interact, they may seem terse, curt, and uninterested. Because effective leadership depends on relationship building, this communication style can limit a leader's ability to approach and be approached by others.

The first two subscales speak to the social aspects of Reserved. They tend to negatively correlate with the Sociability and Interpersonal Sensitivity scales of the HPI. The Tough subscale is a bit different and really speaks to the notion of heart, or more specifically, heartlessness when it comes to leader behavior. Too high or too low scores have obvious drawbacks from a leadership standpoint. Too high and the leader may develop a reputation for being heartless, which can diminish follower-ship. Too low and the leader may develop an "old softy" reputation as a person who is easily hornswoggled.

Risk Summary

	Low Scores	High Scores
Career	May avoid making tough but important decisions	May miss opportunities to network and build relationships
	May avoid interpersonal conflicts or confrontations that are necessary for advancement	May misread situations that have a large people component
Performance	Superiors may see excessive people concerns as soft on performance issues	Superiors may resist engaging a loner in important initiatives
	Peers may employ aggressive or confrontational tactics as a means of influence	Peers may not reach out to network because of aloofness
	Direct reports may misread messages that are too diplomatic and not sufficiently direct	Direct reports may not disclose concerns because of a perceived lack of empathy
	Opponents may use conflict avoidance to gain tacit agreement	Opponents may insert themselves in stakeholder relationships as gatekeepers

LEISURELY

Description: The Leisurely scale concerns appearing to be friendly and cooperative, but actually following one's own agenda and quietly but stubbornly resisting those of others.

Low scorers appear to lack an agenda or direction	Behavior Range	High scorers are passive aggressive and agenda driven

Subscale	Low Score	High Score
Passive Aggressive	Seems steady, cooperative, and forgiving; comfortable expressing feelings and opinions	Overtly pleasant and compliant but privately resentful and subversive regarding requests for improved performance; seems moody and easily upset
Unappreciated	Cooperative, efficient, reliable, and willing to help others; likely to believe hard work will speak for itself	Believes that one's talents and contributions are ignored or underappreciated; perceives inequities in assigned workloads
Irritated	Open to feedback, willing to assist others; easily distracted or too readily agrees to help others and loses focus on own agenda	Privately but easily irritated by interruptions, requests, or work-related suggestions; not easily coached

Leadership and Reputation Implications

Effective leaders have explicit agendas. The real question concerns whether their agendas serve the needs of the organization or their own needs. Behaviors at the low end tend to over-serve the needs of the organization, or worse, the needs of a given individual, such as a manager. In essence, this scale is a marker for some of the negative aspects of followership, namely, following others simply because one has no agenda that offers any resistant or alternative direction. A further downside to low Leisurely behaviors is the lack of resistance to agenda change, which can create a reputation as a leader who just goes with the flow.

It is interesting to consider how high Leisurely behaviors play out for a leader. They seem to be more tolerated if the leader's agenda is in line with the needs of the organization, rather than needs characterized as personal self-interest. In some respects, unwavering adherence to an agenda aligned with the direction of the organization will even garner admiration from followers. Unfortunately, if high Leisurely behaviors are out of sync with the direction of the organization, derailment may be likely regardless of the degree to which the agenda is correct.

The emotional component of the Leisurely scale is often forgotten from an interpretation standpoint. The subscales clearly reinforce this aspect of the scale with respect to leader behavior. All three contain an emotional component, with the Irritated subscale leading the way in terms of visibility from the observer's perspective.

Risk Summary

	Low Scores	High Scores
Career	May be rudderless in seeking career advancement	May resist key opportunities because of adherence to an agenda
	Career decisions may be excessively influenced by others	Paying lip service to offers may diminish future opportunities
Performance	Superiors may tire of wishy-washy or unclear stands on issues	Superiors may become frustrated with passive resistance
	Peers may assume followership regarding their positions on issues	Peers may perceive lip service as political angling
	Direct reports may flounder in the face of an unclear or ambiguous agenda	Direct reports may view stated positions as not credible, conflicts not resolved, or lacking true alignment
	Opponents may seize the lack of an agenda to enlist support for their personal agenda	Opponents may use passive-aggressive behavior as way to park issues they don't want to address

BOLD

Description: The Bold scale concerns seeming fearless, confident, and self-assured, always expecting to succeed, and unable to admit mistakes or learn from experience.

| Low scorers appear to lack self-confidence and resolve | Behavior Range | High scorers seem assertive, self-promoting, and overly self-confident |

Subscale	Low Score	High Score
Entitled	Unassuming, unpretentious, and helpful; lacking in outward confidence; may not actively seek out more challenging work assignments	Feels that one has special gifts and accomplishments and therefore deserves special treatment; seems combative, self-important, and unrealistically expectant of deference from others
Overconfidence	Seems modest and realistic about abilities but may have low standards for work quality or seem to lack focus and drive	Unusually confident in one's abilities; believes that one will succeed in anything; highly organized and systematic, but overestimates one's level of competence and worth
Fantasized Talent	Practical, content, and realistic about abilities; may seem to prefer more routine work or come across as uninventive	Believes that one has unusual talents or gifts and has been born for greatness; seems original and inventive, but arrogant, hypercompetitive, and unrealistic

Leadership and Reputation Implications

The behaviors associated with the Bold scale concern the most visible aspects of a leader's style. Followers look to leaders to instill confidence, especially when it is backed up with a track record of success. Moreover, it is in the toughest of times that these behaviors create memories in followers that become a virtually intractable component of a leader's reputation, which is why the Bold scale offers so much insight into a leader's effectiveness.

Behaviors associated with low Bold scores, particularly when they suggest a lack of self-confidence that is directly measured by the Overconfidence subscale, will cause a leader to rely heavily on position power as a way to motivate others—that is, "do it because I am the boss." High Bold behaviors cause people to believe, and when they believe, they can accomplish more than they imagine. Unfortunately, there is a fine line between confidence and arrogance. Leaders who cross that line can demotivate their followers to the point of tempting them to subvert the leaders' effectiveness. Blaming or credit-grabbing behaviors are among the worst associated with the high end of the Bold scale, and they are virtually assured to diminish a leader's effectiveness.

Risk Summary

	Low Scores	High Scores
Career	Lack of apparent self-confidence will create a follower reputation	Self-promotion may work in the short run, but can do career damage in the long run
	May miss opportunities because of an unwillingness to be assertive	Arrogance can breed resentment and revenge when opportunities arise
Performance	Superiors may overlook views presented without confidence	Superiors may lose confidence when they see an inability to learn from mistakes
	Peers may see insecurity as a sign of weakness or a person easily influenced	Peers may tire of excessive self-confidence or arrogance
	Direct reports may mirror a lack of confidence in ideas or positions	Direct reports may leave when victimized by blaming or credit grabbing
	Opponents may easily sway potential supporters when they see a leader who lacks confidence	Opponents may easily enlist others in efforts to undermine a leader who seems arrogant

MISCHIEVOUS

Description: The Mischievous scale concerns seeming bright, attractive, adventurous, risk-seeking, and limit-testing.

| Low scorers are conservative, compliant, and potentially boring | Behavior Range | High scorers are impulsive, limit-testing, and at times, devious |

Subscale	Low Score	High Score
Risky	Compliant, conservative, and cooperative; avoids unneccesary risk and makes few mistakes; may seem unadventurous or overly conforming	Prone to taking risks and testing limits; deliberately bends or breaks inconvenient rules; may seem unconcerned with risk
Impulsive	Dependable, reliable, and focused; may seem overly reserved, conventional, or predictable	Tends to act without considering the long-term consequences of one's actions; seems disorganized, impetuous, and unpredictable
Manipulative	Seems genuine, straightforward, and trustworthy; may seem overly inhibited; may struggle to gain influence or persuade others	Uses charm to manipulate others and demonstrates no remorse for doing so; may be persusasive and interesting but may potentially seem insincere or deceptive

Leadership and Reputation Implications

Trust is the foundation on which leadership effectiveness depends. Without trust, there is little chance a leader will succeed. If leaders are trusted, many leadership mistakes will be forgiven. On the surface, behaviors associated with the Mischievous scale do not seem to concern trust issues. In fact, it is the cumulative effect of behaviors associated with high-end scores that will erode trust, especially if all three subscales are elevated. Followers do not necessarily trust or distrust a leader at the outset of a relationship. The trust equation is relatively neutral unless a leader has a reputation as trustworthy or devious. In either case, followers have their antennae up to detect whether or not a leader can be trusted.

High-end behaviors accumulate very fast in their ability to diminish trust. These behaviors may appear as interesting, provocative, and even charismatic, but as they are overdone, followers are keeping score. Low-end behaviors will not create an interesting, charismatic reputation for a leader. They might even lead to a reputation for being boring. However, they will not detract from a leader's reputation for being trustworthy. The balance point for behaviors associated with the Mischievous scale is for a leader to be charismatic (or at least interesting) without engaging in the limit-testing, impetuous, or devious behaviors that can contribute to a reputation of untrustworthiness.

Risk Summary

	Low Scores	High Scores
Career	May miss opportunities that exist outside official channels	May erode the trust needed with increasingly responsible positions
	May lack the spirit of adventure necessary to seize opportunities	May create a reputation as a rebel, reducing career opportunities
Performance	Superiors may tire of a rule-compliant, conservative approach	Superiors may see limit-testing as unreliable
	Peers may not network with a dull and boring person	Peers may see devious activities as untrustworthy
	Direct reports may develop a "corporate attitude"	Direct reports may see limit testing as a license for them to break rules
	Opponents may use the conservative mindset to slow or derail progress	Opponents may seek support and cover when their actions appear too risky

COLORFUL

Description: The Colorful scale concerns enjoying being in the spotlight and seeming gregarious, fun, and entertaining.

| Low scorers are modest, unassuming, quiet, and self-restrained | Behavior Range | High scorers are attention-seeking, dramatic, and socially prominent |

Subscale	Low Score	High Score
Public Confidence	Self-restrained, quiet, and controlled; may seem socially reserved, inhibited, and lacking in outward confidence	Outgoing, confident, engaging; presents ideas with energy and enthusiasm, but is attention-seeking, dominates conversation, and talks over others
Distractible	Focused, task-oriented, and methodical; may seem unable to shift gears quickly or multitask effectively	Energetic, curious, and idea-oriented; easily bored, distractible, lacks focus; needs constant stimulation; confuses activity with productivity
Self-Display	Restrained, adherent to social norms and expectations; may not make a strong impression on others	Expressive, entertaining, and dynamic; enjoys the spotlight; uses dramatics to attract attention to oneself; may seem self-absorbed

Leadership and Reputation Implications

Leaders are often the center of attention. Behaviors associated with the Colorful scale predict the degree to which a leader embraces those situations. Leaders who exhibit behaviors at the low end seem to believe that their performance should speak for itself. This is unrealistic because their competitors are more than willing to call attention to themselves and their accomplishments. Being socially reticent can turn a leader into a gray spot on a gray wall—someone who goes unnoticed.

More often, however, leaders need to avoid excessive use of high-end behaviors. It is one thing to discreetly draw attention to oneself and one's accomplishments. It is another thing to suck the oxygen out of a room. From management's perspective, high Colorful behaviors create noise that can diminish a leader's credibility. From the direct reports' perspective, it can be demotivating when a leader constantly upstages them with excessive attention seeking that can be seen as credit grabbing.

It is also important not to forget behaviors associated with an elevation on the Distractible subscale. These behaviors cause leaders to lose focus, or worse, jump from task to task or meeting to meeting, failing to get anything tangible accomplished.

Risk Summary

	Low Scores	High Scores
Career	May be underestimated	May be too self-focused and not a team player
	May seem to lack impact and not appear leader-like	Drama and exaggerations may create mistrust
	Vunerable to others' taking credit for contributions	Self-promotion can cloud real accomplishments
Performance	Superiors may overlook views and opinions	Over-promising may lead to a credibility gap with superiors
	Peers may take the unassuming approach as tacitly supporting them	Peers may tire of being upstaged
	Direct reports may see the unassuming approach as a lack of advocacy	Direct reports may see attention-seeking as credit grabbing
	Opponents may steal the limelight even when it is undeserved	Opponents may use attention-seeking as cover for their own actions

IMAGINATIVE

Description: The Imaginative scale concerns seeming innovative, creative, possibly eccentric, and sometimes self-absorbed.

| Low scorers are practical, rely on routine, and often lack new ideas | Behavior Range | High scorers may seem impractical and unpredictable, and offer unusual ideas |

Subscale	Low Score	High Score
Eccentric	Conventional, practical, and organized; may seem unoriginal or lacking in creativity	Curious and imaginative, but disorganized, distractible, and lacking in follow-through; expresses unusual views that can be either creative or merely strange
Special Sensitivity	Seems open to others' ideas and perspectives, but others may not perceive a strong sense of vision	Belief that one has special abilities to see things others don't and understand complex issues that others cannot
Creative Thinking	Pragmatic and grounded; may seem uninspired or lacking in curiosity and creativity	Highly creative, inventive, and idea-oriented; easily bored, and potentially overconfident in one's problem-solving ability

Leadership and Reputation Implications

Generating ideas, exhibiting creative problem-solving, and seeing around corners are all components of a leader's reputation for being strategic. One of the most common development needs cited for a leader is the need to be more strategic. It is also one of the most misunderstood characteristics of an effective leader. Nonetheless, leaders who offer new ideas (especially when they cause others to think) increase the probability that they will be viewed as strategic. It is also clear that having a reputation for being strategic significantly increases the probability that a leader will be viewed as a high-potential or a candidate for advancement.

Leaders with high Imaginative scores who blather about their ideas and offer impractical solutions will not develop a reputation for being strategic; rather, they may be seen as eccentric or even strange. At the low end of the Imaginative scale, a leader's reputation will likely be one of being excessively practical or stuck in past routines, a particularly salient issue when the Creative Thinking subscale is depressed, indicating a very strong propensity for problem-solving to be grounded in routine, well-known alternatives. Regardless, in a world that sometimes seems to value innovation more than leadership fundamentals, leaders need to overcome low-end Imaginative behaviors without crossing the line into the eccentric in order to avoid the career-limiting label "not strategic."

Risk Summary

	Low Scores	High Scores
Career	May garner a reputation for lacking creativity or strategic thinking	May diminish credibility with eccentric ideas
	May miss chances to inject new thinking	Lack of predictability may cause a reputation as an erratic leader
	May stifle creativity by pursuing routine alternatives	Excessive ideation may confuse those implementing ideas
Performance	Superiors may overlook views when discussing strategy	Superiors may miss the good ideas that are disguised in excessive ideation
	Peers may not seek or may even ignore problem-solving ideas	Peers may dismiss input as often too impractical
	Direct reports may become complacent regarding innovation	Direct reports may be confused by frequent changes of direction
	Opponents may use reliance upon routine to thwart change they fear or don't want	Opponents will cite unusual or eccentric ideas to discredit good ideas

DILIGENT

Description: The Diligent scale concerns being hardworking and detail oriented, and having high standards of performance for self and others.

Low scorers have poor attention to detail and tend to over-delegate	Behavior Range	High scorers are picky and overly conscientious, and tend to micromanage

Subscale	Low Score	High Score
Standards	Seems relaxed and forgiving with respect to performance standards; may seem careless and disorganized	Exceptionally high standards of performance for oneself and others; practical, systematic, and exacting
Perfectionistic	Action-oriented; works quickly; may neglect important details or seem expedient	Perfectionistic about the quality of work products and obsessed with the details of their completion; precise and competitive
Organized	Flexible; able to work comfortably in ambiguous situations; seems inattentive to rules/policies, may not demonstrate strong planning skills or adequate follow-through	Meticulous and inflexible about schedules, timing, rules, and procedures; organized, thorough, and efficient, but management style marked by excessive control

Leadership and Reputation Implications

People are often promoted into leadership roles because they exhibit high Diligent behaviors. It is far less common for people to get promoted because they were not detail oriented or delegated too freely, behaviors common at the low end of the Diligent scale. The behaviors associated with this scale speak to the need for a leader to evolve over time. Early in the career of a leader, high-end Diligent behaviors are quite valued and in many instances essential, given that direct reports may be young or involved in a variety of lower-level tasks. As a leader's career progresses, it is essential to let go of high-end behaviors in favor of greater empowerment of direct reports.

Effective leaders rarely engage in excessive empowerment or what has been called abandonment. They understand how to stay close without taking over. This ability has several important side benefits: (1) it creates a growth environment for subordinates, allowing them to take on more responsibility, and (2) it also frees up the leader to take on more responsibility without sacrificing work-life balance.

An underlying theme related to this scale is the sheer volume of work a leader is able to handle. All three subscales contribute to this theme. At the high end, leaders often cannot keep up with all the challenges that come their way. At the low end, a leader may let go of tasks too soon or fail to adequately follow up on task completion.

Risk Summary

	Low Scores	High Scores
Career	May delegate tasks requiring more oversight	May become overwhelmed with trying to manage everything
	May not give feedback or follow up adequately	True priorities may suffer as all priorities are emphasized equally
	May miss steps or actions essential for successful implementation	Micromanagement may cause work-life balance to suffer
Performance	Superiors may be uneasy with a lack of detail approach	Superiors may see an implementer, not a leader
	Peers may look for more details or substance in projects affecting them	Peers may see the excess focus on details as a bottleneck
	Direct reports may feel cast adrift with little oversight or feedback	Direct reports may be demotivated by micromanagement
	Opponents may use poor follow-up as a way to advance their own agenda	Opponents may rely on conscientiousness to avoid work they should be doing

DUTIFUL

Description: The Dutiful scale concerns seeming to be a loyal and dependable subordinate and organizational citizen.

| Low scorers are overly independent and seem to resent authority | Behavior Range | High scorers are excessively eager to please superiors |

Subscale	Low Score	High Score
Indecisive	Independent and self-sufficient, and may fail to solicit advice or gain buy-in from others when making decisions; may be too quick to dismiss others' input	Overly reliant on others for advice, and reluctant to act independently; careful to seek approval and/or consensus before making decisions
Ingratiating	Self-reliant and tough-minded; may seem insubordinate, may contradict others, or seem unwilling to play politics	Excessively eager to please one's superiors, telling them what they want to hear and never contradicting them; seems overly deferential and hesitant to express strong opinions
Conforming	Challenging; willing to express opinions, but may come across as rebellious, defiant, or disloyal at times; may be inappropriately challenging or contentious	Takes pride in supporting one's superiors and following their orders, regardless of one's personal opinion; seems overly cooperative, obedient, and excessively concerned with compliance

Leadership and Reputation Implications

Leaders need to avoid overly dependent followership behaviors that are associated with the high end of the Dutiful scale. A reputation for high Dutiful behaviors will put a ceiling on a leader's career because of his or her perceived inability to take independent action, or worse, being seen as the "yes person" for the manager. An interesting corollary to the challenges of high Dutiful behaviors is the way a manager might take advantage of the individual by limiting opportunities just to keep the individual in the fold doing the manager's bidding.

Low-end Dutiful behaviors do not seem to be nearly as problematic for a leader. The most significant risk is the potential for friction to develop with authority figures. Leaders exhibiting low Dutiful behaviors may resent management controls and seem rebellious or insubordinate. Managers who have a need for control may be intolerant of these behaviors or even see them as a form of disloyalty. It may seem counterintuitive to consider disloyalty in a conversation about the Dutiful scale, but leaders have a strong need for a degree of followership from direct reports. Decisive, tough, and even rebellious behaviors are inconsistent with behaviors associated with loyalty.

Risk Summary

	Low Scores	High Scores
Career	May miss lessons learned or coaching from those with situational knowledge	May get a reputation as a follower who is best suited doing the bidding of others
	May challenge or dismiss input from the wrong person	May over-promise as the result of being too eager to please
	May exceed latitude of authority in making decisions or taking action	Indecisiveness may slow progress by creating bottlenecks
Performance	Superiors may be uncomfortable with excessive independence	Superiors may tire of dependence or need for guidance
	Peers may question loyalty or trustworthiness	Peers may see a "yes person" incapable of independent action
	Direct reports may lack a role model for organizational citizenship	Direct reports may feel victimized by over-commitments
	Opponents may move into a void created by excessive independence or failure to stay in touch with senior players	Opponents may prey on eager to please attitude to accomplish work they want to avoid

Summary

The HDS is one of the most powerful assessment tools available to leaders and coaches. Its strength lies in providing behavior-based information that will significantly enhance a leader's Strategic Self-awareness and serve as a foundation for continuous improvement through focused development.

This chapter offers evidence regarding why the HDS is seen as an invaluable leadership development tool. The chapter traces the evolution of the HDS from Robert Hogan's early thinking through inventory development to the commercial implementation and continuous improvement of the inventory. Along the way, the discussion highlights some of the science used to develop the inventory to indicate the rigor used throughout the test development process. The chapter concludes with some of the newest thinking about interpreting the HDS. Three key topics include the role of self-monitoring in controlling negative behaviors, the addition of subscales, and the impact of low scores on leader performance. In Chapter 5, we go beyond the interpretation fundamentals by introducing the concept of Situational Context. This concept shifts interpretation of HDS results from a static exercise to a dynamic process, requiring leaders to juxtapose their profile against the realities of their situation.

CHAPTER 5

IMPACT OF SITUATIONAL CONTEXT

INTRODUCTION

Situational Context is not a new idea when it comes to understanding the performance of leaders. There were times in the late 1960s and early 1970s when the notion of situational leadership dominated the literature. Unfortunately, researchers fell off the proverbial cliff by suggesting that the only thing that mattered to leadership performance was the situation—a position that quickly became untenable. In this chapter, we will trace the rise of personality as the dominant predictor of leader performance. But rather than go down the path of suggesting that personality is the only thing that matters, we will introduce the role that Situational Context plays in conjunction with personality in understanding leader performance. We conclude this chapter with a series of nine case studies illustrating the relationship between personality characteristics as measured by the Hogan Development Survey (HDS) and key situational variables. These case studies will serve as the foundation for discussing the coaching techniques covered in Part IV that are aimed at improving leader performance.

EMERGENCE OF INTERPERSONAL THEORY

The early history of personality was dominated by intrapsychic theories of personality where attempting to understand what is going on in a person's head was the only real priority. Perhaps the best known is the Psychoanalytic Theory of Sigmund Freud, which focused on the importance of understanding one's neuroses that were rooted in early childhood. Freud's views were so influential that some people think that all of psychology is little more than Freudian theory (Hogan & Smither, 2008). However, there have been many famous psychologists associated with various intrapsychic theories, including Carl Jung, Alfred Adler, and Karen Horney to name just a few. They all have one quest in common: determining the "why" underpinning all of the behaviors of a person. As a consequence, all of the assessment tools associated with personality theories of this type were designed to diagnose why people do what they do. The tools were notoriously unreliable and even less valid.

The intrapsychic theories of personality did not die with the passing of many of the European stalwarts in the history of psychology. In fact, intrapsychic theories found their way to America in the form of Trait Theory, as proposed by Gordon Allport in the late 1930s (Allport, 1937). Allport believed that personality could be defined in terms of a small number of statistically defined dimensions of individual differences. These traits served both as shorthand descriptions for how a person behaves and as enduring neural psychological structures in the brain. Allport was critical of Psychoanalytic Theory—or any theory of psychology, for that matter—that attempted to reduce people to abstract categories. He was interested in understanding individual uniqueness and compiled an exhaustive list of terms to represent the basic text or language of personality. That list was ultimately reduced to 4,500 traits that, to this day, form the basis for most modern research on the structure of personality.

Allport's work on traits played a very important role with respect to contemporary theories of personality. Researchers in the 1960s and 1970s (e.g., Norman, 1963; Wiggins, 1973) proposed that the 4,500 common traits could be reduced to somewhere between three and seven broad themes or primary dimensions. These themes have subsequently been referred to as the Five-Factor Model (FFM) of personality. Unfortunately, ardent supporters of the FFM persist in their view that even when reduced to five themes, they still just describe consistent patterns of behavior that are controlled by neural psychological structures. In other words, they continue in the tradition of intrapsychic theories, where what goes on in one's head is central to any true understanding of personality. This is the fundamental problem with all intrapsychic theories. It is difficult, if not impossible, to study what goes on inside a person's head. This presents an enormous research challenge and explains why intrapsychic theories in general, and Trait Theories specifically, have done little to advance our understanding of personality beyond elaborate labeling taxonomies.

Intrapsychic theories are not likely to go away any time in the foreseeable future. However, their value in understanding personality is being seriously challenged by Interpersonal Theory. Interpersonal Theory is rooted in the socioanalytic view of human nature. The core of this view is that people are motivated by three broad needs: (1) attention, approval, and acceptance; (2) status and control of resources; and (3) predictability and order in their everyday lives (Hogan & Smither, 2008). These needs can be referred to as getting along, getting ahead, and finding meaning. People meet these needs through social interactions, which are composed of pretexts or agendas and the roles or parts people play. A person's identity guides the social interactions in which that person engages by dictating the roles that he or she will (or will not) play. In short, the behavior that a person demonstrates at any point in time is a function of identity, which determines the role selected in the social interactions in which the person chooses to engage. Social interactions always entail meeting one or more of the basic human needs of getting along, getting ahead, or finding meaning.

The growing popularity of Interpersonal Theory can be attributed to the way it distinguishes between the actor's view of personality and the observer's view of personality. The actor's view of personality is identity; it is the person who *we* think we are. The observer's view of personality is reputation; it is the person who *others* think we are. This distinction is of immense importance because reputation can be reliably measured and accurately described using the FFM dimensions. Furthermore, when reputation is measured with a well-developed personality inventory, the results can be used to predict a wide range of life outcomes, including social acceptance and career success (Hogan & Hogan, 2007).

Interpersonal Theory is a dramatic departure from intrapsychic theories of personality that seek to discover what a person is like way down deep, or to understand the neural psychological structures of the brain. The focus on predicting life outcomes sets Interpersonal Theory apart from all its predecessors. It goes beyond description and establishes a measurement goal that can be tested like any sound theory associated with the sciences. Hogan personality inventories have been built upon Interpersonal Theory in that they are specifically designed to predict the job performance of working adults—a critical life outcome.

PREDICTING JOB PERFORMANCE

The development of a personality inventory that predicts job performance requires the systematic application of formal psychometric techniques. It begins with a clear understanding of what it means when people respond to items on a personality inventory. They are providing self-presentations of their identities, and these self-presentations can be organized using the dimensions of the FFM to form their reputational profiles. A reputational profile can be used to evaluate how a person is perceived by others. The predictive validity of the personality inventory is then determined by correlating reputational profiles with job performance.

In practice, however, it is rarely as simple as the foregoing description might lead one to believe. Determining the predictive validity of a personality inventory is more of a process than an event. It requires the accumulation of validity evidence in the form of data from many studies involving thousands of subjects. The

Hogan approach to test construction, known as Kaizen Psychometrics, was originally created to deal with the challenges of producing well-developed and validated personality inventories. This process involves the continuous improvement of inventories through the use of empirical data. In essence, Hogan inventories never reach an end state of development. Studies are conducted. Items are reviewed and rewritten. The psychometric properties of the inventories are evaluated. The norms are regularly updated. Even the reports that capture reputational profiles undergo regular reviews and edits to improve their accuracy. In fact, it is difficult to imagine the term *valid* being associated with any inventory developed under an approach where test construction was viewed as an event, rather than a process.

An important corollary to the use of Kaizen Psychometrics to improve Hogan inventories is the understanding that has emerged regarding the evaluation of job performance. If the goal is predicting the job performance of working adults, then it is necessary to accurately evaluate performance—it is the only relevant criterion. Unfortunately, accurately evaluating job performance is far from a simple task for the following reasons:

- Evaluating job performance has probably occupied as much journal space as the topic of leadership, and there is still not an agreed-upon model for job performance. Entire books are available on the topic of performance measurement, with no consensus on even a definition.

- No two companies (not even ones with similar jobs) evaluate job performance in the same way.

- The most common method for evaluating job performance is through supervisory ratings, which are consistently unreliable and riddled with personal bias and often bear little relationship to future performance.

- Supervisory ratings are almost always associated with administrative outcomes (raises, promotions, terminations, etc.), which further limit them as true measures of performance.

- When hard measures are used, such as sales figures, number of units produced, service provided, and so on, they are usually confounded with any number of other organizational factors that limit their utility. Corporate auditors even question the value of such hard measures as legitimate indicators of return on investment.

What these job-performance evaluation obstacles demonstrate is that there is no such thing as job performance. There are just ratings of job performance, which are fundamentally dependent on the Situational Context in which the ratings occur. Because of the vagaries of Situational Context, developing an all-encompassing job-performance evaluation instrument could be a real problem if the goal of a well-constructed personality inventory is to predict the job performance of working adults. However, this problem actually presents an important opportunity when test construction is approached as a process using Kaizen Psychometrics.

First, consider that all good criteria measures capture variance in job performance. To the extent that a well-developed personality inventory correlates with the variance in job performance, validity will go up. Hogan inventories consistently outperform the competition in capturing variance in job performance. That is, the Hogan validity coefficients are consistently higher than those of the competition— the inventories are able to successfully meet their intended goal of predicting the job performance of working adults.

Second, effective (or ineffective) job performance is whatever the organization says it is, underscoring the fact that job performance is largely a situational variable, and ratings of it are heavily dependent on contextual factors. The impact on the validity of a well-developed personality inventory is clear. If an inventory is going to be considered robust (i.e., predict performance across many types of jobs and organizations), it has to be able to accommodate the situational vagaries that are inherent in criteria measures and, consequently, job performance.

SITUATIONAL CONTEXT

It is important to consider some of the key situational factors that contribute to ratings of job performance, particularly those factors that relate to the performance of a leader. Three factors are especially relevant to this discussion, including (1) the culture of the organization in which the job is being performed (Culture Context), (2) the personality characteristics of the person doing the rating (Manager Context), and (3) the role in which the individual is performing (Role Context). The following is a brief description of these contextual factors and how they impact ratings of job performance.

Culture Context

This contextual factor includes the norms, values, taboos, and success factors associated with the culture of an organization. No two organizations are alike, regardless of whether they happen to produce competing products or they are part of the same industry. What sets organizations apart from one another is culture. While it can be defined in a variety of ways, Ravasi and Schultz (2006) view organizational culture as a set of shared mental assumptions that guide interpretation and action in organizations by defining appropriate behavior for various situations. One of those situations involves rating job performance for those working for the organization. The combined aspects of the culture will influence the way job performance is rated. For example, in some organizations, the only thing that matters is results. In other organizations, how those results are achieved may be equally important. Even the way rating scales are utilized in an organization can be influenced by the culture. Some organizations are lenient in their ratings, while others can be very tough.

The Culture Context can have a dramatic impact on the success of an employee. Consider a hardworking new supervisor who performs his or her job in a very competent fashion. The new supervisor happens to have a very high score on the Colorful scale of the HDS. The behaviors that the new supervisor demonstrates on the job that are associated with the Colorful scale include being very dramatic, seeking the attention of others, overcommitting on assignments, and generally looking for ways to stand out as a leader.

Let's say that the organization this new supervisor works for happens to have a very strong sales and marketing type of culture. Furthermore, attention-seeking behaviors are quite common among many employees, and employees who fail to call attention to themselves often go unnoticed. In other words, the Culture Context not only supports the Colorful behaviors demonstrated by the new supervisor, they are almost a prerequisite for getting noticed and advancing in the organization. The new supervisor with a reputation for demonstrating high Colorful behaviors would not only survive but may thrive.

In contrast, let's say that our new supervisor joined a different organization. This organization supports a more engineering-oriented culture versus one that is sales and marketing oriented. In this culture, high Colorful attention-seeking behaviors are shunned. Perhaps they are even shunned at what might otherwise be considered an acceptable level in many organizations. The behaviors supported in this organization would look much more introverted, reserved, and even quiet. Despite being hardworking and performing competently, there is every chance that our new supervisor would garner considerable negative attention for demonstrating high Colorful behaviors. At the very least, he or she would likely get feedback to dial back the Colorful behaviors. It might even be the case that without making the appropriate behavior changes, the new supervisor could be let go on the basis of a poor cultural fit.

These two examples illustrate how the Culture Context can play a central role in determining an employee's success. In one organization, the behavioral tendencies associated with a high Colorful score worked to the advantage of the employee. In the second situation, those same behavioral tendencies could result in quite a different outcome. In other words, the rating of job performance of the new supervisor could be dramatically impacted by the Culture Context.

Manager Context

This contextual factor includes the style of the manager doing the ratings and his or her core values and priorities. All managers vary in the way they approach the task of rating performance. Training and sound rating formats can improve consistency across managers, but individual rating differences will always be present. It is interesting that this contextual factor can even come into play within an organization. Employees are often confronted with leadership changes, and their performance may be rated by more than one manager. These types of situations bring the Manager Context into play, which may have an impact on employee success that rivals that of the Culture Context.

The impact of the Manager Context can be illustrated using the previous example of the new supervisor with a high Colorful score. Consider a situation in which the new supervisor reports to a manager who has a similar high Colorful score. It can be expected that the manager would exhibit high Colorful behaviors such as attention-seeking or being overly dramatic. If the new supervisor demonstrates similar high Colorful behaviors, it is likely to go unnoticed by the manager. Interestingly, there may be some additional dynamics at work. For example, the manager may become annoyed with the new supervisor because each is competing for attention. Alternatively, the manager may encourage the new supervisor to demonstrate attention-seeking behaviors as the manager may view them as an essential ingredient for success. Dynamics such as these underscore the awareness challenge employees face on a regular basis. They may not realize it in the concrete terms just described, but these dynamics are quite prevalent throughout the career of an employee.

Now consider what would happen if there was a leadership change for the new supervisor, with the incoming manager having a very low score on the Colorful scale. It is entirely possible that the incoming manager would have disdain for high Colorful behaviors. It may even be the case that such behaviors would elicit negative feedback from the manager in the form of poor performance ratings. In any case, the new supervisor's high Colorful behaviors in relation to the incoming manager's low Colorful behaviors could have serious ramifications for the supervisor's success.

Role Context

This contextual factor is related to the role a person occupies or a role to which the individual aspires. Roles are often not as clear cut as the Culture or Manager contextual factors. In fact, roles can vary by situation and place a significant burden on an individual to maintain a high degree of vigilance regarding behaviors that are appropriate, or more importantly, inappropriate. Again, the example using high Colorful behaviors helps illustrate the impact of this factor. A new supervisor will play a variety of roles as part of his or her job. Two of the most common responsibilities will entail being the leader to those reporting to him or her and a team member working with peers who report to a common manager at the next level up. It may be the case that high Colorful behaviors will be tolerated differently in these two roles. Subordinates may be quite tolerant of some Colorful behaviors in their leader. Peers, on the other hand, may view the Colorful behaviors through a more competitive lens and have little tolerance for them. In either case, it is crucial for the new supervisor to maintain a degree of situational awareness that includes an understanding of the roles that are part of the job and the behavioral expectations that accompany them.

The notion of Situational Context and its relation to employee success can be overwhelming when one considers the myriad possibilities that are ever present in the workplace. Employees confront situational factors daily and find ways to cope with them. It is important to highlight the Culture, Manager, and Role contextual factors because they play such an important part in the success or failure of an employee at every career stage and are ever present in the rating of job performance. In the next section, cases will be presented that pose a situational challenge for an employee based on changes that occur in the contextual factors of Culture, Manager, or Role.

IMPACT OF CULTURE, MANAGER, AND ROLE CONTEXTUAL FACTORS

The following nine cases are designed to illustrate the impact that changes in the Culture, Manager, and Role contextual factors can have on a leader with a given HDS profile. Each case includes a description of the leader's situation before the change, highlights of the leader's HDS profile, a description of the situational change, and potential consequences for the leader as a result of the change. Table 2 provides an overview of each case categorized by the contextual factor and the HDS factor being illustrated. The HDS factor "Moving Away" includes the Excitable, Skeptical, Cautious, Reserved, and Leisurely HDS scales. The HDS factor "Moving Against" includes the Bold, Mischievous, Colorful, and Imaginative HDS scales. The HDS factor "Moving Toward" includes the Diligent and Dutiful HDS scales. We decided to organize the cases in this fashion because the HDS factors have been consistently demonstrated to exist empirically, and it allows for a parsimonious way to accurately portray a very wide range of leader behavior with just nine cases. These nine cases will serve as the foundation for describing how the coaching tips and techniques covered in Part IV can be applied to improve leader performance.

HDS Factor	Contextual Factors		
	Culture	**Manager**	**Role**
Moving Away	**Case 1** **(Low Cautious)** Rex, a risk taker, moves from a small company where he had autonomy to a much larger, more bureaucratic company. The acquiring company was not known for supporting risks, especially in sales.	**Case 2** **(High Skeptical)** Phil, a skeptical logistics person working in a traditional logistics function, has been asked to report to a new head of logistics who has different ideas about the way the function should run.	**Case 3** **(High Reserved)** Robert is an individual contributor who is very quiet and reserved. He has participated on project teams and is now being asked to be the leader of a project.
Moving Against	**Case 4** **(High Mischievous)** Tanya is a crafty insurance professional. She is known for putting together big deals for corporate clients. Her success got her promoted to training manager, reporting to the regional VP.	**Case 5** **(Low Bold)** Janis is a recently promoted customer service manager. She lacks self-confidence, but makes up for it with hard work and attention to detail. Her new manager is an ambitious high-potential leader.	**Case 6** **(High Colorful)** Mark is a district account manager for a consumer products company. Mark's high profile style came under fire when the company expanded his role to include government accounts.
Moving Toward	**Case 7** **(High Dutiful)** James is a marketing manager who worked for the same person in a family-owned business for more than ten years. When the company was sold, James's position was eliminated, forcing him to take a similar position in a technology start-up.	**Case 8** **(Low Diligent)** Courtney just returned to the U.S. from a new plant start-up assignment in Mexico. She was very successful managing a small team of start-up pros. Her new position is assistant operations manager in a manufacturing facility.	**Case 9** **(High Diligent)** Kelly was promoted to CFO for a large clothing retailer. She was known as a detail person who put in long hours and made sure nothing ever fell through the cracks. In her new role, she manages all aspects of the Finance function.

Table 2   Case Studies Categorized by Contextual Factors and HDS Factors

CASE 1—REX, VICE PRESIDENT OF SALES (LOW CAUTIOUS)

Situation

Rex is the vice president of sales for a small start-up company that specializes in the development and sales of natural vitamin supplements. The company has a solid regional presence with impressive growth numbers in a highly competitive market. In addition to the company-developed brand of supplements, Rex's sales team also represents a number of other brands that allow the company to offer a much broader range of products that complement the company's own brand. Rex has been with the company since the very early days of the start-up. He has a great deal of autonomy and is used to making lots of decisions about what brands the company represents and how they are represented to retail customers. Much of the company's growth can be attributed to Rex's aggressive style and willingness to take chances on brands with little or no market presence in their region.

HDS Profile

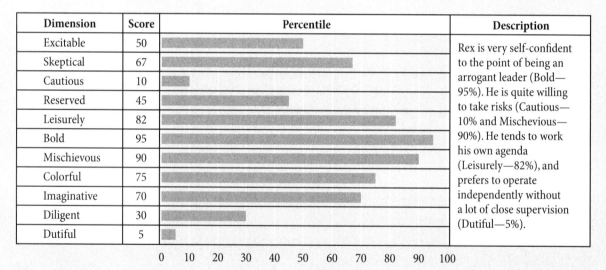

Dimension	Score	Percentile	Description
Excitable	50		Rex is very self-confident to the point of being an arrogant leader (Bold—95%). He is quite willing to take risks (Cautious—10% and Mischevious—90%). He tends to work his own agenda (Leisurely—82%), and prefers to operate independently without a lot of close supervision (Dutiful—5%).
Skeptical	67		
Cautious	10		
Reserved	45		
Leisurely	82		
Bold	95		
Mischevous	90		
Colorful	75		
Imaginative	70		
Diligent	30		
Dutiful	5		

0   10   20   30   40   50   60   70   80   90   100

Situational Change

Six months ago, the company was acquired by a major producer of vitamin supplements. The acquiring company was well established and known for its strong brand recognition and relying upon its size and market presence to drive sales. Rex was asked to stay on as vice president of sales and continue to build business for the company's natural brand of vitamin supplements. Rex continued to operate as he had in the past, relying on his aggressive style and willingness to take risks when the situation called for it. He paid little attention to the growing bureaucracy that was being imposed by the new parent company.

Situational Impact

The acquiring company in this case is described as large with strong brand recognition. It is likely that a company such as this would be somewhat bureaucratic, with established boundaries for decision-making. Rex's entrepreneurial approach, including his tendency to follow his own agenda, take risks, and act independently, is likely to run counter to the prevailing culture of the parent company. The situation is further exacerbated by the fact that Rex's decisions related to sales would be highly visible to others who are used to operating within the cultural guidelines associated with risk.

Case 2—Phil, Logistics Technician (High Skeptical)

Situation

Phil is the lead logistics technician for the western region of a national trucking company. He is known for his careful attention to detail and a heavy-handed approach when it comes to cost control and routing options. He is proud of his ability to sniff out potential problems and call them to the attention of management before they create issues for the company. His current manager often relied upon him to detect problems and to deliver bad news to the field when the situation called for it. The field employees, on the other hand, viewed him as a watchdog, always on the lookout for problems. They only approached him when necessary, and they knew that even relatively minor issues they might raise could be elevated to upper management and draw unwanted attention.

HDS Profile

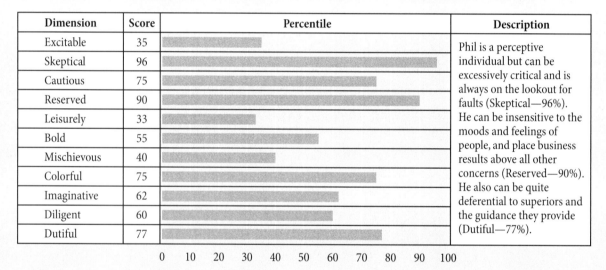

Dimension	Score	Percentile	Description
Excitable	35		Phil is a perceptive individual but can be excessively critical and is always on the lookout for faults (Skeptical—96%). He can be insensitive to the moods and feelings of people, and place business results above all other concerns (Reserved—90%). He also can be quite deferential to superiors and the guidance they provide (Dutiful—77%).
Skeptical	96		
Cautious	75		
Reserved	90		
Leisurely	33		
Bold	55		
Mischievous	40		
Colorful	75		
Imaginative	62		
Diligent	60		
Dutiful	77		

0 10 20 30 40 50 60 70 80 90 100

Situational Change

The head of logistics whom Phil worked for decided to leave and start his own logistics consulting firm. The CEO of Phil's company decided that this was an opportunity to bring in some new leadership talent and create more of a partnership between corporate and the field. The new head of logistics began her tenure by touring the field and gathering input from employees, including the regional logistics teams. During an offsite meeting with the lead technicians, the head of logistics outlined her vision for the function and her plan for implementing it. Key among her plans was an insistence that the logistics function had to move away from the old by-the-numbers mentality and partner with the field employees, much in the same way that the field employees partnered with their customers.

Situational Impact

Phil will likely be faced with two challenges under the new leader. First, he clearly came out of the old by-the-numbers model, where logistics was primarily a corporate watchdog function responsible for monitoring performance, monitoring costs, and enforcing route compliance. Second, it is quite likely that Phil's reputation would have preceded him in any employee-level interviews conducted by the new head of logistics. In other words, the head of logistics could have formed an early impression of Phil based on his reputation, and that impression would likely be in conflict with her vision for logistics to work in partnership with the field employees.

CASE 3—ROBERT, DESIGN ENGINEER
(HIGH RESERVED)

Situation

Robert is a design engineer for a manufacturer of commercial aircraft electronic components. Since graduating from college, he has worked mainly as an individual contributor on a variety of project teams. He is known as a hard worker who attends closely to details. His team members often describe him as a quiet person who rarely speaks up in meetings or offers his own ideas. They also describe him as a very dependable person whom they welcome as a team member because he always comes through in the clutch when the workload becomes demanding. His most recent assignment involved a high-profile project that was critical to the company's future success. Robert worked extensive overtime to see the project through and was seen by upper management as one of the behind-the-scenes guys who helped ensure the success of the project.

HDS Profile

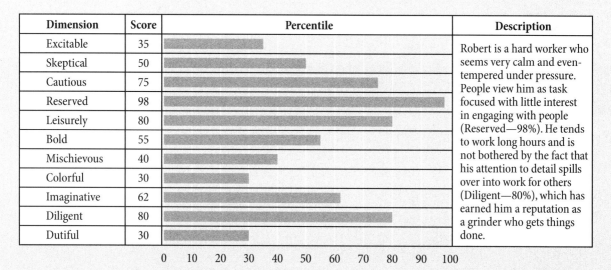

Dimension	Score	Percentile	Description
Excitable	35		Robert is a hard worker who seems very calm and even-tempered under pressure. People view him as task focused with little interest in engaging with people (Reserved—98%). He tends to work long hours and is not bothered by the fact that his attention to detail spills over into work for others (Diligent—80%), which has earned him a reputation as a grinder who gets things done.
Skeptical	50		
Cautious	75		
Reserved	98		
Leisurely	80		
Bold	55		
Mischievous	40		
Colorful	30		
Imaginative	62		
Diligent	80		
Dutiful	30		

0 10 20 30 40 50 60 70 80 90 100

Situational Change

Robert's hard work and willingness to put in the hours needed to help ensure the success of his most recent project caught the attention of upper management. After considerable discussion, management concluded that Robert was ready to take on a project leadership role. The new project to which he was to be assigned involved the development of a new cabin security system. If the project was successful, there was a high probability that the system would become a requirement for a wide array of commercial aircraft. The project team was slated to be cross-functional in nature and would even include external team members from the Transportation Security Administration. The design-build timeline for the project looked to be demanding and well suited to Robert's no-nonsense, get-it-done approach.

Situational Impact

One of Robert's biggest challenges will be to moderate his quiet, reserved style and make sure his team members see him as approachable. The new role will also require him to be more proactive in his communications, given the cross-functional nature of the project and the involvement of an external government agency. Finally, the project looks to be quite demanding, which seems well suited to Robert's hardworking approach. However, Robert could easily slip into becoming an overly demanding leader with little regard for the toll his behavior may take on his team members.

CASE 4—TANYA, INSURANCE PROFESSIONAL (HIGH MISCHIEVOUS)

Situation

Tanya is a successful insurance professional for a medium sized corporation. For years, the company relied on the entrepreneurial spirit of its insurance professionals for growth. In fact, Tanya's success in putting big deals together resulted in her promotion to training manager, with the hope that she could impart her knowledge to up and coming pros. Tanya viewed the promotion as an opportunity to advance her own career and to teach young professionals how to get ahead in the business using her unique strategies for closing big deals. She knew the position would require her to teach the basic blocking-and-tackling aspects of the business; however, she felt her knowledge of how to stretch the envelope in putting together deals could be a real asset in developing new professionals.

HDS Profile

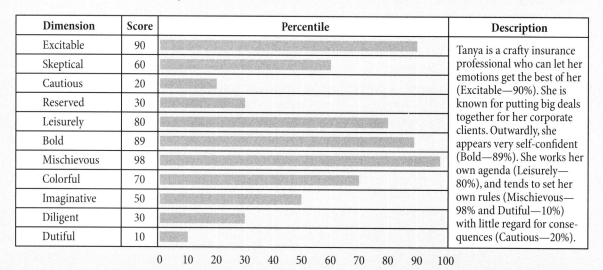

Dimension	Score	Percentile	Description
Excitable	90		Tanya is a crafty insurance professional who can let her emotions get the best of her (Excitable—90%). She is known for putting big deals together for her corporate clients. Outwardly, she appears very self-confident (Bold—89%). She works her own agenda (Leisurely—80%), and tends to set her own rules (Mischievous—98% and Dutiful—10%) with little regard for consequences (Cautious—20%).
Skeptical	60		
Cautious	20		
Reserved	30		
Leisurely	80		
Bold	89		
Mischievous	98		
Colorful	70		
Imaginative	50		
Diligent	30		
Dutiful	10		

0   10   20   30   40   50   60   70   80   90   100

Situational Change

The insurance industry has always come under scrutiny by government agencies. About the time Tanya was promoted to training manager, the company was inundated with a number of new government regulations. These regulations forced company leaders to embark on a culture-change initiative to ensure compliance with the new regulations. The initiative was viewed as critical because violations could result in heavy fines or worse. One of the most important components of the culture-change initiative was to ensure that new insurance professionals were well acquainted with the regulations and were scrupulous in their adherence to them in completing their jobs.

Situational Impact

Tanya's business approach prior to the new regulations was likely seen as simply stretching the envelope to meet customer needs. Her promotion resulted in her approach being put on stage in front of new professionals. The culture-change initiative presents a significant challenge for Tanya. First, she will come under careful scrutiny because of the importance of the right message being conveyed to the new professionals. Second, some aspects of her success formula could go beyond stretching the envelope and cross into areas that could challenge regulatory compliance. There are also risks associated with how Tanya will react to the regulatory constraints that were not in place when she accepted the position as training manager.

CASE 5—JANIS, CUSTOMER SERVICE MANAGER (LOW BOLD)

Situation

Janis is a newly appointed customer service manager who works for a software company that sells and supports a variety of tax-preparation software packages. Since joining the company, she worked closely with a regional manager who mentored her and was instrumental in getting her promoted from team member to team leader and, most recently, customer service manager. Janis is best known for being a very energetic person who has a knack for defusing difficult customer-service situations. Customers consistently describe her as a positive person who did not over-promise and did a great job keeping them informed. Team members describe her as very conscientious and extremely loyal to the company. There were also rumblings that she sometimes did not stand up to people and could be easily manipulated.

HDS Profile

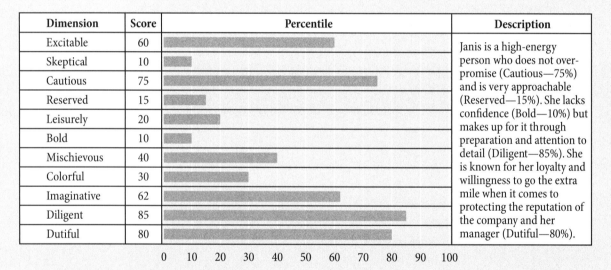

Dimension	Score	Percentile	Description
Excitable	60		Janis is a high-energy person who does not over-promise (Cautious—75%) and is very approachable (Reserved—15%). She lacks confidence (Bold—10%) but makes up for it through preparation and attention to detail (Diligent—85%). She is known for her loyalty and willingness to go the extra mile when it comes to protecting the reputation of the company and her manager (Dutiful—80%).
Skeptical	10		
Cautious	75		
Reserved	15		
Leisurely	20		
Bold	10		
Mischievous	40		
Colorful	30		
Imaginative	62		
Diligent	85		
Dutiful	80		

0   10   20   30   40   50   60   70   80   90   100

Situational Change

Janis's long-time regional manager was promoted shortly after her promotion to customer service manager. The new regional manager is viewed as hard charging, very confident, and charismatic. He is young for his position and is known for being very demanding of his team members. He is also known for being like Teflon in that he always seems to be in the right place when there is good news and always seems to avoid blame or deflect it to those around him when there is bad news. Some have questioned his trustworthiness, but the results he achieves seem to override the negatives associated with how he achieves them.

Situational Impact

Janis's dutiful nature could make her an early favorite of the new regional manager. She will probably accept his demanding requests and will work very hard to see that they are achieved. The impact will likely be two-fold. First, she may end up driving her team beyond acceptable limits, which could result in turnover. Second, her inability to push back could result in diminishing her own quality of life. The long-term career impact could be even more significant for her. If problems, even those beyond her control, should arise, it is likely the new regional manager could make her a target for the blame. Furthermore, her lack of self-confidence could be seen as weakness by the new regional manager, diminishing her prospects for future leadership opportunities.

Case 6—Mark, District Account Manager (High Colorful)

Situation

Mark is a district account manager for a consumer products company. He has been with the company for more than 20 years. Mark is regarded as a very loyal employee but a bit of a character. He has managed most of his accounts for years and is on a first-name basis with many of his customers. He tends to be a larger-than-life person who can take most of the oxygen out of a room. He is known for telling jokes but at the same time has a somewhat boorish interpersonal style. He can often exaggerate problem situations to elevate his own importance and likes to draw attention to his accomplishments, even those that are rather meager in their true importance. Those around him have grown accustomed to his style and have even learned to deal with his lack of attention to detail.

HDS Profile

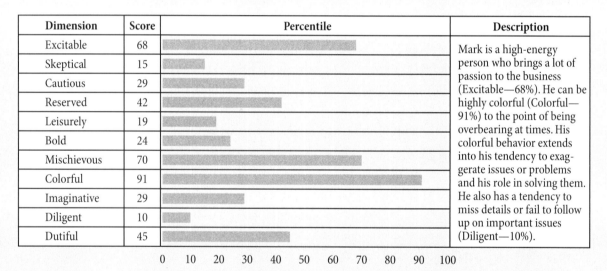

Dimension	Score	Percentile	Description
Excitable	68		Mark is a high-energy person who brings a lot of passion to the business (Excitable—68%). He can be highly colorful (Colorful—91%) to the point of being overbearing at times. His colorful behavior extends into his tendency to exaggerate issues or problems and his role in solving them. He also has a tendency to miss details or fail to follow up on important issues (Diligent—10%).
Skeptical	15		
Cautious	29		
Reserved	42		
Leisurely	19		
Bold	24		
Mischievous	70		
Colorful	91		
Imaginative	29		
Diligent	10		
Dutiful	45		

0 10 20 30 40 50 60 70 80 90 100

Situational Change

An economic downturn seriously impacted the company, creating the need for a number of changes. The first sign of trouble was when the company had to lay off 20 percent of the workforce. Mark survived the first round of layoffs because of his tenure in the company. The next major change involved the consolidation of government accounts with all other accounts. The consolidation significantly changed Mark's role by adding a number of large, new government accounts to those he was already managing. It was also a big change because of the type of customers he had to deal with on a day-to-day basis. Many were no-nonsense government employees who were used to doing business by the book and had little interest in relationship building.

Situational Impact

Mark's existing customers knew him quite well and had grown accustomed to his high-profile, colorful style. However, the new accounts he took over were large, government accounts with customers who had little interest in jokes or stories. They approached the business by the book. Mark's approach, using his colorful interpersonal style, is unlikely to be effective with the new customers and may even alienate some of them. Plus, the transactional nature of the government accounts will require high attention to detail, which is not Mark's strength. The economic challenges faced by the company underscore the urgency for Mark to hit the ground running and avoid customer complaints.

Case 7—James, Marketing Manager (High Dutiful)

Situation

James held the position of marketing manager for 10 years in a relatively small, family-owned technology business. He gained a lot of knowledge in his role because the owners relied on him to execute anything they needed from a marketing standpoint. His calm, even-tempered demeanor was perfect for the company because he never overreacted to requests by the owners regardless of how eccentric the requests might be. He also played a gatekeeper role by critically evaluating marketing requests from other parts of the organization and making very sure he had all the due diligence complete before bringing something to the owners. The owners really appreciated James because of his willingness do what they asked and, at the same time, keep what they viewed as distractions off the table.

HDS Profile

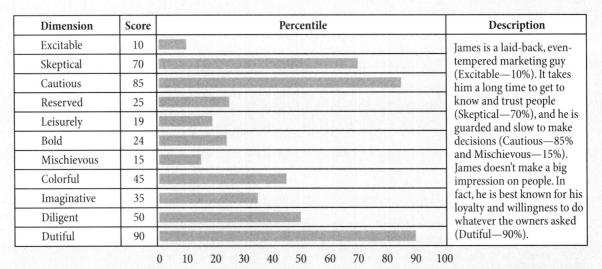

Dimension	Score	Percentile	Description
Excitable	10		James is a laid-back, even-tempered marketing guy (Excitable—10%). It takes him a long time to get to know and trust people (Skeptical—70%), and he is guarded and slow to make decisions (Cautious—85% and Mischievous—15%). James doesn't make a big impression on people. In fact, he is best known for his loyalty and willingness to do whatever the owners asked (Dutiful—90%).
Skeptical	70		
Cautious	85		
Reserved	25		
Leisurely	19		
Bold	24		
Mischievous	15		
Colorful	45		
Imaginative	35		
Diligent	50		
Dutiful	90		

0 10 20 30 40 50 60 70 80 90 100

Situational Change

The owners received a nice offer for the business from a well-established technology company and decided to accept the offer and take early retirement. The acquiring company had well-established staff functions, so a number of people were let go as the result of the acquisition, including James. The owners did help James find a new position with a local technology start-up company. It was a small company but was growing very fast. New employees were often asked to wear multiple hats, and the fast-paced nature of the business forced people to make decisions without a lot of guidance or management support.

Situational Impact

Perhaps the biggest change for James was that he had to make a lot of important decisions on his own. Most of the people in the company knew very little about marketing, but they were more than willing to offer their thoughts and ideas. James's tendency to carefully analyze ideas and only make decisions once he had all the facts was likely not going to be received well in this fast-paced environment. Furthermore, his lack of guidance contributed to his inability to make decisions; in the previous company, he typically relied on the owners to tell him what needed to get done. His early life in the new start-up company looked more like a data-collection exercise than a newly established marketing function in which steps were being taken to build a high-profile brand.

CASE 8—COURTNEY, ASSISTANT OPERATIONS MANAGER (LOW DILIGENT)

Situation

Courtney has been viewed as a high-potential employee since the day she joined this electronics manufacturing company. She was placed on the fast track and given plenty of opportunities to develop her skills. In her last position, she was put in charge of a team of start-up professionals responsible for opening a new manufacturing facility in Mexico. The assignment was a good fit for her because she had a great deal of freedom to make decisions, and the folks working for her were equally independent and went about their jobs with little need for guidance. There were plenty of ups and downs, mostly due to government involvement. Courtney's ability to use her charm and influencing skills played an important role in keeping the project on track and getting the plant open on time.

HDS Profile

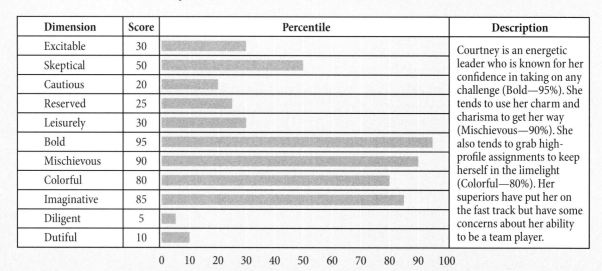

Dimension	Score	Percentile	Description
Excitable	30		Courtney is an energetic leader who is known for her confidence in taking on any challenge (Bold—95%). She tends to use her charm and charisma to get her way (Mischievous—90%). She also tends to grab high-profile assignments to keep herself in the limelight (Colorful—80%). Her superiors have put her on the fast track but have some concerns about her ability to be a team player.
Skeptical	50		
Cautious	20		
Reserved	25		
Leisurely	30		
Bold	95		
Mischievous	90		
Colorful	80		
Imaginative	85		
Diligent	5		
Dutiful	10		

0 10 20 30 40 50 60 70 80 90 100

Situational Change

Despite her strong track record and successful plant start-up, Courtney's superiors had lingering questions about her ability to be a team player. They decided to assign her to one of their best plant managers as the assistant operations manager. Her new manager was the type of woman who never let things fall through the cracks. She worked long hours in her role as plant manager and was well known as a person who demanded the same from her team, but her team always responded well to her leadership style. Courtney's superiors viewed this move as an opportunity for her to learn from a seasoned professional, build her day-to-day management skills, and take some of the burden off the plant manager in keeping up with many operational details.

Situational Impact

The position of assistant operations manager is likely to be quite a challenge for Courtney. She is being asked to work closely with a seasoned leader who has a reputation for carefully managing the business. Her management responsibilities will be expanded to include not only a much larger team of people but responsibility for handling much of the burden for day-to-day operations. She will have to get work done through a lot of people while maintaining visibility to the details of the business. Her charismatic leadership style might be helpful in building relationships; however, it will likely not carry much weight with her new manager, who is focused on the performance of the plant.

CASE 9—KELLY, CHIEF FINANCIAL OFFICER (HIGH DILIGENT)

Situation

Kelly spent five years as the controller for a large clothing retailer. She managed the books with microscopic precision. She followed a set routine to close the books that took many hours of overtime but ensured that costs were fully accounted for down to the last penny. She had a reputation for being a bit cold interpersonally. More importantly, she could be quite probing or questioning of employees when it came to expenses or cost overruns. Employees did not necessarily fear her. In fact, they admired how hard she worked and watched out for the company. However, her interpersonal style did tend to get in the way of her building relationships. Even her team members treated interactions with her in a somewhat mechanical manner, almost like a financial transaction.

HDS Profile

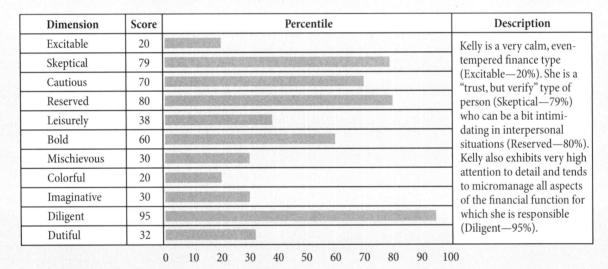

Dimension	Score	Percentile	Description
Excitable	20		Kelly is a very calm, even-tempered finance type (Excitable—20%). She is a "trust, but verify" type of person (Skeptical—79%) who can be a bit intimidating in interpersonal situations (Reserved—80%). Kelly also exhibits very high attention to detail and tends to micromanage all aspects of the financial function for which she is responsible (Diligent—95%).
Skeptical	79		
Cautious	70		
Reserved	80		
Leisurely	38		
Bold	60		
Mischievous	30		
Colorful	20		
Imaginative	30		
Diligent	95		
Dutiful	32		

0 10 20 30 40 50 60 70 80 90 100

Situational Change

Kelly's approach to the business was well suited for the role of controller. The role required a high degree of attention to detail, did not suffer from her micromanaging tendencies, and did not require extensive relationship building. When the CFO passed away suddenly, it created a big gap in the company's leadership team. There was a lot of concern about putting Kelly in the role of CFO, but the company had little choice given the needs of the business and the lack of adequate succession planning. When Kelly took over the role, her responsibilities expanded to all aspects of the finance function. Plus, she had to work closely with the other members of the leadership team to pull together the annual budget.

Situational Impact

Kelly was known well enough by members of the leadership team that her somewhat cold, argumentative interpersonal style did not get in the way. However, her new management responsibilities were a different matter. In the short term, keeping up with the work was a matter of putting in more hours. In the long term, it is likely that her tendency to micromanage everything is going to derail her with her team and cause her to burn out. Kelly will likely also struggle with contributing to the strategic aspects of the business. First, the vast amount of her time will be spent on details. Second, her low Imaginative and high Cautious thinking style may limit her big-picture perspective.

SUMMARY

The emergence of personality inventories from an Interpersonal Theory standpoint was an important step forward. It made these inventories relevant in terms of predicting critical life outcomes, such as job or career success. Instead of focusing on what is going on inside a person's head, inventories like those developed by Hogan provide a reputational snapshot of an individual's behavioral tendencies on the job. Furthermore, these behavioral tendencies drive real behaviors that can be observed and measured (i.e., an individual with a high Colorful score on the HDS is likely to seek the attention of others, be overly dramatic, etc.—all of which can be observed in day-to-day job performance). It is at the point of observation and measurement where the Situational Context really does matter. Success (or failure), when ratings of job performance are used as the primary criteria measure, has a number of situational components. We have highlighted three components that have important implications for success as a leader, including the Culture, Manager, and Role contexts. While it is true that there is considerable stability in the behavioral tendencies of a leader as measured by an inventory like the HDS, it is also true that the behaviors driven by these tendencies will have greater (or less) success depending on the Situational Context—an extremely important point from a leadership development perspective. A leader who is aware of his or her behavioral tendencies (HDS profile) and the Situational Context is well positioned to control (develop) behavior on the job and, ultimately, impact performance success.

PART III

BUILDING THE COACHING FOUNDATION

In Part III, we begin to move away from a discussion of the theory and information that can be gleaned from Hogan inventories to a discussion of the Hogan approach to helping leaders make meaningful performance improvements. What sets the Hogan approach to coaching apart from other approaches is our firm belief that a leader's reputation should be the target for performance improvement. Personality characteristics drive behavior, and the accumulation of behaviors results in a reputation. It is a pretty simple but highly effective equation when helping leaders improve their performance. Consider the following example:

> A leader who is high on the Excitable scale can get overly emotional and animated in stressful situations. These behaviors could earn the leader a reputation for lacking executive disposition, which definitely can be career limiting. Expanding the leader's Strategic-Self-awareness regarding excitable behaviors and providing some coaching tips for controlling these behaviors will result in the leader's appearing to others as more calm and even-tempered. Because appearing calm and even-tempered is central to a reputation for having an effective executive disposition, the leader's reputation will move in the direction of a more effective executive disposition. As the calm and even-tempered behaviors accumulate, the leader's reputation for effective executive disposition will grow.

The foundation for the Hogan approach to coaching grew out of this notion that reputation change is real change. We have spent decades demonstrating it through empirical research and convincing those with an interest in leadership development that our approach is very effective. Along the way, two things have happened. First, we have worked with and learned from some of the best executive coaches in the world. We have invited the best of the best to be part of the Hogan Coaching Network (HCN). The coaches in the HCN come from all walks of life and have been trained in a wide range of coaching protocols. We welcome this diversity in the HCN and consider it to be a towering strength as we have developed the Hogan approach. Second, the coaches in the HCN have taught us that an approach with no standards is not an approach at all. In fact, in a world where anybody can hang a shingle on the door that says *Executive Coach*, standards are essential for quality control.

Therefore, we developed the following 10 standards we require coaches to adhere to if they are to be part of the HCN.

HOGAN COACHING STANDARDS

- **Certification in Assessment Technology**—Coaches using assessment tools should be able to clearly demonstrate that they possess the qualifications necessary to use those tools.

- **Certification in Coaching Best Practices**—No two coaches provide coaching services in exactly the same way. However, there are proven best practices. Coaches should be able to demonstrate their awareness of those practices.

- **Mentor or Consortium Support**—Coaches are constantly being presented with new and challenging coaching situations. Coaches should have confidential resources available to discuss challenges they may not have encountered in the past.

- **Participant Team**—The most successful coaching engagements rely on a strong team model that includes the participant, the coach, the manager, and human resources.

- **Coaching Agreement**—All coaching engagements should include a written agreement describing the roles and responsibilities of the entire participant team.

- **Defined Protocol**—Coaching engagements should not be made up extemporaneously. The engagement should begin with a defined protocol that provides a basic outline of how the engagement will progress.

- **Communications Plan**—The effective involvement of a participant team means that a clear communications plan is outlined, and it fully describes how confidential information will be handled.

- **Coaching Agenda**—Regularly scheduled meetings should follow a written agenda, which will help avoid having sessions turn into unproductive discussions.

- **Reenergizing Mechanism**—Almost all coaching engagements run out of steam after a few successes or setbacks. A reenergizing mechanism should be established at the outset of the engagement to ensure long-term success.

- **Engagement Closeout**—One of the most difficult things about coaching engagements is ending them. Closing out a coaching engagement does not mean the coach and the participant never talk again. It simply means that a mechanism should be in place to summarize the engagement at its formal conclusion.

These standards are purposely broad to give clear guidance in terms of the quality we demand in the Hogan approach. At the same time, the standards are designed to be inclusive to allow our HCN coaches and all coaches to use their unique skills in helping leaders improve their performance.

The following chapters expand on these standards by addressing four key areas that need focused attention to ensure that our approach reaches its full potential in terms of success: the coaching agreement, the personality of the learner, feedback, and the development plan.

Chapter 6 outlines what may be the single most important success factor in our approach: the coaching agreement. Chapter 7 addresses what personality says about the learner. It has been our experience that the characteristics of the learner are forgotten in preparing to give feedback or coaching. The Hogan inventories are unique in the kind of information that they can provide for a coach in preparation for working with a learner. Chapter 8 outlines our approach to delivering effective personality-based feedback. Chapter 9 concludes Part III with a discussion of the key ingredients in an effective development plan. Our recommendations throughout Part III are central to the Hogan approach, and they account for the unique challenges presented by the use of personality data in improving leader performance.

CHAPTER 6

THE COACHING AGREEMENT

INTRODUCTION

A clear coaching agreement is not just an administrative detail. It is an important and integral part of the coaching itself. Creating a document that focuses on specific goals and responsibilities of key stakeholders in the engagement is an important coaching intervention in itself. This emphasis on planning and purpose is especially true in the Hogan approach to coaching because it is anchored in a specific set of assumptions and processes that can make it distinctly different from other types of coaching. While many of the interventions a Hogan coach might use appear similar to other types of coaching, Hogan interventions are almost always rooted in a goal of helping participants close the gap between their identity and the actual reaction others have to them. Most practicing coaches today would probably describe their approach to coaching as eclectic, drawing on a wide range of techniques and theories. But the Hogan approach to coaching has a particular theoretical underpinning and objectives derived from years of careful personality-based research. For this reason, although every coaching engagement will have unique elements, there will also be some common components. If the key stakeholders involved in a coaching engagement understand this concept from the beginning, they can all contribute to the process in more coordinated and constructive ways.

EXECUTIVE COACHING IN GENERAL

As executive coaching has become a more popular and accepted part of most executive careers, it has also raised the potential for greater confusion of what coaching is all about. Coaching is often confused with mentoring, counseling, consulting, sponsoring, or other forms of executive development. The executive development literature itself has multiple definitions of these terms (cf. Kram, 1988; Hart & Kirkland, 2001; Luecke, 2004). Moreover, a useful distinction can be made between coaching interventions that are *remedial* (where the individual has identifiable problems in behavior that need correction or elimination) and initiatives that are *augmentative* (where the focus is to add to or further refine the repertoire of existing behaviors or experience in order to accelerate the individual's development). The Hogan inventories provide opportunities to address both kinds of coaching interventions.

Another element sometimes contributing to the confusion can be the different messages communicated about coaching between an individual and his or her manager. Participants in coaching often have opinions about their bosses and their organizations that they will share confidentially with a coach but not with others. Similarly, managers are often inarticulate or deliberately reluctant to share with their subordinates the unvarnished truth about what they think are the developmental issues. Also, many organizations today have a matrix structure, which results in the individual having more than one manager. Different managers may disagree about developmental needs or the priority of those needs. It is also not uncommon for the human resources or talent management partner to have yet another perspective on the key leadership developmental issues.

Another opportunity for confusion about coaching expectations occurs because many coaches now need to sell their services more aggressively than in the past. In the competitive marketplace today, organizations often ask participants to interview several coaches in order to test the interpersonal chemistry between them. While there may be solid reasons for this practice, it also engenders the inevitable conflict between telling potential participants what they want to hear rather than what they need to hear about what will be required of them.

These distinctions may seem trivial at first, and they are often glossed over in initial introductory meetings. But they can have serious implications for any coaching process. Block (2011) makes the point that a good agreement of any kind needs an explicit statement of what the consultant and the client should expect from each other and how they are going to work together (p. 42). A good agreement not only adds clarity, but it also increases the chances of a successful coaching engagement. The beginning of an engagement is the most effective point in time to outline the coaching process, define roles and responsibilities, confirm understandings about confidentiality, describe the pace of the program, and define the criteria for success. This framing of the coaching process will color everything else that follows over the ensuing months.

Setting expectations, defining roles, and gaining consensus about goals from the key stakeholders are some of the most important and helpful steps in any coaching engagement. The engagement represents a systemic intervention that will be critical for later coaching success. Prioritizing the few critical developmental targets to be worked on brings clarity and focus to the stakeholders who will be most involved in the success of the intervention. It not only engages them but allows them to provide critical guidance as to which kinds of coaching interventions are most likely to be accepted and successful within the culture and business needs of the organization. Insiders will usually be much more expert than the coach in determining what are the most critical business needs, which key competencies are needed by the participant, and what aspects of the participant's reputation will have the most impact. That discussion itself is an extremely helpful developmental intervention. The key stakeholders are the people who will be the ultimate arbiters of whether a coaching engagement was successful or not, so they need to be included in setting the criteria for success.

As a practical matter, there is another good reason for developing well-defined agreements about the parameters of the coaching at the beginning. Most executive coaching engagements last between 3 and 12 months. Much can happen to an individual and an organization in that timespan. Participants can and often are promoted, transferred, or demoted; assigned a new manager; or given a new set of business goals.

If goals and objectives are not clearly defined, it is very easy for "mission creep" to enter in. Mission creep occurs when other new issues, duties, and responsibilities occur during the coaching engagement that were not considered or in existence at the beginning of the engagement. No consultant likes to end an engagement with issues hanging; consequently, many coaching engagements often far exceed the timespan anticipated initially. Coaches, as well as client organizations, need to be reminded periodically about the original parameters of the engagement and when they have been fulfilled.

Ultimately, the goal of setting up the initial coaching agreement is to have all the relevant parties agree on a limited number of clearly articulated goals, methodologies, roles, criteria for success, and the approximate length of the engagement. If circumstances change during the course of the coaching engagement, these goals, objectives, and timeframes will need to be renegotiated but with a new set of clear coaching targets.

THE HOGAN APPROACH AND THE COACHING AGREEMENT

The issues just discussed are true in any coaching engagement, but especially so when the Hogan suite of inventories is used as a primary assessment vehicle for the coaching. The inventories' focus on building greater Strategic Self-awareness, using that awareness to modify specific behaviors, getting feedback, modifying one's reputation, and eventually internalizing these behaviors will shape the parameters of an engagement. Years of careful observation of how people are successful or not in jobs have yielded a logical framework of steps for feedback, developmental planning, and the coaching process. This kind of coaching, while behaviorally focused, work centered, and time limited, can have longer term effects. Personality profiles are relatively stable over time, but it is also true that behavioral changes can result in changes of reputation, which in turn can result in internalized personality changes over the long run (Hogan et al., 2007, p. 268). This specific approach makes it necessary to have a written agreement spelling out the roles and responsibilities of each stakeholder in the coaching process (Hogan et al., 2007, p. 295).

The Hogan Development Cycle (see Hogan Development Cycle, page 27) prescribes a sequence of steps:

- Building greater awareness regarding the participant's impact on others.

- Targeting a limited number of behaviors to modify for greater effectiveness (usually two to three).

- Getting feedback.

- Making appropriate adjustments in behavior to be more effective and that address reputational issues.

- Internalizing these changes so that they can be a sustained part of the behavioral repertoire (changes in identity can occur over time, although they may be modest and may take an extended period of time to occur).

Because there is a predictable framework in coaching, it is important for all the relevant parties to be aware of how the process unfolds and the rationale behind it. This methodology aligns everyone to a common understanding of how the developmental goals are identified. It also sets the stage for all parties to understand how they can play a constructive role in the process.

What follows is a shopping list of the useful items that might be included in a coaching agreement:

- Names of participant, manager(s), human resources or talent management partner, and coach.

- Roles and responsibilities of each person.

- Length of engagement, including the start date and projected end date.

- Parameters of confidentiality—when, to whom, and what kind of information will be reported to anyone other than the participant and the coach.

- Where data about the participant will ultimately reside (e.g., with the participant, in the individual's personnel file, etc.).

- Expectations regarding the availability of all parties.

- Frequency of reporting progress in coaching and to whom.

- Key milestones or other means of gauging progress at critical points.

- Expected frequency of contact.

- Specific goals of the coaching engagement as can be best identified at the time of the agreement (later data may require renegotiation of the original goals).

- Methods of assessing progress at the end of the program.

- Financial investment (e.g., coach's fee, how travel and miscellaneous expenses will be billed, session cancelation policy, etc.).

- What the coaching process is not (e.g., counseling, therapy, training, etc.).

As noted in the final bullet, sometimes it is well advised to include language in an agreement about what the coaching is *not*. In order to be clear about what the coach's role will be, it may be necessary to state explicitly that coaching is not counseling, psychotherapy, drug counseling, mental health care, substance abuse treatment, or financial counseling. Often, participants may already be engaged in a separate counseling or mentoring process with someone else, and this only underscores the need to keep coaching as a distinct process different from the others. This "not" clause not only clarifies what should be part of the appropriate work of the Hogan coach and participant, it also provides a measure of legal protection for the coach. Processes like counseling and psychotherapy, or titles like therapist, counselor, or psychologist, are normally controlled by legal statute.

What follows are several sample coaching agreements that are specifically geared to the coaching process when Hogan inventories are involved. The first several objectives are automatically included because they would be intrinsic to any coaching process grounded in the Hogan approach. Additional space is included to define other objectives that may be uncovered through discussion with the participant's manager, with human resources, or as part of the assessment process. Completion of this document specifies the deliverables for the coaching engagement. Asking for signatures may be optional, but signing on the dotted line adds a level of formality that ensures that all parties will take the process and their roles seriously.

AGREEMENT FOR COACHING SERVICES (SAMPLE 1)

Participant   Coach
Name: _____   Name: _____

Participant's   Human Resources
Manager:_____   Partner:_____

Below is an outline of the coaching process to be undertaken by_____ for a period of approximately six months, beginning on_____ and ending _____.

It is understood by all participating parties that the process of coaching is not a replacement for counseling, mentoring, organizational consulting, therapy of any kind, or legal/financial advice.

Objectives of the Coaching Process

- To provide the participant greater self-awareness of his or her effective and less effective behaviors in the workplace.

- To provide greater understanding of situations that may trigger unproductive behavior in the workplace.

- To identify high-priority developmental goals that will make the participant more effective in the workplace.

- To discuss collaboratively specific behavioral actions that may enhance future work performance.

- To determine other goals after the initial assessment phase.

- To substantiate progress toward the goals before and after the coaching process.

The Process

Before identifying additional developmental goals, a thorough assessment will be conducted, including the following deliverables:

Assessment

- Administration of the Hogan suite of inventories (the Hogan Personality Inventory; the Hogan Development Survey; and the Motives, Values, Preferences Inventory).

- Review of any existing, additional multi-rater sources of data (e.g., multi-rater assessments, performance appraisals, etc.).

- Job analysis to identify current or future critical job demands.

- Interviews with six to eight colleagues of the participant, centered on observed strengths, developmental opportunities, critical relationships, leadership style, and other factors that may be relevant to work performance.

- Feedback to the participant in order to collaboratively integrate all the data and begin identifying developmental goals.

Goal Confirmation

- The participant and coach will meet for one or more sessions to review the data and integrate it into two to three developmental goals.

- A goal confirmation meeting will be set, which will include the participant, coach, manager, and representative from HR, to present the goals and modify them, if needed, based on the discussion at that time.

Ongoing Coaching

- Coaching will proceed for the remaining length of the engagement.

- The exact nature of the coaching will be dependent on the goals identified and may take the form of discussions, regular face-to-face meetings, telephone sessions, direct observation, videotape rehearsals and feedback, readings, role playing, or other generally accepted coaching methods of developing new or more effective behaviors.

- During this time, the coach will periodically check in with the manager and human resources representative to give updates on the status of the coaching and to solicit observations from them that might be relevant to the coaching process.

Endpoint Evaluation

- In the sixth month of the program, the coach will conduct follow-up interviews with the original sample of colleagues to obtain their input about progress made since the initial interview.

- A wrap-up meeting will be held, which will include the participant, coach, manager and human resources representative to discuss progress, longer-term developmental goals, and any additional issues that have emerged in the six-month period.

Confidentiality

It is understood from the above outline that all parties will be in communication with each other from time to time. Data such as assessment scores, interview notes, or session notes will be held in confidence by the coach. The participant will have the discretion of sharing this information with others should he or she choose to do so.

The general information gleaned from interviews the coach may conduct will be shared with the participant, but no individual attributions will be made to any of the individuals interviewed.

It is understood that the material from these sessions, other than that which is already part of the participant's official personnel file, will not be kept in any official record of his or her service.

Frequency of Meetings

The expectation is that the participant and coach will meet on a weekly or semi-weekly basis, whether in person or by telephone. Both parties will make reasonable efforts to be available unless other events preclude this (e.g., business travel, vacations, holidays, major business initiatives, etc.).

Approximately once a month, the participant's manager and human resources representative will make every effort to be available for consultation about the progress of the participant.

Roles and Responsibilities

The participant agrees to make himself or herself reasonably available most weeks during the course of the engagement and to complete mutually agreed-upon assignments that are developed during the course of the coaching. The manager agrees to provide ongoing feedback and support on a timely basis.

The human resources (HR) representative agrees to provide regular feedback regarding critical events or perceptions about the participant's progress to the coach and the participant.

The coach agrees to proactively check in with all parties to get their ongoing perceptions of behavioral change.

All parties recognize that because one of the goals of coaching is reputational change, advocacy for the participant, when warranted, is crucial. The manager and HR representative will make proactive efforts to talk to others about positive changes the participant may make during the course of the coaching process.

Fees and Expenses

Payment of (enter dollar amount) is due in three installments: one-third at beginning of project, one-third at the midpoint, and one-third upon completion of project. It is understood that expenses for assessment instruments, surveys, documents, phone charges, and so on will not be billed back. Extraordinary expenses such as travel outside this metropolitan area, international calls, and so on will be billed back at cost with prior authorization by the participant's manager.

Agreed to by:

_____   _____
Participant   Date

_____   _____
Coach   Date

_____   _____
Manager   Date

_____   _____
Human Resources/Talent Management Representative   Date

AGREEMENT FOR COACHING SERVICES (SAMPLE 2)

Services to Be Provided

The coaching engagement will span (X) months, and the coach will provide customized services to the participant including:

- Initial assessment, which will include administration of the following inventories: the Hogan Personality Inventory; the Hogan Development Survey; and the Motives, Values, Preferences Inventory.

- Review of existing multi-rater assessment data, performance appraisals, and performance improvement plans.

- Consultation with participant's manager and human resources representative.

- Creation of a customized development plan targeting two to three key areas for the participant to be coached on that are agreed to by the key stakeholders.

- Ongoing coaching sessions at intervals agreed upon by the coach and participant from the period of (enter timeframe).

- Interactive assessment interviews with up to nine individuals at the end of the coaching process to document progress against initial goals and to identify future developmental opportunities.

Coaching Objectives

- To provide the participant greater self-awareness of the participant's effective and less effective behaviors in the workplace.

- To provide greater understanding of situations that may trigger unproductive behavior in the workplace.

- To identify appropriate developmental goals that would make the participant more effective in the workplace.

- To collaboratively discuss specific behavioral actions that may enhance future work performance.

- To determine other goals after the initial assessment phase.

Confidentiality

- It is understood that the coaching process requires a free flow of communication between the coach and the participant. It is also understood that communication with other parties, such as the participant's manager, HR, or other key stakeholders will be occasionally required in order to gauge the effectiveness of coaching interventions during the length of the program. Psychological test data from the above-mentioned process will not be released to the organization unless the participant clearly grants permission. In addition, multi-rater assessment data (either already in existence or collected by the coach) will be made available to all stakeholders because this material requires evaluation by not only the participant but also by others familiar with the organization who can evaluate its significance.

- During the course of this coaching process, the coach may obtain information about the company not available to the general public. In recognition of this, the coach agrees to not disclose any information to outside parties. Further, the coach will not engage in any activity, such as direct purchase of company stock, which might be construed as capitalizing on inside information. Further, the coach agrees not to use the name of the company in any advertising, marketing materials, promotional activities, etc.

Sessions

- Coaching sessions may take the form of face-to-face interactions, phone conversations, or e-mails. Their length may vary from short, ad hoc discussions of under 10 minutes to longer sessions up to 60 minutes in length.

- One-hour sessions will be billed at the rate of (enter dollar amount). Shorter, ad hoc sessions will not be charged. Sessions canceled or rescheduled with less than 24 hours' notice will be billed at fifty percent of the hourly rate. It is expected that during the course of the coaching process, a maximum of (X) sessions will be required.

- Consultation discussions with the participant's manager or with human resources/talent management will not be billed unless the meeting extends beyond 30 minutes.

- If required, stakeholder interview sessions will be billed as regular sessions at the hourly rate of (enter dollar amount).

- No fees will be charged for preparation time, creation of preliminary development plans, etc.

- Expenses incurred for assessment will be billed back to the company at cost.

- Travel expenses will be billed back to the company at cost. Expenses outside the immediate metropolitan area will require prior approval by the participant's manager.

Stakeholder Responsibilities

- The coach will provide expert feedback regarding the Hogan assessments.
- The coach will act as an expert resource to the participant to collaboratively interpret the implications of the assessment data and to develop actions to address developmental opportunities or augment existing strengths.
- The coach will collaboratively generate with the participant and other stakeholders two to three target developmental areas.
- The participant will faithfully work on developmental activities that were collaboratively developed.
- The manager and the human resources representative will make themselves regularly available to both the coach and the participant for discussions of progress against agreed-upon coaching goals.
- The manager and the human resources representative agree to make sure that progress made by the participant is known to other key stakeholders in the organization.

Scope of the Coaching Process

It is understood that coaching is a process designed to help individuals who are emotionally and psychologically healthy. It is not a substitute for therapy, counseling, or other services normally provided by other licensed or accredited professionals.

Agreed to by:

_____   _____
Participant   Date

_____   _____
Coach   Date

_____   _____
Manager   Date

_____   _____
Human Resources/Talent Management Representative   Date

Summary

The coaching agreement examples here may look overly detailed and cumbersome. Many organizations have their own forms that contain many of the elements listed here or other criteria not considered here. The salient point is that topic areas covered in the examples presented should be explicitly understood by all parties, preferably in writing. A clear understanding of the overall objectives of the coaching process, its goals, the processes by which those goals will be pursued, and the role each stakeholder needs to play is central to success and will increase the likelihood of the satisfaction of key stakeholders.

CHAPTER 7

WHAT PERSONALITY SAYS ABOUT THE LEARNER

INTRODUCTION

For years, personality was thought to be outside the realm of leadership development; however, this restrictive philosophy has changed dramatically over the past 20 years. The personality characteristics of a leader are now recognized as a vital ingredient in effective leadership development. In this chapter, we will take this concept one step further and look at what personality tells us about the learner (i.e., the leader or feedback recipient or participant) and how we can use these insights to enhance the feedback, coaching, and development processes. Learning is central to Strategic Self-awareness and, ultimately, to changing behaviors to be a more effective leader. It makes sense that if we can determine how a person best learns, we can use these insights to inform feedback, coaching, and development activities for a better outcome.

This chapter focuses on how personality insights obtained through the Hogan inventories can be invaluable to coaches in the following three key areas of the leadership development process:

- Enhancing the learner's receptivity to feedback and coaching.
- Matching feedback and coaching approaches to the learner's preferred learning style.
- Promoting engagement and action toward the execution of the development plan with the intent of producing positive behavioral change.

These three areas will be discussed in detail. Two case studies will be used to illustrate how the personality of the learner can impact each of these areas.

BACKGROUND

We are all wired differently, and these differences in our personalities show up in everything that we do, including how we learn and how we apply what we learn. Personality can play a pivotal role in determining how a learner is likely to engage in and respond to feedback and coaching. The role of personality in the behavior of a leader, while perhaps under-researched, is unquestioned and widely recognized. Various research studies have considered the potential influence that personality can have on reactions to feedback, goal setting, and responses to multi-rater assessment (Smither, London, & Reilly, 2005). Among the many observations made by various researchers is that the personality of the individual receiving the feedback can play a meaningful role in his or her reactions and responses to feedback. As we gain a deeper understanding of the learner, we can unlock many insights to further assist him or her throughout the feedback, coaching, and implementation processes.

It also makes sense that a coach's effectiveness can be enhanced by better understanding the personality profile of a learner. Sometimes, coaches approach feedback or coaching sessions in a highly structured, process-driven manner, without much (if any) consideration of the learner's personality, preferences, or individual differences. Coaches who take this approach may overlook a great deal of potential value that can be realized through a more individualized and tailored approach that is based on a clear understanding of the learner's personality.

A highly tailored approach toward feedback and development, which includes a deep understanding of the learner's personality and preferred learning style, can create the optimal environment for learning and development. In her 2003 *Harvard Business Review* article, "Personalize Your Management Development," Natalie Shope Griffin spoke about why it was important to adopt a tailored approach to leadership development and the success that could be realized in doing so. According to Griffin,

> Companies don't recognize the degree to which personal characteristics, ideologies or behaviors affect an individual's ability to learn . . . people don't check their individuality at the door before leaping into the great corporate melting pot, nor do they all fit a single leader-in-training profile. (para. 4)

She went on to suggest that, in her work with Nationwide Financial,

[H]ad we not developed a tailored approach [to development], we would be setting our managers up for failure. While one type of person responds very well to one form of "treatment," the same approach backfires with someone else. (para. 38)

It is also helpful for coaches to understand the lenses and filters through which the learner views the world. We each have a unique view of the world around us that is, in many ways, shaped by our personalities. As we deal with the many stimuli that we experience at any given time, we continually attend to information differently, draw unique conclusions, make decisions, and take various actions based on the filters and lenses through which we interpret information. Therefore, it is important for coaches to take the learner's lenses and filters into account to promote a clear understanding of any feedback being provided. Take, for example, two individuals with greatly divergent political views. It is likely that the same world event will be perceived and integrated differently by each person based on the lens through which it is viewed. These filters can be quite strong in determining how we view the world and others around us, and how we react to them.

A coach should understand the learner's lenses and filters not only to better frame feedback and coaching, but also to assist the learner in recognizing his or her own biases and how they color perceptions, judgment, decisions, and actions. Learners interpret events through their strongly held beliefs, and this can lead to self-deception. In a book titled *Leadership and Self-Deception*, by The Arbinger Institute (2010), the authors discuss the concept of self-deception and why they believe that it is one of the most significant challenges facing leaders. They explain how leaders are often blinded by self-deception, which "obscures the truth about ourselves, corrupts our views of others and our circumstances, and inhibits our ability to make wise and helpful decisions." Through the process of assisting leaders in enhancing their Strategic Self-awareness, coaches can play a pivotal role in helping leaders see themselves as others see them, thus better equipping them to improve their performance over time.

As a result, feedback, coaching, and development activities should be tailored to the unique needs and personality of the learner, as opposed to using a one-size-fits-all structured model. The more that coaches understand about the individual's personality and preferences, the greater the impact they can have in helping that person attend to, successfully integrate, and act upon relevant information.

UTILIZING PERSONALITY INFORMATION

This section outlines three ways a coach can leverage knowledge of the learner's personality to drive success across the key areas of feedback, coaching, and development activities: (1) enhancing the learner's receptivity to feedback and coaching, (2) matching feedback and coaching approaches to the learner's preferred learning style, and (3) promoting engagement and action in executing the development plan.

Enhancing the Learner's Receptivity to Feedback and Coaching

When preparing for a feedback or coaching session, it is advantageous for the coach to identify how best to enhance the recipient's openness to receiving the feedback and coaching. When interacting with very busy and highly successful professionals, it is often quite difficult to gain their full attention without first helping them recognize the value to be gained. As a result, one very important initial step in engaging participants in any feedback or learning process is to help them answer the question, "What's in it for me?" Once a coach has created the hook that causes the participant to recognize the value of the process, the person is much more likely to be engaged and committed.

In addition to creating a hook, the coach needs to understand what style or approach to providing feedback and coaching will resonate best with the learner and, consequently, be the most impactful. Simply anticipating how the learner might react and tailoring the style and approach accordingly can produce dramatically different results even in a single session.

The learner's results across the three Hogan inventories can provide an excellent source of possible hooks, styles, or approaches that might be most effective, and the kinds of reactions to expect from the learner. Examining the scales on all three inventories, especially the scales that are very high (above 90%) or very low (below 10%), can give coaches strong leads as to what will be important to the learner, what will frustrate the learner, and what will motivate the learner. Further, the coach can determine the recipient's preferred style and pace, likely hot buttons, and interests and aversions. Then, presenting the feedback through this lens will likely better hold the learner's interest, prompt the learner to see the value of the feedback, and ultimately, motivate the learner to modify his or her behaviors.

One of the first places a coach can look for insights into how to motivate someone to pay attention to the feedback and coaching is the Motives, Values, Preferences Inventory (MVPI). Gaining a deeper understanding of what a leader truly values can be quite helpful in motivating him or her to be engaged in a feedback-related discussion.

For example, if the MVPI suggests that a leader clearly values recognition (i.e., a high score on the Recognition scale), that individual might be more deeply engaged in the leadership development process if he or she understands how behavior changes can lead to greater recognition through enhanced performance. If a leader values helping and nurturing others (i.e., a high Altruistic score), he or she may be more motivated to enhance performance based on an expectation that more effective performance can be beneficial to others (e.g., direct reports, peers, the broader organization, customers, etc.).

Similar to using the MVPI, a coach can use the Hogan Personality Inventory (HPI) and Hogan Development Survey (HDS) to obtain broader information about personality characteristics, including how the learner approaches others, pursues goals, makes decisions, and deals with stress. Such information will provide valuable insights into some of the factors that can facilitate or inhibit learning, including possible hooks, ideas for the coaching approach to use, and the learner's reactions to feedback.

Consider the insights that can be gained from the HPI. As a hook example, if a leader is high on the Ambition scale, positioning the feedback in terms of "this will help you get promoted" or "this will help you achieve your goals" will get the leader's attention. As an example of what approach to use, consider a leader who scores very low on the Prudence scale. Such an individual is probably not going to be interested in a lot of detail, so the coach needs to keep the feedback at a bigger picture level or risk losing the learner's interest. As a reaction to feedback example, a leader who scores very low on the Adjustment scale might be expected to be stressed or overwhelmed by feedback or focused only on the negative information that is provided.

Equally useful information can be obtained from the HDS. A hook example from the HDS can be seen in working with a leader who scores high on the Dutiful scale (80% or higher). A leader with such a score could easily have his or her interest piqued by positioning the feedback in terms of "these behavior changes will please your boss." As an example of deciding which approach to use, a coach might find that leaders with high Skeptical scores present a challenge in terms of gaining their trust in the process and in recognizing the potential value of the feedback and coaching. As a result, the coach might be wise to emphasize the rules concerning confidentiality of the feedback and related discussions. An example of anticipating the reaction from the learner can be found in a leader with a high Bold score. Such a leader can be expected to be indifferent or even resistant to feedback from a coach (or from most others, for that matter).

These examples present just a few of the possibilities that can be gleaned from a leader's personality profile regarding his or her openness to feedback and coaching. Coaches who use the Hogan inventories in preparation for feedback or coaching are, in essence, drawing up a battle plan for how information should be deployed to maximize impact. This approach should in no way be interpreted as deceptive or manipulative. Rather, it should be thought of as presenting information in a way that has the highest probability of increasing a learner's Strategic Self-awareness.

Matching Feedback and Coaching Approaches to the Learner's Style

Just as personality insights can assist a coach in preparing to deliver feedback and coaching, Hogan inventories can also help a coach determine a leader's preferred learning style. This awareness can result in greater engagement in the learning process and more interest on the part of the learner in actually applying the knowledge gained.

One of the most important roles that a feedback provider or coach can play is that of awakening the Strategic Self-awareness of the learner. To fulfill this role most effectively, the coach needs a keen understanding of the learner and how to best engage the individual in the learning process. A great deal of research has been conducted to better understand learning styles and how to utilize insights into one's preferred learning style to enhance the learning process. Smith (1982) defined learning style as "the individual's characteristic ways of processing information, feeling, and behaving in learning situations" (p. 2). It is widely recognized that people bring their own predispositions and preferences to the learning process (Kolb, 1986; Honey & Mumford, 2006). In addition, one's preferred learning style is influenced by personality characteristics. Therefore, any insights that a coach can gain regarding personality characteristics and their impact on a leader's preferred learning style can greatly enhance the effectiveness of the learning process.

Many theorists have proposed learning-style models that group and describe the most common ways that people prefer to learn (Smith & Kolb, 1986). The HPI provides a Learning Approach scale to provide insights into the preferred learning approaches that someone might have. Regardless of the model employed, establishing a learning environment that is comfortable, engaging, and familiar for the learner (i.e., based on the learner's personality) is likely to lead to a positive and more productive learning experience.

The purpose of this discussion is not to provide an exhaustive review of various learning models, but rather to demonstrate how the insights from the Hogan assessments, including the Learning Approach scale, can be used in concert with these models to optimize the feedback, coaching, and development experience. One model that is frequently employed and well regarded is Kolb's learning model (Kolb, 1984). Kolb's model outlines four learning styles that can be employed to help better understand individual differences in how people acquire knowledge. The four learning styles are Accommodators, Divergers, Assimilators, and Convergers.

- **Accommodators** prefer hands-on learning. They trust their instincts versus relying on logic. They tend to solve problems intuitively and may be flexible in their approaches. These people use other people's analysis and prefer to take a practical, experiential approach. They are attracted to new challenges and experiences and to carrying out plans. They commonly act on gut instinct rather than on logical analysis. Accommodators tend to rely on others for information rather than conducting their own analysis. This learning style is prevalent and useful in roles requiring action and initiative. People with an Accommodating learning style prefer to work in teams to complete tasks.

- **Divergers** employ reflective observation to analyze information from various perspectives. They are likely to generate a broad range of ideas, and may be motivated to do so in group settings. These people are able to look at things from different perspectives. They are sensitive. They prefer to watch rather than do, tending to gather information and use their imaginations to solve problems. Divergers perform well in situations that require idea generation, such as brainstorming. People with a Diverger learning style have broad cultural interests and tend to be strong in the arts. They are interested in people and often prefer to work in groups, to listen with an open mind, and to receive personal feedback.

- **Assimilators** are known for taking abstract information and synthesizing it into concrete ideas based on logic and practical analysis. They prefer a concise, logical approach. Ideas and concepts are more important than people. Assimilators require a good, clear explanation rather than the practical value of something. They excel at understanding wide-ranging information and organizing it in a clear, logical format. They are less focused on people and more interested in ideas and abstract concepts. In formal learning situations, Assimilators prefer readings, lectures, exploring analytical models, and ample reflective time.

- **Convergers** tend to use logic and structured processes to evaluate information and ideas and to solve problems that have a practical application. They may also prefer to work with data and information, as opposed to opinions and viewpoints, so they often prefer independent learning and problem approaches as opposed to group discussion. Convergers like to apply their learnings to find solutions to practical issues. They prefer technical tasks and are less concerned with people and interpersonal aspects. A Converger learning style enables specialist and technology abilities.

Based on Kolb's model, it can be seen how insights gained through the Hogan inventories can be beneficial in promoting a productive learning environment. Table 3 maps the relevant Hogan scales to Kolb's model and can be used to provide insights into an individual's learning style.

		Hogan Scales		
		HPI	**HDS**	**MVPI**
Kolb Learning Style	**Accommodator**	Low Learning Approach Low Prudence • Low Impulse Control • Low Not Spontaneous High Sociability	Low Cautious Low Diligent	Low Science High Affiliation
	Diverger	High Learning Approach High Inquisitive • High Generates Ideas High Sociability	High Imaginative	High Aesthetics High Affiliation
	Assimilator	High Learning Approach Low Sociability High Prudence	High Diligent	High Science Low Affiliation
	Converger	Low Learning Approach High Prudence • High Impulse Control Low Inquisitive Low Sociability	Low Imaginative High Cautious High Diligent	High Science Low Affiliation High Security

Table 3   Kolb's Model with Related Hogan Scales

If learners are **Accommodators**, the coach needs to keep the discussion fast paced and determine what the learner thinks or feels, as opposed to laying out a methodical set of data to prove a point. When engaged in development planning, the Accommodator will like action items that are practical and involve other people. One challenge for the coach might be to keep the learners on task as they will likely be easily distracted.

With **Divergers**, the coach needs to keep the pace up, or the learners will lose interest. The coach should be prepared for the learners to have lots of ideas about what to work on and what would improve performance. The Divergers might want to gather additional input prior to creating a development plan. A challenge for the coach might be getting the learners to narrow down the number of development areas to address.

When working with **Assimilators**, the coach should take a concise, logical approach when explaining information. The learners will most likely want some time to process the feedback and then synthesize the data into a logical development plan of well-defined items. A challenge might be ensuring that the learners recognize the impact that their behaviors have on other people.

With **Convergers**, the coach should emphasize the value of the feedback from a practical standpoint. Convergers will want to create a development plan with actions that are pragmatic. A challenge could be that the learner might overlook input from others unless it has a practical application.

Coaches can use the foregoing approaches to more closely match the preferred learning style of their learners, thereby enhancing the impact of the discussion. In his classic *Harvard Business Review* article "Teaching Smart People How to Learn," Chris Argyris (1991) suggests that effective learning is dependent upon the way people recognize and understand their own behavior. He points out that, in order to facilitate impactful learning, organizations have to help individuals better recognize their own behaviors and contributions to situations while breaking down the defensiveness that often gets in the way of true learning. This approach supports the importance of increased Strategic Self-awareness and the value of using preferred learning styles to facilitate it.

Promoting Engagement and Action in Executing the Development Plan

As a coach, it is important to motivate the learners to effectively execute the development plan. As noted previously, most people are open to input and coaching that they believe will benefit them; the challenge is to help them clearly recognize the potential value to be gained by engaging in new approaches and alternative behaviors. It can be challenging to engage successful professionals in changing their behaviors or approaches—particularly when these behaviors and approaches are what have taken them to their current levels of success. In addition to experiencing a high level of achievement, most executives have often been told how smart, strategic, and insightful they are. As a result, it may be easy for a successful executive to believe that there is very little need for change or growth, even during times of changing circumstances. It is incumbent upon the coach to help the learners recognize the value in positive change even when they are currently performing quite well. The coach has to help them understand that "what got you here won't get you there" in today's ever-evolving business environment.

Once again, the filters or lenses through which a learner views the world come into play and can lead him or her to fall back on what is believed as opposed to what is reality. This "performance trap" also includes relying too heavily on what has led to success in the past, with the expectation that such behavior will yield similar positive results in the future. Finkelstein (2004) points out how unsuccessful people tend to stubbornly rely on what worked for them in the past. He offers examples of how many CEOs inappropriately fall back on a "default response" or answer that was positively reinforced in the past. Such automatic or default responses may be triggered by the learner's personality or by the lens through which he or she views various situations. One of the greatest gifts that a coach can provide to a learner is the ability to clearly see a situation for what it is. In other words, the coach helps the learner recognize biases and filters and (rather than relying on predisposed responses) then consider a range of approaches (perhaps even new ones) relevant to the situation at hand. In essence, the coach can be instrumental in providing a learner with a call to action.

The Hogan inventories can provide a coach with the insights necessary to build a call to action that will inspire learners to apply what they have learned. The previous points covered can be used as a starting point, with attention given specifically to those tendencies that can lead to future success. For example, if a person scores high on Ambition, Power, and Commerce, then the call to action might be that the behavior change will result in getting promoted, having more influence, or receiving additional compensation. This call to action will probably not be appealing at all to the learner who has high scores on Sociability, Colorful, Recognition, and Affiliation. This person's definition of future success might be to work with a broader base of constituents and to receive the kudos that he or she so rightly deserves.

The coach should also use insights about the learner's preferred learning styles to prompt action. For example, learners who are Convergers will be engaged with behavior changes that are practical for everyday use because they will want to see some quick wins. On the other hand, Assimilator learners will be more engaged with behavior changes if there is an opportunity to think them through in logical steps.

It can be quite challenging and often counterproductive to propose new behaviors to learners that differ greatly from their personality or natural tendencies. When making behavior-change suggestions, the coach must clearly consider the preferences of the learner. For example, if coaching is being provided to someone with a profile that reflects high Reserved, low Sociability, low Colorful, and low Recognition, it may not be helpful to merely recommend developmental actions that are highly extroverted or outgoing in nature. The learner will need to clearly understand the need for behavioral change and the potential downsides to not changing and then be eased into some of these non-preferred actions that may benefit performance. Coaches should not try to change the identity of leaders because there are many ways that leaders can be successful. Rather, coaches need to teach new behaviors, approaches, and skill sets that learners can add to their toolkits. The underlying notion here is to expand the behavioral repertoire of learners to allow them to become better equipped to approach people and situations in even more impactful ways.

Case Studies

The following two case studies demonstrate how coaches can use insights into the learner's personality to (1) enhance the learner's receptivity to feedback and coaching, (2) match feedback and coaching approaches to the learner's preferred learning style, and (3) promote engagement and action in executing the development plan. These case studies were selected because the natural tendencies of the learner represented a significant barrier to success, and insights into the personality of the learner were instrumental in overcoming this barrier.

Carol, Research and Development Scientist

Background

Carol is a well-respected research and development scientist who has been with her organization for more than 15 years. She has worked her way up the hierarchy over that time by being a recognized expert across many of the technical areas in her organization. Her career has grown primarily through a deep level of technical expertise and innovative approaches to research and development. She often leads through her expertise and is frequently sought out by others as a technical expert.

Carol is at a stage in her career where she is well established and has very little to prove in terms of her expertise or ability to add value to the organization. However, some key stakeholders, including her direct manager, believe that Carol has a number of growth opportunities to address before she can be truly considered a highly effective leader. In the past, Carol did not pay much attention to feedback she was given. Her boss asked her to participate in a coaching initiative that included the Hogan inventories in the hope that this time she might be more open to the feedback and recommendations for behavior changes. The following are notable aspects of Carol's Hogan results that are important to driving greater effectiveness across the three key areas: feedback, coaching, and development.

Notable MVPI Results

High Scores
- Science (96th percentile)
- Commerce (92nd percentile)
- Power (90th percentile)
- Recognition (87th percentile)

Low Scores
- Hedonism (8th percentile)
- Security (10th percentile)
- Tradition (12th percentile)
- Affiliation (15th percentile)

Notable HPI Results

High Scores
- Ambition (100th percentile)
  - Competitive (5/5)
  - Self-confident (3/3)
  - Leadership (6/6)
- Prudence (96th percentile)

Low Scores
- Sociability (25th percentile)
- Adjustment (8th percentile)
  - Trusting (0/3)
- Interpersonal Sensitivity (12th percentile)
- Learning Approach (16th percentile)
  - Education (1/3)
  - Reading (0/4)

Notable HDS Results

High Scores
- Bold (100th percentile)
- Mischievous (95th percentile)
- Excitable (92nd percentile)
- Leisurely (90th percentile)
- Colorful (82nd percentile)
- Dutiful (92nd percentile)

Low Scores
- Cautious (8th percentile)
- Reserved (15th percentile)

Preparing for Carol's Feedback and Coaching Sessions

Before providing Carol with feedback or coaching, it is important for the coach to understand how the process can be tailored to fit her personality, including the possible hooks, her lenses and filters, her possible reactions, her preferred learning style, and possible calls to action. In doing so, the coach can structure the feedback and coaching processes to allow Carol to be more deeply engaged in receiving the information and insights.

On the MVPI, Carol's high score on the Science scale indicates that she is likely to value analytical problem-solving, curiosity, and objective decision-making. So, the coach might want to take an approach that allows Carol to explore and uncover the meaning of the feedback. More specifically, she could be invited and encouraged to be an integral part of the discovery process, as opposed to the coach's merely delivering the feedback to her along with an interpretation and assessment of the potential implications. The consultation could be structured as a feedback session in which Carol plays a very active role in the interpretation of the data while being guided by the coach. As a feedback provider, it can be challenging at times for a coach to step out of the expert role—that is, to hold back on providing deep and rich insights. However, this circumstance might be one of those situations in which the feedback provider may want to lead into the insights, rather than presenting them, in order to allow Carol the opportunity to play an important role in the data analysis and interpretation processes.

In addition, the coach may be able to further incent Carol to attend to the feedback and its potential implications by helping her recognize the link between enhanced leadership effectiveness and some of the outcomes that she might value, such as being able to make more money and to get ahead (high Commerce), or by identifying ways that she could gain even greater control through improved approaches (high Power). These are just a few of the insights revealed through Carol's MVPI results that could assist the coach in tailoring the feedback and coaching session.

Exploring Carol's HPI and HDS results more deeply reveals that Carol is highly driven to succeed (high Ambition) and may have a strong desire to please her key stakeholders (high Dutiful). Carol also appears to be quite comfortable working independently (low Sociability) and is likely to be quite confident in her knowledge and expertise (high Bold).

Further, her high Bold score, coupled with a low score (0/3) on the Trusting subscale, suggests that she may not be open to (or may push back on) the feedback or opinions of others. This possible intransigence could be a potential challenge for the coach to consider before providing feedback to Carol. In this case, it may be important to dedicate some time up front to establishing a degree of trust and helping Carol become comfortable with the coach and the feedback process. If Carol is resistant to the feedback, the coach may need to revisit some of Carol's strong values to identify ways to help her recognize and accept the value of the feedback.

Engaging Carol in the Learning Process

With regard to her preferred learning style, Carol's Hogan results indicate that she is a Converger. Although this is not an exact match on the relevant Hogan scales,

Carol scored low on Learning Approach, low on Sociability, and high on Science, which are all related scales for a Converger style preference. These results indicate that Carol has a practical preferred learning style.

Carol's low Learning Approach score suggests that she might not desire an academic type of feedback session that results in an assignment of books and articles to read. She might also be more interested in the application of the feedback as opposed to merely understanding it. It may be important to help her answer the question, "So why should this matter to me?" In addition, her high Ambition and high Dutiful scores provide insights that she might be highly motivated to understand and take action on the feedback if she feels that it is expected of her and that it will help her achieve future success.

Also, Carol's low Interpersonal Sensitivity score may indicate that the coach can engage in a tell-it-like-it-is feedback session as opposed to having to position things in a more sensitive manner (i.e., Carol might appreciate a more direct approach).

Motivating Carol to Act Based on the Feedback and Coaching

After Carol has received her feedback and coaching, the Hogan insights can also be invaluable in understanding how she can be motivated to act on the feedback that she has received. Carol's high Ambition score suggests an opportunity to use the development planning objectives as a challenge to her to grow and achieve. Her high Dutiful score suggests that she may be likely to take action if she believes that this is what her key stakeholders (perhaps her upper management) want and expect her to do. In addition, based on these insights, it may be helpful to encourage Carol to directly share these developmental objectives with her direct manager or a key stakeholder in the organizational hierarchy. Involving others will allow Carol to be able to keep score through someone else regarding her developmental objectives, while also being dutiful in the accomplishment of these objectives.

David, Marketing Director

Background

David is a highly successful marketing director who has previously been passed over for promotion to vice president. David is widely recognized for his technical excellence and is often seen as one of the smartest people in the room. However, the feedback about David is that he is often viewed as not having a strong presence in group discussions and operating in ways that are seen as being under the radar. Despite his vast knowledge and deep expertise, David does not express his opinions much in group settings and rarely pushes back on others even when it might be appropriate to do so. While he is highly talented, David appears to be undervalued and underutilized in his role. David's boss wants to help him develop so he can be a viable candidate for a vice president position. With that purpose in mind, she has recommended a coaching initiative that includes the Hogan inventories. To prepare for the initiative, the coach noted the following:

Notable MVPI Results

High Scores

- Altruistic (98th percentile)
- Tradition (96th percentile)
- Security (92nd percentile)
- Aesthetics (88th percentile)

Low Scores

- Hedonism (9th percentile)
- Power (15th percentile)
- Recognition (23rd percentile)

Notable HPI Results

High Scores

- Learning Approach (100th percentile)
- Interpersonal Sensitivity (86th percentile)
    - Easy to Live With (4/5)
    - Sensitive (4/4)
    - Caring (4/4)
    - No Hostility (3/3)
- Adjustment (82nd percentile)
- Inquisitive (78th percentile)

Low Scores

- Sociability (5th percentile)
    - Likes Parties (0/5)
    - Experience Seeking (2/6)
    - Exhibitionist (1/5)
    - Entertaining (1/4)

Notable HDS Results

High Scores

- Dutiful (98th percentile)
- Skeptical (88th percentile)
- Cautious (86th percentile)
- Reserved (76th percentile)
- Diligent (75th percentile)

Low Scores

- Bold (5th percentile)
- Leisurely (12th percentile)
- Excitable (18th percentile)

Preparing for David's Feedback and Coaching Sessions

In reviewing David's MVPI results, the coach noticed he has high scores on Altruistic, Tradition, Security, and Aesthetics. Based on his high Altruistic score, it might be helpful for David to recognize how he could better serve others by first helping (developing) himself. His high Tradition score suggests that he would react well to hearing some of the rules and best practices associated with the feedback processes. In addition, it might be possible for the coach to leverage David's desire for security by helping him see how improved performance, based on feedback, could serve to reduce risk.

David's high Interpersonal Sensitivity score, coupled with his high Dutiful score, suggests someone who will approach the feedback session in an open, polite, and accepting manner. It might be important to push deeply to uncover any areas of confusion or concern because he might not initiate that type of questioning or pushback. His low Bold and Excitable scores may also suggest that he is unlikely to react to the feedback in a very direct or emotional way.

Engaging David in the Learning Process

With regard to his preferred learning style, David's Hogan profile indicates that he is a Diverger. Although this is not an exact match on the relevant Hogan scales, he has a high Learning Approach score, a high Inquisitive score, and a high Aesthetics score, all related scales for a Diverger learning style preference. As a Diverger, David will learn better when he is allowed to observe and collect a wide range of information. He will most likely need time to process the information as well.

David's high score in Learning Approach further suggests that he is likely to value education and learning. He may also be very open to receiving coaching and developmental feedback if he thinks it will lead to learning opportunities.

David enjoys the opportunity to help others (as evidenced through his high Altruistic score). One way to engage him to work on his developmental opportunities may be to position them as a chance to add value for others. As an example, if he is working on speaking up more and expressing his opinions openly, it might be helpful to highlight the positive impact that sharing his ideas could have on others, as he will be stimulating their thoughts, which may lead to better decisions.

Motivating David to Act Based on the Feedback and Coaching

The context that the coach was given regarding the reason for the coaching—that David does not speak up, does not voice his opinions, and does not have a strong presence—is supported by his low Sociability score and high Cautious score, coupled with his high Interpersonal Sensitivity score and low Bold score. In David's case, the behaviors that will help his performance the most involve being more extroverted and learning to take stands. These behaviors will not be easy for David, given his profile, and he will have to work outside of his comfort zone to attempt them. Therefore, it is even more important that the coach find a call to action that will convince David that he really does need to change his behaviors to be successful in the future. The coach can leverage the scales discussed earlier and also appeal to David's high Dutiful nature by positioning the behavior changes as something that upper management wants him to do. It will also be useful to help David understand that the extroverted behaviors do not have to be turned on 100 percent of the time. The key to David's willingness to use them will rest with the selective identification of key events in which he can employ the behaviors and change the trajectory of his introverted reputation. Building in downtime or time to quietly recover from such events will also be quite welcomed by David as part of the development plan. Introverts are often more willing to take on extroverted roles when they can anticipate downtime that allows to them to recover from situations with extensive social pressure.

SUMMARY

Throughout the leadership development process, enhancing feedback receptivity, matching approaches to ensure greater understanding, and promoting higher levels of commitment to implementing the development plan all play a significant role in the coaching success equation. The learner's personality is central to each of these areas, and effectiveness of the development initiative is often determined by the ability of the coach to use personality insights to tailor the coaching engagement to the learner. Hogan inventories provide a wealth of information to help coaches better understand the learner's styles, preferences, filters, hot buttons, and the like. Coaches interested in improving their effectiveness can use this type of personality information to promote a more stimulating, meaningful, and impactful development experience for the learner.

CHAPTER 8

DELIVERING EFFECTIVE PERSONALITY-BASED FEEDBACK

INTRODUCTION

Hogan consultants and coaches have more than two decades of experience in delivering feedback based on Hogan inventory results. Over this time, Hogan has conducted research that includes objective ratings of thousands of feedback recipients who have evaluated the effectiveness of their feedback sessions. We have also gathered best practices in giving feedback from the highly qualified experts in the Hogan Coaching Network (HCN). Both of these sources of information tell us that the best-rated and most valuable feedback consists of interpretations that account for and are grounded in the Situational Context of the leader, identify developmental themes and appropriate developmental goals, and result in specific behavioral actions to take to achieve those goals.

Such feedback offers more than a mere recounting of where a person fits in terms of scale score percentiles and static descriptors. Rather, it is better characterized as a process of collaborative interpretation that accounts for the leader's context and goals, his or her attempts to influence and cope with that context, and his or her level of Strategic Self-awareness. High quality feedback is a dynamic interplay between the reputational and identity components of personality and between the leader and the coach. It is a balance between art (the ability of a skilled coach to orchestrate the feedback) and science (the technical validity of the inventories). In this chapter, we share how to achieve the marriage of these to provide meaningful and actionable feedback by discussing the Framework (p. 141) needed for the session and by describing the salient Coach's Skills and Attributes (p. 156).

Background

The goal of Hogan feedback is rarely, if ever, for leaders to leave with some high-level ideas about themselves. The goal is to increase a leader's Strategic Self-awareness *in service of* enhanced job performance. Hogan feedback should help the leader become better equipped to take effective action that will improve career success. This complex task requires the coach to synthesize the Hogan data into meanings, check those meanings with real-world meanings (either multi-rater assessment data or the leader's real-world experience), identify developmental themes (the places where the leader can improve performance, such as developing others or staying out of the weeds), identifying which developmental themes are most important now, and then identifying a few simple and specific actions to start. Again and again, leaders report to us that this full cycle of action—this process of feedback that begins with data and concludes with meaningful themes, goals, and action items—is impactful and even life altering.

Coaches, organizational development professionals, and human resource professionals have typically worked two ends of the human development continuum. They have become very good at identifying big, broad (and often dichotomous) labels and descriptors for people (e.g., this person is strategic, or that person is detail oriented). They have also become very good at providing lists of things to do and boxes to check with the hope that the activities reflected in the boxes will help people develop in a way that matches the goals. Unfortunately, these professionals do not often fluidly connect the dots between the assessment data, the lived world of the individual, and the themes, goals, and actions of the development plan. Developmental feedback is one of the important connectors between these dots, and this chapter will help coaches think both philosophically and concretely about the process of translating assessment data into development themes and actions.

This transformation of data into action is a complex task requiring integration and interpretation of multiple data points and individualization for each specific leader. The complexity can be intimidating and overwhelming for users who are new to the Hogan inventories. Thus, in this chapter, we describe the all-important framework that the HCN coaches have developed based on thousands of feedback sessions in an effort to break this complex task down into five smaller components:

- Explaining the logistics.
- Providing an overview of the Hogan inventories.
- Interpreting the scales.
- Individualizing the feedback.
- Identifying developmental themes and pivot points.

Like the Hogan scales, these factors are interconnected and often take place simultaneously, but for the sake of clarity, we will discuss them separately. We will then turn to the qualifications and attributes that are critical for the coach to possess to successfully orchestrate the session. It is this combination of framework and coaching skills that enables the marriage of art and science, resulting in a stellar feedback session.

THE FRAMEWORK

Hogan feedback sessions have lots of moving parts, and it is extremely helpful for the coach to delineate up front to the leader what will happen during the session and what the expected outcomes are—in other words, establish a framework. The coach, as the feedback provider, sets the framework to ensure that the purpose and goals of the feedback session are clear to the leader, to help organize the mass of assessment data to be covered, and to help contain the emotions that often emerge when leaders see a new or less-than-flattering view of themselves. The framework creates a clear roadmap for the session and a safe base for reflection, allowing the leader to be more open to the data and to the development process and to formulate and try out alternative behaviors. While the framework is established at the beginning of the session, it is useful to remind the leader of the framework at each transition and during the introduction of new material during the session. It is imperative to return to the framework for closure. An old adage in public speaking is "tell them what you're going to tell them—then tell them—then tell them what you told them." A similar sequence occurs in setting the framework: the coach explains to the leader what is going to happen, then it happens, then the coach and leader summarize what happened, and then the coach and leader agree on what should happen next.

Explaining the Logistics

Even though many of the logistics about the session have likely been communicated ahead of time, recapping them is imperative to set the framework. After a brief introduction, the coach can review some or all of the following to help the leader feel grounded, respected, and secure:

- How long the feedback will take (and that the feedback will have a beginning, a middle, and an end).
- The purpose of the feedback (i.e., increased Strategic Self-awareness).
- Expected outcomes (e.g., identification of two to three major takeaways—either strengths to leverage or development areas to improve—and accompanying actions and behavior modifications that will increase effectiveness as a leader).
- Whether or not the feedback is confidential.
- What will happen to the data after the feedback.

- Whether or not the organization has any expectations of the leader after the feedback (e.g., sharing the feedback or completing a development plan).

- The leader's understanding of why he or she took the Hogan inventories.

- A brief recap of the leader's history and expectations or hopes for the feedback session.

Although these items are simple to cover, they go a long way toward helping an individual feel in control of his or her destiny, particularly if the feedback has been mandated or is a part of a remediation process. People often come to a feedback session having no idea what to expect, so reviewing at least some of these parameters is important to garner alignment with the leader, to pace the session, and to build rapport. It is an absolute necessity that the coach have clarity around each of these logistical items, even if the coach does not choose to review all of them with the leader.

Providing an Overview of the Three Hogan Inventories

Once the leader is clear about what is going to happen in the time allotted, it is important to provide a basic understanding of what is being measured by the Hogan inventories. Clear understanding of what the data are measuring saves enormous amounts of time, reduces confusion during feedback, and sets the groundwork for more accurate interpretations of the data (especially because Hogan data is quite different from other types of commonly used assessments). Given that a good part of the two-day basic Hogan Assessment Certification Workshop is spent discussing the topic of what is measured by the Hogan inventories, it is not an easy task to summarize in just a few minutes. For this reason, we have provided both a description of and a framework for a three-minute "elevator speech" about Hogan data that can be given at the outset of the feedback session. If the coach is also reviewing multi-rater feedback or performance reviews, he or she may want to add a few sentences to explain why the multi-rater feedback information is useful and how it relates to the Hogan inventories. One description is that the Hogan inventories provide information (statistical likelihoods) about how a person is likely to show up, and the multi-rater feedback gives information about how a person shows up in the real world as described by real people who know the person being assessed.

The Elevator Speech

The coach should start the elevator speech by explaining that there is a lot of information to cover but that it is worthwhile to take five minutes to explain what is being looked at in terms of data. The coach explains that even though the suite of inventories is often called "the Hogan," which suggests that it is one big assessment, it is actually three inventories, including the Hogan Personality Inventory (HPI); the Hogan Development Survey (HDS); and the Motives, Values, Preferences Inventory (MVPI). There are actually three different types of data that lend three different views of the person (i.e., the Bright Side, the Dark Side, and the In Side). This brief commentary gives the coach an opportunity to advise that the feedback discussion will address the way the inventories work together and that the scales always operate in combination, interacting and buffering each other, highlighting and shadowing each other. To keep things clear, the coach specifically discusses what is measured and what is predicted by each of the three inventories.

HPI in Elevator Speech Version

The HPI data provide information about an individual's strengths. It is information that reflects how other people are likely to see the individual in everyday situations. When establishing this section of the framework, the coach needs to explain seamlessly and quickly to the leader the concepts of identity (how we see ourselves) and reputation (how others see us). The Hogan measures reputation because it is the best predictor of future behavior, and this is also why the inventory suite has such strong predictive validity and resonates so strongly with real life experiences and descriptions.

The topic of reputation raises a second and equally important point about Hogan data: the data may or may not resonate with the leader's self-perception (identity). The coach needs to alert leaders to this fact and advise them that when a gap between identity and reputation is uncovered, it will be explored during the feedback session.

A gap between identity and reputation as measured by the Hogan can occur for four general reasons. First, it is possible that the person has a blind spot about how others see him or her. Identification of a blind spot is often great news from a development perspective because increasing Strategic Self-awareness can lead to developmental gain. The second reason for the gap is that when we interpret scales one scale at a time and at the most basic level, the scale may not resonate fully with a leader. When this disconnect happens, we have to account for the way that other scales come into play. In real life, the scales do not show up as singular qualities but as a gestalt of qualities that highlight and shadow each other. Third, while the scales give general information about reputation and core personality characteristics, the scales do not give concrete information about developmental efforts and behavioral modifications that the leader has undertaken. Fourth, and finally, as with any testing situation, there is always the possibility of testing error. Acknowledging the possibility of testing error often reduces defensiveness and increases the individual's faith in the coach's competence as a scientific practitioner.

Once the coach establishes that the HPI is reputational data, it is useful to explain that the graph depicts a bell curve, where high scores and low scores are both strong scores and thus reflect strong personality characteristics. Those strong characteristics can be leveraged but are also prone to overuse, especially if they are above the 90th or below the 10th percentile. Letting leaders know these factors up front can go a long way in helping them understand and relate to their Hogan data on a more intimate and friendly level, rather than in a reactive or dismissive manner.

Incorporating all of this material may sound like an enormous amount of information to cover on the front end of a feedback session, but if this information is articulated in a succinct manner, it will save time answering questions and dealing with resistance later on. Also, when the conversation moves to the HDS and MVPI, the differences between identity and reputation do not have to be covered again, and those discussions will go faster.

HDS in Elevator Speech Version

HDS data are designed to inform leaders about the ways that they might overuse strengths—to such excess that the strength can become a derailer. In this sense, the HDS represents the Dark Side of personality. Like the HPI, the HDS data represent how others are likely to describe the leader. The differences between the HPI and the HDS are that the HDS scores are more likely to become problematic when the leader is under stress and pressure, has become complacent, or is not able to self-monitor. Further, the HDS scales can be viewed as coping styles, and they are built up over a lifetime when the individual has had to cope with a stressful situation or an unknown. Although it is useful to think of the HDS characteristics as more likely to be problematic when one is not monitoring one's own behavior, it is helpful for leaders to know that the HDS characteristics do not disappear altogether. Rather, they recede into a general background of personality characteristics instead of being on the surface as highlighted, annoying characteristics. It is also worth mentioning that HDS scales need to be interpreted in light of the context in which the leader works. Elevations in HDS scales are only problematic in light of cultural norms. For example, a moderate risk on the Colorful scale is likely more problematic in a culture of highly focused statisticians and less problematic in the entertainment industry.

MVPI in Elevator Speech Version

The MVPI is designed to capture the motives, values, and preferences of an individual. In setting up a feedback session, coaches need to explain that the MVPI reflects the leader's values and desires and often reflects reputation as well as identity. MVPI data suggest the kind of culture in which an individual will thrive. The MVPI also predicts the kind of culture an individual will strive to create as a leader, and it provides some understanding of how the HPI and HDS data are likely to show up in the real world. For example, if two leaders have high Ambition and high Sociability scores on the HPI, but one leader is low on the MVPI scales of Recognition, Power, and Commerce and the other leader is high on these MVPI scales, the leaders are likely to look quite different in the real world. The high Ambition–high Sociability combination is likely to play out very differently when the combination is fueled by different values. Giving examples (such as this) before the feedback alerts the leader that the interpretation will work across the Hogan inventories and across all of the data to create textured meanings rather than black-and-white, fail-safe descriptions.

The elevator speeches provide the details of what leaders need to know in general about the Hogan data before the coach starts to tell them the specifics of their particular profiles. Leaders who feel well informed and secure and who are clear about the data will be less resistant and better able to follow along as the coach bobs and weaves through the scales. Most importantly, when leaders realize how complex and multifaceted the data are and realize that the coach can guide them through a clear, yet nuanced, interpretation of the data, they will become curious and interested in how the coach will make sense of the results.

While the foregoing discussion has highlighted very practical benefits of the data overview, there is an additional reason the overview is important. When the coach and the leader are very clear about what is being measured and the technical aspects of the data, this clarity can set limits and guardrails for interpretations. Coaches want to help create meaning out of the data but have to remain true to the technical meanings of what is being predicted. Therefore, the technical meaning of the scales is an important part of the framework.

Coaches can use the following information to create their own elevator speeches:

HPI

The main points about the HPI are as follows:

1. It reflects the Bright Side of personality.

2. It is about how others are likely to see the leader in everyday situations.

3. It reflects reputation.

4. It may or may not relate to the way the leader sees himself or herself (identity). There are four basic ways to account for when the Hogan reputational data and identity are disconnected:

    a. Leaders sometimes have blind spots (gaps between identity and reputation).

    b. Scales nuance and buffer each other.

    c. Developmental gain could have occurred (i.e., the leader has modified the behavior through active development).

    d. Testing errors may have occurred.

5. The graphic view of the inventory results are conveyed on a bell curve:

    a. Both high and low scores are strong scores.

    b. Strong scores are strong personality characteristics, and have both advantages and disadvantages.

    c. Very strong scores are more likely to be overused than average scores.

HDS

The main points about the HDS are as follows:

1. The HDS represents risk factors for derailment—that is, the Dark Side of personality. These risk factors are usually overused strengths; however, very low scores can suggest potential problems as well (see Chapter 4).

2. Risk factors can show up in everyday situations but are more likely to become problematic when the leader is under stress and pressure (after all, they are the ways the leader copes with stress), or conversely, when the leader is not monitoring self-presentation.

3. Higher scores suggest a greater likelihood of problematic behavior.

4. HDS scales are statistically related to HPI scales.

5. Scale relationships can improve accuracy when interpreting results.

MVPI

The main points about the MVPI are as follows:

1. The MVPI data reflect the leader's drivers, values, and unconscious biases.

2. The data are good predictors of the type of culture in which the leader will thrive.

3. The data are a good predictor of the type of culture the leader is likely to create in his or her sphere of influence.

4. The data help us understand potentially unconscious biases of the leader.

5. The data help us understand the impact of the HPI and HDS data in the real world.

At this point, the coach has discussed the first two components of the framework—a review of feedback session logistics and a basic overview of the Hogan inventories. These two components of the framework create rails in which the middle section of feedback (the actual interpretations, individualization, and design of interventions) takes place. It can be helpful to insert reminders about the framework throughout the feedback session to keep the feedback session on track.

Interpreting the Scales

Once the coach establishes the framework and sets expectations, he or she is ready to provide the actual interpretation. Because of the massive amount of information and the dynamic interplay that goes on between the coach and the leader in Hogan feedback, a funnel approach is recommended to describe the scales themselves. This funnel approach helps the coach convey information about the scales with crystal clarity, starting with the most basic, general information about the scale and progressing to the more personal and contextualized interpretations.

During the conversation, it is easy to forget that the leader usually does not have an understanding of what each scale measures. For this reason, it is helpful to start with a sentence stating what the scale is about, such as "the Prudence scale is about conscientiousness." The coach is then set to convey information about the leader's score and make a very basic interpretation. "Your score falls in the high range on Prudence, and that means that others are likely to see you as . . . ." The coach should have a robust set of descriptors for each scale. Not every descriptor associated with a scale score will fit every leader, so it is the coach's job to help the leader understand as many aspects of the scale as possible in a time-efficient manner. This juncture is also where the coach can begin to add nuance to the scale interpretation by using subscales or by integrating contextual information about the leader, including commentary about subscale trends and deficits; context about the leader's role, goals, and organizational culture; and so on. Examples of basic contextualization might include these statements:

- "I can see how your high Prudence could really help you with your current goal of better organizing the work flow of your group."

- "I can see how your high Ambition works well for you at Company X, as Company X is known for its competitive spirit."

- "Your 99th percentile Prudence probably helped you early in your career, but now that you have reached the executive level, we may want to question whether it keeps you too far in the weeds when you need to be more strategic."

These statements do not need to be lengthy interpretations or commentary, just a brief comment followed by a question about whether or not the interpretation connects to the leader's experience. Often, leaders start to get enthusiastic about the feedback at this point, as this is where the data start to come alive for them. If scales are really resonating with the leader's experience and time permits, the coach can request a few examples. However, we just want to add a cautionary note about time management: while we want to engage the leader as much as possible, we also need to contain the session in the time allotted.

If the contextualized interpretation falls flat with the leader, the coach can check for other scales that might mitigate the description provided, as illustrated by the following example:

The leader is a 99 percent on Inquisitive and works as an accountant. During feedback, the coach notes that the 99 percent Inquisitive suggests that others may see the leader as open-minded and with lots of ideas but possibly impractical. However, the leader is unable to relate to the descriptors. It is certainly possible that this leader has a blind spot, but the coach needs to check out alternative explanations for the leader's inability to relate to the feedback. The coach might hypothesize that the high Inquisitive is held in check or even covered over by high scores on Cautious and Diligent and no risk on either Imaginative or Mischievous.

Although the funnel schema may seem excessively formulaic in the context of integrating so much data (including information shared by the leader), it helps the leader follow the process structure, and it helps the coach avoid overwhelming the leader. Throughout the feedback session, coaches tend to inundate leaders with information. Anything that can be done to help leaders maintain clarity and a sense of structure will help them stay engaged. Again, to make interpretive leaps, both the coach and the leader have to understand the most basic components of the interpretation as singular elements. Sometimes it helps to use language markers to assist the leader in moving through the layers of complexity. A coach might start by saying something such as "let's look at the most basic level of this scale" and then describing what the scale is about. Then the coach might add, "Before I ask if that resonates for you, let me just add that we also need to consider the way that these other scales might impact the scale." The main goal is always clarity for the leader, and it is the coach's responsibility to assess how much complexity the leader is able to digest and then adjust the discussion accordingly.

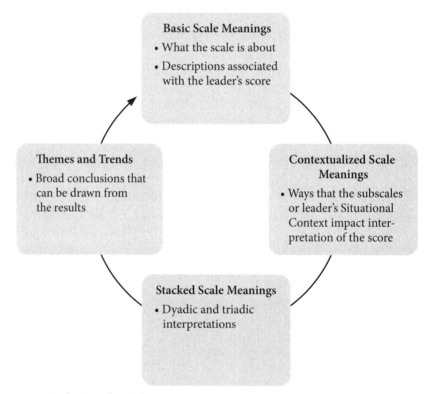

Figure 7   Explaining the Scales

Figure 7 explains how meaning is built using Hogan data and how the coach should always return to the basic, validated descriptors of the scales to maintain the integrity of the process.

The coach can apply these basic concepts for interpreting scales to many different ways of structuring a feedback session. The choice of structure should be informed by the coach's level of comfort as a feedback provider, the leader's Hogan profile, and the reason that the leader took the Hogan inventories in the first place. Coaches should consider their own Hogan profiles when deciding on a feedback structure. For example, coaches who are more comfortable with ambiguity and have greater openness to ideas should double-check whether they are providing their leaders with enough structure. Conversely, coaches who are less comfortable with ambiguity and have a strong desire for structure and predictability should double-check whether they are providing their leaders with enough leeway for new and unforeseen interpretations to emerge during the feedback session. The leader's Hogan profile should also inform the choice for structuring the feedback session (see Chapter 7). Leaders whose Hogan profile suggests comfort with ambiguity and openness to new ideas can tolerate less structured feedback while leaders with less comfort with ambiguity and a strong desire for order and predictability appreciate greater structure and clarity.

Following are three (non-exhaustive) types of feedback structure from least to most complex:

Assessment-Based Structure

Assessment-based Structure is the simplest feedback structure and is organized around the Hogan inventories. This feedback structure starts with the HPI or the MVPI and progresses through each inventory, scale by scale (typically covering every scale for the HPI and the highest and lowest scales for the HDS and MVPI), and builds a complete picture of strengths and opportunities. This feedback structure builds meaning out of blocks of information. This is the easiest form of feedback to deliver for newer coaches and feedback providers because it is the most linear of the three structures presented here. The benefits of the assessment-based structure are that it is clear, it can be quick, and it is easy to manage. The downside of this structure is that it may be harder to develop robust themes, and it may miss nuances that would help identify developmental opportunities.

Integrated Developmental Structure

The Integrated Developmental Structure approach is based around the HPI *and* the statistically correlated or thematically interrelated scales. In this feedback structure, the coach typically starts with the Adjustment and Ambition scales and then checks the statistically correlated or thematically related HDS and MVPI scales and subscales to see what meaning they add. The coach then weaves these elements together as a gauge of how the leader approaches his or her world and goals. Further, the coach uses this information as an indicator of the type of role the leader is likely to assume with others (e.g., is this person driven to lead or to follow?). The goal is to integrate meaning *across* the Hogan inventories to identify salient personality themes. In this approach, the coach discusses every HPI scale but picks and chooses relevant HDS and MVPI scales. With this structure, themes emerge out of three broad areas rooted in the HPI: (1) self-regulation and the leader's approach to getting ahead (Adjustment and Ambition), (2) social wiring (Sociability and

Interpersonal Sensitivity), and (3) the leader's approach to solving problems and how the leader views the world (Prudence, Inquisitive, and Learning Approach).

The caveat with using this type of feedback structure is that it necessitates maintaining a very strong framework and providing a clear forewarning to the leader that the feedback will ramble across the inventories. Coaches should master the assessment-based, more linear structure for feedback before attempting an integrated, developmental approach. The benefit of the integrated structure is a depth of interpretation that usually resonates with the leader. The potential downside is that the leader may not know what to do with the depth of information unless the coach is prepared to create clear goals and behavioral recommendations or the leader has the opportunity for continued coaching and mentoring. A variation on this model is fully described by Hogan et al. (2007), in which the Hogan Performance Model is used as the foundation for structuring feedback.

Specific Need Structure

This approach structures the feedback session to address a specific, pre-identified need that was the impetus for the leader's taking the Hogan inventories and perhaps participating in subsequent coaching. If the coach is working with a leader on a very specific issue, the coach can use the Hogan results to help hone in on it. For example, the HR generalist advised the coach that the leader to whom the coach will provide feedback (Joe) presently has a reputation for strong performance on the execution of projects and for getting things done quickly and efficiently. This performance led to Joe's promotion, his first into the executive level. The HR generalist recommended coaching to him both to increase his ability to build his team and to manage his tendency to do the work himself. Knowing this, the coach can customize the feedback to address these issues. While the feedback will cover all of the HPI scales and many of the HDS and MVPI scales, the coach is going to go to great lengths to specifically address the ways that his Hogan data inform his two developmental needs. Whatever the specific need, this approach tailors the Hogan feedback to it. While to some degree all feedback draws connections to the developmental needs of the leader, this approach draws an even tighter connection.

The coach does not need to talk about every aspect of a person's personality in every feedback session, and in fact, there are many feedback sessions where it is appropriate to leave interesting and important information out of the session based on relevance. Whatever structure the coach applies, it needs to be a conscious choice, and the coach needs to plan the interpretations around that structure and explain it as he or she sets the frame for feedback.

Individualizing the Feedback

Coaches are asked to debrief a wide variety of people from a wide variety of situations. While it is possible to accurately interpret Hogan scales without the Situational Context and without information about a leader's experience in his or her world, much of the developmental richness of Hogan data and opportunities for developmental intervention are lost without these elements (see Chapter 5). People never show up for their Hogan feedback *ex nihilo*. They show up with all of their experiences, their baggage, and the stories that they have told themselves about those experiences. Those experiences and stories help coaches understand the Hogan scales from the inside out and provide great insight into the way scale-related behaviors show up in the leader's present world and how they might play out in the future. Thus, it is important that the coach take a brief history from the leader and proactively include it in the feedback conversation. The leader's history and perspective constitute the identity components of personality, which are invaluable for individualizing Hogan feedback and for identifying pivots points and behavioral shifts (discussed in the next section).

Often, time does not permit a lengthy discussion of the leader's history, but at a minimum, the coach should ask the leader to describe the reason for the feedback, the current situation (including the leader's perception of key strengths and weaknesses), and the leader's future goals and desires. Asking the leader to describe these elements offers several pieces of information that the coach can draw on to connect how the leader sees the world to the reputational data.

- When leaders describe their current role and future goals, they are explaining how they see themselves, the world, and others. The coach needs to take note of things such as whether they sound positive or negative. Do they mention other people? If so, is there a trend in the way they describe people; are people allies, adversaries, or something else? Can they describe their goals with plans to reach them, or are they far in the distance and fantastical? Do they describe their plans in a way that casts them as agents or as passive passengers in their lives? This kind of quick analysis is important in establishing a baseline of identity against which to compare the reputational data.

- When leaders describe their current goals and challenges, the coach gains insight into how leaders see themselves and their problems. Are the key strengths and watch-outs that they describe consistent with their Hogan profile? This self-description can provide insights into their Strategic Self-awareness. Do they articulate vague places where they are unhappy or feel stuck? Do they describe general areas of difficulty, or do they identify specific circumscribed problems? Do they have a development plan or goals for dealing with these challenges? This kind of analysis is very important in helping to create specific and actionable goals.

- When leaders describe general information such as hometown, education, work experience, hobbies, and the like, the coach can identify potential entry points for connecting scales to the real world to make them come alive for the leader. For example, a leader who describes doing volunteer work with Big Brothers and taking a leadership role with the choir provides real-life content to connect to the leader's 100th percentile score on the Altruistic scale, a high Ambition score, and high levels on the Power and Recognition scales.

Once the coach has a conversation about a leader's real life and starts to connect it with Hogan insights, it allows for a basic understanding that is essential for realistic goal setting and development planning. Initial understanding can be refined by specific questions about how the leader manages to cope when under stress and the personal hot buttons that may evoke an emotional response. These are triggers that are critical for the leader to recognize in order to modify behavior in the future.

When the coach gathers this kind of information at the beginning of the session and then weaves it into the discussion of specific scales, the coach is individualizing the session. This makes Hogan feedback extremely powerful in that it is an accurate reflection of a leader's reputation, and one that is connected to the real life world of the leader. The coach needs to engage in an interpretive process that remains a valid description of reputation yet addresses the current experience of the leader. To do this, the coach must continually check the reputational data to see how it relates to the other pieces of data (usually multi-rater assessment data, but also development plans) as well as to the experience of the leader. The use of questions is extremely important here as it keeps the leader engaged in the session and also causes personal reflection to provide real-world examples. This process of checking sounds easy enough, but the actual act of checking the data against other data involves elements from the previous section that are worth reiterating here:

- First, the back-and-forth movement of making comparisons and drawing meaning from myriad sources of data necessitates that the coach create a framework that helps to clarify the reason for the feedback, what is reflected in the various types of data, and the goals of the feedback.

- Second, the coach needs to make a choice about how to structure the feedback. That structure will help highlight the data that is most relevant to the individual leader's needs in the here and now. The coach just cannot address every aspect of the Hogan data in a single feedback session, so he or she needs to make choices about focus. Those choices should directly reflect the goals of the feedback.

- Third, the coach is always interested in and looking for ways that the scales play together and form into themes and subthemes. In real life, the scales never function in isolation but are always present in combinations with different situations calling forth and activating different behavioral responses. While it is possible to interpret the scales in combination without any information about the leader, or his or her ways of viewing the world, this information makes it much easier to bring the scales to life. The leader's answers to the coach's ongoing questions go a long way to facilitating this.

- Fourth, the coach individualizes interpretations by exploring whether or not the leader can relate to the interpretations being made about him or her and by making connections between Strategic Self-awareness and the scales. For example, many executives with low Prudence scores will have developed ways of maintaining a handle on low prudent behaviors. They are often able to give examples of the kinds of things they do to help mitigate any negative repercussions of low Prudence (e.g., relying on their administrative assistant, hiring team members with higher Prudence, using commercially distributed planners and systems). Often, multi-rater assessment data or collateral interviews for executives low on Prudence indeed reflect that they have learned how to deal with behavioral issues such as impulsivity, lack of attention to details, and lack of planning.

In summary, we individualize Hogan data by setting a structure that allows the exploration of the relationship between identity and reputation without doing a disservice to either, and in a way that themes, goals, and specific actions emerge.

Identifying Development Themes and Pivot Points

At this point, we have created a research-based, yet leader-centric understanding and interpretation of the Hogan data. So what? Now what?

Unless these questions are answered in the feedback session, chances are high that either the leader is going to want the coach to write an individual report capturing the interaction and co-created recommendations, or the leader will file the notes and forget much of what was discussed. Both are bad options and call for the need to collaborate with the leader during the feedback session to identify key development themes and to create a few simple behavioral interventions.

By now, the coach should have an understanding of the leader's goals (the ones he or she came to the feedback session with), an understanding of the leader's reaction to the scales, and the leader's input on how the scales play out in the real world. The coach should have engaged in a conversation with the leader to determine the best interpretation of scales into themes. This conversation relies heavily on the coach's understanding of the Hogan data, additional data such as multi-rater assessments or performance goals, and the leader's real life and real-world experience.

The coach should always prepare a list of potential development themes in advance of the feedback session. However, this list is based solely on insights from the leader's Hogan profile and any other information (e.g., multi-rater assessment data) that the coach has prior to the session. As the session progresses and the coach learns more about the leader and his or her real-world situation, the coach should edit the list to reflect the most relevant development themes. As the leader talks, the coach can contribute ideas and ask for the leader's reactions so that soon they are weaving their ideas together. This collaboration is not only respectful of the leader, but it makes him or her responsible for personal development and growth.

At this juncture, we have everything needed to pare down the themes, to identify two to three development goals that are material to the leader's success, and to identify some specific behavioral changes (actions) that the leader can apply as soon as the feedback session is complete. More than ever, this section of the feedback requires the coach to ask questions and help the leader take responsibility and become an agent in his or her own learning and development. One way to do this is for the coach to refer to the framework and let the leader know that the time has come to create a summary of development goals with supporting actions to be taken. It is a good idea to start with the leader's thoughts about the most important pieces of the feedback. A simple way to unearth the leader's thoughts is by asking the question, "What were the most important developmental themes that you heard today, and which ones do you think are most important to work on now?"

Once the development themes are identified, the coach can ask the leader about potential "pivot points." Pivot points are places or openings where a leader can make shifts in behavior to start to pivot away from ineffective behaviors or add new behaviors. Adding even a small behavior shift affords the leader the opportunity to see things from a different vantage point, experience different behaviors, and then identify further behaviors to continue the progress of the pivot. The pivot point is a rotation that changes the leader directionally and toward a broader set of choices for interpreting situations and reactions. Specific behaviors fuel the pivot and build momentum for development. As an example, let's take the case of Jim:

Situation

Jim, an executive in a scientific area, had a development theme of difficulty relating to others. He reported a long history of difficulty connecting with others and a tendency to go in his office and shut the door. Jim was incredibly smart, very good with analytical tasks, and known as one of the best scientists in the organization. These features had been the key to his success. Others were willing to work with Jim because of his expertise. Not surprisingly, Jim had high scores on Ambition but very low scores on Sociability and Interpersonal Sensitivity; high risk scores on Reserved and Skeptical; and low scores on Recognition, Affiliation, and Altruistic. He had never been truly motivated to improve his people skills or his communication skills, but he was now within five years of retirement, and suddenly he was, for the first time ever, experiencing a desire to develop others and, most importantly, to develop a successor to continue his important scientific work.

Coaching

In Jim's case, his new desire to develop others to carry on his work was a huge pivot point. It was an opening where he was willing to try out a few new behaviors. Jim's coach began with one very specific task. He was to find out something new about three people with whom he worked. He had to perform this task in face-to-face, one-to-one conversations (not by eavesdropping on conversations in the lunch room as he initially suggested). In a way, the simplicity of this intervention was mind numbing, especially in light of Jim's scientific contributions. In another way, the simplicity of the task made it unavoidable.

When the coach saw Jim after the first attempt, he was sitting at his desk, waiting for her. As soon as she walked in the room, he started smiling in a way that made her think that he was going to fire her as his coach. But he did not. Instead, he told her about how he learned that his administrative assistant had a twin who just lost a baby and who was working harder than ever for him because he gave her the afternoon off to be with her sister. He told the coach that he found out that his colleague, like him, had a son with Asperger's, and he now saw this colleague in a totally different way. He said, "I don't know how trying to find out one thing about a person led to these kinds of discussions, or why things turned out this way, but it worked. I have a different view of them." Jim went on to get to know many people in his organization in a way that he had never experienced. On his own, Jim applied this new attitude and skill to members of his board of directors and garnered great support for his continued development of the organization. His colleagues helped him identify a successor and began assisting him in developing the successor to be ready. The cascade of positive transitions that emerged out of a pivot point and one behavioral shift was incredible. While the changes were hard for Jim through many points in his coaching, and he had a few points of regression, both Jim and his coach were able to hold on and return to the idea of working with a development theme, identifying an opening (pivot point), and utilizing one behavior to start improving performance.

Finding pivot points is not as hard as it might seem. The coach needs to ask questions concerning the identified development themes the leader considers most crucial for his or her enhanced effectiveness and continued success. The coach should also ask about the leader's greatest desires for the next year. Desire for something is the greatest motivator for leaders to pivot. But the changes are not all about desires and ideas; change is about concrete actions (sometimes small ones) to make progress toward achieving a goal. While suggestions from books and guides are helpful, the best action items and the most specific ones usually come from leaders themselves. Typically, they know what to do; coaches just have to help them find it.

Although it is easy to feel pressure to come up with grandiose interventions for the leader, many times the coach needs to start with extraordinarily practical and simple steps. Change is hard when trying to tackle everything at once; it is made much easier by breaking changes down into simple steps that can potentially build into greater development shifts.

While there is not time to do an actual development plan in a single feedback session, the coach can certainly get the leader off to a solid start through the discussion of development themes, pivot points, and behavior modifications. Using the discussion as a basis, the leader can then refine the information to be included in the development plan. The leader should identify two to three development goals that will move the needle the most on improving performance, and then identify one to two action items (including pivot points and behavior changes) to support each goal. If the coaching initiative is multiple sessions, then the coach can assist in providing input to the development plan that the leader creates and in checking progress versus the plan. (For more on Development Planning, please see Chapter 9.)

If the development themes and next steps discussion has occurred at the end of the session, then the coach can close on that note. However, if the development themes and next steps have unfolded throughout the session, the coach will want to summarize with the leader what has been agreed to collaboratively as far as development themes, pivot points, action items, and specific next steps.

It is now time to say goodbye. Not every leader will engage with the coach in an interpretive dance about his or her data. Some leaders just are not interested in development, and some are distracted no matter how enticing the invitation to engage. Many, however, are thrilled at the opportunity to have someone *really* listen and help them understand the richness of Hogan data. For these leaders, it is often difficult to end the session—they want more! While this is great, it is a good idea to know in advance if there is a possibility to continue working with the leader or to identify who could subsequently help the leader. The usual choices for this work are a coach, mentor, or HR generalist. A note of caution here is that when identifying follow-up support people, it is worthwhile to recommend that the leader only share the full Hogan data with individuals who have been through Hogan certification. If follow-up support people are not certified, it is recommended the leader share thematic interpretations and action items.

THE COACH'S SKILLS AND ATTRIBUTES

In using "the Hogan" for development planning, the feedback provider must make interpretations of the data that relate to the leader's current world and the ways that the leader might improve performance. There are three main ingredients of this kind of interpretation. First, interpretations should be grounded in the scientifically validated descriptors associated with the scales themselves. While the coach may be interested in the ways the scales impact and nuance each other, remaining true to the validated descriptors themselves is also important. Interpretations should not overreach. Second, interpretations should also be informed by and grounded in relevant background information from psychology, human development, business, and other fields pertaining to the reason for the assessment. Third, interpretations should be made in the context of the leader's specific history and situation, such as the leader's job, organizational culture, goals, prior efforts at development, pertinent personal factors, and current level of Strategic Self-awareness. Navigating the delicate balance of these ingredients leads to the most accurate, current, and useful interpretations but is an art even for the most seasoned coach. This section describes coach qualifications and skills that enhance the interpretive process.

Technical Expertise in the Hogan Inventories

To begin, it is important that coaches giving feedback and using the Hogan inventories for development have familiarity with psychological testing in general, the limits of assessment, and the technical characteristics of the Hogan inventories specifically. Coaches can develop this familiarity through Hogan Assessment Certification Workshops (both Basic and Advanced), through the Hogan Development Feedback Certification Course, by reading the technical manuals for each of the inventories, and by reading and referencing *The Hogan Guide: Interpretation and Use of Hogan Inventories* (Hogan et al., 2007).

It is also important for coaches to understand that different uses of testing call for slightly different interpretative processes of the data. Hogan data are widely used for both selection and development, and it is worth noting a few of the interpretive similarities and differences here. Both tasks rest on the fact that personality can be validly measured when considered from the perspective of reputation. Both tasks also rest on the idea that personality assessment from this perspective is useful: Personality predicts likely future behaviors. Hogan data rest on these two basic assumptions no matter what the data are used for: (1) The core personality characteristics that create a leader's reputation can be measured, and (2) these characteristics are a useful predictor of future behaviors.

Interpretive differences show up when the coach considers the goals of using the Hogan inventories for development and using them for selection. When Hogan data are used to aid the selection process, the goal is to predict which candidates are most likely to exhibit certain behaviors. As such, the coach is not concerned with the person sitting behind the data and instead interprets the data based on statistical likelihoods of whether or not the applicant is likely to exhibit the behaviors associated with the criteria for job success. These are very technical, research-based interpretations that rely on careful analysis of the criteria (i.e., the behaviors needed) for job success and the Hogan scales that best predict which individuals will exhibit those behaviors. The coach can think of interpretations for selection as a set of impersonal, statistical likelihoods designed to show whether or not the leader is likely to succeed in a particular role.

When assessment is used for coaching and development, the coach not only needs to remain true to the validated predictive meaning of the scales but also needs to help the individual leader understand how the data relate to his or her history, present performance, and envisioned future. The goal here is to predict reputation in general *and* to help the individual understand his or her assessment data in order to expand his or her behavioral repertoire and ways of viewing, reacting to, and acting in the world. While the coach is still using statistically based descriptors, he or she is called on to personalize and nuance the information pertaining to the individual leader. The leader is not just a set of statistical likelihoods, but another person who has a history of experiences, a set of subjective hopes and desires, and an ability to learn and engage in action. When giving feedback, the coach must engage the leader as a part of the interpretive equation and help the leader understand how Hogan scales not only reflect how others see him or her but also reflect the behaviors he or she is likely to exhibit. At the deepest level, the way the leader views and understands the world; the way he or she views, understands, and interacts with others; and the way he or she creates expectations about what will happen are all behaviors that are, in a complex way, predicted by the Hogan inventories.

Finally, it is important that the coach recognize and become comfortable with the relationship between stable personality characteristics and developmental gain. Hogan inventories measure stable personality characteristics that are unlikely to significantly change over time. At the same time, people develop. While personality characteristics are relatively stable, people live them differently as they have life experiences, integrate feedback, and try out new behaviors. As people develop, they are more capable of expanding their repertoire of responses, their capacity to hold multiple meanings, and their ability to navigate competing agendas. An individual who is empathic and able to tolerate disappointment, who can hold opposing thoughts and feelings simultaneously, and who can create strategies for dealing with complex situations involving competing goals and desires will exhibit his or her core personality characteristics differently than an individual who cannot tolerate disappointment and falls back into black-and-white thinking. The former individual brings out the best of the characteristics and works hard to mitigate the negative qualities. The latter individual is likely to display more negative qualities associated with the characteristics. The characteristics themselves are not good or bad. The way the characteristics are exhibited can have positive or negative implications. A leader can exhibit characteristics like high Ambition and high Bold by running people over for immediate gratification and to get his or her own way, or the leader can learn to negotiate, delay gratification, and build consensus to lead others to attain the goal.

To equip coaches to deal with these many moving parts, a strong knowledge base is essential. As we've already discussed, coaches must have a strong facility with using the Hogan inventories. This proficiency starts with fluency in each of the Hogan inventories and the unique perspective offered by each. Coaches must have fluency with each of the specific Hogan scales and subscales and a clear understanding of common coaching issues and interventions associated with each. Coaches must have a clear understanding that the scales always function in combinations (e.g., leaders do not exhibit their high scores on Ambition as pure ambition; their ambition is tempered or enhanced by other scales and flavored by values), and they must develop experience with interpreting dyadic and triadic groupings. Coaches must understand that multiple scales are always needed in order to constitute trends and themes. Finally, coaches must understand that in any given situation, not all the scales are displayed at the same time, but neither are they completely hidden.

Strong Coaching Skill Set

In addition to familiarity with the Hogan scales, effective feedback is supported by a strong coaching skill set. First, the coach must have good verbal skills, including the ability to build rapport, to engage the leader in dialogue, and to convey complex ideas in a clear and compelling manner. Additionally, the coach needs to be able to create powerful questions. Questions can sometimes be the best tool to help leaders connect Hogan data to their lived experiences. Questions that foster this connection are not necessarily brilliant, clever, or well spoken; rather, they need to hit the core of the leader's experiential world and open the possibility that the experience is related to the characteristic.

Second, the coach must have good listening skills to hear what is being said beyond the stories and examples to the essential meanings. The coach must be able to attune to a wide variety of leaders. Third, the coach must be able to connect the multiple data points (Hogan inventories, multi-rater assessments, prior development plans, etc.) into a story and then interpret the data in light of what the leader presents as his or her history and ability to understand the coach's feedback. There is a unifying meaning under the din of all the information. The coach needs to be able to find that meaning. Fourth, the coach must demonstrate flexibility and be able think on his or her feet. This is true not only in the sense of shifting interpretations as the leader presents information but also in the sense of the coach's ability to shift his or her feedback style to meet the leader's learning style and personality characteristics. Fifth, and finally, the coach needs to be able to tolerate ambiguity and contain a wide variety of emotional reactions from leaders.

In using the Hogan inventories for development and coaching, interpretation of the results becomes a back-and-forth movement between the statistically based descriptors and the application to the real-life world of the leader. Effective interpretation draws on both reputational and identity components of personality and is grounded in the expertise of the feedback coach and the framework. Not all interpretations of Hogan data are equal. Some feedback coaches are more adept than others, and some leaders are more willing to participate than others. The bare minimum, however, is that the feedback should be fair to the current experience of the leader without doing injustice to the statistically correlated descriptors of the scales themselves.

Summary

The most effective Hogan feedback sessions are a marriage of art and science. The science utilizes the technical meanings of the data to create nuanced interpretations about strengths and development needs. The art is brought to bear by a coach who is experienced in the technical meanings of the Hogan scales, who possesses superior coaching abilities, and who is able to bring the leader's Hogan results to life. The coach needs to utilize a strong framework to help organize the data and manage the feedback session. Hogan feedback for development explores the relationship between reputation and identity in the service of professional and personal development. The interpretation and individualization of data take place in the form of a dialogue between the coach and the leader. Within this dialogue, there is a back-and-forth movement in which the coach and the leader create meaning, identify development themes and goals, and pinpoint specific, behaviorally based action steps to reach the goals. The leader leaves an effective feedback session with greater Strategic Self-awareness that will lead to improved performance and continued career success.

CHAPTER 9

DEVELOPMENT PLANNING, MONITORING, AND CALIBRATION

INTRODUCTION

A solid development plan, complete with specific action items, a clear definition of success, and appropriate measurements, is the *sine qua non* for behavior change. If the assessment results are the "what" (What do these say about me?) and the feedback session is the "so what" (So what are the implications for my effectiveness as a leader?), then we now come to the all-important "now what" (Now what do I do?). The development plan is the "now what"—done correctly, it turns a haphazard joy ride into a well-mapped journey with a specific destination in sight.

In this chapter, we will address the elements of an effective development plan, how to operationalize the development plan, how to monitor and modify the plan, and how to measure results.

ELEMENTS OF AN EFFECTIVE DEVELOPMENT PLAN

There are four elements that need to be addressed to ensure an effective development plan, as follows:

- The *scope* needs to be clearly identified as to what will benefit the leader and organization the most.

- The plan must be *customized* to the leader within the leader's Situational Context.

- There must be *goal clarity*, including specificity of actions, a definition of success, and the desired impact on the leader's reputation.

- There must be *active commitment, involvement, and support* on the part of the leader's manager.

Each of these elements is described in detail in the sections that follow.

Scope

Too often, development planning is viewed solely as fixing something that is wrong or needs to be improved. However, that is much too narrow a perspective, and individuals and organizations that have this view miss a huge opportunity. While improving areas of weakness is crucial, development planning also includes leveraging key strengths that the leader already possesses. Many times, an organization can benefit much more from a person's leveraging a key strength that will have a broad impact than from a person's trying to improve an area of weakness that is relatively inconsequential.

> The power of a change in emphasis was illustrated in the case of Joe, a very creative and innovative leader who was being groomed for greater responsibility. He absolutely detested details, and in an organization that was engineering and project management oriented, this was a huge barrier. For several years, Joe's development plan focused on honing his project management skills and attention to details. He read books, took courses, and headed up projects to gain on-the-job experience, all to no avail. Joe was unhappy, and the organization suffered through missed due dates and incorrect data on the projects he led. Finally, Joe and his manager agreed that he was much more valuable to the business as a strategist and innovator. He focused on leveraging his strengths by leading a think tank to develop new products, and he willingly nurtured and mentored new hires to teach them the competitive landscape. This career shift was a win-win for Joe and the organization, as he was happy doing what he did best, and the organization benefitted from the new ideas and the pipeline of new leaders he encouraged.

Development planning can also include the leader's venturing into the world of untested and untried competencies. This journey into the unknown is particularly important for high-potential leaders who will need skills at the next level that they might not have had an opportunity to demonstrate or develop in their current job.

Lauren, who was relatively quiet and shy, was a marketing manager for a medical devices company. She aspired to be a field sales person, but she just did not know if she was outgoing and persuasive enough to interface with doctors and their staffs, as she had never really tried her wings in these areas. As a development assignment, Lauren's manager arranged for her to spend a month in the field with a seasoned sales rep. At first, Lauren was an observer on the sales calls, but by the end of the month, she was closing sales. She was convinced she had what it took to be successful, and so was her manager. When a field sales position opened up, Lauren was selected for the job and regularly exceeded her sales quota.

In addition to improving areas of weakness, leveraging strengths, and trying untested competencies, there are other compelling reasons for development planning:

- To maximize the effectiveness of both the individual and team.
- To enhance performance on the current job.
- To prepare for a future job.
- To differentiate oneself from others.
- To enhance one's reputation and brand.
- To serve as a role model for direct reports in their development journeys.
- To create and encourage a culture of growth and development.

Customized to the Leader

Just as feedback must be tailored appropriately for each individual, so too must the development plan, due to the fact that leaders have diverse needs as far as areas to leverage and develop and the most appropriate ways to approach them.

Although the development plan needs to be customized, it certainly is not I-centric ("all about me"). Leaders work in organizations; therefore, development cannot occur in a vacuum. As we saw in Chapter 5, the Situational Context of the leader is critical, especially three components: the organizational culture, the leader's manager, and the leader's role. The development plan needs to be created within the person's Situational Context because the same level of competency or the same behavior that is considered a key strength within one context might be considered a derailer in another.

The development plan also needs to consider the current perceptions of the leader held by others—that is, his or her reputation. The plan is where the Hogan foundational concept of Strategic Self-awareness, discussed throughout this book, is translated into behavior change and skill building that will enhance a leader's reputation, thereby making the leader more effective.

Choosing the Most Impactful Areas to Leverage and Develop

Too often, development plans address too many areas, resulting in the dilution of the time, resources, and focus directed to the goals. Selecting too many areas to work on is a recipe for delivering disappointing results: developing a new skill or modifying a behavior is hard work, and people have a finite amount of energy to expend. Therefore, the development plan should be limited to two to three areas that are crucial for the leader to be more successful. In identifying the areas of focus that will be the most impactful, it is helpful to think of them in terms of *deal breakers* and *game changers*. A deal breaker is a behavior or skill gap that will sideline a leader and severely hamper success. A game changer is a behavior or skill, usually already somewhat of a strength, that if leveraged or developed further will differentiate the leader from others, providing a competitive edge.

- **Deal Breaker**—Bill was a mid-level manager in a manufacturing company. He was viewed by all as extremely competent from a technical standpoint, and he routinely delivered solid business results. Both employees and vendors alike thought he was a "genuinely nice guy," and therein was the deal breaker: Bill was too nice. He tended to sugarcoat constructive feedback to his direct reports to a degree that the message was obscured. He caved in negotiations with vendors, which cost the company thousands of dollars. He began to get the reputation of being a pushover. Bill had aspirations of being promoted, and he could not understand why he was passed over, given his good results. His boss advised him that no matter how good his results or how much people liked him, he would not be promoted until he demonstrated that he could handle conflict effectively because the ability to do so was not optional at the next level of leadership. Bill took the feedback to heart and built his development plan around eliminating his deal breaker.

- **Game Changer**—Kay was a highly regarded marketing leader who was known for her successful brand-building campaigns. Although she had spent her entire career in the creative side of marketing, she had been a math major in undergraduate school, and she loved numbers. She was the unofficial numbers cruncher in the marketing department. Her colleagues came to her if they wanted data analyzed or profit-and-loss assessments made. Repeatedly, she displayed keen business insights (not just marketing insights), and this became a key strength for her. Her boss recognized this aptitude and advised her that this business acumen could be a real game changer for her. If she could demonstrate it to other departments, and they saw that she had an overall business perspective, she could differentiate herself for cross-functional assignments, task forces, and the like.

Link Development Areas to the Business

The development areas selected should be tightly linked to the business and should be in alignment with one or all of the following:

- The business goals the leader has to achieve.
- The competencies associated with the current position or the next position to which the leader aspires.
- The needed reputation changes or enhancements.

How Big Is the Gap?

A critical assessment to make is "How big is the gap?" between how the leader behaves now and how the leader should behave, or between the current level of competence and the needed level, or between the way the leader is currently perceived and the desired perception. The size of the gap will help clarify the development goal, the actions needed to support the goal, and the time and resources required. Goal clarity is absolutely critical for effective development.

Goal Clarity

A well-recognized framework within the development-planning literature is that of creating SMART goals (Specific, Measurable, Achievable, Relevant, and Time-bound).

Using the insights about Strategic Self-awareness gained from the Hogan inventories, we can make SMART goals SMARTER. The "ER" stands for "Enhanced Reputation," and that is exactly what a development plan should do: address the behaviors and skills that will enhance the reputation and brand of the leader to make him or her more effective. A well-crafted development plan should include a definition of success as to what the modified behavior or improved skill looks like, what the business results will be, and what the impact on the leader's reputation will be.

As long as the development plan contains the elements of SMARTER goals, the format of the plan itself can vary from simple (a few columns) to more complex. At the end of this chapter, we have included several different examples of development plan formats, but they all have goal clarity, including a definition of success.

Commitment

Critical to the success of the development plan is that the leader's manager commit to an active, involved, and supportive role. The manager must agree to be an ongoing source of feedback for the developing leader. In addition, the manager must seek opportunities for the leader to practice the development areas, and if those opportunities are not readily available, the manager must create them. Too often the manager's role is not clearly defined, and too much is left to chance. As can be seen in the remainder of this chapter, the leader's manager plays a pivotal role in the success of the development plan.

Operationalizing the Development Plan

A development plan is of no use if it just sits on a shelf and is updated once or twice a year at the time of the mid-year or end-of-year performance reviews. To facilitate progress, the action items and developmental assignments supporting the goals should be practical real-world activities that are related to the person's day-to-day job so that they have these qualities:

- Able to be repeated often (practice makes perfect).
- Observable by others who can provide ongoing feedback.

Because "leadership is a contact sport" (Marshall Goldsmith), the majority of the activities that support the goals should be ones that can be practiced in the context and situations of the leader's everyday job. It is fine to have an action item of a book to read or a course to attend, but these types of activities should not compose the entire plan. Neither should a leader select a development area that he or she just will not have ample opportunity to develop. For example, if a leader makes one presentation every six months, he or she should not select "enhancing presentation skills" as a goal because he or she will not have sufficient venues to practice, or, if "enhancing presentation skills" truly is a critical skill to develop, then the leader's manager will need to find opportunities for the leader to make presentations on a more frequent basis.

Conventional wisdom on how leaders learn has recommended that a good development plan consists of the following:

- 70 percent job and task content, including experiences that stretch and test capabilities.
- 20 percent people to study, listen to, and work with, including relationships with people who challenge and stimulate learning.
- 10 percent courses and readings, including structured education and leadership development programs.

The foregoing items can comprise both formal and informal learning experiences to ensure exposure to a wide range of approaches and perspectives. This also keeps the momentum of the development plan alive and prevents people from getting bored with monotonous tasks. For example, if the person needs to develop relationship-building skills to be successful, he or she could perform a stakeholder analysis of key colleagues as part of the formal job-and-task category. On an informal basis, the person could attend more functions and work on networking skills. In the people-to-study category, a formal mentor could be assigned, and on an informal basis, the individual could have lunch with an expert in a certain subject. Likewise, in the courses-and-readings category, the individual could attend a formal week-long, instructor-led workshop, and on an informal basis, he or she could participate in a one-hour webinar. With the rise of social media, blogs, Massive Open Online Courses (MOOCs), and other online venues, there are an ever-increasing number of alternatives for both formal and informal learning.

The findings from DDI's "Global Leadership Forecast 2014/2015" revealed that the actual ratio of time spent by leaders in various types of learning is as follows:

- 55 percent job and task content.

- 25 percent people to study, listen to, and work with.

- 20 percent courses and readings.

This distribution puts more emphasis on formal learning and learning from others and deemphasizes the on-the-job learning. However, the important point is to integrate learning across the three areas so they are complementary.

Developmental Assignments

Typically, the assignments that provide the greatest growth and development for a leader are the ones that are stretch assignments—the ones that require the leader to step out of his or her comfort zone. Here are some examples of stretch assignments:

- Start-ups.

- Fix-its.

- Special projects.

- Line to staff or staff to line.

- Rotation to a different department or function.

- Taking an enterprise-wide view.

- Task forces.

- Developing others.

- Being a change agent.

- Implementing a new technology.

- Managing direct reports who are located remotely.

- Leading a merger or acquisition.

- Working in a foreign country.

- Participating in activities away from work.

- "Battlefield promotions"—moving people into uncomfortable roles early in their careers or prematurely.

Developmental Activities

If a stretch assignment is not a viable option for the individual, then stretch activities within the individual's own job can provide growth:

- Handling unfamiliar responsibilities.
- Proving oneself to others.
- Starting something from scratch.
- Taking a business in a new direction.
- Fixing inherited problems.
- Making tough decisions about staff.
- Dealing effectively with problem performers.
- Dealing with high pressure situations.
- Managing multiple, diverse functions.
- Working across cultures (either organizational cultures or country cultures).
- Dealing with job overload.
- Handling external pressure.
- Influencing without authority.
- Getting the job done without support.
- Dealing with a difficult boss.
- Gaining consensus around projects with multiple, competing constituencies.
- Participating in projects where one has to take the line perspective simultaneously with the staff.
- Working with a coach (either an external or internal coach, but someone different from the immediate manager).
- Working with a mentor.

MONITORING AND MODIFYING THE DEVELOPMENT PLAN

"No news is good news" definitely does not apply in development planning, as individuals need ongoing feedback and checkpoints to determine their progress versus their development goals. In addition, development plans do not exist in a vacuum, and they need to be flexible. Often, business conditions change, and the development plan needs to change accordingly. Perhaps a behavior that the leader thought would be effective turns out not to work, and the leader needs to dial it up or dial it down. Several tools to monitor progress and determine the need for modifications follow.

Ongoing Feedback

In Chapter 2, we saw the Hogan Development Cycle (see Hogan Development Cycle, page 27), and learned that ongoing feedback is essential. Ongoing, timely feedback serves the following key purposes:

- Reinforces the importance of Strategic Self-awareness and Situational Context.

- Gives the leader insight into the differences between Identity (self-perception) and Reputation (perception of others).

- Allows the leader to modify the development plan actions and behaviors as needed on an almost real-time basis.

On an informal basis, feedback should certainly come from the boss, but it is helpful for the leader to seek feedback from trusted others (peers, direct reports, colleagues, etc.) as well. These casual evaluations typically occur on an ad hoc basis and can be quite helpful in identifying which new behaviors are working and which need modification. It is also helpful to seek feedback from people in other functions and areas of the business to ensure that various perspectives are considered.

On a more formal basis, many people find it helpful to identify an advocate. They take the advocate into their confidence and explain to the advocate the behavior changes they want to make, and they ask the advocate to consciously observe their behavior and give them feedback, both good and bad. In addition to being trusted by the leader, an advocate needs to be someone who is in a position to observe the leader on a regular or frequent basis—by attending the same meetings, for example. Ongoing contact provides the venue for the advocate to give real-time feedback regarding behavior modifications. It is essential that an advocate is someone whose opinion the leader values so the leader will accept the feedback and suggestions and act on them.

Two leading indicators (obtained from timely feedback) can be helpful in determining the efficacy of the development plan and in identifying any needed behavior modifications. These are "early returns" and "over-correction."

- **Early Returns**—Just as exit polls during an election can give candidates an indication of how they are doing, so too can feedback received early in the implementation of the development plan inform leaders of which new behaviors are working well and which ones need to be modified. This early feedback is best obtained on a casual or informal basis by the leader, the manager, or the advocate. Trusted colleagues whose input is valued by the leader can be asked how the leader is doing. The leader can ask, "Did I appear to be listening better in the meeting this morning?" followed by "What could I do to be even more effective?" Or, the manager or advocate can make similar inquiries to determine if people are noticing the leader's behavior changes and if the changes are having the desired impact on the leader's effectiveness: "Have you noticed a change in the clarity of Bob's written communications?" "What do you think he still needs to do?"

- **Overcorrection**—It is not at all unusual for a leader to overcorrect when first trying a new behavior. The old adage "be careful what you wish for, you just might get it" applies here as sometimes people are so anxious to improve, they take the new behavior to an extreme. The behavior change should not be so extreme that the person becomes a joke. That said, in some cases, especially development areas that concern interpersonal skills such as being too aggressive or too quiet, an overcorrection is necessary in the beginning so that people will notice that the leader has changed. Reputations die hard, and people continue to play old tapes regarding the leader's behavior unless the change is quite noticeable. Ultimately, though, the leader needs to strike a balance regarding the behavior, and early returns feedback can help him or her do that.

Progress Reviews

As part of formal feedback, the leader's manager and leader should conduct a formal review of progress as measured against the development plan at least every six months—or more frequently if the development goals are shorter term in nature or if the development plan is part of a time-bound performance improvement program. Results should be documented on the development plan, and modifications to the plan should be noted as needed.

Key Milestones

The key milestones identified on the development plan are another gauge of progress. These are typically dates or numbers and are easily quantified as "made" or "missed." The development plan can then be modified if needed (e.g., a due date has slipped because of funding and through no fault of the leader), or remedial action can be taken (e.g., a due date was missed because the leader did not fulfill his or her responsibilities).

Coaching Oneself

A very effective tool for monitoring progress and keeping development top of mind is the "Week in Review," which allows the leader to self-coach. It prompts the leader to engage in self-reflection at the end of every week and to evaluate the progress made and what needs to be done differently. The following are the types of questions that could be included in a "Week in Review" of one's development plan progress:

- What strengths did I leverage?
- What areas for development did I address?

- What actions did I take (e.g., accomplishments, progress versus plan, dates met or missed, etc.)?
- What interactions did I have (e.g., with direct deports, peers, boss, others, in meetings, etc.)?
    - What new skills did I use?
    - What went well?
    - What would I change?
- What feedback did I receive from others?
- What insights did I have? What did I learn?

Modifications to the Development Plan

Many times, the foregoing monitoring tools of ongoing feedback, review of key milestones, and self-coaching reveal that modifications to the development plan are necessary. Additionally, modifications might be driven by business reasons, such as a change in the leader's role, a reorganization, or a change in business strategy. Further, a leader might have reached or exceeded a development goal, resulting in the need to retire it and replace it with another development goal. Regardless of the reason, *the development plan needs to be a living document* that is not cast in concrete. As long as the leader and his or her manager agree on what the modifications are and why they are needed, and they follow the practices just outlined, then development should continue successfully.

This approach is consistent with the ongoing nature of the Hogan Development Cycle that we introduced in Chapter 2 (see Hogan Development Cycle, page 27). One mnemonic that supports the Hogan Development Cycle and that captures the essence of a solid development plan is spelled as "FIRST":

- **F**ocus on priorities; identify critical issues and goals.
- **I**mplement something often; stretch the comfort zone.
- **R**eflect on what happens; extract maximum learning from experiences.
- **S**eek feedback and support; learn from others' ideas and perspectives.
- **T**ransfer learning into next steps; adapt and plan for continued learning.

MEASURING THE RESULTS OF DEVELOPMENT PLANNING

The bottom line of development planning is the answer to the question, "Is the leader more effective?" Results can be measured at two levels: the Individual Level and the Process Level. The Individual Level is relatively straightforward and easy to measure, while the Process Level is more macro and can be quite difficult to measure.

Measuring Effectiveness at the Individual Level

There are multiple ways to measure the success of a leader against his or her development plan at the individual level:

- **Definition of Success**—As noted earlier, sound development plans include a definition of success that describes what success looks like. So, a key measure is whether the person is now behaving in the manner articulated as success.

- **Multi-rater Assessment Following the Development Plan**—Before-and-after multi-rater assessments are frequently administered to determine if the leader has moved the needle in his or her development areas. The multi-rater assessment need not be a time-consuming, multiple-item sophisticated survey. It can be an informal, verbal multi-rater interview consisting of just a few key questions conducted by the leader's boss or coach to see if there is perceived behavior change and increased effectiveness.

- **Anecdotal "Buzz"**—Multi-rater assessment as just described often does not need to be solicited as stakeholders will proactively comment on the person's changed behavior or increased effectiveness. Similar to Chief Justice Potter Stewart's infamous "I know it when I see it" comment regarding obscenity, people know behavior change and increased effectiveness when they see it. If the word on the street is positive, then that is a positive sign of reputation enhancement.

- **Success of the Leader's Team and Organization**—Generally, when a leader becomes more effective as a result of successful development, there is a pull-through effect for team members and the broader organization. This can be seen in both hard numerical business objectives and in the morale within the team and the reputation of the team as viewed by outsiders.

Measuring Effectiveness at the Process Level

While there is not a body of research on the effectiveness of development planning per se, there is quite a bit of evidence on the effectiveness of coaching. Because coaching typically involves development planning, we can look at the results of coaching studies as a surrogate, as follows:

- **The ROI of Coaching**— The watershed study on the return on investment (ROI) of coaching was published by Manchester Consulting (McGovern et al., 2001). Prior to this study, coaching, still in its infancy, was measured by anecdotal evidence, if at all. The Manchester study was the first to quantify the results of coaching in monetary terms. In addition, the Manchester study isolated the impact of coaching from other factors that could have improved the leader's performance (e.g., a process or technology improvement, a new boss, etc.). The Manchester study included 100 mid-level and executive-level leaders who were coached between 1996 and 2000. Through a rigorous process designed to isolate the impact of the coaching and to consider confidence level, executives and key stakeholders were asked to quantify the dollar value of the coaching. Forty-three of the 100 executives could provide quantitative evidence, and the result was an ROI of 570 percent (i.e., the benefit attributable to the coaching was 5.7 times greater than the amount of the investment).

- **Total Value**—All 100 leaders participated in the Total Value measurement that Manchester created. The leaders were asked to rate their coaching experience on a scale of −5 to +5.

  - A "+5" indicated the value of coaching was far greater than the time and money invested.

  - A "0" indicated the coaching paid for itself.

  - A "−5" indicated the value of the coaching was far less than the time and money invested.

  Twenty-seven percent of the participants rated the coaching as +5, 27 percent rated it as +4, and 23 percent rated it as +3. In other words, 77 percent of the participants rated it as +3 or above. When key stakeholders were included in the survey, 75 percent rated the coaching as +3 or above.

- **Goal Achievement**—The Manchester study asked the coaching participants and key stakeholders about how effectively the participants had achieved their goals. Seventy-three percent of the coaching participants said they had "very effectively" or "extremely effectively" achieved their goals. Fifty-four percent of the key stakeholders assigned these ratings, and 83 percent gave ratings of "effectively" or better. The coaching goals that these ratings address are development-planning goals by another name, so certainly these results support the efficacy of development planning.

In addition to the Manchester study, several other studies have calculated the ROI of coaching, and they have revealed similar significant paybacks. A study conducted by Merrill Anderson (2001) showed an ROI of 500 percent. A study conducted by Booz Allen Hamilton (Parker-Wilkins, 2006) showed an ROI of 689 percent. Thus, the coaching surrogate for measuring development planning shows it to be a clear winner.

SAMPLE DEVELOPMENT PLANS

What follows are several sample development plans that are specifically geared to the coaching process when Hogan inventories are involved. Although the formats and columns are different, each plan addresses development areas that are crucial to enhancing the leader's reputation and future success.

Sample 1—Jane Barnes Development Plan

Jane Barnes was a senior director of marketing for a Fortune 100 consumer products company. She was the brains behind numerous successful product launches, gaining her a reputation of being one of the best creative minds in the business. However, her organization and implementation skills were sorely lacking, causing her direct reports to flounder due to lack of task clarity, causing her boss to be completely frustrated due to budget overruns, and causing her peers to be disgusted with continual last-minute appeals by Jane to borrow resources to keep the project on track. Her stellar reputation for a "creative mind" was being outweighed by a reputation as "Calamity Jane" as far as implementation was concerned. One of her development goals concerning this is shown in the following table.

Name: Jane Barnes   **Title:** Senior Director, Marketing

Development Goal	Supporting Goals	Actions	Outcome/Measures	Results

Enhance my organization and execution skills to ensure smooth implemetation of my projects.
 	
Reputation Impact:
 	
I am known not only as an "idea" person but as a reliable implementer as well.
	1. Establish operating plans for the ABC project, including owners, milestones, completion dates, and metrics for the goals to ensure success.
	
	2. Determine clear roles and accountabilities for direct reports, delegate accordingly, and empower them to achieve results.
	
	3. Implement additional personal and organziational structure and management routines (e.g., processes, progress checks, follow-up, etc.) to ensure focus remains on priorities.
		1. ABC Project:
		  a. Ask DRs to provide their input to me by 3/8.
		  b. Refine their input and present plan to my manager by 3/15.
		  c. Finalize by 3/22.
		
		2. Discuss and gain buy-in from key stakeholders once plan is finalized:
		  a. With DRs by 4/1.
		  b. With peers by 4/5.
		
		3. Process activities:
		  a. Conduct bi-weekly one-on-one meetings with DRs to check progress against goals. Utilize tracking form.
		  b. Utilize tracking form.
		  c. Re-assess my administrative assistant's role to leverage her capabilities.
		  d. Review routines and processes currently in place.
			1. & 2. Clarity around goals, priorities, accountability, metrics, and milestones. Measured by actual results versus plan (e.g., did we successfully implement the project on time and on budget) and by feedback from key stakeholders.
			
			3. Measures include:
			  a. & b. Better communication and organization measured by feedback from direct reports.
			  c. More personal time to focus on implementation; more discipline applied to administration. Measured by feedback from stakeholders.
			  d. Documented, clear routines/processes; better organization and productivity.	

Sample 2—Leah Minton Development Plan

Leah was a high-potential employee in the corporate communications department of a large franchised food company. Her reputation was one of being very hardworking and collaborative—always ready to help her colleagues and to do whatever needed to be done to ensure a quality work product. She was promoted to director, and, for the first time, she had a team of direct reports. She began to struggle with the transition from individual contributor to leader, as she was not demonstrating leadership presence, especially as far as speaking her mind. One of her development goals is shown in the following table.

Name: Leah Minton   **Title:** Director, Corporate Communications

Goal	What Success Looks Like	Action Steps/Due Date/Progress	Resources/Tools/Approaches
Demonstrate director-level leadership, confidence, and influence by being more vocal in taking stands and expressing my views.	I am seen as clear leader with a strong point of view to advance business goals.	• Think through issues in advance and develop my point of view so I can clearly articulate and support it.	• Make a list of talking points so I'm clear on the points I want to make.
		• Speak up at key opportunities: my manager's direct report meetings, officer/director meetings, editorial board meetings, etc.	• My manager is to provide opportunities for me to attend at least one meeting a week in which I can practice this.
		• Don't hesitate to weigh in on issues even when I'm not an "expert."	• Develop a list of phrases that enable me to stick my toe in the water of conversations in which I'm not comfortable with the subject matter.
		• Consciously develop my views through a team leader lens as opposed to a team member lens.	• Use my manager and mentor as sounding boards; share my views with them to ensure that I'm taking a leader's perspective.
		• Don't be afraid to say "no."	• Reframe this so I know I'm saying "no" in order to better address my top priorities.
		• Make sure I'm not defensive to feedback or input.	• Remind myself to truly listen to what people are saying; get feedback from my manager and a trusted colleague as to how I'm coming across.
		• Make sure that being overly cautious doesn't slow down decision-making.	• Start thinking in terms of how material a decision is to the business; how much does it matter?
		NOTE: All of the above are ongoing activities.	

Sample 3—Jose Sanchez Development Plan

Jose Sanchez was a VP of operations for a mid-sized pharmaceutical company. He was known as a subject-matter expert in numerous manufacturing processes, and executive management considered him the go-to guy to lead difficult projects that they needed to make sure were successful. Over the years, Jose's interpersonal style had gained him the reputation of being tough and direct, but his technical skills and his ability to deliver results always outweighed his people issues. Now, however, his poor interpersonal skills were standing in the way of his getting promoted as his peers were complaining about his abrupt manner to the point of not wanting to work with him. Members of the executive team were reluctant to take him into their organizations on a lateral basis, much less as a promotion. Jose's manager made it clear to him that the people skills issue was a deal breaker, and Jose was determined to correct it. One of his development goals to address this issue is shown in the following table.

Name: Jose Sanchez   **Title:** VP, Operations

Development Goal	Action/Due Date	Progress/Results
Maintain strong relationships by "reading the audience" and being more interpersonally sensitive and tuned in to stakeholders' needs, goals, and styles. *Success and Reputation Impact:* **Key stakeholders view me as a trusted advisor.** **Key stakeholders reach out to me proactively.** **Other VPs want me to rotate into their organizations.** **Manager and others provide positive feedback.**	1. Complete the Stakeholder Analysis tool for key stakeholders to: a. Better understand their needs, goals, styles, and "hot buttons" to tailor my style. b. Evaluate existing relationships with key stakeholders in terms of build/maintain/repair and develop plans to address. Key stakeholders to include are: exec. team and selected peers to start with. *Complete analysis by June 1 and implement on an ongoing basis* 2. Identify ways to increase interfaces with key stakeholders (either face-time or phone time) so we get to know each other better. *Starting now and ongoing* 3. Enhance my Emotional Intelligence so that I might be more empathetic to others: a. Read and understand EI materials supplied by my coach. b. Complete the EI self-assessment to identify low areas that are most critical to my success and subsequently address them. c. Start viewing actions through an EI lens, and modify my behavior accordingly. *Complete self-assessment by June 1 and implement on an ongoing basis* 4. Ensure that I have a people focus vs. strictly a task focus (even if I have to overcorrect for a while) so that I take into account how my communications and actions will be perceived by others. (Keep my sense of urgency without being perceived as pushy.) *Ongoing* 5. Slow down, take a breath, and consider the consequences of my actions prior to acting. *Ongoing*	1. Ongoing—productive conversations held with exec. team members; seeking feedback on an ongoing basis from them and peers. 2. Having more face-to-face meetings where possible and teleconferences when travel is not an option. 3. Completed the tool and identified the area of EI where I need to focus most (it was Social Awareness—Empathy); now working on it daily. 4. Consciously reviewing how my communications (both oral and written) will be perceived by others. 5. Consciously thinking about this. Positive feedback so far.

SUMMARY

Because quality leadership is a key differentiator in achieving superior business results, then surely, quality development planning for those leaders should be a top priority of organizations. Development plans that are orchestrated using the methodology we have outlined in this chapter can facilitate this foremost priority. In fact, DDI's "Global Leadership Forecast 2014/2015" revealed that organizations that have high-quality, effective development plans in place increase their bench strength of "ready now" leaders by 9 percent.

Part III covered the foundation components of the Hogan approach to improving leader performance. In Part IV, we turn our attention to development content that has been proven to be effective in addressing personality-based performance challenges.

PART IV

COACHING TECHNIQUES FOR THE DARK SIDE

Once a leader has received feedback on the Hogan Development Survey (HDS) results, coaching can play an extremely important role in helping the leader make the necessary behavior changes to minimize the impact of potential derailers. With effective coaching, a leader can develop a deeper understanding of the derailer and the impact it can have on leadership effectiveness and long-term career success. Coaching can then enable the leader to identify effective behavior changes and development actions.

Part IV provides some suggested coaching strategies and tips for coaching leaders whose scores on HDS scales indicate a potential for derailment. The focus is on both high scores and low scores for the HDS scales:

- High HDS scores (defined as 80% or above for this discussion) indicate a potential for certain behaviors to be overused and expressed in negative or counterproductive ways. Because these behaviors are often memorable, they can have a significant negative impact on a leader's overall reputation and on the leader's near-term effectiveness.

- Low scores on a scale (defined as 20% or below for this discussion) may indicate a significant underuse or even absence of the behaviors associated with a scale. As a result, the leader's efforts often go unnoticed, and the leader can have minimal impact and less overall effectiveness.

The coaching strategies and tips provided are intended to enable leaders to make behavioral change that is sustainable over time. In general, the strategies and tips include (1) questions to pose to a leader to deepen the leader's awareness and understanding of the behavior and its impact on others, (2) exercises to engage in with a leader in a coaching session or for the leader to do outside of a coaching session to further enhance understanding and learning, (3) tips and techniques a coach can use to help a leader improve performance, and (4) readings and other suggested learning resources for the leader. The following is an example of how we will use the cases outlined in Chapter 5 to illustrate the use of coaching strategies and tips.

Case 2—Phil, Logistics Technician

Phil (Case 2—Phil, Logistics Technician, page 90), the lead logistics technician for a national trucking company we introduced in Chapter 5, provides an example of how the information contained in Part IV can be used to address performance challenges arising from the Dark Side of personality. Phil's HDS results indicate three high-risk behaviors: Skeptical (96%) (being excessively critical and on the lookout for problems and faults); Reserved (90%) (being insensitive to the moods and feelings of people and placing business results above all other concerns); and Dutiful (77%) (being quite deferential to superiors). While these behaviors may have been highly valued by the previous leader of Phil's organization, the new leadership is seeking to establish a culture centered around strong partnerships between corporate and the field.

After debriefing the HDS results with Phil, his coach began the coaching discussion by asking him a series of questions intended to help him understand the overall impact of his highly skeptical behavior:

- Can you describe the behaviors you believe others see when you are being highly skeptical?

- Are there ways these behaviors have contributed to your success? How?

- What are some circumstances where these behaviors have interfered with your ability to achieve a goal or build a relationship?

- How could being less skeptical positively impact your overall effectiveness as a leader? How could it contribute to the new "partnership" culture your new leader is working to create?

- What specific behaviors associated with being highly skeptical would be most important for you to stop or dial back? What new behaviors would be most important to start?

Through these questions, Phil revealed that while his high skepticism enabled him to identify some significant problems or opportunities for the company, his high degree of cynicism and high level of intensity impeded his collaborating effectively with others in identifying and implementing solutions. Specifically, he spoke to a situation where he had an urgent issue to address within a very tight timeframe. In deciding on colleagues to consult on the issue, he selected those he trusted and knew well. He excluded a colleague who he believed would not engage collaboratively and would only resist potential solutions. Because this individual's perspective and ideas were not considered, not only was a less-than-optimal solution identified, it was poorly implemented because of the lack of engagement of this key colleague. In speaking with her after the implementation, Phil came to see she was collaborative and, in fact, had some very creative solutions to offer. He realized that his lack of trust in this individual resulted in a significant missed opportunity for the company and may have damaged his relationship with his colleague and his reputation as a leader. The discussion of the situation also caused Phil to recognize the role his high score on the Reserved scale may play. Because of the stress associated with the urgency of this situation, Phil limited the number of people he involved and excluded others who could have added value to the process. It became clear to Phil that to be successful in this new culture, he needed to behave in a more open-minded and less cynical fashion so that he could build trusting relationships and effectively engage others. He recognized why a partnership culture was critical to the company's success and why it was important for him to play a role in that change.

Phil and his coach agreed that in their second session, they would debrief the situation with the colleague and identify what Phil would do differently were the situation to occur again. As homework, Phil's coach asked him to identify leaders who he believed demonstrate open-mindedness and approachability. The coach also asked him to observe as many of those leaders as possible and make note of the behaviors they demonstrate that contribute to their open-mindedness and approachability.

In their second session, Phil and his coach did the following:

- Defined the triggers that cause Phil stress and, ultimately, the excessive degree of skepticism he exhibited in that circumstance.

- Brainstormed specific ways to demonstrate more open-mindedness to others' perspectives, including asking open-ended questions, listening actively, and identifying solutions collaboratively.

- Identified actions Phil will take informally and outside of meeting situations to get to know this colleague (and others) better and help them get to know him.

To enhance Phil's ability to lead effectively by building and leveraging trusting relationships, his coach also recommended he read Chapter 4, "Can People Trust You?: Influence Begins with Trust—Why Earning the Trust of Others Is Key to Becoming a Great Boss," from the book *Being the Boss: The 3 Imperatives for Becoming a Great Leader* (Hill & Lineback, 2011).

Part IV is dedicated to providing the most comprehensive development content available to date that can be used to successfully address performance challenges related to the Dark Side of personality like those faced by Phil. The content is based on the experiences of the Hogan Coaching Network (HCN) coaches. The coaching questions, activities, and tips for each of the HDS scales (including both high and low scores) have been utilized with success in actual coaching cases. The content is organized around the HDS scales and presented in reference guide format.

If we have conveyed anything up to this point in the book, it is that every leader is different. Personality characteristics combine with Situational Context in ways that epitomize the notion of *equifinality* when it comes to the ways in which a leader can achieve career success. What we have attempted to do in Part IV is use the structure of the HDS to organize development content proven to be effective in addressing the barriers to success commonly encountered by leaders. Our purpose here is to provide leaders and the coaches who work with them the development content necessary to customize a development program that will lead to performance improvement.

CHAPTER 10

EXCITABLE

HIGH EXCITABLE

Detecting When It Is a Problem

High Excitable behaviors are easily observed in the workplace, and even one incident can have a devastating impact on a leader's reputation. Perhaps one of the best examples comes from the U.S. political world involving a presidential candidate named Howard Dean. Mr. Dean had to deliver a concession speech following a third-place showing in an important primary election. He proceeded to go on stage in front of his supporters and explode into an emotional rant that culminated in screaming uninterpretable phrases, and he was red-faced and frothing at the mouth. Needless to say, Mr. Dean was not elected and has drifted into political obscurity.

It is rare for leaders not to be able to detect the fact they exhibit high Excitable behaviors. They see themselves getting overly emotional. They may even feel their emotionality at a visceral level. Admitting that these behaviors are having a negative impact on their reputation may be difficult, and controlling them, even more difficult. But these behaviors are easily observed and quickly accumulate to the detriment of the leader's reputation.

Tanya from Case 4—Tanya, Insurance Professional on page 94 provides a good example of an individual with a high Excitable profile. Tanya's highest derailer is her Mischievous score (98%), but the Excitable score is not far behind (90%). The following is Tanya's profile summary.

Tanya's Situational Summary			
Tanya was a successful insurance professional for a medium-sized corporation who was promoted into the role of training manager. The new role looked to be quite challenging because it required a new skill set to be successful, and the insurance industry as a whole was evolving into a highly regulated industry with many new government regulations. Tanya's new role as training manager could potentially be quite stressful given the job demands and industry changes.			
Dimension	**Score**	**Percentile**	**Description**
Excitable	90		Tanya is a crafty insurance professional who can let her emotions get the best of her (Excitable—90%). She is known for putting big deals together for her corporate clients. Outwardly, she appears very self-confident (Bold—89%). She works her own agenda (Leisurely—80%), and tends to set her own rules (Mischievous—98% and Dutiful—10%) with little regard for consequences (Cautious—20%).
Skeptical	60		
Cautious	20		
Reserved	30		
Leisurely	80		
Bold	89		
Mischievous	98		
Colorful	70		
Imaginative	50		
Diligent	30		
Dutiful	10		

0   10   20   30   40   50   60   70   80   90   100

Tanya's case is an interesting one in that her Mischievous score and the situational information presented in the case suggest that her Mischievous behaviors may present the more immediate concern from a coaching standpoint. However, Tanya is at a transition point in her career, having just received a promotion. High Excitable behaviors come under increasing scrutiny as a leader rises through increasingly more responsible positions. Furthermore, it is likely that future career roles for Tanya could involve people management responsibilities. It is likely that she will have more contact and greater need to rely upon her peers as her career progresses. At the very least, her high score on the Excitable scale suggests the need for probing regarding Excitable behaviors on the job. It may be the case that an early coaching intervention could help her avoid any negative Excitable behaviors and the associated damage to her future reputation.

Evaluating the Need for Change

The following behavioral questions should be considered in conjunction with a leader's high Excitable score (as exhibited by Tanya) when evaluating the need for a change in behavior. A "yes" response to three or fewer items suggests that there is no imminent need for behavioral changes. A "yes" response to four to six items suggests that a high score on the Excitable scale should be a watch-out for a leader. A "yes" response to more than six items suggests that a leader should take active steps toward making behavioral changes.

Does the leader:

1. Quickly get visibly angry when frustrated or annoyed by the actions of others?   **Yes   No   Not Sure**

2. Demonstrate emotional outbursts, such as yelling at employees, vendors, or customers?   **Yes   No   Not Sure**

3. Appear to fuel the emotions in a situation by failing to exert emotional control?   **Yes   No   Not Sure**

4. Appear to be on an emotional roller coaster with highs and lows associated with various colleagues?   **Yes   No   Not Sure**

5. Get easily disappointed or disenchanted with employees who do not live up to expectations?   **Yes   No   Not Sure**

6. Regularly convey disappointment in others through emotional reactions?   **Yes   No   Not Sure**

7. Express an excessive amount of emotional regret regarding the way challenging situations are handled?   **Yes   No   Not Sure**

8. Make it difficult to determine values or beliefs because of emotional highs and lows?   **Yes   No   Not Sure**

9. Create directional uncertainty because of unpredictable emotional reactions?   **Yes   No   Not Sure**

These items should be considered as behavioral indicators. Similar or associated behaviors to any of those listed that are exhibited by a leader likely suggest a "yes" response. They provide additional support that a leader may be at risk for the negative reputational consequences associated with those scoring high on the Excitable scale, such as Tanya.

Impact of High Excitable Behaviors

High Excitable behaviors can create reputational concerns for leaders among their direct reports, peers, and managers. While there are examples of high Excitable leaders who are able to differentially manage their emotions among certain constituencies, it seems to be more the exception than the rule. The more likely explanation for emotional responses varying by constituencies is the degree to which self-monitoring goes up and consequences decline. For example, leaders may do a much better job maintaining emotional control in front of their managers, especially if the consequences for an outburst could mean permanent reputational damage. By contrast, such outbursts in front of direct reports may have fewer short-term consequences, but the long-term consequences could be equally problematic. The following are some of the consequences of high Excitable behaviors, broken out by three constituencies: managers, peers, and direct reports.

Managers

Managers often have little patience for high Excitable behaviors. They will associate these behaviors with a lack of maturity and see them as having little positive value when it comes to performance. It does not take much for a manager to form a negative reputational image of a person who displays these behaviors. Even a single instance can leave a lasting impression. Furthermore, most managers have little to no idea how to coach such behavior short of telling the person to quit it.

Peers

Peers will deal with these behaviors by limiting their interactions with high Excitable leaders. If they have to interact with them because of a business issue, they will do their best to avoid creating an emotional situation. They may maintain a cordial relationship with respect to nonbusiness interactions, or they may avoid interactions with these types of leaders all together. Interestingly, peers may seize upon these behaviors as a weakness and exploit them by creating circumstances designed to lure a person into exhibiting Excitable behaviors in front of others in positions of authority. Such actions are often political in nature. Their purpose is to create a negative reputation incident for a perceived competitor.

Direct Reports

Generally speaking, direct reports will engage in mood-management behaviors when working for leaders who exhibit high Excitable behaviors. The direct reports will attempt to discern the mood of these individuals and find ways to work around them if the probability is high that an excitable moment is on the horizon. The behavior of direct reports may range from simple avoidance to hiding bad news. Paradoxically, direct reports may develop strong loyalties to high Excitable leaders if they have developed solid coping strategies for dealing with the high Excitable behaviors. The reason for loyalty lies in the notion of disclosure and trust. High Excitable leaders often wear their emotions on their sleeve and over-disclose their feelings. Such disclosure shows vulnerability, and when people display vulnerability, they become easier to trust.

Coaching Focus

Excitable behaviors work very much in a wave fashion, vacillating between highs and lows over time because mood swings are found in almost all people. The difference is that amplitude and wavelength differ depending on the degree of excitability. Individuals who are highly excitable tend to have greater amplitude in their emotions, as well as shorter wavelengths. Figure 8 illustrates this description.

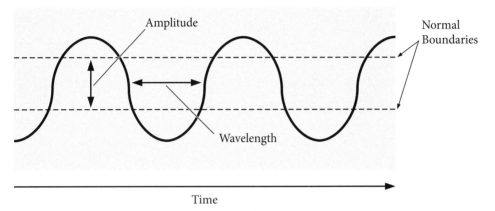

Figure 8   Model of High Excitable Behavior

Based on this model, emotional behavior vacillates between highs and lows over time. The amplitude represents the highs and lows. High Excitable individuals have highs and lows that often exceed the normal boundaries. The time between the highs and lows may also be shorter than what might normally be expected, meaning excitable moments happen with greater frequency.

The coaching focus for those exhibiting high Excitable behaviors is to bring the amplitude of the highs and lows within normal boundaries and increase the wavelength (time) between the highs and lows. In essence, the focus should be to flatten the wave to the point that others do not perceive or experience the emotional highs or lows. A persistent question will be whether leaders can internalize control over their emotional highs and lows. While that might be preferable, the starting point is to reduce behavioral manifestations so that reputational damage is kept to a minimum and more even-tempered behaviors emerge over time.

Coaching Strategy

There are five basic steps associated with the coaching strategy for high Excitable behaviors:

1. Increase the leader's self-awareness regarding what the behaviors look like in public. The coach should ask the individual to catalog behavioral examples and the circumstances surrounding them.

2. The behavioral examples should provide the basis for analyzing the themes, situations, people, and so on that act as triggers.

3. Pre-trigger activities that can reduce the probability of an excitable moment should be identified.

4. The leader should begin to implement the activities with an eye toward those excitable moments that appear to create the most reputational damage.

5. The leader should engage in evaluation and calibration of activities to determine which activities are most effective or impactful.

Strategy Refinements Using Subscale Information

The subscales offer insights as to how the coaching strategy might be refined to improve the effectiveness of the intervention. The subscales for Excitable include Volatile, Easily Disappointed, and No Direction. They offer insights as to the trigger points for excitable moments. If the subscales are elevated, the coaching strategy should focus on those trigger points that elicit the most damaging excitable moments.

Volatile

An elevation on the Volatile subscale often indicates that a particular event triggers an emotional moment. Plus, it may indicate that the amplitude of the moment may rise well above or fall well below normal boundaries. A strategy refinement here could involve placing a strong emphasis on understanding trigger points, helping the leader to anticipate the trigger points, and putting active steps in motion to control the amplitude of the behavior. Success when this subscale is elevated often depends on the number of trigger points and awareness the leader has of them. If there are many trigger points with new ones arising regularly, the coaching strategy may have to revert to helping the leader identify internal cues (e.g., increased heart rate, rise in blood pressure, facial flushing, etc.) to put into motion active steps to control the amplitude of the behavior.

Easily Disappointed

The Easily Disappointed subscale very much concerns the people in the leader's life. The vacillation between emotional highs and emotional lows is directly related to the leader's perceived actions of others. It is important to point out that these are perceived actions, and may or may not be related to actual performance. The point is that the leader builds up an expectation for certain actions on the part of others. When those expectations are met, the emotional moment may involve overly effusive expressions of support. When the expectations go unmet, there may be no effusive expressions, and the emotional moment may instead include negative or critical behaviors. The key to coaching elevations on this subscale is working with the leader to set realistic expectations and to help the leader predetermine reactions that fall within normal or acceptable boundaries.

No Direction

The No Direction subscale involves verbal expressions made by the leader indicating dissatisfaction with self-worth, accomplishments, or contributions. It is a harbinger of behaviors like wearing emotions on one's shirtsleeve and making statements that have a strong feeling of doom and gloom. Others will see these behaviors as inappropriate self-disclosure. Furthermore, these behaviors run the risk of diminishing the leader's credibility because they are typically more severe than reality suggests, and they may alternate with overly optimistic disclosures, further diminishing credibility. The coaching refinement here involves controlling the leader's need for disclosure or creating a safe outlet for disclosure that will help the leader avoid credibility hits.

Coaching Tactics

Coaching tactics cover a range of approaches and resources that have been found useful in addressing high Excitable behaviors. These tactics are typically used in combination to form a custom plan suited to the specific learning needs of a leader. The tactics are divided into four categories: (1) thought-provoking questions for a leader to consider, (2) exercises a leader can engage in to improve performance, (3) tips and techniques a coach can use to help a leader improve performance, and (4) support resources that can be consulted to gain additional insights in addressing high Excitable behaviors.

Thought-Provoking Questions for a Leader

- What can you do to pause in a situation and consider your impact on others?
- How do you build a long-term view of success and key milestones?
- How can you be selective about sharing emotional responses?
- Reflect back on observations of a high Excitable leader and ask, "Would you want to work with this person?"
- How do you handle situations when your emotions have gotten the best of you?

Exercises for a Leader

- Assess situations where you have dealt with stress effectively and have not dealt with it effectively.
- Begin each coaching session by practicing pausing and breathing to create a calmer emotional state.
- Give a colleague permission to issue a volatility alert.
- Keep track of the cues that seem to trigger an emotional response.
- Evaluate a situation prior to becoming involved in terms of how an emotional response by you might be triggered and how you plan to handle it.

Tips and Techniques for a Coach

- Help the leader prepare for potentially stressful situations by anticipating challenges ahead and doing what-if planning.

- Preview the leader's Outlook calendar to flag potentially stressful events, and work with the leader to plan ahead regarding how the events should be handled.

- Strengthen the leader's awareness of the emotional style associated with a high Excitable score, and work with the leader to understand the emotional styles of others who pose a challenge. Develop, obtain buy-in, and communicate plans, timelines, and measures of success.

- Help the leader develop a visual cue to think "calm and peaceful" that can be incorporated into a routine used as preparation for stressful events.

- Debrief stressful events with the leader, and evaluate the triggers and responses that were elicited.

Support Resources

Bradberry, T. (2014, February). **How successful people stay calm.** *Forbes.* Retrieved from http://www.forbes.com/sites/travisbradberry/2014/02/06/how-successful-people-stay-calm/

Bradberry, author of a best-selling book on emotional intelligence and cofounder of an organization that serves 75 percent of Fortune 500 companies, describes tactics successful people use when faced with stressful situations.

Contu, D. (2002, May). **How resilience works.** *Harvard Business Review.* Retrieved from https://hbr.org/2002/05/how-resilience-works

Harvard Business Review senior editor Diane Coutu discusses why resilience is currently a "hot topic" in the business world, the unexpected relationship between resilience and optimism, resilience's building blocks, and what resilience looks like in today's world.

Daft, R. L. (2010). *The executive and the elephant: A leader's guide for building inner excellence.* San Francisco, CA: John Wiley & Sons.

Leadership expert Daft posits that, despite having clear intentions, leaders often fall prey to their instincts. His book offers real-life examples and case studies to help readers find balance between their intentions and their instincts.

Gordon, J. (2011). *The seed: Finding purpose and happiness in life and work.* Hoboken, NJ: John Wiley & Sons.

Wall Street Journal best-selling author Jon Gordon uses an engaging parable to inspire and guide people through the process of finding meaning in and sparking passion for their work.

Harvard Business Review (2014). *HBR guide to managing stress at work.* Boston, MA: HBR Press.

HBR's guide teaches readers how to channel tension productively, avert stress-inducing circumstances, set realistic expectations, manage anxiety when it inevitably arises, and bounce back after succumbing to stress and pressure.

McGonigal, K. (2013). How to make stress your friend [Video file]. Retrieved from http://www.ted.com/talks/kelly_mcgonigal_how_to_make_stress_your_friend

Based on research suggesting that stress is detrimental only if people believe the preceding is true, psychologist Kelly McGonigal urges listeners to see stress as beneficial and introduces them to an under acknowledged mechanism for stress reduction—reaching out to others.

Seldman, M., & Seldman, J. (2008). *Executive stamina: How to optimize time, energy, and productivity to achieve peak performance.* Hoboken, NJ: John Wiley & Sons.

Gleaned from top executive coaches and world-class athletes' training tactics, this book offers overextended executives readily applicable tips and tools to help optimize their career potential, sustain physical health, and live true to their personal values.

Sample Coaching Program (Case 4—Tanya)

Tanya's profile indicates an Excitable score of 90 percent. An examination of her subscale scores indicates that the Volatile subscale is elevated to the maximum level, while the Easily Disappointed and No Direction subscales are only moderately elevated. The case information presented about Tanya clearly indicates that Excitable behaviors may not be the top priority for her success in her current position. However, upon reflecting on Tanya's comments during feedback, it is clear that she has excitable moments related to her ability to control emotional outbursts and raising her voice to colleagues who do not agree with her as means of getting them to listen. Given that Tanya has career potential and aspirations beyond her current role, an early coaching intervention on her Excitable behaviors, emphasizing the behaviors associated with the Volatile subscale, would be valuable. The following are the proposed steps for this aspect of a coaching engagement with Tanya:

- Have Tanya participate in a self-reflection exercise to identify incidents where she exhibited volatile behavior. The incidents should include a description of the situation and the details of what was said, including her affect and her perception of the impact she had on the others involved.

- Review the incidents of the self-reflection exercise with Tanya, and help her identify the themes, trigger points, and other cues that would help alert her to future situations that could cause an emotional moment.

- Work with Tanya to develop a set of alternative behaviors that she can use to avoid such emotional moments, as follows:

  - Take a 10- to 15-minute walk before entering a situation that has a high probability of eliciting an emotional moment. Use the time to control breathing, and self-talk emotionally neutral statements that could be used to diffuse the situation.

  - Upon entering the situation, have in place a behavioral reminder to use neutral self-talk statements that were practiced during the walk.

  - (Optional) Forewarn those who may be in the meeting or interaction that this is an issue that she is passionate about or has strong feelings regarding it.

  - (Optional) Follow up with those who were a part of the meeting or interaction to determine if she was appropriately passionate without excessive emotions.

- Have Tanya maintain a journal cataloging incidents that could have elicited or did elicit an emotional moment on her part. The journal will serve as a point of discussion during follow-up coaching discussions.

Summary

Keep Doing

Act with passion, energy, and enthusiasm.

Stop Doing

Lose emotional control, allowing emotions to run away, yelling.

Start Doing

Recognize and handle situations that cause frustration and emotional moments.

High Excitable behaviors are extremely visible to all constituencies who are a part of a leader's work environment. A leader who demonstrates these behaviors can quickly develop a reputation for lacking executive maturity, presence, and the ability to handle workplace pressure. These behaviors can be difficult to control. They stem from what has been called the "caveman brain" and require discipline and significant effort on the part of the leader to prevent them from creating reputational damage. Coaching that involves an active self-monitoring program and the substitution of appropriate alternative behaviors can correct or even prevent their negative reputational consequences.

LOW EXCITABLE

Detecting When It Is a Problem

Low Excitable behaviors are typically difficult to observe in the workplace and are often mistaken for other characteristics. For example, it is not uncommon for a low Excitable person to be mistaken for an introvert or even someone who is arrogant or above it all emotionally. People use the emotional responses of their leaders as a barometer of the seriousness of a situation. When there is an absence of an emotional response or the leader has a flat affect, people tend to fill in the emotional gap with their own take on the situation. It is difficult to cite a memorable example of low Excitable behaviors because they are anything but memorable. One high-profile example that illustrates low Excitable is Prince Charles. He is often described in his public appearances as coming off as intelligent, aloof, and a bit awkward. He is almost never described as inspirational or able to motivate others through his passion. In fact, it is often discussed in the tabloids that Prince Charles may be passed over in favor of Prince William as the heir to the British throne. While there is a panoply of reasons offered as to why something that flies against a tradition that goes back centuries may occur, one cannot help but speculate that Prince Charles's inability to be inspirational could be a contributing factor. A flat affect and the inability to inspire others are the hallmark behaviors that can impact the career of a low Excitable leader.

James from Case 7—James, Marketing Manager on page 100 provides a good example of a low Excitable profile. James's highest derailer is his Dutiful score (90%), but his Excitable score is very low (10%) and worth examining in terms of his long-term leadership potential. The following is James's profile summary.

James's Situational Summary			
James was the marketing manager for a small family-owned business that was sold to a well-established technology company. After the sale, James moved on to a small, fast-moving start-up technology company. He had clear challenges with his ability to get things moving in the new company. His low Excitable score tended to exacerbate the problem because he seemed to lack passion and urgency around the challenges confronting him in a fast-moving start-up company.			
Dimension	**Score**	**Percentile**	**Description**
Excitable	10		James is a laid-back, even-tempered marketing guy (Excitable—10%). It takes him a long time to get to know and trust people (Skeptical—70%), and he is guarded and slow to make decisions (Cautious—85% and Mischievous—15%). James doesn't make a big impression on people. In fact, he is best known for his loyalty and willingness to do whatever the owners asked (Dutiful—90%).
Skeptical	70		
Cautious	85		
Reserved	25		
Leisurely	19		
Bold	24		
Mischievous	15		
Colorful	45		
Imaginative	35		
Diligent	50		
Dutiful	90		

0   10   20   30   40   50   60   70   80   90   100

Notice the descriptive language associated with James' profile. He is described as "laid back" and "does not make a big impression on people." These are not the kind of descriptions that are commonly associated with an effective leader, especially one in a high-profile function like marketing. James may be very competent and could achieve a degree of success based on his competence. However, his inability to summon his emotions and inspire others with what has often been called "fire in the belly" could be a limiting factor in his future career success. He also runs the risk of displaying what others may perceive as a lack of urgency because of his laid-back emotional style. Start-up companies, especially those in a highly competitive industry like technology, tend to be populated with people who enjoy a fast-paced lifestyle. James may actually enjoy the pace, but his emotional demeanor conveys otherwise.

Evaluating the Need for Change

The following behavioral questions should be considered in conjunction with a leader's low Excitable score (as exhibited by James) when evaluating the need for a change in behavior. A "yes" response to three or fewer items suggests that there is no imminent need for behavioral changes. A "yes" response to four to six items suggests that a low score on the Excitable scale should be a watch-out for a leader. A "yes" response to more than six items suggests that a leader should take active steps toward making behavioral changes.

Does the leader:

1. Remain calm or subdued even when the situation calls for an emotional reaction?	Yes No Not Sure
2. Show little to no emotional reaction even when others create an obvious annoyance?	Yes No Not Sure
3. Demonstrate little to no emotional reaction regardless of the situation or circumstances?	Yes No Not Sure
4. Appear to lack any emotional reaction even when clearly disappointed by the performance of others?	Yes No Not Sure
5. Rarely or never seem disappointed or disenchanted with employees who fail to live up to expectations?	Yes No Not Sure
6. Avoid conveying any disappointment with others through emotional reactions or demeanor?	Yes No Not Sure
7. Express little to no emotional regret when challenging situations are not handled effectively?	Yes No Not Sure

8. Demonstrate such a lack of emotion that core principles and beliefs are very difficult to read by others?   **Yes   No   Not Sure**

9. Create directional uncertainty because of a lack of emotional reaction or even passion?   **Yes   No   Not Sure**

These items should be considered as behavioral indicators. Similar or associated behaviors to any of those listed that are exhibited by a leader likely suggest a "yes" response. They provide additional support that a leader may be at risk for the negative reputational consequences associated with those scoring low on the Excitable scale, such as James.

Impact of Low Excitable Behaviors

Low Excitable behaviors can have a more subtle impact than do high Excitable behaviors. There is almost a flattening of emotions to the extent that they do not vary greatly from situation to situation or even between constituencies. It is fundamentally at the heart of why low Excitable behaviors can have a negative impact on a leader's career. Leaders regularly encounter situations that should elicit a range of emotions. Low Excitable leaders have a very limited range of emotions. Their reputations are impacted more by what they did not do in a given situation, rather than what they did do. In some ways, the reputational impact can be more career limiting than the behaviors exhibited by high Excitable leaders. In most cases, high Excitable leaders are required to dial back on emotional behaviors. Low Excitable leaders are required to read situations and dial up the appropriate emotional behaviors, and these behaviors often do not come naturally. Therefore, even if low Excitable leaders read situations correctly and attempt to dial up the appropriate emotional behaviors, they still run the risk of their behavior looking awkward and insincere. The following are some of the consequences of low Excitable behaviors, broken out by three constituencies: managers, peers, and direct reports.

Managers

Managers are often unconcerned about low Excitable behaviors. In fact, these behaviors may be a welcome relief in many circumstances as such behaviors require little in the way of attention when it comes to accomplishing many tasks. The real danger, with respect to a manager's perspective, is that the leader develops a reputation for not having fire in the belly or the ability to inspire others. The consequences of these negative reputational descriptions for a leader are most severe when the individual is considered for future opportunities. Behavioral descriptions like "no fire in the belly" or "uninspiring" can become reasons for the manager to conclude that the leader might not be right for a higher-level position.

Peers

Peers can have a much different reaction to low Excitable behaviors. Peers are in the business of making sure they are on sound political ground with those around them. Among the most important cues they rely upon in trying to read others are emotional behaviors. Low Excitable individuals are inherently difficult to read. The vacuum of information can create questions in the mind of a peer as to where a low Excitable individual stands on an issue, or worse, can result in the peer simply not trusting the individual.

Direct Reports

Direct reports present a much different challenge for a low Excitable leader than either a manager or a peer. Direct reports generally appreciate working for a calm, even-tempered leader, where mood-management demands are at a minimum. However, leaders must motivate and inspire those they lead. Emotions are as essential as the message when it comes to motivating and inspiring people. Imagine the "I Have a Dream" speech delivered by a low Excitable leader instead of by Martin Luther King, Jr., and the point becomes obvious.

Coaching Focus

Low Excitable behaviors work very much in a wave fashion like high Excitable behaviors, vacillating between highs and lows over time. The difference between a low Excitable person and a high Excitable person exists in the amplitude and wavelength of the emotional highs and lows. Individuals who are low on the Excitable scale tend to have much less amplitude in their emotions and a much longer wavelength between high and low changes. The following figure illustrates this description.

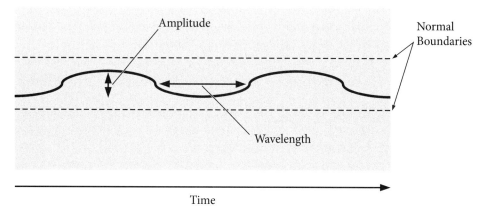

Figure 9   Model of Low Excitable Behavior

Notice that a wave pattern is illustrated in both Figure 8 (page 187) and Figure 9. The primary difference is that the amplitude of the wave for a low Excitable individual falls well below normal boundaries, allowing the emotional swings to go largely undetected. Furthermore, the wavelength is longer, making emotional swings even more difficult to detect. Presented with an emotionally charged situation, a low Excitable leader will be slower to react emotionally, the reaction will rarely climb to a detectable level, and the reaction will dissipate quietly.

The coaching focus for a low Excitable leader is far different than that for a high Excitable leader. For the most part, the low Excitable behaviors will be welcomed by those around the leader. The challenge exists in developing the low Excitable leader's ability to summon the appropriate level of emotion when a situation calls for it. Interestingly, if the leader can develop this ability and use it effectively, it can have a tremendous "wow" factor simply by virtue of the contrast with the low Excitable leader's natural, steady state of being calm and even-tempered.

Coaching Strategy

There are three fundamental components necessary for an effective coaching strategy with low Excitable leaders: situational recognition, behavioral substitution, and emotional sincerity. None of these is easy to effectively implement. Situational recognition refers to the need for the leader to determine those few key situations in which a strong emotional response will have a positive impact both on those involved in the situation and on the leader's reputation. Behavioral substitution refers to the development of the content of the message without regard to the affect with which it is delivered. Emotional sincerity refers to the ability to deliver the message with the appropriate affect. These components can only be demonstrated successfully with practice; as a result, the coaching should begin by introducing them in low-risk situations where a degree of awkwardness will not result in substantial reputational damage.

Strategy Refinements Using Subscale Information

The subscales offer insights into how the coaching strategy might be refined to improve the effectiveness of the intervention. The subscales for Excitable include Volatile, Easily Disappointed, and No Direction. They offer insights as to how to address the challenges of situational recognition, the content of behavioral substitution, and emotional sincerity.

Volatile

A depression on the Volatile scale often indicates a real flattening of emotions. In other words, the leader typically appears very calm and even-tempered to the point that many see the leader as cold, emotionally detached, or lacking urgency. When the Volatile scale is very low, it presents a significant challenge in helping the leader demonstrate an emotional response that others perceive as sincere. Even when well practiced, the emotional sincerity component may come off as awkward to the point that others might describe the behavior as being faked. It is important that the leader practice the new behaviors in low-risk situations to avoid negative reputational consequences such as diminished trust or loss of credibility.

Easily Disappointed

The concern with the Easily Disappointed subscale is with the leader's ability to demonstrate real "fire in the belly" when things go particularly well or particularly badly. Leaders who are low on this subscale tend to show few emotions when others are reacting to the highs or lows of a situation. It can appear to others that the leader just does not care. For example, in a situation that most would view as disappointing, the leader's lack of emotion conveys an attitude of "so what" or "no big deal." In contrast, a lack of emotion conveyed during a celebratory moment can be demotivating and destructive to morale. In both cases, others, who are expecting an emotional response and get none, begin to question whether or not the leader really cares about anything or has any sense of urgency. Coaching can be refined here by getting the leader to combine message content with some acknowledgment that, despite the appearance of little emotion, he or she has genuine concern or delight, depending on the circumstances.

No Direction

The No Direction subscale presents a challenge from a coaching standpoint. Behaviors associated with this subscale are not unlike the obtuse reaction to negative feedback one often sees with individuals who have very high scores on the Adjustment scale of the HPI. Leaders who are very low on this subscale miss cues (especially emotional ones) and feedback to the point that they are oblivious to the need for an appropriate emotional response in a given situation. Failure to demonstrate an appropriate emotional response can be particularly damaging because there is information out there to be had, but the lack of situational recognition prevents or inhibits the ability of leaders low on this subscale to effectively use the information. Furthermore, their stilted emotional responses offer few clues as to their own emotional state. The coaching here needs to focus on raising situational recognition and the information value that it may contain. It can also be useful to encourage these leaders to give those around them a glimpse into the emotions they are feeling about the situation as those emotions are likely difficult for others to read.

Coaching Tactics

Coaching tactics cover a range of approaches and resources that have been found useful in addressing low Excitable behaviors. These tactics are typically used in combination to form a custom plan suited to the specific learning needs of a leader. The tactics are divided into four categories: (1) thought-provoking questions for a leader to consider, (2) exercises a leader can engage in to improve performance, (3) tips and techniques a coach can use to help a leader improve performance, and (4) support resources that can be consulted to gain additional insights in addressing low Excitable behaviors.

Thought-Provoking Questions for a Leader

- What emotional cues in others do you find most helpful in reading a situation?
- What do you find most difficult when trying to bring your emotions into a situation?
- What are some of the cues you might consider to help you detect how you feel about a situation or an issue?
- How would you go about circling back with people to make sure they know your position on critical issues?
- How will adding more emotional range to the way you address groups help your career?

Exercises for a Leader

- Identify the situations in which you think you need to utilize more emotional range in order to successfully navigate them.
- Describe leaders who communicate emotions effectively, including what emotions they convey.
- Practice verbalizing descriptive language for communications with your team members or other key stakeholders.
- Exercise your emotional range in front of a safe audience prior to rolling it out in a critical situation.
- After a key presentation, ask for feedback from key stakeholders on your effectiveness in conveying emotions.

Tips and Techniques for a Coach

- Review the career implications of using greater emotional range in critical situations.
- Identify situations, issues, or people who do elicit emotional peaks from the leader (as small as they may be) and determine what they have in common.
- Develop a list of situations, from easy to hard, where emotional range can be practiced without negative reputational impact.
- Develop an outline illustrating the leader's as-is emotional range with a to-be emotional range.
- Provide the leader with an emotional mirror in practice situations leading up to a critical talk or speech.

Support Resources

Chamorro-Premuzic, T. (2014). *Confidence: Overcoming low self-esteem, insecurity, and self-doubt.* New York, NY: Penguin.

Chamorro-Premuzic argues that, contrary to popular belief, confidence is capable of thwarting achievement, employability, and likability. Among other topics, this book discusses the silver linings of low confidence, teaches readers how to identify when to feign self-assurance (and how to do so effectively), and offers tactics for improving physical and emotional health.

Goleman, D., Boyatzis, R., McKee, A., & Finkelstein, S. (2015). *HBR's 10 must reads on emotional intelligence.* Boston, MA: HBR Press.

Ten thoughtfully selected articles written and identified by experts in the field of emotional intelligence.

Gordon, J. (2007). *The energy bus: 10 rules to fuel your life, work, and team with positive energy.* Hoboken, NJ: John Wiley & Sons.

Gordon takes readers on a thought provoking and inspirational ride, sharing 10 tactics for approaching work and life with the type of optimistic, forward thinking that facilitates true accomplishment both professionally and personally.

Sanborn, M., & Maxwell, J. C. (2004). *The Fred factor: How passion in your work and life can turn the ordinary into the extraordinary.* Colorado Springs, CO: WaterBook.

Sanborn summarizes four principles intended to "release fresh energy, enthusiasm, and creativity" in readers' careers and lives.

Schneider, B. (2007). *Energy leadership: Transforming your workplace and life from the core.* Hoboken, NJ: John Wiley & Sons.

Renowned coach Bruce Schneider teaches readers how to understand and harness their most valuable personal resource—energy.

Toastmasters International (https://www.toastmasters.org/)

Toastmasters International is a global network of clubs devoted to helping members improve their communication and leadership skills.

Sample Coaching Program (Case 7—James)

James's profile indicates an Excitable score of 10 percent. An examination of his subscale scores indicates that all three—Volatile, Easily Disappointed, and No Direction—are depressed. The case information presented about James indicates that Dutiful (90%) may be a more immediate development priority. However, his reputation for being "laid back" and failing to "leave a big impression on people" indicates that his long-term success as a leader will be impacted by his low Excitable score. James's situation offers a fairly low-risk environment for addressing the low Excitable aspect of his profile. The company is small, fast moving, and likely forgiving as long as there is a perception that James is making progress. Given that his early days in the organization were spent collecting information from people who do not have a great familiarity with marketing, it would make good sense to have James craft a presentation for the troops outlining the vision and direction for marketing. It would give James the opportunity to build content based on his technical background, present an opportunity to make sure he is aligned with his manager, and challenge his low Excitable demeanor to deliver a passionate statement about the direction of marketing. The following are the proposed steps for this aspect of the coaching engagement with James:

- Have James craft a draft presentation about the direction he wants to take marketing, based on the information he has gathered and his technical competence.

- Review the presentation with James on two levels. First, does it contain content that he truly believes in? Second, are the logic and flow of the presentation sound?

- Have James gain support from his manager, and then prepare James for the delivery of his message:

  - Once the draft is in solid form, James should set up a meeting with his manager to do a preliminary review. Prior to the meeting with his manager, complete several test-runs on the presentation by role playing his manager in the meeting.

  - Encourage James to leave the meeting with any modifications to the presentation and a commitment from his manager to create a forum for James to present it to the troops.

  - Assuming modifications to the presentation have been made and presentation to the troops is set, begin working with James on the delivery.

  - Become James's emotional mirror during practice sessions, preparing him to deliver the presentation in an inspiring manner.

- Follow up with several meeting participants to gather information regarding the presentation from both a content and delivery standpoint. Provide feedback to James based on the information.

- Establish a follow-up plan with James that offers update opportunities with the troops and that further reinforces the lessons learned during his initial presentation.

SUMMARY

Keep Doing

Maintain a calm, even-tempered demeanor when others lose control of their emotions.

Stop Doing

Respond to others in ways that they may infer a lack of urgency or "fire in the belly."

Start Doing

Practice bringing passion, energy, and enthusiasm to public speeches or presentations.

Low Excitable behaviors are often difficult to detect, and it is even more difficult to determine if they are having a negative impact on a leader's reputation. Often, a leader only finds out that these behaviors might be a problem when a promotion has been missed or a plum opportunity has been offered to someone else. Changing a leader's reputation once it includes labels like "laid back" or "no fire in the belly" can be difficult but not impossible. Furthermore, once a low Excitable leader learns to use emotions selectively and with sincerity, the impact on others can be quite significant because of the contrast with the leader's natural tendencies.

CHAPTER 11

SKEPTICAL

HIGH SKEPTICAL

Detecting When It Is a Problem

Leaders with high Skeptical scores are generally perceptive, but they look at others' actions through a lens of distrust. These leaders question the motives behind others' actions and assume the worst. They are highly critical, do not easily build trust, and expect to be mistreated. The collaborative relationships required in today's heavily matrixed organizations suffer with high Skeptical leaders. These leaders are unlikely to forget or forgive a wrong and will hold these memories ever-present.

The North Korean dictator Kim Jong-Un serves as a good illustration of a leader who does not trust. This wariness holds Kim Jong-Un back from even considering international alliances that otherwise might be in the best interests of his country. In certain environments and circumstances, this highly skeptical approach may be seen as being savvy. However, in most environments and circumstances, this potential derailer can get in the way of building productive, sustainable relationships and can have even broader consequences, as with Kim Jong-Un.

Phil from Case 2—Phil, Logistics Technician on page 90 provides a good example of a high Skeptical profile. Phil's HDS results indicate two high-risk behaviors: Skeptical (96%) (being excessively critical and on the lookout for faults) and Reserved (90%) (being insensitive to the moods and feelings of people and placing business results above all other concerns). The following is Phil's profile summary:

Phil's Situational Summary
Phil is a lead logistics technician for a national trucking company. Phil's approach to his job generally has been one of a watchdog who tries to identify problems and deliver bad news. A new incoming leader for whom he will be working in the future has a decidedly different view of how the function should run. The leader believes technicians should take more of a partnership approach with field employees, treating them as internal customers.

Dimension	Score	Percentile	Description
Excitable	35		Phil is a perceptive individual but can be excessively critical and is always on the lookout for faults (Skeptical—96%). He can be insensitive to the moods and feelings of people, and place business results above all other concerns (Reserved—90%). He also can be quite deferential to superiors and the guidance they provide (Dutiful—77%).
Skeptical	96		
Cautious	75		
Reserved	90		
Leisurely	33		
Bold	55		
Mischievous	40		
Colorful	75		
Imaginative	62		
Diligent	60		
Dutiful	77		

0   10   20   30   40   50   60   70   80   90   100

Under the prior leadership in logistics, Phil's highly skeptical behavior might have been encouraged. Phil was expected to be alert for problems and function as a watchdog. However, his environment has shifted with the change in leadership. The new head of logistics is taking an approach that engages other departments and builds partnering relationships. Trust is often at the core of such relationships and partnerships. High Skeptical leaders do not trust readily and hold negative expectations of others. While these behaviors may have been valued by the previous leader of Phil's organization, the new leader is seeking to establish a culture centered on partnerships between corporate and field. It will be challenging for Phil to shift his reputation and interactions with others as his new manager will expect. Phil will need to repair existing relationships and establish new partnerships. With the added challenge of his high Reserved score, Phil is likely to find it difficult to build relationships in general, and his high Skeptical behaviors may hinder his ability to pivot to a different approach.

Evaluating the Need for Change

The following behavioral questions should be considered in conjunction with a leader's high Skeptical score (as exhibited by Phil) when evaluating the need for a change in behavior. A "yes" response to three or fewer items suggests that there is no imminent need for behavioral changes. A "yes" response to four to six items suggests that a high score on the Skeptical scale should be a watch-out for a leader. A "yes" response to more than six items suggests that a leader should take active steps toward making behavioral changes.

Does the leader:

1.	Have difficulty accepting a compliment without questioning the motives?	Yes	No	Not Sure
2.	Assume people have questionable or suspicious motives when they offer to do a favor?	Yes	No	Not Sure
3.	Regularly question what management is up to or planning?	Yes	No	Not Sure
4.	Express distrust for coworkers even when there is no reason to think they are untrustworthy?	Yes	No	Not Sure
5.	Indicate that people will cheat you if given the opportunity?	Yes	No	Not Sure
6.	Not take feedback due to a lack of trust for those offering ideas or input?	Yes	No	Not Sure
7.	Have a hard time forgiving people even for minor issues?	Yes	No	Not Sure
8.	Express concerns that most people are only motivated by their own self-interests?	Yes	No	Not Sure
9.	Write people off or suggest that some people should never be forgiven?	Yes	No	Not Sure

These items should be considered as behavioral indicators. Similar or associated behaviors to any of those listed that are exhibited by a leader likely suggest a "yes" response. They provide additional support that a leader may be at risk for the negative reputational consequences associated with those scoring high on the Skeptical scale, such as Phil.

Impact of High Skeptical Behaviors

High Skeptical behaviors can get in the way of forming solid, trusting relationships that are essential to influencing others and having long-term success in organizations. High Skeptical leaders develop reputations that put people off and limit their willingness to engage or interact with them. These leaders will often be seen as negative, cynical, and judgmental. They must develop greater awareness of their underlying belief system and be willing to question it if they are able to shift their behaviors and, ultimately, improve their reputation. The following are some of the consequences of high Skeptical behaviors, broken out by three constituencies: managers, peers, and direct reports.

Managers

In most organizations, collaboration is necessary. Managers may find that high Skeptical individuals have difficulty establishing collaborative partnerships. While they might be practiced at weighing both sides of an issue and playing bad cop, this behavior may not be welcomed in all instances. High Skeptical individuals will be seen as highlighting what is wrong, what is not being done, and what will not work. Managers may tire of these negative or cynical responses from high Skeptical individuals. These leaders are less likely to tell a positive story or acknowledge contributions and will generally be a drag on morale. Managers who are challenged daily to motivate people and get the best out of them will have little patience for those who are only capable of seeing the glass half-empty.

Peers

Peers may find it difficult to partner with high Skeptical individuals, even though they may value highly skeptical individuals' ability to identify issues and spot political dynamics that the peers might otherwise have overlooked. The mistrustful behaviors of the high Skeptical leaders make it difficult for other teams to engage and interact with them. Peers will be reluctant to look to high Skeptical leaders for input or accurate feedback given these leaders' proclivity for always seeing the downside when offering their views. Peers will also be less likely to share ideas or express their views because they do not want to appear vulnerable to the negative perspective the highly skeptical leaders bring to the table. In fact, politically savvy peers may leverage the negativism and let the high Skeptical individuals be the ones to highlight problems or shoot down new ideas.

Direct Reports

High Skeptical leaders will be seen by their direct reports as critical and less likely to acknowledge their positive contributions or improvements. Furthermore, the morale of direct reports may suffer because of the negative, low-trust environment that these leaders create. Developmentally, direct reports may not reach their full potential because high Skeptical leaders often show little trust in allowing them to take on stretch assignments, or these leaders are so overly critical that their direct reports shy away from such assignments. Additionally, the lack of trust demonstrated by these leaders in the way they collaborate can spill over to the way their direct reports work with other individuals or teams.

Coaching Focus

Leaders who fall into the high end of the Skeptical scale tend to approach relationships from a negative perspective. These leaders are not easily deceived, but their wariness also makes building productive, positive relationships difficult. High Skeptical leaders are unlikely to question their own assumptions about others and generally will not probe to get a different understanding or viewpoint. They will attribute intent to the behaviors they observe, and this often-distorted view becomes their truth. They may find themselves becoming increasingly isolated, and their networks may become more limited in scope. Consequently, building the collaborative relationships that are valued by so many organizations will be a challenge and a key developmental need for these leaders.

Coaching high Skeptical leaders is demanding as they are likely to question the coaching process or the need for change. If they will accept coaching, the coaching process can be leveraged to help these leaders reframe the way they assess situations and colleagues. High Skeptical leaders will need to practice this reframing and retelling of stories to build their positive frame of reference or mindset. Their internal belief system may not change or may shift slowly, but they can be encouraged to behave in ways that facilitate relationship development and trust building.

Coaching Strategy

An essential aspect of coaching high Skeptical leaders involves linking a behavioral shift to the achievement of their key goals. If these leaders acknowledge that they need to build relationships or shift the relationships they have, they may be more willing to try some new approaches. Until they experiment and experience success, they are likely to remain skeptical about the value of or need for change.

A starting point for a coaching initiative with a high Skeptical leader is to have the leader explicitly state his or her short-term and longer term goals. The coach can also help by asking probing questions about how the leader plans to accomplish those goals, and then the coach can highlight the role that relationships play. Once a high Skeptical leader acknowledges the importance of relationships to achieving his or her goals, the next task is to consider how best to build trusting relationships. To facilitate this, the coach may ask what value each potential stakeholder offers and what value the high Skeptical leader can provide to each stakeholder. To make this exercise even more meaningful, the high Skeptical leader may need to be pushed to consider alternative versions of the intentions of others. This encouragement to be more open-minded will help a high Skeptical leader develop a more positive lens through which to view colleagues.

Strategy Refinements Using Subscale Information

The subscales offer insights as to how the coaching strategy might be refined to improve the effectiveness of the intervention. The subscales for the Skeptical scale include Cynical, Mistrusting, and Grudges. When the subscales are elevated, they offer insights into how the high Skeptical behaviors will be manifested in the workplace.

Cynical

The Cynical subscale concerns a leader's interactions with other people. An elevation on this subscale suggests a leader who ascribes negative motives to others. Second-guessing every action and interaction with others has a negative impact on relationships. Moreover, the individual's behavior may be seen as moody. A leader high on this subscale will question every interaction and make assumptions about why others do what they do. This conviction can make a leader seem suspicious and will get in the way of building the trust that forms the foundation of strong relationships. An effective approach to coaching a leader elevated on this subscale is to ask the individual to consider possible positive intents that could be motivating the behavior of colleagues. In other words, the coach should help a high Skeptical leader move away from his or her negative belief system.

Mistrusting

An elevation on the Mistrusting subscale often indicates that a leader is prone to having a general feeling of uncertainty toward others, which leads to a tendency to be on the lookout for signs of mistreatment. This heightened sense of mistrust may cause rifts in long-standing relationships and may make it challenging to develop new ones. In addition, mistrust begets mistrust. A leader who enters a relationship with mistrust is far more likely to have that relationship proceed down the path of greater and greater mistrust. This downward spiral is nothing more than relationship dynamics at work. People who feel they are not trusted in turn become more wary.

Grudges

The Grudges subscale involves holding grudges and withholding forgiveness about real or perceived prior wrongs. A leader high on this subscale is likely to recall every real (or perceived) slight or instance of mistreatment by others; consequently, this preoccupation with past grievances will impact the way these individuals will be engaged with in the future. For this type of leader, a grudge is like a scar; even if the wound has healed, the scar is an ever-present reminder of the offending event. Successfully coaching this type of leader often means increasing the utilitarian value of the offender. By taking this approach, a coach can help a leader refocus the relationship on the achievement of tasks or goals. The scar itself may not go away, but the relationship may reach a functional level, and mutual success has a way of mitigating grudges.

Coaching Tactics

Coaching tactics cover a range of approaches and resources that have been found useful in addressing high Skeptical behaviors. These tactics are typically used in combination to form a custom plan suited to the specific learning needs of a leader. The tactics are divided into four categories: (1) thought-provoking questions for a leader to consider, (2) exercises a leader can engage in to improve performance, (3) tips and techniques a coach can use to help a leader improve performance, and (4) support resources that can be consulted to gain additional insights in addressing high Skeptical behaviors.

Thought-Provoking Questions for a Leader

- In what ways has being highly skeptical helped you? In what circumstances has it interfered with your ability to achieve a result or build a relationship?

- How could being less skeptical positively impact your overall effectiveness as a leader? How could it enhance your career?

- What specific behaviors associated with being highly skeptical would be most important for you to stop or dial back? What new behaviors would be most important to start?

- What might you gain by assuming a positive intent on the part of others? What do you risk?

- How can you allow space for others to vet their ideas without being dismissed?

Exercises for a Leader

- Practice reframing a challenging scenario by retelling the story, assuming the colleague's positive intent.

- Identify the value and contributions of someone with whom you have difficulty.

- Create two lists: List 1 should be a list of people you trust and also who are important to your success and your team's success. List 2 should be a list of people you do not trust and who are important to your success and your team's success. Discuss who from list 2 needs to be on list 1. Develop an action plan to engage in small experiments to build trust gradually (e.g., pick one person a month from the second list and work to establish a relationship and move that person to the first list).

- Think back to why you hold a grudge against an important stakeholder. Determine what it would take to build a functional working relationship with the individual over time.
- Identify and deliver at least one positive or uplifting statement you could make to a coworker each day.

Tips and Techniques for a Coach

- Identify a situation where the leader can assume positive intent, and record observations of outcomes.
- Ask the leader to role play giving balanced, motivational feedback to a colleague, team, and so on.
- Ask the leader to recognize when a conversation is about to start or evolve into an argument. Practice helping the leader to pause and ask, "Is this a battle worth fighting?"
- Work through a list of the positive attributes key stakeholders bring to the table when completing tasks or assignments.
- Work with the leader to identify a specific relationship that has been damaged due to a trust issue. Put a strategy in place for rebuilding trust with the individual over time.

Support Resources

Brown, B. (2010, June). The power of vulnerability [Video file]. Retrieved from http://www.ted.com/talks/brene_brown_on_vulnerability?language=en

Brené Brown, researcher and expert on the topic of human connection, discusses what true vulnerability is and why it should be fostered and celebrated instead of avoided and disdained.

Caruso, D. R., & Salovey, P. (2004). *The emotionally intelligent manager: How to develop and use the four key emotional skills of leadership.* San Francisco, CA: Jossey-Bass.

Caruso and Salovey challenge the notion that emotions do not have a place in the workplace, arguing that emotions are fundamental to our intelligence as well as our thinking and reasoning capabilities. The authors teach readers how to quantify, learn, and hone each component of their hierarchy of emotional skills.

Covey, S. M. R. (2006). *The speed of trust: The one thing that changes everything.* New York, NY: Simon & Schuster.

Covey asserts that trust is the linchpin of the new global economy and demonstrates that trust—and the speed at which it can be developed with employees, clients, and constituents—is a defining factor within successful, high-performance organizations.

Ferrazzi, K. (2009). *Who's got your back: The breakthrough program to build deep, trusting relationships that create success—and won't let you fail.* New York, NY: Broadway Books.

Best-selling author, consultant, and coach Ferrazzi provides a convincing argument why one cannot "win" alone and offers a step-by-step guide for lowering one's guard, using "sparring" as a productive tool, and building deeper and more trusting relationships.

Hill, L. A., & Lineback, K. (2011). *Being the boss: The 3 imperatives for becoming a great leader.* Boston, MA: Harvard Business Review Press.

Hill and Lineback explain why and how your reputation impacts the people you manage, the quality of their work, their loyalty and commitment, and their willingness to make personal sacrifices for the good of their teams and organizations.

The Arbinger Institute. (2010). *Leadership and self-deception: Getting out of the box.* San Francisco, CA: Berrett-Koehler.

The Arbinger Institute argues that self-deception determines one's experience in every aspect of life. The extent to which it does the preceding and, in particular, the extent to which it is the central issue in leadership, is the subject of this best-selling book.

Sample Coaching Program (Case 2—Phil)

Phil's profile indicates a Skeptical score of 96 percent. The subscale scores associated with this—Cynical, Mistrusting, and Grudges—are all elevated to the maximum level. In the past, Phil's Skeptical scale score and the associated behaviors were rewarded. His previous boss appreciated that Phil could anticipate every potential problem and deliver bad news. However, as the situation shifted and Phil's boss was replaced, the goals for Phil's role also shifted. The associated Skeptical behaviors made it challenging for Phil to adjust to the new priorities and style of a different boss, one who values collaboration and partnering. Phil will need to change the way he approaches his role and, as important, will need to repair and redefine existing relationships. Phil's high Reserved score will make engaging in these new behaviors even more challenging.

The starting point in this coaching relationship is for the coach to establish trust with Phil. The coach can begin by encouraging Phil to talk about what his goals are for the coaching engagement, as well as his broader career aspirations. The coach should also determine Phil's perspective on the best way he can be supported. This information should be included in the formal, written agreement outlining the coaching engagement.

The approach to Phil's coaching should include the following:

- Have Phil outline the priorities of his role so they align with his new boss's priorities. Ask Phil to look at the role as a vacant position. Ask the question, "What attributes would you look for in a person to fill this role?" Help Phil build the perspective that his role has changed significantly and is essentially a new position. Ask him, "What will you need to do to meet the challenges of the role?"

- Ask Phil to identify the strengths and capabilities he brings to this redefined role that will support his success. Help Phil reflect on how he will demonstrate these attributes and how he intends to build trust with his new boss.

- Review various interactions with Phil and ask him to retell stories while working to assume and demonstrate positive intent. Help Phil expand the possibilities that come with this shift.

- Have Phil build a list of key stakeholders and reflect on the value he can get from each one. Ask Phil to push himself to identify at least one point of added value for each person.

- Role play various scenarios with Phil to help him practice shifting his emphasis from what might be wrong to what is right. Help him develop questions that can lead others to see issues on their own and make adjustments before there is a problem.

- Ask Phil to practice taking a moment to pause in tense situations and ask, "Is this a battle worth fighting? Is it important to be right in this instance?"

SUMMARY

Keep Doing

Analyze and try to understand the motives and intentions of others.

Stop Doing

Approach the world in a negative, cynical, glass-half-empty fashion.

Start Doing

Look for the positive aspects in people and situations.

High Skeptical behaviors can hinder leaders from being effective and progressing in their careers. Highly skeptical individuals generally are seen as negative and do not build a foundation of positive relationships, resulting in difficulty building followership, alliances, and collaboration—all of which are required for long-term career success. Changing these behaviors requires highly skeptical leaders to shift their belief system about people or, at the very least, work to see people through a different lens—a lens that is not as tainted by mistrust and an expectation that others are out to do them wrong. Coaching these leaders can be challenging because their natural tendency is to look at the world and other people from a glass-half-empty perspective. It takes considerable effort for these leaders to go beyond behavior change and make a change in their belief system, which is essential for long-term career success.

LOW SKEPTICAL

Detecting When It Is a Problem

Low Skeptical behaviors may not be readily evident early in a leader's tenure and may, in fact, result in a leader's being seen as open, approachable, and willing to see the best in everyone. Gandhi might be an example of a low Skeptical individual. Gandhi was known for his trusting nature and proclivity to see the positive in each individual and every situation. While Gandhi may have been an inspiration to many, one might wonder how successful his outlook would have been inside a Fortune 500 company. Leaders in organizations must be able to navigate the political environment. While they need not be overly cynical or paranoid, they do need to evaluate the range of consequences in situations rather than assume the best outcome or that all involved have the noblest of motives. Being overly naïve can result in missing potential problems, being taken advantage of, and not being as aware of the undercurrents of the organization as necessary for a savvy leader. Additionally, leaders with low Skeptical scores may have difficulty accurately assessing team members, seeing only the best in individuals who may or may not be performing effectively. Over time, these leaders can develop a reputation for being poor at evaluating talent or unwilling to address performance problems.

Mark from Case 6—Mark, District Account Manager on page 98 provides a good example of a low Skeptical profile. The following is Mark's profile summary:

Mark's Situational Summary				
Mark is a long-tenured district account manager for a consumer products company. A significant change in his account portfolio brought a number of new government accounts under his control. These customers were no-nonsense type customers who had little interest in his affable nature and tendency to exaggerate to garner attention.				
Dimension	**Score**	**Percentile**		**Description**
Excitable	68			Mark is a high-energy person who brings a lot of passion to the business (Excitable—68%). He can be highly colorful (Colorful—91%) to the point of being overbearing at times. His colorful behavior extends into his tendency to exaggerate issues or problems and his role in solving them. He also has a tendency to miss details or fail to follow up on important issues (Diligent—10%).
Skeptical	15			
Cautious	29			
Reserved	42			
Leisurely	19			
Bold	24			
Mischievous	70			
Colorful	91			
Imaginative	29			
Diligent	10			
Dutiful	45			

0 10 20 30 40 50 60 70 80 90 100

Mark provides an example of the pitfalls of being a low Skeptical leader. Over the course of his career, Mark built trusting relationships with his clients. They knew him well, knew what to expect from him, and tolerated his high Colorful behavior. His organization viewed Mark as a loyal employee, and Mark trusted and supported the leadership team. When the company revenues began dropping, layoffs commenced. Mark seemed unaware of the impact of these developments. He survived the initial round of cuts, but then his role was changed, and he was asked to assume responsibility for government accounts. Mark's low Skeptical score may present some challenges in his new circumstances. Mark may be too ready to assume that his new customers will be transparent, and he may not be aware of the politics of working with the government bureaucracy. He is likely to approach and interact with his new customers in exactly the same way he dealt with his previous customers and not see the downside of one-size-fits-all approaches. Additionally, Mark seems to have missed the cues about the urgency behind the recent changes in his organization. The leadership team might have supported him in the past while he produced the requisite bottom-line results. But now, Mark needs to carefully consider how best to navigate the new political landscape of his organization. Assuming that the leadership will continue to support him may be naïve. Mark may be in danger of being included in the next round of layoffs.

Evaluating the Need for Change

The following behavioral questions should be considered in conjunction with a leader's low Skeptical score (as exhibited by Mark) when evaluating the need for a change in behavior. A "yes" response to three or fewer items suggests that there is no imminent need for behavioral changes. A "yes" response to four to six items suggests that a low score on the Skeptical scale should be a watch-out for a leader. A "yes" response to more than six items suggests that a leader should take active steps toward making behavioral changes.

Does the leader:

1. Appear overly optimistic even when the situation suggests otherwise?	Yes	No	Not Sure
2. Accept people at face value without ever questioning their motives?	Yes	No	Not Sure
3. Ignore or deny the existence of politics in the workplace?	Yes	No	Not Sure
4. Appear to trust people even when their behavior suggests that they have ulterior motives?	Yes	No	Not Sure
5. Seem to get taken advantage of by others?	Yes	No	Not Sure

6. Appear to be naïve when it comes to the motives of others?   **Yes   No   Not Sure**

7. Forgive people even when they have done nothing to warrant forgiveness?   **Yes   No   Not Sure**

8. Fail to recognize when people are only out for their own self-interests?   **Yes   No   Not Sure**

9. Take people at their word even when their past actions suggest otherwise?   **Yes   No   Not Sure**

These items should be considered as behavioral indicators. Similar or associated behaviors to any of those listed that are exhibited by a leader likely suggest a "yes" response. They provide additional support that a leader may be at risk for the negative reputational consequences associated with those scoring low on the Skeptical scale, such as Mark.

Impact of Low Skeptical Behaviors

Successful leaders acknowledge the politics present in every organization and learn how to navigate political waters to achieve high-impact results. Politically savvy leaders build strategic relationships and develop strong advocates and alliances. While being overly political is problematic, not being political at all often results in a leader who is ineffective in many arenas. Low Skeptical individuals are likely to miss the political cues in an organization and assume that they have support where none may exist. These individuals may also be described as unable to make the tough calls or too nice and unaware of the unstated issues. They are less likely to enforce performance standards and will accept excuses from underperforming employees. At the same time, these individuals may not be able to advocate for and support their employees (or their own careers) with opportunities, resources, or endorsements. The following are some of the consequences of low Skeptical behaviors, broken out by three constituencies: managers, peers, and direct reports.

Managers

Managers may view low Skeptical leaders in a positive way, highlighting their likeability factor and appreciating their loyalty. However, managers may also view leaders of this type as gullible and naïve. Because most senior-level roles require a significant degree of political savvy, low Skeptical leaders who have a reputation for being gullible and naïve will not be considered qualified or ready for such roles. Furthermore, managers are unlikely to turn to these individuals to handle politically sensitive situations or assignments that involve organizational savvy. Low Skeptical leaders also run the risk of being too trusting of their managers when it comes to support or career advocacy. They simply believe that their managers will have their best interests at heart, and that very well may not be the case.

Peers

Peers may view low Skeptical leaders as easy to get along with or likeable. However, peers will also recognize the overly trusting nature of low Skeptical individuals and use it to their benefit. For example, peers may choose to take advantage of these leaders to gather more resources, obtain high-profile assignments, or, more often, duck onerous assignments by passing them along to these gullible, naïve individuals. Most organizations have politically savvy employees. These employees inevitably seek out peers who exhibit low Skeptical behaviors and do their best to subjugate them in pursuit of their own self-interests.

Direct Reports

Direct reports may find that a general lack of accountability makes it easy to offer excuses to low Skeptical leaders without repercussions. Missed deadlines or low-quality work may be accepted by a low Skeptical leader if it comes with a personal plea by the direct report. Other team members may see that lower standards are tolerated and begin to model similar behaviors. Additionally, team members will recognize these leaders are not adept at navigating the organization to garner support and resources for their teams, resulting in frustration and low morale. An interesting corollary to the way low Skeptical leaders treat underperforming team members is the way they defend these individuals to peers and superiors. Defending team members when their behavior suggests they do not deserve it further reinforces the reputation of these leaders as being gullible and naïve.

Coaching Focus

Leaders who exhibit low Skeptical behaviors are typically relationship oriented, good-natured, and overly optimistic. The coaching focus should be to support these leaders to enhance their self-awareness and more clearly see the problematic aspects of these behaviors. Being able to understand the negative impact of these behaviors on relationships and team vitality might be instrumental in motivating the leaders to make some changes.

Coaching Strategy

Helping low Skeptical leaders understand the impact of their behavior and become more aware of their optimistic lens will enhance self-awareness and set the stage for new behavioral strategies. Gathering feedback from their colleagues can help them better understand their impact or lack of impact. Because these individuals often accept things as presented, they are likely to receive feedback that they need to exhibit more behaviors typically associated with raising standards and expectations. To facilitate changes of this type, these individuals should be asked to develop a set of tools that will help them look below the surface of interactions and verbal messages. Continued practice with these tools will make new behaviors more routine.

A starting point with a low Skeptical leader would be to review some recent, impactful interactions—interactions that may have had serious, negative consequences. The purpose of the review is to help the leader consider what more could have been uncovered from these interactions or how the outcomes may have shifted with a deeper level of understanding of the stakes involved. The leader should consider how doing this might enhance relationships even further. Examples of behavior that led to negative consequences or outcomes can help illustrate for the leader the importance of accurate situational awareness and the career-limiting impact of benign, superficial situational acceptance. The leader should also be encouraged to ask "what if" with the coach regularly modeling this approach when situations are reviewed or discussed. Modeling the what-if and what-else questions will help the leader see the value in them and can help the leader learn to ask these questions in a way that avoids creating defensiveness. Additionally, the leader should be encouraged to develop a set of questions that can be used in many situations to trust, but verify.

Strategy Refinements Using Subscale Information

The subscales provide clues as to where to put the coaching emphasis. The subscales for Skeptical include Cynical, Mistrusting, and Grudges. At the extreme low end of these subscales, there are likely to be behaviors that can result in a reputation for being overly optimistic, naïve, and lacking in managerial toughness. The consequences of this set of behaviors will likely be cumulative and point to a leader who may not be seen as having courage and clarity of purpose.

Cynical

With no elevation on the Cynical subscale, it is likely that a low Skeptical leader is overly optimistic with an expectation that things will turn out well. This positivity may result in being less likely to plan for contingencies and being seen as not anticipating potential issues, which can culminate in a reputation for being caught off-guard when problems arise or for not seeing around corners on complex issues. The coaching refinement here involves having the leader develop a practice of asking what-if questions and building contingency plans, regardless of the leader's perceived need for such planning.

Mistrusting

Lower subscale results on Mistrusting generally point to an individual who assumes positive intent. Although this seems like an attribute that would facilitate relationships, the consequence is that the low Skeptical leader may not appreciate the need to hold people accountable. Even when experience indicates otherwise, a leader low on this subscale will continue to accept reassurances to the point of being seen as just plain naïve. A sound coaching refinement with respect to this subscale involves helping the low Skeptical leader view holding people accountable as a positive, not punitive, measure that will promote team productivity.

Grudges

No elevation on the Grudges subscale indicates an individual who may be taken advantage of repeatedly. Regardless of how a prior interaction may have concluded, a leader low on this subscale will anticipate that this time it will be different; this time it will be successful. This positive outlook further contributes to a reputation of naiveté. The classic comic strip "Charlie Brown" comes to mind with respect to this subscale. No matter how many times Lucy encouraged him to take a run at kicking the football—only to have her yank it away at the last second—good ole' Charlie Brown just kept saying to himself, "This time, it will be different!" The key coaching emphasis with respect to this subscale involves working with the leader to develop a checklist of questions he or she can use to better assess situations and relationships and thereby engage differently with those who have been problematic in previous interactions or encounters.

Coaching Tactics

Coaching tactics cover a range of approaches and resources that have been found useful in addressing low Skeptical behaviors. These tactics are typically used in combination to form a custom plan suited to the specific learning needs of a leader. The tactics are divided into four categories: (1) thought-provoking questions for a leader to consider, (2) exercises a leader can engage in to improve performance, (3) tips and techniques a coach can use to help a leader improve performance, and (4) support resources that can be consulted to gain additional insights in addressing low Skeptical behaviors.

Thought-Provoking Questions for a Leader

- Describe a decision or action that did not turn out positively that could have had a better outcome if you had asked more questions ahead of time. If you had asked more questions, how would the outcome have been more positive? What will you do differently next time?

- Using what you learned from the preceding bulleted item, identify an upcoming project where probing more deeply upfront will have a positive impact the outcome. What questions will you pose?

- How do you know when you can trust someone, and how do you verify that?

- What words come to mind when we talk about "influencing" or "political savvy"?

- How do you know when someone has earned your trust? How do you know when someone has earned your distrust?

Exercises for a Leader

- Think about a leader who effectively demonstrates the concept of "trust, but verify." What do you admire about this leader's approach?

- List some bullet points that describe critical feedback. List some bullet points that describe the impact on the team and team members when this type of feedback is not provided.

- Design a set of questions that elicit information needed to evaluate and check on projects and identify potential roadblocks to success (for example, "Are you sure you can do this?" or "Is there enough time?").

- Develop a "political savvy" map listing key influencers and indicating their potential impact on your career, along with the level of support you believe you receive from them.

- Develop a personal set of what-if questions that you can easily use to enhance your situational understanding as opportunities arise.

Tips and Techniques for a Coach

- Ask the leader to select an upcoming project or assignment. Work with the leader to develop a set of questions that can be used to gain an appropriate level of situational understanding. Include with the questions the names of the stakeholders from whom input is needed on the project or assignment. After the leader has had an opportunity to use the questions, ask the leader what information he or she obtained through the questions, and what impact the information had on the leader's situational understanding.

- Role play a negotiation scenario in which the leader needs to achieve a balanced outcome or a win-win solution.

- Role play a performance review in which the leader has to deliver negative feedback and set appropriate expectations for an improvement in performance.

- Work with the leader to identify a situation where critical feedback would be valuable. Create and implement a plan to provide that feedback.

- Work with the leader to identify an individual in the organization who makes effective use of political skills or demonstrates political savvy. Define the political behaviors demonstrated by this individual and how the leader might incorporate similar behaviors to achieve a political advantage.

Support Resources

Browne, M. N., & Keeley, S. M. (2014). *Asking the right questions* (11th ed.) [Kindle edition]. Retrieved from Amazon.com

Browne and Keeley's concise book provides readers actionable guidance for enhancing critical thinking skills and identifying inconsistencies.

Connors, R., & Smith, T. (2011). *How did that happen?: Holding people accountable for results the positive, principled way.* **New York, NY: Penguin.**

Experts on workplace accountability and authors of the best-selling book, "The Oz Principle," Connors and Smith tackle the next crucial step everyone and anyone (e.g., managers, supervisors, CEOs, or individual contributors) can take in "How Did That Happen?"—instilling greater accountability in all the people you depend upon.

DeLuca, J. R. (2002). *Political savvy: Systematic approaches to leadership behind the scenes.* **Berwyn, PA: EBG Publications.**

DeLuca describes tactics employed by ethical leaders, helps readers identify their own political styles, and offers an efficient and actionable guide to navigating murky political waters.

Grimshaw, J., & Baron, G. (2010). *Leadership without excuses: How to create accountability and high-performance.* **New York, NY: McGraw Hill.**

Grimshaw and Baron detail how leaders can help generally good (but less-than-fully accountable) employees drastically decrease their use of excuses and markedly improve their performance.

Hanson, T., & Hanson, B. Z. (2007). *Who will do what by when? How to improve performance, accountability and trust with integrity.* **Tampa, FL: Power Publications.**

True to their book's title, Hanson and Hanson present a holistic system for improving trust, accountability, and performance within the context of an engaging parable.

Marquardt, M. J. (2014). *Leading with questions: How leaders find the right solutions by knowing what to ask.* **San Francisco, CA: Jossey-Bass.**

Marquardt describes how asking the right questions can encourage participation and teamwork, foster forward thinking, empower people, build relationships, and solve problems. Both directly and indirectly via interviews with thirty esteemed leaders, Marquardt's book helps readers determine which questions can spark solutions to their most challenging problems.

Maxwell, J. C. (2014). *Good leaders ask great questions: Your foundation for successful leadership.* **New York, NY: Hachette.**

Maxwell makes a strong case for the power of questions and why questioning should not be underutilized. He explains how questions can have a marked impact on leadership and discusses the questions leaders should be asking their teams.

Sample Coaching Program (Case 6—Mark)

Mark's Skeptical scale indicates a score of 15 percent. An examination of his subscale scores indicates that Cynical and Mistrusting are at the very low end of the scale. The case information presented about Mark indicates that his addressing his low Skeptical score may not be the top priority for his success in his current position. However, for Mark to continue in his role, be successful, and help his company sustain their business, he will need to shift some of his low Skeptical behaviors. Based on prior results, Mark has demonstrated sales capability, and it is likely that his organization is looking to him to contribute significantly to revenue production. The following are the proposed steps for this aspect of the coaching engagement with Mark:

1. Ask Mark to reflect on how his low Skeptical behaviors have supported his success and when they have created difficulties for him in achieving his goals.

2. Ask Mark to describe how he views other individuals when engaging in a relationship. Ask what might be important to the individual that Mark may not see or be aware of. Have Mark practice with different scenarios to ascertain what might be important to know besides what is right on the surface of an interaction.

3. Ask Mark to look ahead and assess what it takes to be successful in his organization—what might be obvious and what might not be obvious?

4. Have Mark build a list of key organizational decision makers and assess the state of his relationships with each. From this assessment, Mark can design an action plan to enhance needed support.

5. Have Mark do some work between sessions to identify someone who demonstrates the concept of trust, but verify, and ask Mark to consider how he might best employ this approach.

SUMMARY

Keep Doing

Be open to seeing the positive in people and building trust-based relationships.

Stop Doing

Naïvely make the assumption that all is well in every circumstance.

Start Doing

Practice looking below the surface and probing to consider alternative possibilities.

The risks associated with a low Skeptical score often emerge over time. The negative consequences of low Skeptical behaviors tend to have a cumulative effect. As time passes, the low Skeptical leader is more and more often labeled as less effective. The self-awareness necessary to develop a repertoire of alternative approaches and behaviors can be developed over time. They often require the leader to recognize that these behaviors, while appearing negative or even questioning others' trustworthiness, often have a positive outcome. Furthermore, the leader needs to learn that developing political or organizational savvy can be accomplished without becoming deceitful or untrustworthy.

CHAPTER 12

CAUTIOUS

HIGH CAUTIOUS

Detecting When It Is a Problem

High Cautious behaviors are common in the corporate world and may even be encouraged by leaders in corporate cultures that value accuracy, compliance, top-down decision-making, and the avoidance of mistakes.

Individuals with elevated Cautious scores are likely to appear timid, unassertive, indecisive, and lacking in confidence. These high Cautious behaviors can impact people's perceptions of the leaders' competence, credibility, and overall leadership presence. Team members at all levels—including their bosses—are likely to be frustrated with the inability of high Cautious leaders to make timely decisions as well as their inability to take a firm stand when needed.

One recent example of a high Cautious individual involves former Japanese Prime Minister Yukio Hatoyama. Hailing from a Kennedy-like Japanese political family—and having served in a variety of government roles as a career politician—Hatoyama would have seemed to possess the perfect background for the top leadership role in his country's government. In fact, he was swept into office in

September 2009, with an unprecedented majority of the vote. However, he resigned his office in disgrace in June 2010, barely nine months into his term.

What was the cause of his demise? In a nutshell, it was his indecisiveness as a leader, along with changing his initial opinions on key issues when faced with any kind of opposition or setbacks. Early decisions were often reconsidered and then changed. Hatoyama was seen as being a flip-flopper on key domestic issues. Soon, the voting public lost faith in his credibility as a leader.

People want leaders who are capable of making tough decisions and who then lead them forward. People will often forgive leaders who make the occasional mistake, but they insist on leaders who are decisive. Hatoyama failed to appreciate the importance of decisiveness in determining the credibility of a leader.

While Prime Minister Hatoyama provides an international, high-profile example of high Cautious behavior, what form does this behavior take in day-to-day corporate settings? James from Case 7—James, Marketing Manager on page 100 provides a good example of a high Cautious profile. James's highest score on the HDS is on the Dutiful scale (90%), but his score on the Cautious scale is close behind at 85 percent. Taken together, these elevations underscore a lack of decisiveness, an unwillingness to take a stand, overall unassertiveness, and an elevated need to require affirmation or support from others before moving forward. The following is James's profile summary.

James's Situational Summary			
James was the marketing manager for a small family-owned business that was sold to a well-established technology company. After the sale, James moved on to a small, fast-moving start-up technology company. He had clear challenges with his ability to get things moving in the new company. His high Cautious score will have a direct impact on the speed with which he makes decisions that may be in conflict with a fast-moving start-up company.			
Dimension	**Score**	**Percentile**	**Description**
Excitable	10		James is a laid-back, even-tempered marketing guy (Excitable—10%). It takes him a long time to get to know and trust people (Skeptical—70%), and he is guarded and slow to make decisions (Cautious—85% and Mischievous—15%). James doesn't make a big impression on people. In fact, he is best known for his loyalty and willingness to do whatever the owners asked (Dutiful—90%).
Skeptical	70		
Cautious	85		
Reserved	25		
Leisurely	19		
Bold	24		
Mischievous	15		
Colorful	45		
Imaginative	35		
Diligent	50		
Dutiful	90		

          0   10   20   30   40   50   60   70   80   90   100

As detailed in the situational information above, James's elevations on both the Cautious and Dutiful scales are likely to be problematic in his new role with the fast paced technology company that is in start-up mode. While these elevations may not have been major concerns in his previous company, where his meticulous nature and emphasis on avoiding mistakes were actually rewarded, his inability to make quick decisions and make strong recommendations will likely result in negative outcomes in his new role.

Evaluating the Need for Change

The following behavioral questions should be considered in conjunction with a leader's high Cautious score (as exhibited by James) when evaluating the need for a change in behavior. A "yes" response to three or fewer items suggests that there is no imminent need for behavioral changes. A "yes" response to four to six items suggests that a high score on the Cautious scale should be a watch-out for a leader. A "yes" response to more than six items suggests that a leader should take active steps toward making behavioral changes.

Does the leader:

1.	Have a hard time expressing opinions that are unpopular or out of the mainstream?	Yes	No	Not Sure
2.	Have difficulty expressing views in front of strangers or unfamiliar groups?	Yes	No	Not Sure
3.	Seem reluctant to ask others for favors or support even when it is clearly needed?	Yes	No	Not Sure
4.	Worry about making a mistake or hesitate in taking action when the risk of a mistake exists?	Yes	No	Not Sure
5.	Lack self-confidence or vacillate when the time for a decision is due (or overdue)?	Yes	No	Not Sure
6.	Use excessive data collection or ask employees for additional legwork in order to avoid making a decision?	Yes	No	Not Sure
7.	Fail to take a stand or voice an opinion when there is disagreement or controversy regarding a decision?	Yes	No	Not Sure
8.	Seem to take a backseat when important decisions are being discussed or being made?	Yes	No	Not Sure
9.	Easily back down when an opinion is challenged or contrary views are expressed?	Yes	No	Not Sure

These items should be considered as behavioral indicators. Similar or associated behaviors to any of those listed that are exhibited by a leader likely suggest a "yes" response.

They provide additional support that a leader may be at risk for the negative reputational consequences associated with those scoring high on the Cautious scale, such as James.

Impact of High Cautious Behaviors

High Cautious behaviors not only negatively impact an individual's day-to-day performance; they also negatively impact a leader's reputation because such a leader is likely to be viewed as somebody who simply cannot get things done. In addition to being seen as indecisive, highly cautious individuals are likely to be resistant to change and also likely to focus on the negative outcomes associated with taking risks. Those with high Cautious scores may also be overshadowed in meetings by those who are more action-oriented and direct, who in turn will find work-arounds to avoid involving high Cautious individuals in key projects and activities. The following are typical perspectives of three of the high Cautious leader's constituents: managers, peers, and direct reports.

Managers

Most managers will become frustrated with the inability of high Cautious employees to make independent and timely decisions as well as their general lack of assertiveness. Frequently, those with high Cautious scores need constant reassurance from a manager before making a decision, and even then may have a hard time being decisive.

Managers may inadvertently encourage high Cautious behaviors if they are overly critical of the mistakes made by their staff or if they lapse into micromanagement of their team. Managers need to critically examine their own behaviors to ensure that they are not encouraging any of the high Cautious behaviors among their direct reports or other team members.

Peers

Peers are quick to recognize high Cautious leaders as nonentities when it comes to important decision-making. If the high Cautious leader is in a position to slow down or block the progress of a key initiative, peers will find ways to avoid involving the leader in that initiative. As a result, communication and coordination between and within departments suffer. Frequently, peers will begin making their own decisions in areas that should be addressed by the high Cautious leaders.

Direct Reports

Direct reports of high Cautious leaders are likely to feel disempowered as they quickly recognize that their leader will not be an advocate for them or their ideas. While some direct reports will assert themselves and start making more independent decisions, others will actually use their leader's reticence to make decisions as an excuse for their own low levels of initiative. Frequently, high Cautious leaders lack respect among their direct reports.

Coaching Focus

High Cautious behaviors can be part of a leader's natural tendencies, in which case the coaching focus can be on the individual. Sometimes the highly cautious behaviors can be the result of organizational factors, which may require an organizational intervention. The most challenging situation is when the leader's high Cautious behaviors are reinforced by organizational factors. In any case, organizational factors that may increase the number of high Cautious behaviors being exhibited by an individual should be investigated. Does the individual have a boss who is controlling or a micromanager? Is the organization (or the person's manager) unforgiving about mistakes? Is there a culture where it is better to not make a decision than to make a decision that is incorrect? Are there major consequences for errors made by the individual, either because of specific job duties or the specific industry?

Coaching Strategy

There are five basic steps associated with the coaching strategy for those scoring high on the Cautious scale. First, increase the leader's self-awareness of what form the cautious behaviors take at work, including documenting specific examples of behavior and the circumstances contributing to the behavior. Second, analyze the themes, situations, corporate culture factors, people, and so on that trigger high Cautious behaviors. Third, identify strategies that reduce the probability of exhibiting these behaviors. Fourth, ask the leader to implement the strategies, with an emphasis on those situations where being indecisive and unassertive are having the most negative impact. Fifth, the coach and leader should evaluate the strategies that have been implemented for effectiveness and impact.

Strategy Refinements Using Subscale Information

The subscales offer insights as to how the coaching strategy might be refined to improve the effectiveness of the intervention. The subscales for Cautious include Avoidant, Fearful, and Unassertive. Coaches can use this subscale information to focus their follow-up questions about a leader's specific behaviors, and should also use this information to tailor their developmental recommendations.

Avoidant

Individuals with high scores on the Avoidant subscale avoid new people and new situations due to general awkwardness. They may avoid speaking up or participating in meetings with people they do not know well, or with whom they are not comfortable. These high Cautious individuals may avoid taking on new projects or assignments and may be less willing to push themselves to accomplish goals in areas with which they are not familiar. The key to coaching behaviors associated with this subscale involves identifying opportunities for the leader to interact with others more frequently and actively participate in meetings, task forces, committee assignments, and so on. Particular attention should be given to putting the leader in situations that are outside of his or her normal comfort zone (i.e., stretch assignments) involving both different tasks and different people.

Fearful

Individuals with high scores on the Fearful subscale avoid making independent decisions out of a fear of making mistakes and a fear of being judged or criticized. These individuals may not only be seen as indecisive, but they may also be seen as relying too much on data and analysis and not using their own judgment and experience when making decisions. Coaching those with high scores on the Fearful subscale generally involves analyzing past successes and failures and the criticism that resulted from those failures. Coaches can also reinforce the successes the leader has had and use those successes as a basis for encouraging more independent decision-making. Further, coaches can take steps to ensure that key stakeholders (such as the leader's manager) will be supportive of the leader's efforts even if all decisions do not turn out to be totally correct.

Unassertive

Individuals with high scores on the Unassertive subscale are reluctant to assert themselves and will not stand up for what they believe. This behavior can occur even in areas where the individual is a subject-matter expert, and in situations where corroborating information exists that supports the individual's point of view. These individuals are also prone to be exploited by others. Coaches should identify two to three areas where the leader can take a more active and assertive role and provide guidance on how to demonstrate greater involvement in or influence over these areas.

Coaching Tactics

Coaching tactics cover a range of approaches and resources that have been found useful in addressing high Cautious behaviors. These tactics are typically used in combination to form a custom plan suited to the specific learning needs of a leader. The tactics are divided into four categories: (1) thought-provoking questions for a leader to consider, (2) exercises a leader can engage in to improve performance, (3) tips and techniques a coach can use to help a leader improve performance, and (4) support resources that can be consulted to gain additional insights in addressing high Cautious behaviors.

Thought-Provoking Questions for a Leader

- What steps do you take when assessing risk? Are you more likely to focus on the negative aspects resulting from unsuccessful change or focus more on the positive impact from change?

- What areas have been described by your leadership team and other key stakeholders as areas in need of change?

- Are your manager and your organization in general receptive to change? Does your corporate culture facilitate or inhibit risk taking?

- How can you best identify areas where change is needed? What types of change are important to you, and what positive outcomes could you see from such changes?

- Do others see you as a decisive leader? Why or why not?

- Do you have a clear understanding of where your decision-making authority starts, and where it stops? Do you know the decisions that you have the authority to make versus those decisions your manager wants to review before action is taken?

- How do you handle situations where you need to make a quick decision when facts or data are not available?

- Do you always need to get a second—or third—opinion before moving forward with a decision?

Exercises for a Leader

- Reflect on past successes. Make a list of the decisions you made that turned out to be correct and the special insights that you brought to these decisions. Use this list to build confidence in your decision-making abilities.

- Prioritize and set deadlines. Identify three to four critical decisions that you need to make, and then set deadlines for when you will make them. Use these deadlines as a way of limiting the amount of time that you spend on data-gathering and analysis.

- Identify and articulate your worst case scenario. What is the worst outcome that can occur if you make an incorrect decision? Sometimes articulating a worst-case scenario can allow for a more realistic assessment of the negatives associated with an incorrect decision.

- Identify two to three areas where you can display a higher level of assertiveness in your current role. List specific behaviors that you will engage in to help with assertiveness, and get feedback from colleagues on whether they see improvement in your assertiveness.

- Identify a meeting situation in which you would normally be reluctant to express your opinion. Ahead of time, outline a specific position or opinion that you believe needs to be expressed and discussed. Follow your outline and assert yourself in the meeting. Then, after the meeting, ask a trusted source for feedback about your performance.

Tips and Techniques for a Coach

- Help the leader understand there are costs associated with either delaying or not making a decision. These may involve opportunity costs as well as a cost to the leader's reputation and perceived competence by others.

- Ensure the leader has not overestimated the negative consequences associated with an incorrect decision.

- Work with the leader and the manager to ensure there is a clear understanding of where the leader's decision-making authority starts and where it stops. In a joint meeting, identify a few areas where the leader will take a more active and decisive role.

- Discuss how enhanced learning and experience can come with decisions that turn out to be incorrect. Take steps to ensure the leader's manager will be supportive of decisions even if they should turn out to be incorrect. Meeting separately with the manager to verify his or her support may be necessary.

- Identify a mentor or role model who can provide informal feedback on key decisions, and take steps to ensure the leader uses this information to supplement decision-making efforts.

Support Resources

Farber, S. (2004). *Radical leap: A personal lesson in extreme leadership.* Poway, CA: Mission Boulevard.

Hailed as one of the "100 Best Business Books of All Time," Farber describes a leadership model to aspire to—one that does not frighten leaders into shunning risks, avoiding mistakes at all costs, or, despite good intentions, paying lip service to employee input.

George, M. L., & Wilson, S. A. (2004). *Conquering complexity in your business: How Wal-Mart, Toyota, and other top companies are breaking through the ceiling on profits and growth.* New York, NY: McGraw Hill.

Six Sigma and Lean production experts, George and Wilson, make a convincing case that every business harbors unnecessary cost-inflating and profit-draining complexity, and offer methods for increasing efficiency, cutting costs, and improving resource use in corporate environments.

Heath, R. (2009). *Celebrating failure: The power of taking risks, making mistakes, and thinking big.* Pompton Plains, NY: Career Press.

Heath offers readers tactics they can employ to reframe failure as a valuable learning tool and convincingly argues that "positive failures" can be springboards to beneficial change and success.

Jiang, J. (2015). *Rejection proof: How I beat fear and became invincible through 100 days of rejection.* New York, NY: Penguin.

Jiang offers practical lessons learned during his "100 days of rejection experiment," including secrets of successful requests, strategies for picking targets, how to determine when an initial "no" can be transformed into a "yes," techniques for handling rejection, and confidence-building strategies.

Klein, M., & Napier, R. (2003). *The courage to act: 5 factors of courage to transform business.* Palo Alto, CA: Davies-Black.

Based on fieldwork conducted across four continents, Klein and Napier offer a simple yet elegant model for gauging, promoting, teaching, and embodying courage. Readers will benefit from a thorough description of the factors needed to effectively manage ambiguity, face adversity, capitalize on fleeting opportunities, and work through conflict.

Patterson, R. J. (2014). *The assertiveness workbook: How to express your ideas and stand up for yourself at work and in relationships.* Oakland, CA: New Harbinger.

Patterson's highly rated workbook explains how to establish and sustain personal boundaries without becoming unapproachable, and offers readily applicable cognitive behavioral techniques capable of fostering increased assertiveness.

Tichy, N. M., & Bennis, W. G. (2009). *Judgment: How winning leaders make great calls.* New York, NY: Penguin.

Tichy and Bennis, consultants and advisors to prominent CEOs, offer a framework for making tough calls when stakes, pressure, and ambiguity are high. Their book teaches readers how to identify pivotal moments during the decision-making process, determine when decisive action is vital, and how to effectively execute and move forward once key decisions have been made.

Sample Coaching Program (Case 7—James)

James from Case 7 provides an example of a high Cautious profile. His high score on the Cautious scale (85%) is exceeded only by his elevated score on the Dutiful scale (90%). An analysis of his subscale scores shows maximum elevations on the Fearful and Unassertive subscales with no elevation on the Avoidant subscale. Therefore, James's reticence to make key decisions in his role with the new company is not due to general unease when interacting with his new coworkers but is, instead, due to his fear of making mistakes and his overall unassertiveness. The case information shows that a lack of specific guidance from the new leadership team greatly contributed to James's lack of decisiveness. As such, the coaching program should focus on role clarification, on setting clear expectations on the issues that James is expected to handle on his own, and on actions designed to boost James's confidence. The following steps will be beneficial in this situation:

- Ask James to outline areas where he can take on a leadership role, including being more assertive and more decisive.
- Have James list the current areas where he is facing key decisions, and then have him provide a suggested course of action for each.
- Meet with James and his manager to review the information gleaned from steps 1 and 2, and jointly decide on a course of action for each.
- Ask the manager to outline additional areas where James can be more decisive, including support the manager is willing to provide when decisions need to be made.

- Ask the manager to explain his or her approach to risk taking and dealing with mistakes. James is now part of a newer and fast-growing organization, and chances are the corporate culture is more forgiving of mistakes. Gain clarity on this in a discussion with the manager.

- Ask James to compile a list of his major successes, with a particular emphasis on those situations where he had unique insights or where he demonstrated decisiveness. Ask James to review this list regularly as a way of increasing his self-confidence about his decision-making abilities.

SUMMARY

Keep Doing

Review plans and proposals thoughtfully for feasibility and unnecessary risks.

Stop Doing

Hold up progress due to indecisiveness and a lack of assertiveness.

Start Doing

Provide suggestions and solutions instead of simply raising objections.

High Cautious behaviors are readily observable, and leaders who exhibit these behaviors are often passed over for promotions or surpassed by peers who are more action-oriented and dynamic. Changing a leader's reputation in this area involves identifying and structuring situations where the leader can be more assertive and more decisive. Success often begets success, and once the high Cautious leader begins making progress in this area, future progress will rapidly follow. Gaining the support of the leader's manager is an integral step when working with a high Cautious leader, and an assessment of the degree to which the corporate culture supports risk and change is also an important step. It is more difficult to enact behavioral change in a high Cautious leader if the organizational dynamics do not support risk taking or change. However, once the boundaries or limits are known, the behavior of a high Cautious leader can be stretched to make the most of decision-making opportunities.

LOW CAUTIOUS

Detecting When It Is a Problem

Low Cautious behaviors—including making rapid decisions without an appropriate level of data-gathering, analysis, or reflection—are not only difficult to detect but may be encouraged by corporate cultures that reward action-oriented and decisive behavior.

Low Cautious leaders often escape being held accountable for the outcome of their decisions. The rapidity with which individuals change roles in organizations—let alone the speed with which people change organizations—may mean that low Cautious leaders are long gone by the time the ramifications of their decisions become apparent. The leader-like behaviors that these individuals display (action-orientation, assertiveness, decisiveness, etc.) are frequently remembered, but the actual outcome of their decisions is often given scant attention.

When low Cautious leaders' behaviors are recognized, the damage to their reputations can be disastrous. They might be labeled as a "loose cannon" or "not a team player," resulting in a loss of credibility and impacting relationships.

One historical example of a leader, who probably would have had a low Cautious score, is Captain Edward Smith of the RMS *Titanic*. As all movie lovers and history buffs are aware, the *Titanic* was a luxury ocean liner that sank on its inaugural voyage after hitting an iceberg. Captain Smith, who was making his final scheduled voyage as a captain before retirement, was at the helm of the fastest and most luxurious ship of its time. In the hubris of the day, the construction of the ship led it to be labeled as being "unsinkable." It is speculated that Smith's motivation to not just beat, but smash, the existing time record for a trans-Atlantic crossing led him to ignore iceberg warnings and run the Titanic's engines at an accelerated rate. With the ship having lifeboats for only one third of the passengers she carried, over 1,500 people lost their lives when she sank on April 15, 1912.

While not as dramatic a tale as Captain Smith of the RMS *Titanic*, Rex from Case 1—Rex, Vice President on page 88 provides a good example of a low Cautious profile. The following is Rex's profile summary.

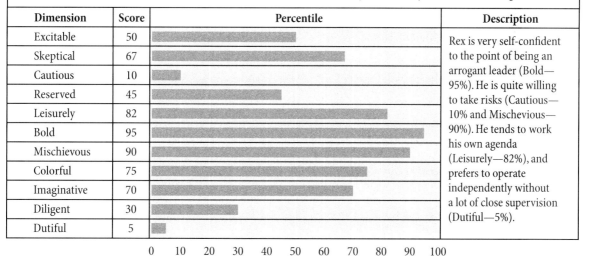

Rex's Situational Summary			
Rex worked in a small company as vice president of sales. In his role, he had considerable autonomy and freedom to make decisions. The company was acquired by a much larger, well-established company with rules, processes, and procedures that often accompany a large bureaucracy. Rex's willingness to take risks and make fast, independent decisions runs counter to the culture that exists in the new company. This issue could be exacerbated by his tendency to follow his own agenda.			
Dimension	**Score**	**Percentile**	**Description**
Excitable	50		Rex is very self-confident to the point of being an arrogant leader (Bold—95%). He is quite willing to take risks (Cautious—10% and Mischevious—90%). He tends to work his own agenda (Leisurely—82%), and prefers to operate independently without a lot of close supervision (Dutiful—5%).
Skeptical	67		
Cautious	10		
Reserved	45		
Leisurely	82		
Bold	95		
Mischevious	90		
Colorful	75		
Imaginative	70		
Diligent	30		
Dutiful	5		

0   10   20   30   40   50   60   70   80   90   100

Rex has a combination of scores (low Cautious and low Dutiful, and high Mischievous and high Leisurely) that will exacerbate both his tendency to make quick decisions and his tendency to be very independent and resistant to supervision or control. These characteristics are likely to be troublesome in his new work environment with its emphasis on agreed-upon processes and standardized operations.

Evaluating the Need for Change

The following behavioral questions should be considered in conjunction with a leader's low Cautious score (as exhibited by Rex) when evaluating the need for a change in behavior. A "yes" response to three or fewer items suggests that there is no imminent need for behavioral changes. A "yes" response to four to six items suggests that a low score on the Cautious scale should be a watch-out for a leader. A "yes" response to more than six items suggests that a leader should take active steps toward making behavioral changes.

Does the leader:

1. Express an opinion even when it is unpopular or politically unwise?   Yes   No   Not Sure

2. Willingly express views regardless of the people present or the potential for negative consequences?   Yes   No   Not Sure

3. Comfortably make requests or ask for favors from people known only casually?   Yes   No   Not Sure

4. Rarely express concern about or reflect on past mistakes?   Yes   No   Not Sure

5. Demonstrate excessive confidence in decisions made or decision-making ability in general?   Yes   No   Not Sure

6. Make decisions even when it is clear that additional data or input from others would be helpful?   Yes   No   Not Sure

7. Take rigid stands on issues even without data to support the positions taken on issues?   Yes   No   Not Sure

8. Seem to get out in front with an opinion even when the issue or decision is controversial?   Yes   No   Not Sure

9. Fail to back down on an opinion even when faced with data or evidence suggesting it may be wrong?   Yes   No   Not Sure

These items should be considered as behavioral indicators. Similar or associated behaviors to any of those listed that are exhibited by a leader likely suggest a "yes" response. They provide additional support that a leader may be at risk for the negative reputational consequences associated with those scoring low on the Cautious scale, such as Rex.

Impact of Low Cautious Behaviors

Leaders with low Cautious scores may be seen as being action-oriented and leader-like. They may come across as having a can-do attitude and may actually be rewarded for the behaviors they exhibit. They may overshadow those who take a more thoughtful and analytical approach—at least until the ramifications of their poorly planned decisions become apparent. Once poor decisions start to unravel in the form of negative outcomes or problematic consequences, low Cautious leaders will garner a reputation for having poor judgment. Just like the positive attributes that often accumulate early on for these leaders, the negative attributes start accumulating rapidly once these leaders have their judgment questioned. Furthermore, there are few reputational consequences more difficult to shake off than that of being a leader with poor judgment. The following are typical perspectives of three of the low Cautious leader's constituents: managers, peers, and direct reports.

Managers

Managers may initially be impressed with the decisiveness and energy levels of low Cautious leaders but may eventually come to feel these individuals need to be reined in or controlled. Managers may find low Cautious leaders assert themselves in situations where they should not be involved. Managers may also find these leaders take the liberty of making key decisions on their own without involving them. Astute managers may see these behaviors unfold before they create problems and early enough to set boundaries to bring the behaviors under control. Once issues start cropping up and problems emerge, managers will begin to lose trust in low Cautious leaders and take actions beyond simple boundary setting to prevent future problems.

Peers

Peers are likely to find those with low Cautious scores to be independent and action oriented and even a bit cavalier. Those serving on teams with low Cautious leaders may find the low Cautious leaders are not always in alignment with team decisions or priorities. They may go along with the team's direction initially, but then they switch gears and make different decisions than what was agreed upon. Peers may feel they have made a compelling case for the decisions they propose (complete with supporting facts and data) but may find this information falls on deaf ears. Peers will lose trust in low Cautious leaders, especially when their behavior has a direct, negative impact on those peers. Politically savvy peers may use the behavior of low Cautious leaders against them by painting them as reckless and then touting their own views as representing the voice of reason.

Direct Reports

The direct reports of low Cautious leaders often find themselves in a quandary. They enjoy working for an independent and decisive leader, and they enjoy having a leader who can get things done. However, they may find themselves being isolated when the actions of their leader are not aligned with the direction of the organization. In addition, the direct reports' reputations may suffer from being associated with a leader whose decisions are ultimately not successful. In some cases, low Cautious leaders may even put their direct reports in ethical binds by involving them in actions that go beyond the accepted boundaries established by the organization.

Coaching Focus

A major area of focus for a coach should be to illustrate the effect low Cautious behaviors have on others and on the organization. Have the leader's decisions had a positive impact on the organization? Have the leader's decisions affected other people in a positive way or negative way? What outcomes could have been achieved with a more inclusive and analytical decision-making process? Frequently, those with low Cautious scores have a blind spot when it comes to evaluating the impact of their decisions. The most serious consequence arising from such a blind spot is that the leader develops a reputation for poor judgment. The coaching focus is quite different for a leader who has not been tagged with the poor judgment label versus one who has. The difference is essentially one of designing a coaching engagement around preventive steps versus one involving reputational repair.

Coaching Strategy

An initial coaching strategy should first involve an evaluation of corporate culture issues, specifically whether or not the existing corporate culture or the leader's direct manager encourage low Cautious behaviors. Second, an objective analysis of any low Cautious behaviors that have been displayed should be undertaken—have there been negative ramifications from these behaviors or possible negative consequences from the behaviors? Third, the coach should evaluate the degree to which the leader is open to self-reflection and learning from past experiences. Finally, the coach should investigate the degree to which low Cautious behaviors could be career limiting for the leader and use this information to underscore the need for change.

Strategy Refinements Using Subscale Information

The subscales for Cautious include Avoidant, Fearful, and Unassertive. Each subscale contributes to an overall Cautious scale score and provides interpretation refinements beyond those that can be achieved from a scale score alone. These interpretation refinements can have implications for specific behavioral changes that may improve leader performance. They may also help in refining the coaching strategy that would be most effective in producing positive behavioral changes.

Avoidant

Leaders scoring low on the Avoidant subscale are eager to meet new people, but do so in an uninhibited manner that likely overpowers others. They also have a tendency to insert themselves in situations in ways that are not warranted. Coaches working with a low Avoidant leader need to ensure that the leader can recognize situations where more subtle and low-key behaviors are called for. Then, the coach needs to ensure that the leader is actually capable of displaying these lower-key behaviors. For example, leaders may be advised to do equal amounts of listening versus talking when in meetings. They can also be encouraged to use more "seeking" behaviors as their natural tendencies cause them to lean too far in the direction of "tell" behaviors.

Fearful

Those with low scores on the Fearful subscale are quick to make independent decisions, whether data or information supports their position or not. Low scoring leaders frequently underestimate the costs of a poor or ineffective decision, and may not have patience with those who want to take a more thoughtful approach on issues and problems. Low scores on this subscale put leaders at the most risk for negative reputational consequences. Their propensity to be impulsive and make decisions without proper due diligence is easily observed by others. Such behaviors will play a prominent role in these leaders' developing a negative reputation if negative outcomes start to accumulate. Coaches need to ensure that low-scoring leaders make use of available data when making decisions, and should also ascertain that these leaders actually recognize situations where gathering additional data is needed to make a quality decision. Coaches should also ensure these individuals actively collaborate with others when making important decisions.

Unassertive

Low scorers on the Unassertive subscale look forward to stating their opinions and beliefs and often do so with great confidence. Low scorers actively look for ways to make things happen and are usually very action-oriented. Coaches should take steps to ensure these leaders are asserting themselves at the appropriate times and in the appropriate manner. Often, those with low scores in this area are seen as being overly assertive and domineering. They appear to lack impulse control when it comes to offering their views. Others may see them as always needing the last word or as individuals who needlessly extend conversations to get their opinions on record.

Coaching Tactics

Coaching tactics cover a range of approaches and resources that have been found useful in addressing low Cautious behaviors. These tactics are typically used in combination to form a custom plan suited to the specific learning needs of a leader. The tactics are divided into four categories: (1) thought-provoking questions for a leader to consider, (2) exercises a leader can engage in to improve performance, (3) tips and techniques a coach can use to help a leader improve performance, and (4) support resources that can be consulted to gain additional insights in addressing low Cautious behaviors.

Thought-Provoking Questions for a Leader

- List the major decisions you made that have been successes, and then list those that were not successes. For the non-successful decisions, would you have made a different decision had you spent more time researching and evaluating this issue? Why or why not?

- On average, have your independent decisions turned out to be effective and correct? List examples to justify your answer.

- How has your decision-making style affected others in the organization and your relationships with others in the organization?

- How do you determine which decisions you have the authority to handle on your own as opposed to those that require input or approval from your manager?

- Is your decision-making style collaborative and inclusive? Do you actively incorporate the ideas and viewpoints of others when making decisions?

- What decisions do you wish that you could redo? How would your decision—and the process you undertook to make it—be different the second time around?

- How do you determine when to be assertive and push for results versus adopting a more subtle approach? Provide examples of when you have been successful with both styles.

Exercises for a Leader

- Do a postmortem on a decision that did not go well, and identify any additional data you should have gathered (and coworkers whom you should have involved) when making this decision.

- Identify some role models in your organization who are decisive, but who also demonstrate high levels of collaboration and coordination with others when making decisions. Spend time with these individuals, and gain insights from them on how you can improve in this area.

- Faced with a key decision, make a list of the key stakeholders involved in the decision, and make a concerted effort to communicate and coordinate with them during the decision-making process.

- Take the time to list the pros and cons of the different courses of action you are considering. Find a person whose judgment you trust, and use him or her as a sounding board for the decisions you are considering.

- Make sure that you are comfortable with analytics and data. If this is not an area of strength for you, find a coworker who can assist in this area. Make sure that you make appropriate use of data and information when making decisions.

- Maintain a journal covering the decisions that you think are critical in your job or career. Because outcomes often take time to determine, update your decisions with information about outcomes as it comes available.

Tips and Techniques for a Coach

- Make sure the leader understands the impact of any decisions that have not been well thought out or that have been incomplete. Make sure that the leader understands the impact that these decisions have had on coworkers and the organization overall.

- Enlist the manager of the leader in your efforts, including obtaining a clear picture on what decisions the leader is empowered to make individually versus those requiring additional input or approval from the manager.

- Make sure the leader has access to, and an understanding of, the data and information that are available when making key decisions.

- Ensure that the leader recognizes when there is a need to gather additional information and research issues more fully before making a decision.

- Find internal people who can serve as a sounding board and help the leader make more effective decisions. Also, serve as a sounding board yourself.

- Find sources to provide real-time feedback to the leader as to his or her behavior in meetings, such as whether the leader is being too assertive, dominating discussions, and so on.

- Have the leader practice different decision-making styles (such as, decisive, flexible, hierarchic, integrative, etc.) under safe circumstances to increase the leader's range of decision-making styles and comfort in using them.

Support Resources

Bartkus, V. O., & Conlon, E. (2008). *Getting it right: Notre Dame on leadership and judgment.* San Francisco, CA: Jossey-Bass.

The authors present a problem-solving framework that has served as the basis of Notre Dame's business education and has been tested in corporate settings. The model encompasses three overarching themes: discovering solutions, moving from analysis to action, and driving solutions through the organization.

Bazerman, M. H., & Moore, D. A. (2008). *Judgment in managerial decision-making* (7th ed.). Hoboken, NJ: John Wiley & Sons.

Bazerman and Moore examine judgment in a variety of organizational contexts, describe practical strategies for changing and improving readers' decision-making tactics, and offer abundant examples and hands-on decision-making exercises.

Hoch, S. J., & Kunreuther, H. (2001). *Wharton on making decisions.* New York, NY: John Wiley & Sons.

Based on a compilation of perspectives on decision-making from leading researchers at The Wharton School, Hoch and Kunreuther describe how to apply the latest approaches in decision-making from four angles: personal, managerial, negotiator, and consumer.

Lowy, A., & Hood, P. (2010). *The power of the 2 × 2 matrix: Using 2 × 2 thinking to solve business problems and make better decisions.* San Francisco, CA: Jossey-Bass.

Based on an examination of hundreds of the most effective and original business minds, Lowy and Hood describe how 2 × 2 matrices can be used within essentially any scenario to deeply (but efficiently) analyze situations and identify the best possible course of action.

Nutt, P. C. (2002). *Why decisions fail: Avoiding the blunders and traps that lead to debacles.* San Francisco, CA: Berrett-Koehler.

Nutt analyses fifteen notoriously bad decisions, describes how these mistakes could have been avoided, and explains how to improve organizational decision-making tactics to avoid similar failures.

Sundheim, D. (2013). *Taking smart risks: How sharp leaders win when the stakes are high.* New York, NY: McGraw-Hill.

Sundheim reconceptualizes risk, suggesting that, instead of fearing risk, leaders should be more fearful of what could be lost if "good" risks are not pursued. "Taking Smart Risks" helps readers identify, anticipate, and pursue the type of intelligent, savvy risks capable of moving organizations forward.

Tassler, N. (2009). *The impulse factor: An innovative approach to better decision making.* New York, NY: Simon & Schuster.

Tasler, a researcher and director at the pioneering think tank TalentSmart, guides readers through a process of analyzing their decision-making styles, helps readers understand why they make the choices that they do, and offers tools designed to help readers maximize their unique decision-making styles.

Sample Coaching Program (Case 1—Rex)

Rex from Case 1 provides a good example of a low Cautious profile. As previously noted, Rex has a combination of scores (low Cautious and low Dutiful; high Mischievous and high Leisurely) that will exacerbate his tendency to make quick decisions and his tendency to be very independent and resistant to supervision or control. These characteristics are likely to be troublesome in his new work environment, with its emphasis on standardized operations and efficiency.

An analysis of Rex's Cautious subscale scores indicates lower scores in all three areas—Avoidant, Fearful, and Unassertive. Therefore, Rex is very eager to participate in meetings and have an impact, he is not afraid of making mistakes, and he is very comfortable being assertive. Each of these behaviors was previously rewarded in his sales role in his old organization.

As a coach, one of your major challenges will be to find a proper balance point for Rex to display these behaviors in the new corporate culture. Some possible steps to accomplish this are as follows:

- Work with Rex and his manager to clearly outline the areas where Rex has the autonomy to make independent decisions versus those areas that need additional levels of discussion or approval before acting.

- Help Rex learn more about the corporate culture of the acquiring organization. Find a mentor or role model who can meet regularly with Rex and give him insights into key cultural issues and who can provide feedback to both you and Rex on Rex's interactions with others.

- Make sure that Rex understands the operations of the acquiring company, including its rules, policies, procedures, and modes of operation. This knowledge should help Rex work more effectively in the new corporate culture.

- Evaluate whether Rex is comfortable with analytics and data, and whether he has the ability to recognize when additional fact-finding and analysis are needed before making a decision.

- Identify strategies that can help Rex when he encounters roadblocks or setbacks. Help him develop alternatives to simply acting independently and making his own decisions.

- Make sure that Rex is actively participating in planning meetings and progress report meetings. Make sure he stays updated with the current status of projects, etc.

- Identify individuals who can give Rex real-time feedback on how he is coming across to others in meetings, with particular emphasis on situations where he has come across as being too assertive or domineering.

- Conduct regular follow-up meetings with Rex to discuss the key decisions he is making and alternative courses of action that he might take. Include a postmortem of the decisions that he does make, with a critical eye on whether he could have involved others, whether he could have made more effective use of available data, etc.

SUMMARY

Keep Doing

Be open and receptive to both change and new ideas.

Stop Doing

Overlook the risks associated with decisions, and minimize concerns raised by others.

Start Doing

Ensure due diligence when evaluating the positive and negative aspects of risk.

Low Cautious behaviors may be rewarded in the short term, but they usually catch up with an individual over time. Changing a leader's behavior in this area takes time and frequent follow-up as this quick-decision mode is often a highly ingrained behavior. There may also be the added coaching challenge of reputation repair if the leader has accumulated a history of making bad decisions. Getting the low Cautious leader's manager actively involved in the coaching effort is one of the keys to success. In addition, the degree to which the leader's low Cautious behaviors have been rewarded needs to be assessed. If the organization currently rewards low Cautious behaviors, the leader needs to be aware of the impact of these rewards on his or her behaviors. Long-term career success rarely follows individuals who exhibit low Cautious behaviors even when they are rewarded. Leaders who are aware that existing reward structures may be fueling their low Cautious behaviors can also recognize that as their careers evolve and their decisions have greater impact, their mistakes will not be easily forgotten and rewards can disappear in hurry.

CHAPTER 13

RESERVED

HIGH RESERVED

Detecting When It Is a Problem

High Reserved behaviors are not readily apparent in the workplace and often go unnoticed for long periods of time, especially in tough or low social environments. As such, these behaviors can be difficult for others to describe and name. The reason for this is because high Reserved behaviors are as much about what leaders *are not* doing as what they *are* doing. For example, classic high Reserved behaviors, such as pulling back, being cold and aloof, or being uncommunicative, are often described by others as making them feel awkward, disconnected, or nervous. Others may also suggest that these leaders appear to lack warmth, compassion, or a sense of social connection. In other words, interacting with high Reserved leaders causes others to feel a level of discomfort and to sense that something is missing in these individuals.

High Reserved leaders may exhibit overt behaviors that are problematic such as being tactless, socially clumsy, or blunt. These behaviors add to the inability of these individuals to build social relationships or establish social networks, which are fundamental skills for successful performance in senior-level positions. Coaching high Reserved individuals involves helping them dial down high Reserved behaviors while adding more effective social skills that will improve their ability to form and maintain connections with others. High Reserved individuals with self-awareness and average social skills perform better than those with low self-awareness and poorly developed social skills. Therefore, it is critically important to address the behaviors high Reserved leaders *are* demonstrating as well as those they *are not* demonstrating.

One example of a fictional high Reserved individual is the infamous Michael Corleone from Mario Puzo's best-selling *Godfather* novels and *The Godfather* film trilogy. Michael's reserved behavior is apparent in comments such as "never hate your enemies, it affects your judgment" and "never let anyone know what you're thinking," as well as in his brutal actions, such as dispassionately arranging the murder of his brother Fredo (among many others). While throughout the movies Michael has his passionate moments, his cold, logical toughness is his defining characteristic. While most high Reserved individuals are not as callous as Michael Corleone, descriptors such as dispassionate, ruthless, cold, and calculating certainly can apply.

Robert from Case 3—Robert, Design Engineer on page 92 provides a good example of a high Reserved profile. Robert's highest derailer is his Reserved score (98%), but his Leisurely and Diligent scores (both 80%) may add to his reputation as a tough, stubborn man of few words and high expectations. The following is Robert's profile summary.

Robert's Situational Summary			
Robert is a design engineer for a manufacturer of commercial aircraft electronic components. He has worked primarily as an individual contributor and was known for getting things done. His hard work resulted in a promotion to project leader on a cross-functional team. His new role will be highly demanding and require effective leadership skills that will be a challenge for his quiet, reserved nature, and tendency to fade into the background in social situations.			
Dimension	**Score**	**Percentile**	**Description**
Excitable	35		Robert is a hard worker who seems very calm and even-tempered under pressure. People view him as task focused with little interest in engaging with people (Reserved—98%). He tends to work long hours and is not bothered by the fact that his attention to detail spills over into work for others (Diligent—80%), which has earned him a reputation as a grinder who gets things done.
Skeptical	50		
Cautious	75		
Reserved	98		
Leisurely	80		
Bold	55		
Mischievous	40		
Colorful	30		
Imaginative	62		
Diligent	80		
Dutiful	30		

0   10   20   30   40   50   60   70   80   90   100

The foregoing description highlights the challenge that will face Robert in his new role as project leader. As a design engineer, Robert was only responsible for his own work, and the social interaction component of his job was likely quite minimal. As a leader, the social interaction demands on Robert will increase significantly. In fact, the biggest challenge may not come from managing his direct team members, as they will have ample opportunity to become accustomed to his interpersonal style. It may come from the cross-functional aspects of his new role and the networking that will likely be necessary. This new emphasis on social connections will put Robert in the position of having to initiate social interactions to build relationships and to use a range of social skills to persuade and influence constituents who will be essential to the success of the project. Putting his head down and relying on his hard work, attention to detail, and high standards will not be enough for him to succeed.

Evaluating the Need for Change

The following behavioral questions should be considered in conjunction with a leader's high Reserved score (as exhibited by Robert) when evaluating the need for a change in behavior. A "yes" response to three or fewer items suggests that there is no imminent need for behavioral changes. A "yes" response to four to six items suggests that a high score on the Reserved scale should be a watch-out for a leader. A "yes" response to more than six items suggests that a leader should take active steps toward making behavioral changes.

Does the leader:

1. Often work behind closed doors or in locations that ensure social contact is kept to a minimum?   **Yes   No   Not Sure**

2. Have difficulty interacting with strangers, casual acquaintances, or unfamiliar colleagues?   **Yes   No   Not Sure**

3. Appear to be too socially guarded or maintain social barriers that limit approachability?   **Yes   No   Not Sure**

4. Interact with few friends, colleagues, or associates at work?   **Yes   No   Not Sure**

5. Put up interpersonal barriers to keep people out or put people off?   **Yes   No   Not Sure**

6. Appear to lack social skills, or come off as awkward in social situations?   **Yes   No   Not Sure**

7. Act indifferent to the plight or problems of others?   **Yes   No   Not Sure**

8. Tend to treat employees as replaceable parts in a machine rather than as people?   **Yes   No   Not Sure**

9. Seem to be unconcerned about reputational issues, especially those related to interpersonal skills?   **Yes   No   Not Sure**

These items should be considered as behavioral indicators. Similar or associated behaviors to any of those listed that are exhibited by a leader likely suggest a "yes" response. They provide additional support that a leader may be at risk for the negative reputational consequences associated with those scoring high on the Reserved scale, such as Robert.

Impact of High Reserved Behaviors

High Reserved behaviors can often be hard to precisely pinpoint, and it may take time for them to have a serious impact on a leader's reputation. However, once these behaviors become part of a leader's reputation, it can be very difficult to achieve reputational change because the very behaviors needed to achieve such change (e.g., social skills, networking, etc.) may be poorly developed or absent altogether. Additionally, once high Reserved individuals have been labeled as aloof, cold, or unsupportive, others may not want to engage with them and may not be receptive to their attempts to connect and repair the relationship. At the extreme, others may even report feeling uncomfortable, intimidated, or even afraid around them. As with all potential derailers, the Situational Context will play a large role in determining the likelihood of derailment. The following are some of the consequences of high Reserved behaviors, broken out by three constituencies: managers, peers, and direct reports.

Managers

Managers may have great patience with high Reserved leaders because these individuals tend not to seek much support, usually do not complain, and possess the toughness needed to handle difficult situations. The challenge for managers comes into play when they need these individuals to engage with others, to develop others, to support others, and to be active team participants. When managers try to coach high Reserved individuals, they may find it difficult to connect or develop sufficient trust with them to facilitate the necessary behavioral change. There is also an interesting side note to the way managers can take advantage of high Reserved individuals. It is not uncommon for managers faced with difficult people problems (such as a downsizing or firing) to have these individuals handle the dirty work. High Reserved individuals often have little regard for the "human" in "humanity" and are not bothered by being tough on people.

Peers

Peers often find high Reserved leaders to be tough and self-reliant. As such, in tough environments, peers may appreciate the ability of these individuals to plow through work without requiring a lot of support and assistance. However, in highly social work cultures, in decentralized and egalitarian groups, or in other situations that require people to work interdependently, peers may find high Reserved leaders to be difficult to engage in collaborative, coordinated efforts. Thus, peers may describe high Reserved individuals as lacking in social skills and being unsupportive of colleagues and team members. Interestingly, while the toughness may seem to help these individuals emotionally weather many difficult challenges in the workplace, their lack of social connectivity may allow politically savvy peers to achieve greater organizational success.

Direct Reports

High Reserved leaders often fail to demonstrate much concern when it comes to people. Competent, self-reliant direct reports may enjoy the freedom that comes from the distance these leaders put between themselves and others. In contrast, direct reports who need a lot of support and direction or those who want to be actively engaged in their professional development may become frustrated and disillusioned with these types of leaders. They may feel that these leaders do not care about them or their contributions. Such feelings could eventually cause these direct reports to disengage or leave their teams entirely. Also during stressful times, direct reports may feel a lack of direction and support from high Reserved individuals to the point they may feel they are on their own or set adrift to fend for themselves.

Coaching Focus

High Reserved behaviors relate to the need for managing the social distance between self and others. The initial focus of coaching high Reserved leaders should be to help these leaders gain an understanding of how high Reserved behaviors damage relationships and how damaged relationships can damage careers. This coaching should include the identification of triggers for the high Reserved behaviors and the use of alternative behaviors that build relationships. It can also be helpful to equip high Reserved leaders with a set of skills that can be employed to repair relationships where damage has already occurred. The long-term coaching focus needs to address the strategic communication skills of these leaders. They need to recognize the importance of politically savvy communication skills and the positive career impact those skills can have when effectively employed.

Coaching Strategy

It is important for the coach to help the high Reserved leader understand that the goal is not for the leader to interact with others all the time. Rather, the goal is to effectively communicate when the situation calls for it and to be able to disengage from interactions without damaging relationships. There are three general steps associated with the coaching strategy for a high Reserved leader:

- The first step is for the leader to become proficient at identifying his or her need and desire to pull away from others and the triggers that elicit this need. This step, in and of itself, can be difficult, because when people pull away, they often defend themselves with statements such as, "What are you talking about? I'm not doing anything!"

- The high Reserved leader needs to become adept at asking others for a time-out when he or she needs to take to a break and think through an issue alone. The time-out request should be accompanied by a follow-up plan or timeframe to reengage on the issue. This is extremely important as it helps mitigate the potential negative impact of the high Reserved leader's disconnecting from others. Unless others understand what the Reserved leader is up to, they can attribute almost any motivation (including malevolent ones) to the leader's disengagement from them.

- The high Reserved leader should learn how to reengage with others after a disengagement incident. This bridge can be as basic as a set of scripts for different scenarios, or as complex as helping others understand the cues for disconnecting and reconnecting.

Strategy Refinements Using Subscale Information

The subscales for the Reserved scale include Introverted, Unsocial, and Tough. Each subscale contributes to an overall Reserved scale score and provides interpretation refinements beyond those that can be achieved from a scale score alone. These interpretation refinements can have implications for specific behavioral changes that may improve leader performance. They may also help in refining the coaching strategy that will be most effective in producing positive behavioral changes.

Introverted

An elevation on the Introverted subscale suggests that the high Reserved leader values private time and prefers to work alone. Trigger points may include situations where the leader is forced to work in one-on-one or group settings for long periods of time. It can cause a high Reserved leader to respond by seeming uninterested, aloof, or by physically leaving. Internally, high Reserved individuals who are high on the Introverted subscale may feel exhausted by social contact. When the Introverted subscale is elevated, strategy refinements can include helping the leader establish the need for downtime and communicating this need in such a way that group members understand that the need to pull away is not personal. These leaders become more effective at handling situations involving extensive social interactions when the situations have clear time limits.

Unsocial

An elevation on the Unsocial subscale suggests the high Reserved leader may limit close relationships and actively keep others at a distance to prevent physical and emotional closeness. Internally, high Reserved leaders with high scores on the Unsocial subscale lack the need and motivation for social interaction, leading to a reputation for being detached, cold, and unapproachable. While similar to the Introverted subscale, scoring high on this subscale can lead to a reputation for being uncaring, unfriendly, calculating, or even mean. The two keys to working with a leader with a high score on the Unsocial subscale are to help the leader understand the cost of the unsocial behaviors and to help the leader explore the ways that being a bit more social could benefit, comfort, or please others.

Tough

The Tough subscale relates to a focus on work rather than people and a seeming indifference to others. An elevation on the Tough subscale suggests a leader may have a reputation for being cold, uncaring, and indifferent to the problems of others. Under heavy workloads, tough leaders can become caustic and show their lack of tolerance for whining and complaining. While tough leaders are often star performers in terms of delivering results, many times they leave a wake of bodies in their path. Two keys goals for leaders who have an elevation on the Tough subscale are developing greater tolerance and compassion for self and others, and developing a balance between people issues and getting things done (including learning how to get things done through others). Like the other two subscales, the potential danger of being too tough must be presented clearly as the benefits of being kinder or gentler will certainly not be apparent or appealing to a toughminded leader. Further, while behaviors that are too tough are detrimental in the long run, they are often rewarded by fast-paced managers and organizations in the short run because they can achieve results.

Coaching Tactics

Coaching tactics include a range of approaches that have been found useful in addressing high Reserved behaviors. These tactics are typically used in combination to form a custom plan suited to the specific learning needs of the leader. The tactics are divided into four categories: (1) thought-provoking questions for a leader to consider, (2) exercises a leader can engage in to improve performance, (3) tips and techniques a coach can use to help a leader improve performance, and (4) support resources that can be consulted to gain additional insights in addressing high Reserved behaviors.

Thought-Provoking Questions for a Leader

- Why would it be helpful for you to engage others to garner support and build alliances?
- In what circumstances have specific high Reserved behaviors worked for you?
- What's the potential risk of not engaging with others?
- What can you do to occasionally share genuine emotional responses?

- Is there any benefit to just chatting and interacting with others?

- How do you build trust? Are there any relationships that might benefit you or your work if you could build trust with others? How might you do this?

- How did you build your closest relationships, and how do people get into your inner circle? What aspects of this can be applied to work relationships?

- What would it take for you to accept that feelings are important and that other people can be hurt easily?

Exercises for a Leader

- Learn the key elements of EQ and how to apply them to specific relationships.

- Develop your personal time-out message that you can use to gracefully exit social situations that have become tiresome.

- Establish specific quiet times during the course of the workday in which others know you are not to be interrupted.

- Establish a set of quiet time activities that you can engage in after situations involving extensive interactions.

- Identify situations in your past where others have exploited your toughness (such as asking you to fire someone, lead a downsizing, deliver bad news, etc.) and become vigilant regarding those types of situations in the future.

Tips and Techniques for a Coach

- Build a stakeholder matrix and then discuss with the leader how to engage each stakeholder.

- Have the leader build access points for others, such as office hours or pro-active social engagements.

- Videotape the leader to help identify behaviors and body language that others might describe as smug and aloof.

- Have the leader take time after meetings to check with others to gauge the overall message that was communicated (e.g., ask them what they heard).

- Have the leader practice asking others about themselves, and reflect privately on what was learned. Ask how this information might inform the way the leader builds trust with and communicates with others.

- Maintaining a connection with a high Reserved leader is an important aspect of the coaching engagement. The coach should engage the leader in a discussion of how the connection between them should be maintained. This discussion should include a commitment to attend scheduled coaching sessions and a mechanism for the leader to appropriately reschedule sessions when conflicts arise.

- Coaching the high Reserved leader should include enormous emphasis on why connecting with others is important and the ways in which a lack of connection with others can be detrimental.

- Coaching is often much more effective with a high Reserved leader when behavior change is approached in terms of baby steps because of his or her propensity to withdraw or disengage.

Support Resources

Cain, S. (2013). *Quiet: The power of introverts in a world that can't stop talking.* New York, NY: Crown.

Cain discusses the "Extrovert Ideal," how it has contributed to the devaluation of introverted qualities, and the risk we as a society take when we underestimate what introverts have to offer. "Quiet" highlights groundbreaking achievements of introverts from past and present, and likely will leave readers seeing themselves and other introverts in a different light.

Carnegie, D. (2010). *How to win friends and influence people.* New York, NY: Simon & Schuster.

This business classic has helped countless now celebrated figures achieve success, both professionally and personally, for over sixty years.

Conant, D., & Norgaard, M. (2011). *TouchPoints: Creating powerful leadership connections in the smallest of moments.* San Francisco, CA: Jossey-Bass.

Based on Conant's tenure as CEO of Campbell Soup Company and Norgaard's extensive consulting experience, the authors make a convincing case for the argument that a leader's impact and legacy are created via hundreds of interactions that, in the moment, seem inconsequential.

Cuddy, A. J. C., Kohut, M., & Neffinger, J. (2013, July–August). Connect, then lead. *Harvard Business Review.* Retrieved from https://hbr.org/2013/07/connect-then-lead

HBR's 10 must reads on emotional intelligence.

Dotlich, D. L., & Cairo, P. C. (2003). *Why CEO's fail: The 11 behaviors that can derail your climb to the top and how to manage them.* San Francisco, CA: Jossey-Bass.

The authors alternate high profile cases with compelling examples from their coaching practice. The Aloofness chapter offers coaching tactics for Reserved tendencies.

Ferrazzi, K. (2014). *Never eat alone, expanded and updated: And other secrets to success, one relationship at a time.* New York, NY: Crown Business.

After distinguishing genuine relationship building from "networking," this best-selling business classic describes the specific steps (as well as the mentality) needed to make meaningful connections, both in general and in the digital realm.

Fishbein, M. (2013). *How to build an awesome professional network: (Meet new people and build relationships with business networking)* [Kindle edition]. Retrieved from Amazon.com

Based on extensive research and his own personal experience, Fishbein thoroughly but succinctly offers practical and actionable tips that will help readers develop and sustain relationships with people capable of facilitating career and business growth.

Sample Coaching Program (Case 3—Robert)

Robert's profile indicates a Reserved score of 98 percent and a Diligent score of 80 percent. An examination of his subscale scores indicates that all three subscales are elevated. The case information clearly indicates that Robert's detail orientation and diligence have helped him advance to where he is and that his quiet reserved nature has not hindered him. In the new role, however, these former strengths could quickly become liabilities as he will be required to motivate and inspire a cross-functional team to deliver top-notch, accurate results while staying out of the weeds himself, and without overworking the team. Given that the project will be high profile and demanding, there is a high risk for Robert to communicate too little and try to do too much of the work himself. Robert's coaching intervention should first clarify the need for a behavioral shift and then assist him in learning the necessary skills to proactively communicate with his team, create and communicate a compelling vision and strategy for the project, set clear expectations with his team (to maximize the likelihood that they will meet his high standards), and create a system for coordinating work and managing the project to include a feedback loop to monitor his team's engagement and energy level. The following are the proposed steps for the coaching engagement with Robert:

- Ask Robert to perform an analysis of the best ways to get the work done and how to create a vision and strategy for the project.

- Help Robert identify challenges associated with his personality and work style in this Situational Context. Make sure he understands that he cannot do all the work himself and that he will need to lead others in order for the project to be successful.

- Collaboratively create a plan for Robert to meet each member of the new team for the purpose of identifying what each member can contribute and the ways in which the team might work together. This task may require some basic social skill building on Robert's part.

- Help Robert create and implement a plan for communicating his vision and strategy. Have Robert reflect on why it is important for his team to know the vision and strategy, and have him regularly communicate and reinforce his vision and strategy with all the stakeholders and people working on the project. This task may require educating Robert about how much others need to know about the strategy. It would be worthwhile for

Robert to explore if there are others who can help him communicate his messages about the strategy.

- Given Robert's track record of working independently, help him reflect on the benefits of having the team collaboratively set the goals and tactics for implementing his strategy.

- Guide Robert to meet with each member of his team to identify individual responsibilities and communicate his expectations. Have him set up regular meetings during which the team can communicate progress.

- To combat his higher Diligent score (and the potential for him to become a micromanager), have Robert set up a dashboard to monitor progress. Have him create checkpoints to determine when he needs to get involved in team problems. This will help him make conscious decisions about when to let his team members handle things.

SUMMARY

Keep Doing

Show steadiness when others are becoming emotional and overwrought.

Stop Doing

Tune other people out, and ignore their concerns.

Start Doing

Check for understanding after important interactions or meetings.

High Reserved behaviors involve pulling away and disconnecting from others. The internal motive for pulling away varies across leaders and may range from a need for solitude to gather thoughts, to emotional parsimony, to pleasure in watching others squirm or attempt to connect with them. The Reserved subscales of Introverted, Unsocial, and Tough are important in helping determine how others are likely to see the high Reserved behaviors. While high Reserved behaviors may sometimes assist individual contributors to be productive in tough environments and with high workloads, these behaviors become problematic when these individuals are expected to lead and develop others.

Coaching should include social skill building as well as interventions aimed at building comfort in being with others. High Reserved leaders should be reassured that the goal is not to take away all private time or solitary work, but rather to determine where and when these behaviors are not in their best interests.

LOW RESERVED

Detecting When It Is a Problem

If high Reserved behaviors are not readily apparent in the workplace, low Reserved behaviors are even less obvious. Low Reserved leaders are frequently described as friendly, warm, engaging (and engaged), and interpersonally skilled. The problems that these leaders encounter are associated with their lack of awareness or ability to emotionally, socially, or even physically pull back when situations are overheated, toxic, or politically detrimental. Their social boundaries are poorly defined, which often results in excessive concern for the feelings of others and a strong level of discomfort with conflict. In the workplace, these individuals miss cues about the intentions of others, have a difficult time saying "no," and often do not stand up for themselves. They can appear to others as naïve and are quite vulnerable to being manipulated.

A great example of a low Reserved individual can be found in the first film of *The Godfather* trilogy. During the wedding scene at the opening of the movie, Johnny Fontane (a singer and actor) goes before Don Corleone and pleads for help in dealing with a mean movie producer. Johnny Fontane appeared weak, soft, and very conflict averse. Don Corleone, annoyed with Johnny Fontane's low Reserved behaviors, slapped him around and demanded that he toughen up. It was clear from the interaction that Don Corleone had lost respect for Johnny Fontane because of his inability to stand up for himself. While workplace situations may not be as dramatic, loss of respect is potentially a real consequence of low Reserved behaviors.

Janis from Case 5—Janis, Customer Service Manager on page 96 provides a good example of a low Reserved profile. The following is Janis's profile summary:

Janis's Situational Summary			
Janis is a newly promoted customer service manager who works for a software company. Her long-time regional manager was recently promoted, and her new manager is described as young, hard-charging, and very demanding. Janis is very conscientious and works hard to keep everybody happy. Her new manager will likely test her ability to push back, or she will find herself challenged to keep up with his demands. Her lack of self-confidence will also be readily apparent to her new manager.			
Dimension	**Score**	**Percentile**	**Description**
Excitable	60		Janis is a high-energy person who does not over-promise (Cautious—75%) and is very approachable (Reserved—15%). She lacks confidence (Bold—10%) but makes up for it through preparation and attention to detail (Diligent—85%). She is known for her loyalty and willingness to go the extra mile when it comes to protecting the reputation of the company and her manager (Dutiful—80%).
Skeptical	10		
Cautious	75		
Reserved	15		
Leisurely	20		
Bold	10		
Mischievous	40		
Colorful	30		
Imaginative	62		
Diligent	85		
Dutiful	80		

```
        0   10   20   30   40   50   60   70   80   90  100
```

Janis's case is an interesting one in that her Reserved score is at the 15th percentile, but her Skeptical score is even lower, at the 10th percentile. These two scores together suggest that Janis could be quite naïve about the intentions of others and organizational politics. She will have difficulty delivering tough messages or correcting problematic behavior of others. She might also overexpose herself to others socially and emotionally, allowing others to know too much too quickly about her.

Combining these behaviors with her tendency to overwork to please others (high Diligent) and her intense loyalty (high Dutiful), a profile emerges of a very vulnerable leader. It suggests that Janis will be easy prey for those who may not have her best interests at heart or who use politics to advance their own agendas. She will not push back even if work requests are unreasonable, she will not notice when she is being used to gain a political advantage, and she will not raise concerns even when she observes (or is asked to participate in) behaviors that stretch the limits of good business ethics.

Evaluating the Need for Change

The following behavioral questions should be considered in conjunction with a leader's low Reserved score (as exhibited by Janis) when evaluating the need for a change in behavior. A "yes" response to three or fewer items suggests that there is no imminent need for behavioral changes. A "yes" response to four to six items suggests that a low score on the Reserved scale should be a watch-out for a leader. A "yes" response to more than six items suggests that a leader should take active steps toward making behavioral changes.

Does the leader:

1. Openly welcome discussions or interactions even when they disrupt work that is under way?   Yes   No   Not Sure

2. Exhibit too much ease and comfort when interacting with strangers?   Yes   No   Not Sure

3. Prefer to work in meetings or in group situations compared to working alone to accomplish tasks?   Yes   No   Not Sure

4. Rely excessively upon a network of colleagues or associates to discuss routine business issues?   Yes   No   Not Sure

5. Open up to the point that others may become too familiar with personal information unrelated to work?   Yes   No   Not Sure

6. Lack the verbal and bodily cues to signal others to back off?   Yes   No   Not Sure

7. Exhibit an excess of concern over and involvement in the plight or problems of others?   Yes   No   Not Sure

8. Delay or fail to make difficult people calls because the individual involved may be negatively impacted?   **Yes   No   Not Sure**

9. Display an excess of concern regarding reputational information or the perceptions of others?   **Yes   No   Not Sure**

These items should be considered as behavioral indicators. Similar or associated behaviors to any of those listed that are exhibited by a leader likely suggest a "yes" response. They provide additional support that a leader may be at risk for the negative reputational consequences associated with those scoring low on the Reserved scale, such as Janis.

Impact of Low Reserved Behaviors

Low Reserved behaviors can create reputational vulnerabilities. While leaders with low Reserved scores may have difficulty setting firm boundaries with almost everyone, the low Reserved behaviors manifest themselves differently across three particular constituencies in the work place: managers, peers, and direct reports.

Managers

Effective managers often enjoy working with low Reserved individuals, as they are engaged and responsive, and conflict avoidant. Managers are often impressed by the way low Reserved individuals work with other team members, work cross-functionally, and build supportive networks. Problems arise, however, when managers need their low Reserved leaders to make tough calls, take action on business and people problems, or engage in interactions that involve conflict. In cases such as these, low Reserved leaders may appear weak in negotiations, unclear with requests, unwilling to take tough stands on issues, and too soft on direct reports. Unfortunately, these behaviors result in a reputation for the low Reserved leaders as being too nice, soft, weak, or even not leader-like.

Peers

Well-intentioned peers often enjoy working with their low Reserved colleagues and often describe them as kind, collegial, willing to help, and good team players. However, peers can become frustrated with these leaders when they avoid situations that call for critical feedback or the need for holding others accountable. Ambitious or politically savvy peers may use the vulnerabilities of low Reserved leaders to gain an advantage over them. For example, savvy peers may sidestep unwanted or undesirable work, allowing it to fall into the laps of low Reserved individuals because of their inability to say "no." Savvy peers looking to gain a political advantage over low Reserved leaders will also talk up the negative reputations of these individuals to superiors, with little fear of a conflict developing.

Direct Reports

Low Reserved leaders are often pleasant and rewarding to work for because they are friendly and caring, and cognizant of the needs of their direct reports. It is easy for low Reserved leaders to develop friendly relationships with their direct reports, but therein lies the problem. These relationships can become overly friendly and lack the boundaries necessary to deliver critical feedback or hold people accountable. This unwillingness to be candid can lead to frustration for direct reports who truly want to improve performance through feedback, as well as for high performers who may be forced to cope with poorly performing team members. Finally, low Reserved leaders, to their own detriment, can be overly giving to others of their time and energy. As leaders, they may ultimately lose credibility because of their reluctance to set limits.

Coaching Focus

Reserved behaviors are all about social and emotional connectivity. High Reserved individuals have difficulty maintaining social and emotional connections with others and can easily pull away from others, appearing tough and even insensitive. On the other hand, low Reserved individuals run the risk of being overly connected with others such that they have difficulty delivering tough messages and are uncomfortable being in conflict with others, resulting in a reputation for being overly soft, dithering, and weak. Leaders who are overly connected to others may also reveal too much information about their own thoughts and ideas, thus losing power and putting themselves at risk for "idea theft."

In the broadest sense, the coaching focus for those exhibiting low Reserved behaviors is to help them develop flexible, yet firm, boundaries and limits with others. The strong social and emotional ties these leaders tend to create are fine as long as they do not go too far. From a coaching perspective, these ties have gone too far when the leader is unable to pull back and evaluate others objectively, deliver clear messages and critical feedback, and make and uphold tough decisions.

Coaching Strategy

The coaching strategy for low Reserved leaders is to increase their flexibility in connecting with others, particularly as it relates to setting boundaries, saying no, and gaining control over how much access others have to them. The coaching strategy should also address how much they expose their thoughts and inner workings to those around them. This strategy has three basic components:

- The first component is to evaluate how the low Reserved behaviors might negatively impact the leader. In Janis's situation (Case 5—Janis, Customer Service Manager, page 96), for example, her promotion to customer service manager, accompanied by her reporting to a new regional manager who was very demanding, significantly increased the potential for her low Reserved behaviors to become problematic. Analyzing the situational risk is essential to tailoring an effective coaching intervention for a low Reserved leader.

- The second component of the strategy is to help the leader identify situations that are likely to elicit derailing, low Reserved behaviors. This part of the coaching involves exploration of situations in the past when derailing behaviors have been displayed by the leader. This component should include a clear understanding of the triggers and consequences of these behaviors.

- The third component of the strategy is to design interventions that effectively shield the leader from the negative reputational consequences of low Reserved behaviors but that do not destroy the positive aspects of a low Reserved score. This can be challenging because of the need to balance the leader's positive pro-social behaviors with the need to maintain appropriate social distance. This may involve very simple and subtle cues to others that the leader is less available, or it may involve more overt actions on the part of the leader such as creating office hours, scripting difficult interactions, and learning to say "no."

Strategy Refinements Using Subscale Information

The subscales for Reserved include Introverted, Unsocial, and Tough. Each of these subscales provides interpretation refinements beyond those that can be achieved from a scale score alone. These refinements can have implications for specific behavioral changes that may improve leader performance. They may also help in determining the coaching strategy that will be most effective in producing positive behavioral changes.

Introverted

A lack of elevation on the Introverted subscale suggests that the leader is socially engaging, enthusiastic, and enjoys being around others. While these are all positive behaviors, a strategy refinement would involve determining if the low Reserved leader is so socially outgoing that it negatively impacts performance in other areas, such as task performance or productivity in general. The strategy refinement is two-fold. First, individuals with a low score on this subscale have to learn to restrict the way they initiate social contact. Second, because it is likely that they have established a reputation for being highly approachable, they have to control the degree to which others feel they can socially engage them. Success, in both cases, can be accomplished through scheduling closed-door work. An important aside is that in an age where social media is everywhere, this strategy will have to be augmented by a commitment to stay off social media during closed-door work.

Unsocial

A lack of elevation on the Unsocial subscale suggests that the low Reserved leader is relationship oriented, accessible to others, warm, highly cooperative, and conflict averse. With this subscale, the strategy refinement hinges on whether or not the leader has an appropriate level of executive presence and is able to stand up to unreasonable requests or demands. Over-accessibility can decrease respect, and over-friendliness and familiarity can decrease professionalism and undermine executive presence.

Tough

A lack of elevation on the Tough subscale suggests that the leader is overly diplomatic, too sympathetic and sensitive to the feelings of others, and too soft on people issues. The strategy refinement with this subscale involves determining whether or not the leader can deliver tough messages when necessary and in a timely manner. When a leader is low on this subscale, situations that include business negotiations, performance reviews, and conflict resolution are all at risk for a poor outcome. One of the best coaching strategies is to have the leader script the information to be covered well ahead of any challenging situation.

Coaching Tactics

Coaching tactics cover a range of approaches and resources that have been found useful in addressing low Reserved behaviors. These tactics are typically used in combination to form a custom plan suited to the specific learning needs of a leader. The tactics are divided into four categories: (1) thought-provoking questions for a leader to consider, (2) exercises a leader can engage in to improve performance, (3) tips and techniques a coach can use to help a leader improve performance, and (4) support resources that can be consulted to gain additional insights in addressing low Reserved behaviors.

Thought-Provoking Questions for a Leader

- Do you think it is possible for leaders to be overexposed, and for others to know too much about them, their thought process, their vulnerabilities, and their feelings? What is the risk?

- How do you think your pro-social behavior (such as putting others ahead of your own interests, helping others, extending kindness, etc.) is sometimes abused by others?

- What do you think are some of the benefits to others when you give them direct feedback?

- How do you think others would describe your executive presence as a leader?

- How has your inability to say "no" affected your work-life balance?

- Are there any negative implications when you withhold critical feedback?

- What is the value of giving positive or negative feedback in the moment?

- Does it ever decrease your power (or do you ever lose respect from others) when you are overly engaged and friendly with others?

- Do you ever pay a personal price when others have access to you all the time?

Exercises for a Leader

- Practice setting parameters about when and for how long you are available to be interrupted.

- Describe a team member who would benefit from feedback. Consider the adverse impact on this individual by delaying the feedback or not giving it at all.

- Develop a script for an upcoming interaction that you anticipate will be difficult. During the interaction, follow the script. After the interaction, evaluate how it went and what was achieved.

- Create an incremental plan to increase communication about expectations and disappointments and to share feedback.

- Practice saying "no" in a way that shows self-respect and respect for others.

Tips and Techniques for a Coach

- Help the leader engage in rigorous calendar management that leaves time for reflection, thinking strategically, and business planning.

- Work with the leader to develop a list of acceptable high Reserved behaviors that serve to increase the leader's executive presence. Develop an implementation plan to help the leader incorporate these behaviors into regular use to build a more commanding executive presence.

- Have the leader practice giving difficult feedback through role play.

- Have the leader role play a difficult negotiation in which tough stands are required, as well as saying "no" in response to unreasonable demands.

- Assess if the leader has socially fulfilling connections outside of work. If the social connections outside of work are lacking, help the leader devise a plan to build a greater network of friends and acquaintances outside of work. That is, make sure that the leader is not meeting all of his or her social and emotional needs at work.

- Review incidents in the leader's past where he or she accepted work assignments or commitments that should have been turned down or at least modified to something more reasonable. Discuss how these incidents came about and how they could have been handled differently to achieve a more reasonable outcome.

- Strengthen the leader's awareness of politics within the organization, and help the leader develop a plan to manage those politics.

Support Resources

Brandon, R., & Seldman, M. (2004). *Survival of the savvy: High-integrity political tactics for career and company success.* New York, NY: Free Press.

Two of the nation's most successful corporate leadership consultants reveal their proven, systematic program for using the power of "high-integrity" politics to achieve career success, maximize team impact, and protect the company's reputation and bottom line.

Fisher, R., Ury, W., & Patton, B. (1992). *Getting to yes: Negotiating agreement without giving in.* New York, NY: Penguin.

Getting to Yes has a 30-year history of helping people negotiate smarter and more strategically. Based on the work of the Harvard Negotiation Project, "Getting to Yes" offers readers an established and systematic strategy for achieving mutually satisfactory agreements regardless of the circumstances at hand.

Patterson, K., Grenny, J., McMillan, R., & Switzler, A. (2011). *Crucial conversations: Tools for talking when stakes are high.* New York, NY: McGraw-Hill.

This best-selling book offers readers concrete and actionable advice about how to communicate when circumstances are less than ideal: when the stakes are high, all parties are on different pages, and emotions are heightened.

Rosenberg, M. B. (2003). *Nonviolent communication, a language of compassion.* Encinitas, CA: PuddleDancer Press.

Rosenberg offers an easy to implement model for communicating non-aggressively, compassionately, and in a manner that "fosters respect, attentiveness, and empathy."

Stone, D., Patton, B., & Heen, S. (2010). *Difficult conversations: How to discuss what matters most.* New York, NY: Penguin.

Based on fifteen years of research at the Harvard Negotiation Project, "Difficult Conversations" walks readers through a step-by-step, proven approach to having less-than-welcome conversations with "less stress and more success."

Ury, W. (2007). *The power of a positive no: Save the deal save the relationship and still say no.* New York, NY: Bantam Dell.

Saying no the right way is critical because, according to Ury, no is quite possibly the most powerful word in our language. Based on his acclaimed Harvard University course for leaders and executives, Ury offers readers specific and actionable advice about how to effectively say no in any situation, defend their interests, resist challenges, and ultimately reach the target—yes.

Sample Coaching Program (Case 5—Janis)

Janis has a Reserved score of 15 percent. Her subscale scores indicate that she is low on the Introverted and Tough subscales. Further, she is low on the Skeptical, Leisurely, and Bold scales, and she has elevations on the Cautious, Diligent, and

Dutiful scales. In combination, these scales portray an individual who is warm, engaging, friendly, and hardworking. More problematic characteristics include the likelihood that she is conflict avoidant, people pleasing, and overly soft in tough situations. Additionally, the combination of these scores suggests she is naïve about both organizational politics and the downside of overexposure.

The case information presented regarding Janis suggests that her low Reserved score is part of a pattern that will need to be addressed for her to succeed with the new hard-driving and charismatic regional manager. The following steps are recommended for coaching Janis:

- Help Janis understand that while her energy, positivity, conscientiousness, and ability to diffuse difficult customer service issues are all positive in many situations, the landscape (including the management) has changed. She now needs a new set of strategies and a new repertoire of behaviors.

- Help Janis understand that the new landscape calls for firm limits with her new manager about the workload for herself and her team and for careful consideration of what she discloses to the new manager.

- Discuss ways for Janis to redirect her social skills into "targeted charisma" to project a confident presence to her new manager, to her peers, and to her direct reports.

- Given her low score on the Leisurely scale, Janis may need to clearly define her own mission and objectives so that her new charismatic and driven regional manager does not usurp her agenda.

- Sell the fact that projecting a confident image and clear agenda will help Janis negotiate her workload, thus protecting her team and her work-life balance. Reinforce this throughout the coaching process. Stress that a confident person is less likely to become a target for blame and more likely to be considered for promotion in the future.

- Prompt Janis to reflect on her criteria for trusting others. This may lead to the need for additional help in reading the intentions of others.

SUMMARY

Keep Doing

Use positive social skills and the ability to connect productively with others.

Stop Doing

Allow others to abuse your time or have unlimited access to you.

Start Doing

Project confidence in setting boundaries with others and saying "no" when necessary.

Reserved behaviors are all about social, emotional, and even physical connections with others. A low Reserved score predicts friendly, warm, and engaging behaviors that are often beneficial in building relationships, developing others, and creating team cohesion. Unfortunately, these same behaviors when overdone can become problematic for the leader and the organization. Subscales help determine how and where the more troublesome low Reserved behaviors are likely to create problems. Contextual elements can help gauge how big a problem these behaviors are likely to create. Low Reserved behaviors are most likely to become problematic in environments or situations that require social and emotional toughness. They are also more likely to be problematic when a low Reserved individual, lauded for his or her warmth and social skills and for being a good team player, becomes a leader who needs to develop firmer social boundaries. In cases of this type, open door policies and displaying overly chummy behaviors can drain the leader's time and energy, lead to overexposure, and reduce the executive presence necessary to appear leader-like.

CHAPTER 14

LEISURELY

HIGH LEISURELY

Detecting When It Is a Problem

The impact of high Leisurely behavior is not immediately apparent. The leader may initially be perceived as capable, cooperative, and friendly. As time passes, however, and stresses intensify, cracks may appear in the façade. High Leisurely leaders do what they want, when they want, rather than meet the expectations of their managers and the organization. They consistently say one thing and do another—even after verbally agreeing to deliver exactly what the manager needs. Time and time again, they follow their own agenda, leaving a trail of unmet commitments in their wake. The pattern eventually becomes obvious. Trust is lost; credibility is compromised.

The disconnect that high Leisurely leaders create with the larger organization has repercussions for all of the leaders' stakeholders. But the biggest impact is on their direct reports, who are left without a connection to the work of the larger organization. This disconnect is exacerbated by the tendency of high Leisurely leaders to be uncommunicative. They keep their agendas to themselves and cut off questions with monosyllabic answers. They seem unwilling or unable to share information. So not only do high Leisurely leaders operate outside the objectives of the larger organization, but they also leave their followers without any communication about the larger organizational goals. Further, high Leisurely leaders do not like to be hurried or interrupted, and become irritated or aggressive if requests persist, creating yet another barrier to effective communication.

Another characteristic of high Leisurely leaders is passive aggression, or the indirect expression of hostility. The list of passive-aggressive behaviors is too long to recount here, but among the more obvious behavioral signs are:

- Not doing what they say they will.

- Procrastinating.

- Unwillingness to confront others.

- Blaming others for situational outcomes.

- Lacking empathy for the urgency of others.

George W. Bush (43) is an example of a high Leisurely leader. In the book *Decision Times*, he alludes to several missteps during his presidency. However, in spite of his role as president, he expresses no accountability for these. Rather, he named those who influenced his decisions as the ones with sole responsibility for those decisions. High Leisurely behaviors were also evident in his decisions about the Iraq war. Despite enormous pressure to change his war strategy and move in a different direction, he held steadfast to his own agenda. An important aspect of high Leisurely leaders is that they firmly believe in their own agenda despite the prevailing zeitgeist.

The high Leisurely leader's manager needs to be alert for signs of any missed deadlines and miscommunications and deal with them as soon as possible to mitigate the negative impact the high Leisurely leader may have on the organization. At the same time, the manager also needs to be aware that the high Leisurely leader may be both stubborn and hard to coach.

Rex from Case 1—Rex, Vice President of Sales on page 88 provides an illustration of a high Leisurely profile.

Rex's Situational Summary
Rex worked in a small company as vice president of sales. In his role, he had considerable autonomy and freedom to make decisions. The company was acquired by a much larger, well-established company with rules, processes, and procedures that often accompany a large bureaucracy. Rex's willingness to take risks and make fast, independent decisions runs counter to the culture that exists in the new company. This issue could be exacerbated by his tendency to follow his own agenda.

Dimension	Score	Percentile	Description
Excitable	50		Rex is very self-confident to the point of being an arrogant leader (Bold—95%). He is quite willing to take risks (Cautious—10% and Mischievous—90%). He tends to work his own agenda (Leisurely—82%), and prefers to operate independently without a lot of close supervision (Dutiful—5%).
Skeptical	67		
Cautious	10		
Reserved	45		
Leisurely	82		
Bold	95		
Mischievous	90		
Colorful	75		
Imaginative	70		
Diligent	30		
Dutiful	5		

0   10   20   30   40   50   60   70   80   90   100

Rex's profile is reminiscent of the lone cowboy syndrome—a man who lives life on his own terms and by his own rules. This maverick mentality is an asset in a small start-up, but is more of a liability in a larger organization with a well-established code of conduct and brand. Now that he is part of such an organization, Rex will have to make significant adjustments to his *modus operandi*.

In this situation, Rex would benefit from a mentor or an experienced coach to help him thrive under the new regime. Unfortunately, Rex's profile indicates that he is likely to be resistant to feedback, coaching, and advice. An elevated Leisurely score (82%) alone suggests this. The combination of a high Leisurely score with high Bold (95%) and Mischievous (90%) scores and with low Dutiful (5%) and Cautious (10%) scores only exacerbates this tendency. If Rex proves open to feedback and coaching, the initial coaching focus should be on his high Leisurely behaviors, specifically his tendency to ignore rules, procedures, and processes. This rebellious behavior will not be acceptable in a more bureaucratic organization.

Evaluating the Need for Change

The following behavioral questions should be considered in conjunction with a leader's high Leisurely score (as exhibited by Rex) when evaluating the need for a change in behavior. A "yes" response to three or fewer items suggests that there is no imminent need for behavioral changes. A "yes" response to four to six items suggests that a high score on the Leisurely scale should be a watch-out for a leader. A "yes" response to more than six items suggests that a leader should take active steps toward making behavioral changes.

Does the leader:

1. Put off or delay completing tasks that are viewed as less important than personal agenda items?	**Yes**	**No**	**Not Sure**
2. Appear to suppress anger even when it is obvious that a request creates an annoyance?	**Yes**	**No**	**Not Sure**
3. Often agree to a course of action, even when there is no intention of taking action, just to avoid a conflict?	**Yes**	**No**	**Not Sure**
4. Appear to be "put upon" when others ask for help or assistance?	**Yes**	**No**	**Not Sure**
5. Express discontent with the way others express or fail to express gratitude that is perceived to be deserved?	**Yes**	**No**	**Not Sure**
6. Leave the impression that personal agenda items should supersede the agenda items of others, even superiors?	**Yes**	**No**	**Not Sure**
7. Come across as insincere or even annoyed when others ask for help or assistance?	**Yes**	**No**	**Not Sure**
8. Get annoyed when his or her personal agenda is challenged by those wanting to go in a different direction?	**Yes**	**No**	**Not Sure**
9. View interruptions or distractions, regardless of how important, as unnecessary and annoying?	**Yes**	**No**	**Not Sure**

These items should be considered as behavioral indicators. Similar or associated behaviors to any of those listed that are exhibited by a leader likely suggest a "yes" response. They provide additional support that a leader may be at risk for the negative reputational consequences associated with those scoring high on the Leisurely scale, such as Rex.

Impact of High Leisurely Behaviors

Disillusionment, distrust, and loss of credibility are likely to be the result of the leader's high Leisurely behavior, which most clearly affects those with whom the leader most frequently interacts: manager, peers, and direct reports. What makes high Leisurely leaders even more of a puzzle to deal with is their propensity to engage in pleasant, friendly, and straightforward behavior at random intervals, punctuated by sudden bursts of internal anger or impatience. This emotional fluctuation leaves their colleagues confused, and makes the leader's underlying ambivalence toward others obvious. The following are some of the consequences that could result from high Leisurely behavior, broken out by the three key constituencies: managers, peers, and direct reports.

Managers

Managers will be frustrated due to their inability to predict the timeliness, thoroughness, consistency, and accuracy of what a high Leisurely leader delivers. The leader's behavior may create embarrassment as well as anger and anxiety. The manager is regularly left to wonder if this is another instance of being left in the lurch. Over time, the perception of the high Leisurely leader as someone who does not deliver will be cemented in the manager's mind. The career reality for high Leisurely leaders is that managers may eventually decide to let them go, ignore them, or move them elsewhere in the organization unless they have highly valued and unique skills or make frequent highly valuable contributions to the organization. In that case, the high Leisurely leader often becomes a "fair-haired" favorite of the higher-ups.

Peers

Peers will likely stop communicating, interacting, and, eventually, working with a high Leisurely leader because of a lack of trust. These defensive actions on the part of peers are meant to shield them from the negative consequences that could befall a high Leisurely leader. However, these actions may or may not preclude the negative impact the leader can have on the organization as a whole. It is also important to point out that more savvy peers may conspire to create circumstances that tempt the high Leisurely leader into demonstrating leisurely behaviors in front of other organizational members as a means of gaining political advantage.

Direct Reports

The high Leisurely leader can provide direct reports with a negative role model that may result in serious consequences for them. For example, they may inadvertently pick up some of the high Leisurely leader's behaviors or simply follow the misguided agenda of the leader. It is also possible that they recognize the misguided agenda and go around the leader to accomplish tasks, putting themselves in harm's way of the leader. In any case, poor communication and misalignment with the rest of the organization could very easily damage the reputations of the direct reports. Unfortunately, they are not left with a lot of great options for correcting the situation short of confronting the leader directly or escaping the situation entirely.

Coaching Focus

Coaching first and foremost must focus on the leader's acting in alignment with the rest of the organization. Continuing to act as an individual and pursuing a personal agenda with little communication and with no sense of accountability to the manager or to the organization will lead to certain failure for the leader. The importance of acting as an organizational member, regaining credibility and trust, practicing open communication, and tending to stakeholder relationships cannot be overestimated. Trust and credibility are the "coins of the realm," and the leader needs to regain lost ground by delivering on commitments and sharing information consistently.

High Leisurely leaders tend to be quite stubborn when it comes to their agenda. Coaching them is a challenge because admitting faults is anathema to them; consequently, they are not prone to accepting advice. To overcome this barrier, the coach should spend time up front helping high Leisurely leaders identify, clarify, and acknowledge the negative effect of their behavior on their reputation, on organizational relationships, and on the performance of their team. If the problem is not understood by the leader, the likelihood of a successful coaching outcome is slim.

Coaching Strategy

The steps involved in coaching a high Leisurely leader are as follows:

- Helping the leader understand and acknowledge the issues and their repercussions.
- Identifying the specific situations and behaviors that have been problems in the past.
- Scanning the environment and using as positive role models those who exhibit few high Leisurely behaviors and identifying negative role models and then tracing some of the exhibited behaviors to their ultimate outcome.
- Partnering with the leader to prioritize issues and develop plans to build trust (activities must have as their primary focus increasing alignment with the manager and the organization).
- Defining how success will be measured.
- Monitoring effectiveness of the behavioral changes and refining the new behaviors as needed.

Strategy Refinements Using Subscale Information

The subscales for Leisurely include Passive Aggressive, Unappreciated, and Irritated. Each subscale contributes to an overall Leisurely scale score and provides interpretation refinements beyond those that can be achieved from a scale score alone. These refinements can have implications for specific behavior changes that may improve leader performance. They may also help in determining which coaching strategy will be most effective in producing positive behavioral changes.

Passive Aggressive

High Leisurely leaders who are elevated on the Passive Aggressive subscale are publicly compliant and pleasant but privately resentful of others. This Janus-faced facade is most clearly demonstrated in a conflict situation. Individuals who are high on the Leisurely scale value reaching their personal goals more than maintaining their relationships. However, because they want to maintain an affable persona and are reluctant to reveal their true thoughts and feelings, they tend to agree with whatever their stakeholders want and then go about doing what they wanted to do anyway. High Leisurely leaders' behavior is characterized by making commitments and not keeping them. The coaching strategy should include a discussion about why trust is important in an organization and how trust and credibility are built.

Unappreciated

High Leisurely leaders who are elevated on the Unappreciated subscale feel that their contributions, efforts, and outcomes are unrecognized. In many ways, they create these issues for themselves. They are reluctant to share their agendas as well as share information, so they are often not recognized for making a contribution. No one knows what their contribution has been. Here the coaching strategy should revolve around communication, especially focusing on sharing information. The leader's contributions stand a much better chance of being recognized when those contributions are communicated effectively and are aligned with the manager and the organization.

Irritated

High Leisurely leaders who are elevated on this subscale are frequently irritated by interruptions or requests for information. Interruptions interfere with the leader's personal agenda and so are unwelcome. Also, the interruptions are often accompanied by requests for information that leaders do not particularly want to share or see the necessity for sharing. Coaching for these leaders should emphasize the responsibilities of a leadership role in an organization and how to structure interruptions into their schedules. Interestingly, these leaders often do not realize that their irritation is showing and that others actually recognize that the leaders would prefer to pursue their personal agendas. Agenda alignment can also be helpful with respect to this subscale in that misalignment is often the origin of the irritation in the first place.

Coaching Tactics

Coaching tactics cover a range of approaches and resources that have been found useful in addressing high Leisurely behaviors. These tactics are typically used in combination to form a custom plan suited to the specific learning needs of a leader. The tactics are divided into four categories: (1) thought-provoking questions for a leader to consider, (2) exercises a leader can engage in to improve performance, (3) tips and techniques a coach can use to help a leader improve performance, and (4) support resources that can be consulted to gain additional insights in addressing high Leisurely behaviors.

Thought-Provoking Questions for a Leader

- What situations cause you to be stubborn or to procrastinate? How do these behaviors impact your effectiveness? What do you think they are doing to your reputation?

- How often do you make commitments and then not meet them? What situations are more likely to result in this happening? Does this ever create problems for your credibility?

- What situations make you feel as if people do not value your contributions? Do you feel underappreciated? Do you have any ideas about how to get the recognition you think you deserve?

- Under what circumstances do you question the competence of others? Direct reports? Peers? Bosses? How do you handle this? How could you handle it more effectively?

- What impact are high Leisurely behaviors having on your career?

Exercises for a Leader

- Scan the organization and identify others who exhibit high Leisurely behaviors. List the consequences or negative impact of these behaviors and how the problems they created could have been averted.

- Generate a list of questions that are designed to understand rather than to undermine the directions or agendas of others.

- Identify a trusted colleague in the organization, and ask the colleague to help track high Leisurely behaviors including the *tells* that indicate irritation.

- Schedule project review meetings with the manager to ensure that expectations are clearly communicated and agendas are aligned.

- Identify examples when you should have spoken up when you disagreed or when things were not going according to your agenda. List some alternative ways these situations could have been handled to avoid people thinking you were in agreement when you really were not.

Tips and Techniques for a Coach

- Work with the leader's manager to gain a clear understanding of the manager's priorities and objectives. Go through this list with the leader to see where alignment and misalignment between both sets of priorities exist. In those areas where the manager's and leader's priorities are misaligned, meet with them jointly to gain alignment and to determine an acceptable way forward.

- Have the leader generate two lists. One list includes commitments that the leader has met in the last six months, and the other list includes commitments that have not been met. What distinguishes the lists from one another? Are there any consistent patterns or themes?

- Work with high Leisurely leaders to help them learn how to pause and think before making a commitment. Have them consider if making a particular commitment is something they really want to do. Point out that it is better to refuse right away than to disappoint the person to whom they have made a commitment that they do not keep. Continue to emphasize the difference between necessary commitments and optional commitments.

- Does the leader have trouble saying no? Look around for a role model who is able to say no smoothly and without giving offense. Also, here it would be important for the leader to learn to differentiate between a trivial request and an urgent request.

- Help the leader understand the *tells* he or she exhibits when irritated. The point here is to help the leader recognize that *tells* are important. Others will pick up on them.

Support Resources

Braiker, H. B. (2002). *The disease to please: Curing the people-pleasing syndrome.* New York, NY: McGraw Hill.

After discussing why people pleasing is more than just a "benign problem," Braiker offers readers a self-assessment, describes the roots of people pleasing tendencies, and provides simple, subtle, and easy-to-implement tips for breaking free of the "Disease to Please Triangle."

Brandt, B., & Rothschild, B. (2013). *Keys to eliminating passive aggressiveness.* New York, NY: W.W. Norton & Company.

Brandt and Rothschild discuss the often benign roots of communication labeled as passive-aggressive and teach readers how to subtly change their communication tactics so that they come across as assertive, transparent, and constructive.

Butler, G., & Hope, T. (2007). *Managing your mind: The mental fitness guide.* New York, NY: Oxford University Press.

Based on time-tested management advice and proven clinical psychology tactics such as Cognitive-Behavior Therapy, Butler and Hope describe how readers can develop the "mental fitness" necessary to be fulfilled and productive, both personally and professionally.

Cooper, R. (2014). *Difficult people: Ultimate dealing with difficult people guide!* [Kindle edition]. Retrieved from Amazon.com

Difficult People helps readers discover how to effectively and constructively interact with challenging people in professional and non-professional settings. Among many other topics, Cooper discusses the roots and precursors of people's behavior, how to respond to passive aggression, and how to quickly and effectively defuse conflict.

Runion, M. (2010). *Speak strong: Say what you MEAN. MEAN what you say. Don't be MEAN when you say it.* New York, NY: Morgan James.

Filled with real-life examples and practical, actionable advice, "Speak Strong" teaches readers how to find their voices, express their true sentiments, create boundaries, set and maintain higher communication standards, and overcome less-than-constructive communication tendencies, among many other valuable lessons.

Simon, G. K. (2010). *In sheep's clothing: Understanding and dealing with manipulative people.* Little Rock, AR: A.J. Christopher & Company.

Simon's succinct but example-laden book helps readers understand what they can do to decrease the odds that they are targets for manipulators and offers easy-to-implement tactics readers can employ when interacting with controlling or manipulative people.

Sample Coaching Program (Case 1—Rex)

Two of the Leisurely subscales were elevated for Rex, so coaching needs to address Rex's Passive Aggressive and Irritated subscales. His feelings of Unappreciated were not elevated. These are Rex's priorities:

- Rebuilding trust and credibility.

- Accepting his role as an organizational citizen, which includes doing what he says he will (acting in alignment with the rest of the organization), openly communicating his perspectives, and building relationships with stakeholders.

The first step in modifying behavior is accepting feedback. Given that Rex tends to discount feedback, getting him to take the feedback seriously is of utmost importance. The coach should ask Rex to identify those people in the organization whose opinions he respects and include them in the multi-rater assessment process. Simultaneously, the coach should ask Rex's manager who should be included. In Rex's case, stakeholder interviews supplemented by questionnaires would be ideal. As many critical incidents and the repercussions of these incidents as possible should be part of the feedback. The intention here is to provide Rex with airtight and undeniable feedback.

In Rex's case, the coach might also consider a more intensive coaching experience. Taking him off-site for three or four days and having two coaches work with him at the outset of the coaching engagement is an option that would be more likely to produce success. This initial immersion experience would need to be followed by regular on-site coaching (once a week or once every two weeks for at least six months with the lead coach).

Coaching should address Rex's Passive Aggressive behavior (specifically, teaching him to do what he says he will) and his Irritated behavior (teaching him alternative ways of dealing with interruptions).

Passive Aggressive

Rex does want to maintain smooth relationships with stakeholders. Once he receives *and* accepts the feedback that his stakeholders do not trust him, his motivation for change will most likely be activated. These steps should be taken:

- Helping him recognize that one of the most important trust builders is doing what he says he will.

- Realizing that accepting a role as a leader in an organization indicates that Rex is willing to act in alignment with that organization. His new position does not mean that he cannot have a different perspective, but it does imply that he will be willing to openly express his perspective and will ultimately act in accordance with the organization's point of view. It is important to review this point repeatedly with Rex especially when he exhibits behaviors that suggest a misalignment with the direction of the organization.

- Noting the congruity between Rex's body language and his words during the coaching and pointing out to him when they are incongruent. This recognition is essential because the likelihood of acting during the coaching session as he does normally is high (i.e., agreeing to something with no intention of delivering on it). The coach will let Rex know that he or she is aware when Rex is not committed to making changes. This coaching should occur at those moments when Rex is giving lip service to change as opposed to expressing wholehearted commitment to change.

- Considering carefully before he agrees with any request whether or not he really intends to comply. If he is not in agreement, he needs to say so.

- Saying "no" while role playing high-stakes situations. This exercise will probably take several role plays before it becomes natural to Rex to say "no" in a way that is not likely to be offensive to his stakeholders.

- Reviewing with him, at each coaching session, his progress in this area.

- Emphasizing that consistently doing what he says he will is the only way to rebuild trust.

- Scheduling a meeting with each one of his stakeholders to make amends for his past behavior. These meetings should be carefully planned with guidance from the coach.

Irritated

Behavioral Approach: From a purely behavioral perspective, this issue is much more easily changed than "doing what you say you will." It involves planning ahead and scheduling time for interruptions and times when there will be no interruptions except for emergencies. Medical doctors and other professionals sometimes schedule calling times for their clients when they plan to make themselves available as needed and other times when office hours or project work takes precedence. These same techniques can be employed to help Rex.

Mind Management Approach: In conjunction with dealing with the behavioral aspects of this issue, the coach should also approach it from a mind management perspective:

- Identify the thoughts that Rex is thinking when he is interrupted that directly affect his mood and cause him to be irritated. For example, is he thinking "Doesn't this person realize how important my work is?" or "This person should not be interrupting me or wasting my time!"

- Help Rex reframe the situation once he identifies these unrealistic or dysfunctional thoughts. Reframing is a way to help Rex look at a situation from a variety of perspectives and learn to substitute different emotional reactions to the situation. For the first example above, he might substitute "There is no way that person knows the importance of what I am working on," and for the second example the substitution, "I am sure this must be urgent for this person to be interrupting me."

- Practice reframing so that it becomes a useful tool. The coach might suggest that Rex keep a journal between coaching sessions. Rex records any time he becomes irritated, frustrated, impatient, or upset, what his thoughts were at the time, and how he might reframe the situation. The coach and Rex can then review these records at each session until reframing becomes second nature to Rex.

- Help Rex set realistic expectations for controlling his tendency to become irritated. Instruct Rex to initially use the reframing process with minor emotional upsets. Once success is achieved here, Rex can start slowly using reframing with more difficult emotional situations. Start with situations where there is a high probability of success.

Unappreciated

Although the Unappreciated subscale was not elevated for Rex, as coaching progresses and Rex works diligently on changing his behavior, he may start to feel unappreciated, especially if no one notices his progress. The coach and Rex's manager will probably make positive comments. However, other people probably will not as most people are quite self-involved. One strategy that may prove useful is for Rex to let trusted associates know about the behavioral changes he is trying to make. This information increases the probability that they will notice the changes.

Summary

Keep Doing

Foster positive relationships by using effective social skills.

Stop Doing

Make commitments that may not be met.

Start Doing

Be candid regarding agenda disagreements or conflicts.

The negative impact of high Leisurely behaviors is sometimes hard to recognize because it may take a while for repercussions to occur. Managers who repeatedly experience high Leisurely behaviors on the part of a subordinate will, over time, recognize the signals and lose trust in the person. High Leisurely leaders tend to feel misunderstood and, as a result, may be quite stubborn and hard to coach. Critical to coaching high Leisurely leaders is understanding that they often do not recognize the negative impact of their behavior on others. Consequently, they need to become more aware. Patience is a requirement for the coach because high Leisurely behaviors may be well entrenched and resistant. However, these behaviors are not impossible for a motivated leader to change.

Low Leisurely

Detecting When It Is a Problem

Low Leisurely leaders only want to please and have no personal agenda. They are people pleasers and completely "other-directed." Low Leisurely leaders are easy to spot. One or two interactions and coworkers have them pegged.

Low Leisurely leaders are patient when interrupted, regardless of whether the interruption is trivial or urgent. They will agree to anything, which often leads to overload. But no problem, they will trudge through, almost always deliver on time, and exceed the requestor's expectations. They are overly cooperative and put others' needs before their own. Because they do this, they seldom delegate and are always willing to step in and help an overwhelmed colleague, manager, or direct report.

Good examples of low Leisurely leaders can be found among one's past or present colleagues. They accept whatever level of performance their staffs deliver, never setting "stretch" goals or expecting improvements in performance. They find it difficult to correct average or low-performing direct reports, or to encourage and urge high performers to excel. They are overly focused on whether or not their direct reports like them and tend to accept the status quo and overly value and praise mediocre results.

Reality TV offers copious examples of low Leisurely scores in action. Watch any of the shows with multiple participants, such as *Celebrity Apprentice* or *Survivor*, and note that there is always at least one person who is overly agreeable and looks to others for leadership.

Janis from Case 5—Janis, Customer Service Manager on page 96 provides a good example of a low Leisurely profile. The following is Janis's profile summary.

Janis's Situational Summary
Janis is a newly promoted customer service manager who works for a software company. Her long-time regional manager was recently promoted, and her new manager is described as young, hard-charging, and very demanding. Janis is very conscientious and works hard to keep everybody happy. Her new manager will likely test her ability to push back, or she will find herself challenged to keep up with his demands. Her lack of self-confidence will also be readily apparent to her new manager.

Dimension	Score	Percentile	Description
Excitable	60		Janis is a high-energy person who does not over-promise (Cautious—75%) and is very approachable (Reserved—15%). She lacks confidence (Bold—10%) but makes up for it through preparation and attention to detail (Diligent—85%). She is known for her loyalty and willingness to go the extra mile when it comes to protecting the reputation of the company and her manager (Dutiful—80%).
Skeptical	10		
Cautious	75		
Reserved	15		
Leisurely	20		
Bold	10		
Mischievous	40		
Colorful	30		
Imaginative	62		
Diligent	85		
Dutiful	80		

0   10   20   30   40   50   60   70   80   90   100

With a new ambitious and demanding manager, Janis's low Leisurely score (20%) may prove to be problematic. As a low Leisurely leader, Janis's desire to please is likely to result in her accepting a workload that is unrealistic. Further, she will probably neither feel nor express frustration or irritation at such demands. As always, she will put her own needs behind the needs of her manager and the organization. Given her new manager's tendency to place blame on others for any failure to deliver, Janis may find herself in a precarious position.

Janis's other scores increase the likelihood of an undesirable career outcome. Her Dutiful score (80%) indicates a person who tries hard to do what she is expected to do. Given Janis's high Cautious score (75%), she wants these expectations to be spelled out in minute detail. Because they seldom are, Janis is often indecisive and resistant to change. Her high Diligent score suggests that she is attentive to detail and that she will provide others with structure and direction, but she may be reluctant to delegate. With a hard-charging new manager, these characteristics will not be valued and may rebound to damage Janis's reputation.

While Janis has numerous strengths, including her attention to detail and her loyalty (Dutiful), she lacks initiative and leadership energy, as indicated by her low Bold, Mischievous, Colorful, and Imaginative scores. She also may be overly trusting, given her low Skeptical score, which is not an asset for leaders. This lack of potential for leadership is exacerbated by her low Leisurely score, indicating that she has no agenda of her own. For Janis, this lack of an agenda may become a major obstacle to her career success.

Evaluating the Need for Change

The following behavioral questions should be considered in conjunction with a leader's low Leisurely score (as exhibited by Janis) when evaluating the need for a change in behavior. A "yes" response to three or fewer items suggests that there is no imminent need for behavioral changes. A "yes" response to four to six items suggests that a low score on the Leisurely scale should be a watch-out for a leader. A "yes" response to more than six items suggests that a leader should take active steps toward making behavioral changes.

Does the leader:

1. Agree to unrealistic timeframes for requests regularly, with little or no push back?   **Yes   No   Not Sure**

2. Put his or her own agenda aside or have it supplanted completely in fulfilling the requests of others?   **Yes   No   Not Sure**

3. Comply with requests, even when they appear to run counter to his or her own views or beliefs?   **Yes   No   Not Sure**

4. Maintain a demeanor of gratitude even when requests are unreasonable? **Yes   No   Not Sure**

5. Appear excessively appreciative in situations where such emotions are inappropriate or should be tempered? **Yes   No   Not Sure**

6. Happily acquiesce to the agenda of others without offering any challenge or resistance? **Yes   No   Not Sure**

7. Appear excessively compliant or agreeable when others make requests of them? **Yes   No   Not Sure**

8. Suppress negative emotions even in situations that would test the patience of most people? **Yes   No   Not Sure**

9. Accommodate interruptions or distractions, regardless of how trivial, without showing signs of irritation? **Yes   No   Not Sure**

These items should be considered as behavioral indicators. Similar or associated behaviors to any of those listed that are exhibited by a leader likely suggest a "yes" response. They provide additional support that a leader may be at risk for the negative reputational consequences associated with those scoring low on the Leisurely scale, such as Janis.

Impact of Low Leisurely Behaviors

Low Leisurely leaders often wind up being discounted. They become leaders without followers. Paradoxically, they have earned the appellation of "leader," while in reality they have none of the qualities required for leadership. They quickly become characterized as pushovers, wishy-washy, or wimps. Typically, they are promoted because they have had managers who were impressed by their ability to over-deliver and who really did not want input on issues anyway. The following are some of the consequences of low Leisurely behaviors, broken out by three constituencies: managers, peers, and direct reports.

Managers

Managers learn that low Leisurely leaders will deliver under any circumstances. If managers are highly autocratic, they may take advantage of this and pile on the work. If managers are more participative, they may quickly tire of the low Leisurely individual's ambiguous or unclear answers and agendas and may be unable to determine why the leader is consistently overcommitted. Low Leisurely leaders hide behind their "busy-ness," thus freeing them from having to contribute an opinion or idea.

Peers

Peers soon realize that low Leisurely leaders have no agenda and no opinions and tend to assume a role of follower in group settings. Peers begin regarding these leaders as unimportant and possessing no organizational power or influence. Peers quickly stop soliciting low Leisurely leaders' opinions and participation and may perceive them as pushovers. Peers may even co-opt these leaders into their own agenda as a way of gaining political advantage.

Direct Reports

Low Leisurely leaders work hard to maintain a nice persona and, as a result, do not give their staff feedback or hard-hitting performance appraisals when called for. This absence of candid criticism is perceived positively by those who are sliding by and will annoy those who perform well. Importantly, direct reports may not be aligned with the rest of the organization and may perceive their leader as not supporting and defending them. Such leaders also fail to delegate and thus neglect developing as well as supporting and defending their direct reports. More ambitious or politically savvy direct reports may even manipulate low Leisurely leaders. It is not uncommon for direct reports to get low Leisurely leaders to do their work for them. It is also not uncommon for direct reports to use these leaders as stepping stones to advance their own careers.

Coaching Focus

The coaching focus for low Leisurely leaders will initially be on clarifying values, beliefs, feelings, needs, and wants in order to define their leadership identity and goals. The focus will then switch to appropriately assertive behavior.

Coaching Strategy

Low Leisurely leaders need to learn a new set of behaviors to replace their current passive behavior. This understanding will involve learning and practicing how to express feelings, thoughts, needs, wants, disagreements, and opinions appropriately. A large number of commonly encountered situations require assertiveness, including expressing opinions, setting limits, refusing requests, and resolving disagreements and disputes. The steps for coaching low Leisurely leaders are the following:

- Helping them become aware of their behavior and the impact it has on their colleagues and their reputation.
- Collecting behavioral data from their colleagues.
- Identifying themes and prioritizing target behaviors.
- Discussing roadblocks that they encounter in practicing the new behaviors.
- Exploring underlying beliefs or values that may be hindering their progress.
- Monitoring progress and refining plans as needed.

Strategy Refinements Using Subscale Information

The subscales for Leisurely include Passive Aggressive, Unappreciated, and Irritated. Each subscale contributes to an overall Leisurely scale score and provides interpretation refinements beyond those that can be achieved from a scale score alone. These interpretation refinements can have implications for specific behavior changes that may improve leader performance. They may also help in refining which coaching strategy will be most effective in producing positive behavioral changes.

Passive Aggressive

A low score on the Passive Aggressive subscale indicates that low Leisurely leaders are neither aggressive nor assertive. They could be characterized as selfless. They routinely put the needs of the organization before their own personal needs. They will agree at the last minute to take on assignments that are seemingly impossible and then consistently over-deliver, inevitably leading to additional impossible requests of them as colleagues and managers realize that these individuals will always come through. The coaching focus with a low Leisurely leader with a low Passive Aggressive subscale should be on practicing to identify and assert needs in a constructive manner. The alternative of always serving others' needs first will eventually take its toll on the leader's professional and personal life.

Unappreciated

A low score on the Unappreciated subscale indicates that low Leisurely leaders feel that their contributions, efforts, and outcomes are much appreciated by others. However, in seeking to gain the approval and appreciation of everyone, these leaders suppress their own emotional wants and needs and might be out of touch with their feelings. They lose sight of themselves in their effort to be all things to all people. These leaders have trouble identifying their own emotions. The coaching focus should be on helping these leaders identify and become aware of their feelings (particularly their "negative" feelings) so that they can then focus on their own wants and needs. The coaching needs to emphasize the importance of the leader's becoming aware of and expressing his or her feelings appropriately.

Irritated

A low score on the Irritated subscale indicates leaders who are unlikely to feel or show irritation. These leaders do not mind adhering to their managers' or their organizations' agendas because they have none of their own. They welcome interruptions because dealing with the needs of others keeps them from having to identify and deal with their own needs. Coaching these leaders involves helping them to determine their values and beliefs. Who are they? What do they stand for? What is truly important to them?

Coaching Tactics

Coaching tactics cover a range of approaches and resources that have been found useful in addressing low Leisurely behaviors. These tactics are typically used in combination to form a custom plan suited to the specific learning needs of a leader. The tactics are divided into four categories: (1) thought-provoking questions for a leader to consider, (2) exercises a leader can engage in to improve performance, (3) tips and techniques a coach can use to help a leader improve performance, and (4) support resources that can be consulted to gain additional insights in addressing low Leisurely behaviors.

Thought-Provoking Questions for a Leader

- What is most important to you at work? What sort of reputation would you like to have? Is there anything you would like to do differently?

- When is it important to take a stand? How do you express this?

- How do you set limits with colleagues? How and when do you say "no"?

- When there is a difference of opinion with a colleague, how do you resolve the situation?

- Do you find yourself doing the work of others or doing more than your fair share? How can you push back to avoid this circumstance in the future?

Exercises for a Leader

- Identify and observe colleagues who are good role models for assertiveness.

- Generate a list of appropriate phrases that can be used when encountering situations that provide an opportunity for assertiveness.

- Describe the characteristics you admire in great leaders, and compare those characteristics with your areas of strength and weakness.

- Identify situations in which other leaders use their emotions effectively to achieve their goals and objectives. How does that compare with the way you use your emotions?

- Are your contributions to the organization being noticed or recognized? How could you go about raising awareness regarding the value you bring to the table?

Tips and Techniques for a Coach

- Have the leader role play expressing a definitive opinion to peers. As the coaching proceeds, have the leader role play refusing a request constructively, expressing disagreement, resolving a dispute, and providing feedback to a direct report.

- Ask the leader to develop a personal statement describing values, needs, and wants, and then discuss the statement. As the next step, ask the leader to craft a description of what he or she wants to stand for as a leader in the organization.

- Keep in mind that low Leisurely leaders are inveterate people pleasers, and be aware of this in your interactions with them.
- Point out in-the-moment low Leisurely behaviors.
- Look for opportunities to remind low Leisurely leaders that assertiveness requires appropriate body language, which makes points clearer and more effective.
- Emphasize the need to "practice, practice, practice" assertive behaviors.

Support Resources

Breitman, P., & Hatch, C. (2001). *How to say no without feeling guilty: And say yes to more time, and what matters most to you.* **New York, NY: Broadway Books.**

Based on the premise that anyone can learn how to say no with self-assurance, grace, and kindness, Breitman and Hatch teach readers five simple techniques that make saying no easier and less guilt-inducing regardless of the circumstances.

Chamorro-Premuzic, T. (2014). *Confidence: Overcoming low self-esteem, insecurity, and self-doubt.* **New York, NY: Penguin.**

Chamorro-Premuzic argues that, contrary to popular belief, confidence is capable of thwarting achievement, employability, and likability. Among other topics, this book discusses the silver linings of low confidence, teaches readers how to identify when to feign self-assurance (and how to do so effectively), and tactics for improving physical and emotional health.

Craig, N., George, B., & Snook, S. (2015). *The discover your true north fieldbook: A personal guide to finding your authentic leadership* **[Kindle edition]. Retrieved from Amazon.com**

Based on the best-selling book *True North*, this workbook walks leaders through a series of exercises that help them identify their leadership objectives and facilitate the development of authentic leadership skills.

Klaus, P. (2004). *Brag!: The art of tooting your own horn without blowing it.* **New York, NY: Warner Business.**

Renowned communication expert Klaus offers readers a "subtle but effective" plan for selling themselves without seeming self-promoting or overeager to impress.

Murphy, J. (2011). *Assertiveness: Stand up for yourself and still win the respect of others* **[Kindle edition]. Retrieved from Amazon.com**

Based on a list of principles she calls the "Bill of Rights of Assertiveness," Murphy helps readers understand how to be assertive without crossing the line to aggressiveness and offers numerous examples and exercises designed to help readers practice being assertive in a variety of contexts.

Patterson, R. J. (2014). *The assertiveness workbook: How to express your ideas and stand up for yourself at work and in relationships.* **Oakland, CA: New Harbinger.**

Patterson's highly rated workbook explains how to establish and sustain personal boundaries without becoming unapproachable and offers readily applicable cognitive behavioral techniques capable of fostering increased assertiveness.

Smith, M. J. (2000). *When I say "No," I feel guilty* (Vol. 2). N.p.: A Train Press.

This classic assertiveness training book offers readers immediately implementable tips for saying "no" without guilt or regret, staying calm when people are trying to push their buttons, and standing up for themselves and their best interests.

Sample Coaching Program (Case 5—Janis)

Janis's Leisurely score is 20 percent. An examination of her three subscale scores indicates that her Passive Aggressive and Irritated scores were low, while her Unappreciated score was not low. Because Janis works tirelessly at pleasing others, this is not surprising. Initially, more attention needs to be paid to Janis's low Passive Aggressive and Irritated scores. Once Janis gets more in touch with her emotions, her Unappreciated score may turn out to warrant coaching as well. Most importantly, the coach needs to be aware that Janis wants to please and will probably agree with anything the coach says. Follow up probes may result in more valid information from Janis. The following are suggested coaching approaches for the subscales.

Passive Aggressive

- The coach might begin the initial session by asking Janis what she wants from the coaching process. Most likely, she will be unable to answer this question. If follow-up probes do not elicit a response, try asking questions such as, "Imagine you were your more successful twin sister. How would she answer this question?" The coach should be persistent in getting a response.

- The coach should follow up with psychological tests, a family and career history, stakeholder interviews, and surveys to ensure a thorough assessment process. This process is particularly important in Janis's case as it will provide a platform for future sessions.

- The coach, in future sessions, should have Janis provide her reactions to the feedback, continuing to be patient and persistent in having Janis articulate her wants, needs, values, motivations, and opinions.

- Once Janis begins to get in touch with herself, the coach and Janis will work on anticipating situations that are likely to occur and planning how Janis will behave. The goal is to have Janis begin to act in a manner that is consistent with her needs but not offensive to others. In other words, she will start learning how to handle situations in an assertive manner.

- The coach, if possible, should observe Janis in her day-to-day interactions in order to help her fine-tune her behaviors and to brainstorm alternatives to interactions with others who do not meet her expectations.

Irritated

Janis is always willing to turn her attention to the needs of others, even when their needs interfere with her own needs. When interrupted, Janis should start to think of herself first and what might be sacrificed if she allows the interruption. If the interruption will result in an inconvenience to her, she needs to communicate this in a firm but tactful manner. Role playing interruptions with her coach will be necessary for her to learn to do this. Saying "no" in this situation is a great opportunity for Janis to practice setting limits and boundaries so that she is not as vulnerable to the whims of others.

Unappreciated

As Janis begins saying "no" to others, they may respond by withdrawing from her to some degree. Furthermore, the extent to which others express their appreciation may also decline as she begins to stand up for herself. As she becomes more and more aware of her own feelings and acts accordingly, she will recognize the changes in the behavior of others and may start to feel less appreciated. The coach needs to help her to anticipate this reaction and brainstorm mechanisms to deal with it.

SUMMARY

Keep Doing

Maintain positive and agreeable attitudes and behaviors.

Stop Doing

Say "yes" to every request no matter how daunting or unrealistic.

Start Doing

Use more assertive behavior when appropriate.

Low Leisurely leaders are people pleasers. They are unassertive and can be easily manipulated. Changing a leader's reputation once colleagues have concluded that the leader is a pushover and wishy-washy can be challenging. A motivated leader can undergo a dramatic transformation and achieve an enhanced reputation by taking advantage of coaching for assertiveness that includes multiple role playing sessions. The most challenging aspect of reshaping the reputation of a low Leisurely leader is establishing a toughminded attitude to build an agenda and stick with it. The natural tendency to revert to pleasing others is powerful. Low Leisurely behaviors can be quite career limiting in a world that values strong-willed leadership. These behaviors may not get an individual fired, but they certainly can contribute to the individual's being passed over.

CHAPTER 15

BOLD

HIGH BOLD

Detecting When It Is a Problem

Individuals who have high scores on the Bold scale are typically described by others as being arrogant, being overconfident, acting in an entitled way, and seeing themselves as being destined for greatness. This pattern becomes a problem when the behavior starts breeding resentment in others or drives the individual to engage in reckless activities. High Bold behavior can be a serious problem if it becomes so extreme that it borders on delusional and is impervious to a reality check.

Moderate elevations on the Bold scale can sometimes be useful. Most leaders of organizations need to have at least a moderate degree of self-confidence in order to assume positions of leadership and convey confidence to the people who must follow them. The optimal point for the Bold characteristic depends on the situation or challenge that must be faced. What constitutes confident, decisive leadership behavior in one situation or organizational culture may appear unrealistic or reckless in another context.

A good example of a high Bold individual is the World War II general George S. Patton. Patton languished for over 16 years as a major in the U.S. Army prior to the war and was even briefly demoted back to captain. An early evaluation of Patton stated that "he would be invaluable in a time of war, but is a disturbing element in time of peace." He failed to be selected for Command and General Staff School, which was a prerequisite for advancement. When war broke out, though, his unusual combination of self-confidence, ambition, and excitability catapulted him into a generalship. Eventually, he became a four-star general, but during his tenure as general, he came perilously close to being drummed out of the service and was sidelined from several important battles owing to his arrogance, competitiveness, and lack of interpersonal sensitivity. By the end of the war, Patton was once again in danger of derailing his career owing to a series of incidents. Eventually fate intervened and he was killed in a peace-time accident, so we will never know if he would have been able to make the transition back to a world not at war.

One of the distinguishing features of individuals with high Bold behaviors is that they are impervious to negative feedback or events. Donald Trump, the well-known businessman, could be a poster child for this phenomenon. Although he has had many successful business ventures over his career, he has also had many failures, which he seems unwilling to acknowledge. Several years ago, *Time* magazine documented his many failed business ventures, which included Trump Airlines, Trump Vodka, Trump Mortgages, a Trump Monopoly game, various Trump casinos, and several bankruptcies. When asked about why he was filing for bankruptcy for a third time in a New Jersey bankruptcy court, he responded, "I don't like the B word."

What makes this profile especially difficult to coach is that people who are high on the Bold scale are often very successful and do, in fact, gain status among their peers. If we think about life's challenges as getting along, getting ahead, and making sense out of life, high Bold people often do quite well, at least at the getting ahead part.

Rex from Case 1—Rex, Vice President of Sales on page 88 is a good example of a high Bold individual whose situation has recently changed dramatically. Factors that previously made him successful may now conspire to derail him. The following is Rex's profile summary.

Rex's Situational Summary
Rex worked in a small company as vice president of sales. In his role, he had considerable autonomy and freedom to make decisions. The company was acquired by a much larger, well-established company with rules, processes, and procedures that often accompany a large bureaucracy. Rex's willingness to take risks and make fast, independent decisions runs counter to the culture that exists in the new company. This issue could be exacerbated by his tendency to follow his own agenda.

Dimension	Score	Percentile	Description
Excitable	50		Rex is very self-confident to the point of being an arrogant leader (Bold—95%). He is quite willing to take risks (Cautious—10% and Mischievous—90%). He tends to work his own agenda (Leisurely—82%), and prefers to operate independently without a lot of close supervision (Dutiful—5%).
Skeptical	67		
Cautious	10		
Reserved	45		
Leisurely	82		
Bold	95		
Mischievous	90		
Colorful	75		
Imaginative	70		
Diligent	30		
Dutiful	5		

0   10   20   30   40   50   60   70   80   90   100

In addition to his high Bold scores, Rex's profile displays several extreme scores that could spell trouble for him in the workplace. A score of 90 percent on the Mischievous scale indicates someone with a proclivity to test the limits and chafe under bureaucratic rules and regulations. His elevated score on the Leisurely scale might also predict that he will be stubborn about accommodating rules with which he does not agree. Exceedingly low scores on the Cautious and Dutiful scales also would predict someone who may act impulsively and not be good at following orders.

As we saw with Patton, in the right set of circumstances a high Bold pattern can drive ambitious, energetic leadership. For Rex, as vice president of sales for a small company, this high Bold pattern contributed to a large part of the company's growth. But six months ago, the Situational Context for Rex changed when the company was acquired by a larger and more bureaucratic organization. The autonomy he previously enjoyed is likely to be greatly restrained. Rex was a major contributor to the growth of his organization before it was acquired, so he may have feelings of entitlement that are not entirely unjustified. He has continued to operate in an aggressive and risk-taking manner that will not be a good fit with the new organization. His extremely high Bold score, coupled with elevations on the Leisurely and Mischievous scales, will increase the likelihood that he will run afoul of the new, more bureaucratic culture.

Evaluating the Need for Change

The following behavioral questions should be considered in conjunction with a leader's high Bold score (as exhibited by Rex) when evaluating the need for a change in behavior. A "yes" response to three or fewer items suggests that there is no imminent need for behavioral changes. A "yes" response to four to six items suggests that a high score on the Bold scale should be a watch-out for a leader. A "yes" response to more than six items suggests that a leader should take active steps toward making behavioral changes.

Does the leader:

1.	Appear to take liberties beyond those approved or appropriately sanctioned?	**Yes**	**No**	**Not Sure**
2.	Insist on a level of respect that is beyond that which has been earned?	**Yes**	**No**	**Not Sure**
3.	Express disdain or even refuse to accept assignments considered more appropriate for those of lesser status?	**Yes**	**No**	**Not Sure**
4.	Display arrogance when it comes to the probability of success, regardless of the challenge?	**Yes**	**No**	**Not Sure**
5.	Always accept the credit, but never accept the blame?	**Yes**	**No**	**Not Sure**
6.	Lack humility when it comes to abilities or accomplishments?	**Yes**	**No**	**Not Sure**
7.	Proclaim unusual talent and the greatness that will result from it?	**Yes**	**No**	**Not Sure**
8.	Have an inflated self-image when it comes to skills or abilities?	**Yes**	**No**	**Not Sure**
9.	Complain about personal talents that are under-utilized or that career opportunities should be more forthcoming?	**Yes**	**No**	**Not Sure**

These items should be considered as behavioral indicators. Similar or associated behaviors to any of those listed that are exhibited by a leader likely suggest a "yes" response. They provide additional support that a leader may be at risk for the negative reputational consequences associated with those scoring high on the Bold scale, such as Rex.

Impact of High Bold Behaviors

Patton initially was loved and admired by his men, partly because he instilled confidence in them and backed it up by winning battles. But as the war dragged on, his men started referring to him as "Blood and Guts Patton—our blood, his guts." This change in regard is a very familiar pattern with high Bold leaders. Initially, they are charismatic and inspiring to be around. But with time, and particularly if the individual does not spread recognition around to others, what is initially seen as dynamic leadership will be viewed as insensitive self-aggrandizement. There is often a narcissistic quality to high Bold individuals who fail to acknowledge the contributions of others. Daring, bold behaviors can morph into being seen as recklessness, particularly when others are put at risk.

In Rex's case, this pattern of behavior will probably be dramatically exacerbated because the work environment in which he has successfully operated for years has changed literally overnight. Rex's tendency to operate independently is not likely to be tolerated in the more bureaucratic environment in which he now finds himself. The fact that he is in a very visible role as vice president of sales probably means that he will run afoul of organizational norms sooner rather than later.

The following are some of the consequences of high Bold behaviors, broken out by three constituencies: managers, peers, and direct reports.

Managers

Managers may initially appreciate the aggressiveness and dynamism of high Bold individuals, especially if they produce good results. Ultimately, however, high Bold individuals can be a disruptive influence in a number of ways. Their tendency to act impulsively can make them hard to manage within a traditional corporate setting. Even when they are successful, their competitiveness and presumption of special status may be very disruptive to team cohesion. A major task of any manager is to build a high-performance, coordinated team, and the high Bold person's need for individual recognition will usually work against this. When an individual is high on the Bold scale, coupled with being low on the Cautious scale and high on the Mischievous scale (as Rex is), the manager will have to pay close attention to ensure that the individual remains within prudent limits and that the person does not circumvent rules and regulations. Furthermore, high Bold individuals tend to discount or ignore feedback, which makes them particularly hard to coach. Even when the impact of their actions is pointed out to them, they may not believe it, rationalize it away as jealousy, or assume that as long as they keep producing results, their actions will be forgiven.

Peers

High Bold individuals on a team are likely to encourage competition and rivalry, not cooperation or collaboration, among team members. High Bold leaders make assumptions of entitlement, which often lead to resentment from others. Their peers may ignore occasional instances of high Bold behavior, but in more extreme cases of resentment, their peers may even try to minimize or sabotage their efforts. Sooner or later everyone makes mistakes. High Bold leaders who are prone to making risky, impulsive moves will probably make a mistake sooner rather than later. When they do make a mistake, they are likely not to have a base of support or forgiveness among their peers. In fact, their peers may even get a sense of gratification in seeing such leaders finally get what was coming to them.

Direct Reports

Followers are naturally attracted to bold, confident, decisive leaders. Confidence can be infectious and spur people on to greater efforts and achievements than they would otherwise accomplish. But unless direct reports eventually get some recognition for their efforts, at least some of them will become disenchanted. This self-promotion without acknowledging others explains the change in Patton's reputation to one of "our blood, his guts." When high Bold leaders also have a low Cautious score, their followers may additionally resent these leaders for taking excessive risks that put them in jeopardy or push them to the breaking point. Some direct reports may also figure out that the best way to work with a high Bold leader is to use flattery, setting the stage for a dysfunctional pattern of the leader's being surrounded by people who reinforce preexisting feelings of entitlement and superiority. It is also a recipe for building a team of blind followers who refuse to tell the emperor he has no clothes.

Coaching Focus

High Bold behaviors become most problematic when they antagonize others and lead to unrealistic risk taking. As noted earlier, some behaviors related to moderate Bold scores may even be desirable. As such, the focus of coaching needs to be to dial down but not eliminate these behaviors. Because coaching is not therapy, it should focus on behavioral change.

Coaching Strategy

High Bold individuals see themselves as special and entitled. Their high self-esteem is not an episodic thing; they may hide the assumption much of the time, but it is there all the time, lying under the surface. High Bold leaders are acutely interested in how they come across to others. They may be oblivious to the negative reputational impact of their behaviors, but they do not think reputation is unimportant. They want and expect to be acknowledged for their special qualities. Challenging this underlying assumption is unlikely to be successful in a coaching relationship. The general strategy needs to be to guide the leaders to be more self-aware of how their actions are perceived and then induce them to change their behavior in order to be perceived as positively as they know they should be. Because they see themselves as special, coaching need not challenge that directly; however, the session will be more successful if it looks at what behaviors might be blocking the attainment of that special status they feel they deserve. Ideally, coaching should increase the frequency and accuracy of their self-monitoring.

This approach does not necessarily mean an abandonment of a central goal of Hogan coaching: to facilitate greater self-awareness. In fact, this approach capitalizes on that goal. The high Bold leader's intense need for recognition creates an ideal entry point for behavior change and self-monitoring, which over longer periods of time *may* lead to greater self-awareness.

Strategy Refinements Using Subscale Information

The subscales for Bold include Entitled, Overconfidence, and Fantasized Talent. Each of these subscales contributes to an overall Bold scale score and provides interpretation refinements beyond those that can be achieved from a scale score alone. These interpretation refinements can have implications for specific behavior changes that may improve leader performance. They may also help in refining the coaching strategy that would be most effective in producing positive behavioral changes.

Entitled

The Entitled subscale focuses on the beliefs that one deserves special treatment and should be recognized for one's special qualities. It is a central aspect of people who score high on the Bold scale, which usually translates into self-promoting behavior and a reluctance to share credit for accomplishments. Rather than challenge the fundamental assumption of specialness, it may be more productive to collaboratively engage the individual in discussions about appropriate behaviors that can be used to achieve recognition. A person may come to see that being magnanimous and awarding credit to others is actually a much more effective way to gain status than personal aggrandizement.

Overconfidence

Elevations on the Overconfidence subscale can indicate that the individual believes that he or she can succeed at any task and will make overly optimistic projections of success. When failures occur, the high Bold individual will usually blame others or external events for the failure. High scorers on this subscale not only bite off more than they can chew, they will select tasks that may be beyond the capability of their team. Coaching discussions about exercising greater caution will be more effective if they are framed in terms of the limitations of the leader's team, not the leader.

Fantasized Talent

Leaders with an elevation on the Fantasized Talent subscale believe they have unusual gifts or talents or some special destiny for greatness. While these leaders tend to blame others when things go badly, when things go right, they interpret that as further confirmation of their special talents. They have a no lose approach to life. When things go well, it is their doing. When things go badly, it is the fault of others or circumstances. Coaching discussions are likely to be more productive if they center on how dialing down some of the high Bold behaviors will ultimately increase the chances of attaining the greatness they believe they deserve.

Coaching Tactics

Coaching tactics cover a range of approaches and resources that have been found useful in addressing high Bold behaviors. These tactics are typically used in combination to form a custom plan suited to the specific learning needs of a leader. The tactics are divided into four categories: (1) thought-provoking questions for a leader to consider, (2) exercises a leader can engage in to improve performance, (3) tips and techniques a coach can use to help a leader improve performance, and (4) support resources that can be consulted to gain additional insights in addressing high Bold behaviors.

Thought-Provoking Questions for a Leader

- How can you ensure that others will perform to your expectations?
- What steps can you take to increase the likelihood of others' success?
- If others fail, how will that reflect on you?
- What might go wrong that is beyond your control?
- As the leader and developer of the team, how will recognizing the contribution of the team reflect positively on you as well?
- How can you be successful in a way that gets the support and recognition of your peers and manager?
- If you are entitled to special privileges or considerations, how are your colleagues likely to react?
- From whom should you get input in order to build commitment to your agenda?
- How can you leverage your confidence to inspire others most effectively?
- How can you drive your agenda in such a way that others do not feel dominated?
- How can you create win-win situations in your dealings with others?
- Because everyone has blind spots, whom can you select as a truth teller to give you feedback about how you come across to others?
- What could derail you from achieving the goals and recognition you feel you deserve?
- What is the best way you can show the humility a true leader would display?
- Which of your special abilities can you use to get others to cooperate, collaborate, or follow you?

Exercises for a Leader

- Discuss where people have failed implementing your plans before. With hindsight, how could you have ensured success?

- Discuss your experience setting goals that might ensure success in the future.

- Role play having a discussion with someone about how to best ensure success for your ideas.

- Anticipate resistance you might get from others about a project and prepare arguments you can present about "What's in it for them?"

- Role play how you might engage your team in a discussion of "What could go wrong?" on a project.

- List two or three ways you can best fulfill your role as an inspirational leader for the team and set them up for success.

Tips and Techniques for a Coach

- Engage in what-if planning with the leader.

- Rehearse how the leader will give people constructive feedback if things do not go well.

- Rehearse how the leader will give people pats on the back if things go well.

- Discuss the ways that using positive reinforcement with others can build commitment to and enthusiasm for the leader.

- Discuss how admitting to some vulnerabilities or uncertainties may make the leader more appreciated as a leader.

- Discuss with the leader how the best leaders spread credit for success around to others but put failures on their own shoulders.

Support Resources

Bolton, R. (1986). *People skills: How to assert yourself, listen to others, and resolve conflicts.* New York, NY: Simon & Schuster.

In this communication skills handbook, Bolton describes the twelve most common barriers to effective communication and teaches readers how to better listen, assert themselves, resolve conflicts, and find mutually agreeable compromises.

Burg, B. (2011). *The art of persuasion: Winning without intimidation.* Mechanicsburg, PA: Tremendous Life Books.

Based on an in-depth examination of some of the most influential people across history, best-selling author Burg distills and shares key principles of persuasion in clear and, often, entertaining terms.

Burg, B., & Mann, J. D. (2011). *It's not about you: A little story about what matters most in business.* New York, NY: Penguin.

Presented in the form of an engaging parable, best-selling authors Burg and Mann help readers understand the power of subtle influence tactics.

Connors, R., & Smith, T. (2011). *How did that happen? Holding people accountable for results the positive, principled way.* New York, NY: Penguin.

Experts on workplace accountability and authors of the best-selling book *The Oz Principle*, Connors and Smith tackle the next crucial step everyone and anyone (e.g., managers, supervisors, CEOs, or individual contributors) can take in *How Did That Happen?*—instilling greater accountability in all the people you depend upon.

Dotlich, D. L., & Cairo, P. C. (2003). *Why CEO's fail: The 11 behaviors that can derail your climb to the top and how to manage them.* San Francisco, CA: Jossey-Bass.

The authors alternate high profile cases with compelling examples from their coaching practices. The Arrogance chapter addresses coaching tactics for Bold.

Hunter, J. C. (2006). *The servant leadership training course: Achieving success through character, bravery, and influence* [Kindle edition]. Retrieved from Amazon.com

The acclaimed author of the best-selling book *The Servant* teaches listeners about the servant leadership tactics employed in over one-third of Fortune Magazine's "100 Best Companies to Work For."

Salvador, T. (2013). The listening bias [Video file]. Retrieved from http://www.ted.com/watch/ted-institute/ted-intel/tony-salvador-the-listening-bias

Salvador shares tactics for becoming a better listener; for example, doing away with preconceptions, allowing vulnerability, and challenging the fear of hearing unwelcome messages.

Sample Coaching Program (Case 1—Rex)

An analysis of Rex's subscales suggests that he is particularly elevated in the Overconfidence subscale. Therefore, the coaching program should particularly target getting him to rein in his tendency to set unrealistic goals for himself or his team. Further, Rex should practice sharing credit when things go well and refrain from blaming others when things go badly.

- Acknowledge Rex's past contributions to the former organization, which allowed it to grow and eventually be purchased.

- Engage Rex in a "motivated abilities exercise," (i.e., those times and accomplishments when he was not only successful but felt that he was using his abilities to their fullest).

- Engage Rex in a discussion of when he over-committed or set goals that turned out to be beyond his or his team's abilities. How could he have assessed his and the team's capabilities more accurately?

- Ask Rex to identify his direct reports' key strengths and capabilities, and likewise, the areas where they struggle. In the past, has he fully considered these when he committed to a deliverable?

- Have Rex make a list of his key business goals. Are the goals realistic given his and his team's abilities? If not, what can he do to develop his team members so that they can succeed?

- Engage Rex in a discussion of what he will need to do differently as a leader in the new organization. What does the organization value? How can he modify his behaviors to be successful? What are the organization's priorities? Are his goals in alignment?

- Appeal to Rex's need for status by reframing his leadership role as one where he can develop and mentor others and be recognized for his guidance. Address with him the fact that he will gain more respect by sharing credit with his team than by taking it all for himself. Likewise, he can demonstrate leadership by shouldering blame when projects hit a snag.

Make sure that other key stakeholders, such as Rex's manager and HR, provide positive feedback about any changes Rex makes to set more realistic goals for himself and his team, to share credit when appropriate, and to shoulder blame when appropriate.

Summary

Keep Doing

Be a role model for a positive attitude toward challenges and problems.

Stop Doing

Overpromise, and blame others when a plan or project fails.

Start Doing

Share credit with your staff for successes and missions accomplished.

Leaders who are high on the Bold scale exhibit a constellation of behaviors that can include confidence, ambition, high levels of energy, dominance, competitiveness, entitlement, arrogance, impulsivity, and self-promotion. These individuals represent a particularly difficult coaching challenge because they are often unwilling or unable to see the destructive aspects of their behavior. Direct attempts at moving them to acknowledge their shortcomings are not likely to be successful, at least not early in a coaching engagement. Instead, the coaching focus should be on using appropriate behaviors that will lead to the success and recognition these leaders feel they deserve. Additionally, by building self-reflective questions into their repertoire, these leaders may eventually gain a better understanding of the consequences of high Bold behaviors.

Low Bold

Detecting When It Is a Problem

It is always harder to observe something that is not happening than something that is happening. Individuals who are high on the Bold scale normally stand out to others. Individuals who are low on this scale usually do not stand out from the crowd in any noticeable way. People who score low on this scale are often described as modest, lacking in self-confidence, laid back, restrained, reluctant to lead, non-confrontational, and self-effacing. They often are the good, reliable workers who follow orders and do not make waves. Prominent examples of low Bold people are hard to come by because, almost by definition, they are followers, not leaders. They are more likely to take orders than to give them, particularly if they are also high on scales such as Diligent or Dutiful. When low Bold people also have a high Cautious score, the fear of failure can paralyze them from taking action.

Like so many potential derailing tendencies, the Situational Context can play a significant role in determining the degree to which low Bold behaviors impact an individual's career. For example, low Bold individuals may thrive in subordinate roles but derail when they are thrust into leadership positions that require confidence, independent thinking, and action.

A good example of a low Bold leader is General George McClellan during the American Civil War. McClellan had been a successful general in peacetime, but the demands of the job changed when the North and South went to war. While McClellan played an important role in raising a well-trained and organized army for the Union, his extreme unwillingness to take bold action by engaging in battle brought the North perilously close to losing the war in the first year of the conflict. McClellan's timid, restrained style in battle hampered him greatly in a fast-moving battlefield environment. He chronically overestimated the strength of enemy units and was reluctant to engage the enemy troops unless he was almost certain of victory. Eventually, President Lincoln had to replace him with another general, Ulysses S. Grant, who was a bolder, decisive leader and willing to take risks. It is also worth noting that Grant was frequently accused of being overly bold and reckless.

Janis from Case 5—Janis, Customer Service Manager on page 96 provides a good example of someone who has a low Bold profile combined with higher potential derailers in her Diligent and Dutiful scores. The following is Janis's profile summary:

Janis's Situational Summary				
Janis is a newly promoted customer service manager who works for a software company. Her long-time regional manager was recently promoted, and her new manager is described as young, hard-charging, and very demanding. Janis is very conscientious and works hard to keep everybody happy. Her new manager will likely test her ability to push back, or she will find herself challenged to keep up with his demands. Her lack of self-confidence will also be readily apparent to her new manager.				
Dimension	**Score**	**Percentile**		**Description**
Excitable	60			Janis is a high-energy person who does not over-promise (Cautious—75%) and is very approachable (Reserved—15%). She lacks confidence (Bold—10%) but makes up for it through preparation and attention to detail (Diligent—85%). She is known for her loyalty and willingness to go the extra mile when it comes to protecting the reputation of the company and her manager (Dutiful—80%).
Skeptical	10			
Cautious	75			
Reserved	15			
Leisurely	20			
Bold	10			
Mischievous	40			
Colorful	30			
Imaginative	62			
Diligent	85			
Dutiful	80			

0   10   20   30   40   50   60   70   80   90   100

Janis's situation has changed recently. She has a new boss, and she is now in a new position of authority. Up until now, the biggest criticism of Janis was that she was not assertive enough in some situations. For the most part, however, her high scores on service-related scales, such as Diligent and Dutiful, may have contributed to her being well liked and successful in a customer service job where defusing unhappy customers was critical. But now, she has a new boss in addition to a new job. Her new boss is described as charismatic, confident, and hard-charging. He also seems to have a knack for avoiding responsibility when bad things happen. We can imagine that, in the beginning, the new boss will appreciate Janis's careful planning, attention to detail, loyalty, and conscientiousness. But over the longer term, his hard-charging style is likely to be incompatible with Janis's more conservative way of working. She also would likely make a good target for taking the blame when bad things happen because of her reluctance to push back. In other words, she could end up being the new manager's whipping boy.

Evaluating the Need for Change

The following behavioral questions should be considered in conjunction with a leader's low Bold score (as exhibited by Janis) when evaluating the need for a change in behavior. A "yes" response to three or fewer items suggests that there is no imminent need for behavioral changes. A "yes" response to four to six items suggests that a low score on the Bold scale should be a watch-out for a leader. A "yes" response to more than six items suggests that a leader should take active steps toward making behavioral changes.

Does the leader:

1. Avoid any appearance of taking personal advantage of the perks offered by the system?	**Yes**	**No**	**Not Sure**
2. Pass up challenging assignments that would be helpful in terms of future career opportunities?	**Yes**	**No**	**Not Sure**
3. Accept tasks that are better suited for individuals at a lower level in the organization?	**Yes**	**No**	**Not Sure**
4. Exhibit excessive self-doubt or concern when it comes to accepting what should be routine assignments?	**Yes**	**No**	**Not Sure**
5. Consistently set the bar low in terms of goal setting or career aspirations?	**Yes**	**No**	**Not Sure**
6. Appear excessively humble to the point others may perceive a lack of self-confidence?	**Yes**	**No**	**Not Sure**
7. Gravitate toward the status quo when presented with new opportunities or career options?	**Yes**	**No**	**Not Sure**
8. Espouse a poor self-image when it comes to personal skills or abilities?	**Yes**	**No**	**Not Sure**
9. Defer to others despite possessing superior knowledge or the skill necessary to address an issue?	**Yes**	**No**	**Not Sure**

These items should be considered as behavioral indicators. Similar or associated behaviors to any of those listed that are exhibited by a leader likely suggest a "yes" response. They provide additional support that a leader may be at risk for the negative reputational consequences associated with those scoring low on the Bold scale, such as Janis.

Impact of Low Bold Behaviors

Low Bold behaviors are characterized by a reluctance to take leadership positions, deference to others, and a reluctance to challenge colleagues. Low Bold leaders will be reluctant to volunteer for challenging projects, preferring to play it safe. They are often well liked by others, as they are cooperative with requests for help and abhor conflict with their peers. The following are some of the consequences of low Bold behaviors, broken out by three constituencies: managers, peers, and direct reports.

Managers

Managers who like "yes" people may initially like low Bold individuals. Managers will appreciate the fact that low Bold individuals are "good corporate citizens," but their reluctance to try more challenging or innovative tasks will ultimately prove frustrating. Managers are usually reluctant to advocate higher level positions for low Bold individuals unless the managers also happen to be low on the Bold scale or they see such individuals as pawns in their future career aspirations.

Low Bold individuals will follow orders and probably not push back, especially if they are also high on the Diligent or Dutiful scales. Eventually, though, managers often become annoyed with these individuals, whom they view as incapable, reluctant to think outside of the box, or hesitant to take on more challenging assignments. Also, managers who want to get lots of things done may be exasperated with the slow, timid pace at which low Bold individuals proceed. Because low Bold individuals are reluctant to act independently, they require more direct supervision, which limits the amount of work that can be delegated by the manager. Managers who abhor micromanagement will ultimately be dissatisfied with low Bold individuals.

Peers

Initially, peers may appreciate the low Bold leader's tendency to cooperate and avoid conflict with them. They may especially appreciate the fact that low Bold leaders do not assert themselves well or argue their points of view aggressively. They usually defer to the wishes of others, but their tendency to dither on issues may eventually prove exasperating to peers. Ultimately, peers may determine that the best strategy for working with low Bold individuals is to let them know about actions or decisions after the fact or, in fact, ignore them completely. It is also possible that peers will co-opt these individuals in achieving their own agendas or use them as scapegoats when things go bad. Peers who value true collaboration with a colleague will be disappointed by low Bold individuals.

Direct Reports

Direct reports may initially appreciate that they are not being aggressively pushed by their low Bold leader, but, over the longer term, they may come to not respect their leader. Direct reports may become disgruntled, especially if they are more action oriented. Because low Bold individuals are rarely good at asserting positions aggressively, direct reports may feel that they do not have a strong advocate in the organization to compete for needed resources or to advocate for their careers. Some members of the team may like the fact that they are not being pushed for stronger performances. Other more aggressive or career-oriented members of the team may want to leave for better opportunities or the sponsorship of a more forceful leader.

Coaching Focus

The focus of coaching low Bold individuals is to get them to see that nothing is risk free, even plodding along at a snail's pace. Being low on the Bold scale has its own risks, including being passed over, being a scapegoat, being demoted, or not being respected. The coaching must entail boosting the self-esteem of these individuals so that they become emboldened to take on more aggressive projects, to advocate for themselves more effectively, and to be more optimistic about their ability to be successful.

Coaching Strategy

The basic strategy in coaching is to get the individual to progressively act more assertive and decisive. It is a building strategy based on taking baby steps that set the leader up for successes. Early successes can then be built upon to increase the leader's assertiveness and decisiveness. Because low Bold leaders are doubtful about their ability to succeed, it is important for the coaching strategy to build in a lot of positive reinforcement along the way.

At this point, the personal relationship with the coach can be of major assistance, but other key stakeholders such as the individual's manager or others can also be valuable. When the leader takes one of these baby steps, the coach may want to make sure that there are people around the person who will catch them doing something right and then provide a lot of positive feedback about it. At the very least, a cooperative arrangement can be worked out with specific colleagues whereby critical incidents (positive and negative) are passed along to the coach to review and evaluate with the leader.

The coach needs to engage the low Bold leader in a realistic discussion of career accomplishments that engender a sense of pride and possibilities for the future. Also, the coach can work with the individual to anticipate situations where he or she may need to act in a more assertive manner. These situations can then be role played, with the coach suggesting more assertive responses and allowing the individual to try new behaviors that may result in a reputation for being more confident.

An important point here is to define in advance what success will look like. Initially, success may be defined in a very limited way, such as just being able to express one's opinion. If this initial goal is accomplished, the method of successive approximations can be subsequently used to gradually build on each new level of assertiveness until it reaches a desirable point. A key aspect of this approach is the development of a reputation for a degree of confidence in public. It may well be the case that the leader still has internal self-doubts, but change begins with the public persona.

Strategy Refinements Using Subscale Information

The subscales for Bold include Entitled, Overconfidence, and Fantasized Talent. Each subscale contributes to an overall score on the Bold scale, and provides interpretation refinements beyond those that can be achieved from a scale score alone. These interpretation refinements can have implications for specific behavior changes that may improve leader performance. They may also help in refining the coaching strategy that would be most effective in producing positive behavioral changes.

Entitled

Leaders who are low on the Entitled subscale feel as if they are not entitled to any special rights or privileges and may even feel like they are being treated too well. It is important to review the person's history with the organization with a special emphasis on past contributions. It is important for leaders low on this subscale to accurately evaluate their contributions and learn to accept the commensurate praise or rewards. These individuals often have a very tough time accepting praise and think that their excessive humility is valued by others. While that may be true to a certain extent, there is a difference between being humble and appearing meek or timid.

Overconfidence

A low score on the Overconfidence subscale often indicates that the leader is reluctant to take on a leadership role when it comes to challenging assignments but will readily cooperate with requests to help others. These behaviors cement a reputation as a follower. Leaders at the very low end of this subscale often have to learn to say "no" to projects if they are out of the scope of their responsibilities. They may also be reluctant to challenge or disagree with others. They will need to learn to interrupt appropriately and to challenge or even criticize others. With rehearsal, successful experiences, and reinforcement from others, these leaders can be encouraged to gradually take on progressively more challenging tasks and assignments.

Fantasized Talent

Leaders who are high on the Fantasized Talent subscale believe they have some special skill or destiny. In contrast, low Fantasized Talent individuals see nothing special about themselves. They may even see themselves as less worthy than their peers. Individuals who feel this way are prone to the "impostor syndrome" of not believing they are worthy of the role they have. The coach may need to encourage them to begin fantasizing about opportunities or projects that they previously would not have considered. It is also important to help these leaders develop an accurate accounting of the skills and abilities they bring to the table and where these skills and abilities can be leveraged to contribute to organizational success. Again, the point here is to help these individuals develop a more leader-like public persona.

Coaching Tactics

Coaching tactics cover a range of approaches and resources that have been useful in addressing low Bold behaviors. These tactics are typically used in combination to form a custom plan suited to the specific learning needs of a leader. The tactics are divided into four categories: (1) thought-provoking questions for a leader to consider, (2) exercises a leader can engage in to improve performance, (3) tips and techniques a coach can use to help a leader improve performance, and (4) support resources that can be consulted to gain additional insights in addressing low Bold behaviors.

Thought-Provoking Questions for a Leader

- What is the cost to your reputation for not asserting yourself?
- What is the worst that can happen if you try this new way?
- What might be some of the positive consequences of asserting yourself more often?
- If you repeatedly assert yourself, do you think it will gradually become easier to do?
- Do you feel like you are being ignored by key people?
- How will you feel if people more junior or with less experience get promoted over you?
- What is the effect on your direct reports of not speaking up?
- Do you have a responsibility to assert yourself for the good of the organization, your people, or yourself?
- Can you think of times when not pushing back caused things to not go well?
- What is one thing for which you could take a very limited but innovative approach that might also improve things in your area of responsibility?
- What would be a modest next step in your career?

Exercises for a Leader

- Discuss how others may react to your unassertiveness.
- Reenact actual situations that occurred and how they might have been handled differently.
- Rehearse alternate ways of responding to those situations.
- Identify individuals by whom you may feel particularly dominated and develop new tactics about how to deal with these individuals.
- Pick a situation that is coming up and rehearse more assertive ways of dealing with it.

- Pick an area where you have to compete with a peer for resources. Plan how you would make your case.

- Have your coach model how you might assert yourself more effectively.

- Identify several role models in the organization whom you admire. What qualities make them so admirable?

Tips and Techniques for a Coach

- The coach needs to remember that the relationship with the leader will be a key lever to encourage the leader to try out new behaviors.

- Set criteria for success at very minimal levels in the beginning. Initially, just trying new behaviors should be the standard for success, regardless of their outcome.

- Remind the leader often that continually avoiding potential failure carries with it the potential for disapproval or ridicule by others.

- Use positive reinforcement extensively to encourage new behavior, and then build on that to shape even more appropriately assertive behaviors.

- Enlist the aid of others (e.g., manager, HR, other key stakeholders, etc.) as additional sources of encouragement for the leader.

Support Resources

Alter, C. H. (2012). *The credibility code: How to project confidence and competence when it matters most.* Meritus Books.

Alter describes how readers can use body language, posture, eye contact, intonation, and many other actively controlled cues to project more self-assurance and an aura of credibility and competence.

Beckwith, H., & Clifford, C. (2011). *You, inc.: The art of selling yourself.* New York, NY: Hachette.

Based on the premise that "the most important part of the sale is you," Beckwith and Clifford offer practical, readily-applicable advice for marketing oneself (along with a healthy dose of humor).

Bolton, R. (1986). *People skills: How to assert yourself, listen to others, and resolve conflicts.* New York, NY: Simon & Schuster.

In this communication skills handbook, Bolton describes the twelve most common barriers to effective communication and teaches readers how to better listen, assert themselves, resolve conflicts, and find mutually agreeable compromises.

Cuddy, A. (2012). Your body language shapes who you are [Video file]. Retrieved from http://www.ted.com/talks/amy_cuddy_your_body_language_shapes_who_you_are

Social psychologist Amy Cuddy explains how "power posing"—using confident body language—can impact mechanisms in the brain capable of positively impacting the likelihood of being successful.

Cuddy, A. (2015). *Presence: Bringing your boldest self to your biggest challenges.* New York, NY: Hachette.

Rather than try to make a fundamental transformation of an individual, Cuddy argues that small tweaks in body language, behaviors and mind-set can produce more assertive and effective behaviors.

Dotlich, D. L., Cairo, P. C., & Rhinesmith, S. H. (2006). *Head, heart, and guts: How the world's best companies develop complete leaders.* San Francisco, CA: Jossey-Bass.

The authors rely heavily on high profile case studies while discussing the crucial capabilities required of today's leaders and offering readers an actionable plan for stepping outside their "leadership comfort zone."

Harris, R. (2011). *The confidence gap: A guide to overcoming fear and self-doubt.* Boston, MA: Trumpeter Books.

Harris posits that, rather than attempting to "get over" fear and insecurity, readers should try to reconceptualize and stop fighting these emotions. Borrowing liberally from tenets of the well-respected and proven-effective Acceptance and Commitment Therapy (ACT), Harris offers readers a practical plan designed to minimize missed opportunities stemming from insufficient confidence.

Patterson, K., Grenny, J., McMillan, R., & Switzler, A. (2013). *Crucial accountability: Tools for resolving expectations, broken commitments, and bad behavior* (2nd ed.). New York, NY: McGraw Hill.

The authors of the best-selling book *Crucial Conversations* offer readers strategies for dealing with unmet expectations in a manner capable of strengthening, not damaging, relationships.

Sample Coaching Program (Case 5—Janis)

Janis is not only low on the Bold scale, she also scores high on several other combinations of scales that might portend future conflict with her manager. Her elevated score on the Diligent scale (85%) predicts that she will work very hard for her new boss, and because he is a hard-charger, this pair will be a good fit, at least initially. Her score of 80 percent on the Dutiful scale predicts that she will be a loyal direct report and eager to please.

But the fact that she is also elevated on the Cautious scale may mean that her hard-charging boss will eventually find her conscientiousness and attention to detail too slow and plodding for his style. Her low Bold score makes it unlikely that she will push back, and her Dutiful and Cautious scores predict that she will have difficulty saying no to him. She may push her team of people beyond their limit in an attempt to please the new boss, but it is just as likely that she will diminish the quality of her personal life by taking too much on herself.

This is probably not a scenario that will be sustainable over the long run. Things inevitably fall through the cracks, and when they do, Janis's new boss, who is described as "Teflon," will probably deflect the blame to someone else. Janis's low Bold score makes her a prime target.

Janis's scores on all the Bold subscales were low, so a coaching initiative for her needs to address low Bold behaviors in general and include the following steps:

- Janis needs to ramp up assertiveness to a more reasonable level. She needs to fully understand that if she does not, her prospects for future leadership opportunities will be greatly diminished.

- Janis needs to review the successes she has had in her career in order to bolster themes normally found in a high Bold profile, such as becoming more confident, recognizing her particular talents, and feeling comfortable and entitled to some credibility in the organization where she has been successful for years.

- Janis needs to practice saying "no" to unreasonable requests; however, she will probably need to build up to this in gradual steps because it is unlikely she can be assertive enough in one fell swoop.

- Janis and her coach need to identify specific situations that present problems for her self-confidence. The coach can work with her using role play rehearsals to prepare for these situations in the future. Janis and her coach should draw up two lists: a to-do list of things she and her team need to get done and a not-to-do list of things they are not going to do. The not-to-do list can include things that other people outside of Janis's group need to handle, as well as things that do not need to be done at all.

- Janice should practice with her coach how to disagree with others or offer an alternate point of view in a polite but effective way.

- Janis should practice applying the good customer skills she has with the outside world to her job internally. She should keep her manager and other key stakeholders regularly informed of both the work she and her team are doing and the work they have decided they cannot do.

- Janis should practice assertiveness in a safe forum, such as role playing with her coach or in a program like Toastmasters.

- Janice has an elevated Diligent profile, so, she and her coach should discuss whether she is delegating enough and fully leveraging the resources of her team. She and the coach should identify specific situations where she will have to delegate projects to others and hold them accountable.

SUMMARY

Keep Doing

Exhibit good team behaviors like listening, collaborating, and acknowledging others.

Stop Doing

Avoid confrontations, let others take credit for your work, and fail to state opinions.

Start Doing

State your own opinions, and advocate for your own positions on issues.

While leaders who are high on the Bold scale often run the risk of being fired, leaders who are low on the scale run the risk of being passed over or unrecognized for their contributions. Many times they have much to offer an organization, but their full potential goes untapped. However, assertiveness is a skill that can be coached, just like any other skill. If low Bold individuals can be encouraged to take successively more assertive actions, eventually this assertiveness may become part of their normal behavioral repertoire. The key success with coaching these leaders is changing their public reputation from one of a lack of self-confidence to one of effective assertiveness. Many times this simple change opens the door for these individuals, allowing others to see their potential for contributing to the success of the organization.

CHAPTER 16

MISCHIEVOUS

HIGH MISCHIEVOUS

Detecting When It Is a Problem

Mischievous behaviors concern the tendency to appear charming, friendly, and fun-loving, but also to seem impulsive, excitement-seeking, and nonconforming. High scorers usually make a favorable first impression, but others find them hard to work with because they tend to test limits, ignore commitments, and take risks that may be ill-advised. Although those with high scores on the Mischievous scale may seem to be decisive, they tend to make fast and loose decisions because they are often motivated by pleasure and do not fully evaluate the consequences of their choices. They can gain a reputation for being flighty, for not taking business issues seriously enough, or even for lacking the gravitas needed to be a leader.

Sir Richard Branson, who owns more than 300 companies under the umbrella of The Virgin Group, lives a life and espouses a business vision that illustrate the essence of a high Mischievous character: "In the end, you have to say screw it. Just do it." From the music industry to the airplane industry to commercial space travel and exploration, Branson has made technological leaps. He has also experienced numerous failures, earning him membership in the coveted "famous failures" entrepreneurial club. He says there are two techniques that free him from dreaded routine (which is anathema to the high Mischievous leader): breaking world records and making bets. One striking aspect of Sir Branson's public persona is that he is often thought of as a charismatic leader. High Mischievous leaders are often thought of as charismatic because they approach life with an adventuresome spirit that followers admire.

Tanya from Case 4—Tanya, Insurance Professional on page 94 provides a good example of a high Mischievous profile (98%).

Tanya's Situational Summary
Tanya was a successful insurance professional for a medium-sized corporation who was promoted into the role of training manager. The new role looked to be quite challenging because it required a new skill set to be successful, and the insurance industry as a whole was evolving into a highly regulated industry with many new government regulations. Tanya's new role as training manager could potentially be quite stressful given the job demands and industry changes.

Dimension	Score	Percentile	Description
Excitable	90		Tanya is a crafty insurance professional who can let her emotions get the best of her (Excitable—90%). She is known for putting big deals together for her corporate clients. Outwardly, she appears very self-confident (Bold—89%). She works her own agenda (Leisurely—80%), and tends to set her own rules (Mischievous—98% and Dutiful—10%) with little regard for consequences (Cautious—20%).
Skeptical	60		
Cautious	20		
Reserved	30		
Leisurely	80		
Bold	89		
Mischievous	98		
Colorful	70		
Imaginative	50		
Diligent	30		
Dutiful	10		

0   10   20   30   40   50   60   70   80   90   100

Tanya's high Mischievous profile contributed to her success in prior jobs that required an entrepreneurial spirit, but in her new position as training manager, this profile can be a derailer, especially because the company has been inundated with a number of new government regulations. These regulations forced company leaders to embark on a culture change initiative to ensure compliance with the new regulations. One of the most important components of the culture change initiative was to ensure that new insurance professionals were well acquainted with the regulations and were scrupulous in their adherence to them in completing their jobs. The culture change initiative presents a significant challenge for Tanya. First, she will come under careful scrutiny because of the importance of the right messages being conveyed to new professionals. Second, it is reasonable to assume that some aspects of her success formula could go beyond stretching the envelope and cross into areas that challenge regulatory compliance. There are also risks associated with how Tanya will react to the regulatory constraints that were not in place when she accepted the position as training manager.

Evaluating the Need for Change

The following behavioral questions should be considered in conjunction with a leader's high Mischievous score (as exhibited by Tanya) when evaluating the need for a change in behavior. A "yes" response to three or fewer items suggests that there is no imminent need for behavioral changes. A "yes" response to four to six items suggests that a high score on the Mischievous scale should be a watch-out for a leader. A "yes" response to more than six items suggests that a leader should take active steps toward making behavioral changes.

Does the leader:

1. Regularly bend the rules of the organization to advance personal agenda items?   **Yes   No   Not Sure**

2. Fail to consider the downside when taking actions that have unknown consequences?   **Yes   No   Not Sure**

3. Push limits to the point it makes other people uncomfortable with the consequences or outcomes?   **Yes   No   Not Sure**

4. Take fast action on the basis of intuition without the necessary facts or contingencies?   **Yes   No   Not Sure**

5. Use charm or charisma as a means of avoiding personal responsibility when things go wrong?   **Yes   No   Not Sure**

6. Appear to be too impetuous in situations that would likely benefit from a more measured approach?   **Yes   No   Not Sure**

7. Rely excessively on political skills or charisma to persuade or influence others?   **Yes   No   Not Sure**

8. Stretch the truth or embellish the situation in order to look more effective in the eyes of others?   **Yes   No   Not Sure**

9. Tend to pursue personal self-interests to the point that it results in a trust or credibility gap?   **Yes   No   Not Sure**

These items should be considered as behavioral indicators. Similar or associated behaviors to any of those listed that are exhibited by a leader likely suggest a "yes" response. They provide additional support that a leader may be at risk for the negative reputational consequences associated with those scoring high on the Mischievous scale, such as Tanya.

Impact of High Mischievous Behaviors

The most distinctive traits of high Mischievous individuals are charm, self-assurance, verbal facility, and a tendency to be a bit flirtatious with those they try to influence. However, at their worst, high Mischievous individuals are impulsive, reckless, faithless, remorseless, and exploitative. They can be manipulative and can think and talk their way out of any problem. To work with these leaders, one must be prepared to fill in behind them, to help them follow through with commitments, to urge them to pay attention to details, and to encourage them to think through the consequences of their actions or consider alternate scenarios. The following are typical perceptions of these individuals on the part of three constituencies: managers, peers, and direct reports.

Managers

Managers may see limit testing and rule breaking as unreliable behavior, potentially requiring damage control. Managers may also see this behavior as diminishing the trust required for increasingly responsible positions and for the people alliances that must be built to get work done. Persistent Mischievous behavior and gambits may create a corporate rebel reputation for a leader, reducing opportunities for career development and advancement. Trust in the high Mischievous individual is diminished because of his or her tendency to finesse mistakes by denying or covering them up. Mischievous individuals may deflect attention from themselves by raising other, more compelling issues or by parsing words or shifting to discussing their intentions and not their actual behavior.

Peers

Peers may see limit testing and cleverness as a kind of self-confidence that leads to a sense of entitlement, special giftedness, and the projection of invulnerability. While peers may find high Mischievous individuals to be attractive and often rewarding to deal with, there is also a strong sense of unpredictability. The high Mischievous leader often pledges support for a variety of initiatives, but the support may be short-lived. Projects and other initiatives are sometimes left to flounder because of some newer, more exciting project. To work with high Mischievous people, peers must be prepared to pick up the loose pieces, help them finish projects while checking for missing parts, and encourage them to be more circumspect when considering the end results. Peers must also be wary of the tendency for high Mischievous leaders to try to gain an advantage when it comes to office politics.

Direct Reports

Direct reports may see rule breaking and manipulative behavior as untrustworthy and exploitative. The high Mischievous leader's facile charm and persuasive manner wears thin, and direct reports come to see these individuals as using and manipulating people, ignoring commitments, displaying poor follow-through, and creating doubt about their personal integrity. Direct reports may feel alienated and confused at the high Mischievous leader's inability to understand how his or her statements and actions affect others. Direct reports may also be dismayed by the fact that these leaders can put them into compromising situations through no fault of their own. Such actions further diminish trust to the point that existing team members may look for a way out, and potential future team members who become aware of the leader's mischievous reputation will be reluctant to get involved.

Coaching Focus

In order to set the stage for coaching, it is worthwhile to recap several important qualities of the high Mischievous leaders: they are often selfish and self-centered, they see others as toys or tools to be used, and they have little ability to identify with others' feelings. They have low tolerance for boredom and become impatient to move on to new projects and people. Finally, they often revel in their various limit-testing activities.

The essential coaching focus is not to eliminate impulsivity, risk taking, and manipulative tendencies. Rather, it is to reduce these potentially derailing behaviors to a level that is productive and sanctioned within the Situational Context of the leader. For example, managing spontaneity and rule bending involves helping the leader become aware of the Situational Context and where the line is drawn as to when these behaviors are acceptable and when they will not be tolerated. This "line awareness" involves making qualitative judgments about the impact of these tendencies and when they cross the line, as illustrated in Figure 10.

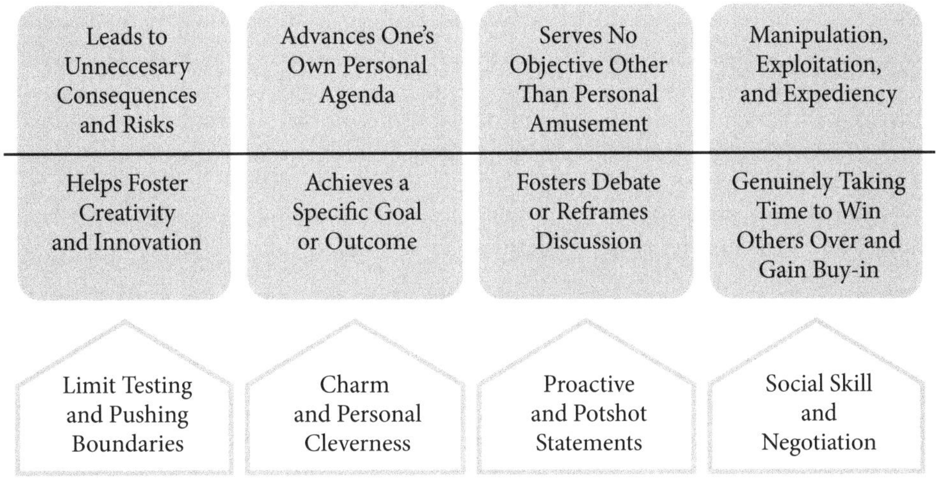

Leads to Unneccesary Consequences and Risks	Advances One's Own Personal Agenda	Serves No Objective Other Than Personal Amusement	Manipulation, Exploitation, and Expediency
Helps Foster Creativity and Innovation	Achieves a Specific Goal or Outcome	Fosters Debate or Reframes Discussion	Genuinely Taking Time to Win Others Over and Gain Buy-in
Limit Testing and Pushing Boundaries	Charm and Personal Cleverness	Proactive and Potshot Statements	Social Skill and Negotiation

Figure 10   Crossing the High Mischievous "Line"

Exhibiting many of these high Mischievous behaviors often meets an arousal need for these leaders in ways that may not be met in more socially accepted forms. Because this type of leader operates so much from a gut level, the coach can offer a more systematic, scientific alternative of testing the advantages and disadvantages of these behaviors. But beware—high Mischievous leaders may engage in coaching in a superficial manner. In other words, the same charm and manipulation these leaders employ with their constituents may be used to persuade or influence a coach.

Coaching Strategy

High Mischievous individuals tend to be suspicious of developmental feedback, viewing it as an attempt to make them adhere to meaningless rules and expectations. While they will be superficially charming and interested in feedback, they will covertly reject many of the ideas offered by the coach. They often blame past errors or missteps on others or rationalize the blunders away. As a result, it is important for the coach to be assertive in identifying areas of concern, while highlighting the personal challenges inherent in developmental feedback. It is also important these individuals recognize that the diminished trust resulting from their high Mischievous behaviors can be career limiting. They are often oblivious to their faults until a promotion opportunity passes them by. Therefore, it is important to heighten their awareness about trust issues and the subtle signs that they are walking a very thin line.

Strategy Refinements Using Subscale Information

The subscales for Mischievous include Risky, Impulsive, and Manipulative. Each of these subscales contributes to an overall Mischievous scale score and provides interpretation refinements beyond those that can be achieved from a scale score alone. These interpretation refinements can have implications for specific behavior changes that may improve leader performance. They may also help in refining the coaching strategy that would be most effective in producing positive behavioral changes.

Risky

The Risky subscale identifies the propensity to take ill-advised risks, test limits, and take enjoyment in bending or breaking the rules. When high Risky leaders exhibit these behaviors, others begin to view their risk taking as a liability, not an asset. One of the first strategy refinements for coaching leaders on risk taking is to encourage them to quit viewing every tempting scenario as a personal challenge—picking one's battles or rule breaking should be approached with more circumspection and purpose. Is the limit testing meant to expose inefficiency, hypocrisy, or uncritical assumptions, or is it based more on the leader's identity or self-image of being a rebel without a cause? Ask the high Risky leader to identify specific objectives and end-points that he or she thinks can be achieved through risky behaviors. Then, work with the leader to explore alternative, more socially acceptable ways of achieving those desired objectives or endpoints. It is also beneficial to help the leader develop a habit of doing a simple cost/benefit analysis around key decisions. This type of analysis is often an afterthought for the high Mischievous leader.

Impulsive

The Impulsive subscale identifies the tendency to act spontaneously with little regard for the consequences of the action. High Impulsive leaders often act without considering consequences, and they risk developing a reputation for making snap judgments and unpredictable decisions. Interestingly, these leaders believe in their ability to charm their way out of mistakes, which can exacerbate the situation because the damage is done and is often quite visible. A critical coaching refinement for impulsivity is the interruption (or disruption) of the impulsive stimulus-response chain. As much as their spontaneity and seat-of-the-pants behavior make them seem daring, high Impulsive leaders often should consider a timeout before acting. They should invite feedback, if possible, with someone (including the coach) about the potential constructive or destructive effects of their anticipated impulse to act. Impulsive leaders are often non-introspective and unaware of the ramifications of their impulsive behavior. Discussing these impulsive acts with them can reduce the likelihood of their committing destructive acts unknowingly.

Manipulative

The Manipulative subscale identifies the tendency to use social skills to persuade others. High Manipulative leaders rely on charm or deceit to achieve their goals. They may seem insincere or deceptive, and they run the risk of developing a reputation for being so slick that they are untrustworthy. Who can forget the moniker "Slick Willy" attached to President Bill Clinton? Manipulative leaders have underdeveloped behaviors in three areas: empathy, reciprocity, and social sensitivity. Role playing can be a very effective coaching tool to use with high Manipulative leaders who do not grasp how their statements and interpersonal tactics affect others. Role playing that puts the high Manipulative leader on the receiving end of manipulative behavior or ploys can help challenge a core belief of this person: Other people are weak or naïve and *deserve* to be manipulated or exploited.

Coaching Tactics

Coaching tactics cover a range of approaches and resources that have been found useful in addressing high Mischievous behaviors. These tactics are typically used in combination to form a custom plan suited to the specific learning needs of a leader. The tactics are divided into four categories: (1) thought-provoking questions for a leader to consider, (2) exercises a leader can engage in to improve performance, (3) tips and techniques a coach can use to help a leader improve performance, and (4) support resources that can be consulted to gain additional insights in addressing high Mischievous behaviors.

Thought-Provoking Questions for a Leader

- What are the triggers for you to test limits or make potshot or provocative statements?

- In what circumstances does taking a risk work well for you?

- Describe a time that you made an impulsive choice that did not turn out well. What would you have done differently?

- How do you ensure you are seeking and getting enough substantive input to your decisions?

- How would you describe the risk tolerance of the organization? How does that align with your risk tolerance? For you to achieve your business and career goals, how might you need to adapt your style?

- How might your credibility change if you enlisted others in arriving at a course of action?

Exercises for a Leader

- Examine key stakeholders associated with your role, and grade them in terms of the degree to which they trust you.

- Evaluate a key mistake you made in terms of how you handled the aftermath. Consider how that situation could have been handled differently as a trust-building opportunity.

- Take an idea or proposal and analyze the pros and cons from two perspectives: (1) your point of view and (2) others' points of view.

- Consider the challenge and fun of engaging others and moving them from non-supporters or neutral to supporters. How could this benefit you? Your team? The organization?

- Generate a list of all the positive attributes that might be associated with a high Mischievous person. Look at these attributes through a different, less positive lens, and consider how others may view these attributes.

Tips and Techniques for a Coach

- There are a number of key messages that a coach might use to help high Mischievous leaders become less impulsive and manipulative:

  - Slow down decision-making to afford time for a realistic appraisal of the likely consequences of alternative courses of action.

  - Recognize career success depends on the support of others. Consider their ideas from their point of view, not yours.

  - Demonstrate loyalty to others by following through on the commitments you made to them.

- Identify and apologize to those who may have been hurt or disappointed by past actions, rather than trying to explain the situation away.

  - Leverage spontaneity and charm carefully to become a good team player who seeks success for all members of the organization.

- Identify a critical decision-making situation that will occur in the near future. Discuss with the leader how this situation could be handled including ways that differ from those used in the past.

- Work with the leader to design a process to create a pause before acting on decisions or impulses. Find a trusted partner for feedback.

- Identify a decision tree process the leader can use to assess possible options for action and pros and cons. Use this process to evaluate decisions during coaching sessions.

- Role play with the leader how to accept negative feedback and learn from it, instead of using charm and manipulation to side step it.

Support Resources

Covey, S. M. R. (2006). *The speed of trust: The one thing that changes everything.* New York, NY: Simon & Schuster.

Covey asserts that trust is the linchpin of the new global economy and demonstrates that trust—and the speed at which it can be developed with employees, clients, and constituents—is a defining factor within successful, high-performance organizations.

Dotlich, D. L., & Cairo, P. C. (2003). *Why CEO's fail: The 11 behaviors that can derail your climb to the top and how to manage them.* San Francisco, CA: Jossey-Bass.

The authors alternate high profile cases with compelling examples from their coaching practices. The Mischievousness chapter addresses coaching tactics for Mischievous.

Hogan, J., Hogan, R., & Kaiser, R. B. (2010). *Management derailment: Personality assessment and mitigation.* In S. Zedeck (Ed.), *APA handbook of industrial and organizational psychology, Vol. 3: Maintaining, expanding, and contracting the organization* (pp. 555–576). Washington, DC: American Psychological Association.

A substantive chapter (also available via Hogan's website) with four main points. First, leadership literature offers few useful generalizations about the distinguishing characteristics of good leaders. Second, the behaviors associated with managerial derailment are well documented. Third, private and public sectors are rife with bad managers. Finally, organizations that observe principles of good management, including how they manage their managers, are more profitable.

Hogan, R., & Warrenfeltz, R. (2011). **Educating the modern manager.** *Academy of Management Learning and Education, 2,* 74–84.

This Hogan Press article discusses key terms associated with learning and education often left unspecified, offers a taxonomy of learning outcomes associated with self-knowledge, and concludes noting that executive education proceeds most efficiently and productively when it is preceded by an assessment of capabilities relative to role responsibilities.

Horsager, D. (2012). *The trust edge: How top leaders gain faster results, deeper relationships, and a stronger bottom line.* New York, NY: Free Press.

Based on research likely to resonate with today's leaders, Horsager's highly rated book describes the eight pillars of trust and explains how to build them.

Kouzes, J. M., & Posner, B. Z. (2011). *Credibility: How leaders gain and lose it, why people demand it.* San Francisco, CA: Jossey-Bass.

Building on research described in their best-selling book, *The Leadership Challenge*, Kouzes and Posner describe six key disciplines that "strengthen a leader's capacity for developing and sustaining credibility" and provide poignant examples of credible leaders in action.

Maxwell, J. C., & Covey, S. R. (2007). *The 21 irrefutable laws of leadership: Follow them and people will follow you.* Nashville, TN: Thomas Nelson.

While some leadership books encourage leaders to break all the rules, Maxwell and Covey's best-selling leadership book provides readers with specific rules to abide by, in addition to a self-assessment tool and exercises designed to facilitate personal growth.

Sample Coaching Program (Case 4—Tanya)

Tanya's high Mischievous score (98%) shows high elevation on all three subscales: Risky, Impulsive, and Manipulative. While others may find Tanya to be charming, friendly, and fun-loving, they may also find her hard to work with because of her tendency to test limits, ignore commitments, and take risks that may be ill-advised. Coaching approaches, then, include strategies to curb or redirect these potentially derailing tendencies.

- Use the newly implemented regulatory environment to help Tanya differentiate and identify a new "success profile."

  This case is an exploration of the adage "what got you here may not get you there." With respect to Tanya's creative initiative and mischievous resourcefulness, she will have to clearly understand the range of behaviors that will be successful in her upcoming role; moreover, she must understand what will not be tolerated. Have Tanya develop a two-column chart that lists "Former Regulatory Environment" and "New Regulatory Environment." She should list responsibilities, behaviors, explicit rules, regulations, decision-making latitude, and so on to contrast the difference in the two environments of the training manager position. What shifts will she have to make to meet expectations and adjust to the constraints in the newly defined environment? Specifically, with respect to working style, decision-making, creative boundaries, and dealing with impediments or roadblocks, how do the two contexts differ and what will that require for success? What are the boundaries in both versions of the role for the ability to challenge or act expediently? What are the collaborative realities in both scenarios?

- Manage impulsivity and risk taking by transferring those behaviors to a more appropriate activity where creative resourcefulness is an asset.

This is a sublimation or redirection strategy—transfer undesirable or intolerable behavior to another, more acceptable setting. For example, training presentations are greatly enriched and more memorable with a training style that incorporates charismatic behavior, including mischievous ploys.

Have Tanya identify and compile a list of ways that she might use her seat-of-the-pants, shake-things-up mentality to liven up what could be staid and formal training content. How could she deliver training with a degree of cleverness and creativity to accomplish learning objectives?

Tanya would be natural at role playing. She could develop role play exercises where rule compliance comes into play, with her playing her natural limit-testing and rule-busting self. These sessions could be easily practiced with the coach as a participant experiencing Tanya's behavior and providing feedback.

- Develop a flexible style of expression where a level of mischievous behavior can be used in a way that is appropriate to the situation.

This tactic is an incorporation of the "Crossing the High Mischievous Line" into the awareness and thinking of the high Mischievous person. Extinction of impulsivity, risk taking, and manipulative savvy is not necessarily desirable, but part of the moderation of these elements is consciously assessing whether these behaviors are invoked for a productive benefit or not. Tanya must make qualitative judgments about the impact of these behaviors and when they cross the line.

Have Tanya identify a scenario where she thought she was at her best in making a risky decision, acting opportunistically, being cleverly resourceful and creative, gaining confidence from others quickly, or simply beating the system. Then have Tanya evaluate her behavior along four dimensions of mischievous behavior:

  - Did my limit-testing and pushing boundaries (a) help foster creativity and innovation in the end or (b) lead to unintended or unnecessary consequences and risks?

  - Did I use my charm and persuasion to (a) achieve a specific, legitimate goal or outcome or (b) show off my personal, engaging style of interacting?

  - Did my provocative or cleverly insightful statements or challenges (a) foster a more vigorous, focused debate or help reframe the discussion, or (b) did they really serve no objective other than my own personal amusement of goofing on others?

  - When I turn on the charm, is it to (a) genuinely deepen trust and comfort in order to get others comfortable with working with me, or is it to (b) use my ability to talk others into something or convince them about something in the speediest manner possible?

Have Tanya tabulate the number of "a" answers versus "b" answers, with "a" representing appropriate uses of mischievous behavior, and "b" representing crossing over the line into reckless, risky, overly manipulative territory. How might this kind of post-scenario dissection help Tanya become more deliberate and aware of her mischievous tendencies?

SUMMARY

Keep Doing

Take prudent risks, and appropriately challenge the status quo.

Stop Doing

Ignore warnings, cautions, and feedback about your unnecessary risk taking.

Start Doing

Avoid impulsive behavior by slowing down and evaluating the consequences of decisions.

Individuals with high scores on the Mischievous scale expect that others will like them and find them charming. Consequently, they expect to be able to extract favors, promises, money, and other resources from people with relative ease. They see others as individuals to be exploited. As a result, they have problems maintaining commitments and are unconcerned about violating expectations. At their best, Mischievous individuals are self-confident and have an air of daring that others find attractive and even intriguing. At their worst, they are impulsive, reckless, faithless, exploitative, and manipulative. Their self-confidence and recklessness lead to many mistakes, but they seem unable to learn from experience. A lack of trust is at the core of the problems they create for themselves. The career consequences for being perceived as untrustworthy include missed opportunities, being passed over for promotion, or even being fired. The essential coaching focus is not to eliminate the impulsivity, risk taking, and savvy influencing skills but to curb these behaviors and help the leader better use them to achieve productive, trust-building outcomes.

LOW MISCHIEVOUS

Detecting When It Is a Problem

The low Mischievous individual can be summed up with two words: unassuming and responsible. Low Mischievous people tend to avoid unnecessary risks and play by the rules, which make them valued corporate citizens. Bosses appreciate their dependability and trust them to think through the consequences of proposed actions. They are cautious by nature and tend to make few mistakes in managing their careers. However, they may not take many chances. When formulating business strategy, they remember past mistakes and try to minimize risk. Warren Buffett, the legendary investor, typifies low Mischievous attributes. Buffett is known for thinking carefully when those around him lose their heads; his low-key, conservative attributes permeate his investing philosophy—he's noted for his adherence to value investing and for his personal frugality despite immense wealth ($65 billion).

What gets low Mischievous leaders in trouble or causes them to be ignored are the attributes on the low end of the charisma dimension: an unwillingness to be adventuresome or try new things, a lack of cleverness or charm, and an inability to influence others. Restrained and muted, these individuals typify the corporate survival rule regarding derailers: "High scores get you fired, low scores get you passed over."

The 1980 presidential debate between Ronald Reagan and Jimmy Carter provides a salient and memorable example of risk taking and quick wit versus risk aversion and personal restraint: Carter stumbled, citing his young daughter Amy's advice that nuclear weapons were the most important issue. Reagan lived up to his reputation for delivering lines, deflating one of the president's criticisms with a chuckling, "There you go again." And Reagan summed up his argument in the end by asking voters in what would become a classic campaign question: "Are you better off now than you were four years ago?"

James's profile from Case 7—James, Marketing Manager on page 100 provides a good example of a low Mischievous profile (15%).

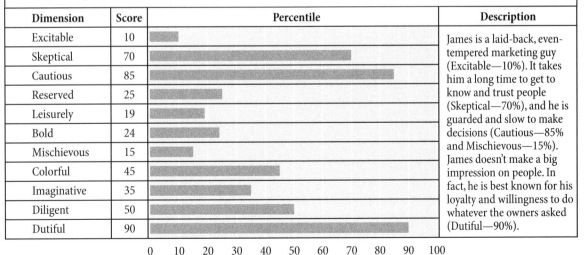

James's Situational Summary			
James was the marketing manager for a small family-owned business that was sold to a well-established technology company. After the sale, James moved on to a small, fast-moving start-up technology company. He had clear challenges with his ability to get things moving in the new company. Combined, his high Cautious score with a low Mischievous score will have a direct impact on the speed with which he makes decisions that may be in conflict with a fast-moving start-up.			
Dimension	**Score**	**Percentile**	**Description**
Excitable	10		James is a laid-back, even-tempered marketing guy (Excitable—10%). It takes him a long time to get to know and trust people (Skeptical—70%), and he is guarded and slow to make decisions (Cautious—85% and Mischievous—15%). James doesn't make a big impression on people. In fact, he is best known for his loyalty and willingness to do whatever the owners asked (Dutiful—90%).
Skeptical	70		
Cautious	85		
Reserved	25		
Leisurely	19		
Bold	24		
Mischievous	15		
Colorful	45		
Imaginative	35		
Diligent	50		
Dutiful	90		

With the sale of his former company and downsizing, James was relocated to a small, high-tech start-up. Unlike his former business, this start-up was a fast-paced business that forced people to make decisions without a lot of guidance or management support. Perhaps the biggest change for James was the fact that he was left to make a lot of important decisions on his own. James's low scores on the Risky, Impulsive, and Manipulative scales contributed to his tendency to carefully analyze ideas and only make decisions when he had all the facts. His slow, methodical approach is likely not to be received well in the new fast-paced environment. Furthermore, James's lack of guidance contributed to his inability to make decisions, as he typically relied on the owners in his previous company to tell him what needed to get done. His early life in the new start-up looked more like a data collection exercise than a newly established marketing function in which steps were being taken to build a high-profile brand. Furthermore, James's low Mischievous score indicated a very unassuming individual who could easily be lost in the entrepreneurial environment of a fast moving start-up.

Evaluating the Need for Change

The following behavioral questions should be considered in conjunction with a leader's low Mischievous score (as exhibited by James) when evaluating the need for a change in behavior. A "yes" response to three or fewer items suggests that there is no imminent need for behavioral changes. A "yes" response to four to six items suggests that a low score on the Mischievous scale should be a watch-out for a leader. A "yes" response to more than six items suggests that a leader should take active steps toward making behavioral changes.

Does the leader:

1. Rigidly follow the rules of the organization, even when they should be appropriately challenged?   **Yes   No   Not Sure**

2. Devote an excessive amount of attention and energy to what might fail rather than what might succeed?   **Yes   No   Not Sure**

3. Stay so far within established organizational limits that it stifles creativity or innovation?   **Yes   No   Not Sure**

4. Fail to act, even when the evidence is overwhelming that action is called for and needed?   **Yes   No   Not Sure**

5. Accept blame or become a scapegoat when things go bad due to the actions of others?   **Yes   No   Not Sure**

6. Exhibit an excessive degree of caution in taking action even when the negative consequences are minimal?   **Yes   No   Not Sure**

7. Seem to lack the necessary political skills to persuade or influence others?   **Yes   No   Not Sure**

8. Speak with candor in situations where a more guarded approach would be more appropriate?   **Yes   No   Not Sure**

9. Set aside personal self-interests to the point that others see this as a weakness and take advantage of it?   **Yes   No   Not Sure**

These items should be considered as behavioral indicators. Similar or associated behaviors to any of those listed that are exhibited by a leader likely suggest a "yes" response. They provide additional support that a leader may be at risk for the negative reputational consequences associated with those scoring low on the Mischievous scale, such as James.

Impact of Low Mischievous Behaviors

Low Mischievous leaders strike others as lacking in creative initiative and charisma. While it is important to follow rules and procedures, sometimes expediency and resourcefulness are important, appropriate, and career enhancing. And though low Mischievous leaders are seen as trustworthy, they are also viewed as restrained in taking initiative, especially as it relates to challenging the current business assumptions or conventions. Low Mischievous behaviors do not create interesting, charismatic reputations for a leader. Indeed, they might even lead to a reputation for being boring, unassuming, safe, and not a provocateur. Low Mischievous leaders are less likely to motivate others through inspiration. The balance point for behaviors associated with the Mischievous scale is for a leader to be charismatic (or at least interesting) without engaging in the limit testing, devious behaviors that can contribute to a reputation of untrustworthiness.

Low Mischievous behaviors can create reputational concerns for a leader among three constituencies: managers, peers, and direct reports.

Managers

While bosses appreciate the low Mischievous leader's dependability and prudence to think through the consequences of proposed actions, they may tire of a rule-compliant, overly conservative approach on every occasion. The low Mischievous leader may lack the spirit of adventure necessary to seize opportunities, especially opportunities that exist outside official channels. The natural cautiousness of these individuals often causes them to miss opportunities to enhance their career. They may be relegated to handling routine, lower-profile projects and businesses. Interestingly, some limits on their careers are created by their own lack of action, but equally career limiting is the impression they leave on superiors as not appearing very leader-like.

Peers

Though low Mischievous leaders are reliable and trustworthy, peers may find networking and partnering with these somewhat dull and boring individuals less than rewarding, especially when a collaborative spark is needed for creative problem-solving or innovative thinking. In fact, opponents may use the conservative mindset of a low Mischievous leader as a way to slow or derail progress. Peers often prefer team members who are willing to take on projects or assignments that have a degree of risk associated with them. The key here is making sure the degree of risk has been appropriately assessed. By taking some appropriate risks, especially toward innovation and strategic advantage, the low Mischievous leader could benefit the team and the organization.

Direct Reports

Direct reports may develop a corporate attitude by emulating the rule-abiding behavior and rigid adherence to procedures and policies of their low Mischievous leader. While adhering to rules and procedures is important, sometimes it can stifle the creativity and resourcefulness of the low Mischievous leader's direct reports. Furthermore, direct reports may use the hesitance of a low Mischievous leader to take action as a way of avoiding work. They hope that the slow, cautious decision-making process of the leader will take over, and the work will be put off.

Coaching Focus

Coaching the low Mischievous leader—helping a leader manifest a new behavior that is contrary to his or her natural tendency and display the new behavior in a way that does not appear insincere to others—is a challenge.

The coaching focus should frame the dimensions of Mischievous behavior as existing on a continuum, with implications for high-, low-, and mid-range performance. The coach should have the low Mischievous leader view Risk Aversion (vs. Risk Taking), Self-Control (vs. Impulsivity), and straightforward Sincerity (vs. Manipulation) as a spectrum of behaviors. The coach should discuss what behavior at either end of the spectrum looks like and in which circumstances or contexts this behavior might be productive. The coach should help the leader determine where he or she falls on the spectrum. Then, the coach should assist the leader to identify the potentially positive outcomes of moving slightly further along the spectrum, perhaps toward the mid-range as a sweet spot. The essential focus of this exercise is to encourage the leader not to operate on the extreme ends of the Mischievous scale.

Low Mischievous leaders may be reluctant to take action in situations where they have had little or no experience. The coach's role is to help them be less afraid of failure and pushing limits. Getting the low Mischievous leader to work with a mentor who has a track record and reputation for success can provide a development opportunity. The control board analogy illustrated in Figure 11 represents some of the behaviors that can be dialed up by a leader to be more adventuresome without taking excessive risk or being perceived as impulsive or manipulative.

Figure 11 also indicates a rough sweet spot that the low Mischievous leader should strive to achieve on each scale of the control board.

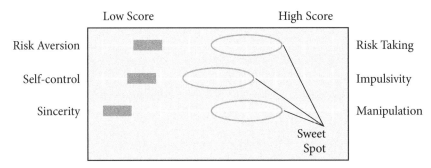

Figure 11   The Inner Mischief Control Board

Coaching Strategy

The low Mischievous leader will likely not receive a great deal of specific, actionable feedback from superiors. When feedback is provided, it will probably be associated with the need for the leader to take greater initiative or demonstrate a stronger bias for action. In fact, the way low Mischievous leaders often get on the radar screen for coaching is that their managers get frustrated with trying to motivate these individuals to do something—anything. It is unlikely coaching these individuals will result in greater charisma or a more adventuresome spirit. The goal should simply be to increase their bias for action in ways their superiors see greater autonomy, resourcefulness, and measured risk taking. These individuals will usually respond well to coaching that helps them define decision-making boundaries and provides positive feedback for their attempts to function more autonomously, taking prudent risks within the defined boundaries.

Strategy Refinements Using Subscale Information

The subscales for Mischievous include Risky, Impulsive, and Manipulative. Each of these subscales contributes to an overall Mischievous scale score and provides interpretation refinements beyond those that can be achieved from a scale score alone. These interpretation refinements can have implications for specific behavior changes that may improve leader performance. They may also help in refining the coaching strategy that would be most effective in producing positive behavioral changes.

Risky

The Risky subscale indicates the propensity for taking ill-advised risks and testing limits and for finding enjoyment in bending or breaking rules. Low scoring leaders are compliant, conservative, and cooperative; they avoid unnecessary risk, make few mistakes, and often appear unadventurous or overly conforming. Coaching involves getting these leaders to consider the risk of not changing anything and the lost possibilities due to their hesitation. Ask the question, "What possibilities could you open up?" Also, have these leaders describe the ways in which they are risk averse. These leaders need to raise their awareness regarding how low-risk behaviors impact team members and their own overall effectiveness.

Impulsive

The Impulsive subscale indicates the tendency to act spontaneously and follow temporary impulses. Low scoring leaders are dependable, reliable, and demonstrate behavior that may seem overly structured, conventional, or predictable. Leaders who score low on this subscale are seen as good at execution; however, they are not able to adapt to changing priorities or deal with ambiguous issues or situations. This lack of flexibility may diminish their reputation as being ready for more senior leadership roles. Ask these leaders to describe their openness to new ideas or to approaches suggested by others. Have them extend their boundaries by trying something new or different in their routine and behavior. Part of the reluctance of low Impulsive leaders to act impulsively or opportunistically is their wariness of the unfamiliar. Changes in their behavior can occur in increments, with ever-increasing experiences of testing the waters. There is a truism in the CEO world: most senior leaders who led a major change initiative have nearly uniformly wished that they had moved faster and sooner. Encouraging low Impulsive leaders to act in accordance with this truism is critical in helping open future opportunities for them.

Manipulative

The Manipulative subscale indicates a leader's tendency for using charm, or otherwise manipulating others to reach desired goals. Low scoring leaders seem genuine, straightforward, and trustworthy, but they may also seem overly inhibited, and they struggle to gain influence or persuade others. With respect to charisma, low scoring leaders are less likely to motivate others through inspiration because they lack a certain flair or wit that is engaging. While it is unlikely that a coach is going to infuse a low scoring leader with charisma, it is possible to help the individual develop a degree of executive presence. This effort begins with helping the leader identify and observe a person considered to have executive presence. What behaviors create this presence? Have the leader describe the person's body language, confidence level, storytelling ability, empathy, and listening proficiency. Contrast that with someone who is not perceived as having executive presence. What's missing? The discussion should focus on how these leaders compare to one another, and what behaviors the low Manipulative leader could model to increase his or her executive presence.

Coaching Tactics

Coaching tactics cover a range of approaches and resources that have been found useful in addressing low Mischievous behaviors. These tactics are typically used in combination to form a custom plan suited to the specific learning needs of a leader. The tactics are divided into four categories: (1) thought-provoking questions for a leader to consider, (2) exercises a leader can engage in to improve performance, (3) tips and techniques a coach can use to help a leader improve performance, and (4) support resources that can be consulted to gain additional insights in addressing low Mischievous behaviors.

Thought-Provoking Questions for a Leader

- In what situations are you most likely to stick with the tried-and-true, and a less risky course of action? What does this indicate about your leadership brand?

- How would you describe the risk tolerance of the organization? How does that align with your fairly low level of risk tolerance? For you to achieve your business and career goals, how might you need to adapt your style?

- How would you describe the "balance point" for leadership behaviors associated with being daring, creative, and charismatic (or, at least, interesting) without engaging in the limit testing, deviousness, and provocative behaviors that can contribute to a reputation of untrustworthiness?

- In what circumstances does avoiding risks or not experimenting with a creative approach work well for you?

- Describe a time when you had to sell others on an idea or secure their buy-in. How did you do that? Provide a camera-ready (i.e., details that a camera would have captured) example of what you did and said.

Exercises for a Leader

- Define a list of behaviors that contribute to executive presence, and identify those you want to incorporate into your leadership style.

- Consider the challenge and fun of engaging others and moving them to be supporters. How could this benefit you? Your team? The organization?

- Map where the organization and specific leaders fall on the risk spectrum, and the impact their behavior has had on their careers. Where do you fall in comparison to them?

- Create a Tell-a-Story vignette about a personal experience or business experience, one where you learned something about yourself. The story can even be self-deprecating, but share an experience where you took a risk or went outside conventional boundaries, or did something that might have been embarrassing.

- Identify a situation in your past where you believe others have taken advantage of you. What could you do differently in the future to avoid these situations?

Tips and Techniques for a Coach

- If you can achieve a working alliance with the leader, you can encourage and coach the low Mischievous leader through a number of skill-building steps, including:

- Identifying circumstances or contexts in which the leader behaves in a cautious and restrained manner, and describing the impact of this behavior on his or her team and overall effectiveness as a leader.

- Helping the leader consider the risk of not changing anything and the lost possibilities that result from hesitation. Ask what possibilities could be opened up by changing this behavior.

- Asking the leader to identify how and what might be done to strengthen his or her executive presence. The discussion should include behaviors the leader could model, starting with the easiest and progressing to those behaviors that are more sophisticated.

- Having the leader role play a scenario where others have to be sold on an idea that is somewhat risky and where there is hesitance for buy-in.

- Work with the leader to view risk as a spectrum. Discuss what the behavior at both ends of the spectrum looks like. Identify where the leader falls on the risk spectrum. Ask the leader to identify the potentially positive outcome of moving slightly further along the spectrum.

- Have the leader generate a list of positive attributes that might be associated with a low Mischievous individual, and the impact these attributes have on team members. Now, have the leader generate another list that describes the high Mischievous leader's approach. Examine the contrasts between the two approaches, and identify the mid-range or productive blend of the two approaches.

- Help the leader think about how to build a "Leadership Legacy," including how the leader would want to be described by others in the future with respect to his or her leadership style and accomplishments. Identify the low Mischievous behaviors that can stand in the way of the leader's achieving the desired legacy and how they could be overcome.

- Help the leader develop a stump speech on a specific area of interest or topic of concern. Work with the leader to infuse the speech with anecdotes, humor, and so forth. Identify venues where the leader can give the speech and a plan to get feedback on the delivery and audience perceptions.

Support Resources

Cain, S. (2013). *Quiet: The power of introverts in a world that can't stop talking.* New York, NY: Crown.

Cain discusses the "Extrovert Ideal," how it has contributed to the devaluation of introverted qualities, and the risk we as a society take when we underestimate what introverts have to offer. "Quiet" highlights groundbreaking achievements of introverts from past and present and likely will leave readers seeing themselves and other introverts in a different light.

Cooper, R. (2014). *Decision-making: The ultimate guide to decision-making!* [Kindle edition]. Retrieved from Amazon.com

"Decision Making" offers practical and proven tactics capable of helping readers efficiently evaluate options, decisively and confidently make decisions, and maintain the self-restraint necessary to see decisions through to fruition.

Glei, J. K. (Ed.). (2013). *Maximize your potential: Grow your expertise, take bold risks & build an incredible career.* Las Vegas, NV: Amazon Publishing.

In addition to offering wisdom from 21 leading creative minds, this book provides guidance on how to create new opportunities, build creative expertise, cultivate relationships, and take bold, strategic, growth-promoting risks.

Grenny, J., Patterson, K., Maxfield, D., McMillan, R., & Switzler, A. (2013). *Influencer: The new science of leading change,* (2nd. ed.). New York, NY: McGraw-Hill.

Grenny and colleagues offer readers science-based insights about successful influence tactics, inspiring stories about influencing against all odds, and concrete, step-by-step recommendations for enhancing influence skills.

Houpert, C. (2014). *Charisma on command: Inspire, impress, and energize everyone you meet* [Kindle edition]. Retrieved from Amazon.com

Based on a thorough analysis of some of today's most charismatic leaders, "Charisma on Command" teaches readers how to tap into their "charismatic potential" and develop the mannerisms and mentality that others perceive as magnetic and memorable.

Kahnweiler, J. (2013). *The introverted leader: Building on your quiet strength.* San Francisco, CA: Berrett-Koehler.

After discussing common workplace challenges faced by introverts and offering a self-assessment, Kahnweiler provides concrete and readily applicable strategies introverted leaders can apply when on stage, managing up, leading projects, and in many other scenarios.

Pillay, S. (2014, December). A better way to think about risk. *Harvard Business Review.* Retrieved from https://hbr.org/2014/12/a-better-way-to-think-about-risk

Pillay presents a compelling argument for reframing "risk" in a more favorable (and productive) light.

Sample Coaching Program (Case 7—James)

James's low scores on the Risky, Impulsive, and Manipulative subscales helped to explain what caused him to be perceived by others as rule-bound, predictable, and overly corporate. These perceptions resulted in his reputation of being unadventurous and overly compliant. The coaching challenge is how to help him manifest new, more adventuresome behaviors contrary to his natural tendencies and to do so in a sincere manner. The intervention should include the following activities:

- Identify and evaluate the aspects of the new organizational context that will likely require new behaviors.

James should plan a number of lunch meetings with various members of his new organization, ostensibly to get to know them, but also to learn as much as possible about the start-up culture, employee climate, the start-up's story, etc. James should be well prepared for these meetings. He should do the following:

  - Have a well-rehearsed, three-minute infomercial about himself, including who he is, his career highlights, and what excites him about being with the new start-up.

  - Ensure he opens each meeting with a full disclosure of his need to better understand the organization, to see how he can contribute, and to build his network in the company.

  - Have some prepared questions that he can use to gain an understanding of what is expected from the marketing function and from him as the leader of the function.

- Collaborate with key members of the new organization to align with work culture expectations and business objectives.

After collecting and evaluating data from his initial networking efforts, James should do the following:

  - Develop a profile of strengths he can leverage and weaknesses or shortcomings he may have to address, specifically assessing risk taking, flexibility, building an image, and other interpersonal dimensions of leadership.

  - Formalize a job position statement and share it with his boss and key decision makers. When sharing this statement, he should again query these individuals on their expectations for an effective marketing function.

- Identify the important behaviors that must be demonstrated in order to build a reputation for being an effective leader of the marketing function.

With intelligence gathering complete for this stage, James should deploy and demonstrate behaviors and a working style commensurate with that needed for an effective leader of the marketing function. He should do the following:

  - Refine and formalize the descriptive profile of what the company deems an ideal marketing person for the enterprise at this stage in its development.

  - Identify an in-house confidant or on-boarding mentor that he can use as a sounding board.

  - Keep a log of situations that come up weekly in business operations, including how he handled the scenarios, what seems to be working well, and what needs adjustment.

• Seek agenda time, if appropriate or available, for any meetings where successes can be celebrated, and where any adjustments need to be made.

SUMMARY

Keep Doing

Be a valued corporate citizen who is dependable and thinks through consequences.

Stop Doing

Be overly cautious, and minimize risk taking.

Start Doing

Take some appropriate risks in terms of being more proactive and innovative.

Leaders with low scores on the Mischievous scale have a reputation for being compliant and risk averse; they conscientiously follow rules and established procedures. They remember past mistakes and incorporate those lessons into their behavior going forward. These leaders are resistant or unwilling to try new, innovative, or experimental approaches to solving problems or attaining objectives. This lack of resourcefulness means they miss opportunities that are outside the box for the team and for themselves. They are unassuming and responsible in their work approach, but less likely to motivate others through inspiration due to a muted and restrained personal demeanor. They can be depended upon to handle routine, lower-profile projects with efficiency, but with a lack of fanfare.

Coaching the low Mischievous leader—helping the leader manifest new behaviors that are contrary to his or her natural tendencies and also help him or her display these new behaviors in a sincere manner—is a challenge. Core to the approach is teaching the low Mischievous leader to view risk, impulsivity, and manipulation as a spectrum of behaviors, with the goal of moving slightly further along the spectrum.

CHAPTER 17

COLORFUL

HIGH COLORFUL

Detecting When It Is a Problem

High Colorful behaviors are readily observed by others, and if not reined in, can earn the leader a reputation as a show-off or a blow-hard in pretty short order. In addition, it can be exhausting to be around high Colorful individuals for an extended period of time due to their high-energy levels and constant chatter. At their best, high Colorful leaders are articulate, friendly, and many times draw followers like moths to a flame. However, when their behaviors are over the top, their larger-than-life personalities can alienate their constituents.

A good example of a high Colorful leader is Cristina Fernandez de Kirchener, the former high-profile president of Argentina. During her years as a senator and then as president, she constantly drew attention to herself through both her appearance and her actions. Perfectly coiffed, heavily made-up, and dressed in designer clothes (she was rumored to have over 200 "mourning black" dresses in her wardrobe following the death of her husband), she was routinely seen front-and-center in photographs with other world leaders. She was notoriously vain, and the very public discussion of her cosmetic surgery and collagen injections to ensure she stayed youthful earned her the moniker "The Botox Queen." Quite outspoken and known for dramatics, she sometimes brought her followers to tears through her passionate speeches, while at other times, she shook her fist at her adversaries. She maintained her flamboyant lifestyle despite the fact that her policies brought the Argentinian economy to its knees and she was the subject of a personal financial scandal. Prone to over-sharing, Cristina once tweeted over 61 times in a 9-hour period. Even as she left office (her term ended at midnight), she maintained her penchant for high drama as she quipped, "I can't talk much because after midnight, I'll turn into a pumpkin."

Similar to Cristina Kirchener, most high Colorful individuals thrive on their attention-getting behaviors. That is why convincing a high Colorful leader to dial it down can be so difficult. Typically, high Colorful leaders have received praise and compliments on their outgoing personalities over the years, and they just do not realize when they are over the top with their antics. They find themselves very entertaining, and think everyone else does, too.

Mark from Case 6—Mark, District Account Manager on page 98 provides a good example of a high Colorful profile. The following is Mark's profile summary.

Mark's Situational Summary				
Mark is a long-tenured district account manager for a consumer products company. A significant change in his account portfolio brought a number of new government accounts under his control. These customers were no-nonsense type customers who had little interest in his affable nature and tendency to exaggerate to garner attention.				
Dimension	**Score**	**Percentile**		**Description**
Excitable	68			Mark is a high-energy person who brings a lot of passion to the business (Excitable—68%). He can be highly colorful (Colorful—91%) to the point of being overbearing at times. His colorful behavior extends into his tendency to exaggerate issues or problems and his role in solving them. He also has a tendency to miss details or fail to follow up on important issues (Diligent—10%).
Skeptical	15			
Cautious	29			
Reserved	42			
Leisurely	19			
Bold	24			
Mischievous	70			
Colorful	91			
Imaginative	29			
Diligent	10			
Dutiful	45			

0 10 20 30 40 50 60 70 80 90 100

Mark is a district account manager whose high Colorful behaviors, while earning him a reputation of being a bit of a character, have not been problematic in the past. In fact, they have endeared him to his work colleagues and customers because he is so outgoing. However, given the transactional nature of the work with his new by-the-book government accounts, his high Colorful behaviors, compounded by his low Diligent, low Cautious, and slightly elevated Mischievous and Excitable scores, are likely to become derailers. Further, although Mark has survived a couple of downsizings already, he is not likely to survive the next ones if he alienates his large government accounts.

So, it is crucial that Mark modify his high Colorful behaviors with his customers. He also needs to be mindful of his interactions with his colleagues as his jokes and bravado might not play as well as they did in the past, and his lack of attention to detail might matter more given the austere financial situation that the company is experiencing.

Evaluating the Need for Change

The following behavioral questions should be considered in conjunction with a leader's high Colorful score (as exhibited by Mark) when evaluating the need for a change in behavior. A "yes" response to three or fewer items suggests that there is no imminent need for behavioral changes. A "yes" response to four to six items suggests that a high score on the Colorful scale should be a watch-out for a leader. A "yes" response to more than six items suggests that a leader should take active steps toward making behavioral changes.

Does the leader:

1.	Consistently grab the stage or the limelight when opportunities arise in public settings?	Yes	No	Not Sure
2.	Appear to be compelled to be the first to speak in group situations?	Yes	No	Not Sure
3.	Exhibit poor listening skills because of an excessive desire to express views or opinions?	Yes	No	Not Sure
4.	Lose focus on the task at hand because of an excessive need to engage others in conversation?	Yes	No	Not Sure
5.	Become easily bored when the task at hand involves extensive details or the need for a high degree of focus?	Yes	No	Not Sure
6.	Exhibit an excessive need to interact with people even when it results in the neglect of task assignments?	Yes	No	Not Sure
7.	Demonstrate the need to stand out in a crowd or be the center of attention?	Yes	No	Not Sure
8.	Exhibit behaviors or actions that seem intended to draw the attention of anyone within close proximity?	Yes	No	Not Sure
9.	Garner so much public attention that even those who are observing the situation seem to cringe?	Yes	No	Not Sure

These items should be considered as behavioral indicators. Similar or associated behaviors to any of those listed that are exhibited by a leader likely suggest a "yes" response. They provide additional support that a leader may be at risk for the negative reputational consequences associated with those scoring high on the Colorful scale, such as Mark.

Impact of High Colorful Behaviors

Larger-than-life, high Colorful behaviors are typically seen by all constituencies—direct reports, peers, and managers—but the intensity of the behaviors displayed to each group may vary. For example, a high Colorful leader might laugh and joke much more with direct reports than with a group of senior executives. Likewise, the audience's perceptions of the high Colorful individual may vary by group. For example, a manager of a high Colorful person may see unshakable self-confidence as executive presence, peers may see it as strutting like a peacock, and direct reports may perceive it as intimidating.

Regardless of the constituency, one of the major derailers of high Colorful leaders is that it can be exhausting to be around them. When they are in high Colorful mode, their energy, enthusiasm, verbosity, and demands for attention can overwhelm people, suck the oxygen out of a room, and cause an audience to wonder if there is an off button. The following reactions are broken down by constituency: managers, peers, and direct reports.

Managers

Managers are often more tolerant of high Colorful leaders because they have more limited exposure to these individuals and see the strong personality characteristics as leader-like. The high Colorful person's confidence, energy, and interesting anecdotes can be seductive in small doses. However, managers can soon tire of too much of a good thing and view a high Colorful leader as a self-centered show-off who is not a team player. The manager might feel threatened by the high Colorful leader and not take the individual to meetings for fear of being upstaged. High Colorful individuals' exaggerations and lack of attention to detail can wear thin and create trust issues as to whether they will really deliver on their promises.

Peers

Typically, peers initially enjoy being around high Colorful individuals because of the energy and excitement they generate. Outgoing and gregarious, high Colorful leaders keep things interesting. However, their constant need to be the center of attention and to take credit for accomplishments can gain them the reputation of not being a team player or of being overly competitive. Peers can wind up resenting them and not wanting to work with them. If his or her Distractible subscale is elevated, the high Colorful leader can annoy peers with constant interruptions while they are trying to work.

Direct Reports

At first, direct reports can be seduced by the high Colorful leader's energy and gregariousness. However, the larger-than-life personality can overwhelm direct reports and intimidate them. They might feel that they cannot get a word in edgewise due to the high Colorful individual's constant chatter and failure to listen. If the high Colorful leader is also elevated on the Distractible subscale, the behaviors typically displayed can result in false starts and frequent changes of direction that can confuse and frustrate direct reports. In addition, because it is all about themselves, high Colorful leaders might fail to share credit with the team or recognize them at all, and this lack of recognition can cause resentment. It is as if the high Colorful leader walked out on the branch of a tree and left a saw in the hands of the direct reports. As the resentment builds, the likelihood of the direct reports' sawing off the branch to bring down the leader increases.

Coaching Focus

The coaching focus for high Colorful individuals is to help them realize not everyone has an unlimited appetite for their over-the-top behaviors. They may find themselves totally charming, but they must recognize that not everyone does, and therefore must dial down their antics depending upon the audience and the situation. Convincing the high Colorful leader of the need to regulate his or her Colorful behaviors can be an exceptionally tough sell for a coach because, many times, these are exactly the behaviors that have gotten the leader promoted in the past. The leader has been complimented and rewarded for exhibiting confidence, charm, energy, a winning personality, and the like. High Colorful behaviors truly are strengths run amok, and it is often difficult for the high Colorful leader to accept that "people just are not into you as much as you might think."

The coach needs to recognize that the high Colorful leader might like the coaching at first, because the individual will enjoy being the center of attention. However, the leader might soon tire of it and be concerned that his or her Colorful behaviors have been found out. The leader may very well try to charm the coach as a way to divert attention away from the development needs. So, it is important for the coach to remain task-focused.

It is also important for the coach to recognize that high Colorful leaders need to shine in some way. If the high Colorful leader is being asked to dial it down at work, then the coach needs to help the individual find another place to redirect the energy where the high Colorful behaviors are more appropriate. Perhaps it could be something outside of work, such as leading a volunteer project.

Coaching Strategy

There are six steps associated with the coaching strategy for a high Colorful leader:

1. Increase the leader's self-awareness regarding what is perceived by others as over-the-top Colorful behavior. Ask the high Colorful leader for instances when others have commented that the Colorful behaviors were a distraction that negatively impacted performance effectiveness. The coach can provide examples from multi-rater assessment data or behavioral interviews as the high Colorful leader might struggle to come up with examples via reflection.

2. Look for themes, situations, people, etc., to determine when derailment is most likely to occur.

3. Help the leader recognize situational demands (i.e., this situation calls for focus) and identify what level of behavior would be acceptable and appropriate (i.e., determine what people would not find over-the-top; what behavior is suitable for the audience or situation).

4. Identify what activities and tools will enable the high Colorful leader to dial the behavior down to an appropriate level.

5. Implement the activities.

6. Evaluate and calibrate the activities to determine which are the most effective.

Strategy Refinements Using Subscale Information

The subscales for Colorful include Public Confidence, Distractible, and Self-Display. Each of these subscales contributes to an overall Colorful scale score and provides interpretation refinements beyond those that can be achieved from a single scale score alone. These interpretation refinements can help identify specific behavior changes that may improve the leader's performance. The subscales may also help in refining the coaching strategy that would be most effective in producing positive behavioral changes.

Public Confidence

An elevation on the Public Confidence subscale is typically manifested by high Colorful leaders' wanting a lot of air time and monopolizing the conversation. They come across as extremely articulate and convincing, but they will not let others speak. These leaders are so busy talking that they do not listen or pick up on others' needs. A coaching refinement for leaders elevated on this subscale is to make sure they listen at least twice as much as they talk, and that they do not constantly take over a conversation. Another refinement is for these leaders to divide the length of the meeting by the number of people attending, allot everyone a certain amount of time to talk, and then make sure that they themselves do not exceed their share of air time.

Distractible

Leaders who are elevated on the Distractible subscale are the classic crisis managers. There is considerable drama concerning issues that arise and how to address them. Further, their constituencies can become confused with the constant change of direction. The leader's credibility can suffer because of missed commitments due to a lack of attention to details. The coaching emphasis for leaders who are elevated on the Distractible subscale should be on staying focused, keeping priorities straight, meeting due dates, and seeing things through to completion. The coach should also consider the leader's score on other Hogan Personality Inventory and Hogan Development Survey scales, including low Prudence, high Inquisitive, high Excitable, high Mischievous, high Imaginative, and low Diligent scores to see if they have compounded the derailing behaviors associated with the high Distractible leaders.

Self-Display

Of the three subscales, perhaps behavior related to the Self-Display subscale is the most noticeable and draws the most negative reactions from those who witness it. When the score on the Self-Display subscale is elevated for a leader, it typically suggests an all-about-me attitude. These leaders use dramatic and even outlandish means to draw attention to themselves. Keep in mind that the means these leaders use to draw attention to themselves can come in many forms (e.g., voice level, dress, gestures, outlandish statements, taking on high-profile projects, etc.). These behaviors are damaging, not only because nobody likes a show-off, but also because the Self-Display behaviors can be more interesting than what the leader is actually saying or doing (i.e., style overshadows the substance or content). The coaching refinement here should focus on explaining to the leader just how different the Self-Display behaviors are from the norm and having the leader try to mirror the behavior that is accepted in the organization's culture.

Coaching Tactics

Coaching tactics cover a range of approaches and resources that have been found useful in addressing high Colorful behaviors. They are typically used in combination to form a custom plan suited to the specific learning needs of a leader. The tactics are divided into four categories: (1) thought-provoking questions for a leader to consider, (2) exercises a leader can engage in to improve performance, (3) tips and techniques a coach can use to help a leader improve performance, and (4) support resources that can be consulted to gain additional insights in addressing high Colorful behaviors.

Thought-Provoking Questions for a Leader

- How socially generous are you? Do you suck the air out of a room, or do you share the floor with others? Do you proactively try to include them?

- How do you focus on listening to others?

- Do you find yourself encouraging others to speak (e.g., bringing them out) or shutting them down?

- How do you learn from others?

- How do you step back to let others step forward? What is the value of this for you?

- How can you shine the light on others?

- How can you make sure you stay focused and meet commitments?

Exercises for a Leader

- Observe your participation in meetings. How often do you speak first, and what percentage of the time are you speaking?

- Try counting to 10 to give others time to jump in before you respond.

- Make sure you respond to what others have said before you shift gears to what you want to talk about.

- Practice focusing on listening and not speaking. Take notes on the situation, what you observed, and what you learned as a means of controlling your need to immediately interject your views.

- Be curious about the thoughts and perceptions of others. Use open-ended questions that encourage others to express their views, and listen carefully to what they are saying.

- Before you speak up in a meeting, think about the type of contribution that is really needed at that moment and whether what you intend to say will add value.

- Think of the benefits of allowing others to be in the limelight.

- Identify situations where your efforts could be better spent following through on previous commitments or focusing on more strategic issues versus engaging with others.

- Share your development goals with a trusted colleague, and ask for observations of your behaviors in key situations.

Tips and Techniques for a Coach

- Help the leader determine why he or she demonstrates high Colorful behaviors. What need is being met? Are these behaviors an attempt to impress people? Are they being used to gain approval or admiration? Identifying the underlying need will assist in finding other ways the need can be met that are less disruptive.

- Discuss the concept of "social generosity" with the leader—that there is give and take in any social situation and that it is the leader's responsibility to make sure the views of others are heard in an atmosphere of respect without unnecessary distractions.

- Ask the leader to describe a situation where his or her Colorful behaviors dominated a group discussion. Review the purpose of the interaction, the outcomes, and what the leader contributed. Also ask the leader what others were able to contribute. Discuss what may have been achieved by providing opportunities for others to contribute more. What could the leader have done differently to achieve that?

- Identify a critical situation that is going to occur in the near future. Rehearse how the leader will approach the situation differently than he or she would have in the past.

- Help the leader identify venues where high Colorful behaviors will add value (or at worst, not detract from others' experiences). Perhaps the venue may be a volunteer project or other non-work related opportunity.

Support Resources

Bolton, R., & Bolton, D. G. (1984). *Social style/management style: Developing productive work relationships.* New York, NY: AMACOM.

Based on their extensive research uncovering four predominant social styles (amiable, analytical, expressive, and driver), management experts Robert and Dorothy Bolton explain how to assess behavior patterns and use the resulting information to capitalize on strengths, minimize weaknesses, and achieve the desired results during the course of interactions.

Cain, S. (2012, February). The power of introverts [Video file]. Retrieved from https://www.ted.com/talks/susan_cain_the_power_of_introverts

Susan Cain makes a passionate argument that introverts bring "extraordinary talents and abilities to the world, and should be encouraged and celebrated."

Fotinos, J. (2014). *My life contract: 90-day program for prioritizing goals, staying on track, keeping focused, and getting results.* Charlottesville, VA: Hampton Roads.

Based on his popular class, Joel Fotinos provides an easy-to-use, example-based blueprint for helping people achieve their goals.

Nichols, M. P. (2009). *The lost art of listening: How learning to listen can improve relationships* (2nd ed.). New York, NY: Guilford.

Mike Nichols offers true-to-life examples, readily applicable techniques, and practical exercises for enhancing listening skills and communicating more effectively, productively, and empathically.

Tichy, N. (2007). *The leadership engine: Building leaders at every level.* New York, NY: HarperBusiness Essentials.

Based on decades of research and extensive firsthand experience, acclaimed faculty member and consultant Noel Tichy describes a proven system for creating dynamic leaders at every organizational level, emphasizing why the successful organizations of today require nimble, adaptable, and forward-thinking leaders capable of anticipating change and responding decisively.

Treasure, J. (2011). 5 ways to listen better [Video file]. Retrieved from http://www.ted.com/talks/julian_treasure_5_ways_to_listen_better?language=en

In his brief TED talk, sound expert Julian Treasure describes five ways people can "retune" their ears for "conscious listening."

Sample Coaching Program (Case 6—Mark)

An examination of Mark's scores on the Colorful subscales reveals that he is high on the Distractible and Self-Display subscales and low on the Public Confidence subscale. Thus, his greatest risks with his new accounts will most likely involve his lack of attention to detail, his failure to deliver on promises, and his coming on too strong with his jokes and anecdotes, as opposed to his having to have the floor all the time. Given the precarious financial situation of Mark's company and the reality that his job could be at stake, coaching around the Distractible and Self-Display behaviors is imperative to get him off to a good start with his new low Colorful accounts. The steps for coaching Mark should address his Self-Display and Distractible behaviors.

Distractible

- Ask Mark to provide examples of when he missed due dates or failed to give sufficient attention to details. Have him think about the consequences of his actions, both from a business standpoint (e.g., he provided incorrect information) and from a relationship standpoint (e.g., he disappointed a client). What were both the short-term implications and the long-term implications?

- Ask Mark to describe the circumstances under which the foregoing situations occurred in order to identify any triggers.

- Ask Mark what should have happened. How should he have behaved?

- Identify tools to help Mark deal with details and stay focused:
  - Create a to-do list with electronic reminders.
  - Use a time-management and priority-management system.
  - Find an assistant who is good with details to help keep him organized.
  - Suggest that Mark review the details of a project with a direct report, enabling Mark to interact with someone else, rather than having to focus on the tedious details by himself. It will also give Mark the opportunity to see how the direct report thinks and handles things.

- Identify upcoming events where Mark can practice his behavior modifications.
- Seek feedback from others to gauge the effectiveness of Mark's behavior changes.

Self-Display

- Ask what Mark hopes to gain by being the center of attention. Does he want to impress people? Does he want to be admired? Does he feel people will not remember him unless he does *x*, *y*, *z*, and so on? He has some personal need that he must satisfy, and understanding that personal need can help him identify other more socially constructive ways it can be met. Also, ask him to think about other people he knows who operate in a similar fashion. How does he react to being with them and battling for floor time? Is he annoyed by their behavior?

- Ask Mark to provide examples of situations when he has been told that his behavior was over the top and annoyed others. The coach might have to supplement Mark's examples with a multi-rater assessment or behavioral interview feedback as high Colorful individuals just do not realize that their behavior is not the norm. Mark's examples should include a description of the situation, what he said (including, if possible, the tone and volume of his voice, and his facial expressions), and how others reacted.

- Look for common themes in the situations that Mark describes to identify any specific triggers for his high Self-Display behavior.

- Ask Mark how his behavior compares to how others in the organization who are respected and viewed as leader-like would have behaved. How would his customers have behaved? Have Mark identify how he could have modified and dialed down his behavior to be less annoying to others. How could he mirror the behavior of the leaders? What behavior would be acceptable in the customer's organization?

- Develop ways Mark can control his Self-Display behavior going forward:
    - Perform a Stakeholder Analysis to identify the styles and business goals of Mark's key stakeholders so that Mark can determine how best to interact with them.
    - Get ahead of situations, and decide how to behave based on the audience.
    - Use a "cut-it-in-half" or "don't-do-it" mantra, at least initially, to focus on the behavior modifications required. Mark should try to be half as expressive, or not tell any jokes at all, and so on and see what the reactions are.

- Identify upcoming situations where Mark can practice modifying his behavior and use role plays if necessary.

- Seek feedback from others to gauge the effectiveness of Mark's behavior changes.

SUMMARY

Keep Doing

Relate to clients and colleagues with verve and enthusiasm.

Stop Doing

Talk past your allotted time, and interrupt others while they are working.

Start Doing

Listen rather than talk, and share the limelight with others.

An individual's high Colorful behaviors are highly visible to his or her constituents. Because of the positive aspects of Colorful behavior, and the positive feedback that the leader often receives about having a great personality, it can be difficult for the leader to accept that his or her Colorful behavior can cross the line. It is important that the coach help the leader calibrate the level of "personality" needed in a given situation, and recognize when his or her high Colorful behaviors are too much of a good thing. Typically, overcorrection is needed for the leader to get in the habit of reining in derailing behaviors. Overcorrection is also important because it helps to convince constituents that the leader is serious about behavior change. In fact, the behavior change itself is likely to draw positive attention for the leader and reinforce the effort to dial back the negative Colorful behaviors.

LOW COLORFUL

Detecting When It Is a Problem

The greatest risk for low Colorful leaders is being overlooked. These leaders are quiet, unassuming, and unassertive. A low Colorful individual's good ideas and contributions can go unnoticed because of his or her nonobtrusive, low-key personal demeanor. A stereotypical example of a low Colorful individual is Caspar Milquetoast, the character introduced in the 1920s in "The Timid Soul" comic strip. Caspar was so weak and ineffectual that the term *"milquetoast"* has been incorporated into everyday language to mean bland, plain, unadventurous, and easily overlooked. Low Colorful leaders run the risk of being perceived as "quiet" at best, and "invisible" at worst. Typically, they view their more Colorful colleagues as showboats, and convincing them to become more colorful themselves can be a challenge for a coach.

Another good example of a low Colorful leader is President Gerald Ford. He was picked for U.S. vice president after the resignation of Spiro Agnew essentially because of his low Colorful, unobtrusive style. Then, when Ford became president after the resignation of Richard Nixon, he served out his term in virtual anonymity. He is the only person in U.S. history to serve as vice president and president without ever being elected by the American people. While it is true he won his party's nomination for president in 1976, he ran what could only be described as a boring campaign. He was beaten by perhaps the second lowest Colorful president in U.S. history, Jimmy Carter. Ford's entire career was built on the notion that he was an everyday guy to whom anyone could relate and trust. His career success is a testament to the fact that leadership success can be achieved despite a low Colorful profile.

Robert from Case 3—Robert, Design Engineer on page 92 provides a good example of a low Colorful profile. The following is Robert's profile summary.

Robert's Situational Summary				
Robert is a design engineer for a manufacturer of commercial aircraft electronic components. He has worked primarily as an individual contributor and was known for getting things done. His hard work resulted in a promotion to project leader on a cross-functional team. His new role will be highly demanding and require effective leadership skills that will be a challenge for his quiet, reserved nature, and tendency to fade into the background in social situations.				
Dimension	**Score**	**Percentile**		**Description**
Excitable	35			Robert is a hard worker who seems very calm and even-tempered under pressure. People view him as task focused with little interest in engaging with people (Reserved—98%). He tends to work long hours and is not bothered by the fact that his attention to detail spills over into work for others (Diligent—80%), which has earned him a reputation as a grinder who gets things done.
Skeptical	50			
Cautious	75			
Reserved	98			
Leisurely	80			
Bold	55			
Mischievous	40			
Colorful	30			
Imaginative	62			
Diligent	80			
Dutiful	30			

0   10   20   30   40   50   60   70   80   90   100

Robert's Colorful score is 30 percent, and we typically use a score of 20 percent or below as a red flag that a low HDS score might be problematic. However, when viewed in the context of Robert's new situation as a project leader, along with the rest of his HDS profile, a score of 30 percent on the Colorful scale can definitely derail him. In combination with his extremely high score on the Reserved scale (98%), and his elevated scores on the Diligent (80%) and Cautious (75%) scales, Robert is likely to be seen as task-focused, quiet, unassuming, unapproachable, and having little time for small talk. In his new position as the project leader, his low Colorful behaviors could be disastrous as he will need to communicate with his team, build alignment, generate excitement and energy about the project, and be more visible and leader-like. Given the tight timeframe of the new project, his team will probably experience quite a bit of stress, and the team could use some levity and cheerleading from Robert. Further, Robert will need to be a successful advocate for his team so they receive credit for their hard work.

Evaluating the Need for Change

The following behavioral questions should be considered in conjunction with a leader's low Colorful score (as exhibited by Robert) when evaluating the need for a change in behavior. A "yes" response to three or fewer items suggests that there is no imminent need for behavioral changes. A "yes" response to four to six items suggests that a low score on the Colorful scale should be a watch-out for a leader. A "yes" response to more than six items suggests that a leader should take active steps toward making behavioral changes.

Does the leader:

1. Shy away from the stage or limelight when opportunities arise in public settings?   **Yes   No   Not Sure**

2. Blend in to the crowd to the point of going virtually unnoticed by others?   **Yes   No   Not Sure**

3. Appear awkward or unable to engage in small talk that would put others at ease in public settings?   **Yes   No   Not Sure**

4. Appear to remain task focused and unable to change directions even when others are creating significant distractions?   **Yes   No   Not Sure**

5. Tend to get immersed in a task to the point that distractions appear to be easily blocked out?   **Yes   No   Not Sure**

6. Exhibit little to no tendency to become bored with a task, regardless of the details involved?   **Yes   No   Not Sure**

7. Over-prepare for situations that require speaking to a group or in a public setting?   **Yes   No   Not Sure**

8. Leave little to no impression upon others he or she encounters in public settings?   **Yes   No   Not Sure**

9. Appear embarrassed or uncomfortable when others call attention to actions or contributions in public?   **Yes   No   Not Sure**

These items should be considered as behavioral indicators. Similar or associated behaviors to any of those listed that are exhibited by a leader likely suggest a "yes" response. They provide additional support that a leader may be at risk for the negative reputational consequences associated with those scoring low on the Colorful scale, such as Robert.

Impact of Low Colorful Behaviors

The greatest risk of low Colorful behaviors is that the leader is invisible to others and, therefore, ineffectual. The low Colorful person blends in with the woodwork and fails to make an impression. The impact of low Colorful behaviors can vary with three key constituencies: managers, peers, and direct reports.

Managers

Managers often appreciate low Colorful employees, as they are quiet, unassuming, and focused on the job, and they do not try to make themselves look good. However, these behaviors can work to the low Colorful individuals' disadvantage as they might be assigned dull, routine tasks, or they might not have much influence over the manager due to their quiet demeanor. Managers might not consider them for high-profile assignments, leadership roles, or promotion when doing rating and ranking because low Colorful individuals are not memorable or leader-like.

Peers

Peers generally find it easy to work with low Colorful individuals because they stay focused on the task at hand without any fanfare. In addition, peers do not feel threatened by low Colorful leaders, as they do not try to steal the limelight or practice one-upmanship. However, peers can take advantage of them by taking credit for the low Colorful individual's work. Further, peers might discount the individual's input or opinion because it is generally so low key.

Direct Reports

The low Colorful leader's greatest risk for derailment in relationships with direct reports is that the direct reports feel a lack of advocacy and support from the leader. Many times, due to the low Colorful individual's low-key style, direct reports feel that the boss is not going to bat for them—either to promote their ideas proactively or to defend them when under attack. Further, it can be pretty dull working for low Colorful leaders, due to their lack of energy around the work or their failure to provide recognition to the team, resulting in morale erosion.

Coaching Focus

The coaching focus with low Colorful leaders is to help them show more personal presence, including being more assertive and more lively. This demonstrative demeanor can be quite difficult for low Colorful leaders because these behaviors are so unnatural to them. Many times, low Colorful individuals perceive their higher Colorful colleagues as insincere or fake, and they certainly do not want to be perceived that way. Thus, coaching can be a challenge.

Further, sometimes low Colorful individuals do not want to have more influence or get promoted, so there's not much motivation to change. In this case, it is helpful to look at the individual's MVPI scores to find a hook that will prompt the behavior change. For example, if an individual is high on the Altruistic scale, dialing up the colorful behaviors can be positioned through the lens of helping others.

Coaching Strategy

There are five steps associated with the strategy for coaching low Colorful individuals:

1. Help the low Colorful leader understand that a lack of positive affect and presence can negatively impact his or her effectiveness as a leader. Ask for examples of times when the leader has been overlooked and times where being more assertive and motivational would have been important. Ask how the outcomes to the situations described would have been different with a livelier discussion, a more energetic approach, etc. Supplement this information with examples from a multi-rater assessment or performance feedback regarding low Colorful behaviors.

2. Ask the leader what behaviors could be modified in the foregoing examples to be more effective.

3. Identify approaches and tools to help the leader dial up behaviors to be more noticeable in a way that is acceptable.

4. Identify upcoming, low-risk situations where the leader can practice the new behaviors.

5. Ask for feedback from key stakeholders to evaluate which new behaviors are working and which need further modification. It is important to start slowly and build on each success. Big setbacks or embarrassing moments will significantly hinder the willingness of a low Colorful leader to try new, more Colorful behaviors.

Strategy Refinements Using Subscale Information

The subscales for Colorful include Public Confidence, Distractible, and Self-Display. Each of these subscales contributes to an overall Colorful scale score and provides interpretation refinements beyond those that can be achieved from a scale score alone. These interpretation refinements can have implications for specific behavior changes that may improve leader performance. They may also help in refining the coaching strategy that would be most effective in producing positive behavioral changes.

Public Confidence

Leaders who score low on the Public Confidence subscale are typically quiet, controlled, and outwardly lacking in confidence. Thus, the coach needs to work with them on inserting themselves into conversations, offering their opinions, showing conviction, and being more expressive in their delivery. Further, these individuals need to understand the concept of affirmation—the notion that their audiences need some sort of reaction from them, be it positive or negative, to know where they stand on issues. Audiences are not mind-readers, so in the absence of a reaction from the leader, they draw their own conclusions, and the leader loses the opportunity to influence others.

Distractible

Leaders who score low on the Distractible subscale are usually focused, task-oriented, and unable to shift gears quickly. A deficit on this subscale is not as big a derailer as with the other two subscales because the leader will be task-focused and persistent. However, there is a danger that the leader will become known as a plodder and end up with grind-it-out kinds of jobs that no one else wants. It is also possible that excessive task focus involving low Distractible behaviors like working behind closed doors will limit networking and the overall visibility of the leader. Such behaviors can only further serve to diminish the leader's future career opportunities.

Self-Display

A low score on the Self-Display subscale indicates that the leader is restrained and adheres to social norms. When Self-Display is low, the leader is at serious risk of blending in with the woodwork and being overlooked because the individual is doing nothing to make an impression. In essence, the leader becomes a gray spot on a gray wall. Coaching should focus on increasing the leader's positive affect, including facial expressions, body language, and inflection and tone of voice. Additionally, the leader should look for opportunities to promote personal and team successes. These opportunities do not have to come with great fanfare. In fact, leaders who strategically promote their successes and the successes of their team tend to be far more effective and reduce their risk of being seen as taking victory laps.

Coaching Tactics

Coaching tactics cover a range of approaches and resources that have been found useful in addressing low Colorful behaviors. These tactics are typically used in combination to form a custom plan suited to the specific learning needs of a leader. The tactics are divided into four categories: (1) thought-provoking questions for a leader to consider, (2) exercises a leader can engage in to improve performance, (3) tips and techniques a coach can use to help a leader improve performance, and (4) support resources that can be consulted to gain additional insights in addressing low Colorful behaviors.

Thought-Provoking Questions for a Leader

- How do you contribute in team settings?
- How would you like to be seen, and what is necessary to accomplish this?
- What do you do to display executive presence?
- How do you show affirmation so your audience knows where you stand on an issue?
- How can you promote your own and your team's accomplishments?
- What is necessary to achieve your business or career goals?

Exercises for a Leader

- Prepare for meetings by summarizing key points you want to make in bullet points.
- Arrive at the meeting early to secure a visible seat in the room.
- Find regular opportunities to brag about an individual or team accomplishment.
- Lead or become involved in a project or initiative that will make it necessary for you to demonstrate a strong presence.
- Keep track of your accomplishments and the accomplishments of your team. Plan strategic moments to insert statements about these accomplishments in the presence of superiors.
- Develop a list of interesting stories, anecdotes, or jokes that you can draw upon in social situations.
- Identify a high profile task or assignment that is within your capabilities. Put a strategy together to advocate to the decision-makers that you are the right person for the assignment.

Tips and Techniques for a Coach

- Help the leader reframe the dialed-up Colorful behaviors as necessary for accomplishing business goals and being effective as a leader.
- Help the leader determine, "what is executive presence in your company?" Develop a list of behaviors that the leader can incorporate to build a stronger executive presence.
- Have the leader practice using the word "I" in describing an accomplishment.
- Help the leader prepare a 30-second elevator speech that can be used to describe his or her role and contribution to the organization in a clear and compelling way.

- Have the leader observe and practice mannerisms of high Colorful people who effectively promote themselves within the organization. Identify situations where the leader can experiment with these mannerisms and observe the reactions of others.

- Have the leader practice the more Colorful behaviors in a low-risk, non-work environment where it will not matter if things do not go smoothly.

Support Resources

Cabane, O. F. (2013). *The charisma myth: How anyone can master the art and science of personal magnetism.* New York, NY: Penguin Group.

Drawing on techniques she originally developed for Harvard and MIT, Cabane breaks charisma down into its components and describes how people can become more influential, persuasive, and inspiring.

Clark, B., & Crossland, R. (2002). *The leader's voice: How your communication can inspire action and get results.* New York, NY: SelectBooks.

Based on over 20 years of communication research and an examination of over 1,100 examples of leadership communication, Clark and Crossland describe their simple but elegant leadership communication model and offer communication principles capable of helping readers communicate authentically, powerfully, and in a manner that inspires others' confidence.

Hedges, K. (2011). *The power of presence: Unlock your potential to influence and engage others.* New York, NY: AMACOM.

Executive and CEO coach Kristi Hedges demystifies the elusive quality often referred to as "presence" and shows readers how they can strengthen their impact irrespective of their personality or hierarchical position.

Hodgkinson, S. (2005). *The leader's edge: Using personal branding to drive performance and profit.* Lincoln, NE: iUniverse.

Based on current research about impression management, executive development, and social networking, Hodgkinson uses familiar language to offer readers profound insights and a readily applicable plan for creating their own personal brands.

Maxwell, J. C. (2010). *Everyone communicates, few connect: What the most effective people do differently.* Nashville, TN: Thomas Nelson.

Based on the premise that anyone can learn how to turn communication into an opportunity for powerful connection, Maxwell guides readers through the process of developing the crucial skills necessary to connect with others.

Weiner, A. N. (2006). *So smart but…: How intelligent people lose credibility and how they can get it back.* San Francisco, CA: John Wiley & Sons.

Weiner describes how anyone can find ways to make measurable, credibility-enhancing improvements in how they present themselves.

Sample Coaching Program (Case 3—Robert)

Robert's profile indicates a Colorful score of 30 percent. His subscale scores reveal that he is low on all three subscales, so coaching should address his general need to be more visible and demonstrate more personal presence now that he is a project leader.

- Have Robert reflect on recent situations with his team that he thinks would have had a better outcome if he had been more confident, energetic, emotive, assertive, etc.

- Ask Robert how he could have demonstrated more assertiveness or emotion. Ask him to identify leaders whose styles he admires and think about what they would have said or done.

- Ask Robert to recall a time when he was more assertive or emotive. What was the situation (e.g., helping his people, discussing business results, etc.)? What did he feel physically (e.g., excited about the topic, etc.)? How did his tone modulate? What was his body language? How did his audience react? How can he tap into these positive feelings in more situations?

- Help Robert identify ways he can be more visible and approachable:
  - Communicate with team members proactively, including managing by walking around.
  - Lighten up by including humor or anecdotes in interactions with people.
  - Make sure he speaks up at least twice in each meeting he attends.
  - Share the team's accomplishments with senior management.

- Identify upcoming situations where Robert can practice these behaviors by role playing with him what he will say, how he will say it, and so on. If he is reluctant to try these at work, ask him to try them in a low-risk, non-work situation (e.g., chatting with someone in line at the grocery store, speaking up at a PTA meeting, etc.).

- Have him select an advocate to give him ongoing feedback. Evaluate the success of his changed behaviors not by how he feels (he will be uncomfortable), but by their impact on others or on the outcome of the situation.

Summary

Keep Doing

Be a good team player, and use good listening skills.

Stop Doing

Be so quiet and unassuming that you forfeit your opportunity to influence others.

Start Doing

Speak up with more self-confidence, and promote team accomplishment.

The greatest risk for low Colorful leaders is being overlooked. Not only might they be overlooked personally (e.g., for a promotion or a high-profile assignment), but their good ideas and their team's good work might be overlooked due to lack of strong advocacy. This lack of acknowledgement results in a lose-lose situation for all individuals involved and the organization. Leader "emergence" is perhaps one of the most significant variables in career success. Effective use of Colorful behaviors is one of the hallmarks of leaders who have strong emergent profiles. Coaching around confidence, energy, and presence in general can help leaders display a more Colorful persona that will raise their emergent profile and increase the probability of greater career success.

CHAPTER 18

IMAGINATIVE

HIGH IMAGINATIVE

Detecting When It Is a Problem

Most organizations today are striving to develop leaders who, among other leadership characteristics, have the ability to be strategic and lead innovation. In doing so, they are usually seeking leaders who can think outside the box and can creatively develop strategies or solutions by generating different and new perspectives and ideas. Leaders who score very high on the Imaginative scale, however, can negatively impact their effectiveness and reputation through an excessive number of unconventional ideas and a preoccupation with their own ideas. Further, they can acquire reputations for being impractical and for being disconnected from the business.

A good example of a leader with high Imaginative behaviors is Ron Johnson, a former Target and Apple executive who is known as a retail genius. Johnson joined J. C. Penney as CEO in 2011 and was subsequently ousted in fewer than two years. He set out to transform J. C. Penney by completely changing the customer shopping experience and introducing pricing strategies brand new to this segment of the retail industry. His radical ideas were developed without a solid understanding of the J. C. Penney customer base, and suggestions by others that these ideas be tested prior to implementation were dismissed. The pricing schemes alone were found to be very confusing and alienated many customers, resulting in a significant drop in sales and the stock price. Johnson was fired and immediately replaced by the former CEO, Myron Ullman.

High Imaginative leaders often consider visionary leadership and creativity essential to success and believe strongly in their own ideas. This mindset makes it very challenging for them not to push their ideas, particularly in stressful and critical circumstances. Their idea generation can also be perceived as very random and confusing. Hence, they are often seen as eccentric and impractical and are unable to articulate ideas in a way that engages others.

Courtney from Case 8—Courtney, Assistant Operations Manager on page 102 is a good example of a high Imaginative profile. She also has high scores in the Bold (95%) and Mischievous (90%) scales. The following is Courtney's profile summary.

Courtney's Situational Summary
Courtney successfully completed a plant start-up in Mexico for an electronics manufacturing company. Despite being considered a high potential leader, her superiors had lingering questions about her leadership ability. As a result, she was given the role of assistant operations manager working for one of the best plant managers in the company. Courtney's new manager is known for her high standards, careful attention to detail, hard work, and putting in long hours.

Dimension	Score	Percentile	Description
Excitable	30		Courtney is an energetic leader who is known for her confidence in taking on any challenge (Bold—95%). She tends to use her charm and charisma to get her way (Mischievous—90%). She also tends to grab high-profile assignments to keep herself in the limelight (Colorful—80%). Her superiors have put her on the fast track but have some concerns about her ability to be a team player.
Skeptical	50		
Cautious	20		
Reserved	25		
Leisurely	30		
Bold	95		
Mischievous	90		
Colorful	80		
Imaginative	85		
Diligent	5		
Dutiful	10		

0   10   20   30   40   50   60   70   80   90   100

Courtney's high Imaginative score (85%) has probably been a helpful aspect of her profile thus far in her career. However, she is now working for a plant manager who appears to be a very pragmatic, detail-oriented person who does not take big risks or make big changes without a lot of due diligence. Courtney will have plenty of big ideas, given her high Imaginative score. She will also feel an obligation to put them on the table as she would see that as one way of contributing to the business. Unfortunately, what she considers brainstorming could be seen by her new manager as wild ideas coming from a person who has not thought through how things work in an established plant. Similar to Ron Johnson, Courtney will not be inclined to go through careful due diligence on her ideas before offering them publicly. Her low Diligent score (5%), low Cautious score (20%), and high Mischievous score (90%) will contribute to a tendency to be impulsive and willing to take risks. This could easily run afoul of her new manager's style and damage Courtney's reputation with the new manager.

Evaluating the Need for Change

The following behavioral questions should be considered in conjunction with a leader's high Imaginative score (as exhibited by Courtney) when evaluating the need for a change in behavior. A "yes" response to three or fewer items suggests that there is no imminent need for behavioral changes. A "yes" response to four to six items suggests that a high score on the Imaginative scale should be a watch-out for a leader. A "yes" response to more than six items suggests that a leader should take active steps toward making behavioral changes.

Does the leader:

1. Make statements that others find shocking or just plain weird?   Yes   No   Not Sure

2. Exhibit behaviors that others would fine peculiar or unconventional?   Yes   No   Not Sure

3. Appear to be unaware, or at least unconcerned, about how unconventional actions affect others?   Yes   No   Not Sure

4. Profess an ability to anticipate what others may say before they actually say it?   Yes   No   Not Sure

5. Profess to have special talents or abilities that others do not possess?   Yes   No   Not Sure

6. Point out things that tend to go unnoticed by others?   Yes   No   Not Sure

7. Often put forth ideas that others find strange or difficult to grasp?   Yes   No   Not Sure

8. Tend to leap from one idea to the next, leaving the impression of erratic or irrational thinking?   Yes   No   Not Sure

9. Offer ideas that are impractical or undoable to the point that it negatively impacts his or her personal credibility?   Yes   No   Not Sure

These items should be considered as behavioral indicators. Similar or associated behaviors to any of those listed that are exhibited by a leader likely suggest a "yes" response. They provide additional support that a leader may be at risk for the negative reputational consequences associated with those scoring high on the Imaginative scale, such as Courtney.

Impact of High Imaginative Behaviors

Leaders with high Imaginative scores often view themselves as highly creative, visionary, and open to new ways of doing things. In certain situations, however, their colleagues can become highly frustrated, impatient, and confused by those behaviors. If these tendencies are not effectively managed, they can impact a leader's reputation, current performance, and future career potential. To effectively manage these behaviors, it is essential that the leader be aware of the situations that trigger the behavior and fully understand and appreciate the impact of the behavior on others and on the leader's overall performance and reputation. The following are some of the consequences of high Imaginative behavior, broken out by three constituencies: managers, peers, and direct reports.

Managers

Managers may be concerned about a high Imaginative leader's ability to drive or contribute to rational problem-solving and decision-making. The high Imaginative individual's results orientation may also be called into question, which can negatively impact the manager's willingness to tap that individual for significant opportunities going forward. Because people with high Imaginative scores often communicate their ideas poorly, a manager may have concerns about their ability to effectively direct, influence, and engage others, culminating in the manager's perception of the high Imaginative leader as not being able to achieve results through others, which can significantly affect his or her career potential.

Peers

Leaders with high Imaginative scores can lose credibility with their peers quickly. These leaders are often seen as overly committed to their own ideas and not open to alternative ways of thinking or to others' ideas. Their behavior can also be seen as counterproductive in meetings (e.g., consuming a lot a time without productive outcomes, digressing, being distracted, offering too many ideas for others to digest, etc.). As a result, peers often stop listening to these individuals and do not sufficiently consider the ideas proposed. Peers also will avoid involving these individuals in new opportunities, believing the input will not be practical and the interaction will not be productive. This isolation can negatively impact near-term performance as well as long-term career potential because peers are often consulted regarding a leader's suitability for a promotion or broader role in the organization.

Direct Reports

Direct reports of high Imaginative leaders can often feel confused by these leaders, primarily because of their inability to clearly communicate ideas. Communicated ideas can often feel to direct reports like stream-of-consciousness thinking that changes moment to moment. Direct reports can also be frustrated by the high Imaginative leader's need to excessively explore new ideas with no sense of marching orders or prioritization. This absence of organization can result in a lack of alignment around key priorities and a lack of team member engagement. Often, a team with a high Imaginative leader will need to regroup without the leader present to clarify key decisions and next steps. High Imaginative behaviors can reduce a leader's ability to attract and retain key talent, build an effective team, and limit promotion opportunities.

Coaching Focus

The coaching focus for leaders exhibiting high Imaginative behaviors is not to completely eliminate their innovative thinking and problem-solving, but instead to help these leaders identify the right degree of idea generation and imagination.

Coaching Strategy

The four basic steps associated with the coaching strategy for high Imaginative behaviors are:

1. Increase the leader's self-awareness of what the behaviors look like in public. Often, it can be helpful to characterize these behaviors as a light that is shining so brightly that it is blinding others, and by turning the dimmer switch down, it can be more comfortable for others.

2. Make note of those situations where these behaviors surface and the circumstances surrounding them to help the leader reflect on those situations. Ask the leader to analyze the themes, situations, people, etc. that triggered the behaviors.

3. Identify and implement pre-trigger activities to reduce the probability that these behaviors will surface.

4. Ask the leader to evaluate the activities and identify those that are most effective or impactful.

Strategy Refinements Using Subscale Information

The subscales offer insights as to how the coaching strategy might be refined to improve the effectiveness of the intervention. The subscales for Imaginative behavior include Eccentric, Special Sensitivity, and Creative Thinking. They offer insights as to the trigger points for imaginative moments. If they are elevated, the coaching strategy should focus on those trigger points that elicit the most damaging imaginative moments.

Eccentric

Leaders who are elevated on the Eccentric subscale are likely seen as unusually un-conventional or idiosyncratic in their thoughts and ideas. In addition, the way in which they communicate their ideas may come across as disorganized, which in turn may cause others to have a hard time following or understanding the practicality of their ideas. Over time, these leaders will be known as being eccentric and unusual in their thought processes. They may also struggle with focusing on what matters, as well as with follow through, given their nonlinear thought processes. As a result, it is important that the coaching strategy identify trigger points and focus on ways to avoid the damaging behaviors. Leaders can improve their leadership effectiveness by anticipating potential triggers and controlling their unconventional thinking.

Special Sensitivity

Leaders with an elevation on the Special Sensitivity subscale believe that they have an unusually strong ability to read people and an ability to notice things that would likely be overlooked by others. When this subscale is elevated, it is important for leaders to identify the impact that these beliefs can have on their ability to effectively engage and collaborate with others. These leaders must find ways that they can avoid jumping to conclusions about people, especially in the absence of real data. Additionally, they should strive to better understand the knowledge, perspective, and ideas of others.

Creative Thinking

Leaders who are elevated on the Creative Thinking subscale are often unusually inventive and use their imaginations to creatively solve problems. These leaders are at risk of being seen as not focused on business realities, as impractical, and as not open to others' ideas—all of which can damage their credibility. The coaching strategy should focus on helping these leaders define the circumstances where their creative thinking behavior becomes excessive, or their ideas appear too unconventional. Once these circumstances have been identified, these leaders can then learn to control their need to offer an excessive number of creative ideas or ideas that others may find weird. The solution can be as simple as the leader's clarifying the situation as a brainstorming session. Additionally, the leader can be encouraged to use more seeking behavior rather than telling behavior.

Coaching Tactics

Coaching tactics cover a range of approaches and resources that have been found useful in addressing high Imaginative behaviors. These tactics are typically used in combination to form a custom plan suited to the specific learning needs of a leader. The tactics are divided into four categories: (1) thought-provoking questions for a leader to consider, (2) exercises a leader can engage in to improve performance, (3) tips and techniques a coach can use to help a leader improve performance, and (4) support resources that can be consulted to gain additional insights in addressing high Imaginative behaviors.

Thought-Provoking Questions for a Leader

- What is your purpose in sharing ideas? How do you get satisfaction from this?

- How do you communicate that a discussion is intended for brainstorming purposes? How do you communicate that a discussion is intended to focus on identifying and implementing solutions?

- How do you let your team know which ideas represent out-loud thinking and which are to be acted on?

- How do you assess ideas before presenting them in high stakes situations?

- What cues do you look for to assess understanding and to gauge reactions from others?

Exercises for a Leader

- Find a partner with whom to vet ideas. Practice discussing all the implications and the necessary steps for implementation of the ideas. Practice staying focused.

- Think through an idea you are about to propose and design follow-up questions to check for understanding regarding the idea and the implications associated with implementing it.

- Keep a record of the important ideas you present during meetings. Track which of those ideas are actually implemented and taken to completion. Critically evaluate the ideas in terms of their success and your role in the implementation process.

- Establish operating guidelines for team members to challenge new ideas and push back on ideas that are unclear or inconsistent with the direction of the team.

- Maintain a list of ideas that have been implemented on a whiteboard and track them regularly in terms of progress.

Tips and Techniques for a Coach

- Review and discuss other related scale results and their impact on the appearance of high Imaginative behaviors (e.g., Prudence, Inquisitive, Cautious, Mischievous, and Aesthetics).

- Discuss the impact of excessive idea generation on group decision-making. Ask for specific circumstances when that occurred. Identify alternative approaches.

- Review and discuss the leader's journal of situations where high Imaginative behaviors surfaced. Identify key patterns, themes, and triggers. Identify ways to prevent these behaviors in the future.

- Role play a situation where the leader presents a new, groundbreaking idea to you with the goal of influencing you to adopt that idea.

- Work with the leader to slow down his or her ideation process by evaluating each idea. The remedy could be as simple as putting each idea on a flipchart and rating the idea on its potential impact and practicality. The goal is to get the leader to self-monitor ideation using more mental evaluation before public disclosure.

Support Resources

Burkus, D. (2013). *The myths of creativity: The truth about how innovative companies and people generate great ideas.* San Francisco, CA: Jossey-Bass.

Based on the latest research on successful creative individuals and organizations, Burkus reconceptualizes the concept of creativity and teaches readers how to employ "a practical approach, grounded in reality, to find the best new ideas, projects, processes, and programs."

Drucker, P. F., Christiansen, C. M., & Govindarajan, V. J. (2013). *HBR's 10 must reads on innovation.* Boston, MA: HBR Press.

A thoughtfully curated group of articles from the *Harvard Business Review* offer insight about, for example, identifying ideas worth pursuing, innovating "through the front lines" (not just from the top), and how to avoid stifling innovation.

Duarte, N. (2010). *Resonate: Present visual stories that transform audiences.* Hoboken, NJ: Wiley.

"Resonate" teaches readers how to convey messages with "passion, persuasion, and impact," energize and move audiences to "transformative action," and make meaningful connections with people, even from on stage.

Manning, J., & Roberts, K. (2015). *The disciplined leader: Keeping focused on what really matters.* Oakland, CA: Berrett-Koehler.

Manning and Roberts offer 52 concise lessons designed to help leaders hone in on the "vital few" activities that truly drive results instead of chasing the countless things they "could do."

Palmer, S. A. (2008). *Good in a room: How to sell yourself (and your ideas) and win over any audience.* New York, NY: Doubleday.

Palmer, former Director of Creative Affairs at MGM, uncovers the tactics used by Hollywood's top producers, directors, and writers to win buy-in and financing, and describes how readers can apply the same approaches to sell themselves and their ideas in the business world.

Shank, J. K., Niblock, E. G., & Sandalls Jr., W. T. (1973, January). Balancing 'creativity' and 'practicality' in formal planning. *Harvard Business Review.* Retrieved from https://hbr.org/1973/01/balance-creativity-and-practicality-in-formal-planning

This HBR classic uses multiple examples to demonstrate how creativity and practicality need not be at odds during the planning process.

Smith, P. (2012). *Lead with a story: A guide to crafting business narratives that captivate, convince and inspire.* New York, NY: AMACOM.

Smith makes a passionate and convincing case, based heavily on real-world examples in companies like Nike, Merrill-Lynch, 3M, and Proctor & Gamble, for the power of storytelling in corporate settings. *Lead with a Story* teaches readers how to do just that—craft powerful narratives capable of, among other things, energizing people around a vision, marketing ideas, or generating commitment.

Sample Coaching Program (Case 8—Courtney)

Courtney has an elevated score on the Imaginative scale, combined with high scores on the Bold and Mischievous scales. Given that success in her role requires close management of the business and effectively engaging a broader team of people than she has led previously, managing her high Imaginative tendencies is an important area of focus for the coaching program. This coaching focus is further reinforced by her high Bold and Mischievous scores, which may be contributing to the existing concern that Courtney is not a team player. With respect to her subscale scores, she scores very high on the Special Sensitivity subscale but scores at lower levels on the Eccentric and Creative Thinking subscales. Based on this, the coaching engagement should include the following key steps:

- Ask Courtney to complete a self-reflection exercise in which she will identify situations in the past where she has demonstrated high Imaginative behaviors. It is important for her to look at those situations objectively and make note of each situation and its specific details, such as the purpose of the meeting, people in attendance, and what may have prompted the high Imaginative behavior. She should also describe the behaviors she demonstrated and the impact she believes they had on the effectiveness of the discussion, on others around her, and on her own effectiveness.

- Review these situations with Courtney to identify themes or patterns in the circumstances where these behaviors tend to surface. This identification will help Courtney better prepare for those circumstances and reduce the probability that these behaviors will surface.

- Help Courtney identify some alternate behaviors that she can use that will reduce her tendency to engage in high Imaginative behaviors. The following are some examples:

  - Clarifying in advance the specific objectives or outcomes expected from an interaction or meeting with others.

  - Making a list of the ideas or solutions she wants to bring to the discussion and conducting a preliminary assessment of their relevance to the issue at hand.

  - Identifying questions to ask others in the meeting to gather more input and perspectives and listening effectively to responses.

- Allowing others to offer their ideas before offering hers and acknowledging the value in those ideas.

- Having a way to communicate to the group that she is shifting to out-of-the-box thinking.

- Asking a trusted colleague to give her a signal during the meeting when her high Imaginative behaviors appear.

- Asking a trusted colleague for feedback on her behavior after the meeting.

- Ask Courtney to identify at least one person with whom she is having difficulty communicating on new ideas. Define the specific challenges with that individual and develop some alternate approaches.

- Encourage Courtney to keep a journal of situations where her high Imaginative behaviors appeared. Ask her to include a description of the situation, how she responded (effectively or ineffectively), the impact her behavior had on the effectiveness of the interaction, and what she would do differently next time. The goal is to enable Courtney to learn from her own critical incidents.

SUMMARY

Keep Doing

Provide ideas, insights, and original solutions to everyday business problems.

Stop Doing

Offer ideas or solutions without being asked or before the problem has been identified.

Start Doing

Check with colleagues about the practicality of ideas before taking them public.

Leaders who have the ability to think creatively and get others to think creatively can be a tremendous asset to their organizations. However, creative thinking must be demonstrated to the right degree and balanced with the realities of an organization. When leaders exhibit excessive ideation or impractical ideation, they can be seen as unfocused, distracting, and even eccentric. If these high Imaginative behaviors can be brought under control by the leader through coaching and greater self-awareness, they can become an important asset in the leader's achieving career success. If these behaviors go unchecked, the leader's credibility will suffer and career limitations will follow.

Low Imaginative

Detecting When It Is a Problem

The ability to think strategically and innovatively has become an important competency for leaders in many organizations. The Imaginative scale provides an assessment of the degree to which an individual thinks and acts in interesting and unusual ways. While those who score high on this scale demonstrate a strong potential to be derailed because of developing a reputation for an excessive amount of idea generation, those who score low also demonstrate a strong potential to be derailed but for different reasons. When leaders score low on the Imaginative scale, they are often seen as lacking creativity, failing to contribute new ideas, and being inflexible. Their major derailment risks stem largely from missing opportunities to innovate, blocking innovation, or not seeing the need for innovation, and from being labeled as "not strategic."

Classic examples of this are Jim Balsillie and Mike Lazaridis, former co-CEOs of RIM/Blackberry. Dan Pontefract, author of *Flat Army: Creating a Connected and Engaged Organization*, wrote about the failure of Balsillie and Lazaridis to create a new and innovative platform for Blackberry when Apple introduced the iPhone. Pontefract described the situation at Blackberry this way: "To many, RIM seemed to morph from an innovative and flexible organization to one that was rigid, blind, egocentric, and hierarchical. The situation at RIM was a lack of perception, and many of its leaders were culpable. The situation has become a vortex with close-minded behavior at the root."

Leaders with low Imaginative scores may be highly successful as long as their roles require them to remain focused on tasks and key metrics, and results can be achieved through a clear, predictable leadership style. If, however, these leaders are required to lead the development of innovative ideas, methodologies, or processes, they may become quite challenged. The challenge at the low end of this scale is particularly strong because it necessitates demonstrating new behaviors that the leader has not likely exhibited before. Taking on or acquiring new behaviors is generally much more difficult than dialing back a behavior. In the case of low Imaginative leaders, the challenge is particularly daunting because ideation (an important behavior lacking in these individuals) is a difficult skill to learn and an even more difficult skill to coach.

Kelly, the CFO of a large clothing retailer from Case 9—Kelly, Chief Financial Officer on page 104, is a good example of the potential impact of low Imaginative. The following is Kelly's profile summary.

Kelly's Situational Summary				
Kelly was successfully performing in the role of controller for a large clothing retailer. The CFO passed away suddenly, leaving a big gap on the leadership team. Kelly was promoted into the CFO position despite concerns about her readiness. The new role required expanded job responsibilities, effective working relationships with other members of the leadership team, and a more strategic approach to the business.				
Dimension	**Score**	**Percentile**		**Description**
Excitable	20			Kelly is a very calm, even-tempered finance type (Excitable—20%). She is a "trust, but verify" type of person (Skeptical—79%) who can be a bit intimidating in interpersonal situations (Reserved—80%). Kelly also exhibits very high attention to detail and tends to micromanage all aspects of the financial function for which she is responsible (Diligent—95%).
Skeptical	79			
Cautious	70			
Reserved	80			
Leisurely	38			
Bold	60			
Mischievous	30			
Colorful	20			
Imaginative	30			
Diligent	95			
Dutiful	32			

```
0   10   20   30   40   50   60   70   80   90   100
```

Kelly's Imaginative score is 30 percent. A score of 20 percent or below is typically used as a red flag that a low HDS score might be problematic. However, when viewed in the context of Kelly's new situation as a CFO, accompanied by the rest of her HDS profile, a score of 30 percent on the Imaginative scale can definitely derail her. Scores on three other scales are particularly problematic for Kelly, including Diligent (95%), Skeptical (79%), and Reserved (80%). These high scores combined with her low Imaginative score show a strong potential for Kelly to be seen as very focused on detail, not creative in her thought process, and cynical or mistrusting of others and new ideas or approaches. In her new role as CFO, being successful necessitates that she think flexibly and contribute meaningfully to developing the long-term business strategy, build trusting collaborative relationships with her peers, and lead the development of innovative ideas and solutions. It will be critical for Kelly to understand the significant negative impact that her low Imaginative behaviors, if unchanged, could have on her ability to be a credible leader and successful at the CFO level.

Evaluating the Need for Change

The following behavioral questions should be considered in conjunction with a leader's low Imaginative score (as exhibited by Kelly) when evaluating the need for a change in behavior. A "yes" response to three or fewer items suggests that there is no imminent need for behavioral changes. A "yes" response to four to six items suggests that a low score on the Imaginative scale should be a watch-out for a leader. A "yes" response to more than six items suggests that a leader should take active steps toward making behavioral changes.

Does the leader:

1.	Refrain from offering ideas in situations associated with brainstorming or problem-solving?	**Yes**	**No**	**Not Sure**
2.	Avoid the appearance of being out of the mainstream or unconventional in any way?	**Yes**	**No**	**Not Sure**
3.	Exhibit an excessive concern for how others may react to ideas or thoughts offered on an issue?	**Yes**	**No**	**Not Sure**
4.	Appear easily impressed by the ideas of others, when most people would find the ideas pretty conventional?	**Yes**	**No**	**Not Sure**
5.	Display a great deal of humility when others point out his or her personal talents or abilities?	**Yes**	**No**	**Not Sure**
6.	Appear firmly grounded in reality, to the point of appearing boring or uninteresting to others?	**Yes**	**No**	**Not Sure**
7.	Consistently put forth ideas that others consider practical or blatantly obvious?	**Yes**	**No**	**Not Sure**
8.	Lock in on practical solutions to problems in a way that stifles creativity or innovation?	**Yes**	**No**	**Not Sure**
9.	Often get described as someone who is a poor or weak strategic thinker?	**Yes**	**No**	**Not Sure**

These items should be considered as behavioral indicators. Similar or associated behaviors to any of those listed that are exhibited by a leader likely suggest a "yes" response. They provide additional support that a leader may be at risk for the negative reputational consequences associated with those scoring low on the Imaginative scale, such as Kelly.

Impact of Low Imaginative Behaviors

Leaders who score low on the Imaginative scale will be quite challenged in organizations that are striving to grow, change, and innovate. These leaders may also be a source of frustration to their colleagues due to their lack of contribution to strategy and new ways of thinking. Low Imaginative leaders may be seen as "not strategic," resistant to the achievement of organizational goals, or unable to deal with complexity, which can have a negative impact on a leader's performance and long-term career growth, and on the performance of the team. The following are some of the consequences of low Imaginative behavior, broken out by three constituencies: managers, peers, and direct reports.

Managers

Some managers appreciate having individuals with low Imaginative behaviors on their team. Low Imaginative leaders are seen as practical, sensible, task-oriented, and willing to go along with the plan as defined. They also are willing to allow their managers to receive all of the visibility and recognition, making a manager very happy. On the other hand, managers who rely on and value team members who bring independent thinking and a broad perspective to the table will view individuals with low Imaginative scores as missing opportunities to contribute. These individuals may be seen as performing at an acceptable level in the near term. However, their persistent low Imaginative approach to change and innovation can limit their opportunities to be considered for more complex, higher level, and more visible roles in the future. Nothing stops a leader's potential for promotion faster than being labeled as "not strategic." Managers commonly use this label for those exhibiting low Imaginative behaviors.

Peers

Peers may consciously avoid individuals who demonstrate low Imaginative behaviors because they may interpret their lack of idea generation as a lack of support or resistance to new thinking. Peers may even develop an unconscious bias to not seek opinions from these individuals because of their reputation for not bringing forward any new perspectives or ideas. Peers will more likely gravitate to others who will add value with respect to innovative or creative thinking. Building relationships and networking with peers are critical interpersonal behaviors for career success. These interpersonal behaviors will be among the first to be negatively impacted when peers begin to restrict their interactions with a low Imaginative leader.

Direct Reports

Direct reports often find it challenging to sell new ideas to low Imaginative leaders or engage them in thinking differently and making decisions that go beyond those that are straightforward and safe. This difficulty can negatively impact the morale of direct reports, especially if they are ambitious and looking for ways to meaningfully contribute to the business. A collateral problem for direct reports is they often get painted with the same brush as a low Imaginative leader. Low Imaginative leaders can create a bottleneck for innovation when they squelch the new ideas that come from their direct reports as they perpetuate their own rigid adherence to past routines. Direct reports who might otherwise get recognized for bringing innovative ideas to the business are instead mired in executing the comfortable routines of the leader.

Coaching Focus

As with other low scale scores, coaching individuals with a low score on the Imaginative scale can be more challenging than coaching individuals with high scores due to the higher level of difficulty associated with acquiring a new behavior or skill rather than toning down a behavior. The overall goal of the coaching should be to help the individual develop a higher degree of idea generation and imagination, consistent with the organization's culture and goals. Short of that, these individuals can at least learn to be facilitators of the ideas of others.

Coaching Strategy

The coaching strategy for low Imaginative behaviors should be centered on three key phases:

1. The first phase is to help leaders understand the impact of their behaviors on their near-term performance and reputation, as well as on their long-term career potential. In this phase, the coach should be specific about how these behaviors might be perceived by various stakeholder groups and the impact of those perceptions on the leader's ability to achieve individual and organizational goals. MVPI results may reveal some key motivators that can help leaders embrace the need for change.

2. In the second phase, leaders should identify circumstances where demonstrating more flexibility and willingness to innovate could significantly enhance their performance.

3. The third phase consists of developing new behaviors and identifying low-risk situations where they can be practiced. The new behaviors should take two forms. First, these leaders should work to identify and articulate their own ideas. Experience and taking deep dives into understanding a topic or issue can be very helpful here. Second, these leaders need to learn to be idea facilitators, not idea killers. If a leader is not very good at generating ideas, the next best thing is to be a leader who nurtures the ideas of others.

Strategy Refinements Using Subscale Information

The subscales for Imaginative include Eccentric, Special Sensitivity, and Creative Thinking. Each of these subscales contributes to an overall Imaginative scale score and provides interpretation refinements beyond those that can be achieved from a scale score alone. These interpretation refinements can have implications for specific behavioral changes that may improve leader performance. They may also help in refining the coaching strategy that would be most effective in producing positive behavioral changes.

Eccentric

When the score on the Eccentric subscale is low, these leaders may be perceived as individuals who think about issues and problems in a typical or conventional way. They offer tried-and-true ideas that provide practical solutions to the issues at hand. Varying from their conventional thinking may feel like a significant risk to their reputation. As a result, behavior change should occur over time and be initiated in low-risk situations. A simple exercise these leaders can practice to break out of conventional thinking is to privately ask themselves what-if questions before taking their views public. This type of exercise will help these leaders stretch their thinking.

Special Sensitivity

Leaders who score low on the Special Sensitivity subscale tend to hold back on offering insights that may diverge from those offered by others. This hesitancy can be perceived as a lack of confidence, or a reluctance or inability to bring forward new or independent thoughts. The coaching should focus on helping these leaders rely on intuition more and take more risk in offering opinions or ideas. On a positive note, leaders who score low on this subscale often recognize and value the ideas of others and have no problem believing that others may have special abilities beyond their own. Properly leveraged with good facilitation skills, this positive attribute can be parlayed into a leadership style of being willing and able to build on the ideas of others—a style that is highly valued in most organizations.

Creative Thinking

A low score on the Creative Thinking subscale indicates an inability or unwillingness to explore creative solutions to problems. These leaders can be hesitant to take risks and have a propensity to put up strong resistance to potential problem solutions that vary from convention. While these leaders may be more pragmatic in nature, they may struggle to devise outside-of-the-box solutions. Leaders who fail to offer creative solutions to problems often get labeled as weak strategic thinkers—the death knell in the evaluation of leadership ability. Furthermore, these leaders can come off as uninspired or lacking in curiosity and creativity. The coaching focus should be on helping these leaders stretch their thinking beyond their typical pragmatic solutions. Understanding the motivation of leaders low on this subscale can be quite important. For example, there is a big difference between coaching a leader who is fearful and risk averse versus one who is simply resistant. Understanding these differences can dictate the coaching focus.

Coaching Tactics

Coaching tactics cover a range of approaches and resources that have been found useful in addressing low Imaginative behaviors. These tactics are typically used in combination to form a custom plan suited to the specific learning needs of a leader. The tactics are divided into four categories: (1) thought-provoking questions for a leader to consider,

(2) exercises a leader can engage in to improve performance, (3) tips and techniques a coach can use to help a leader improve performance, and (4) support resources that can be consulted to gain additional insights in addressing low Imaginative behaviors.

Thought-Provoking Questions for a Leader

- What are the potential negative implications of not engaging in more creative and flexible thinking?
- How can you give yourself permission to explore new ideas that may not have a practical application?
- What might the benefit be of encouraging your team to be more creative? How would you want to encourage your team to be more creative?
- Think about times when you are creative. What are the circumstances? What enabled you to be creative?
- What resources or support do you feel you need to be more creative?
- What causes you to avoid offering new ideas or innovative solutions when you have them? What would make it easier for you to offer them?
- How do you go about preparing in advance to discuss a problem or issue that is likely to come up in discussions with your colleagues?
- When you are convinced that a tried and proven approach to solving a problem is the best, how do you go about building your case to win support?
- How do you define "strategic thinking," and what are your strengths and weaknesses with respect to it?
- What are some alternatives you could pursue to gain a fresh perspective on a problem or issue that you have been unable to successfully address?

Exercises for a Leader

- Determine when it is best to inject brainstorming into your work and define guidelines you can follow to allow the flow of ideas.
- Identify colleagues who have reputations as innovative and strategic thinkers. Develop a plan to meet with each periodically to learn more about their thought processes and approaches to creative thinking.
- Find new sources of information for one initiative you are working on.
- Identify a problem or issue that has been plaguing your business unit. Set up and facilitate a brainstorming session to identify potential alternatives for addressing the problem or issue. Establish an implementation team to evaluate and implement a plausible solution from among the alternatives.
- Build a what-if journal in which you keep track of problems or issues with which you are challenged. Keep track of what-if ideas that come to you for these problems or issues, and make it a habit to ask others to contribute their what-if thoughts.

Tips and Techniques for a Coach

- Review and discuss other Hogan inventory results and their impact on the appearance of low Imaginative behaviors, (e.g., Prudence, Inquisitive, Cautious, Mischievous, and Aesthetics).

- Engage the leader in a creative brainstorming session, challenging the leader's thinking and forcing the leader to consider alternatives.

- Ask the leader to describe circumstances where he or she injected brainstorming into the situation. What worked well? What impact did it have on the outcome? What did not work well? What would the leader do differently in the future?

- Pick a problem or issue that is challenging the leader. Work with the leader to conduct background research and benchmarking to identify potential alternatives or solutions. Work with the leader to develop an implementation plan to address the problem or issue.

- Work with the leader to build the "strategic" component of his or her leadership style. Begin by identifying the key stakeholder meetings in which strategic topics are likely to come up. Use a role play approach to prepare the leader to make specific "strategic" contributions in these meetings.

Support Resources

Bryan, M., Cameron, J., & Allen, C. A. (1999). *The artist's way at work: Riding the dragon.* **New York, NY: William Morrow.**

Bryan and Cameron, the creators of the country's most successful course on creativity, collaborated with Allen after receiving feedback that their teachings were tremendously helpful in business settings. Underpinned by innovative principles of organizational behavior, the arts, and human development, the authors teach readers how to "release their creative spirit at work and tap reserves of energy, vision, and passion."

Buckingham, M., & Coffman, C. (1999). *First, break all the rules: What the world's greatest managers do differently.* **New York, NY: Simon & Schuster.**

Based on a large-scale and in-depth examination of exceptional managers working across a wide variety of contexts, the authors identified managers who excelled at harnessing their employees' capabilities and studied them extensively, finding that these exceptional managers all consistently did one thing—break all the conventional "rules." This book explains why, and how readers can learn from their findings.

De Bono, E. (2008). *Creativity workout: 62 exercises to unlock your most creative ideas.* **Berkeley, CA: Ulysses.**

De Bono, a leading creativity expert, reconceptualizes creativity as a skill anyone can learn, cultivate, and capitalize upon and offers readers 62 exercises designed to elicit a creative mindset and more original thinking.

Gibson, R. (2015). *The four lenses of innovation: A power tool for creative thinking*. Hoboken, NJ: Wiley.

Based on input from some of the world's most prolific innovators (e.g., Steve Jobs, Richard Branson, Jeff Bezos), best-selling author Rowan Gibson offers readers a series of innovation-promoting business perspectives and teaches readers how to "reverse engineer creative genius and make radical business innovation an everyday reality."

Pink, D. (2006). *A whole new mind: Why right-brainers will rule the future*. New York, NY: Berkeley.

Pink makes a strong and convincing case that "right-brained" thinkers will be the successful leaders of tomorrow, describes six research-based abilities required for success and fulfillment in the days ahead, and describes how to develop and enhance the aforementioned abilities in easy-to-digest terms.

Sample Coaching Program (Case 9—Kelly)

The role of CFO presents a tremendous opportunity for Kelly to enhance her understanding of her low Imaginative behaviors on her effectiveness as a leader. While these behaviors did not appear to get in Kelly's way in her role as controller, they could become a derailer in the CFO role. This role will necessitate a stronger ability to think and lead strategically as well as collaborate effectively with other leadership team members. Her low score on the Imaginative scale (30%) combined with her relatively high scores on the Diligent (95%) scale and the Skeptical (79%) scale would imply the need for significant behavior change for her to be seen as contributing to the strategic aspects of the business. Kelly's scores on the Eccentric and Creative Thinking subscales are particularly low, suggesting that helping Kelly expand her willingness and ability to consider new and unusual ways of thinking will be an important coaching focus. The following is a proposed approach to the coaching engagement with Kelly.

- To help Kelly understand the need for change in these behaviors, ask her what impact contributing more actively in discussions about strategy and innovation could have on her success in the CFO role. How could her contribution in these areas impact her relationships with her peers? How could it impact the performance of her team? What are the consequences of not changing her behaviors in these areas?

- Examine with Kelly past experiences where she had the opportunity to contribute to the development of new ideas. What behaviors did she demonstrate that contributed productively? In what ways did she resist new ideas or decline to help move an idea forward? What would she do differently next time?

- Ask Kelly to identify a key business issue she has an interest in that requires new ways of thinking. How can she become involved or change the way she is contributing to help advance the innovative thinking of the group?

- Work with Kelly to practice the behaviors she wants to demonstrate in that setting. In a role play, act as one of her team members and discuss innovative ideas so she can practice her reactions, the questions she could pose to challenge ideas or encourage further development, and any other behaviors that may be challenging for her. The goal is not only to help Kelly demonstrate the behaviors effectively, but also to help her feel authentic in doing so.

- Identify a specific opportunity for Kelly to demonstrate some of the new behaviors with her team members. Then, review the experience with her, asking her what went well, what the key outcomes from the discussion were, what did not go as she hoped, and what she will do differently next time.

SUMMARY

Keep Doing

Offer practical and grounded advice in appropriate problem-solving situations.

Stop Doing

Act as an unnecessary roadblock to innovation that could improve results.

Start Doing

Contribute and facilitate ideas and strategies that will help grow the business.

Low Imaginative behaviors can often result in missed opportunities to contribute new ideas and, in some cases, contribute to the broader organizational direction and strategy. At some organizational levels and in some roles, these behaviors may not negatively impact the leader's performance. However, as a leader advances in his or her career, effectively demonstrating these behaviors becomes essential to being seen as strategic and contributing in a meaningful way to the growth of the business. Leaders with low Imaginative scores must consistently challenge their thinking about innovation and risk taking. They also must work to become good facilitators of strategic thinking among their colleagues and with their teams. It is not essential for them to be the source of great ideas or strategies. However, it is essential for them to be associated with great ideas or strategies. The association alone will help them build a stronger reputation for being a strategic thinker.

CHAPTER 19

DILIGENT

HIGH DILIGENT

Detecting When It Is a Problem

High Diligent leaders are hardworking, careful, detail oriented, superb at follow-through, and able to get results. However, when these behaviors are overused, high Diligent leaders have a tendency to be extreme perfectionists who micromanage their team members and are reluctant to delegate even the simplest of tasks. They often believe that there are only two options when completing tasks: perfection or failure. This all-or-nothing stance leads them to believe that they must do everything equally well. Early in their careers, high Diligent individuals are often rewarded and promoted for the high quality of their work. As their careers progress, these same behaviors can limit their success.

The fundamental problem with high Diligent behaviors is the wasted effort that they cause and the negative effect they have on the morale of team members. High Diligent leaders are typically inflexible, which limits their ability to change when change is needed. Often they think their way is the only way, and they are not open to new approaches. They also do a poor job prioritizing, treating all tasks with equal importance. By making everything a priority, they create situations in which mission-critical objectives are lumped into everything else and, therefore, do not get the attention they deserve.

Steve Jobs is an example of a high Diligent leader. He was obsessed with details his entire professional life. For example, he was concerned about the color of screws used inside products, even though they were not visible to the customer. He was fired from his initial stint with Apple because he was a tyrant and because of his obsessive level of diligence. Most people found him impossible to deal with as a manager. It was only after he surrounded himself with team members who understood his behavior that he became the leader who enabled Apple's success.

Leaders with high Diligent scores see themselves as caring about quality. "We have to get the details right" is something one would hear from high Diligent individuals. Because of their overreliance on their own abilities, they are poor at delegation, which is a critical skill required for being a successful leader. Team members find high Diligent leaders to be demanding, fussy, excessively critical micromanagers. For these leaders, opportunities are lost because their obsession with details prevents them from seeing the big picture. They become mired in the process instead of focusing on the goal.

Perhaps the most damaging behavior associated with high Diligent leaders is their tendency to micromanage their team members. Micromanagement often results in the team members' becoming alienated. When that happens, the team members soon refuse to take any initiative and simply wait to be told what to do and how to do it. Team members with growth potential will not get the development opportunities they need because of the lack of delegation. Top-performing team members will consider leaving the organization because they feel their abilities are being underutilized and unappreciated.

Kelly from Case 9—Kelly, Chief Financial Officer on page 104 provides a good example of an individual with a high Diligent profile. The following is Kelly's profile summary.

Kelly's Situational Summary

Kelly was successfully performing in the role of controller for a large clothing retailer. The CFO passed away suddenly, leaving a big gap on the leadership team. Kelly was promoted into the CFO position despite concerns about her readiness. The new role required expanded job responsibilities, effective working relationships with other members of the leadership team, and a more strategic approach to the business.

Dimension	Score	Percentile	Description
Excitable	20		Kelly is a very calm, even-tempered finance type (Excitable—20%). She is a "trust, but verify" type of person (Skeptical—79%) who can be a bit intimidating in interpersonal situations (Reserved—80%). Kelly also exhibits very high attention to detail and tends to micromanage all aspects of the financial function for which she is responsible (Diligent—95%).
Skeptical	79		
Cautious	70		
Reserved	80		
Leisurely	38		
Bold	60		
Mischievous	30		
Colorful	20		
Imaginative	30		
Diligent	95		
Dutiful	32		

0   10   20   30   40   50   60   70   80   90   100

Kelly's high Diligent behavior, which served her well in her role as controller, will become problematic in her new role as CFO. It could derail her in two ways. First, if she continues to micromanage her staff and fails to delegate, both she and her staff will experience burnout, and she will not have the time to function as a CFO. Second, the combination of her high score on the Diligent scale, her elevated score on the Cautious scale (70%), and her lower score on the Imaginative scale (30%) predict that she will be detail focused and miss the big picture. As CFO, Kelly will be expected to bring strategic thinking to the table that will contribute to the achievement of organizational goals. Failure to rise above the details and add strategic value could derail her in the role as CFO.

Evaluating the Need for Change

The following behavioral questions should be considered in conjunction with a leader's high Diligent score (as exhibited by Kelly) when evaluating the need for a change in behavior. A "yes" response to three or fewer items suggests that there is no imminent need for behavioral changes. A "yes" response to four to six items suggests that a high score on the Diligent scale should be a watch-out for a leader. A "yes" response to more than six items suggests that a leader should take active steps toward making behavioral changes.

Does the leader:

1. Establish performance requirements that are well beyond those necessary for a job to be well done?   Yes   No   Not Sure

2. Appear to be overly picky or critical when it comes to evaluating the work done by others?   Yes   No   Not Sure

3. Seem difficult to work with because nothing is ever good enough?   Yes   No   Not Sure

4. Focus so much on the details of tasks or assignments that the big picture is often missed?   Yes   No   Not Sure

5. Take over or redo tasks assigned to others because of dissatisfaction with the work completed?   Yes   No   Not Sure

6. Miss deadlines or fail to stay on schedule because of excessive attention to detail?   Yes   No   Not Sure

7. Appear to be rigid or inflexible in the way work is completed, to the point of being viewed as change resistant?   Yes   No   Not Sure

8. Often fail to determine the importance of a task or assignment to the point that everything is a top priority?   Yes   No   Not Sure

9. Create unnecessary stress or pressure because of a meticulous approach to work?   Yes   No   Not Sure

These items should be considered as behavioral indicators. Similar or associated behaviors to any of those listed that are exhibited by a leader likely suggest a "yes" response. They provide additional support that a leader may be at risk for the negative reputational consequences associated with those scoring high on the Diligent scale, such as Kelly.

Impact of High Diligent Behaviors

High Diligent leaders like Kelly are often meticulous, picky, critical, overly conscientious, and perfectionistic. They are reluctant to try anything new, and when they do try to innovate, it is usually in small incremental steps. Although they appear to be polite, detail oriented, and hardworking, they can be very hard to please and come off as demanding, with unrealistically high standards. These leaders make everything a priority and want all projects and tasks done equally well. Because of their high standards, many times they believe the only way things get done right is to do it themselves. They create elaborate processes or engage in excessive checking of work to ensure that things are done right. This intricate, obsessive mindset often results in the need to work long hours, overworked team members, and an overall reduction in team efficiency. Furthermore, high Diligent leaders become so focused on details that they overlook the big picture and miss many opportunities, particularly the opportunity to develop team members through effective delegation.

The following are some of the ways high Diligent behaviors are typically viewed, broken out by three constituencies: managers, peers, and direct reports.

Managers

Managers see high Diligent leaders like Kelly as good at execution but not able to adapt to changing priorities or ambiguous issues or situations. Managers may conclude such individuals are only capable of implementing, not leading, and therefore question their readiness for more senior leadership roles. The inability of high Diligent leaders to develop team members also works against them in being considered for difficult or challenging projects and promotions. Managers often conclude that these individuals are best suited for executing the day-to-day operational aspects of the business, rather than activities of a more strategic nature. High Diligent leaders develop a reputation for working solely *in* the business as an implementer, rather than being capable of working *on* the business as a strategic leader.

Peers

Peers may view the high Diligent leader's excessive focus on detail as a bottleneck and lose trust in the leader's ability to deliver commitments on time and build sound working relationships. High Diligent leaders do not work well with others because everything has to be done their way, creating a lack of cohesion and friction with their peers. Because high Diligent leaders develop a reputation for getting in the weeds, peers may not seek their input on strategic issues. In addition, peers will tire of the high Diligent leader's incessant tendencies to bring up details, to fall prey to analysis paralysis, and to cause unnecessary delays in making decisions.

Direct Reports

High Diligent leaders who micromanage their direct reports stifle the team's ability to learn, create, and grow. Without being delegated tasks, the team members do not develop, are not empowered, and are not given the leeway they need to use their skills and contribute at a high level. Because high Diligent leaders are demanding and critical in nature, their direct reports may learn to avoid criticism and default to waiting to be told rather than feeling empowered to act or be proactive. High-performing team members may get frustrated with being micromanaged and leave the organization.

Coaching Focus

Micromanaging takes a huge toll on both the leader and the team members who are victimized by this management style. Leaders will collapse under the sheer volume of work that they create for themselves, especially as they move into increasingly more responsible positions. Team members simply become lazy, disempowered, or quit if they have employment alternatives. Therefore, the coaching focus for high Diligent leaders is to move them into the Delegation Zone, as shown in Figure 12. Moving into the Delegation Zone means that they have to learn to get work done through others, thereby freeing up their time to work on assignments appropriate to their level in the organization.

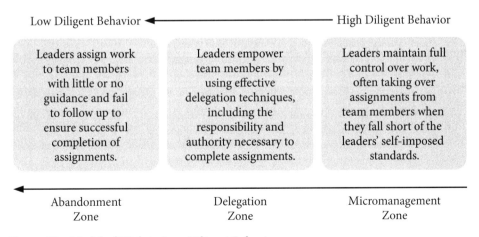

Low Diligent Behavior ◀━━━━━━━━━━━━━━━━ High Diligent Behavior

| Leaders assign work to team members with little or no guidance and fail to follow up to ensure successful completion of assignments. | Leaders empower team members by using effective delegation techniques, including the responsibility and authority necessary to complete assignments. | Leaders maintain full control over work, often taking over assignments from team members when they fall short of the leaders' self-imposed standards. |

◀━━━━━━━━━━━━━━━━━━━━━━━━━━━━━━━━━

Abandonment Zone   Delegation Zone   Micromanagement Zone

Figure 12   Model of High to Low Diligent Behavior

Coaching Strategy

Coaching for high Diligent leaders should address three critical areas, which are (1) identification of key priorities, (2) effective delegation, and (3) strategic thinking:

- Help leaders understand the need to prioritize tasks and place the emphasis on the critical few projects or tasks that need to be done really well and that are aligned with organizational goals and objectives. True priorities may suffer if all priorities are pursued equally. Team members may be confused and overworked if they do not know which objectives are the true priorities. A discussion of categories of tasks, such as "nice to do," "need to do just well enough," and "need to do really well," is necessary to help high Diligent leaders understand where they are wasting time. A good question to ask is "Have you checked priorities with your stakeholders, manager, and peers?" A full understanding of priorities will set the stage for effective delegation by the high Diligent leader by identifying tasks or assignments that team members should reasonably be expected to handle.

- Help high Diligent leaders realize that they must learn to delegate and utilize team members effectively. Delegation is the key to effective time management, and allows leaders to more broadly leverage their skills, and become more valuable to their organizations. Delegation is also critical in motivating and developing team members so that their skills become more valuable to their organizations. Leaders who are obsessed with details will eventually get overwhelmed with trying to manage everything. Leaders who build a strong understanding of their priorities and learn to use an effective delegation model will vastly increase the amount of work they can accomplish. Simultaneously, as they learn to stay close to the work without taking over, they will improve the satisfaction and work-life balance of their team members.

- High Diligent leaders need to build awareness of the big picture of what the organization is trying to achieve and how they can contribute to the strategic aspects of the business. One approach is to help leaders understand the concept of "bifocal vision." This concept refers to balancing activities working *in* the business with strategic activities working *on* the business. High Diligent leaders are often quite good at seeing the up-close details of their jobs. In fact, they spend the bulk of their time working *in* the business, as was mentioned earlier. Leaders with bi-focal vision are able to maintain their effectiveness working *in* the business by appropriately delegating assignments to their team members. Effective delegation will free up time for them to find ways to work *on* the business by contributing at the strategic level.

Strategy Refinements Using Subscale Information

The subscales for Diligent include Standards, Perfectionistic, and Organized. Each of these subscales contributes to an overall Diligent scale score and provides interpretation refinements beyond those that can be achieved from a scale score alone. These interpretation refinements can have implications for specific behavior changes that may improve leader performance. They may also help in refining the coaching strategy that would be most effective in producing positive behavioral changes.

Standards

High Diligent leaders with elevations on the Standards subscale will set exceptionally high standards for themselves and others for all work performed. They are practical and systematic when approaching tasks, to an exacting point. Furthermore, they expect others to live up to their standards and complete tasks with the same practical, systematic approach to which they are committed. As a result, they are very hard to please, and others will find them very demanding and critical. These leaders need help in recognizing that all tasks do not need the same level of priority, standards, or attention. It is important to help these leaders work through a ranking process to determine which objectives are most critical to their organization's success and warrant the highest priority. The focus is to get them to realize the importance of matching the priority and quality standards to the criticality of the task. One way to do this is to engage these leaders in a discussion of task categories such as "nice to do," "need to do just well enough," and "need to do really well." This approach not only helps them recognize where they can make the best use of their time but also helps them understand where delegation is the most appropriate course of action.

Perfectionistic

High Diligent leaders who are elevated on the Perfectionistic subscale are obsessive about attending to every possible detail because they assume that all details are equally critical. They prefer to take their time and evaluate all angles of each situation because, for them, precision is job one. Their exacting approach to situations or tasks often causes others to become extremely frustrated. In fact, individuals who are less diligent than these leaders will have trouble even recognizing the minutia these leaders have identified as important and will consider the excessive attention to be overkill. The high Diligent leaders' exacting, detailed nature will slow down work, limit the amount of work the team members can actually complete, and demoralize the team. Coaching these leaders begins with getting them to avoid diving into the details of a task before the objectives or desired outcomes for the task have even been defined. While "the devil may be in the details," these leaders need to learn to differentiate between situations where diving into the details adds value versus situations where it is viewed as derailing progress.

Organized

An elevation on the Organized subscale indicates a tendency to be meticulous and inflexible about schedules, timing, rules, and procedures. High Diligent individuals with this subscale elevated want to control everything and are often viewed as unable to be flexible when the situation calls for it. Their preference to plan ahead causes them extreme frustration when something unexpected comes up. Their solutions to problems are also well calculated, so much so that they have a hard time stepping outside of their own approach to consider alternative solutions. These individuals need help to realize that "tried-and-true" solutions may not offer the highest payback, and they should be coached to solicit alternative solutions from others. Coaches can open the discussion by exploring what is preventing the leader from trying new ideas and approaches. Asking these leaders to define multiple paths to success for less critical tasks will help them move away from their rigid adherence to a set path and focus on outcomes.

Coaching Tactics

Coaching tactics cover a range of approaches and resources that have been found useful in addressing high Diligent behaviors. These tactics are typically used in combination to form a custom plan suited to the specific learning needs of a leader. The tactics are divided into four categories: (1) thought-provoking questions for a leader to consider, (2) exercises a leader can engage in to improve performance, (3) tips and techniques a coach can use to help a leader improve performance, and (4) support resources that can be consulted to gain additional insights in addressing high Diligent behaviors.

Thought-Provoking Questions for a Leader

- What are your key priorities at this time? How do you prioritize work on the objectives that are strategic and highly important? How do you reach agreement with key stakeholders?

- What is your model for delegation? How important is this to you? Do all your team members need the same level of oversight?

- Where have you experienced success or failure when delegating to others, and what did you learn from these experiences?

- Think about your focus on details. What are the missed opportunities resulting from this behavior?

- Reflect on the term "micromanager" and the behaviors that are associated with the term. Would you like to work with a person who exhibited these behaviors?

- Do all your tasks and objectives deserve the same amount of attention and focus?

- Do you often get lost in the weeds (details) and not see the bigger picture? Do you sometimes miss the obvious?

- What are your key goals for the future? How will you let go of enough of your current workload to free up time to contribute in new areas?

- Is your pay commensurate with the work you are doing?

- Do you impose or create structure in every situation in order to reduce ambiguity and uncertainty?

- Do you spend so much time micromanaging people that their development needs become secondary or overlooked?

- Do you hold on to work or fail to delegate tasks for fear that they will not be done correctly or the right way? Are you very demanding and hard to please?

- What is the worst thing that could happen if you let go of some control?

Exercises for a Leader

- Look at the tasks that you and your team perform, and place them into the following three categories:

  - Nice to do.

  - Need to do just well enough.

  - Need to do really well.

- Create a delegation guide and checklist to provide necessary structure while you build your delegation skills.

- Consider a time when the best solution may not have been cost effective, and "good enough" may have been perfectly acceptable.

- Think about a time when the work of your direct reports did not meet your standards. Were your standards unrealistic?

- Ask your manager to create a list of leaders who are good delegators and people developers. Interview them for insights and opportunities to improve your skill in these areas.

- Draw a circle representing the total time in your work day. Indicate where you currently spend your time—supervising the activities of others, doing work yourself, building relationships, and focusing on long-term goals. How do you want to shift where you spend your time?

- Set a limit on the time you spend at work. Choose an activity that gets you out of your office.

- Determine where strengths and weaknesses lie among your team members. Then, identify which tasks currently on your to-do list could be fully delegated to team members, and which ones you could work on with team members to help them develop new skills.

Tips and Techniques for a Coach

- Work with the leader to build a delegation guide and checklist.

- Discuss the difference between working *on* the business and working *in* the business. Work with the leader to determine the percentage of time currently spent working *on* the business versus working *in* the business and how time should be allocated in the future.

- Build the leader's awareness that effective leaders strive to develop skilled team members who are motivated and exhibit personal initiative. Ask how the effective delegation of meaningful assignments could help develop team members who exhibit these characteristics.

- Talk about work-life balance and what the impact on the leader's available time would be by improving prioritization and delegation skills.

- Have the leader outline the level of trust he or she has that each team member is able to independently complete tasks at an acceptable level of performance. Work with the leader to identify safe tasks to delegate to team members that, if completed successfully, will strengthen the trust needed for delegating more work in the future.

Support Resources

Blanchard, K., Oncken Jr., W., & Burrows, H. (1991). *The one minute manager meets the monkey.* New York, NY: William Morrow & Co.

According to the authors, most managers accept and deal with far too many "monkeys"—other people's problems. Experts Blanchard, Oncken, and Burrows offer invaluable advice for managers about how to truly prioritize their priorities, return others' "monkeys," and facilitate their reports' abilities to solve their own problems.

Brown, B. (2010). *The gifts of imperfection: Let go of who you think you're supposed to be and embrace who you are.* Center City, MN: Hazelden.

Brown, renowned speaker, author, and expert on shame, belonging, and authenticity, discusses emotions capable of stifling talent and thwarting courage in this NY *Times* best-selling book about the perils of perfectionism.

Gain, B. (2015). *Stop being controlling: How to overcome control issues, repair your relationships, relieve stress, rebuild your confidence and self-esteem* [Kindle edition]. Retrieved from Amazon.com

Gain describes how to maintain control without being controlling and, among many other topics, teaches readers how to decrease micromanaging, be more trusting, seek help when needed, and improve relationships with others.

Genett, D. M. (2004). *If you want it done right, you don't have to do it yourself!: The power of effective delegation.* Fresno, CA: Linden.

Genett offers readers six simple and practical steps to delegating effectively within the context of a succinct and lighthearted management allegory.

Harvard Business Review (2014). *Delegating work: Match skills with tasks, coach your people, grant them authority.* Boston, MA: HBR Press.

HBR's "Delegating Work" walks readers through the basics of assigning the right work to the right people, effectively handing off responsibility, and overseeing without micromanaging.

Kaplan, B., & Kaiser, R. (2006). *The versatile leader: Make the most of your strengths without overdoing it.* San Francisco, CA: Wiley.

Based on two decades worth of research and extensive executive coaching experience, Kaplan and Kaiser present a cutting-edge approach to diagnosing and remedying "lopsidedness" in leaders. Chock full of real-life examples and practical applications, the authors teach readers how to optimally leverage their strengths while steering clear of "too much of a good thing."

Sample Coaching Program (Case 9—Kelly)

Kelly's profile includes a score of 95 percent on the Diligent scale, and all three subscales are elevated. The tendency to micromanage has been noted by her leadership team but did not seem to inhibit her performance as controller. Her score of 79 percent on the Skeptical scale indicates that she has a mistrustful nature with a need to verify everything. With Kelly's promotion to the CFO role, she will have an expanded set of responsibilities. Kelly will need to pull back from her detail orientation and learn to delegate the "what" and leave the "how" to her team members. If Kelly continues to micromanage her team members, she will burn out and be unable to see the big picture and contribute to the strategic aspects of the business. Her high score on the Diligent scale is exacerbated by her elevated score on the Cautious scale (70%), resulting in a tendency to be conservative and risk averse. Her lower score on the Imaginative scale (30%) indicates a tactical perspective that lacks vision and strategic focus. The coaching initiative for Kelly should help her learn to delegate, stay out of the weeds, and think more strategically. The following are the proposed steps for helping Kelly make improvements in these areas:

- Kelly should not try to do everything equally well and needs to focus on developing her delegation skills so that she can attend to the broader critical objectives. The coach can help her analyze why she does not delegate (e.g., do her team members lack functional skills, the motivation, or the accountability to perform the delegated task?). Help Kelly create milestones and check-in points for each team member to whom she delegates a task so she can keep track of progress without taking over.

- Ask Kelly to interview her fellow leadership team members and the CEO to determine what they expect and need from her in her CFO role. This discussion will assist her in determining her priorities and how she allocates her time. She should employ the "nice to do," "need to do just well enough," and "need to do really well" model to classify her priorities, and then share those priorities with her team.

- Kelly should actively participate in meetings and come to the meetings prepared with open-ended questions that will help her understand the big picture of the organization.

- Kelly should identify a colleague whose key strength is strategic thinking and spend time with that person to gain a better strategic perspective on the business. Kelly could also ask this individual to be a sounding board for her own strategic ideas before taking them public.

Summary

Keep Doing

Provide a role model for hard work, high standards, and quality outcomes.

Stop Doing

Excessively criticize completed work, requiring it to be redone in a certain way.

Start Doing

Effectively delegate tasks to team members, and let them find their own way.

At their best, high Diligent leaders are hard-working, conscientious, detail-oriented implementers. These characteristics, which may have gotten them promoted early in their careers, often lead to perfectionism, micromanagement, failure to delegate, and a lack of the big-picture thinking necessary for today's executives. With coaching, high Diligent leaders can change these behaviors. They can learn to dial back their overused and inefficient high Diligent behaviors. They can develop greater trust in their team members and become more effective delegators. Most important, they can free up their time to focus on and contribute to the strategic aspects of the business. The transition from an implementer to a leader who possesses bifocal vision with the ability to work *in* the business as well as *on* the business is perhaps one of the most difficult to achieve. It epitomizes the age-old business saying: "What got you here won't get you there." It requires giving up behaviors that were once held in high regard and developing new behaviors that do not come naturally. Leaders who make this transition are often among the most valued contributors to the success of their organizations.

LOW DILIGENT

Detecting When It Is a Problem

Leaders with low scores on the Diligent scale are usually relaxed, trusting, undemanding, and action oriented. The speed and impulsiveness associated with their action orientation can result in details being overlooked, a failure to consider or thoroughly evaluate alternatives, and deliverables that miss the mark. These leaders can be very flexible and tolerant of ambiguity, but they may not demonstrate strong planning skills, they may disregard progress monitoring, and they may assume that the results meet the requirements. They are easily distracted, delegate without verification, fail to keep others informed, and are surprised when projects or tasks do not go well.

An example of a low Diligent leader is former Secretary of Health and Human Services Kathleen Sebelius. She was responsible for the rollout of the Affordable Care Act (ACA), perhaps one of the most significant pieces of legislation passed by the U.S. government in the past 50 years. The legislation was designed to reshape the U.S. health care system. It contained more than 2,000 pages of rules, regulations, and procedures. If ever there was a need for a leader with a strong detail orientation, it was the person selected to head up the implementation of this legislation. Ms. Sebelius decided to outsource (delegate) the responsibility for creating the information technology (IT) backbone of the ACA to a Canadian software firm. However, she and her team failed to adequately track progress or test the software before it went live. The cost overruns, delays, and poor service associated with the IT backbone aspect of the ACA continue to this day. Ms. Sebelius was caught completely flatfooted when this failure began to unfold during the initial rollout of the software and user interface. In response to the glitches and failures, she said to Congress in October 2013, "You deserve better. I apologize. I'm accountable to you for fixing these problems and I'm committed to earning your confidence back by fixing the site." It is hard to put into words how much damage the flawed rollout of the ACA did to her reputation as a leader. One certain outcome was that it directly led to her resignation as Secretary of Health and Human Services.

Leaders with low Diligent behaviors are perceived as approachable, flexible, and forgiving with respect to performance standards. They often delegate assignments to team members because they do not want to be bothered with the details and trust that the team members will handle them. They see this approach to delegation as empowering the team members, as opposed to abandoning them. The downside, though, is that their trusting natures, lack of planning, and failure to follow up can lead to a multitude of problems. Their team members, depending on their readiness, may be set adrift and proceed as best they can without adequate oversight. The results can run the gamut from a few missed details to a complete train wreck like what occurred with the ACA. Furthermore, without adequate oversight, team members can begin to view a low Diligent leader as a person who just does not care. Such an attitude can become malignant, spreading throughout the team to a point where the team becomes just a collection of individuals with no common standards for performance.

Courtney from Case 8—Courtney, Assistant Operations Manager on page 102 provides a good example of a low Diligent profile. The following is Courtney's profile summary.

Courtney's Situational Summary			
Courtney successfully completed a plant start-up in Mexico for an electronics manufacturing company. Despite being considered a high potential leader, her superiors had lingering questions about her leadership ability. As a result, she was given the role of assistant operations manager working for one of the best plant managers in the company. Courtney's new manager is known for her high standards, careful attention to detail, hard work, and putting in long hours.			
Dimension	**Score**	**Percentile**	**Description**
Excitable	30		Courtney is an energetic leader who is known for her confidence in taking on any challenge (Bold—95%). She tends to use her charm and charisma to get her way (Mischievous—90%). She also tends to grab high-profile assignments to keep herself in the limelight (Colorful—80%). Her superiors have put her on the fast track but have some concerns about her ability to be a team player.
Skeptical	50		
Cautious	20		
Reserved	25		
Leisurely	30		
Bold	95		
Mischievous	90		
Colorful	80		
Imaginative	85		
Diligent	5		
Dutiful	10		

```
0   10  20  30  40  50  60  70  80  90  100
```

Courtney's low Diligent behavior served her quite well in a fast-paced, entrepreneurial plant start-up in Mexico. She had a good group of independent team members who appreciated her hands-off management style. In her new role, however, poor attention to detail, lack of follow-up, and numerous other behaviors associated with her low Diligent score (5%), may lead to a high probability of running afoul of the management style of the plant manager to whom she now reports. Furthermore, her emergent personality that includes high Bold (95%), high Mischievous (90%), and high Colorful (80%) scores will result in a very visible persona in a manufacturing environment. Such a persona can only serve to magnify her lack of diligence in the eyes of all her constituents, including her manager and peers.

Evaluating the Need for Change

The following behavioral questions should be considered in conjunction with a leader's low Diligent score (as exhibited by Courtney) when evaluating the need for a change in behavior. A "yes" response to three or fewer items suggests that there is no imminent need for behavioral changes. A "yes" response to four to six items suggests that a low score on the Diligent scale should be a watch-out for a leader. A "yes" response to more than six items suggests that a leader should take active steps toward making behavioral changes.

Does the leader:

1. Appear to be lackadaisical when it comes to establishing the requirements necessary for a job to be well done? **Yes   No   Not Sure**

2. Show little or no concern for the details regarding the way delegated assignments are completed? **Yes   No   Not Sure**

3. Seem very relaxed about rules and procedures? **Yes   No   Not Sure**

4. Often take a big picture approach to tasks or assignments, leaving the details to others? **Yes   No   Not Sure**

5. Rarely provide feedback or coaching with respect to the way tasks or assignments are completed? **Yes   No   Not Sure**

6. Disregard the details of tasks or assignments to the point that work quality suffers? **Yes   No   Not Sure**

7. Appear easygoing with respect to timelines and schedules, conveying to others a lack of urgency? **Yes   No   Not Sure**

8. Provide poor guidance regarding the importance of tasks or assignments, creating confusion regarding priorities? **Yes   No   Not Sure**

9. Over delegate without follow-up, to the point that others view it as abandonment? **Yes   No   Not Sure**

These items should be considered as behavioral indicators. Similar or associated behaviors to any of those listed that are exhibited by a leader likely suggest a "yes" response. They provide additional support that a leader may be at risk for the negative reputational consequences associated with those scoring low on the Diligent scale, such as Courtney.

Impact of Low Diligent Behaviors

Low Diligent leaders like Courtney frequently have a frenzy of activity around them. They do not like structure, and they resent situations in which structure is imposed upon them. In conjunction with their lack of detail orientation, they often miss critical commitments and deadlines. Because low Diligent leaders neglect to learn the strengths and weaknesses of their team members and fail to provide proper guidance or oversight, delegated assignments can fall short of the desired outcomes, which often catch these leaders off guard. Low Diligent leaders also do a poor job of keeping others informed, even when their actions have a direct impact on their constituents. Failing to keep others informed can slow progress, create unnecessary obstacles, produce unintended consequences, and reduce the trust that others have in them. The following are some of the consequences of low Diligent behaviors, broken down by three constituencies: manager, peers, and direct reports.

Managers

Managers view low Diligent leaders like Courtney as people who do not deliver on commitments. Further, managers may feel that the deliverables lack the necessary quality due to a lack of attention to details. Thus, managers may not see low Diligent individuals as being able to take on more responsibility, adequately oversee multiple functions, or deliver on key organizational objectives. Low Diligent individuals are often easily distracted and careless about important details. They prefer to think about outcomes rather than details, which can catch up with them if they repeatedly disappoint their managers or make their managers look bad. In addition, managers may find that low Diligent leaders do a poor job of keeping them informed, opening the door for surprises or unanticipated issues. There are very few things that managers hate more than being blindsided because someone who reports to them failed to keep them informed.

Peers

Low Diligent leaders often frustrate peers because of their poor planning and lack of adequate follow-through on assignments. These behaviors can slow down or threaten key priorities and strategies. As a result, peers find their low Diligent colleagues difficult to work with, hard to rely upon, and almost impossible to trust. Peers might ask that other people be assigned to key strategic objectives rather than risk the performance shortfalls of low Diligent colleagues. Peers may also be wary of the tendency of low Diligent leaders to fail to socialize their decisions. In other words, these individuals often neglect to appropriately involve others affected by their decisions which can diminish communication and trust.

Direct Reports

Low Diligent leaders struggle with effective communication and delegation when working with their direct reports. Communication is a problem because these individuals just do things without bothering to inform their direct reports, or they simply forget that their direct reports may need the information to do their jobs. Delegation is a problem because it often looks more like abandonment. Tasks or assignments get handed off by these leaders with few instructions, performance parameters, or effective feedback. Development of their direct reports through delegation is almost completely lost because these leaders typically provide little oversight or coaching along the way. The impact of these behaviors on direct reports can be quite stressful. It is not uncommon for them to feel adrift, abandoned, neglected, or even overwhelmed by their jobs.

Coaching Focus

Low Diligent leaders get surprised due to their trusting style and lack of fol-low-through. Many times, they think they and their teams are doing better than they are. The coaching focus needs to be on empowerment versus abandonment. These leaders need to learn to effectively "trust, but verify" to ensure that key prior-ities and milestones are being met. When delegating, they need to begin by assess-ing the capabilities of those who will be asked to complete the work. This appraisal will dictate the level of leader involvement necessary for success. Next, leaders need to provide guidelines with respect to responsibility, authority, and anticipated out-comes for the work. Once these steps have been taken, leaders should expect a plan from those completing the work that outlines how it will be done and the way prog-ress will be measured. As trust is built, leaders can dial back their level of involve-ment and increase their empowerment when delegating, a move that can be quite motivating to team members if done properly or demoralizing if empowerment is not commensurate with readiness.

Therefore, the coaching focus for low Diligent leaders is to move them into the Delegation Zone, as shown in Figure 13. Moving into the Delegation Zone for these individuals means that they have to learn to get work done through others by pro-viding appropriate oversight and not abandoning team members.

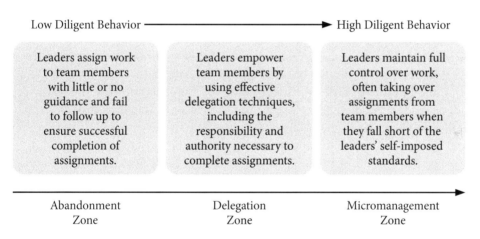

Figure 13   Model of Low to High Diligent Behavior

It is also important for these leaders to recognize the importance of good com-munication with respect to the work they complete themselves or the work they have done through others and to identify what needs to be communicated and to whom. It is something that low Diligent leaders should add to their behavioral repertoire in the form of regular mental checks (i.e., are those affected by the work properly informed?).

Coaching Strategy

Coaching low Diligent individuals should address the following four critical areas: (1) effective delegation, (2) providing oversight, (3) attention to details, and (4) good communication:

- Help low Diligent individuals realize that delegation means more than just the assignment of work and projects. Plans need to be developed and milestones established for all important checkpoints as the work is completed. Regular review of the plans and tactics to achieve goals will avoid the ugly surprises that can plague low Diligent leaders. Helpful in building effective delegation skills are delegation models and checklists, especially ones that include consideration of responsibility and authority that should be part of a good delegation process.

- Work with low Diligent leaders to help them understand that teams and individuals can feel neglected or abandoned if oversight is not provided. Even high performers want recognition that they are doing well and on course. Low Diligent leaders need to understand that their insights and support are critical to developing people, meeting commitments, and helping their teams understand their priorities.

- Low Diligent leaders need to realize that, when assignments are delegated, it is helpful for those doing the work to understand the context (big picture) or broader objectives to which the work contributes. This understanding places greater value on assignments and helps team members understand how their work fits into the bigger picture. However, this type of information is not sufficient on its own. Truly meeting commitments on customer expectations requires implementation and follow-through on all important details. Low Diligent leaders who fail to provide the requisite attention to details can develop a reputation for being sloppy, careless, or incompetent. Constituents will eventually become frustrated by the lack of attention to details, perhaps to the point of losing trust in these leaders.

- One of the most forgotten aspects of the challenges faced by low Diligent leaders is their tendency to under-communicate. When they delegate work, it often looks more like a drive-by handoff. When they talk to their peers, they rarely get into the details of work being performed under their guidance. When they update their managers, they often keep things at a very high level with little mention of key details. There are two basic reasons (aside from those that might be related to interpersonal skills) for under-communication. First, they may not know the details and that has obvious negative consequences. Second, they may consider the details unimportant or harbor the belief that the details are burdensome for others. Under-communication can be solved very easily by establishing guidelines with key constituents. It can be as simple as asking, "How much detail would you like me to cover?" Asking the question alone may avoid

problems down the road as it immediately establishes a willingness to disclose, a behavior that is the cornerstone of a trust-based relationship.

Strategy Refinements Using Subscale Information

The subscales for the Diligent scale include Standards, Perfectionistic, and Organized.
Each of these subscales contributes to an overall Diligent scale score and provides interpretation refinements beyond those that can be achieved from one scale score alone.
These interpretation refinements can have implications for specific behavioral changes
that may improve leader performance. They may also help in refining the coaching
strategy that would be most effective in producing positive behavioral changes.

Standards

With respect to performance standards, leaders scoring low on the Standards
subscale seem relaxed and forgiving but also careless and disorganized. The team
members of leaders low on the Standards subscale are often left without a clear
understanding of what they will be held accountable for, how progress will be
tracked, or how outcomes will be evaluated. Coaches should ask these leaders to
rate their team members on their ability to meet or exceed acceptable performance
standards. Team members who underperform need greater oversight, development,
and "stretch goals" to improve. These team members will test the resilience of low
Diligent leaders to consistently provide the necessary oversight. Team members who
meet or exceed acceptable performance standards do well in working for low Diligent leaders; however, they still need oversight. Very high performing team members
often feed the neglectful behaviors of low Diligent leaders. Oversight with these team
members is more about challenging them than assuring acceptable performance.

Perfectionistic

Leaders who score low on the Perfectionistic subscale are action oriented and work
quickly but may neglect important details in the interest of expediency. While they
tend to get work done quickly, their lack of attention to detail leaves room for errors
and miscommunication. Coaches should help these leaders understand that their action orientation may frustrate people who see the lack of attention to detail as sloppy
work. Others may see the action orientation as impulsive or exemplifying a ready-
shoot-aim approach that disregards a consideration of consequences. Low Diligent
leaders need to slow down and think through the basic details of the actions they are
contemplating. This is particularly true when they delegate the work to team members.
The level of detail that is required largely depends upon the magnitude or importance
of the work and the readiness of team members to handle it. The leaders' inattention
to detail can be motivational (i.e., leaders who are easily bored by attending to details)
or stem from a pure lack of awareness (i.e., leaders who simply miss the trees as they
attend to the forest). In either case, low Diligent leaders can benefit greatly by slowing
down and checking for understanding with their mangers, peers, and team members.

Organized

Leaders who score low on the Organized subscale will be seen as flexible and able to work comfortably in ambiguous situations, but their inattention to rules and policies may not demonstrate strong planning skills or adequate follow-through. These leaders do very well with in-the-moment ideas but lack the follow-through to finish or implement their ideas. Others may have a hard time getting these leaders to plan or define what is ahead. Coaches should help these leaders develop their skills around planning such that all those involved or impacted by the work have an opportunity for an appropriate level of input. This approach will increase buy-in and help ensure that critical steps are not missed and unintended negative outcomes are avoided. It is also important to help low Diligent leaders recognize that rules, policies, and procedures are usually in place for a reason. Disregarding or going around them should only be undertaken with careful consideration of the consequences. It is one thing to approach an assignment with a sense of urgency and a need for action. It is quite another thing to be viewed as a rogue leader who lacks even a modicum of prudence.

Coaching Tactics

Coaching tactics cover a range of approaches and resources that have been found useful in addressing low Diligent behaviors. These tactics are typically used in combination to form a custom plan suited to the specific learning needs of a leader. The tactics are divided into four categories: (1) thought-provoking questions for a leader to consider, (2) exercises a leader can engage in to improve performance, (3) tips and techniques a coach can use to help a leader improve performance, and (4) support resources that can be consulted to gain additional insights in addressing low Diligent behaviors.

Thought-Provoking Questions for a Leader

- How do you delegate and judge when and how to follow up?
- Do you have people on your team who like details?
- What is your assessment of your organizational skills?
- What do your team members need from you to assure that they are working productively?
- How do you create structure and set expectations?
- What would be the result of milestone checkups?
- What is the difference between empowerment and abandonment?
- What is your model for delegation? How important is this to you?
- Do all of your staff need the same level of oversight?
- What are the missed opportunities if you fail to effectively delegate?
- What is the meaning of "trust, but verify"?

- How do you tell the difference between rules and policies that need your close attention versus those you can push to the limit?

Exercises for a Leader

- Evaluate your team members, and determine if you have implementers and detail-oriented people who do not let things fall through the cracks.

- Create a delegation guide and checklist to provide structure while you develop your ability to delegate.

- Work with your manager to create a list of leaders who he or she thinks are good delegators and people developers, and interview them for insights and skills that you can apply with your team members.

- Build a list of questions to ask to determine the processes and milestones necessary to ensure the successful completion of a project or work stream.

- Rank your team members on the basis of their ability to handle delegated assignments and your trust in them to perform delegated assignments successfully. Use this rank ordering as a guide to developing your team members through delegation of assignments.

- Practice mentally checking off the individuals who might be affected by actions you plan to take. Determine how you will communicate with them to help ensure that problems do not arise.

Tips and Techniques for a Coach

- Help the leader understand the following key concepts:

  - **Structure**—Individuals have different needs for structure when completing work assignments. Some individuals find it hard to work without structure, while others prefer to determine their own way of doing things. Understanding these individual differences is an important part of building an effective team.

  - **Communication**—Success in completing assignments is only as good as the communication that accompanies the work. It is of little value to complete work that has an impact on others if they resent not being involved. Similarly, failing to check details or not involving key constituents at an appropriate level of detail can result in failure. It always pays dividends to appropriately involve others.

  - **Follow-up**—Perhaps one of the greatest shortcomings a leader can have is failing to follow up on assignments or work delegated. Making the assumption that something was completed as expected is a recipe for embarrassment or even derailment. Follow-up is not a tacit concept. It should be an explicit step in all assignments but especially those that are mission critical.

- Work with the leader to build a delegation guide and checklist that include the capabilities of team members.

- Discuss the difference between working *on* the business versus working *in* the business. Help the leader determine what percentage of time he or she spends working *on* the business versus *in* the business. Discuss how these percentages should change over time with effective delegation that develops stronger team members.

- Build the leader's awareness that strong, skilled team members are a critical component to his or her future career advancement. Have the leader review the way tasks are delegated to various team members to determine how they could be more effectively delegated to build team member skills.

- Have the leader list the Critical Success Factors (CSFs) and top priorities for the business unit. Discuss the organizational, team, and personal consequences if these priorities are not met. Work with the leader to conduct a team-building session to help all team members understand the success factors and priorities, and where they fit in terms of effort.

Support Resources

Blair, G. R. (2009). *Everything counts: 52 remarkable ways to inspire excellence and drive results.* **Hoboken, NJ: John Wiley & Sons.**

Focused on three realms of achievement (professional, personal, and universal), Blair offers readers concrete strategies for inspiring excellence and achieving noteworthy outcomes.

Chandler, S., & Black, D. (2012). *The hands-off manager: How to mentor people and allow them to be successful.* **Pompton Plains, NJ: Career Press.**

Chandler and Black show managers, tenured and green alike, how to mentor and coach instead of hovering and prodding, allowing employees' strengths to be capitalized upon in a "climate of partnership and mutual goal setting."

Kaplan, B., & Kaiser, R. (2006). *The versatile leader: Make the most of your strengths without overdoing it.* **San Francisco, CA: Wiley.**

Based on two decades worth of research and extensive executive coaching experience, Kaplan and Kaiser present a cutting-edge approach to diagnosing and remedying "lopsidedness" in leaders. Chock full of real-life examples and practical applications, the authors teach readers how to optimally leverage their strengths while steering clear of "too much of a good thing."

Rock, D. (2009). *Your brain at work: Strategies for overcoming distraction, regaining focus, and working smarter all day long.* **New York, NY: Harper Collins.**

Written with humor and fully relevant to everyday life, Rock synthesizes current cognitive neuroscience research and interprets the results in a way that helps readers understand how the brain works and how to make it function more efficiently in personal and professional realms.

Scott, S. (2004). *Fierce conversations: Achieving success at work and in life one conversation at a time.* New York, NY: Berkley.

Scott walks readers through "Seven Principles of Fierce Conversations," helping readers learn how to have meaning-filled and enriched dialogue, increase the clarity and digestibility of their messages, and effectively manage strong emotions that inevitably emerge during the course of authentic conversations.

Tracy, B. (2013). *Delegation & supervision.* New York, NY: American Management Association.

Tracy offers a quick and easy read, written to help readers master the essential skills needed to delegate effectively and with the intent of helping delegates learn, grow, and become more capable.

Sample Coaching Plan (Case 8—Courtney)

Courtney's score of 5 percent on the Diligent scale is "double trouble" given the two changes in her life: a new role (an operations job that requires precision) and a new boss (a woman who is known for her attention to details). Compounding the low Diligent score are Courtney's low score on the Cautious scale (20%) and her high score on the Mischievous scale (90%). These scores indicate that not only will Courtney be inattentive to details, but she will probably be impulsive and make quick and risky decisions that could lead to high-profile disasters. The following are the proposed steps for a coaching engagement with Courtney:

- Help Courtney understand why her low Diligent behavior can be problematic in her new job (even though it has served her well in the past).

- Have Courtney develop a model for delegation that provides the structure needed to ensure her team has adequate oversight and support.

- Review with Courtney the projects she is currently responsible for, and determine the ones that are most critical to the business. Then, help her determine what level of personal involvement is needed from her in each one.

- Review with Courtney that providing oversight is not micromanaging nor is it neglecting. Depending on the situation and the team members to whom she is delegating, the "sweet spot" (see Figure 13 provided in this chapter) is somewhere in the middle. Discuss with her where that "sweet spot" is for each of her projects and each of her team members.

- Have Courtney look at her decision process and determine what she needs to do to perform the due diligence required for critical decisions.

- Have Courtney practice her mental checklist of who needs to be involved in critical decisions or projects and how she plans to communicate with them.

- Help Courtney find a mentor who has well-developed skills in delegation and oversight of projects, so she can learn from this mentor's knowledge and experience.

SUMMARY

Keep Doing

Maintain a big picture perspective without losing sight of the details.

Stop Doing

Be too relaxed about adhering to rules, processes, and procedures.

Start Doing

Practice sound delegation and communication techniques.

At first, low Diligent individuals appear to be trusting leaders who want to develop and empower their people. However, low Diligent behaviors can derail leaders in many ways, including inattention to important details, missed due dates, poor quality deliverables, team members who are adrift because they lack support and oversight, and a failure to build trust with constituents who depend on them. Coaching can help low Diligent leaders understand the problems that can crop up by focusing on the big picture and relying on others to clean up the details they leave behind. Getting work done through others requires effective delegation skills. Low Diligent leaders need to develop team members using a "trust, but verify" mentality. These leaders also need to realize that their effectiveness depends upon their ability to keep others involved and informed; otherwise, they risk alienating constituents who could play a key role in determining their career success.

CHAPTER 20

DUTIFUL

HIGH DUTIFUL

Detecting When It Is a Problem

High Dutiful leaders are very much valued by their managers. They offer little resistance, regardless of what is asked of them. They eagerly look for ways to please their superiors. They will even compromise their own values in their efforts to keep the boss happy. Their high Dutiful behaviors can result in a reputation as a follower who has a difficult time charting his or her own course. However, the more salient aspect of high Dutiful behavior is an exaggerated sense of loyalty and eagerness to please those in authority. Most managers desire and appreciate loyalty from their direct reports. The problem with an exaggerated sense of loyalty is that it places high Dutiful leaders in a position whereby they can be taken advantage of by a manager willing to prey upon their dutifulness.

High Dutiful behavior comes in two basic forms. The first form is what might be called the "Scared Puppy." These are individuals who are timid and fearful. They are loyal and eager to please authority figures, but their high level of dutifulness is often driven by a need for self-preservation. They are typically poorly adjusted and very cautious and may have low scores on the Bold, Mischievous, Colorful, and Imaginative scales. They may also be security oriented and not very interested in power or control. The second form of the high Dutiful leader is the "Good Soldier." These leaders may have a good leadership profile, but their high level of dutifulness causes them to exhibit an exaggerated sense of loyalty and eagerness to please authority.

One of the best historical examples of a "Good Soldier" is Lieutenant Colonel Oliver North. Colonel North was part of the National Security Administration during the Iran Contra scandal in the 1980s. The scandal involved the sale of arms to Iran and the diversion of the proceeds to support the Contra rebel group in Nicaragua. There was a law in place at the time (the Boland Amendment) that specifically prohibited the financial support of the Contras. There are three aspects of this incident that are noteworthy from a high Dutiful standpoint. First, the incident clearly illustrates the lengths to which a high Dutiful leader is willing to go in order to please his or her superiors. Colonel North was well aware of the limits put in place by the Boland Amendment, and yet he broke the law in a clandestine operation that ultimately ended his military career. Second, the public nature of this incident lends considerable insight into the thinking of a high Dutiful leader. Colonel North, during his testimony to Congress, is famously (or rather, infamously) quoted as saying, "I thought it was a pretty neat idea." Finally, Colonel North is credited with the second part of the plan—funneling the proceeds of the arms sales to the Contras. This is important because it illustrates that high Dutiful leaders of the "Good Soldier" variety are capable of taking independent action (although often they choose not to do so). In fact, if they are operating under the impression they are fulfilling the agenda of their superiors, they can initiate all sorts of actions in support of that agenda.

The last point with respect to the "Good Soldier" profile is particularly important from a subscale standpoint. The "Indecisive" subscale speaks to the notion of being reluctant to take independent action. In this case, there is every possibility that Colonel North could have a relatively high Dutiful score and yet score low on "Indecisive." If so, it would account for his ingratiating and conforming behaviors flourishing while opening the door for him to take the actions that he took without the knowledge of his superiors. In some ways, the "Good Soldier" profile could be even more insidious than a maxed-out score on Dutiful typically associated with the "Scared Puppy" profile. History is replete with examples of high Dutiful leaders carrying out the wishes of their superiors using their own initiative and decisiveness in very twisted ways.

More typically, high Dutiful leaders fit the "Scared Puppy" profile. James from Case 7—James, Marketing Manager on page 100 provides a good example. James's highest derailer is his high score on the Dutiful scale (90%). The following is James's profile summary.

James's Situational Summary			
James was the marketing manager for a small family-owned business that was sold to a well-established technology company. After the sale, James moved on to a small, fast-moving start-up technology company. He had clear challenges with his ability to get things moving in the new company. His high Dutiful score will have a direct impact on his ability to act independently in an environment that likely lacks structure.			
Dimension	**Score**	**Percentile**	**Description**
Excitable	10		James is a laid-back, even-tempered marketing guy (Excitable—10%). It takes him a long time to get to know and trust people (Skeptical—70%), and he is guarded and slow to make decisions (Cautious—85% and Mischievous—15%). James doesn't make a big impression on people. In fact, he is best known for his loyalty and willingness to do whatever the owners asked (Dutiful—90%).
Skeptical	70		
Cautious	85		
Reserved	25		
Leisurely	19		
Bold	24		
Mischievous	15		
Colorful	45		
Imaginative	35		
Diligent	50		
Dutiful	90		

0 10 20 30 40 50 60 70 80 90 100

In James's profile, he is described as "laid back" and "does not make a big impression on people." These terms, while not directly tied to high Dutiful, leave the impression of a leader who sits in the backseat waiting for others to initiate or direct action. His conduct is quite different from Colonel North, who saw it as his duty to take action in support of his superior. However, similarities remain between the "Good Soldier" and the "Scared Puppy" profiles in that both involve ingratiating and conforming behaviors. The most telling of these for James can be found in the last line in which he is described as "willing to do whatever the owners ask." It is virtually certain that this type of reputation would be appreciated by those in charge. It is equally certain that those in charge would have a tough time viewing James as a person who could take over and lead in their absence.

Evaluating the Need for Change

The following behavioral questions should be considered in conjunction with a leader's high Dutiful score (as exhibited by James) when evaluating the need for a change in behavior. A "yes" response to three or fewer items suggests that there is no imminent need for behavioral changes. A "yes" response to four to six items suggests that a high score on the Dutiful scale should be a watch-out for a leader. A "yes" response to more than six items suggests that a leader should take active steps toward making behavioral changes.

Does the leader:

1.	Require input from superiors before making a decision or taking action?	**Yes**	**No**	**Not Sure**
2.	Delay decisions until there is certainty that superiors will support the decisions regardless of the outcome?	**Yes**	**No**	**Not Sure**
3.	Appear to go too far when it comes to keeping superiors informed?	**Yes**	**No**	**Not Sure**
4.	Say "yes" to virtually any request made by superiors regardless of the consequences for others?	**Yes**	**No**	**Not Sure**
5.	Spend an inordinate amount of time stroking the egos of those in power?	**Yes**	**No**	**Not Sure**
6.	Tend to tell superiors what they want to hear rather than what they need to hear?	**Yes**	**No**	**Not Sure**
7.	Carefully avoid actions that might rock the boat or go against the wishes of superiors?	**Yes**	**No**	**Not Sure**
8.	Exhibit loyal support for the actions of superiors, even when those actions are wrong?	**Yes**	**No**	**Not Sure**
9.	Often defer personal opinions in favor of those of superiors in order to gain their approval?	**Yes**	**No**	**Not Sure**

These items should be considered as behavioral indicators. Similar or associated behaviors to any of those listed that are exhibited by a leader likely suggest a "yes" response. They provide additional support that a leader may be at risk for the negative reputational consequences associated with those scoring high on the Dutiful scale, such as James.

Impact of High Dutiful Behaviors

High Dutiful behaviors can have reputational impact for a leader that ranges from loyal follower to blind servant. The consequences for a high Dutiful leader's career are often tied to the type of manager for whom the leader works. Some managers relish the notion of having loyal followers who offer little pushback to their agenda. These managers will often bring their dutiful followers along on their journey wherever it may lead. Other managers can be quite averse to being surrounded by dutiful followers, preferring those who will challenge them and push back when the situation calls for it. One thing for certain is that an organization can be at risk when dutiful behaviors are pervasive. These risks include stunted innovation, poor people development, and limited stewardship. For the leader exhibiting these behaviors, the biggest risk is being labeled a "follower." By definition, such a label will be career limiting. The following are some of the consequences of high Dutiful behavior, broken out by three constituencies: managers, peers, and direct reports.

Managers

As just mentioned, managers may have a range of reactions to high Dutiful behaviors. Regardless of how they react, managers are at significant risk when their team includes high Dutiful individuals. If they have too many followers on their team, managers are often insulated from hearing the truth about their ideas, strategies, and actions. Bad news may not reach them in a timely manner because the team may not send up adequate warning signals about potential problems. Plus, the managers may limit their own prospects for promotion because their potential successors end up being viewed as ill-prepared followers. It is certainly a double edged sword for a manager—loyal followers and, at the same time, a troop of "yes" types who could be helping the manager embark on the road to Abilene.

Peers

Peers who are not high Dutiful types themselves will have considerable disdain for leaders exhibiting these behaviors. They will be reluctant to trust such individuals. They will keep their guard up thinking anything they say may end up being used against them by these individuals as part of their ingratiating behaviors. There will be little chance for meaningful *esprit de corps* and a real risk of an in-group/out-group mentality developing among peers. Peers may even take advantage of high Dutiful leaders by passing off work to them, positioning it as "what the manager wants." Managers will often be oblivious to problems arising amongst peers as they are getting their information largely via the individual(s) exhibiting the high Dutiful behaviors. Even more sinister is the possibility of institutional backstabbing that can arise from high Dutiful behaviors. This duplicity can occur when negative information about a peer (accurate or inaccurate) is used by high Dutiful individuals to ingratiate themselves to the manager.

Direct Reports

Direct reports often become the victims of high Dutiful leaders in that they are left with having to handle the workload their leader creates through over-commitment and failing to push back. The result is that direct reports will become disempowered and unwilling to offer their ideas, take initiative, or put in extra effort. They will see their high Dutiful leader as nothing more than a conduit through which the wishes of his or her manager pass. From the direct reports' perspective, the high Dutiful leader has abdicated what they see as the primary responsibility of a leader: to lead. They will feel abandoned and disempowered, perhaps to the point of leaving the team.

Coaching Focus

High Dutiful behaviors are often rewarded and, therefore, can be very difficult to coach. Because leaders with high Dutiful scores are deeply concerned with being accepted and getting along with authority figures, they go out of their way to build bonds that mirror dependency behaviors. They engage in a variety of proactive behaviors they believe will build the bond between them and authority figures, including ingratiating themselves, actively seeking opportunities to be of service, publicly advocating decisions and strategies, undermining adversaries, and supplanting their own values to curry favor. The lengths to which high Dutiful leaders will go largely depend on the strength of the bond they have built (or are trying to build) with authority figures.

In addition to engaging in proactive behaviors to build a bond with authority figures, high Dutiful leaders spend an inordinate amount of time scanning their environment for potential threats to the bond. They are scanning for two basic types of information. First, they are looking for signs of disapproval or any hints that they are doing something that could negatively impact the bond. Should he or she detect any signs, the high Dutiful leader will immediately attempt to remove the threat to the bond. Second, they scan for threats from other constituencies (e.g., peers, direct reports, other superiors, etc.) that could damage the authority figures to whom they are bonded. Should they detect a threat from one or more of these constituencies, they will seek to pass the information along to the authority figure as a sign of where their true loyalty lies.

It might seem from the above description that the coaching focus involves trying to understand the bond that the high Dutiful leader has with the authority figure(s) and trying to break it or at least reduce the level of dependency. That approach may have some short-term benefits and even correct a particular situation. However, it may also damage a valuable relationship the high Dutiful leader has with an authority figure, resulting in negative career consequences. Furthermore, that coaching approach likely will not have long-term benefits in that high Dutiful leaders look to align themselves with authority figures. If the bond with one authority figure goes away, there is every possibility that the high Dutiful individual will bond with another authority figure.

The real coaching focus needs to be on the reputational components of high Dutiful leaders that could negatively impact their career potential. More specifically, the loyalty aspects of Dutiful behavior can be quite valuable from a career standpoint. The key is to maintain a reputation as a person of loyalty, while identifying the negative followership behaviors and minimizing them in the eyes of relevant constituencies (e.g., peers, direct reports, and other authority figures). The challenge is the same for the "Good Soldier" and the "Scared Puppy." The difference lies in the followership behaviors that need to be targeted for positive reputational change.

Coaching Strategy

The challenge with coaching a high Dutiful leader is determining which Dutiful behaviors are career limiting and which may serve to further the leader's career. Perhaps one of the best ways to discern between the two is through a series of stakeholder interviews designed to identify reputational behaviors related to dutifulness. It is important to identify behaviors within each subscale because that will help determine if the leader is a "Good Soldier" or a "Scared Puppy." The coaching strategy should then target the behaviors that most contribute to diminishing the leader's reputation as a person who is independent minded and can fly without cover. It is important to recognize the role the leader's manager may play in the coaching strategy. Without the support of the manager, a coaching strategy aimed at reducing the dependence of the high Dutiful leader could be viewed by the manager as breaking a bond of trust. For example, if a leader consistently receives feedback that he or she does not stand up for employees and suddenly starts standing up for them in public, the change could easily be misperceived by the manager. In other words, the coaching strategy has a far better chance of being successful if the manager recognizes and supports the need for the leader to demonstrate a degree of independence.

Strategy Refinements Using Subscale Information

The subscales offer insights as to how the coaching strategy might be refined to improve the effectiveness of the intervention. The subscales for Dutiful include Indecisive, Ingratiating, and Conforming. The subscales are particularly important in distinguishing between the "Good Soldier" and the "Scared Puppy." They also offer insights into the behaviors that contribute to perceived dependence or limit career success.

Indecisive

From a career standpoint, the Indecisive subscale represents the greatest risk for a leader. Indecisive behavior slows organizational progress, causes direct reports to disengage, frustrates peers, and is often seen by those in authority as a central reason to withhold a promotion. Coaching indecisiveness requires two components: determining the leader's decision-making authority and understanding the leader's decision-making process. Leaders should always work with their managers to firm up their understanding of their decision-making authority. This grasp of the extent of their authority is even more important for high Dutiful leaders and may need to be facilitated with the help of a coach. Once decision-making authority has been established, the coach should familiarize the leader with the process steps associated with decision-making. In particular, information gathering and evaluation of alternatives should receive specific attention. An indecisive leader typically reverts to additional information gathering or excessive evaluation of alternatives as ways to delay making a decision. Coaching the leader at the outset of the decision-making process to set boundaries on information gathering and alternative evaluation will remove two of the most significant tactics leaders employ to delay decisions.

Ingratiating

Ingratiating behaviors involve the use of interpersonal skills in order to curry favor, win approval, or gain an advantage. When ingratiating behaviors are used skillfully, they can be quite powerful in influencing others (Figure 14).

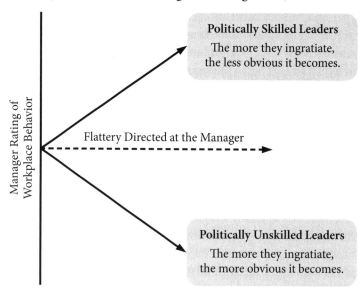

Figure 14   Ingratiating Behavior

High Dutiful leaders use these behaviors in a wide range of inappropriate ways, including overusing them, padding them with superlatives, mistiming them, and so on. Furthermore, they often (but not always) direct them at authority figures. To the observer, these behaviors come off as insincere, smarmy, awkward attempts at praise that could only be offered by a sycophant. Because these behaviors represent "tells," successful coaching involves tracking and substituting statements that are less effusive or even leading with "seeks." Because high Dutiful leaders often have trouble recognizing when they are being ingratiating, it can be helpful to identify a trusted team member who could offer real-time feedback to help raise the leader's self-awareness.

Conforming

Conforming behaviors are those behaviors that violate one's personal beliefs. In other words, there is a difference between a leader's agreeing with a manager because he or she is truly in agreement versus agreeing with a manager simply to avoid confrontation or curry favor. The key is helping a leader high on the Conforming subscale learn ways of expressing disagreement without creating a confrontation with a manager or, worse, a situation in which the manager needs to save face. There are two important points that a high Conforming leader needs to understand with respect to conforming behaviors. First, failing to offer a manager a differing view is not doing the manager a favor. It may, in fact, be a disservice in that the leader is withholding information that might be very useful to the manager. Second, unless the situation is a forum for open dialog, it is likely to be far more effective for the leader to express true beliefs out of the public eye. Not only will it reduce the risk for the high Conforming leader, it demonstrates concern for the manager's image while ensuring the manager sees loyalty versus sycophantic followership.

Coaching Tactics

Coaching tactics cover a range of approaches and resources that have been found useful in addressing high Dutiful behaviors. These tactics are typically used in combination to form a custom plan suited to the specific learning needs of a leader. The tactics are divided into four categories: (1) thought-provoking questions for a leader to consider, (2) exercises a leader can engage in to improve performance, (3) tips and techniques a coach can use to help a leader improve performance, and (4) support resources that can be consulted to gain additional insights in addressing high Dutiful behaviors.

Thought-Provoking Questions for a Leader

- What behaviors are you demonstrating today that may be contributing to a perception that you are just a follower?
- How do you see the leader's responsibility to express independent and perhaps opposing points of view to superiors or those in authority?
- How does supporting your point of view contribute to your organization? What is the impact of not supporting your point of view?
- To what extent do you challenge your superiors currently? As you take on more senior leadership roles, how does that change?
- What impact would supporting your point of view with senior leaders have on your team and your relationship with them?
- What impact would supporting your point of view have on your peers and your relationship with them?

Exercises for a Leader

- Identify some leaders you admire, and discuss what they stand for and how they show this. How does standing up for what they believe in contribute to their leadership image?
- List all the reasons why your manager, your team, and your peers would respond favorably to your being more independent in your point of view.
- Discuss the organization's culture and tolerance for conflict. How does this compare to yours?
- Rehearse assertively expressing a point of view or challenging a superior on an issue.

- Describe a situation in which you disagreed with a superior, but failed to voice your views. What caused you to hold back? Describe an alternative you could have pursued to ensure that your voice was heard.

Tips and Techniques for a Coach

- Identify an issue or an initiative where the leader has control of decision-making authority and the resources necessary to be successful. Work with the leader to outline and execute a plan that places him or her in the position of making the final call on all key steps.
- Have the leader observe and record examples of colleagues or other leaders when they offer challenges or resistance to the ideas of others. Debrief and discuss the effectiveness of the approaches employed with the leader.
- Identify an issue or decision where the leader disagrees with his or her manager. Use a role play exercise to give the leader practice pushing back on the manager and offering a personal perspective.
- Have the leader meet with his or her manager to discuss the scope of decision-making authority, with the goal of establishing a set of boundaries for independent decision-making.
- Work with the leader and the leader's team to establish a decision-making charter covering the commitment and use of team resources.
- As part of a stakeholder analysis, include a power rating for each stakeholder, and use it to help the leader determine the most effective techniques for working with each stakeholder.

Support Resources

Brandon, R., & Seldman, M. (2004). *Survival of the savvy: High-integrity political tactics for career and company success.* New York, NY: Free Press.

Two of the nation's most successful corporate leadership consultants reveal their proven, systematic program for using the power of "high-integrity" politics to achieve career success, maximize team impact, and protect the company's reputation and bottom line.

DeLuca, J. R. (2002). *Political savvy: Systematic approaches to leadership behind the scenes.* Berwyn, PA: EBG Publications.

DeLuca describes tactics employed by ethical leaders, helps readers identify their own political styles, and offers an efficient and actionable guide to navigating murky political waters.

Goulston, M. (2009). *Just listen: Discover the secret to getting through to absolutely anyone.* New York, NY: AMACOM.

Based on his experience as a business consultant, coach, and psychiatrist, Goulston offers readers science- and practice-backed strategies for winning support and collegiality from "unreachable" or unyielding people.

Heffernan, M. (2012). Dare to disagree [Video file]. Retrieved from https://www.ted.com/talks/margaret_heffernan_dare_to_disagree

In her brief TED talk, Margaret Heffernan posits that (a) disagreement is often a precursor to progress and (b) echo chambers are not terribly valuable partners.

Matuson, R. C. (2011). *Suddenly in charge: Managing up, managing down, succeeding all around.* Boston, MA: Nicholas Brealey.

This highly-rated book teaches readers how to manage up as well as down, take steps to maximize their credibility, and take control of their careers and reputations.

McIntyre, M. G. (2005). *Secrets to winning office politics: How to achieve your goals and increase your influence at work.* New York, NY: St. Martin's Griffin.

Organizational psychologist and corporate consultant, McIntyre, offers an actionable strategy for "increasing your personal power without compromising your integrity or taking advantage of others."

Tulgan, B. (2010). *It's OK to manage your boss: The step-by-step program for making the best of your most important relationship at work.* San Francisco, CA: Wiley.

Based on the premise that employees should take greater responsibility for their most important work relationship, Tulgan challenges antiquated beliefs about how employees should manage up and outlines strategies for helping employees get what they need from their superiors.

Sample Coaching Program (Case 7—James)

James's profile indicates that his highest score is on the Dutiful scale at 90 percent, and all three subscales are elevated. The case description indicates that high Dutiful behaviors could be a problem for James in his role as marketing manager—he has joined a technology start-up company in which a premium is placed on employees' acting independently and making decisions on their own. James's history suggests that he was quite effective at executing the instructions of the owners of the company he previously worked for, and they appreciated his willingness to follow through on their requests. In his new job, it is unlikely that James will receive a lot of guidance and, in fact, he will likely be relied upon by others for his expertise in marketing. The initial conversations with James suggested that his early days at the new company were filled with data-collection activities, with little in the way of tangible actions related to building a marketing function. Upon probing, it was clear that James had plenty of ideas but was reluctant to take action for fear of making a mistake or doing something that was inconsistent with the wishes of his manager. It was also clear that he had virtually no idea what his manager actually wanted from him in his new role other than to create an effective marketing function. The following are the proposed steps for a coaching engagement with James that places emphasis on improving his ability to be decisive and take independent action:

- Work through a series of thought-provoking questions with James to raise his self-awareness regarding his high Dutifulness and its impact on his role as the leader of the marketing function:

  - How do you see the leader's responsibility to express independent and perhaps opposing points to his superiors or those in authority?

  - How does stating your point of view contribute to your organization? What is the impact of not supporting your point of view?

- Have James set up a meeting with his manager to establish the Critical Success Factors for his function and discuss the decision-making authority he has in his role.

- Use the initial marketing plan as an initiative to coach James on how to take control of his decision-making authority and the resources necessary to be successful. Work with James to outline and execute the marketing plan, making sure he makes the final call on all key steps.

- Establish a series of follow-up meetings between James and his manager specifically designed for James to keep his manager informed without giving up control of the execution of the marketing plan.

SUMMARY

Keep Doing

Communicate with your boss on relevant business developments and problems.

Stop Doing

Check with others before making decisions that are well within your authority.

Start Doing

Support the decisions of your direct reports once you have delegated responsibility to them.

There is a fine line between dependence and loyalty. High Dutiful leaders tend to err on the wrong side of that line, which can have serious career implications. Managers may see high Dutiful leaders as followers, incapable of taking independent action or standing on their own. Peers may see them as sycophants and seek to marginalize them. Direct reports often feel victimized by high Dutiful leaders because of their willingness to accept directives, regardless of their consequences. Direct reports may also resent the tendency of high Dutiful leaders to disregard their need for support and advocacy. While coaching tactics may vary depending on the way high Dutiful behaviors are manifested, the general approach is to decrease the perception that the leader is dependent on the manager without undermining the bond that loyalty engenders.

LOW DUTIFUL

Detecting When It Is a Problem

Low Dutiful leaders often find themselves operating as if they were on an island, taking actions with little to no cover from their superiors. Their behavior goes beyond the need to act independently. They often have a disdain for their superiors, believing that they themselves possess the knowledge and ability to do things better on their own without any support. Low Dutiful leaders almost view it as a sign of weakness to go to their superiors for help. Problems for low Dutiful leaders can come in spectacular fashion. Their independence can put them into high-risk–high-reward situations that have associated potential for high costs. While managers can embrace independent action, it is only human nature to want to be needed to some extent. Low Dutiful leaders rarely give their managers the sense or feeling that they are needed. When things are going well, low Dutiful leaders can thrive. Derailing potentially comes into play when things go bad and the manager provides no cover.

An interesting example of low Dutiful behavior can be found in the actions of President Barack Obama during his second term. Throughout his first term, his inability to work with Congress was well documented. In fact, you could detect a sense of disdain for Congress and resentment toward Congress's constitutional obligation for oversight, particularly as it related to budgetary matters. President Obama installed a group of czars to oversee many aspects of government, resulting in powerful government agencies that could circumvent the will of Congress. They did this by utilizing rules and regulations to manipulate government spending to help President Obama achieve his agenda (high Dutiful behavior). While these low Dutiful behaviors are not terribly new to presidents trying to get their way, President Obama's in-your-face style in working around Congress is nearly unprecedented in recent history. President Obama's low Dutiful behavior ramped up substantially after being elected to a second term. In a Cabinet meeting on January 14, 2014, he is quoted as saying, "I have a pen and I have a phone." This was a reference (a not-so-veiled threat) to using executive orders to go around Congress to achieve his legislative agenda. There are three important aspects of this example of low Dutiful behavior. First, there is no question as to the president's intent to operate independently of the wishes of Congress. Second, the in-your-face style underscores the notion that he knows best, which he conveys with a degree of disdain. Finally, he has no cover should his initiatives fail or run into trouble. All of these are hallmarks of low Dutiful leaders.

A final point should be made with respect to the impact of low Dutiful behaviors. The importance of failure has been well documented as critical to the growth of a leader. Will Rogers was once quoted as saying, "Good judgment comes from experience, and a lot of that comes from bad judgment." The problem with low Dutiful leaders is that they often do not get second chances. When they fly without cover from a superior, they are exposed, and their mistakes are their own. The ability to recover from a mistake often depends on the willingness of the leader's manager to shoulder a portion of the blame and advocate for second chances. A low Dutiful leader may engender the exact opposite reaction from a manager. This alienation is especially true when the leader's behavior reflects poorly on the manager's judgment. The manager's natural reaction is to put distance between himself or herself and a mistake made by a low Dutiful leader.

Rex from Case 1—Rex, Vice President of Sales on page 88 provides a good example of a low Dutiful profile. Rex's lowest derailer is his score on the Dutiful scale (5%). The following is Rex's profile summary.

Rex's Situational Summary
Rex worked in a small company as vice president of sales. In his role, he had considerable autonomy and freedom to make decisions. The company was acquired by a much larger, well-established company with rules, processes, and procedures that often accompany a large bureaucracy. Rex's willingness to take risks and make fast, independent decisions runs counter to the culture that exists in the new company. This issue could be exacerbated by his tendency to follow his own agenda.

Dimension	Score	Percentile	Description
Excitable	50		Rex is very self-confident to the point of being an arrogant leader (Bold—95%). He is quite willing to take risks (Cautious—10% and Mischievous—90%). He tends to work his own agenda (Leisurely—82%), and prefers to operate independently without a lot of close supervision (Dutiful—5%).
Skeptical	67		
Cautious	10		
Reserved	45		
Leisurely	82		
Bold	95		
Mischievous	90		
Colorful	75		
Imaginative	70		
Diligent	30		
Dutiful	5		

0   10   20   30   40   50   60   70   80   90   100

Rex has a classic sales profile, and it is not uncommon to see a low Dutiful score as part of the profile. He is described as having an entrepreneurial approach, which can be an asset in sales situations. The key to the problems that might emerge for Rex with respect to his low Dutiful behavior lies in his high Mischievous score (90%) and low Cautious score (10%). These scores indicate that Rex is a significant risk taker and may bend rules from time to time. Rex's low Dutiful score suggests that he may not do a very good job of keeping his manager informed. If his risk taking leads to a problem, his manager may be caught off guard and may choose to let Rex stand alone to face the consequences. Further exacerbating Rex's situation is that he is now working for a much larger company. Rex's profile suggests he will quickly try to prove himself, and his new manager may want to keep close tabs on him early on until some trust has been built up in the relationship. The perfect storm is set up for a problem to arise—a low Dutiful entrepreneurial sales person out to prove himself, working for a manager who needs to keep close tabs on him as a new employee.

Evaluating the Need for Change

The following behavioral questions should be considered in conjunction with a leader's low Dutiful score (as exhibited by Rex) when evaluating the need for a change in behavior. A "yes" response to three or fewer items suggests that there is no imminent need for behavioral changes. A "yes" response to four to six items suggests that a low score on the Dutiful scale should be a watch-out for a leader. A "yes" response to more than six items suggests that a leader should take active steps toward making behavioral changes.

Does the leader:

1. Regularly make decisions or take actions without keeping superiors or team members informed?   **Yes   No   Not Sure**

2. Often go out of the way to avoid input from superiors because it may cause his or her actions to be constrained?   **Yes   No   Not Sure**

3. Prefer to ask for forgiveness rather than permission when it comes to taking action or making a decision?   **Yes   No   Not Sure**

4. Display an excessive degree of candor when delivering feedback to superiors?   **Yes   No   Not Sure**

5. Challenge the views of superiors and team members, regardless of those who are present?   **Yes   No   Not Sure**

6. Often display a lack of sensitivity when delivering bad news to superiors?   **Yes   No   Not Sure**

7. Chart a personal course without seeking the guidance or counsel of superiors?   **Yes   No   Not Sure**

8. Cause superiors and team members to feel ignored because of his or her willingness to act independently?   **Yes   No   Not Sure**

9. Often contradict or disagree with the views of superiors when outside of their presence?   **Yes   No   Not Sure**

These items should be considered as behavioral indicators. Similar or associated behaviors to any of those listed that are exhibited by a leader likely suggest a "yes" response. They provide additional support that a leader may be at risk for the negative reputational consequences associated with those scoring low on the Dutiful scale, such as Rex.

Impact of Low Dutiful Behaviors

First and foremost, low Dutiful behaviors can have a negative impact on trust. A low Dutiful leader will diminish trust if he or she acts independently when others expect to be involved or informed. The expectations of the manager play an important role in determining the negative impact of low Dutiful behaviors. Often expectations go unstated or are assumed which opens the door for a trust problem to fester. As low Dutiful behaviors accumulate, more and more social distance is created between the leader and the manager, and less and less trust is possible. The following are some of the consequences that could result from low Dutiful behaviors, broken out by three constituencies: managers, peers, and direct reports.

Managers

Perhaps the most serious impact of low Dutiful behavior occurs between the leader and the manager. It is this relationship where direction is set and expectations should be established. The overarching impact of low Dutiful behaviors on this relationship is diminished trust which can have a range of outcomes. It could be as simple as the manager sees the leader as "me" oriented as opposed to a team player. It could create confusion around direction if the behaviors of the leader are contrary to those of the manager. Or, it could be as direct as an outright abdication of support for the leader and the leader's actions. All of these can result in reputational damage for the leader that could be carried far beyond the point at which they initially impacted the manager-leader relationship.

Peers

Peers can be quite a different matter than managers when it comes to low Dutiful behaviors. The impact likely begins at the point of some type of transaction between the leader and a peer where there has been a violation of the peer's space. For example, the leader disregards an established organization boundary that is within the scope of responsibility of the peer. Infringements of this type tend to diminish trust and contribute to the leader's reputation as not being a team player or as being a maverick. Interestingly, peers do not have to have direct experience with low Dutiful leaders in order to be wary of their behavior. Politically savvy peers pay attention to the leader's reputation and shield themselves from any potential fallout.

Direct Reports

There are two serious issues that a low Dutiful leader can create for direct reports. First, the leader may be displaying low Dutiful behaviors the direct reports think are appropriate to emulate. Emulating the low Dutiful behaviors of the leader could result in the entire team being thought of as a bit rogue. The second impact on direct reports can be the stress a low Dutiful leader can create by putting them in the middle of competing agendas. In other words, if a low Dutiful leader takes actions that are contrary to the direction of the manager (or the organization for that matter), direct reports could become quite conflicted as to how to respond—do they follow the leader or respond with some type of insurrection? Either way, there will be stress involved that cannot be considered healthy.

Coaching Focus

Low Dutiful behaviors can be manifested in many ways. The reason for this is the tension that always exists between demonstrating sufficient independence to be seen as leader-like versus demonstrating so much independence that the trust line is crossed. Furthermore, the tension varies according to the needs of the manager, and these needs can be quite dynamic over time. For example, the experience a manager has with a leader can significantly alter his or her control needs. Even the most ardent micromanagers will give up some control (and the need for Dutiful behaviors) when they have experience with and confidence in a leader. In contrast, new leaders are often subjected to more stringent control by the manager.

The dynamic nature of the impact of low Dutiful behaviors is mirrored by the leader's other constituencies. Peers, direct reports, members of other business units, and even customers have widely varying needs with respect to Dutiful behaviors. The problem with low Dutiful leaders is that they tend to operate across the board with the attitude that everyone believes no news is good news and, to some extent, there is no news in good news. In other words, low Dutiful leaders will forge ahead, leaving an information vacuum behind that others are left to fill. Furthermore, left to their own devices, low Dutiful leaders tend to engage in information sharing under just two specific conditions: victory laps when their efforts culminate with success or cries for help when it becomes clear that no other alternative remains.

The other interesting aspect of a low Dutiful leader from a coaching standpoint is the way risk-taking behaviors interact with the low Dutiful behaviors. Leaders with higher profiles for risk taking tend to have more problems when it comes to low Dutiful behaviors. They take more risks, they are more reluctant to engage in office politics or be ingratiating, and they often revel in their own lack of conformity. It is easy to see how a low Dutiful leader with a high profile for risk taking would earn a reputation as a cowboy, a poor team player, or even a rogue.

The coaching focus for a low Dutiful leader involves heading off the low Dutiful behaviors before the trust bond is broken. The reason should be clear: once the trust bond is broken (regardless of the constituency involved), recovery is difficult if not impossible. People are just not wired to completely forgive a violation of trust. There will always be a nagging voice in the back of their minds reminding them of the situation and reinforcing the negative feelings they have developed for the leader. It is far better to add a few simple behaviors to the low Dutiful leader's repertoire than to rebuild trust with one or more constituencies. It is like putting money in a savings account for an emergency—better to have it and not need it than to need it and not have it.

There are two areas that a coach should focus on to help leaders avoid problems with their low Dutiful behavior: expectations and information sharing. Low Dutiful leaders should always approach a new project or a new management situation by establishing expectations with key stakeholders about how much latitude there is in decision-making authority. The purpose is to establish the guardrails needed to avoid breaking the trust bond. These leaders must also establish information-sharing guidelines. Too often, low Dutiful leaders turn expectations into a license to operate with autonomy. They view the expectations as the final outcome. Activities between when expectations are set and when they are met become the low Dutiful leader's playground within which he or she can operate with impunity. Therefore, the coaching must include some form of calibration that involves information sharing. Keep in mind the dynamic nature of the impact of low Dutiful behaviors. Without calibration using information sharing, there remains a very high probability that problems may develop over time. The coaching focus must include both expectations and information sharing.

Coaching Strategy

The challenge associated with coaching a low Dutiful leader starts with getting the leader to buy in to the coaching in the first place. The coach is not immune to low Dutiful behaviors and may experience the same kind of information vacuum that others feel when working with the leader. Assuming this challenge can be overcome, the Situational Context is the key to developing a strategy that will be effective with a low Dutiful leader. The starting point must be the leader's manager. One of the most effective strategies in working with the manager is to establish mutually agreed upon Critical Success Factors (CSFs). These are the top three to four objectives the leader must accomplish within a specified period of time in order for the manager to consider the leader to be successful. It may sound like a no-brainer, but it is astonishing how often a leader and manager disagree on CSFs, especially when a low Dutiful leader is involved. The CSFs then form the foundation for establishing decision-making authority and an information-sharing protocol. The protocol can serve as the foundation for communicating with other constituencies, including direct reports and peers. The CSFs for the decision-making and information-sharing parameters establish a roadmap for the leader to follow to avoid the pitfalls of his or her low Dutiful behaviors. The remaining challenge is making sure the leader stays on course and executes the information-sharing strategy. The coach should remain in the information-sharing loop throughout the engagement to reinforce the importance of follow-through and head off any lapses as the leader develops an information-sharing habit.

Strategy Refinements Using Subscale Information

The subscales offer insights as to how the coaching strategy might be refined to improve the effectiveness of the intervention. The subscales for Dutiful include Indecisive, Ingratiating, and Conforming. The subscales are *not* created equal when it comes to low Dutiful behavior. Challenges with respect to Indecisive and Conforming tend to create more problems for a low Dutiful leader and should definitely catch the attention of the coach. Problems associated with these subscales can be career ending, not just career limiting.

Indecisive

Leaders low on the Indecisive subscale are excessively decisive. They see it as their role to make decisions and make them independently of the guidance of others. The obvious problem is that the leader runs the risk of stepping outside sanctioned decision-making boundaries. If things turn out well, such a transgression might only result in a rebuke of the behavior. That said, the situation will still have a negative impact on trust with the manager and perhaps others. If things turn out badly, the potential exists for a serious reputation hit or worse depending on the impact of the decision. The key is to ensure the leader and manager are on the same page with respect to decision-making authority. There are decisions that belong to the leader. There are decisions that belong to the manager. And there are decisions that should be discussed and agreed to jointly. Establishing a habit of setting up decision-making parameters will go a long way toward preventing problems associated with the Indecisive subscale.

Ingratiating

Most low Dutiful leaders who also score low on the Ingratiating subscale can see right through ingratiating behaviors. They have little interest in engaging in these behaviors and often have disdain for those who do engage in them. From a coaching standpoint, it is important to make sure that leaders recognize that there is a difference between being politically savvy and being a sycophant who is constantly trying to curry favor with authority figures. It is doubtful that these leaders will incorporate ingratiating behaviors into their repertoire. However, it is quite reasonable to expect them to avoid behaviors that alienate authority figures, such as publicly challenging or contradicting authority figures. Such behaviors are rarely successful and can be quite detrimental. Simply moving an interaction from a public to a private setting to offer up opinions or concerns builds trust among authority figures without the leader's compromising his or her need to be candid.

Conforming

Low Dutiful leaders who score low on the Conforming subscale are anything but conforming. In fact, they often revel in their nonconformist behavior. There are two serious coaching refinements that should be considered here. First, the leader can come across as rebellious and defiant. A little of that behavior goes a long way and can result in a reputation as a leader who is difficult or disloyal. Coaching should focus on making sure the leader has a strong rationale for his or her behavior versus simply taking actions just to enhance a nonconformist reputation. Second, and even more serious, is the tendency of the leader to test limits when it comes to his or her decision-making authority. In other words, low Conforming leaders often chart their own course when it comes to accomplishing objectives. When that course involves exceeding their decision-making authority, there could be serious negative consequences. Coaching here needs to focus on reinforcing established decision-making authority and recognizing organizational norms and the consequences for exceeding the authority the leader has been granted.

Coaching Tactics

Coaching tactics cover a range of approaches and resources that have been found useful in addressing low Dutiful behaviors. These tactics are typically used in combination to form a custom plan suited to the specific learning needs of a leader. The tactics are divided into four categories: (1) thought-provoking questions for a leader to consider, (2) exercises a leader can engage in to improve performance, (3) tips and techniques a coach can use to help a leader improve performance, and (4) support resources that can be consulted to gain additional insights in addressing low Dutiful behaviors.

Thought-Provoking Questions for a Leader

- Are there times when you demonstrate low Dutiful behaviors? What is the impact on your boss, your peers, and your team? Are there times these behaviors work for you? Are there times they work against you?

- How would you describe the cultural norms in your organization relative to acting independently or without close supervision? What are the consequences for not conforming to the cultural norms?

- How do you establish the latitude you have in making decisions? Have you ever exceeded your authority? If so, what were the consequences?

- Have you ever had a dispute with a peer because your actions created a problem for his or her business unit? How did you work through that situation, and what did you learn from it?

- Do you see any advantages to using ingratiating behavior as a means of influencing others?

- Are there any behaviors you are demonstrating today that cause people to think you are not a team player?

Exercises for a Leader

- Identify an individual in the organization with whom you have had a conflict or dispute. Develop and execute an action plan aimed at rebuilding trust with that individual.

- Meet with your team and discuss the key cultural norms and values for your organization and how they should guide all team members in decision-making.

- Develop a team communication report that can be used by all team members as a quick method of updating you on a regular basis on key activities and that you can use to update your manager on key activities.

- Meet with key stakeholders in your organization and discuss their information needs as they relate to your business unit. Develop an information-sharing strategy that will meet their information needs going forward.

- Identify a controversial issue on which you have a strong opinion and want to influence the actions that will be taken on the issue. Identify the other stakeholders with respect to the issue. Develop and execute an influence strategy that will build support among the stakeholders for the actions you want to take.

- Meet with your manager and outline the Critical Success Factors (CSFs) that the two of you agree upon regarding your performance over the next 6 to 12 months. Include in the discussion the manager's needs for an information update on the CSFs and any limits you should be aware of regarding your decision-making authority.

Tips and Techniques for a Coach

- Identify an issue or an initiative where the leader needs to share decision-making authority and the resources necessary to be successful. Work with the leader to outline and execute a plan with the key stakeholders regarding how decisions should be made and what information sharing needs to occur.

- Have the leader observe and record examples of colleagues or other leaders as they offer challenges or resistance to the ideas of others. Debrief and discuss the effectiveness of the approaches employed with the leader.

- Identify an issue or decision where the leader disagrees with the manager. Use a role play exercise to give the leader practice pushing back on the manager and offering a personal perspective in a way that is non-confrontational and maintains the manager's self-esteem.

- Have the leader meet with the manager and discuss the scope of decision-making authority, with the goal of establishing reasonable boundaries that meet the needs of the manager and give the leader opportunities to grow in autonomy.

- Work with the leader and the leader's team to establish a decision-making charter covering the commitment and use of team resources that emphasizes empowering team members and avoiding leader/team member decision-making conflicts.

- As part of a stakeholder analysis, include a power rating for each stakeholder. Use it to help the leader work through the most effective techniques for working with each stakeholder to ensure boundaries and information-sharing needs are clear.

- Have the leader add the coach to the distribution list for formal information-sharing communications, and provide feedback to the leader about the quality and value of the communications.

Support Resources

Brandon, R., & Seldman, M. (2004). *Survival of the savvy: High-integrity political tactics for career and company success.* New York, NY: Free Press.

Two of the nation's most successful corporate leadership consultants reveal their proven, systematic program for using the power of "high-integrity" politics to achieve career success, maximize team impact, and protect the company's reputation and bottom line.

Burg, B. (2013). *Adversaries into allies: Win people over without manipulation or coercion.* New York, NY: Penguin Group.

Best-selling author Burg teaches readers about "Ultimate Influence"—the ability to win people over in a manner that leaves everyone feeling positive about the end result and themselves. Burg describes each component of his five-part framework in succinct but meaty chapters, each rife with actionable tips.

Dotlich, D. L., Cairo, P. C., & Rhinesmith, S. H. (2006). *Head, heart, and guts: How the world's best companies develop complete leaders.* San Francisco, CA: Jossey-Bass.

The authors rely heavily on high profile case studies while discussing the crucial capabilities required of today's leaders and offering readers an actionable plan for stepping outside their "leadership comfort zone."

Gabarro, J. J., & Kotter, J. P. (2005, January). Managing your boss. *Harvard Business Review.* Retrieved from https://hbr.org/2005/01/managing-your-boss?cm_sp=Topics-_-Links-_-Read%20These%20First

Gabarro and Kotter reframe "managing up" in a more favorable, less-deferential light—in their words, "the process of consciously working with your superior to obtain the best results for you, your boss, and the company."

George, B. (2007). *True north: Discover your authentic leadership.* San Francisco, CA: Jossey-Bass.

George helps readers understand that being an authentic leader is as simple as following one's own internal compass. Based on extensive research and interviews with 125 of today's acclaimed leaders, "True North" walks readers through a process of developing their own practical and comprehensive leadership development plan.

Grenny, J. (2014, November). How to disagree with your boss. *Harvard Business Review.* Retrieved from https://hbr.org/2014/11/how-to-disagree-with-your-boss

According to Grenny, even in the most "stultifying" of cultures, there is a subset of people who know how to speak the truth to people in positions of power—he describes the tactics used by these individuals in the above article.

Schrage, M. (2010, April). **Make your boss look good (without becoming a sycophant).** *Harvard Business Review.* Retrieved from https://hbr.org/2010/04/making-your-boss-look-good

This brief article likens managing up to "knowing your customer" and provides several readily applicable examples of how to manage up in a subtle yet effective manner.

Sample Coaching Program (Rex—Case 1)

Rex's profile indicates that he has a very low score on the Dutiful scale (5%), driven by depressed scores on all three subscales, and a strong "Moving Against" profile, which is not uncommon for a successful salesperson. Rex's biggest challenge is that he worked in a relatively small company where his independent style was not only tolerated, it was valued. When his company was acquired by a much larger company, he should have realized that there would be more rules and more processes to follow. Plus, he was going to be working for a new manager who was very unfamiliar with his style or his capabilities. It did not take long for Rex to get sideways with his new manager. He did what might be expected, given his profile, and that was to go out and try to make deals and close business to prove his worth. A key customer to whom Rex was assigned actually called Rex's manager to discuss Rex and what the customer perceived as a very different sales approach in comparison to what he had experienced in the past. It did not take a lot of probing to figure out what was creating problems for Rex. He had simply transferred his aggressive entrepreneurial style from his old company to his new company and assumed it would work just fine. The following coaching program may help get Rex back on the right track in his new company.

- Assign Rex to one of the senior sales associates who will take responsibility for introducing Rex to a number of the company's long-standing customers and help Rex become familiar with the sales style to which the company's customers have grown accustomed.

- Have Rex meet with his manager to establish his Critical Success Factors (CSFs) and Information Sharing plan.

- Review the CSFs and Information Sharing plan with Rex to ensure he understands the boundaries of his decision-making authority and the information needs of his manager.

- Set up an ongoing review process to monitor Rex's information sharing and provide feedback on how to keep it succinct while keeping his manager informed.

- Establish a series of follow-up meetings with the manager for Rex to explore ways in which he could become more independent and use his entrepreneurial style to benefit the company.

SUMMARY

Keep Doing

Take the initiative and drive the business according to sanctioned strategies.

Stop Doing

Venture into unchartered waters without manager knowledge or support.

Start Doing

Set expectations about decision-making authority and information sharing.

Dutifulness and loyalty are closely tied to each other. Unfortunately, low Dutiful leaders often fail to recognize the link. They often see their drive for autonomy and independence as strengths and the hallmarks of great leadership. Under the right circumstances, this view may be quite accurate, but it has to be tempered with the needs of those around the leader. Managers may see the behavior of low Dutiful individuals as a sign of disloyalty or abandonment, which reduces the likelihood that the manager will support those individuals if or when that support is needed. Peers may think that low Dutiful individuals are encroaching on their territory, which creates unneeded friction. Direct reports may emulate these behaviors (potentially creating their own problems), or direct reports may experience excessive stress, which can reduce their ability to perform effectively. Attention to expectations about decision-making and information sharing can go a long way to preventing low Dutiful leaders from creating problems for themselves and others.

PART V

BEYOND THE DARK SIDE

423

In Parts II, III, and IV, we focused our discussion on the results of the Hogan Development Survey (HDS) as the foundation for evaluating the performance improvement needs of leaders and how those needs can be ameliorated with the effective use of coaching techniques. In Part V, we open with two chapters (Chapter 21 and 22) that expand this discussion to include information that can be gleaned from the Hogan Personality Inventory (HPI) and the Motives, Values, Preferences Inventory (MVPI). While we have mentioned HPI and MVPI results throughout the book, these chapters go beyond providing simple reference information to offering specific guidance on how assessment results from these inventories can be used to add value in any effort to improve leader performance.

To accomplish this, we organized the chapters around the Competency Domains outlined by Hogan et al. (2007) and described in Chapter 3 (page 33). The Competency Domains were recommended as an organizing structure for a broad range of competencies that have typically been associated with leader performance. Here we extend this notion to illustrate how the Competency Domains can be used in a similar manner to organize all the scales associated with the HPI, HDS, and MVPI.

Figure 15 represents this organizing structure in the form of a circumplex. The circumplex is divided into quarters, with each quarter representing one of the four Competency Domains. From the center moving to the outer ring of the circumplex, the innermost ring illustrates the scales of the MVPI as they relate to each domain. The next ring covers the HDS scales, followed by the ring illustrating the HPI scales.

Initially, this structure was developed on the basis of expert judgment regarding which scales from each inventory most closely align with a given Competency Domain and, consequently, the associated leadership competencies. After nearly 15 years of research and dozens of validation studies, the empirical support for this alignment continues to mount. In other words, the Hogan Inventory scales associated with a particular Competency Domain are often found to correlate with leadership competencies associated with that domain.

For example, consider a competency like Strategic Thinking. This competency would typically be associated with the Business Domain because it can be done on one's own and requires the ability to process information. Now consider the Hogan Inventory scales that would be useful in predicting a leader's ability to effectively perform the competency of Strategic Thinking. Some obvious possibilities include the Inquisitive scale (openness to new ideas), the Imaginative scale (generating one's own ideas), and the Science scale (using data as part of problem-solving).

Contrast Strategic Thinking with a competency that aligns with the Interpersonal Domain, such as Networking. A Hogan Inventory scale like Interpersonal Sensitivity (the ability to build relationships) is far more likely to predict a leader's ability to network as opposed to a scale like Inquisitive. While it may be true that under certain circumstances these relationships may not always hold up under empirical scrutiny, the purpose of the circumplex is to provide a rational starting point to consider the alignment of Hogan Inventory scales to Competency Domains and their associated leadership competencies.

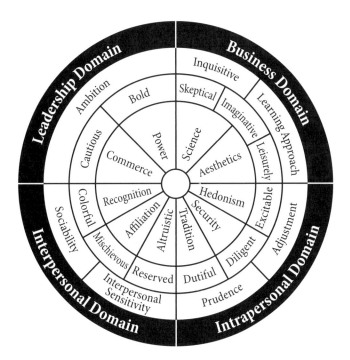

Figure 15   Hogan Inventory Scales Organized by the Domains

The robust nature of the Competency Domains allows nearly any behavior associated with leadership effectiveness to be categorized into one of the four domains. By aligning Hogan Inventory scales to the domains, the emerging structure can be used to describe, at a broad level, an effective leadership profile based on the personality characteristics measured by the scales. The following is a brief description of an effective leadership profile organized by Competency Domains and using personality-based behaviors measured by Hogan Inventories:

- Intrapersonal Domain—A balanced emotional demeanor (moderate Adjustment and low Excitable) with an organized can-do approach (moderate Prudence and Diligent) will be important to success. In addition, those having some respect for authority and possessing integrity (moderate Dutiful and Tradition) with a willingness to add fun to the workplace (moderate Hedonism) and take prudent career risks (low Security) will often advance quickly.

- Interpersonal Domain—It is important for a leader to possess an approachable style with a willingness to take tough stands on important issues (moderate Sociability, Interpersonal Sensitivity, and Reserved). A degree of charisma (moderate Colorful, Mischievous, and Recognition) with a willingness to help others (moderate Altruistic) and take a team approach (moderate to high Affiliation) will be important in motivating team members.

- Leadership Domain—Strength in this domain for a leader is marked by competitiveness (high Ambition), aggressive self-confidence (moderate Bold), willingness to take measured risks (low Cautious), a desire to be in charge (high Power), and an interest in the financial success of the venture (high Commerce).

- Business Domain—Openness to new ideas, creativity and a willingness to learn (moderate to high Inquisitive, Learning Approach, and Imaginative), with a healthy degree of skepticism (moderate Skeptical) and an interest in one's own agenda (moderate Leisurely) are important to success as a leader in this domain. In addition, it is important to value data and creativity (moderate to high Science and Aesthetics).

The circumplex structure provides an excellent heuristic for considering the impact of Hogan Personality Inventory (HPI) and Motives, Values, Preferences Inventory (MVPI) results in conjunction with Hogan Development Survey (HDS) results. We have pointed out that the coaches in the Hogan Coaching Network (HCN) view the Hogan inventories as three sides of a prism. Depending on a leader's profile, viewing performance through the different sides of the prism (i.e., considering HPI and MVPI data in conjunction with HDS data) can have performance implications that range from subtle to profound. There are far too many combinations and permutations to actually enumerate if one were to take into account all scales across the three Hogan inventories. In fact, when considered in light of situational variables, the possible implications border on the infinite. This task is simplified greatly by using the structure of the circumplex in conjunction with the prism notion. For any particular competency that is aligned to its appropriate domain, the number of HPI and MVPI scales to consider because they might impact the HDS scale is reduced by nearly 75 percent. That is not to say that scales other than those found within a particular domain do not impact the performance of a competency, but as a starting point and organizing structure, the circumplex is ideal. Further, leaders who receive feedback on their Hogan inventories say that one of the most valuable aspects is the integration of the data across the three inventories. Through the integration, the feedback is even more impactful because key themes (both strengths and derailers) can be identified. The circumplex readily facilitates this.

Therefore, our intent in Part V is to use the heuristic value of the circumplex to leverage additional data when considering leader performance and structuring effective feedback and coaching interventions. Chapter 21 provides an overview of the Bright Side characteristics as measured by the HPI, while Chapter 22 covers In Side characteristics as measured by the MVPI. These chapters include a brief description of the inventories and their relationship to characteristics measured by the HDS. These chapters also include implications for leadership and coaching broken down into the four domains, with an example of how inventory data beyond the HDS could be leveraged to improve the effectiveness of coaching interventions.

If there are inventory results beyond the HDS that can help coaches improve upon the effectiveness of coaching interventions, then there should be coaching techniques beyond those outlined for the HDS scales that could provide similar value. That is the premise behind Chapter 23. It highlights coaching techniques that are valuable in improving performance regardless of assessment results or performance challenges. These techniques are fairly easy to identify because they are consistently cited as part of coaching interventions regardless of the target behaviors involved. Within the HCN, there are coaches from diverse backgrounds and professional training, yet many of the techniques described in Chapter 23 were cited by these coaches as useful as general behavior-change techniques. Those that were selected to be highlighted in this chapter were consistently found to have considerable utility and a proven track record for increasing the probability of success in coaching outcomes.

It is difficult to summarize a book that covers as much ground as this one with a few concluding thoughts in a final chapter. Therefore, we decided to use the final chapter to highlight what we believe to be the most important takeaways when coaching leaders from a personality perspective. We have taken the position throughout this book that reputation is central to understanding and improving leader performance. Furthermore, reputation is the accumulation of behaviors that are driven by personality characteristics that emerge behaviorally in the form of natural tendencies. Our coaching philosophy is based on a simple concept: reputation change is real change, and reputation is driven by personality characteristics. Chapter 24 is dedicated to this simple concept and why we believe it is the most powerful approach that can be used to produce meaningful improvements in leader performance.

CHAPTER 21

COACHING AND THE BRIGHT SIDE

INTRODUCTION

The Hogan Personality Inventory (HPI) is a measure of normal personality. It was originally designed for use in personnel selection, individualized assessment, and career-related decision-making. The use of the inventory expanded into leadership development in the 1990s, and it is now regarded as a mainstay in a wide range of programs designed to improve leader performance.

The inventory provides detailed information about what is called the Bright Side of personality: characteristics that facilitate or inhibit a person's ability to get along with others and to achieve his or her life goals. Before considering the impact of the HPI on leadership development and coaching efforts, it is important to understand the foundation upon which the inventory is based—the Five-Factor Model (FFM) and the California Psychological Inventory (CPI).

The FFM is closer to settled science in the field of psychology than virtually any other model in the field. Wiggins and Pincus (1992) suggest that most, if not all, well-constructed multidimensional personality inventories can be described in terms of the FFM. Table 4—Five-Factor Model presents these factors with their associated definitions.

Factor	Description
1. Surgency	The degree to which a person needs social attention and social interaction.
2. Agreeableness	The degree to which a person needs pleasant and harmonious relations with others.
3. Conscientiousness	The degree to which a person is willing to comply with conventional rules, norms, and standards.
4. Emotional Stability	The degree to which a person experiences the world as threatening and beyond his or her control.
5. Openness to Experience	The degree to which a person needs intellectual stimulation, change, and variety.

Table 4   Five-Factor Model

The model certainly has some limitations (Hogan et al., 2007); however, it presented a logical starting point for constructing a personality-based inventory for the workplace.

The original model for the HPI was the CPI (Gough, 1975). The feature the Hogans thought was most important about the CPI was that it was designed to predict important social outcomes. Such outcomes did not supplant the importance of formal psychometric considerations in the development of the CPI (or the HPI). Rather, social outcomes became an important design consideration that dramatically broadened the application of multidimensional personality inventories that heretofore were confined to clinical applications.

Both the FFM and the CPI were important influences in the development of the HPI. The FFM provided a useful framework for considering what should be measured. The CPI provided a perspective on measurement goals that was rooted in predicting important social outcomes. Predicting performance outcomes has been an overarching goal for everything that has been done in the development of the HPI.

Design Overview

The purpose here is not to recount decades of design work completed with respect to the HPI. The HPI Technical Manual (Hogan & Hogan, 2007) is the best available source for design information. In this section, we want to highlight some of the most important design facts about the HPI and relate them back to the role they play in improving leader performance.

First, the HPI was originally developed in 1976 and has undergone numerous revisions since that time. Millions of people have taken the inventory, and it has been validated in more than 400 jobs ranging from janitor to CEO. The key to the success of the HPI along this development timeline has been the meticulous maintenance of an extensive research archive. It is this archive that has contributed so much to our understanding of leader behavior that sets the HPI apart from any other Bright Side measure of personality. The archive is also at the core of Hogan's ability to construct norms based on virtually any segment of the workforce, including job types, industry, position level, and even culture.

Second, an increasingly important aspect of the inventory is the fact that there are no practical gender or ethnic differences in scale scores on the HPI. Leaders today come from all walks of life. In fact, many believe there is a leadership shortage on the horizon as baby boomers retire and the economy grows. Inventory biases arising from gender or ethnic differences simply are no longer acceptable. The HPI has led the way in neutralizing these factors when considering leader behavior.

Third, the assessment results from the HPI are available in a wide range of report formats. This scope is important because the report needs of a leader versus those of a coach are typically quite different. Leaders are usually not well versed in personality-based descriptions of behavior. They prefer reports that provide useful, behavioral descriptions of characteristics that allow them to directly consider the implications on performance in the workplace. Coaches, on the other hand, typically want to see assessment results in the most economical form possible. Their training and skill in interpretation of results mediates the need for text-heavy reports. The HPI (and all Hogan Inventories) offers a level of report flexibility that can meet these diverse needs.

Fourth, global portability continues to grow in importance in today's economy. The HPI is available in more than 40 languages. Further, in conjunction with a global network of partners, the norm data and validation research continues to expand to meet marketplace demands. While it is often the case that leaders are multilingual and fully capable of taking our inventories in English, the global portability of the HPI helps to ensure that leaders and coaches can use the inventory with confidence regardless of cultural boundaries.

From almost any design standpoint, the HPI has evolved to become the most versatile measure of Bright Side personality characteristics. The growth of the leadership development market has been an important factor in the evolution of the HPI. As this market has expanded, Hogan has put the necessary design resources in place to make sure the value that HPI data could bring to improving leader performance was at the highest possible level.

Structure

The structure of the HPI has remained relatively stable throughout its history. There are seven primary scales providing full coverage of the FFM. The primary scales comprise 41 subscales, which were originally called Homogenous Item Composites (HICs). The inventory includes a total of 206 items with additional research items that change over time and are used to keep the inventory content up to date. Table 5 from Hogan and Hogan (2007) provides a summary of the scale and subscale definitions with sample items.

Scale	Subscale	Subscale Description	Sample Item
Adjustment— Degree to which a person feels calm and self-accepting	Empathy	Concern for others	I believe people should have a second chance.
	Not anxious	Absence of worry	Deadlines don't bother me.
	No guilt	Absence of regret	I have few regrets about the past.
	Calmness	Not volatile	My coworkers think I am a calm person.
	Even tempered	Patience	I am a patient person.
	No complaints	Complacence	I'm not one to complain.
	Trusting	Belief in others	Most people are basically honest.
	Good attachment	Good relations with authority	In school, teachers liked me.
Ambition— Degree to which a person is leader-like, competitive, energetic, and socially confident	Competitive	Desire to win	I always play to win.
	Self-confident	Self-assurance	I expect to succeed at everything.
	Accomplishment	Personal effectiveness	When I fail at something, I try even harder the next time.
	Leadership	Leadership tendencies	I think I would enjoy positions of authority.
	Identity	Satisfaction with one's life	I am confident in my career choice.
	No social anxiety	Social self-confidence	I am pretty confident about my ability as a public speaker.
Sociability— Degree to which a person seems to need and/or enjoy interactions with others	Likes parties	Affability	I often go to parties in my free time.
	Likes crowds	Affiliativeness	I enjoy crowded sporting events.
	Experience seeking	Needs variety	I like a lot of variety in my life.
	Exhibitionistic	Showing off	I sometimes show off in front of others.
	Entertaining	Being witty and engaging	I always have a good joke to tell.
Interpersonal Sensitivity— Degree to which a person is seen as perceptive, tactful, and socially sensitive	Easy to live with	Being easy-going	I can get along with just about anybody.
	Sensitive	Being considerate	I am sensitive to others' feelings.
	Caring	Social sensitivity	I like helping people who need a break.
	Likes people	Companionable	I am actively involved in my community.
	No hostility	Tolerant	I would rather not criticize people, even when they need it.
Prudence— Degree to which a person is conscientious, conforming, and dependable	Moralistic	Self-righteousness	I always admit it when I make a mistake.
	Mastery	Diligent	I strive for perfection in everything I do.
	Virtuous	Perfectionism	It bothers me when people don't proofread their work.
	Not autonomous	Conformity	I never speak in a group where I have a differing opinion.
	Not spontaneous	Planful	Each morning, I know what I want to accomplish that day.
	Impulse control	Self-discipline	I would never buy the first car that I test drive.
	Avoids trouble	Professed probity	I avoid trouble at all costs.
Inquisitive— Degree to which a person is perceived as bright, creative, and interested in intellectual matters	Science ability	Analytical	Science is the key to our future.
	Curiosity	Investigative	I ask other people a lot of questions.
	Thrill seeking	Stimulus seeking	My friends think I am an adventurous person.
	Intellectual games	Playful cognition	I enjoy solving riddles.
	Generates ideas	Ideation fluency	I enjoy brainstorming.
	Culture	Cultural interests	I enjoy visiting historical landmarks.
Learning Approach— Degree to which a person enjoys academic activities and values education	Education	Academic talent	Doing well in school was important to me.
	Math ability	Numerical talent	Others depend on me to calculate the tip when dining out.
	Good memory	Powers of recall	I have a good memory.
	Reading	Verbal talent	I am always reading.

Table 5   HPI Primary Scales with Subscales

RELATIONSHIP BETWEEN THE HPI AND THE HDS

The HPI has an enormous degree of synergy with the HDS when it comes to understanding leader behavior. As a Bright Side measure of personality, the HPI might best be thought of as those personality characteristics that leaders rely upon on a day-to-day basis to achieve their goals. This view can be contrasted with the HDS as a Dark Side measure in that the HDS identifies the potential barriers that can get in the way of leaders' achieving their goals. This high-level view is quite accurate, but is insufficient when considering the synergies between Bright Side and Dark Side characteristics in understanding leader behavior.

The challenge in describing the synergies is that they are not simply linear. In the past, it has been suggested that the HDS simply measures extreme examples of the characteristics of the HPI. This perspective on the relationship between the HPI and the HDS is largely a linear one. For example, following this line of reasoning, the Excitable scale on the HDS is simply an extension of the Adjustment scale on the HPI. An elevation on the Excitable scale would go hand in hand with a low Adjustment score. This relationship can be described as a linear perspective because the behaviors associated with a high score on the Excitable scale are more extreme extensions of low Adjustment behaviors (i.e., an emotional outburst is an emotional outburst and an indicative behavior for an individual with a high Excitable score and a low Adjustment score).

This perspective is not wrong; it just oversimplifies the synergistic nature of the relationship between the HPI and the HDS. There are three reasons why it can be concluded that the linear perspective is an oversimplification of reality, especially when it comes to leader behavior. First, it has become apparent through literally thousands of feedback sessions, that some of the most valuable interpretive content comes from scale results that on the surface conflict with one another. For example, it is not uncommon to observe a leader with a high Excitable score together with a moderate to high Adjustment score. Behaviorally, a leader with this combination may have good emotional control under most circumstances, but exhibit highly emotional behaviors if the right triggers are present.

Second, the emergence of the importance of low HDS scores seriously compromises the linear view. If successful leader performance depends on certain HDS behaviors being present, then the HDS scales must measure something far more complex than the extremes of the HPI Scales. This notion is further complicated by variables associated with the Situational Context that can dictate, to a certain extent, the types or degree of HDS behaviors that could lead to successful performance.

Third, there is a compensatory component that must be recognized when considering synergies between the HPI and HDS. For example, a high score on the Learning Approach scale may help to compensate for a very low score on the Imaginative scale, or a moderate score on the Prudence scale may hold in check the risk-taking behaviors associated with a very low score on the Cautious scale. These are not unique combinations. They, and many others, are all too common when considering the combination of behaviors that could comprise a success profile.

What can be concluded about the relationship between the HPI and the HDS when it comes to understanding leader performance is that the linear perspective is a useful starting point. However, leaders and coaches need to treat this relationship very much like the layers of an onion. As the layers are peeled back in understanding leader performance, new layers reveal more and more about the relationship between these inventories. The value in using the HPI and the HDS in combination lies in the recognition that the whole is greater than the sum of its parts, and then being able to apply that knowledge to understand leader behavior.

LEADERSHIP AND COACHING IMPLICATIONS

The reputation a leader builds over time is based on the accumulated behaviors he or she exhibits in carrying out day-to-day activities. Reputations do not happen suddenly. They are based on past behavior. Reputations also do not happen in a vacuum. They only form because an observer has seen behaviors and labeled them and then passed along the labels to others. This point is important because it does not take many demonstrations of a behavior for a reputation to form. In fact, it is human nature to reduce people down to a relatively simple reputational view that dictates the way we interact with them.

Bright Side personality characteristics as measured by the HPI provide the foundation or the baseline for the formation of a leader's reputation. They are the characteristics most commonly encountered by others as they form an opinion of an individual. They are also the characteristics most commonly associated with reinforcing an individual's reputation, again because they are the ones most commonly encountered by others. This leads us to three important implications for leadership and coaching based on the personality characteristics measured by the HPI.

First, because these characteristics drive the preponderance of behavior that observers see on a regular basis, the associated reputational labels become quite enduring and stable over time. For example, a high Sociable person will regularly demonstrate high Sociable behaviors over time. Observers will regularly encounter these behaviors and likely form a relatively stable view of the individual as outgoing and easy to engage in an interaction.

Second, because the reputational labels that result from these characteristics are relatively stable and enduring, they can be difficult to change from a coaching perspective. That is not to say that they are impossible to change. It simply means that it will take considerable effort on the part of a leader to exhibit the new or different behaviors over a sufficient length of time for observers to change their view of the leader, thereby driving a reputation change.

Third, Dark Side personality characteristics as measured by the HDS are essentially deviations from the ongoing reputation of a leader. The reputational labels associated with these characteristics are more malleable than those driven by Bright Side characteristics. However, if behaviors driven by Dark Side characteristics are consistent with Bright Side characteristics, changing the reputational label may be just as or even more challenging than a label driven by the Bright Side alone. For example, consider a leader struggling with high Excitable behaviors. Changing his or her reputation for these behaviors will be more difficult for a leader who also happens to be low on the Adjustment scale in comparison to a leader who has a moderate Adjustment score. The behaviors and reputational label arising from a low Adjustment score are in many ways consistent with high Excitable behaviors, making reputational change much more difficult.

These three points underscore the importance of the HPI in improving leader performance. What follows is an overview of the leadership and coaching implications for Bright Side personality characteristics together with Dark Side characteristics. The overview is organized by Competency Domain. For each domain, we will consider the most salient combinations and then provide a coaching example from the previously discussed cases to illustrate how the coaching intervention might be refined based on Bright Side characteristics.

Intrapersonal Domain

The HPI scales most closely aligned with the Intrapersonal Domain are Adjustment and Prudence. These scales fit well in this domain because they have a strong impact on the way leaders approach work in general. They also happen to be the two scales that consistently have the highest validity coefficients across a wide range of job types. They have a very close association with the HDS scales in this domain (Excitable, Diligent, and Dutiful).

The Adjustment scale, depending on how high or low an individual scores, can have a significant impact on all HDS scales. Low scorers tend to have inflated HDS scores, while high scorers tend to have depressed HDS scores. The reason for this impact is likely due to the self-accepting aspect of the Adjustment scale and the way that it is manifested by people in responding to HDS items.

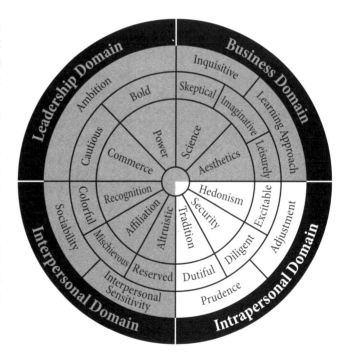

Aside from the broad impact that Adjustment scores can have on HDS scores, there are some very specific implications for the associated HDS scales in the Intrapersonal Domain. The most salient among these implications is for the Excitable scale. The Adjustment scale and the Excitable scale are highly correlated (−.71). They are more strongly correlated than any other combination of HPI and HDS scales. Behaviorally, this strong correlation has significant implications from a coaching standpoint. When the two scales tell a consistent story, it is virtually certain that the negative behaviors associated with either high or low Excitable scores will be observed in the workplace, and making significant changes to improve a leader's reputation will be challenging.

The relationships with the Diligent and Dutiful scales are not nearly as strong. With respect to the Diligent scale, Adjustment behaviors could cause a leader to be more picky (low Adjustment, high Diligent) or even less concerned about details (high Adjustment, low Diligent). The relationship of Adjustment behaviors with the Dutiful scale is not so clear cut. The worrisome aspect of a leader with a low Adjustment score is likely most impactful with this relationship, causing the high Dutiful leader to worry even more about pleasing others, while moderating the tendency to dismiss authority figures that is common to low Dutiful leaders.

The Prudence scale is closely related to Excitable (−.36) and Diligent (.31). Prudence is probably most relevant for a leader with a high Excitable score. Here, high Prudence may help put controls on Excitable behaviors while leaders with a low score on the Prudence scale may have few natural control mechanisms. The Prudence scale's relationship to the Diligent scale is all about the consistency of the scores. Leaders with high Prudence and high Diligent scores are at great risk for being labeled as micromanagers. In contrast, leaders with low Prudence and low Diligent scores can earn a reputation for being careless, disorganized, and incapable of managing details.

On the surface, the Prudence scale does not have a strong relationship with the Dutiful scale (.14). In practice, this relationship deserves a closer look, especially at the low end of scores for both scales. Low Dutiful leaders often fail to keep others informed and tend to act independent of the wishes of those in authority. When these behaviors are combined with low scores on the Prudence scale, they can be dramatically exacerbated. In fact, this is the combination that often puts low Dutiful behaviors on the radar screen of superiors because low Prudence behavior can lead to greater risk taking, and risk taking without keeping superiors informed can lead to disaster.

Leveraging HPI Results in a Coaching Program (Case 1—Rex)

The Prudence-Dutiful relationship provides a good example of leveraging HPI results in a coaching program. We selected Rex (Case 1—Rex, Vice President of Sales, page 88) as a good example of this relationship. The following is Rex's HDS profile summary:

	Rex's Situational Summary

Rex's Situational Summary
Rex worked in a small company as vice president of sales. In his role, he had considerable autonomy and freedom to make decisions. The company was acquired by a much larger, well-established company with rules, processes, and procedures that often accompany a large bureaucracy. Rex's willingness to take risks and make fast, independent decisions runs counter to the culture that exists in the new company. This issue could be exacerbated by his tendency to follow his own agenda.

Dimension	Score	Percentile	Description
Excitable	50		Rex is very self-confident to the point of being an arrogant leader (Bold—95%). He is quite willing to take risks (Cautious—10% and Mischievous—90%). He tends to work his own agenda (Leisurely—82%), and prefers to operate independently without a lot of close supervision (Dutiful—5%).
Skeptical	67		
Cautious	10		
Reserved	45		
Leisurely	82		
Bold	95		
Mischievous	90		
Colorful	75		
Imaginative	70		
Diligent	30		
Dutiful	5		

0 10 20 30 40 50 60 70 80 90 100

Rex's Dutiful score is at 5 percent, so it is reasonable to assume that he enjoys operating with considerable autonomy. His Cautious score (10%) and Mischievous score (90%) suggest that he could test limits and take considerable risks in his decision-making. The coaching program outlined in Chapter 20 on page 421 for Rex has a heavy emphasis on keeping his superiors informed including the establishment of Critical Success Factors (CSFs) and a clear set of reporting guidelines. These steps will undoubtedly be helpful to Rex and improve his chances for success. In addition, Rex's Prudence score (16%) suggests some potential refinements to the coaching intervention that might be worthwhile. The following is a summary of the subscale data associated with Rex's Prudence score.

Subscale	Item Score	Definition	Sample Item
Moralistic	3/5	Self-righteousness	I always admit it when I make a mistake.
Mastery	3/4	Diligent	I strive for perfection in everything I do.
Virtuous	3/5	Perfectionism	It bothers me when people don't proofread their work.
Not autonomous	0/3	Conformity	I never speak in a group where I have a differing opinion.
Not spontaneous	3/4	Planful	Each morning, I know what I want to accomplish that day.
Impulse control	2/5	Self-discipline	I would never buy the first car that I test drive.
Avoids trouble	1/5	Professed probity	I avoid trouble at all costs.

Rex's low Prudence score clearly reinforces the importance of making sure he keeps his superiors informed, using an intervention that includes identifying CSFs and a structure for reporting back to his superiors. The intervention would benefit from a refinement that includes a mechanism for risk management in his decision-making. Two of the subscales, Impulse Control (2/5) and Avoids Trouble (1/5), suggest that Rex may not make the best decisions from time to time, or at least that his decisions may be somewhat impulsive and occasionally get him into trouble. To mitigate this issue, it would be worthwhile to establish clear decision-making limits for Rex with a clear process for obtaining approval when the impact of his decisions could potentially exceed established limits. This addition to the coaching intervention would slow Rex's decision-making down and force a degree of reflection (Impulse Control subscale). It would also help Rex avoid problems with high-risk decisions by including an approval loop (Avoids Trouble subscale).

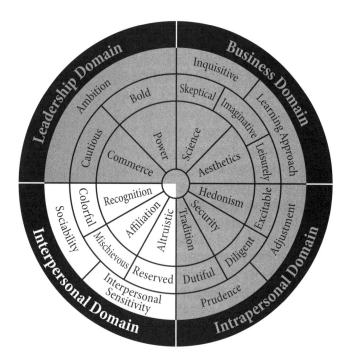

Interpersonal Domain

The HPI scales most closely aligned with the Interpersonal Domain are Interpersonal Sensitivity and Sociability. These scales fit well in this domain because they have a strong impact on the leader's interpersonal style. In fact, using these two scales, one can very quickly sense the way the leader communicates in general. The HDS scales in this domain (Reserved, Mischievous, and Colorful) also have a strong communication component to them and dovetail nicely with the HPI scales.

Of the three HDS scales, the Interpersonal Sensitivity scale has the strongest relationship with the Reserved scale (−.50). This relationship is most problematic from a coaching standpoint for leaders who have high Reserved scores together with low Interpersonal Sensitivity scores. High Reserved leaders are seriously challenged from a communication standpoint. When they are also low on the Interpersonal Sensitivity scale, their communication style is very blunt and direct. Plus, they are imperceptive when it comes to sensing how their communication efforts come across to others. Thus, coaching efforts need to account for the quality of communication as well as the quantity.

The relationships between the Interpersonal Sensitivity scale and the Mischievous and Colorful scales are empirically much weaker than those found for the relationship with the Reserved scale. However, there are some specific implications for the HDS scales, particularly when the leader's score on the Interpersonal Sensitivity scale is low. High Mischievous leaders are often known for testing limits and challenging the status quo. When combined with a low score on the Interpersonal Sensitivity score, the potential exists for leaders to become interpersonally mischievous. They will be provocative in their statements. They will encourage discord in meetings. They will even toss out controversial topics just to get people to argue with one another. These behaviors have obvious implications for a leader's reputation when they are regularly displayed.

The impact of a low Interpersonal Sensitivity score on the Colorful scale is not unlike that found for the Reserved scale. The primary difference is that high Colorful behaviors often occur with high frequency. The lack of a filter that accompanies low Interpersonal Sensitivity behavior presents a tough coaching challenge. Not only might Colorful behaviors occur often, but they may be exhibited with little sensitivity to the impact they have on others.

High scores on the Interpersonal Sensitivity scale basically play a mitigating role with respect to Reserved, Mischievous, and Colorful behaviors. Behaviors at the high end of this scale can serve to soften the impact of the high-end HDS behaviors. Higher Interpersonal Sensitivity behaviors can also influence others to be a bit more tolerant of the high-end HDS behaviors. When these HDS scales are low, leaders run the risk of being perceived as a "nice person, but . . . ." As is usually the case, what follows the "but" contains the real information about the leader's reputation. For example, a low Reserved individual with high scores on the Interpersonal Sensitivity scale might be thought of as a "nice person, but not really tough enough for a leadership role."

Scores on the Sociability scale can impact the HDS scales at either the high end or the low end. High Reserved leaders who are low on the Sociability scale will essentially be socially withdrawn and tend to completely isolate themselves. It is rare to come across a high Reserved leader who also scores high on the Sociability scale. When it does occur, the Reserved behaviors of the leader tend to take a backseat in social situations, but when they are exhibited, the leader will come across as cold and callous with respect to people or the decisions that impact people.

Sociability tends to heighten the degree to which Mischievous behaviors are observed by others. When a leader scores low on both scales, he or she will lack the ability to be interesting and engaging from the perspective of others. When the scores on both scales are high, the Mischievous behaviors are more likely to be displayed publicly because of the need for the leader to engage in social interaction. The high end may be the more problematic of the two relationships mainly because public demonstration of mischievous behaviors is likely to draw considerable negative attention from superiors.

Low scores on both the Sociability and Colorful scales are more problematic for a leader than they might first appear. This is the gray-spot-on-the-gray-wall phenomenon in which an individual can go virtually unnoticed. It will definitely be career limiting in terms of project and promotion opportunities. From a coaching standpoint, the combination of behaviors emerging from these scales will be quite challenging because the leaders will find the alternative behaviors to be draining when they are asked to demonstrate them. The challenge is vastly different when the leader scores high on both scales, which is similar to turning the volume control to the maximum setting. The high Colorful behaviors become magnified in terms of frequency and the attention they draw. The leader will tend to suck the oxygen out of a room, and the coaching challenge will need to focus heavily on dialing back the volume control.

Leveraging HPI Results in a Coaching Program (Case 3—Robert)

The Sociability-Colorful relationship provides a good example of leveraging HPI results in a coaching program. We selected Robert (Case 3—Robert, Design Engineer, page 92) as a good example of this relationship. The following is Robert's HDS profile summary:

Robert's Situational Summary			
Robert is a design engineer for a manufacturer of commercial aircraft electronic components. He has worked primarily as an individual contributor and was known for getting things done. His hard work resulted in a promotion to project leader on a cross-functional team. His new role will be highly demanding and require effective leadership skills that will be a challenge for his quiet, reserved nature, and tendency to fade into the background in social situations.			
Dimension	**Score**	**Percentile**	**Description**
Excitable	35		Robert is a hard worker who seems very calm and even-tempered under pressure. People view him as task focused with little interest in engaging with people (Reserved—98%). He tends to work long hours and is not bothered by the fact that his attention to detail spills over into work for others (Diligent—80%), which has earned him a reputation as a grinder who gets things done.
Skeptical	50		
Cautious	75		
Reserved	98		
Leisurely	80		
Bold	55		
Mischievous	40		
Colorful	30		
Imaginative	62		
Diligent	80		
Dutiful	30		

```
0   10  20  30  40  50  60  70  80  90  100
```

Robert's Colorful score (30%) is only moderately low, but he has a very low Sociability score (9%). Clearly, Robert's promotion was based on his hard work and ability to get things done, rather than on his leadership skills. Such promotions are not uncommon in fields like engineering where people are task focused and interpersonal skills receive minimal attention. Unfortunately, this will change for Robert in his new role for two reasons. First, as a project leader he will need to interact with others a great deal more. Second, his next promotion will likely be much more dependent on his interpersonal skills and his ability to get noticed in his role as a project leader. The following is a summary of the subscale data associated with Robert's Sociability score.

Subscale	Item Score	Definition	Sample Item
Likes parties	2/5	Affability	I often go to parties in my free time.
Likes crowds	0/4	Affiliativeness	I enjoy crowded sporting events.
Experience seeking	3/6	Needs variety	I like a lot of variety in my life.
Exhibitionistic	2/5	Showing off	I sometimes show off in front of others.
Entertaining	0/4	Being witty and engaging	I always have a good joke to tell.

The coaching program outlined for Robert in Chapter 17 covers a number of ways Robert can increase his visibility and demonstrate a more forceful interpersonal presence when dealing with others. His very low Sociability score raises a definite concern about his willingness to actually take steps to engage people in any fashion. His low Sociability score in general and his very low subscale scores for all except the Experience Seeking subscale (3/6) suggest that Robert finds interacting with people to be physically draining. One way to overcome this hurdle is to acknowledge the work it takes for Robert to engage people and to give him a way to recharge when he does have to engage them. One solution could be a simple point system in which Robert starts each day with 100 points. The coach could assign a point value to the various types of interpersonal encounters associated with the coaching tips. Over the course of the day, Robert could deduct points from his total as he engages in interpersonal activities. When the 100 points are used up, Robert would be encouraged to engage in a quiet-time activity that allows him to recharge. Over time, Robert will learn to use this approach as a mental exercise in which he engages in interpersonal activities and recharges as needed. The approach accounts for the draining nature of high Sociability activities and the need for Robert to recover from them.

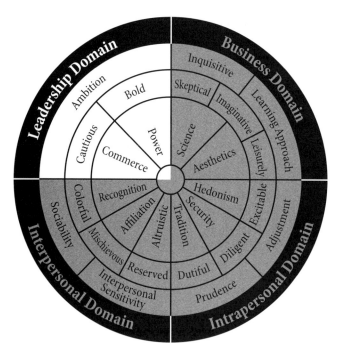

Leadership Domain

The HPI scale most closely aligned with the Leadership Domain is Ambition. It is an interesting scale because it essentially defines the Leadership Domain from an HPI or a Bright Side standpoint. It even contains a subscale that is focused entirely on leadership that provides an excellent source of information on an individual's interest in leading others. The HDS scales in this domain (Bold and Cautious) are also strongly tied to leadership in that they speak to self-confidence and the way an individual conducts business in a leadership role.

The Ambition scale has a strong empirical relationship with the Cautious scale (−.68) and only a moderate relationship with the Bold scale (.14). However, the empirical relationships with the HDS scales are not nearly as important to performance in this domain as is the actual score on the Ambition scale itself. Simply put, individuals with higher scores on the Ambition scale tend to gravitate toward leadership roles, while those with lower scores tend to be content in the role of individual contributor or team member. It should not come as a surprise that in coaching leaders, it is far more common for leaders to have higher rather than lower Ambition scores. This information is important from a coaching standpoint because high Ambition scores are nearly a constant for those in leadership roles and likely would not provide a great deal of information from a Bright Side standpoint in refining a coaching intervention.

The same cannot be said for leaders with lower Ambition scores. Lower scores have very definite leadership implications and implications for coaching interventions associated with the Bold or Cautious scales. Furthermore, the subscale configuration comes much more into play when coaching a leader who has a low score on the Ambition scale because the subscales add greatly to the overall interpretation of the scale. A leader who has low scores on the Competitive or Leadership subscales may not be interested in a leadership role at all and would likely benefit more from career counseling than coaching. A leader who is low on the Accomplishment or Identity subscales may simply be in the wrong leadership role and again benefit from career counseling. However, low scores on the Self-confident or No Social Anxiety subscales have direct implications for coaching interventions on Bold or Cautious behaviors.

A low score on the Self-confident subscale suggests a leader who is not self-assured and may be reluctant to take action. A low Bold score would be consistent with a low Self-confident score and indicate the need for an intervention centered on building self-confidence. A leader with a low Self-confident score and a high Bold score may engage in blaming behavior when things go wrong and avoid taking personal responsibility.

The Cautious scale is associated with risk taking. A low Self-confident score would reinforce a high Cautious score and bring decision-making to a near stop. In contrast, a low Cautious score would suggest a willingness to take significant risks and the low Self-confident behavior would act as a governor, helping to slow risk-taking behavior.

The No Social Anxiety subscale is tied to social confidence. Leaders with low No Social Anxiety scores tend to lack confidence in front of people, especially when the leaders are in front of groups. This subscale has minimal impact on Cautious behavior associated with decision-making. However, a high Cautious leader who has a low No Social Anxiety score will have an even greater propensity to shy away from activities involving groups.

The implications of the No Social Anxiety subscale for the Bold scale are far more profound. Leaders who score high on the Bold scale with low scores on No Social Anxiety will avoid the public bravado that often results in a reputation for being arrogant. Leaders who score low on the Bold scale with low scores on No Social Anxiety run an even greater risk of being labeled as individuals who lack self-confidence to the point it could be seriously career limiting.

It is important to point out that the subscale-level relations described in this section are derived largely from the observations of coaches and not from empirical data. Subscales are great behavioral indicators, but because they employ only three to six items, they are not nearly as stable (or reliable) as scale-level data. From a coaching standpoint, their best use is in reinforcing refinements to an intervention, rather than as the data relied upon to drive an intervention.

Leveraging HPI Results in a Coaching Program (Janis—Case 5)

The Ambition-Bold relationship provides a good example of leveraging HPI results in a coaching program. We selected Janis (Case 5—Janis, Customer Service

Manager, page 96) as a good example of this relationship. The following is Janis's HDS profile summary.

Janis's Situational Summary
Janis is a newly promoted customer service manager who works for a software company. Her long-time regional manager was recently promoted, and her new manager is described as young, hard-charging, and very demanding. Janis is very conscientious and works hard to keep everybody happy. Her new manager will likely test her ability to push back, or she will find herself challenged to keep up with his demands. Her lack of self-confidence will also be readily apparent to her new manager.

Dimension	Score	Percentile	Description
Excitable	60		Janis is a high-energy person who does not over-promise (Cautious—75%) and is very approachable (Reserved—15%). She lacks confidence (Bold—10%) but makes up for it through preparation and attention to detail (Diligent—85%). She is known for her loyalty and willingness to go the extra mile when it comes to protecting the reputation of the company and her manager (Dutiful—80%).
Skeptical	10		
Cautious	75		
Reserved	15		
Leisurely	20		
Bold	10		
Mischievous	40		
Colorful	30		
Imaginative	62		
Diligent	85		
Dutiful	80		

0   10   20   30   40   50   60   70   80   90   100

Janis has a very low Bold score (10%). She has been recently promoted to customer service manager, a promotion that likely is due to hard work and a tendency to under-promise and over-deliver. Her new manager is described as a hard-charger and, in contrast to Janis's profile, likely has a high Bold score. Although Janis probably can continue on a success path that relies upon her hard work, the real questions about her performance will start to arise if she is considered for a higher level position, or if the demands of her current job start to exceed her ability to deal with them through an excess of diligence. Her Ambition score (33%) falls in the low to moderate range, but the subscales suggest that there is more to the story. The following is a summary of the subscale data associated with Janis's Ambition score.

Subscale	Item Score	Definition	Sample Item
Competitive	5/5	Desire to win	I always play to win.
Self-confident	0/3	Self-assurance	I expect to succeed at everything.
Accomplishment	5/6	Personal effectiveness	When I fail at something, I try even harder the next time.
Leadership	6/6	Leadership tendencies	I think I would enjoy positions of authority.
Identity	2/3	Satisfaction with one's life	I am confident in my career choice.
No Social Anxiety	2/6	Social self-confidence	I am pretty confident about my ability as a public speaker.

The first aspect of her Ambition score which should be noted is that Janis is high on both Competitiveness (5/5) and Leadership (6/6). This suggests that she very much enjoys being a leader and the challenges that come with the role. Second, she is very low on the Self-confident subscale, which is consistent with her low Bold score. The coaching program outlined on page 306 has a clear emphasis on building her self-confidence, which will be extremely important as she grows into her role as customer service manager. It is interesting that the program includes a suggestion that Janis get involved with Toastmasters as a safe way to get in front of groups and practice assertiveness. Her somewhat low score on the No Social Anxiety subscale (2/6) indicates that this would be an ideal forum because it would challenge her to become more effective in group situations where she is the least self-confident.

Business Domain

The HPI scales most closely aligned with the Business Domain are Inquisitive and Learning Approach. These scales fit well in this domain because they have a strong impact on the leader's ability to use information in problem-solving and decision-making. The HDS scales in this domain (Leisurely, Imaginative, and Skeptical) also play a strong role in problem-solving and decision-making. These scales combine to provide a clear picture of the way in which individuals processes information commonly associated with leadership roles.

The Learning Approach scale has often been described as a surrogate for cognitive

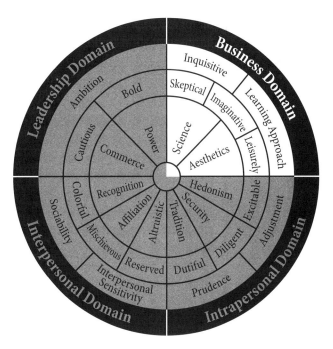

ability because high scores tend to align with success in formal education. Interestingly, the Learning Approach scale does not have a particularly strong relationship with any of the HDS scales. The implications for this scale have more to do with a leader's thinking regarding specific issues driven by the HDS scales rather than the way thinking actually manifests itself in the workplace. For example, leaders who have high Leisurely scores tend to be driven by their own personal agendas. If they happen to have high scores on the Learning Approach scale, it is likely that their personal agendas were formulated to some extent through a more formal process of learning, such as books, business publications, seminars, and so on. In contrast, a leader who has a high Leisurely score and a low Learning Approach score likely relies more on experience-based learning in formulating a personal agenda.

At the high end, all three of the HDS scales associated with the Business Domain—Leisurely (indicating a personal agenda), Imaginative (indicating creative ideas), and Skeptical (indicating a need to evaluate ideas)—involve taking strong positions on issues. From a coaching standpoint, the Learning Approach score can add a degree of understanding in terms of how those strong positions were formed and the extent to which their formation might be biased in the direction of formal education or experience. A coaching refinement that can add value here is making sure that when the leaders take strong positions they are not operating on biased information that resulted from their learning approach. For example, a high Skeptical leader who tends to be quite negative regarding the company's strategic direction because of past experience (indicated by a low Learning Approach score) might become less negative if encouraged to perform due diligence around how that strategic direction was formulated (that is, adopt the behavior of someone with a high Learning Approach score).

At the low end, all three of the HDS scales associated with the Business Domain involve taking weak positions on issues—Leisurely (indicating no personal agenda), Imaginative (indicating few ideas), and Skeptical (indicating the naïve acceptance of ideas). Challenging leaders to get outside their comfort zones from a Learning Approach standpoint is a coaching refinement that can result in strengthening their willingness to take stronger positions. For example, a leader with a low Learning Approach score and a low Imaginative score might be more willing to offer new ideas on a topic if encouraged to get outside the experience comfort zone and do more formal learning around the topic.

The Inquisitive scale is about being open to the ideas of others. While it can be about a leader's own ideation, thinking of it as openness to the ideas of others tends to capture a better picture of the behaviors manifested at either end of the scale than thinking of it as ideation. This perspective also adds tremendous value because of the implications for all three HDS scales in this domain.

Inquisitive scores can impact Leisurely behaviors because of the personal agenda component of the Leisurely scale. Leaders with high Leisurely scores tend to have a firmly established personal agenda. If they score high on the Inquisitive scale, they may be more open to considering or at least hearing the positions of others. Having low Inquisitive scores can indicate the opposite behavior—the leader may be closed to alternatives. Leaders with low Leisurely scores tend to lack a personal agenda. These leaders, if they also have high Inquisitive scores, tend to be mesmerized by the myriad ideas offered by others. A leader with both low Leisurely and low Inquisitive scores simply misses the possibilities that may be offered by others.

If the Inquisitive scale is about openness to the ideas of others, the Imaginative scale is about personal ideation. High Inquisitive in conjunction with high Imaginative create a flood of ideas often resulting in a leader's thinking being labeled stream-of-consciousness. From a coaching standpoint, these leaders need to learn to control their creativity and manage their willingness to put almost any idea on the table. High Inquisitive accompanied by low Imaginative represents a real coaching opportunity. Leaders with this type of profile can be encouraged to build off the ideas of others to enhance their own reputation for being creative.

Low Inquisitive, low Imaginative leaders often get labeled as "not being strategic." This designation can be a death knell to career progress because being strategic (whatever that is) is nearly synonymous with leadership potential. Low Inquisitive, high Imaginative leaders tend to be enamored with their own ideas and have disdain for the ideas of others. In either case, an effective coaching refinement is to focus on increasing the willingness of the leader to be open to the ideas of others. For low Imaginative leaders, it will bring new ideas to the table. For high Imaginative leaders, it will demonstrate a willingness to consider alternatives to their own thinking.

The Inquisitive score may not have as dramatic an impact on Skeptical behaviors as it does on the other two HDS scales in this domain. However, Inquisitive behaviors can significantly alter the perspective others have for Skeptical behaviors. Leaders with high Inquisitive and high Skeptical scores may listen to the ideas of others and simply take pot shots at them, resulting in the leaders' appearing even more negative than they might otherwise. Leaders with low Inquisitive scores and high Skeptical scores may appear unwilling to even entertain the ideas of others which can add to a reputation for being close-minded with a stubborn adherence to a negative outlook. In either case, high Skeptical behaviors, particularly those related to ideas, can be magnified because of a leader's Inquisitive score.

Low Skeptical leaders tend to have reputations for being a bit naïve. Their Inquisitive score may dictate the direction (or bias) of their naiveté. High Inquisitive behaviors may cause them to be excessively open to new ideas, even ideas that have little or no chance for success. Low Inquisitive behaviors may cause them to ask even fewer questions than they might otherwise ask about new ideas, again resulting in ideas being implemented with little or no chance for success. In both cases, Inquisitive behaviors impact the way Skeptical behaviors are manifested with respect to new ideas, processes, or the way work is completed.

Leveraging HPI Results in a Coaching Program (Case 8—Courtney)

The Inquisitive–Imaginative relationship provides a good example of leveraging HPI results in a coaching program. We selected Courtney (Case 8—Courtney, Assistant Operations Manager, page 102) as a good example of this relationship. The following is Courtney's HDS profile summary.

Courtney's Situational Summary				
Courtney successfully completed a plant start-up in Mexico for an electronics manufacturing company. Despite being considered a high potential leader, her superiors had lingering questions about her leadership ability. As a result, she was given the role of assistant operations manager working for one of the best plant managers in the company. Courtney's new manager is known for her high standards, careful attention to detail, hard work, and putting in long hours.				
Dimension	**Score**	**Percentile**		**Description**
Excitable	30			Courtney is an energetic leader who is known for her confidence in taking on any challenge (Bold—95%). She tends to use her charm and charisma to get her way (Mischievous—90%). She also tends to grab high-profile assignments to keep herself in the limelight (Colorful—80%). Her superiors have put her on the fast track but have some concerns about her ability to be a team player.
Skeptical	50			
Cautious	20			
Reserved	25			
Leisurely	30			
Bold	95			
Mischievous	90			
Colorful	80			
Imaginative	85			
Diligent	5			
Dutiful	10			

```
0   10   20   30   40   50   60   70   80   90   100
```

Courtney has a high Imaginative score (85%), which likely contributed to her ability to creatively solve problems in a plant start-up environment. It may even have contributed to her being considered a high-potential employee, as it is not uncommon for leaders who offer new ideas to be thought of as strategic with potential to do a job at the next level. Her new manager appears to be very practical, with a success formula rooted in hard work and with a strong detail orientation. The following is a summary of the subscale data associated with Courtney's Inquisitive score.

Subscale	Item Score	Definition	Sample Item
Science ability	5/5	Analytical	Science is the key to our future.
Curiosity	3/3	Investigative	I ask other people a lot of questions.
Thrill seeking	2/5	Stimulus seeking	My friends think I am an adventurous person.
Intellectual games	3/3	Playful cognition	I enjoy solving riddles.
Generates ideas	5/5	Ideation fluency	I enjoy brainstorming.
Culture	4/4	Cultural interests	I enjoy visiting historical landmarks.

Courtney's Inquisitive score (95%) is very high. Plus, she scores very high on all of the subscales with the lone exception of Thrill Seeking (2/5). Her Inquisitive score is very consistent with her high Imaginative score. When the scores on both the Inquisitive and Imaginative scales are very high, the leader is at great risk for developing a reputation for stream-of-consciousness thinking. Perhaps the most salient behaviors associated with Courtney's profile are the propensity to become enamored with every new idea and a willingness to put new ideas on the table with little or no due diligence with respect to their feasibility. These behaviors would probably be in stark contrast to the behaviors Courtney's new manager is likely to manifest and expect from others. The coaching program outlined on page 363 focuses on helping Courtney control her ideation and willingness to put ideas on the table. The contrast between Courtney, with a high Inquisitive score, and her new manager, who appears to be somewhat practical, is stark. A useful refinement to the coaching intervention for Courtney would be for her to develop an idea filter that mirrors the one used by her manager. This refinement would start with helping Courtney to understand the filter used by her manager in evaluating ideas and then encouraging Courtney to use the same type of filter to evaluate ideas prior to presenting or discussing them with her manager.

SUMMARY

The HPI is the industry leader in measuring Bright Side personality characteristics. When combined with the HDS, results from the HPI often have profound implications for leadership and coaching. In this chapter, we explored many of those implications. While it is nearly impossible to account for the implications of all combinations and permutations of these inventories, especially in light of variables in the Situational Context, we highlighted many of those that could drive coaching refinements. The case studies used throughout the chapter further demonstrate how these refinements can be put into practice. The HPI and the HDS clearly have a powerful synergistic relationship. Combining assessment results from these inventories can enhance any effort to improve leader performance.

CHAPTER 22

COACHING AND THE IN SIDE

INTRODUCTION

The Motives, Values, Preferences Inventory (MVPI) is a measure of values and interests that are motivational concepts. The MVPI is closely related to measures of personality because it taps an aspect of one's identity or self-concept. It differs primarily in item content which tends to be highly transparent and overt in terms of asking about one's specific preferences or interests. The debate as to whether or not interest inventories are, in fact, personality measures dates back as far as the inventories themselves. Holland (1973) specifically addressed the relationship between interests and personality:

> If vocational interests are construed as an expression of personality, then they represent the expression of personality in work, school subjects, hobbies, recreational activities, and preferences. In short, what we have called "vocational interests" is simply another aspect of personality. (p. 7)

To fully appreciate the role of the MVPI in leadership development and in improving leader performance, it is important to have a clear understanding of what is actually being measured by the inventory. One of the best descriptions can be found in two short paragraphs from the MVPI Technical Manual (Hogan & Hogan, 2010):

> [...] when people respond to items on psychological inventories, they behave much as they do during other forms of social interaction. People use their responses to tell others about their idealized self-concept—about how they would like to be regarded by other people. Here, however, we come to a crucial difference between personality and interest inventories. Personality measures ask about a person's typical response in various situations, but interest measures ask about a person's preferred activities, roles, and associates. Interest measures allow people to describe themselves as they would like to be. Thus, interest inventories get much closer to the content of a person's self-concept than do personality inventories.
>
> Interest inventories also allow people to describe themselves in a manner more consistent with their behavior when interacting with strangers. Consider a conversation between two people who have just met in an informal social situation. In response to the inquiry "Tell me about yourself," a person is more likely to say "I like tennis" than "In most situations, I am highly competitive." People are accustomed to talking about themselves in terms of interests; interests are at the core of the language of self-description. (p. 4–5)

The notion that the MVPI is a measure of idealized self-concept is absolutely essential to understanding how this inventory can contribute to improving the performance of a leader. We will return to this role when discussing the implications of the inventory in leadership and coaching. Prior to discussing these implications, it is important to consider the history of the MVPI, some design features, its structure, and its relationship to the HDS.

HISTORY

The 10-scale MVPI taxonomy dates back to a number of key historical figures in psychology, including Spranger (1928); Allport (1961); Murray (1938); Allport, Vernon, and Lindzey (1960); and Holland (1966, 1985). The work of these individuals contributed directly to defining the motives that make up the MVPI taxonomy. Hogan and Hogan (2010) provide a full discussion of the contributions these authors made to the thinking that went in to the inventory and need not be repeated here. However, there are some takeaways from this rich history that should be mentioned.

First, the inventory evolved from a century of work addressing the measurement of interests. On one hand, this is a strength of the inventory because it underscores the importance of the topic and the thoroughness of the measurement research upon which it is based. On the other hand, there is some baggage that comes with such a rich history in that it is accompanied by preconceptions about what is being measured. For example, most people have taken an interest inventory at one time or another, and despite the fact that the MVPI is a unique inventory, there are those who would lump it in with the interest inventories of the past.

Second, the 10-scale taxonomy is unique in the literature. Unlike the HPI, for example, there is no counterpart to the Five-Factor Model (FFM) for motives. The 10 scales that make up the MVPI were rationally derived from the work of previous researchers. Each motive can be traced back to the work of several other authors, but no previous author has proposed the taxonomy that is used in the MVPI.

Finally, and most important, the measurement goals for the MVPI are historically unique. The MVPI permits an evaluation of the fit between an individual and the culture of an organization. This goal is important because of the potential impact fit can have on the success of an individual in a particular organization. No matter how talented or hardworking an individual may be, if his or her values are incongruent with the culture of an organization, there is a strong likelihood that the individual will not be successful in the organization.

Beyond the evaluation of fit, the MVPI is unique among the interest inventories currently available in that it directly assesses a person's motives. All other interest measures allow inferences about a person's motives on the basis of expressed occupational choices. The MVPI provides a direct measure of what precisely motivates an individual (e.g., money, security, fun, etc.). This is a crucial point when considering MVPI results in improving leader performance. Knowing what motivates an individual can add enormous leverage to a program designed to improve performance if that information is properly incorporated into the program.

All of these are important takeaways when considering the history of the MVPI. They serve as a foundation for many of the design decisions that went into the inventory. They also serve as a reminder of how unique the MVPI is in terms of what it measures and the importance of that information in improving leader performance.

DESIGN OVERVIEW

The MVPI is still in its infancy in comparison to many interest inventories. Some of these inventories, such as the Strong Interest Inventory (Campbell & Holland, 1972), have been around for decades and have been fixtures in the educational system helping students with career decisions. Even Holland's model, which is the foundation for many interest inventories, has been around for nearly 50 years (Hogan & Hogan, 2010). Perhaps what sets the MVPI apart is the way it is being used in leadership development programs. There are a number of design features that have helped the MVPI make the transition from a tool primarily associated with the early career search process to one that can add value in improving leader performance and in shaping organizational culture.

First, the MVPI was developed and validated with the adult working population. Like the HPI and HDS, the MVPI has an extensive research archive, which allows for the construction of norms based on virtually any segment of the workforce, including job types, industry, position level, and even culture. Also like the HPI and HDS, there are no practical gender or ethnic differences in scale scores on the MVPI, and it is available in multiple languages with excellent global portability. These features are important requirements that must be met in order for an inventory to have practical application at the leadership level in the emerging global economy.

Second, the MVPI is structured around face-valid content. Leaders know exactly what they are responding to when they answer MVPI items. They are eager to tell you what motivates them. They are honest in their responses with virtually no faking. The results produce very few concerns for the person who completed the inventory, making them of great value for opening a feedback conversation or breaking down any defensiveness that might exist as the result of assessment anxiety.

Third, MVPI results are structured around 10 motives, a construction that is extremely important and unique in the realm of interest inventories. It allows for individual results to be compared to group results. It allows group results to be compared to one another. It even allows for culture building through the selection of team members. At the organization level, the MVPI can help an organization gauge the motives that drive its culture, consider the fit among team members based on their driving motives, and build the culture based on a set of desired motives. At the individual level, the MVPI can provide leaders with important insights into their motives, how they fit with other team members, and how their motives might be leveraged to improve personal satisfaction.

Fourth, the test-retest reliability for the inventory is impressive at both short-term and long-term intervals. For fewer than three months, test-retest reliability ranges from .71 (Power scale) to .85 (Aesthetics scale). Long-term stability ranges from .70 (Hedonism and Tradition scales) to .83 (Security scale). These results demonstrate that the motives assessed by the MVPI are relatively enduring. This consistency is important from a leadership development standpoint because it suggests that what motivates a leader early in his or her career likely plays a motivational role at later stages in the leader's career. Furthermore, given the pace at which Situational Context variables change in today's organizations, the fit between a leader and an organizational culture could be quite a dynamic variable.

These are important design features, but perhaps the most important feature is the way the information can be used to help leaders improve performance. This feature is often overlooked because it is such a simple idea that just seems to unfold naturally when MVPI results are available in conjunction with HPI and HDS results. The MVPI provides a motivational road map for inspiring leaders to make changes that will improve their performance. While this motivational roadmap may not have been a true design feature when the MVPI was initially created, it has become one of the most important design features as the inventory has become more widely used in the leadership development space.

Structure

The MVPI consists of 200 items in the form of statements to which a respondent indicates "agree," "uncertain," or "disagree." This format is different from the forced choice format of the HPI and HDS in which responses are confined to "true" or "false." There are a total of 10 scales, each with 20 items. The items are rationally derived exemplars of likes, dislikes, and aversions. There are five themes per scale, and these form the subscales of the inventory, as follows:

- **Lifestyles**—concern the manner in which a person would like to live.
- **Beliefs**—involve "shoulds," ideals, and ultimate life goals.
- **Occupational Preferences**—include the work an individual would like to do, what constitutes a good job, and preferred work materials.
- **Aversions**—reflect attitudes and behaviors that are either disliked or distressing.
- **Preferred Associates**—include the kind of persons desired as coworkers or friends.

These themes (or subscales) are consistent across all 10 scales and vary only in terms of the content focus of the scale. The following is the list of the scales with a description of the motives addressed by each scale:

Scale	Motives Addressed
Recognition	Motives reflect responsiveness to attention, approval, praise, and a need to be recognized.
Power	Motives are associated with a desire for success, accomplishment, status, competition, and control.
Hedonism	Motives produce an orientation toward fun, pleasure, and enjoyment.
Altruistic	Motives involve concern about the welfare of others, especially the less fortunate and a desire to help them, and in some way, contribute to the development of a better society.
Affiliation	Motives are associated with a desire for social interaction.
Tradition	Motives are typically expressed in terms of a dedication to ritual, history, and old-fashioned values.
Security	Motives reflect a desire for certainty, predictability, order, and control in one's life.
Commerce	Motives reflect an interest in business and business-related matters, such as accounting, marketing, management, and finances.
Aesthetics	Motives are associated with an interest in art, literature, music, the humanities, and a lifestyle guided by questions of culture, good taste, and attractive surroundings.
Science	Motives are associated with a desire for knowledge, enthusiasm for new and advanced technologies, and a curiosity about how things work.

Table 6   The Scales of the MVPI

The items were specifically designed to be easy to read with a high degree of face validity. The following is a sample of items related to the five themes for the Aesthetics scale. These items are indicative of the types of items associated with the other nine scales:

Theme	Sample Item
Lifestyle	I would enjoy touring the great museums of Europe.
Beliefs	Art and literature are the highest forms of expressions of life.
Occupational Preferences	I would like to be an art collector.
Aversions	I dislike people who are always predictable.
Preferred Associates	I like to be around artists and writers.

Table 7   MVPI Sample Items for the Aesthetics Scale

Relationship Between the MVPI and the HDS

Measures of motives, values, and interests are somewhat different from personality measures like the HDS. Personality measures tell us what a person may do in certain situations, while value and interest inventories tell us what a person wants to do (Hogan & Hogan, 2010). This point is at the heart of the relationship that exists between the MVPI and the HDS. For example, a person may want to be recognized for his or her contributions to an organization (high Recognition on the MVPI), but that person's interpersonal style is cold and aloof (high Reserved on the HDS), causing others to avoid offering praise or forms of recognition that involve interpersonal contact.

The positioning of the MVPI as a measure of what people want to do has been used as a foundation for a values-based model for delivering feedback. In this model, the MVPI provides information on "what you want," the HPI addresses "what can get you there," and the HDS highlights "what can get in your way." This view essentially establishes the MVPI as the driving force behind what people want in a job or career, while the HDS stands as an inventory of barriers to success. The problem with this view is that, while it may be useful in certain feedback situations, it is limited in terms of accurately describing the synergies that exist between the MVPI and HDS, especially from a performance improvement standpoint.

Consider what the HDS really has to say about leader performance. In the past, high scores indicated the potential for derailment, and low scores were pretty much ignored. This fits with the notion that the HDS is a measure of the barriers to success. However, this view is outdated. Low scores on the HDS can have a very definite impact on success. Furthermore, at some level, behaviors associated with certain HDS scales can facilitate success and contribute to the realization of values as identified on the MVPI. For example, a leader with a high Power motive might have a very difficult time satisfying that motive if he or she has a very low Bold score, indicating a lack of self-confidence.

The fact that behaviors associated with HDS scales have a much more complex relationship to leader performance than was once thought suggests that perhaps the relationship between the MVPI and HDS deserves further scrutiny. At least three points immediately come to mind.

First, a leader's MVPI profile might dictate the need for certain HDS behaviors to be part of the individual's behavioral repertoire in order for the motive to be satisfied. This point takes us back to the example of the leader with high Power score. It is quite likely that at least a moderate level of Bold behaviors would facilitate success in satisfying a high Power motive. It is also likely that other moderate-level HDS behaviors would be helpful, such as Colorful or Mischievous behaviors.

Second, MVPI motives may play a role in facilitating change that results in performance improvement. If we continue with the Power example, consider a leader who has a high Power score with a low Bold score. The motivating aspect of the Power score could very well drive a leader to strengthen his or her self-confidence. From a development standpoint, the Power motive could be just the leverage a coach needs to encourage a leader to take the steps necessary to improve his or her self-confidence.

Third, it could be equally important to recognize that a motive is *not* present in a leader's profile, and this could actually inhibit change. For example, consider a leader who has a very high Reserved score and exhibits behaviors such as working behind closed doors, failing to network, and avoiding social contact. These behaviors could be career limiting and require development focus. Coaching a leader with low Affiliation motives (especially using action items involving high Affiliation, like large group activities) could be counterproductive. On the other hand, a more successful behavior change effort could take into account the leader's low Affiliation motives. A coach could develop action steps to reduce the leader's high Reserved behaviors based on one-on-one or small group interactions, which are less threatening than high Affiliation, large group activities.

These points illustrate just how much the synergy between the MVPI and the HDS expands when considering the implications of the full range of behaviors associated with HDS scales. Historically, motives have been directly linked to job or career choice. The MVPI opened the door to considering the role motives play in determining the fit of a leader with an organizational culture. It is now clear motives as measured by the MVPI can also play an important role in improving leader performance, especially if they are considered together with development activities.

LEADERSHIP AND COACHING IMPLICATIONS

The HPI and HDS define aspects of normal personality as it pertains to performance in the workplace. They have both been part of the wave of utilizing personality measures in well-designed leadership development programs since the mid-1990s. The MVPI did not really get caught up in the wave. Its utilization in development programs trails that of the HPI and HDS. Furthermore, the use of the information that can be derived from the MVPI about an individual sometimes gets short-shrift in comparison to the HPI and HDS. The reason for the underutilization is because people tend to focus on what has historically been viewed as the strength of the instrument: measuring fit.

Regarding fit, to the extent that an individual's motivation profile fits his or her career or occupational choice, the individual will experience greater satisfaction. Similarly, to the extent that an individual's motivational profile fits the values of an organization, the individual will experience greater satisfaction. These are not insignificant relationships. They have broad implications for perseverance, productivity, turnover, and even team cohesion, all of which are consequential in the workplace.

More recently, MVPI results have been associated with driving the organizational climate. Specifically, Hogan and Hogan (2010) point out that the leaders of an organization dictate the climate (or culture) and that their practices (including hiring, promoting, and rewarding employees) permeate the organization, creating the pillars of the culture. For example, if the leaders of an organization have strong Recognition motives, these motives will be ingrained in their leadership styles and drive Recognition behaviors and activities in others. When Recognition behaviors and activities among the leaders at the top of an organization reach a critical mass, these behaviors and activities will filter down through the organization, establishing a cultural pillar. In more colloquial terms, Darley and Hagenah (1955) put it best in talking about interpersonal similarity: "Birds of a feather flock together."

In this section, we want to go beyond the notions of "fit" and "culture" to consider the role of the MVPI in improving the performance of a leader. This notion has received little attention in the literature because past interest inventories primarily expressed motives in terms of occupational choices. The scale structure of the MVPI allows us to go much further in terms of relating motives to performance and development. In fact, much like the revelation about the HDS that low scores matter, the role of the MVPI in improving leader performance requires a consideration of the motives across the entire range of scale scores. High-end scores have always been thought to indicate strong motivational interest. Low-end scores tend to receive little attention in that they indicate indifference or a lack of interest, but not necessarily demotivation.

Hogan et al. (2007) describe very specific behaviors associated with low scores on the MVPI. Unfortunately, these behaviors are presented in the context of fit and culture. They are not thought of as driving an individual toward something, and largely remain in the shadows in understanding individual behavior. However, from the standpoint of improving the performance of a leader, the motivational aspects of the MVPI scales have implications at both the high end and the low end. For example, consider a leader who has a very low Colorful score and, as a result, fails to call attention to himself or herself and is regularly passed over for promotion. Now add in the motivational qualities of the Recognition scale. If the leader happens to be high on the Recognition scale, behavior change activities can be focused on helping the leader appropriately gain credit and receive recognition for activities. The motivational power of high Recognition could very easily enhance the probability of the leader's changing low Colorful behaviors in order to fulfill his or her recognition need.

Now consider a leader who has a low Recognition score and little interest in being recognized for his or her accomplishments. Often these leaders labor under the impression that their work should speak for itself and that efforts to gain attention for accomplishments are distasteful. Thus, when a leader has both low Recognition and low Colorful scores, a behavior change program that focuses on helping that leader raise his or her profile by using activities aimed at garnering appropriate attention for accomplishments is likely to have little staying power. The leader is simply not motivated by recognition and, therefore, will lose interest in these activities over time, reverting back to the problematic low Colorful behaviors.

A more fruitful set of development activities might play off an entirely different set of motives than the need for recognition. The first place to look would be motives that are in the domain related to the Colorful scale—the Interpersonal Domain. Perhaps the leader has high Altruistic motives. If that is the case, the activities associated with improving low Colorful behaviors could easily be structured around helping others. The chance of sustained behavior change because it fits with the leader's motivational profile has a higher probability of success. Furthermore, the desired result of raising the leader's profile is just as likely to occur with activities arising from an Altruistic perspective as with those arising from a Recognition perspective.

One final point needs to be made with respect to this view of using the MVPI profile as part of the driving force behind behavior change. It is possible that a leader has no elevated motives within a domain where an HDS score suggests a problem. While it may take a degree of creativity, motives in other domains can be called upon to fuel the leader's effort to improve performance. The point that cannot be lost here is behavior change is not easy. Ensuring that there is a motivational component behind the effort to change dramatically improves the probability of success. In the following sections, we again structure the discussion around the four Competency Domains. We will not only focus on the motives tied to the HDS scales within a domain, but we will also offer some suggestions for non-domain-related motives that could be called upon if those motives within the domain prove ineffective. The non-domain MVPI scales were selected on the basis of the magnitude of their correlation with an HDS scale. They should only be considered after fully exploring the potential impact of domain-related relationships.

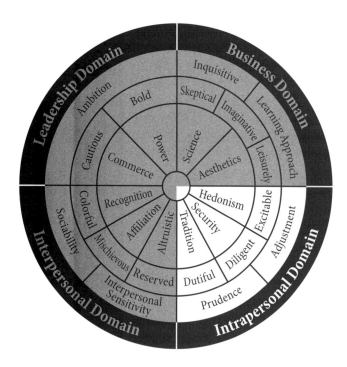

Intrapersonal Domain

The MVPI scales most closely aligned with this Intrapersonal Domain are Hedonism, Security, and Tradition. These scales fit well in this domain because they have deep roots in the way a person grows up and can have a strong influence on the type of work a person will select for a career. Two of the three MVPI scales (Security and Tradition) have strong relationships with the HDS scales associated with this domain (Excitable, Diligent, Dutiful), while Hedonism has a moderate relationship.

Hedonism is perhaps one of the most interesting motives when it comes to leader performance. When leaders have high scores on the Hedonism scale, they tend to take a work-hard, play-hard approach to their jobs, while leaders with low scores on Hedonism tend to be very serious and have a difficult time relaxing, especially when there is work to be done. This MVPI scale has only modest correlations with the HDS scales in this domain. However, the motives associated with the Hedonism scale can seriously impact performance improvement efforts if these motives are strong at either the high end or the low end. For high Excitable leaders, high Hedonism motives can drive near manic fun times or extremely serious, to the point of being dour, low times. For low Excitable leaders, low Hedonism motives can cause the lack of emotion to be even more distinct while high Hedonism motives can moderate a leader's affect in the form of humor or fun.

Leaders with high Diligent scores often work to excess. High Hedonism motives can help a leader ease up on the gas pedal and look for opportunities to add some fun into the workplace. Low Hedonism motives can be a driving force behind the micromanaging behaviors often associated with high Diligent leaders, causing them to be virtually intolerable. Not only will these leaders be highly detail oriented, but they will also be very serious minded about the smallest issues and have little patience for those who do not hold similar views. On the other hand, low Diligent leaders with high Hedonism motives will look for fun when it may be more appropriate to take a more serious approach to mundane activities like following up on delegated assignments. In contrast, if a low Diligent leader has low Hedonism motives, the motives may actually help the leader to be more serious minded about attending to details or following up on assignments.

Low Hedonism motives can drive leaders with high Dutiful behaviors to follow their superiors with a level of conformance that can appear to be near a military level. With leaders with low Dutiful behaviors, their disdain for authority and oversight may extend even into non-work events like dinners or social gatherings. Leaders with high Dutiful scores and high Hedonism scores may simply use fun to further their efforts at ingratiation. In contrast, leaders with low Dutiful and high Hedonism scores might employ fun activities such as dinners or golf outings that are unrelated to work to offset the appearance of their disdain for authority.

Security motives can have a significant impact on HDS behaviors in the Intrapersonal Domain, especially for those who score at the high end of the Security scale. High Security leaders strive to maintain the status quo. If they engage behaviors related to high scores on the Excitable, Diligent, or Dutiful scales that are threatening the status quo, their Security motives can be called upon to motivate behavior change. The behaviors associated with high scores on these HDS scales can be quite visible and draw negative attention from superiors as being less than leader-like. A leader with a high Security motive is much more likely to find a behavior change much less threatening than a status change. Thus, he or she is much more likely to opt for implementing behavior changes if they will help to maintain his or her status.

However, it is important to point out if there is no status threat to the leader, having high Security motives can cause a leader to ignore or avoid any actions with unknown status consequences. This is particularly true with respect to the Diligent and Dutiful scales because they have high correlations with the Security scale (Diligent = .41; Dutiful = .37). In other words, high Diligent and Dutiful behaviors often accompany high Security motives. A status threat not only may be the *best* alternative for motivating change, it may be the *only* alternative.

Having low Security motives can result in the leader's ignoring or avoiding developmental actions regardless of the consequences. For example, a leader may risk losing his or her job due to yelling at employees (high Excitable behavior) or not care about being passed over because of an inability to inspire employees (low Excitable behavior). Similarly, low Security motives can impact high Diligent or Dutiful behaviors in that the leader may not be concerned with the consequences of micromanaging others (high Diligent behavior) or being overly ingratiating (high Dutiful behavior).

Interestingly, low Security motives can have serious organizational consequences when paired with low Diligent or low Dutiful behaviors. These combinations often result in the leader's being more willing to take risks, failing to attend to details (low Diligent behavior), or not keeping superiors informed (low Dutiful), which could result in putting the organization in harm's way. Leaders who are unconcerned about their own security are more likely to test the limits of behaviors associated with low scores on these HDS scales.

The Tradition motives are among the most interesting of those measured by the MVPI. They are often considered to be the volume control on other motives in that an individual who has high Tradition motives tends to have deeply held beliefs, including beliefs associated with other motives measured by the MVPI. The Tradition scale also tends to correlate higher with the HDS scales in the Intrapersonal Domain (Excitable =.13, Dutiful = .30, Diligent = .30) than any of the other HDS scales. Therefore, Tradition motives can have quite an impact with respect to the HDS scales in this domain.

Excitable behaviors are often associated with emotions, either an excess of emotion at the high end of the scale, or a flat affect at the low end of the scale. High Tradition scores tend to offer the most insight from a development perspective with respect to Excitable behaviors. For those scoring high on the Excitable scale, the hot buttons that set in motion emotional outbursts likely align with those motives most deeply driving those individuals. One great example is politics. High Tradition leaders often have deeply held political beliefs. If they engage in a conversation about those political beliefs, and they also happen to have high Excitable behaviors, there is every possibility that the conversation will become emotional. In contrast, high Tradition behaviors can be used to the advantage of a leader trying to overcome low Excitable behaviors because the leader can call upon deeply felt beliefs as a source of passion.

Low Tradition motives do not have as strong an impact with respect to Excitable behaviors as do high Tradition motives. Low Tradition motives neither spark the passion that is missing from a low Excitable leader, nor do they push the hot buttons that can set off high Excitable behaviors. Perhaps the most that can be gleaned from the low Tradition-Excitable relationship is that these individuals will likely expect to receive more tolerance from others for their Excitable behaviors regardless of whether the behaviors exhibited are at the high or low end of the Excitable continuum.

High Tradition motives can moderate the low Diligent behaviors of leaders in ways that can influence them to do the right thing, such as follow up on delegations, fully complete assignments, etc. High Diligent behaviors are another matter. Here, high Tradition motives can lead to a strict attention to detail and an unwavering adherence to high standards. When these behaviors cross the line into micromanagement, they can be nearly intractable. The leader will consider his or her approach to task completion as "there is only one way to do things, and that is the right way."

Low Tradition motives can help ameliorate problems associated with high Diligent behaviors. In performance improvement initiatives, leaders who exhibit these motives and behaviors can be focused on the "what" instead of the "how" when it comes to task completion. For example, a leader with a high Diligent score who might normally micromanage a task from beginning to end can be encouraged to delegate a task to an employee based on what the outcome should be, while giving the employee the flexibility to determine how the task should be done. In the case of a leader with low Diligent behaviors, the leader's low Tradition motives can lead to sloppy work because of the absence of both a reasonable level of detail orientation and a lack of high performance standards. A simple example can be found in the restaurant industry. Restaurant managers with low Tradition motives and low Diligent behaviors may allow standards to slip with respect to cleanliness, which can lead to disaster.

The relationship between the Tradition and Dutiful scales appears to be one of the more logical ones in the Intrapersonal Domain. High Dutiful behaviors are a natural fit with high Tradition motives. Similarly, low Tradition motives are quite compatible with low Dutiful behaviors. When the Tradition motives and the Dutiful scales are not consistent with one another, they can often be used together as leverage to overcome problems. High Tradition motives can be used to drive Dutiful behaviors, such as supporting a company policy. Likewise, low Tradition motives can be used to curb Dutiful behaviors and encourage greater independence.

Leveraging Domain Related MVPI Results in a Coaching Program (Case 4—Tanya)

The Tradition-Excitable relationship provides a good example of leveraging MVPI results in a coaching program. We selected Tanya (Case 4—Tanya, Insurance Professional, page 94) as a good example of this relationship. The following is Tanya's HDS profile summary.

		Tanya's Situational Summary		
	Tanya was a successful insurance professional for a medium-sized corporation who was promoted into the role of training manager. The new role looked to be quite challenging because it required a new skill set to be successful, and the insurance industry as a whole was evolving into a highly regulated industry with many new government regulations. Tanya's new role as training manager could potentially be quite stressful given the job demands and industry changes.
Dimension	**Score**	**Percentile**		**Description**
Excitable	90			Tanya is a crafty insurance professional who can let her emotions get the best of her (Excitable—90%). She is known for putting big deals together for her corporate clients. Outwardly, she appears very self-confident (Bold—89%). She works her own agenda (Leisurely—80%), and tends to set her own rules (Mischievous—98% and Dutiful—10%) with little regard for consequences (Cautious—20%).
Skeptical	60			
Cautious	20			
Reserved	30			
Leisurely	80			
Bold	89			
Mischievous	98			
Colorful	70			
Imaginative	50			
Diligent	30			
Dutiful	10			

0   10   20   30   40   50   60   70   80   90   100

Tanya's score on the Excitable scale is 90 percent. It is clear that Tanya has excitable moments that detract from the perception others have of her executive disposition. These behaviors seemed to be most prevalent in her interactions with colleagues. They may not be terribly disruptive in terms of her ability to perform her new responsibilities as training manager, but they certainly could be career limiting if she is not able to bring them under control. The coaching program outlined on page 191 for Tanya emphasizes the importance of understanding the trigger points that are most often responsible for her emotional outbursts with colleagues. Her MVPI profile indicates a Tradition score of 90 percent. This score suggests two clear-cut refinements that should be considered to strengthen the coaching program. First, Tanya should be strongly encouraged to avoid conversations with colleagues that have a high probability of evoking an emotional response as a result of her high Tradition motives. Conversations involving political or religious topics are common culprits and should be avoided. These triggers could even be leveraged as an indication of poise for Tanya by helping her to learn to appropriately excuse herself from discussions on topics like these. Others will begin to respect the fact that Tanya has a high degree of self-awareness around the emotions such topics evoke in her and is able to excuse herself from the conversation as a way to circumvent potential negative consequences.

Second, it is likely that Tanya's high Tradition motives contribute to other strong feelings she has on topics less obvious than politics or religion. Encouraging Tanya to do some self-reflection and cataloging of these topics will quickly result in the identification of other hot buttons to avoid. While controlling these hot buttons may not eliminate all of Tanya's emotional outbursts, they are low-hanging fruit in starting the process of changing her reputation regarding her Excitable behavior—a very rough reputation for a leader to shake.

Table 8 illustrates some key non-domain relationships between the MVPI and HDS scales that could potentially be leveraged if the domain relationships prove less than helpful in motivating change.

Relationship	r	Description
Affiliation with Excitable	−.46	Affiliation motives (the desire for social interaction) have a strong negative relationship with the Excitable scale. High Affiliation motives can be useful in improving Excitable behaviors. When a leader has a high Excitable score, a high Affiliation score can motivate the leader to control emotions, thereby increasing others' interest in affiliating with him or her. When a leader has a low Excitable score, a high Affiliation score can motivate the leader to have greater affect to increase others' interest in affiliating with him or her.
Commerce with Diligent	.25	Commerce motives (the desire for monetary success) have a moderate positive relationship with the Diligent scale. High Commerce motives can be useful in improving Diligent behaviors. When combined with high Diligent scores, high Commerce scores can provide the rationale for leveraging the talents of others. When combined with low Diligent scores, high Commerce scores can provide the rationale for attending to details and following up on delegated assignments.
Altruistic with Dutiful	.38	Altruistic motives (the concern about the welfare of others) have a strong positive correlation with the Dutiful scale. High Altruistic motives can be leveraged to improve low Dutiful behaviors by encouraging follow-up behaviors as a way of helping others. Low Altruistic motives can be leveraged to reduce high Dutiful behaviors by assisting a leader in recognizing the value of helping those who help themselves.

Table 8   Leveraging Non-Intrapersonal-Domain-Related MVPI Results in a Coaching Program

Interpersonal Domain

The MVPI scales most closely aligned with the Interpersonal Domain are Altruistic, Affiliation, and Recognition. These scales fit well in this domain because they are all people-oriented motives, or more precisely, they often involve an interpersonal component to be adequately fulfilled. The HDS scales in this domain (Reserved, Mischievous, and Colorful) are also people oriented. Therefore, these motives, especially Affiliation and Recognition, could play a strong role in motivating leaders to make performance improvements.

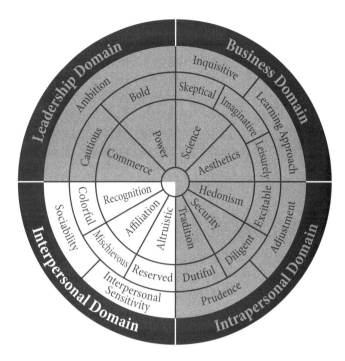

The motives associated with the Altruistic scale can be quite strong. Unfortunately, these motives have at best a tangential influence with respect to the HDS scales in this domain. The strongest relationship can be found between the Altruistic scale and the Reserved scale (−.25). High Reserved individuals who happen to also be high Altruistic might be encouraged to look to their helping behaviors as a means of moderating their Reserved behaviors. Beyond that, the Altruistic scale, when it is consistent with the Reserved scale (i.e., a high Reserved score with a low Altruistic score or a low Reserved score with a High Altruistic score), could actually serve to reinforce Reserved behaviors. For example, a high Reserved and low Altruistic leader could actually point to instances where too much helping went unrewarded or may have even demotivated those receiving help. Such instances could encourage high Reserved leaders to persist in their people-distancing behaviors. Low Reserved leaders might be encouraged to adopt low Altruistic motives, such as offering a hand up instead of a handout, as a means of taking tougher stands with people. But even that is a bit of stretch.

Altruistic motives are likely to be even less helpful with behaviors associated with the Mischievous or Colorful scales. The trust-diminishing aspects of high Mischievous and Colorful behaviors might get in the way of Altruistic endeavors and, therefore, might be used to encourage a high Altruistic leader to reduce these behaviors. For leaders with low Altruistic scores, their motives would likely have little to no influence on Mischievous or Colorful behaviors.

Affiliation motives are a far different matter. They can be quite powerful and are strongly related to all three HDS scales (Reserved = −.64, Mischievous = .34, Colorful = .46). The Reserved scale is negatively related to Affiliation motives. It is quite common for high Reserved individuals to shun social contact. It is equally as common for low Reserved individuals to welcome social contact. Although it is not very common to encounter a high Reserved individual with a high Affiliation score, it does not take extremely strong Affiliation motives to encourage change with respect to Reserved behaviors. In particular, leaders with even moderate Affiliation interests can be encouraged to avoid their tendency to be intimidating from a communication standpoint, resulting in more Affiliation opportunities. Affiliation opportunities can even be incorporated into the change program to help facilitate the improvement of communication skills.

Low Reserved individuals with high Affiliation needs will tend to over-affiliate. Such behaviors can be easily observed in leaders who engage in an excess of meetings or group activities. Moderating Affiliation opportunities through calendar management can be an important ingredient in raising some social boundaries that are important in addressing low Reserved behaviors. Affiliation opportunities can remain at a moderate level to help the leader maintain the positive, approachable aspects of his or her behavior. Selective elimination of superfluous meetings and social interactions tends to work best in improving performance.

High Affiliation motives often create the playground for leaders who have a high Colorful profile. In fact, high Colorful behaviors rarely create a problem in the absence of social interaction. Successfully addressing high Colorful behaviors requires close scrutiny of social interactions. Because those with high Affiliation motives will have many and varied social interactions, the challenge of achieving reputation change for these leaders can be daunting. A useful starting point is identifying those interactions that have the potential for creating the most damage and those that have the most potential for positively impacting the leader's reputation if the Colorful behaviors are brought under control. These situations might not be targeted until low risk practice opportunities have been successful.

For leaders with a low Affiliation score and a low Colorful profile, a successive-approximation approach to affiliating usually works best. The leader is encouraged to engage in social interaction activities that do not create high levels of social pressure. Small group settings with known participants are a good place to start. Here the leader can be challenged to leave an impression on others with respect to one issue or topic. Over time, more difficult situations can be added to gradually increase the leader's comfort level with leaving a positive impression on others.

Affiliation motives can have an impact on Mischievous behaviors similar to that for Colorful behaviors. When leaders have high Affiliation scores, they typically enjoy interacting with lots of people and even larger groups. The size of the audience increases the risk of derailment for those scoring at both the high and low ends of the Mischievous scale as more people experience the Mischievous behavior. For high Mischievous leaders, the risk for creating trust issues increases. Here, the intervention needs to address situational risk. For low Mischievous leaders, the risk of appearing boring or uninteresting increases. Here, the intervention needs to take a successive-approximation approach to ratcheting up the use of behaviors that create a positive impression.

Recognition is another motive that can have a powerful impact in changing leader behavior related to the Interpersonal Domain. Surprisingly, even the Reserved scale can be impacted even though it has a near-zero relationship with Recognition motives ($-.05$). One way to incorporate Recognition motives with respect to Reserved behaviors is to couch recognition in terms of the information it can provide to the leader regarding his or her behavior-change efforts. Those higher on Recognition should simply monitor what others are saying about their efforts. Those lower on Recognition may want to actually seek out feedback from others.

In addition to the information value, Recognition motives have a decidedly different impact on the Mischievous and Colorful scales. The Mischievous scale strongly correlates with the Recognition scale (.52). When the relationship is consistent, high Mischievous leaders are likely to engage in mischievous behaviors simply to gain recognition. Low Mischievous leaders are likely to shun recognition because of their interpersonal awkwardness. A similar relationship exists for Colorful, which also has a strong correlation with Recognition motives (.58). High Colorful leaders are likely to seek out recognition to put their colorful behaviors on display. Low Colorful leaders are likely to avoid recognition because of their discomfort with social attention. The important point for the relationship between Recognition motives and the Mischievous or Colorful scales is that these motives, when consistent, tend to fuel the problems associated with these HDS scales. It is important that any effort to improve performance related to these scales accounts for Recognition motives and ensures that they are not working against the very behaviors a leader is trying to change.

Leveraging Domain Related MVPI Results in a Coaching Program (Case 6—Mark)

The Colorful-Recognition relationship provides a good example of leveraging MVPI results in a coaching program. We selected Mark (Case 6—Mark, District Account Manager, page 98) as a good example of this relationship. The following is Mark's HDS profile summary.

Mark's Situational Summary			
Mark is a long-tenured district account manager for a consumer products company. A significant change in his account porfolio brought a number of new government accounts under his control. These customers were no-nonsense type customers who had little interest in his affable nature and tendency to exaggerate to garner attention.			
Dimension	**Score**	**Percentile**	**Description**
Excitable	68		Mark is a high-energy person who brings a lot of passion to the business (Excitable—68%). He can be highly colorful (Colorful—91%) to the point of being overbearing at times. His colorful behavior extends into his tendency to exaggerate issues or problems and his role in solving them. He also has a tendency to miss details or fail to follow up on important issues (Diligent—10%).
Skeptical	15		
Cautious	29		
Reserved	42		
Leisurely	19		
Bold	24		
Mischievous	70		
Colorful	91		
Imaginative	29		
Diligent	10		
Dutiful	45		

0   10   20   30   40   50   60   70   80   90   100

Mark's score on the Colorful scale is 91 percent. One of his primary issues is that he enjoys telling stories and anecdotes that can sometimes be overbearing and have a negative impact on his credibility. Like most storytellers, Mark has a tendency to exaggerate. In some situations, that might not create an issue, and others might find his exaggerated stories to be amusing and entertaining. Mark also happens to have a high score on Recognition motives (95%). These motives likely fuel Mark's storytelling because he gets plenty of recognition for his stories, which only serves to reinforce the behavior of telling more stories.

In Mark's new role working with government accounts, credibility will be very important, especially in the early stages when Mark is forming new working relationships. It will be important to help Mark understand that being recognized for his storytelling may not be a good thing. It may be especially problematic if Mark starts to be recognized as a storyteller by his new customers, rather than as a good listener interested in the challenges they face. A key refinement to add to Mark's coaching program outlined in Chapter 17 could be situational recognition. For example, it would be helpful for Mark to tone down his storytelling among new customers and spend more time listening. Mark could then meet his Recognition needs by seeking feedback on his improved listening, which is more likely to be welcomed by his new customers than his storytelling.

Table 9 illustrates some key non-domain relationships between the MVPI and HDS scales that could potentially be leveraged if the domain relationships prove less than helpful in motivating change.

Relationship	r	Description
Power with Reserved	−.14	Power motives (the desire for achievement) have a moderately negative relationship with the Reserved scale. High Power motives can be used to entice change in a leader. Combined with high Reserved scores, high Power scores can motivate leaders to consider the "human" in their thinking. Combined with low Reserved scores, high Power scores can motivate greater toughness and its importance in making hard decisions.
Hedonism with Mischievous	.21	Hedonism motives (the desire for good times) have a moderately positive relationship with the Mischievous scale. High Hedonism motives can be useful in improving Mischievous behaviors. Paired with high Mischievous scores, high Hedonism scores can be an important watch-out, as mischievous behaviors could be used to pursue pleasure interests. Paired with low Mischievous scores, high Hedonism scores may be called upon to add interest to an otherwise boring persona.
Aesthetics with Colorful	.20	Aesthetics motives (a concern about good taste) have a moderately positive correlation with the Colorful scale. Colorful behaviors are associated with self-presentation, even in the way a leader dresses. High Aesthetic motives can be called upon to help the leader exercise good taste. Low Aesthetic motives may lead to poor self-presentation and the exercise of bad taste.

Table 9   Leveraging Non-Interpersonal-Domain-Related MVPI Results in a Coaching Program

Leadership Domain

The MVPI scales most closely aligned with the Leadership Domain are Commerce and Power. The scales are consistently associated with leadership positions and play important roles in motivating those interested in leading others. Even the Commerce motive, which could arguably be part of the Business Domain, has a better fit here because of its influence over career choices involving leadership. The HDS scales in this domain (Cautious and Bold) are also closely aligned with leadership roles. These MVPI and HDS scales are cornerstones in understanding and improving leader performance.

Before considering the relationship between the MVPI and HDS scales, it is important to review the relationship between

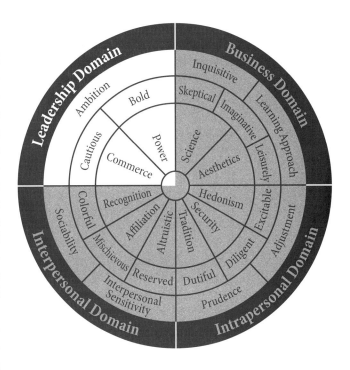

the Commerce and Power scales. These two scales are strongly correlated (.48) despite the different motives these scales tap. Leaders motivated by power or a sense of achievement are also motivated by commerce or the financial success of a venture. This combination turns out to be a relatively common finding when debriefing or providing feedback to leaders. When this relationship is probed, it usually is described in one of two ways. First, those with high Commerce motives are often interested in controlling their own destiny (the Power motive) as a way to achieve their financial goals, and there is no better way to control your destiny than to be in a leadership role. Second, those with high Power motives often see money as the yardstick of success (the Commerce motive), and compensation levels are typically higher in leadership roles. These synergies are striking and should be considered when performance in the Leadership domain is at issue.

Another relationship worth mentioning is the one between the Cautious and Bold scales (−.16). This is not a strong relationship, but it is in the right direction (i.e., cautious leaders tend to be less bold, while bold leaders tend to be less cautious). The magnitude of the relationship does say something about the way these scales play out from a leadership standpoint. Higher Bold scores are often associated with those in leadership roles. In fact, it is behaviors associated with high-end scores like arrogance, blaming others for mistakes, ignoring shortcomings, and so on that are common performance improvement targets. In contrast, the Cautious scale is one of those scales where moderate scores seem to be associated with the most desirable behaviors in a leader. At the moderate level, leaders tend to advocate prudent risk taking, avoiding the traps of excessive caution or poor decisions that can result without adequate due diligence. It is important to understand the behavioral "sweet spot" on these two scales to appreciate how the Commerce and Power motives play out in driving behavior.

Consider the relationship between the Cautious scale and the MVPI scales. A high Power score can be called upon to help motivate a high Cautious leader to take more risks. If the high Power score is accompanied by a high Commerce score, a leader's comfort level in taking more risks can be increased through using financial due diligence. Admittedly, not all risks can be reduced to financial consequences, but many can, and when they can, others tend to view such analyses as rational and leader-like.

Low Cautious leaders tend to take more risks in their decision-making. Power motives at either end can be problematic. A high Power, low Cautious leader will be motivated to take big risks in the hopes of achieving big rewards. These leaders tend to own the consequences of their decisions, good or bad. Leaders with low Power motives may be slow at decision-making, especially when the consequences of a bad decision could have personal ramifications.

Bold behaviors work in a somewhat similar fashion as Cautious behaviors. A high Power score can be used to motivate a leader to let go of the timid behaviors associated with a low Bold score and take more ownership of outcomes. Again, in a coaching program, high Commerce motives can be called upon to increase due diligence and raise the confidence level of a leader.

High Bold behaviors can be strongly reinforced by high Power motives. Leaders with this combination of scores can arrogantly accept responsibility when things go well and just as easily blame others when things go poorly. Low Power motives can reinforce low Bold behaviors and contribute to a pervasive reputation that the individual lacks self-confidence. These individuals often refuse to take ownership of projects or assignments and will persist in raising doubts about their ability to be successful.

High Commerce motives can actually fuel arrogance when accompanied by high Power motives. Of all the combinations of motives and HDS behaviors, this one, especially if accompanied by high risk-taking behaviors like low Cautious or high Mischievous, can produce very serious negative organizational consequences when it is part of the profile of a leader in a position of authority. Many of the corporate meltdowns of the early 2000s, such as Enron or Countrywide, were likely the result of leaders with profiles of this nature. Raising a leader's Strategic Self-awareness is a must when this combination of scale scores is observed.

An important takeaway with respect to this section is the configural impact that can result from the two HDS scales and the MVPI motives associated with the Leadership Domain. They can merge together in combinations that can help a leader build a positive reputation. They can all also combine in ways that can completely derail a leader and produce serious negative consequences for an organization.

Leveraging MVPI Results in a Coaching Program (James—Case 7)

The Cautious-Commerce relationship provides a good example of leveraging MVPI results in a coaching program. We selected James (Case 7—James, Marketing

Manager, page 100) as a good example of this relationship. The following is James's HDS profile summary:

		James's Situational Summary		
	James was the marketing manager for a small family-owned business that was sold to a well-established technology company. After the sale, James moved on to a small, fast-moving start-up technology company. He had clear challenges with his ability to get things moving in the new company. His high Cautious score will have a direct impact on the speed with which he makes decisions that may be in conflict with a fast-moving start-up company.
Dimension	**Score**		**Percentile**	**Description**
Excitable	10			James is a laid-back, even-tempered marketing guy (Excitable—10%). It takes him a long time to get to know and trust people (Skeptical—70%), and he is guarded and slow to make decisions (Cautious—85% and Mischievous—15%). James doesn't make a big impression on people. In fact, he is best known for his loyalty and willingness to do whatever the owners asked (Dutiful—90%).
Skeptical	70			
Cautious	85			
Reserved	25			
Leisurely	19			
Bold	24			
Mischievous	15			
Colorful	45			
Imaginative	35			
Diligent	50			
Dutiful	90			

0   10   20   30   40   50   60   70   80   90   100

James is in a tough situation. He is moving from a family-owned business where he was very familiar with many of the business processes and procedures. If he was not sure about certain decisions, he was surrounded by people who could easily help him with the due diligence needed to make those decisions and even make recommendations that would limit the risks associated with those decisions. However, in a start-up environment, business processes and procedures are often loose or nonexistent. Plus, the kinds of support structure that would likely exist in an established family business would probably not be present.

One aspect of James's profile that could be very helpful to him is his high Commerce score (93%). The motives associated with this score could add three potential refinements to James's coaching outlined on page 231. First, leaders with high Commerce motives often have a strong interest in the financial viability of the companies for which they work. These motives could be called upon as a way for James to gain a degree of credibility by developing a sound understanding of the financial underpinnings of the business. Second, James's self-confidence would likely grow in proportion to the understanding he would gain by studying the business's financial underpinnings. Finally, in the start-up world, the financial impact of all decisions, especially those associated with marketing, receive considerable scrutiny. James would be well served to incorporate a sound financial analysis into his decisions. This integration would raise his confidence level and certainly raise the confidence level others have in his decisions.

Table 10 illustrates some key non-domain relationships between the MVPI and HDS scales that could potentially be leveraged if the domain relationships prove less than helpful in motivating change.

Relationship	r	Description
Affiliation with Cautious	−.48	Affiliation motives (the desire for social interaction) have a strong negative relationship with the Cautious scale. Too often, Cautious behaviors are only associated with task-based decision-making. However, Cautious behaviors can have a definite interpersonal component, which can account for this strong negative relationship. High-end Cautious behaviors with low Affiliation motives can be a watch-out as this could lead to a degree of social isolation for a leader. Low-end Cautious behaviors with high Affiliation motives can result in a leader being overly familiar with others and not respecting information-sharing boundaries.
Recognition with Bold	.68	Recognition motives (a desire to be known) have a stronger correlation with the Bold scale than any other MVPI or HDS scale. When an individual scores at the high end on both scales, it is a potentially lethal combination. These leaders are brimming with self-confidence (arrogance) and go out of their way to make everyone know it. They might as well paint a target on their backs because others will often go out of their way to make sure they "get taken down a notch." When an individual scores at the low end of both scales, he or she simply cannot take a compliment. These individuals appear awkward when recognition comes their way, and this behavior reinforces the fact that these leaders lack self-confidence.

Table 10   Leveraging Non-Leadership-Domain-Related MVPI Results in a Coaching Program

Business Domain

The MVPI scales most closely aligned with the Business Domain are Science and Aesthetics. These scales fit well in this domain because they have a strong impact on the type of information leaders are motivated to use in problem-solving and decision-making. The HDS scales in this domain (Leisurely, Imaginative, and Skeptical) also play a strong role in problem-solving and decision-making. These scales combine to provide a clear picture of the way in which individuals process information commonly associated with leadership roles.

Science motives play a key role in the type of information leaders will bring to the table when they are making their case on an issue or challenging the positions of others. High Science motives tend to be associated with rational, data-driven arguments. When leaders with high Science motives also have high scores on the Skeptical, Imaginative, or Leisurely scales, these leaders will typically come prepared to back up their positions with data. For example, a skeptical individual who is being critical of another person's position is likely to offer arguments based on a rational position that he or she has arrived at after a careful consideration of the available data.

If a leader's Skeptical, Imaginative, or Leisurely scores are low, high Science motives can be used to protect a position a leader might take. This is especially true of Imaginative. Low Imaginative leaders tend to want to stick to known processes or past solutions to problems. Generally, they will be the last ones to the table with innovative or forward thinking approaches. They can employ high Science motives to protect their positions with supportive data that they will selectively employ. Such behavior can reinforce a leader's reputation for being change resistant or a naysayer.

Low Science motives are generally associated with intuitive thinking. It is important to point out that intuitive thinking is not necessarily right or wrong. There are plenty of examples of intuitive leaders who have great ideas, offer good solutions, etc.

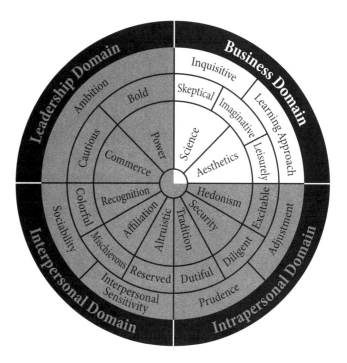

However, low Science motives can reduce the ability of a leader to influence others with respect to criticism (Skeptical), ideas (Imaginative), and personal agenda (Leisurely). This can work in two ways. First, if a leader's position happens to turn out to be wrong, it can damage his or her credibility in the future as there was little rational support for the position to begin with. Second, the absence of rational information makes it much more difficult for a leader to bring others along. These kinds of issues need to be addressed with respect to performance improvement related to high end HDS behaviors associated with this domain.

Low Science motives tend to accentuate the problems leaders have with being dismissed or ignored with respect to low HDS behaviors in the Business Domain. Low Skeptical leaders will appear more naïve, low Imaginative leaders will appear stuck in the past, and low Leisurely leaders will appear to have nothing to contribute to a business agenda. All of these low scores have serious implications for the careers of these leaders. Any performance improvement effort should include a way for these leaders to move in the direction of bringing more data to their positions.

Aesthetic motives range from driving leaders with high scores to be highly creative to causing leaders with low scores to be overly practical. By far, they have their strongest relationship with the Imaginative scale (.33). When these scales are consistent with one another, they serve to accentuate behavior. A high Imaginative leader may be seen as quite eccentric. A low Imaginative leader may be seen as overly practical with nothing to add when innovation needs to be part of the discussion. When the scores conflict with one another, they can be called upon to moderate the negative aspects of the Imaginative scale. High Imaginative leaders with low Aesthetics scores can be encouraged to view their ideas through a practical lens.

Similarly, low Imaginative leaders with high Aesthetics scores can call upon the creative motives to think beyond their tendency to stick with the known.

Aesthetic motives, although not strongly related to Leisurely behaviors, likely play a role in the temperament aspects of the Leisurely scale. High Aesthetic leaders often can be quite temperamental. When these motives are combined with the emotional behaviors that can accompany high Leisurely, the leader's emotions can, in some ways, seem childlike or irrational. Low Leisurely behaviors can seem more emotionally flat (low Aesthetic motives) or can actually provide a foundation for building an agenda based on quality or good taste (high Aesthetic motives).

Aesthetic motives also do not have a strong relationship to Skeptical behaviors (.01). If leaders are high on Aesthetics and Skeptical, they will likely use more creative or quality-oriented views when they challenge others. Leaders with high Skeptical scores and low Aesthetic motives will likely drive more practical or mundane challenges or criticisms. Low Skeptical behaviors associated with the naiveté of a leader will likely drive him or her to look for the good in positions taken by others regardless of whether the leader has a high or low Aesthetics score.

Leveraging MVPI Results in a Coaching Program (Case 2—Phil)

The Science-Skeptical relationship provides a good example of leveraging MVPI results in a coaching program. We selected Phil (Case 2—Phil, Logistics Technician, page 90) as a good example of this relationship. The following is Phil's HDS profile summary.

Phil's Situational Summary
Phil is a lead logistics technician for a national trucking company. Phil's approach to his job generally has been one of a watchdog who tries to identify problems and deliver bad news. A new incoming leader for whom he will be working in the future has a decidedly different view of how the function should run. The leader believes technicians should take more of a partnership approach with field employees, treating them as internal customers.

Dimension	Score	Percentile	Description
Excitable	35		Phil is a perceptive individual but can be excessively critical and is always on the lookout for faults (Skeptical—96%). He can be insensitive to the moods and feelings of people and place business results above all other concerns (Reserved—90%). He also can be quite deferential to superiors and the guidance they provide (Dutiful—77%).
Skeptical	96		
Cautious	75		
Reserved	90		
Leisurely	33		
Bold	55		
Mischievous	40		
Colorful	75		
Imaginative	62		
Diligent	60		
Dutiful	77		

0   10   20   30   40   50   60   70   80   90   100

Phil happens to have a high Science score that accompanies his high Skeptical score. In the past, he called on his rational approach to build his case for criticizing the positions of others or finding fault with the way things were being done. His cogent style made Phil quite a formidable foe. His due diligence was thorough, causing others to shy away from putting up any resistance. A coaching program such as the one outlined on page 211 aimed at helping Phil reduce his negative, fault-finding behavior is on target. However, a simple refinement to the program based on Phil's Science motives could result in more effective behavior change. Phil's new incoming leader has asked Phil to partner with field employees and treat them as customers. Phil's coaching program could focus on having Phil partner with field employees to identify problems and work together to build a case for solutions. In this approach, Phil's Science motives can be fulfilled in partnership with field employees. Furthermore, Phil's Skeptical nature can be ratcheted back because he is now working in partnership with field employees to find workable solutions, as opposed to simply being a critic. In essence, Phil's critical nature can be co-opted to support the challenges faced by field employees.

Table 11 illustrates some key non-domain relationships between the MVPI and HDS scales that could potentially be leveraged if the domain relationships prove less than helpful in motivating change.

Relationship	r	Description
Recognition with Skeptical	.24	Recognition motives (the desire to be known) have a moderate positive relationship with the Skeptical scale. The problem here is what the individual will become known for as a leader. High Skeptical leaders will be known for being cynical and critical. Low Skeptical leaders will be known for being naive and overly trusting. In either case, these leaders need to understand their Recognition motives and how those motives could be contributing to the precise negative aspects of their reputations that they are trying to change.
Security with Imaginative	−.39	Security motives (the desire for stability) have a strong negative correlation with the Imaginative scale. When scores on these scales are consistent, it can cause behavior change with respect to the Imaginative scale to be difficult and should be accounted for in a change program. High Security motives will provide little motivation for high Imaginative leaders to curtail their eccentric behaviors.
Commerce with Leisurely	.22	Commerce motives (the desire for financial success) have a moderate positive correlation with the Leisurely scale. High Commerce motives are common among leaders and can provide the motivation needed to make changes to their Leisurely behaviors. Leaders with high Leisurely behaviors can be encouraged to seek out agenda alignment on the basis that alignment will often facilitate financial success. Low Leisurely leaders can be encouraged to build an agenda that aligns with the financial success of the business.

Table 11   Leveraging Non-Business-Domain-Related MVPI Results in a Coaching Program

SUMMARY

The MVPI is a unique inventory in the way it measures individual motives. These motives can be an important component in any effort to improve leader performance. They can cause a leader to resist change, but more importantly, they can be called upon to motivate a leader to make a change. They can even be used to augment specific change efforts to help ensure they will be implemented and persist over time to produce reputation changes. While it is nearly impossible to account for the implications of all combinations and permutations of the MVPI and HDS scales, especially in light of Situational Context variables, we highlighted many of the combinations that could be of motivational value in helping leaders improve their performance. The case studies provided specific examples of how an individual's motives can be incorporated into coaching programs, and we included some examples where non-domain motives could play a role. Just as the HPI has a powerful synergistic relationship with the HDS, so too does the MVPI. The information covered in this chapter demonstrates unequivocally that motives should be considered if performance improvement efforts are to achieve their full potential for success.

CHAPTER 23

GENERAL TECHNIQUES FOR ANY SIDE

INTRODUCTION

In prior chapters, we have made a solid case that in leadership, personality does indeed matter, Strategic Self-awareness and Situational Context are crucial, and armed with these, leaders can change their behaviors, and subsequently their effectiveness and reputations. We also introduced the Hogan Development Cycle (see Figure 16), which illustrates how ongoing behavior changes and reputation modifications occur.

As powerful as it is, the Development Cycle does not exist in a vacuum. It must be part of an overall strategy for development that, based on both the individual leader and the situation, is best able to enhance the leader's effectiveness. Further, the Development Cycle must be supported by blocking and tackling coaching tips and techniques to help the leader build skills and modify behaviors.

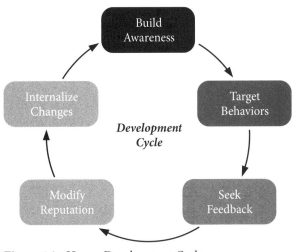

Figure 16   Hogan Development Cycle

477

This chapter describes five general strategies for development that, when tailored to the leader and the situation, have proven to be effective time and again. Then we turn to coaching techniques so widely used that we call them universal.

FIVE GENERAL STRATEGIES FOR DEVELOPMENT

The development strategy is the approach within which skill building, behavior modification, and reputation change occur. Although we often turn to education and training programs as our default development strategy, development is not one size fits all. Many times, a different approach is more appropriate and more effective.

In this section, we outline five development strategies to consider for optimal results depending upon the leader and the situation. These strategies are not mutually exclusive, and they are often used simultaneously to accomplish development. In fact, in the coaching initiatives that are cited as examples in Part IV, a combination of these strategies can often be found. The five strategies are as follows:

- **Develop** through education and training.
- **Leverage** an area of strength.
- **Compensate** with alternative behaviors.
- **Support** the weakness with resources.
- **Redesign** the job or assignment.

Strategy 1: Develop Through Education and Training

A strategy of education and training is well suited for a situation where a leader has an identified skill or competency gap. It is particularly effective when the competencies are part of the Business Domain or the Leadership Domain (see Figure 3 on page 33 for the Hogan Competency Domains). This approach takes many forms—formal programs, classes, or workshops; coaching; mentoring; webinars; or on-the-job training, to name a few—all of which can be viable ways to build and reinforce skills and improve performance. Hard skills, such as data-based decision-making, setting priorities, delegating, public speaking, and the like are readily addressed by this approach. Softer skills, such as building relationships and influencing and motivating others (typically part of the Interpersonal Domain) can be tougher to develop, but this strategy is still effective with a targeted development plan and ongoing feedback.

For example, a leader who struggles with high-quality decision-making can learn and subsequently use a decision-making process that incorporates generating and evaluating alternatives, and then selecting a course of action with the highest probability of success. Or a leader who needs to enhance his or her strategic planning abilities can participate in a strategic planning seminar and then perform an industry Strengths, Weaknesses, Opportunities, and Threats (SWOT) analysis to practice what he or she learned.

Strategy 2: Leverage an Area of Strength

An effective way to compensate for an area of weakness is to leverage an area of strength. Often, an area of strength in one domain, such as the Intrapersonal Domain, can be leveraged to offset a weakness in another domain, such as the Interpersonal Domain.

For example, a leader who wants to improve his or her ability to make an effective public speech (the Interpersonal Domain) can engage and win over an audience by using stories and anecdotes that have their foundation in a good sense of humor (the Intrapersonal Domain).

Another example is a leader who is not creative and innovative (development area), but perhaps is a great team builder and collaborator (strength). The leader can still deliver the desired result of creative and innovative ideas and products through leveraging his or her strength of engaging and encouraging others. In this case, the leader will create an environment that facilitates and nurtures the team's new and different ideas rather than thinking up the new ideas personally.

Strategy 3: Compensate with Alternative Behaviors

This strategy involves using a positive behavior to compensate for a derailing behavior. It can be used to rebuild a reputation of counterproductive behavior. This strategy is most effective when a positive behavior can be identified, incorporated into an ongoing behavioral repertoire, and easily observed by others when it is demonstrated. Repeated demonstration by the leader and observation by others not only helps the leader internalize the new behavior, but it reinforces the leader's reputation change among the observers. Many times, the effectiveness of this strategy increases when the leader uses a physical reminder or awareness builder to ensure frequent and appropriate use of the positive behavior.

For example, a leader who has a reputation for ignoring others' input should make a conscious effort to incorporate nonthreatening "seek" behaviors into team meetings and interactions. As the leader demonstrates the seek behaviors multiple times, his or her reputation will begin to change, and often the new behaviors become the leader's natural behaviors. In this example, as a physical reminder, the leader could change his or her wristwatch from one arm to the other before a meeting as a reminder to engage in the positive behaviors.

Another example is a leader who is known for unstructured free-for-all meetings could start publishing an agenda in advance, keeping the meeting on task and on time, and issuing minutes afterwards. If this process occurs regularly, the leader will gain credibility with the attendees, and his or her reputation will start to change.

Strategy 4: Support the Weakness with Resources

When a leader has a clear weakness that he or she has tried to improve to little or no avail, sometimes the most effective development strategy is to support the individual with resources. Typically, the resource is another team member or employee who possesses the skill the leader lacks. The effectiveness of this strategy increases when the target behavior can be isolated and supported by another person without diminishing the leader's overall effectiveness.

For example, a leader who scores low on Prudence and is disorganized could utilize a well-organized administrative support person to provide a degree of structure and order in the performance of day-to-day responsibilities.

Another example of using this strategy is a leader who struggles with details. This leader could benefit from having a direct report who excels at dotting the *i*'s and crossing the *t*'s, which will free up the leader to focus on his or her strong suits. The organization will run more effectively, and both the leader and the direct report will be happier.

Strategy 5: Redesign the Job or Assignment

To resolve certain problems, it is sometimes possible to alter a leader's job requirements or scope to remove key roles or responsibilities and assign them elsewhere in the organization. Although this might seem drastic, it is preferable to allowing a leader's performance to lag and possibly losing a valuable contributor. This strategy is most effective when a leader's performance in a role or area of responsibility is ineffective, and it is clear that allowing the leader to struggle will diminish his or her effectiveness further and potentially hurt the overall organization. The effectiveness of this strategy increases when the gap created by removing the responsibilities from the position can be backfilled by expanding the leader's responsibilities in areas in which he or she is strong and that are valued by the organization.

For example, a sales manager might be terrific with customers and product sales but inept at managing direct reports. In this case, a good plan might be to reassign the sales force to another manager who has well-honed managerial skills and then expand the number of accounts that the sales manager handles personally to take advantage of his or her strong suit.

Another example is an entrepreneur who excels at new product development and start-up scenarios but who is bored by running an ongoing business. Once the start-up morphs into a stable business, the entrepreneur could hire a professional manager to handle the day-to-day company operations. The entrepreneur could then devote his or her time to developing new ideas.

Universal Coaching Tips

Part IV contains 11 chapters detailing a multitude of coaching tips that are tailored specifically to the high and low ends of each HDS scale. However, there are a number of tried-and-true coaching tips that have proven effective across all the scales, both high and low scores, and indeed, for behavior change in general. For this reason, we call these universal coaching tips. These are the go-to tips, including tools and techniques, which the Hogan Coaching Network coaches use repeatedly, regardless of the coaching issue:

1. **Motivation is half the battle.** A leader who is not motivated to change will not change. A leader who is motivated to change is ready to embrace development and coaching. The question for the leader (and the coach) is "What is the motivation to change?" The only reason to move forward with a plan aimed at improving a leader's performance is if the leader has a clear motivation to change.

2. **Build Strategic Self-awareness**, including acknowledgment of the impact the behavior has on others. Help the leader recognize, accept, and own the behavior that has prompted the coaching. Only by acknowledging that he or she does indeed act in a certain way can the leader begin the journey to modify the behavior. Usually, specific behavioral examples and multi-rater assessment are necessary for the leader to understand the full impact of the behavior.

3. **Camera Check Feedback** is a concept first introduced by Brandon and Seldman (2004). Camera Check Feedback is feedback that is so specific that a video camera would see and hear the feedback that is being delivered. This strategy may sound simple, but in practice it can be quite difficult. It is feedback that cannot be denied when it is delivered with this level of accuracy.

4. **S.M.A.R.T.E.R. goals** are goals that are specific, measurable, achievable, relevant, and time-bound. We have added the "ER," which stands for "Enhanced Reputation." The ER makes these goals even more relevant when a Hogan approach to developing leaders is employed.

5. **Realize the impact** of the behavior on effectiveness, reputation, and, ultimately, career prospects based on the concept of materialism, i.e., how much does the behavior matter? Once leaders understand that the behavior is driving the perceptions of others and limiting their effectiveness and possibly career opportunities, they will likely be more open to coaching.

6. **Determine the triggers of the behavior.** Help the leader identify the people and situations that trigger the derailing behavior. Perhaps it is a particular colleague who gets on the leader's nerves, or perhaps it is all people who are overbearing. The trigger could be meetings in which nothing is decided or a tight due date that must be met. Or it could be a physical phenomenon, such as being tired or hungry. Whatever the trigger, once the leader realizes what it is, he or she can anticipate it and outmaneuver it through various coaching techniques.

7. **Reframe the behavior change.** Behavior change is difficult, and new behaviors are frequently uncomfortable because they are not in the natural "strike zone" of the leader. Many times a leader will say "That's just not the way I am," or "I feel like a fake when I do that." Often, taking the behavior change out of the personal realm and reframing it in terms of the demands of the job or the needs of the team will help leaders feel they are not being untrue to themselves or trying to become someone they are not. For example, if a leader needs to speak up and be more assertive, but feels it is just not in his or her makeup to do this, the coach should position the behavior as something that is part of being a leader. While it might not be the leader's natural behavior, it is certainly behavior that a leader needs to exhibit in order to be effective.

8. **Increase Situational Context awareness.** Going hand in hand with Strategic Self-awareness is awareness of the Situational Context—the need for the leader to be aware of his or her surroundings and decide which behaviors will be potential derailers. The same behavior is not effective in all circumstances. By evaluating the situation and audience, the leader can decide whether to dial a behavior up or down to be effective. A key tool in understanding the Situational Context is a stakeholder analysis. A stakeholder analysis assists the leader in determining which stakeholders are most critical to his or her success. It also helps the leader determine how he or she can best work with each stakeholder from both a style standpoint (e.g., be more or less talkative, focus on results or people, etc.) and a substance standpoint (e.g., discover common goals, determine if there is competition for limited resources, etc.). The stakeholder analysis can help leaders flex their own style to more closely match the style of each stakeholder in an effort to make the stakeholder more comfortable.

9. **Utilize an advocate.** Ongoing, real-time feedback on the effectiveness of a new behavior is key to a leader's success, and an advocate can play a crucial role in providing this feedback. Encourage the leader to select an advocate he or she truly trusts and who sees the leader frequently enough to be aware of and observe new behaviors. The advocate can provide feedback to the leader about how the new behaviors were perceived by others. The leader can then modify the behaviors as needed. The advocate can also be the leader's eyes and ears in the organization regarding the buzz about the leader, including whether colleagues are seeing a positive difference.

10. **Identify best-case and worst-case scenarios.** Sometimes leaders are leery about trying new behaviors for fear that they will fail. An effective way to confront this apprehension is to help them put the consequences of the behavior change in perspective. Ask the leader, "What is the best outcome that could occur?" and have the leader list the positives. Then, ask the leader, "What is the worst outcome that could occur?" and have the leader list the negatives. Typically, the upside potential is far greater than the downside, and the leader will be more willing to try the new behavior.

11. **Use a tangible reminder to keep the behavior change top of mind.** Given the stress associated with today's fast moving workplace, it is easy for leaders to put the need for behavior change on the back burner and to revert to the derailing behavior as an expediency. Further, when a leader is under stress, his or her fallback position is to resort to the old, comfortable behavior. Often, something tangible can serve as an ongoing reminder of the need to practice the new behavior. Putting a rubber band around your wrist, moving your watch from one arm to another, and using a special computer screen saver, are all examples of tangible reminders.

12. **Identify a role model.** It can be both instructive and motivating for a leader to identify a role model who exemplifies the desired behavior. Finding a colleague who is "best in class" at demonstrating the desired behavior takes the behavior out of the theoretical and grounds it in the practical. The leader can actually see what the behavior looks like in the real world and the reactions others have to the behavior. Sometimes, it is powerful to identify a negative role model (i.e., a colleague who exhibits the same derailing behavior as the leader) so that the leader can feel what it is like to be on the receiving end of the behavior. For example, if the leader has trouble controlling his or her temper, ask the leader to identify a "hothead" and think about how he or she would like interacting with that person.

13. **Use a Week-in-Review form.** The Week-in-Review form is a tool designed to help leaders "coach" themselves. At the end of every week, the leader completes the form, which can be customized to the leader's development goals. The form guides the leader through a self-assessment of how he or she did during the week versus the development plan. Typically, items covered include strengths leveraged, new behaviors practiced, reactions by others, feedback from others, key learnings, and behavior modifications needed. After the leader has put pen to paper for several weeks and completed the form, he or she can usually start logging events mentally. The important thing is to make the week in review part of the leader's routine so the development effort stays top of mind.

14. **Evaluate and modify as needed.** The leader and coach should evaluate the effectiveness of the new behavior, and, if necessary, modify it. If a new behavior is delivering the desired results, then the leader should keep it up, thereby internalizing it and reinforcing to others the behavior is going to "stick." However, if the new behavior is off the mark, the leader should modify it. Leaders always need to realize that behavior change is a work in progress, and it might require some adjustment to be maximally effective.

15. **Do not get discouraged!** This mega-tip needs to be repeated frequently. Behavior change is difficult, and changing people's perceptions is even more difficult. Reputations die hard, and sometimes people continue to "play old tapes" long after a leader has modified the derailing behavior. One way to counter this is for the leader to ask people for feedback and "feed-forward" (e.g., "What can I do in the future to be more effective?") so that they feel a part of the leader's success in changing his or her behavior.

Summary

For a leader to modify behavior, increase effectiveness, and ultimately accomplish a reputation change, he or she must actively engage in the Hogan Development Cycle on an ongoing basis. The Development Cycle occurs within one or more of five general strategies for development that have proven successful over time. Development is supported by practical coaching tips and techniques, some of which span multiple strategies and situations and are, therefore, universal. In the sample coaching initiatives described in Part IV, the five strategies and universal coaching tips are often employed with positive results. We strongly believe they should be a part of any effort to improve leader performance.

CHAPTER 24

CLOSING THOUGHTS

INTRODUCTION

Our intent in writing this book was to create the go-to guide for personality-based feedback, coaching, and development. We wanted both to share the Hogan philosophy, which makes a compelling case for the importance of personality in leadership, and to provide practical, proven techniques and tips for applying personality-based information to drive real change in leader behavior and improvement in leader performance.

Throughout this book, we have taken the position that personality truly is important in matters of leadership. Personality drives behaviors, and behaviors accumulate into a leader's reputation. For a leader's performance to improve, behaviors must change, which will lead to a reputation change. Thus, a change in a leader's reputation, as acknowledged by the leader's constituents, is the acid test for whether real change has occurred.

The question "Can leaders change for the better?" always comes up in a book devoted to coaching and development. Our answer to this is a resounding "yes"—if the leader is motivated and is provided with the appropriate feedback, coaching, and development.

Conquering the Dark Side—Let There Be Light!

Using these concepts that leaders can indeed change and that reputation change is real change, we set about describing the most impactful ways to interpret Hogan assessment data and provide feedback and coaching to ensure a successful outcome. Our content is based on extensive Hogan research accumulated over 30 years and on the best practices of more than 40 coaches in the global Hogan Coaching Network (HCN). Our goal is to assist both leaders and the coaches who are guiding them in the pursuit of reputation change and performance improvement. As we looked back over the content covered throughout the book, we thought it would be useful to close with 10 major takeaways we hope were successfully conveyed:

1. Leaders are coaches. Perhaps the most important role for all leaders is that of coach. To be successful, they must pursue their own self-improvement, and they must become proficient in helping those they lead improve their performance. The content of this book is dedicated to all those interested in helping themselves and others become better leaders.

2. Strategic Self-awareness is foundational because without it, the entire development process stalls. Identity is "the you that you know," and reputation is "the you that others know," and it is the latter that is important. It is crucial for leaders to understand how they are perceived by others and why that is the case (e.g., due to their behaviors). Strategic Self-awareness enables them to do this—to understand their key strengths and areas for improvement and how they compare to those of other people. Leaders need to learn to be "awareness consumers" so they are constantly on the lookout for information regarding how they are being perceived by others and can then adjust their behaviors.

3. Situational Context awareness—knowing one's context and being able to adjust behaviors accordingly—is the working partner of Strategic Self-awareness. Leaders must constantly be "reading" the audience or the situation and then dialing up or dialing down behaviors based on what fits the context in which they find themselves. We emphasize three contexts in particular: the role the leader has, the manager to whom the leader reports, and the organizational culture in which the leader works. What is viewed as a key strength in one context might not be one in another. Likewise, what is a derailer in one context might not be one in another. In some instances, a key strength in one context might even be a derailer in another or vice versa. The learning is leaders need to be constantly vigilant as to their context and adapt their behaviors accordingly.

4. The three Hogan inventories (HPI, HDS, and MVPI) play a key role in facilitating leaders' Strategic Self-awareness and Situational Context awareness. Because Dark Side behaviors are the ones that derail leaders and negatively impact their reputations, we focused on the 11 scales of the HDS. Two major concepts emerged from the evolution of the HDS:

- Both high and low HDS scale scores can get leaders into trouble and negatively impact their reputations. While, historically, Hogan has called out higher scores, we have found that lower scores can be problematic as well. Although high-end behaviors are more noticeable and memorable, low-end behaviors can be silent killers for leaders as they typically are not very leader-like. The concept that "high scores will get you fired, and low scores will get you passed over" should be kept in mind whenever HDS scores are addressed. The addition of low-score problematic behaviors and coaching around them adds richness to the Hogan data that was many times overlooked in the past. Coaches and leaders alike should recognize that many times, it is more difficult to dial up a lower score than it is to dial down a higher score, as higher-end behaviors are typically so foreign to the low scoring leader. Each of the 11 scales has a chapter devoted to it that includes in-depth interpretation and coaching tips around both the high and low ends of the scales.

- Subscales have been added to the HDS, and they can be invaluable in determining how derailing behaviors will manifest. Each HDS scale has three subscales that describe different aspects of the major scale, enabling leaders to peel the onion back another layer and specifically target the derailing behaviors. This deeper exploration is particularly helpful if an elevated or depressed subscale is part of a major scale that is neither high nor low and typically would not garner much attention. This subscale elevation or depression allows for the identification of problematic behaviors that would not have been noticed by looking solely at the major scale score. In each of the 11 chapters dedicated to the respective HDS scales, we cover the implications of both high and low scores on the subscales, providing further interpretive nuance.

5. People are all wired differently, and it is essential to the success of a performance improvement effort to consider the personality of the leader, receptivity to feedback, engagement in the development process, and willingness to take action on the development plan. A coach should consider the following elements:

   - The Approach—Coaches must customize the approach they take with their leaders to ensure optimal engagement. Key to this is an understanding of both the personality of the leader and the learning style of the leader. Once these are understood, the coach can tailor his or her style and approach to the leader. The Hogan inventories provide insights into the leader's personality, including likes and dislikes, preferences for pace and level of detail, drivers, what is likely to keep the leader engaged, and the like. Further, if the coach can determine the leader's preferred learning style, using a construct such as the Kolb

Learning Model, additional customization to an approach can be done to maximize impact.

- The Hook—Coaches must identify a hook—the "what's in it for me?" for the leader. This must be something that really matters to the leader and will motivate the leader to change behaviors. Here again, the Hogan inventories can provide excellent insights into what will be important enough to a leader to prompt behavior change.

- The Coach's Own Style—The coach should look at his or her own Hogan inventories and flex his or her style to match the leader's style. This can accelerate building rapport and trust. It can also assist the coach in recognizing where rubs might come in the relationship due to personality differences and avoid those.

6. Leaders' objective ratings of feedback and coaching sessions gathered by Hogan Research and anecdotal data from the coaches of the HCN reveal the most impactful sessions: (1) account for and are grounded in the Situational Context of the leader, (2) identify developmental themes and appropriate developmental goals, and (3) result in specific behavioral actions to take against those goals to enhance performance and effectiveness. To accomplish these requires a highly skilled coach who not only understands the science behind the Hogan inventories and what the results mean, but who also can engage in a back-and-forth discussion with the leader to make the results come alive and be relevant. Coaches need to possess excellent rapport-building skills, solid verbal skills, the ability to ask powerful questions, and certainly, the ability to listen. Further, they need to be able to connect the dots of myriad Hogan data points for the leader, be flexible, be able to deal with ambiguity, and hold the leader accountable for commitments made.

7. A development plan that is well crafted and addresses only two to three areas (either strengths to leverage or watch-outs to improve) is essential to provide structure for improved leader performance. Without a development plan that describes what behavior needs to change, what specific actions need to be taken to accomplish this, and what success looks like in terms of greater effectiveness and enhanced reputation, then the leader's desired behavior changes are no more than a wish list. Further, the leader's manager must be in alignment with what is outlined in the development plan and be committed to providing ongoing feedback to reinforce the leader's behavior change.

8. When coaching the Dark Side, we highly recommend that the comprehensive approach outlined in the 11 chapters dedicated to the respective HDS scales be followed. This approach includes detecting when the behavior is a problem, evaluating the need for change based on the leader's presenting behaviors, determining the impact of the behaviors on various stakeholder

groups, identifying the subscales to target, creating a coaching plan, and utilizing the coaching tips and resources that are delineated.

9. When combined with the HDS, results from the HPI and MVPI often have profound implications for coaching the Dark Side. It is nearly impossible to account for the implications of all combinations and permutations of these three inventories, especially in light of Situational Context variables, but there are closely related scales that can drive coaching refinements. The tool we use to do this is the Competency Domain circumplex that maps the scales of the three inventories to four domains: Intrapersonal, Interpersonal, Leadership, and Business.

10. The Hogan Development Cycle is continuous. Leaders are never finished products but always works in progress, as their context continually changes and with it the need to modify their behaviors to suit the situation. After a development initiative, leaders have come full circle and are back to utilizing their Strategic Self-awareness to understand their reputation and determine what to address next. Nothing takes the place of ongoing feedback in keeping Strategic Self-awareness honed. Too often, especially at higher level jobs, it becomes very difficult for leaders to obtain objective feedback. It is only with the knowledge of how they are being perceived by others (e.g., their reputation) gained through feedback that they can enhance their performance. Leaders need to proactively seek feedback, and if they feel they are not getting the straight scoop anecdotally from their constituents, they should utilize a more formal means such as a multi-rater assessment or stakeholder interviews conducted by a coach.

SUMMARY

In closing, let us recognize that we should never lose sight of *why* we want to enhance leaders' reputations and effectiveness in the first place. It has been shown repeatedly there is a clear line of sight between the quality of an organization's leaders and its business results, including increased financial performance, enhanced employee satisfaction and engagement, less employee turnover, and greater customer satisfaction.

It is our hope that leaders and coaches will take to heart and apply what we have put forth in this book, enabling them to deal with their Dark Side head-on and accomplish real behavior changes, reputation enhancements, and greater leadership effectiveness. More effective leaders vastly improve the quality of their constituents' work lives. Let there be light!

BIBLIOGRAPHY

Allport, G. W. (1937). *Personality: A psychological interpretation.* New York, NY: Holt.

Allport, G. W. (1961). *Pattern and growth in personality.* New York, NY: Holt, Rinehart, & Winston.

Allport, G. W., Vernon, P. E., & Lindzey, G. (1960). *Manual, Study of Values* (3rd ed.). Cambridge, MA: Houghton Mifflin.

American Psychiatric Association (1987). *Diagnostic and statistical manual of mental disorders* (3rd ed., rev.). Washington, DC: Author.

Americans with Disabilities Act of 1990, 102(b) (7), 42 U.S.C.A. 12112.

Anderson, M. C. (2001). *Executive briefing: Case study on the return on investment of executive coaching.* Retrieved from http://www.true-directions.com/downloads/MetrixGlobalCoachingROIBriefing.pdf

Argyris, C. (1991, May–June). Teaching smart people how to learn. *Harvard Business Review.* Retrieved from https://hbr.org/1991/05/teaching-smart-people-how-to-learn

Barney, J. (1991). Firm resources and sustained competitive advantage. *Journal of Management, 17*(1), 99–120. doi: 10.1177/014920639101700108

Barrick, M. R., Day, D. V., Lord, R. G., & Alexander, R. A. (1991). Assessing the utility of executive leadership. *Leadership Quarterly, 2*, 9–22. doi: 10.1016/1048-9843(91)90004-L

Barrick, M. R., & Mount, M. (1991). The Big Five personality dimensions and job performance: A meta-analysis. *Personnel Psychology, 44*, 1–26. doi: 10.1111/j.1744-6570.1991.tb00688.x

Bentz, V. J. (1967). The Sears experience in the investigation, description, and prediction of executive behavior. In F. R. Wickert & D. E. McFarland (Eds.), *Measuring executive effectiveness* (pp. 147–206). New York, NY: Appleton-Century-Crofts.

Bentz, V. J. (1985, August). A *view from the top: A thirty year perspective of research devoted to the discovery, description, and prediction of executive behavior.* Paper presented at the 92nd Annual Convention of the American Psychological Association, Los Angeles, CA.

Bertrand, M., & Schoar, A. (2003). Managing with style: The effect of managers on firm policies. *Quarterly Journal of Economics, 118*(4), 1169–1208. doi: 10.1162/003355303322552775

Block, P. (2011). *Flawless consulting: A guide to getting your expertise used.* San Francisco, CA: Pfeiffer.

Bloom, N., Sadun, R., & Van Reenen, J. (2012). The organization of firms across countries. *Quarterly Journal of Economics*, 1663–1705. doi: 10.1093/qje/qje029

Bloom, N., & Van Reenen, J. (2007). Measuring and explaining management practices across firms and countries. *The Quarterly Journal of Economics, 122*(4), 1351–1408. doi: 10.1162/qjec.2007.122.4.1351

Boudreau, J. W., Boswell, W. R., & Judge, T. A. (2001). Effects of personality on executive career success in the United States and Europe. *Journal of Vocational Behavior, 58*, 53–81. doi: 10.1006/jvbe.2000.1755

Brandon, R., & Seldman, M. (2004). *Survival of the savvy: High-integrity political tactics for career and company success.* New York, NY: Free Press.

Brousseau, K. R. (2005). *The lens of success: perspectives on climbing the spiral staircase.* Thousand Oaks, CA.

Brousseau, K. R., Driver, M. J., Hourihan, G., & Larsson, R. (2006, February). The seasoned executive's decision-making style. *Harvard Business Review*. Retrieved from https://hbr.org/2006/02/the-seasoned-executives-decision-making-style

Campbell, D. P., & Holland, J. L. (1972). A merger in vocational interest research: Applying Holland's theory to Strong's data. *Journal of Vocational Behavior, 2,* 353–376.

Christian, M. S., Garza, A. S., & Slaughter, J. E. (2011). Work engagement: A quantitative review and test of its relations with task and contextual performance. *Personnel Psychology, 64,* 89–136. doi: 10.1111/j.1744-6570.2010.01203.x

Collins, J. (2001). *Good to great: Why some companies make the leap … and others don't.* New York, NY: HarperCollins.

Connellan, T. K., & Zemke, R. (1993). *Sustaining knock your socks off service.* New York, NY: AMACOM.

Crisp, R. J., & Turner, R. N. (2010). *Essential social psychology.* London, UK: Sage.

Darley, J. G., & Hagenah, T. (1955). *Vocational interest measurement: Theory and practice.* Minneapolis, MN: Psychological Corporation.

Day, D. V., & Lord, R. G. (1988). Executive leadership and organizational performance: Suggestions for a new theory and methodology. *Journal of Management, 14*(3), 453–464. doi: 10.1177/014920638801400308

Dirks, K. T., & Ferrin, D. L. (2002). Trust in leadership: Meta-analytic findings and implications for organizational research. *Journal of Applied Psychology, 87*(4), 611–628. doi: 10.1037//0021-9010.87.4.611

Finkelstein, S. (2004). *Why smart executives fail and what you can do to learn from their mistakes.* New York, NY: Penguin Group.

Freud, S. (1913). *Totem and taboo.* New York, NY: Norton.

Gerstner, C. R., & Day, D. V. (1997). Meta-analytic review of leader-member exchange theory: Correlates and construct ideas. *Journal of Applied Psychology, 82,* 827–844.

Gough, H. G. (1975). *Manual for the California Psychological Inventory.* Palo Alto, CA: Consulting Psychologists Press.

Griffin, N. S. (2013, March). Personalize your management development. *Harvard Business Review.* Retrieved from https://hbr.org/2003/03/personalize-your-management-development

Hambrick, D. C., & Quigley, T. J. (2013). Toward more accurate contextualization of the CEO effect on firm performance. *Strategic Management Journal, 35*(4), 473–491. doi: 10.1002/smj.2108

Hart, W. E., & Kirkland, K. (2001). *Using your executive coach.* Greensboro, NC: Center for Creative Leadership.

Harter, J. K., Schmidt, F. L., & Hayes, T. L. (2002). Business-unit-level relationships between employee satisfaction, employee engagement, and business outcomes. *Journal of Applied Psychology, 87,* 268–279. doi: 0.1037//0021-9010.87.2.268

Hill, L. A., & Lineback, K. (2011). *Being the boss: The 3 imperatives for becoming a great leader.* Boston, MA: Harvard Business Review Press.

Hoagland-Smith, L. (2009). Why the movement to license business coaches to executive coaches. Retrieved from http://www.evancarmichael.com/Business-Coach/137/Why-the-Movement-to-License-Business-Coaches-to-Executive-Coaches.html

Hogan Assessment Systems (2014). *HDS technical supplement: Form 5.* Tulsa, OK: Hogan Press.

Hogan, J., & Hogan, R. (2010). *Motives, Values, Preferences Inventory manual: 2010 administrative and norming updates.* Tulsa, OK: Hogan Press.

Hogan, J., Hogan, R., & Busch, C. M. (1984). How to measure service orientation. *Journal of Applied Psychology, 69,* 167–173.

Hogan, J., Hogan, R., & Kaiser R. B. (2010). Management derailment: Personality assessment and mitigation. In S. Zedeck (Ed.), *APA handbook of industrial and organizational psychology, Vol. 3: Maintaining, expanding, and contracting the organization* (pp. 555–576). Washington, DC: American Psychological Association.

Hogan, R. (1983). A socioanalytic theory of personality. In M. M. Page (Ed.), *1982 Nebraska Symposium on Motivation* (pp. 55–89). Lincoln, NE: University of Nebraska Press.

Hogan, R. (2007). *Personality and the fate of organizations.* Mahwah, NJ: Erlbaum.

Hogan Research Division (2011). *Base rate of managerial derailment characteristics in America: Comparisons and implications for leadership development.* Technical Report. Tulsa, OK: Hogan Assessment Systems.

Hogan, R., & Benson, M. J. (2009). Personality theory and positive psychology: Strategic self-awareness. In R. Kaiser (Ed.), *The perils of accentuating the positive* (pp. 115–134). Tulsa, OK: Hogan Press.

Hogan, R., Curphy, G., Kaiser, R., & Chamorro-Premuzic, T. (n.d.). Leadership in organizations. In D. S. Ones (Ed.) [In press].

Hogan, R., & Hogan, J. (1997). *Hogan Development Survey manual.* Tulsa, OK: Hogan Assessment Systems.

Hogan, R., & Hogan, J. (2001). Assessing leadership: A view from the dark side. *International Journal of Selection and Assessment, 9,* 40–51. doi: 10.1111/1468-2389.00162

Hogan, R., & Hogan, J. (2007). *Hogan Personality Inventory manual* (3rd ed.). Tulsa, OK: Hogan Press.

Hogan, R., & Hogan, J. (2009). *Hogan Development Survey manual* (2nd ed.). Tulsa, OK: Hogan Press.

Hogan, R., Hogan, J., & Warrenfeltz, R. (2007). *The Hogan guide: Interpretation and use of Hogan inventories.* Tulsa, OK: Hogan Press.

Hogan, R., & Kaiser, R. B. (2005). What we know about leadership. *Review of General Psychology, 9,* 169–180. doi: 10.1037/1089-2680.9.2.169

Hogan, R., & Smither, R. (2008). *Personality: Theories and applications* (2nd ed.). Tulsa, OK: Hogan Press.

Hogan, R., & Warrenfeltz, R. (2003). Educating the modern manager. *Academy of Management Learning and Education, 2,* 74–84.

Holland, J. L. (1966). A psychological classification scheme for vocations and major fields. *Journal of Counseling Psychology, 13,* 278–288.

Holland, J. L. (1973). *Making vocational choices: A theory of careers.* Englewood Cliffs, NJ: Prentice-Hall.

Holland, J. L. (1985). *Making vocational choices: A theory of vocational personalities and work environments* (2nd ed.). Englewood Cliffs, NJ: Prentice-Hall.

Honey, P., & Mumford, A. (2006). *The Learning Styles Questionnaire: 80-item version.* Peter Honey Publications Limited. Retrieved from https://www.talentlens.co.uk/assets/lsq/downloads/learning-styles-questionnaire-80-item.pdf

Huselid, M. A. (1995). The impact of human resource management practices on turnover, productivity, and corporate financial performance. *Academy of Management Journal, 38*(3), 635–872. doi: 10.2307/256741

Jones, W. H. (1988). *User's manual for PROFILE.* Unpublished manuscript.

Joyce, W. F., Nohria, N., & Roberson, B. (2003). *What really works: The 4+2 formula for sustained business success.* New York, NY: Harper Business.

Judge, T. A., Bono, J. E., Ilies, R., & Gerhardt, M. W. (2002). Personality and leadership. *Journal of Applied Psychology, 87,* 765–780. doi: 10.1037/0021-9010.87.4.765

Kaiser, R. B., & Hogan, R. (2010). How to (and how not to) assess the integrity of managers. *Consulting Psychology Journal: Practice and Research, 62,* 216–234. doi: 037/a0022265

Kaiser, R. B., Hogan, R., & Craig, S. B. (2008). Leadership and the fate of organizations. *American Psychologist, 63,* 96–110. doi: 10.1037/0003-066X.63.2.96

Kantrowitz, T. M. (2014). *Global assessment trends report.* CEB. Retrieved from http://ceb.shl.com/images/uploads/GATR-042014-UKeng.pdf

Kelloway, E. K., Sivanathan, N., Francis, L., & Barling, J. (2005). Poor leadership. In J. Barling, E. K. Kelloway, & M. Frone (Eds.), *Handbook of work stress* (pp. 89–112). Los Angeles, CA: Sage.

Kolb, D. A. (1984). *Experiential learning: Experience as the source of learning and development.* Englewood Cliffs, NJ: Prentice Hall.

Kolb, D. A., (1986). *The learning style inventory: Technical manual.* Boston, MA: McBer.

Kouzes, J. M., & Posner, B. Z. (2010). *The truth about leadership: The no-fads, heart-of-the-matter facts you need to know.* San Francisco, CA: Jossey-Bass.

Kram, K. E. (1988). *Mentoring at work: Developmental relationships in organizational life.* New York, NY: University Press.

Lord, R. G., Foti, R. J., & De Vader, C. L. (1984). A test of leadership categorization theory: Internal structure, information processing, and leadership perceptions. *Organizational Behavior and Human Performance, 34,* 343–378. doi: 10.1016/0030-5073(84)90043-6

Luecke, R. (2004). *Coaching and mentoring: How to develop top talent and achieve stronger performance.* Cambridge, MA: Harvard Business Essentials.

Luthans, F., Hodgetts, R. M., & Rosenkrantz, S. A. (1988). *Real managers.* Cambridge, MA: Ballinger.

Macey, W. H., & Schneider, B. (2008). The meaning of employee engagement. *Industrial and Organizational Psychology: Perspectives on Science and Practice, 1*(1), 3–30. doi: 10.1111/j.1754-9434.2007.0002.x

Mackey, A. (2008). The effect of CEOs on firm performance. *Strategic Management Journal, 29*(12), 1357–1367. doi: 10.1002/smj.708

McCall, M. W. Jr., & Lombardo, M. M. (1983). *Off the track: Why and how successful executives get derailed.* Technical Report No. 21. Greensboro, NC: Center for Creative Leadership.

McGahan, A. M., & Porter, M. E. (1997). How much does industry matter, really? *Strategic Management Journal, 18*, 15–30. doi: 10.1002/(SICI)1097-0266(199707)18:1

McGovern, J., Lindemann, M., Vergara, M. A., Murphy, S., Barker, L., & Warrenfeltz, R. (2001). Maximizing the impact of executive coaching: Behavioral change, organizational outcomes and return on investment. *The Manchester Review, 6*(1), 1–9.

Murray, H. A. (1938). *Explorations in personality*. New York, NY: Oxford University Press.

Nicholson, N. (2013). *The I of leadership: Strategies for seeing, being, and doing*. San Francisco, CA: Jossey-Bass.

Norman, W. T. (1963). Toward an adequate taxonomy of personality attributes: Replicated factor structure in peer nomination personality ratings. *Journal of Abnormal and Social Psychology, 66*, 574–583.

Parker-Wilkins, V. (2006). Business impact of executive coaching: Demonstrating monetary value. *Industrial and Commercial Training, 38*(3), 122–127. doi: 10.1108/00197850610659373

Portfolio (2009). Portfolio's worst American CEOs of all time. Retrieved from http://www.cnbc.com/id/30502091/Portfolio_s_Worst_American_CEOs_of_All_Time

Ravasi, D., & Schultz, M. (2006). Responding to organizational identity threats: Exploring the role of organizational culture. *Academy of Management Journal, 49*(3), 433–458.

Sinar, E., Wellins, R. S., Ray R., Abel, A. L., & Neal, S. (2014). *Ready-now leaders: 25 findings to meet tomorrow's business challenges. Global Leadership Forecast 2014/2015*. Retrieved from https://www.conference-board.org/publications/publicationdetail.cfm?publicationid=2812

Smith, D., & Kolb, D. (1986). *User guide for the learning style inventory: A manual for teachers and trainers*. Boston, MA: McBer.

Smith, R. M. (1982). *Learning how to learn: Applied theory for adults*. Chicago, IL: Follett.

Smither, J. W., London, M., & Reilly, R. R. (2005). Does performance improve following multisource feedback? A theoretical model, meta-analysis, and review of empirical findings. *Personnel Psychology, 58*(1), 33–66. doi: 10.1111/j.1744-6570.2005.514_1.x

Spranger, E. (1928). *Types of men*. New York, NY: Stechert-Hafner.

The Arbinger Institute (2010). *Leadership and self-deception: Getting out of the box.* San Francisco, CA: Berrett-Koehler.

The National Institute for Occupational Safety and Health. (1999). *STRESS ... at work.* DHHS (NIOSH) Publication Number 99–101. Washington, DC: Government Printing Office.

Townsend, J., Phillips, J. S., & Elkins, T. J. (2000). Employee retaliation: The neglected consequence of poor leader-member exchange relations. *Journal of Occupational Health Psychology, 5*(4), 457–463. doi. org/10.1037/1076-8998.5.4.457

Van Vugt, M., Hogan, R., & Kaiser, R. B. (2008). Leadership, followership, and evolution: Some lessons from the past. *American Psychologist, 63*, 182–196. doi: 10.1037/0003-066X.63.3.182

Wiggins, J. (1973). *Personality and prediction: Principles of personality assessment.* Reading, MA: Addison-Wesley.

Wiggins, J. S., & Pincus, A. L. (1992). Personality structure and assessment. *Annual Review of Psychology, 43*, 473–504.

INDEX

ABOUT HOGAN
ASSESSMENT SYSTEMS

We are a premium test-publishing company that uses a comprehensive suite of personality assessments to help companies select employees, develop leaders, and identify talent. We help organizations maximize their human resources through our vast library of research and scientifically based predictive power. We are the science of personality.

Our history is defined by the business applications of personality. This dates back to the 1930s when assessment centers were used to select individuals for dangerous wartime assignments. Rooted in this tradition, Dr. Robert Hogan developed the Hogan Personality Inventory in the 1970s—it was the first measure of normal personality designed specifically for business applications. He spent more than 15 years accumulating mountains of evidence demonstrating that this personality inventory would predict job performance. And he was right. The first commercial applications of the inventory began in the very early 1980s, and in 1987, Drs. Robert and Joyce Hogan founded Hogan Assessment Systems to make this science available to the business community. Today, we continue to build our position as the innovative leader in providing scientifically based personality assessment, development, and talent-management solutions for business and industry.

Quick Facts

- Hogan Assessment Systems was founded in 1987.

- We are a research-based company that is at the forefront of the assessment industry.

- Our research archives cover more than 500 jobs ranging from janitor to CEO.

- Our inventories and services are offered through local distributors throughout the world.

- We have a track record of success working with more than 2,000 companies worldwide.

- Our inventories are currently in use by more than 70 percent of Fortune 100 companies.

Expertise

Employee selection, perhaps more than any other process in an organization, has the power to change a company's destiny. We design and implement selection systems aimed at improving bottom-line business results.

Employee development initiatives provide important insights to help employees develop to their full career potential. Our assessments help companies determine the right fit for each employee and provide feedback to develop each person into his or her most valuable role within the organization. Our highly experienced coaches are available to provide more in-depth feedback and development guidance.

Talent management is now recognized by organizations as a key factor in their future growth. Our talent management expertise helps organizations identify and develop talent, which we define in terms of personality, cognitive ability, and leadership potential.

Our employee selection, development, and talent-management solutions are backed by a team of highly trained professionals dedicated to delivering the quality solutions necessary to achieve a competitive advantage in today's global market.

Learn more about us at www.hoganassessments.com or call 1-800-756-0632.